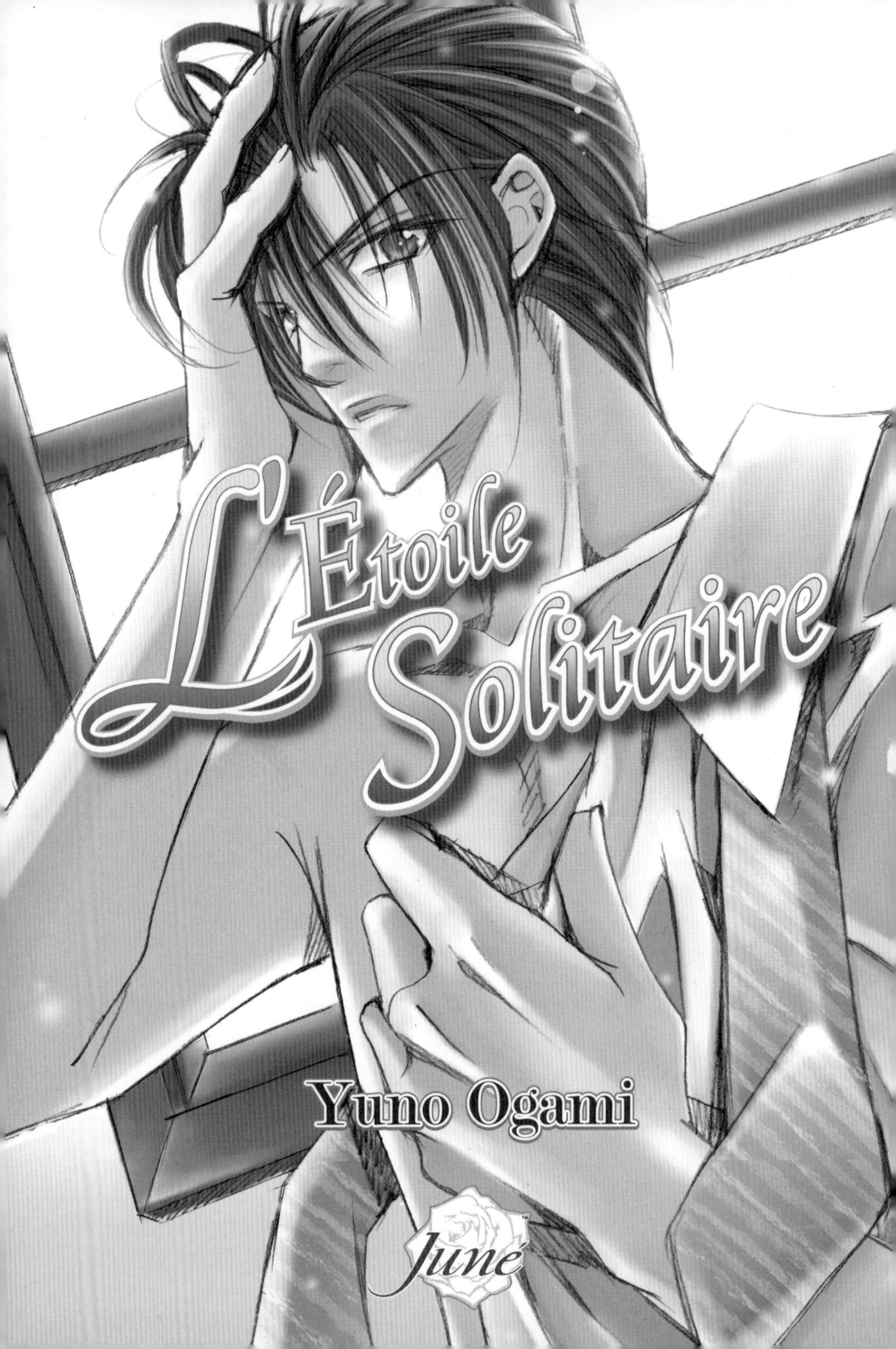
L'Étoile Solitaire
Yuno Ogami
Juné

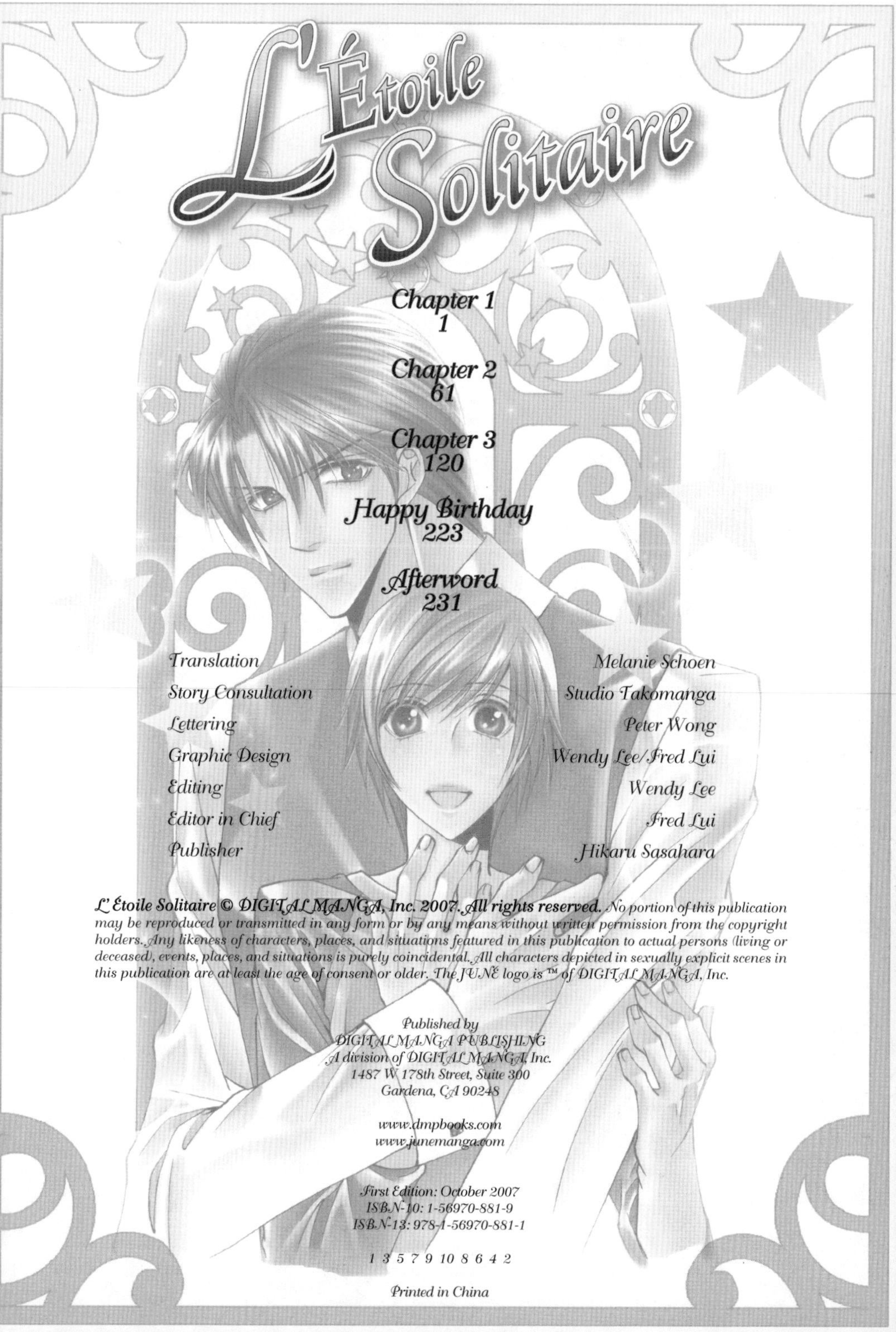

L'Étoile Solitaire

Chapter 1
1

Chapter 2
61

Chapter 3
120

Happy Birthday
223

Afterword
231

Translation — Melanie Schoen

Story Consultation — Studio Takomanga

Lettering — Peter Wong

Graphic Design — Wendy Lee/Fred Lui

Editing — Wendy Lee

Editor in Chief — Fred Lui

Publisher — Hikaru Sasahara

Published by
DIGITAL MANGA PUBLISHING
A division of DIGITAL MANGA, Inc.
1487 W 178th Street, Suite 300
Gardena, CA 90248

www.dmpbooks.com
www.junemanga.com

First Edition: October 2007
ISBN-10: 1-56970-881-9
ISBN-13: 978-1-56970-881-1

1 3 5 7 9 10 8 6 4 2

Printed in China

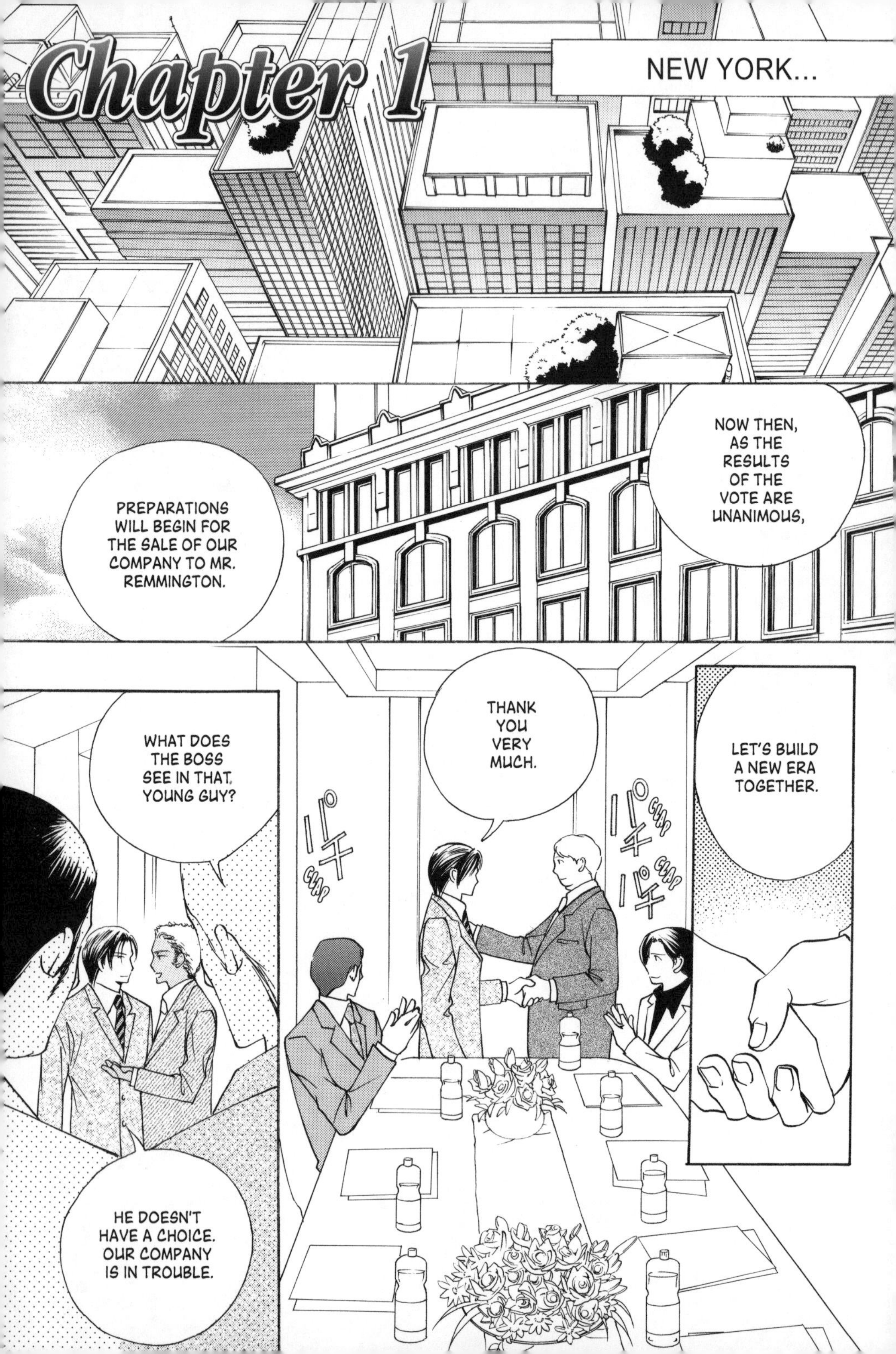
Chapter 1
NEW YORK...
NOW THEN, AS THE RESULTS OF THE VOTE ARE UNANIMOUS,
PREPARATIONS WILL BEGIN FOR THE SALE OF OUR COMPANY TO MR. REMMINGTON.
LET'S BUILD A NEW ERA TOGETHER.
パチ CLAP パチ CLAP
THANK YOU VERY MUCH.
パチ CLAP
WHAT DOES THE BOSS SEE IN THAT YOUNG GUY?
HE DOESN'T HAVE A CHOICE. OUR COMPANY IS IN TROUBLE.

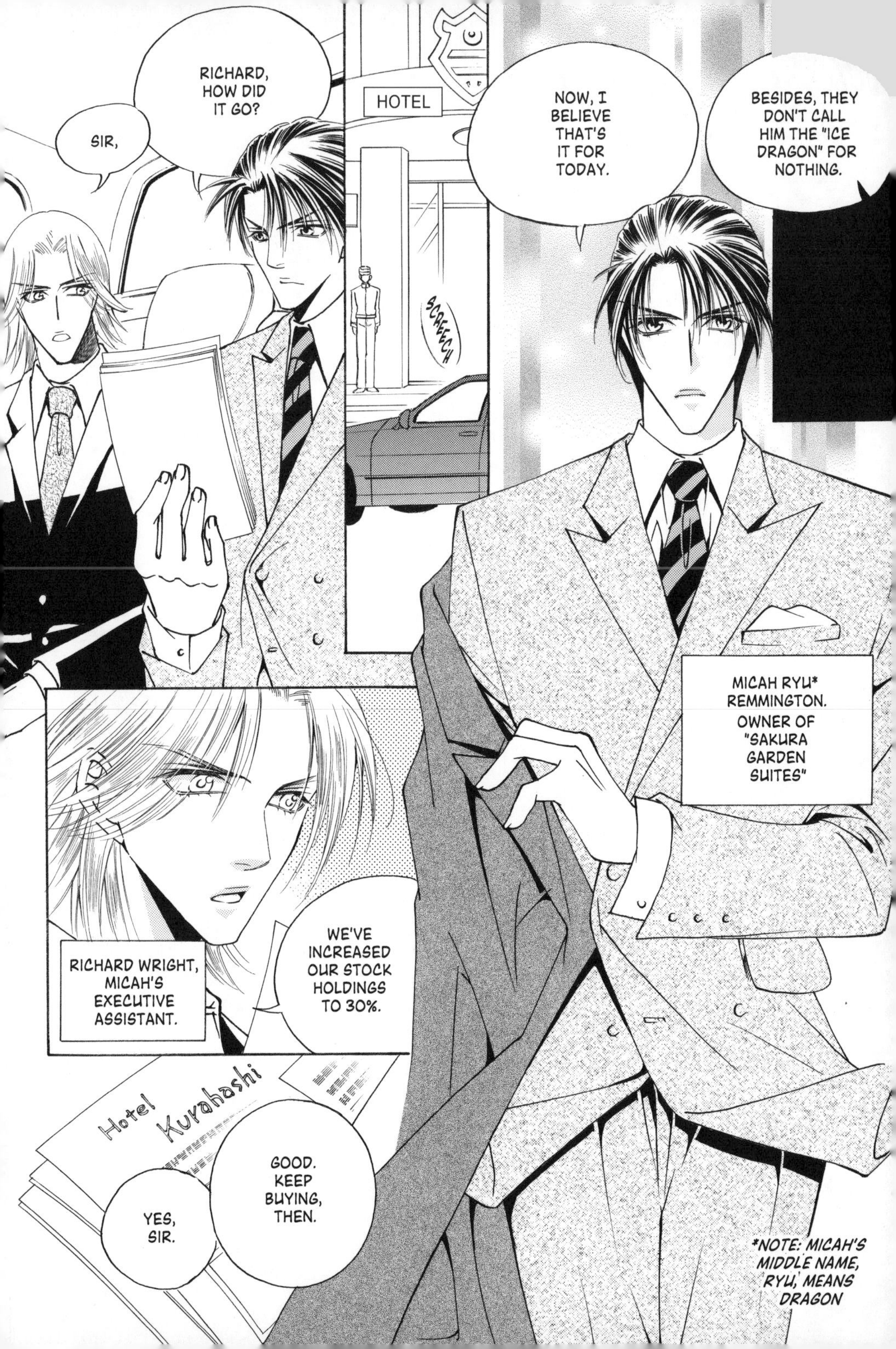

BESIDES, THEY DON'T CALL HIM THE "ICE DRAGON" FOR NOTHING.
NOW, I BELIEVE THAT'S IT FOR TODAY.
MICAH RYU* REMMINGTON. OWNER OF "SAKURA GARDEN SUITES"
*NOTE: MICAH'S MIDDLE NAME, RYU, MEANS DRAGON
HOTEL
SCREECH
RICHARD, HOW DID IT GO?
SIR,
WE'VE INCREASED OUR STOCK HOLDINGS TO 30%.
RICHARD WRIGHT, MICAH'S EXECUTIVE ASSISTANT.
Hotel Kurahashi
GOOD. KEEP BUYING, THEN.
YES, SIR.

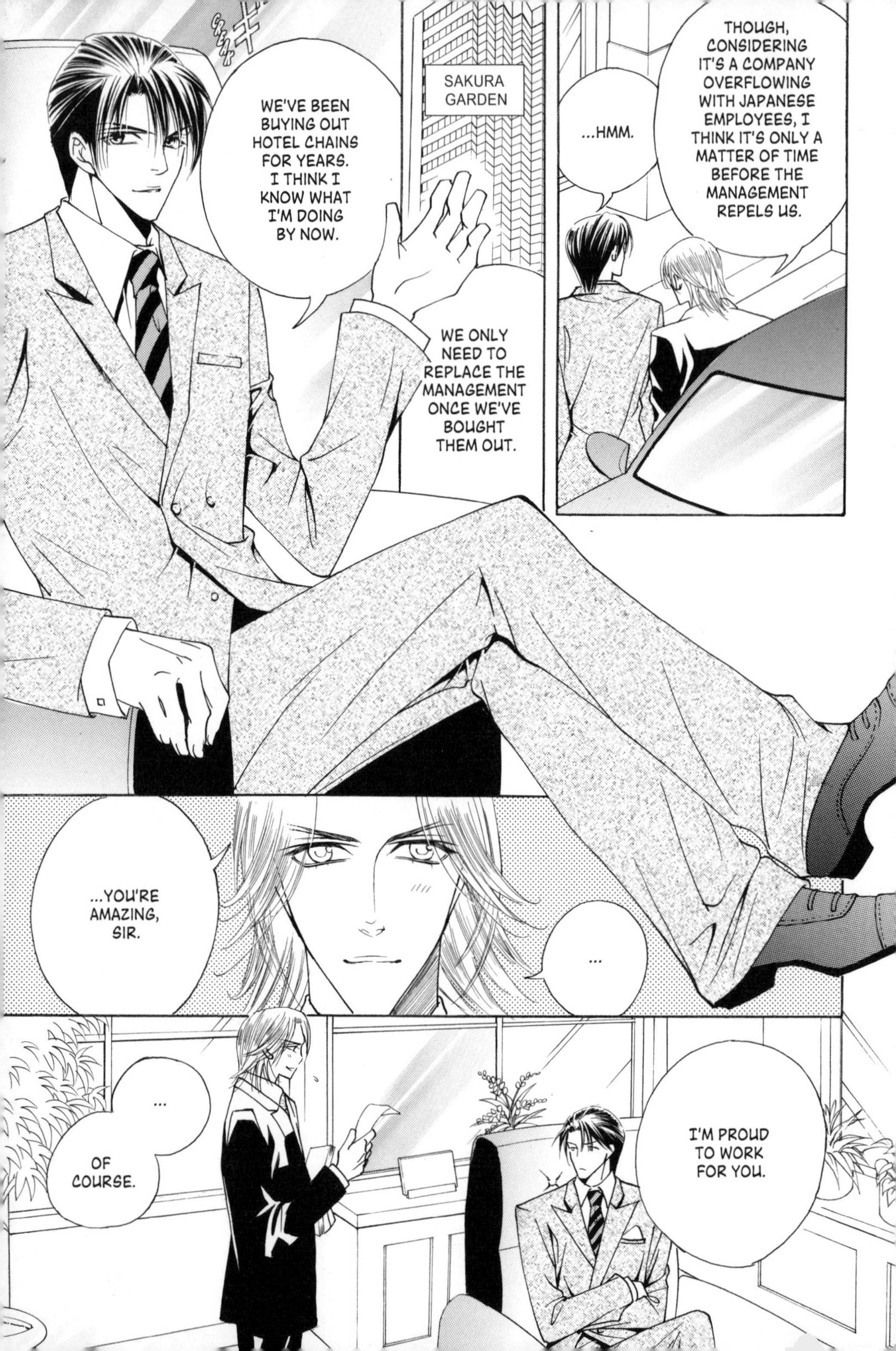
THOUGH, CONSIDERING IT'S A COMPANY OVERFLOWING WITH JAPANESE EMPLOYEES, I THINK IT'S ONLY A MATTER OF TIME BEFORE THE MANAGEMENT REPELS US.
...HMM.
SAKURA GARDEN
WE'VE BEEN BUYING OUT HOTEL CHAINS FOR YEARS. I THINK I KNOW WHAT I'M DOING BY NOW.
WE ONLY NEED TO REPLACE THE MANAGEMENT ONCE WE'VE BOUGHT THEM OUT.
...
...YOU'RE AMAZING, SIR.
I'M PROUD TO WORK FOR YOU.
...
OF COURSE.

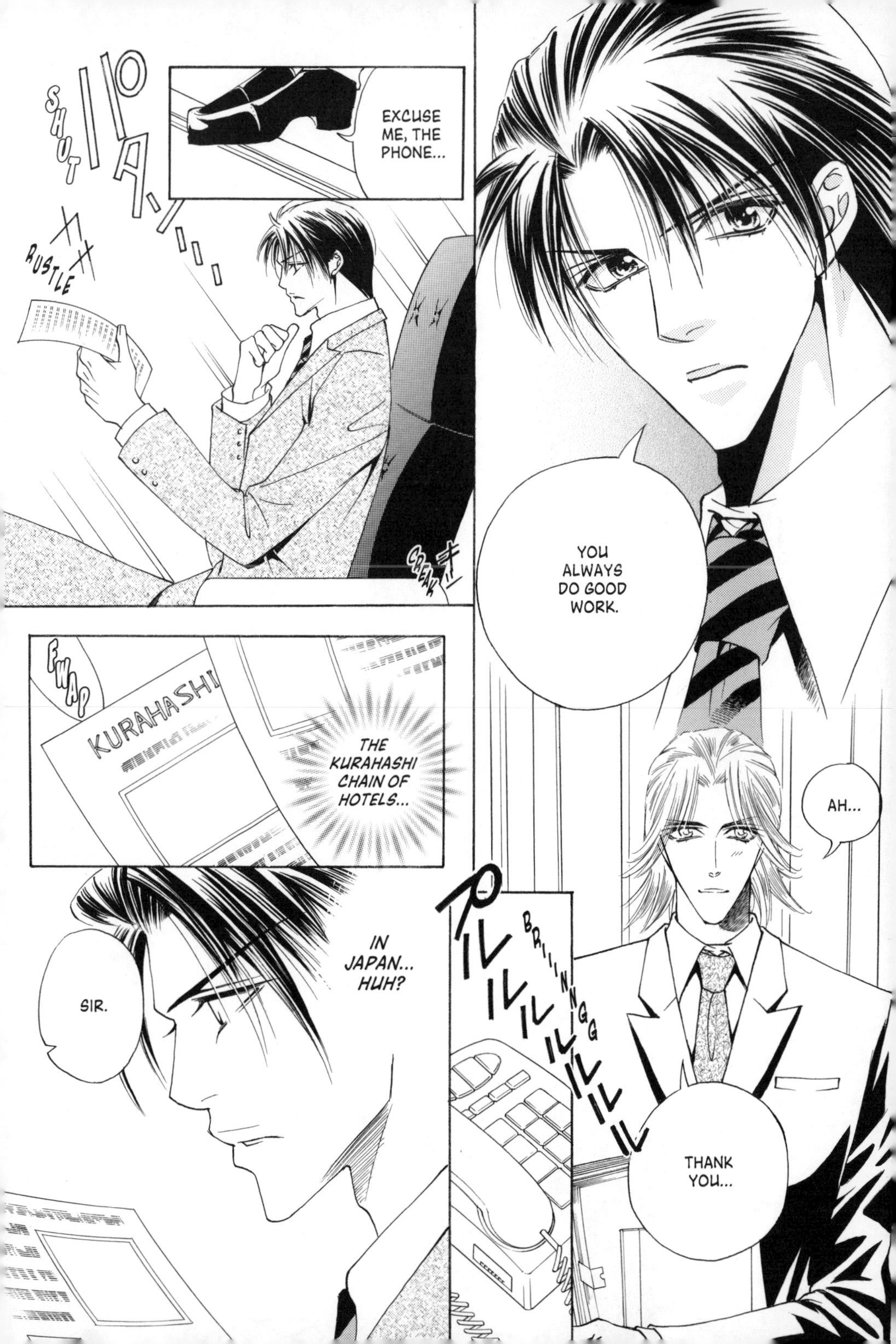
YOU ALWAYS DO GOOD WORK.
AH...
THANK YOU...
BRIIINNGG
EXCUSE ME, THE PHONE...
SHUT
CREAK
RUSTLE
FWAP
KURAHASHI
THE KURAHASHI CHAIN OF HOTELS...
IN JAPAN... HUH?
SIR.

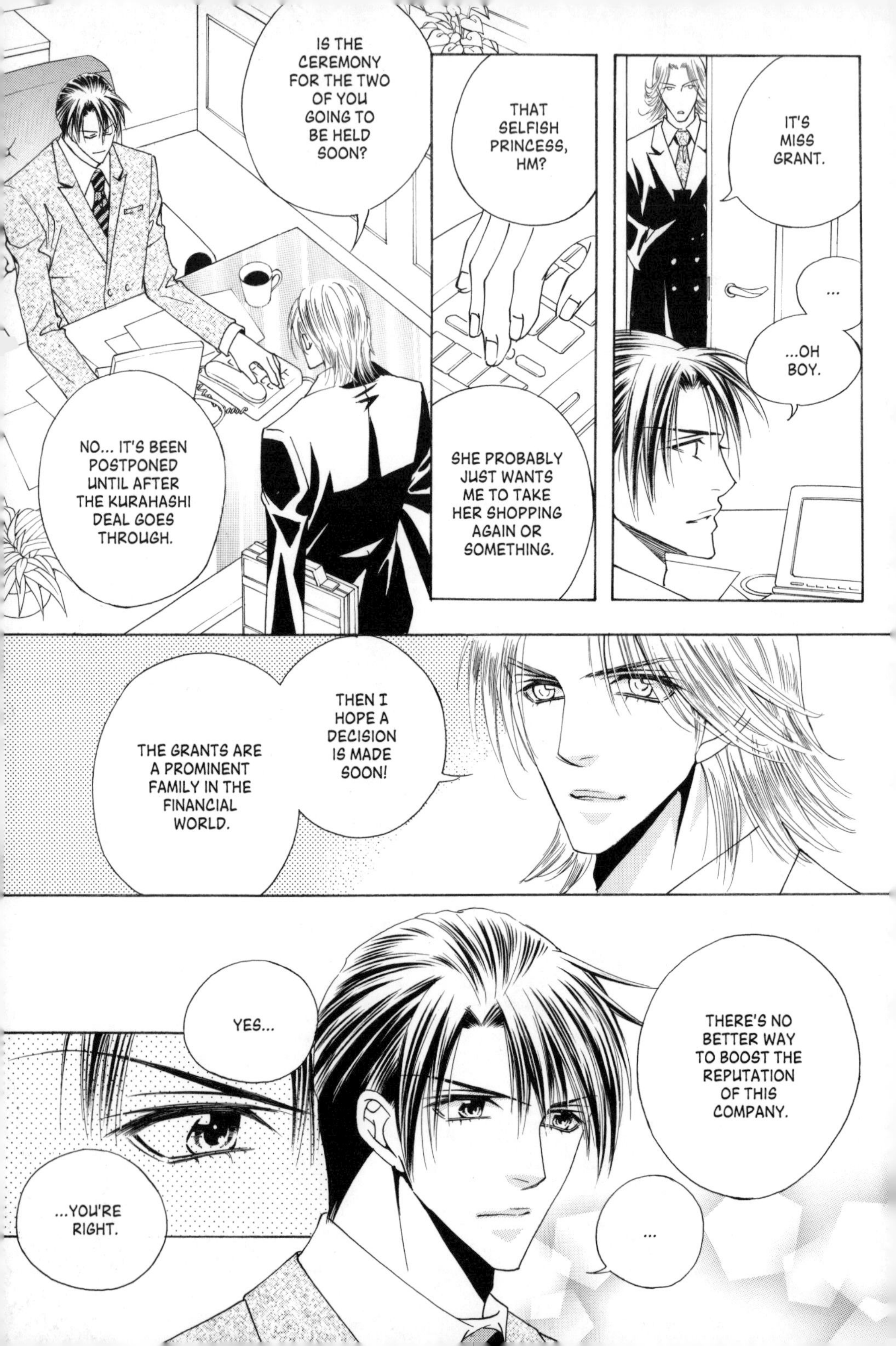
IT'S MISS GRANT.
...
...OH BOY.
THAT SELFISH PRINCESS, HM?
SHE PROBABLY JUST WANTS ME TO TAKE HER SHOPPING AGAIN OR SOMETHING.
IS THE CEREMONY FOR THE TWO OF YOU GOING TO BE HELD SOON?
NO... IT'S BEEN POSTPONED UNTIL AFTER THE KURAHASHI DEAL GOES THROUGH.
THEN I HOPE A DECISION IS MADE SOON!
THE GRANTS ARE A PROMINENT FAMILY IN THE FINANCIAL WORLD.
THERE'S NO BETTER WAY TO BOOST THE REPUTATION OF THIS COMPANY.
YES...
...
...YOU'RE RIGHT.

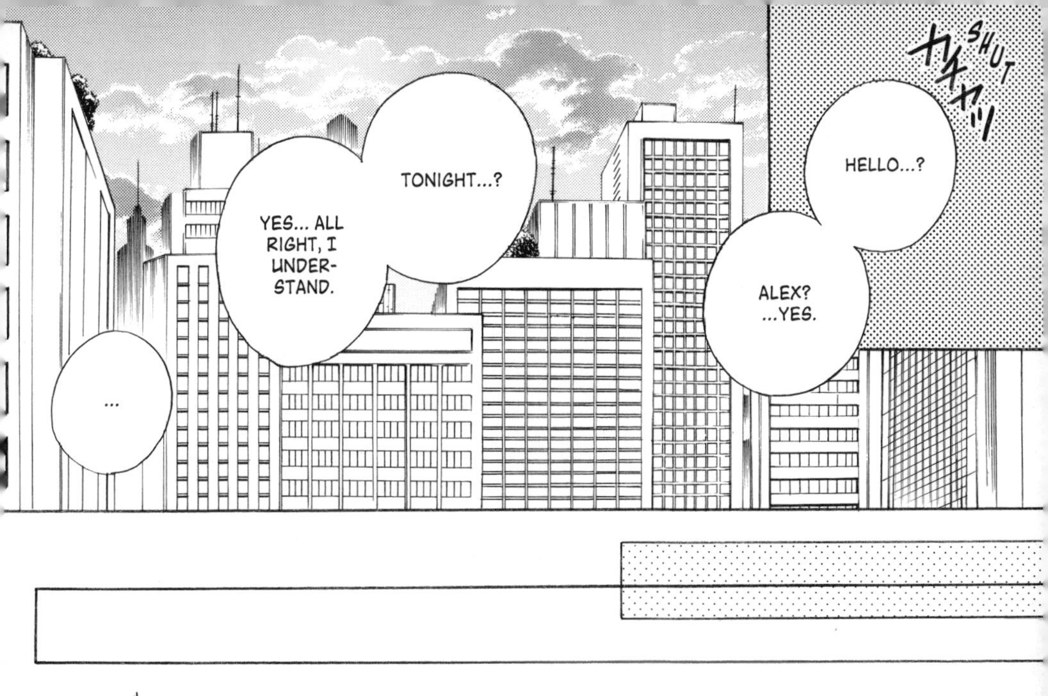
SHUT
HELLO...?
ALEX? ...YES.
TONIGHT...?
YES... ALL RIGHT, I UNDERSTAND.
...

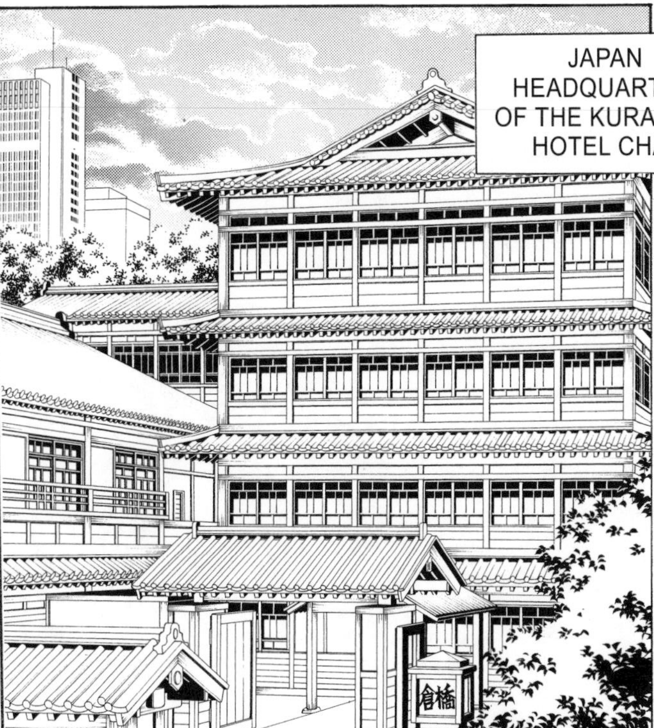
JAPAN HEADQUARTERS OF THE KURAHASHI HOTEL CHAIN.
倉橋

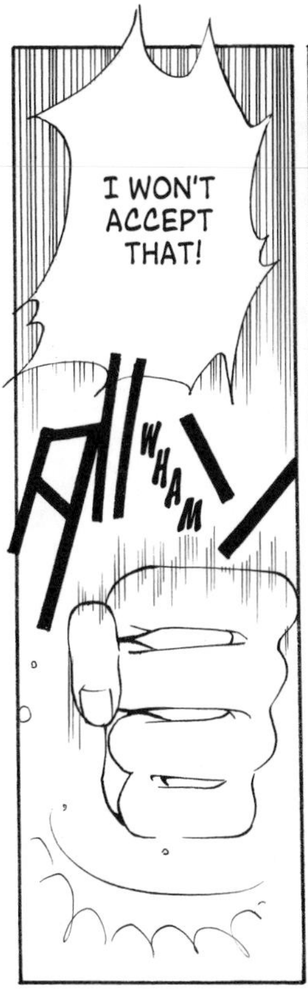
I WON'T ACCEPT THAT!
WHAM

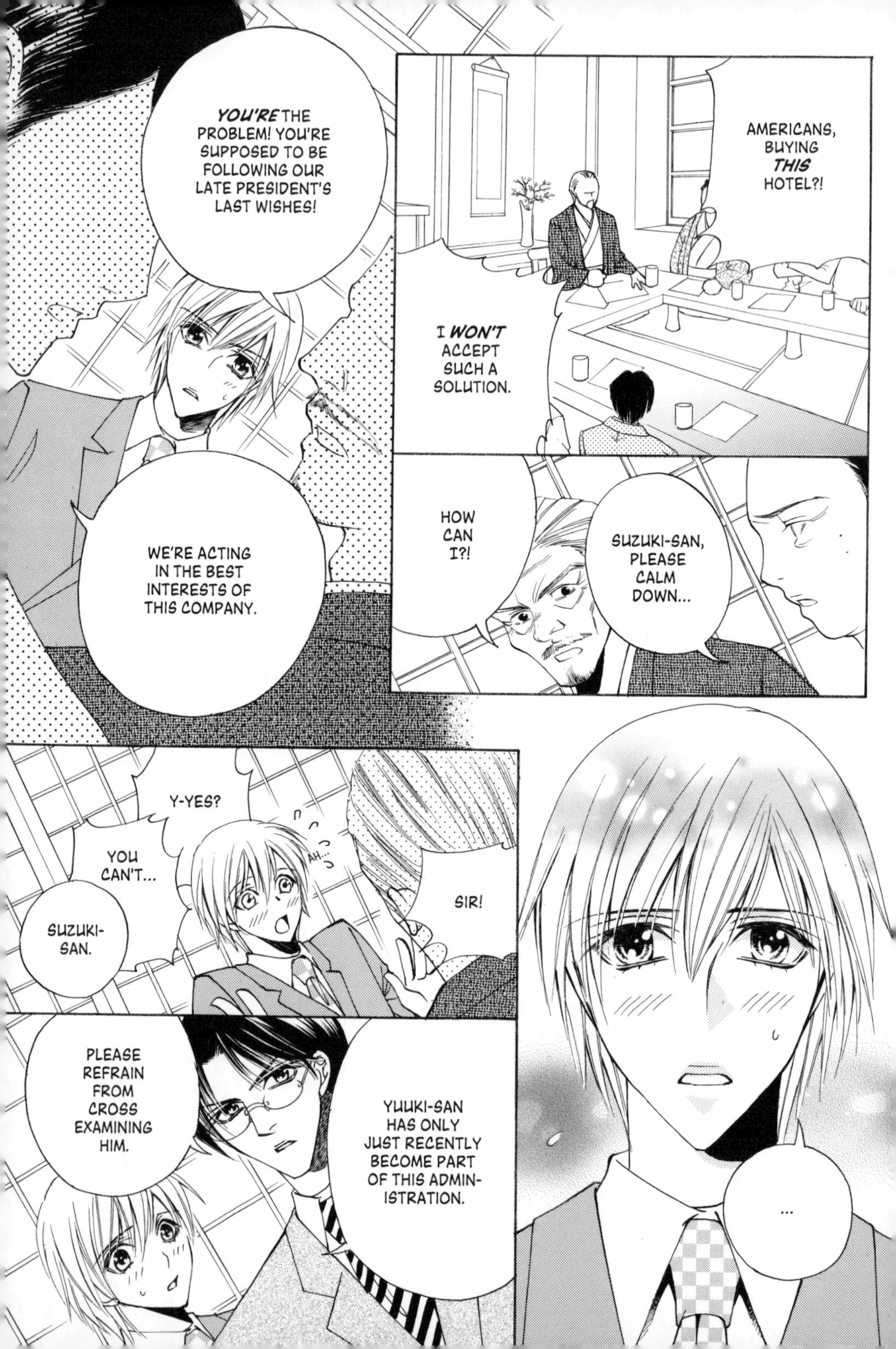
AMERICANS, BUYING THIS HOTEL?!
I WON'T ACCEPT SUCH A SOLUTION.
SUZUKI-SAN, PLEASE CALM DOWN...
HOW CAN I?!
YOU'RE THE PROBLEM! YOU'RE SUPPOSED TO BE FOLLOWING OUR LATE PRESIDENT'S LAST WISHES!
WE'RE ACTING IN THE BEST INTERESTS OF THIS COMPANY.
...
SIR!
AH...
Y-YES?
YOU CAN'T...
SUZUKI-SAN.
YUUKI-SAN HAS ONLY JUST RECENTLY BECOME PART OF THIS ADMIN-ISTRATION.
PLEASE REFRAIN FROM CROSS EXAMINING HIM.

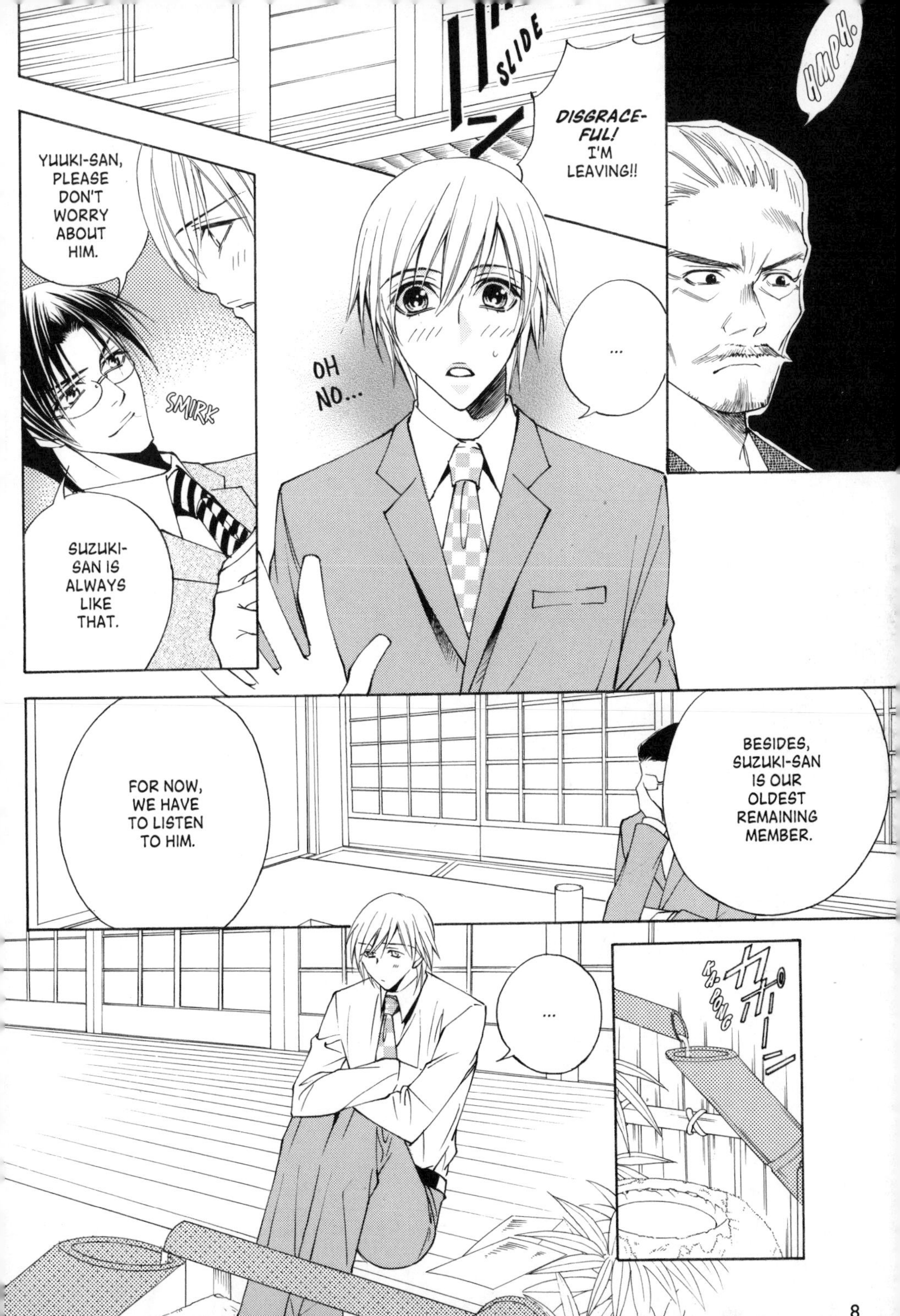
HMPH.
SLIDE
DISGRACE-FUL! I'M LEAVING!!
...
OH NO...
YUUKI-SAN, PLEASE DON'T WORRY ABOUT HIM.
SMIRK
SUZUKI-SAN IS ALWAYS LIKE THAT.
BESIDES, SUZUKI-SAN IS OUR OLDEST REMAINING MEMBER.
FOR NOW, WE HAVE TO LISTEN TO HIM.
KA-PONG
...

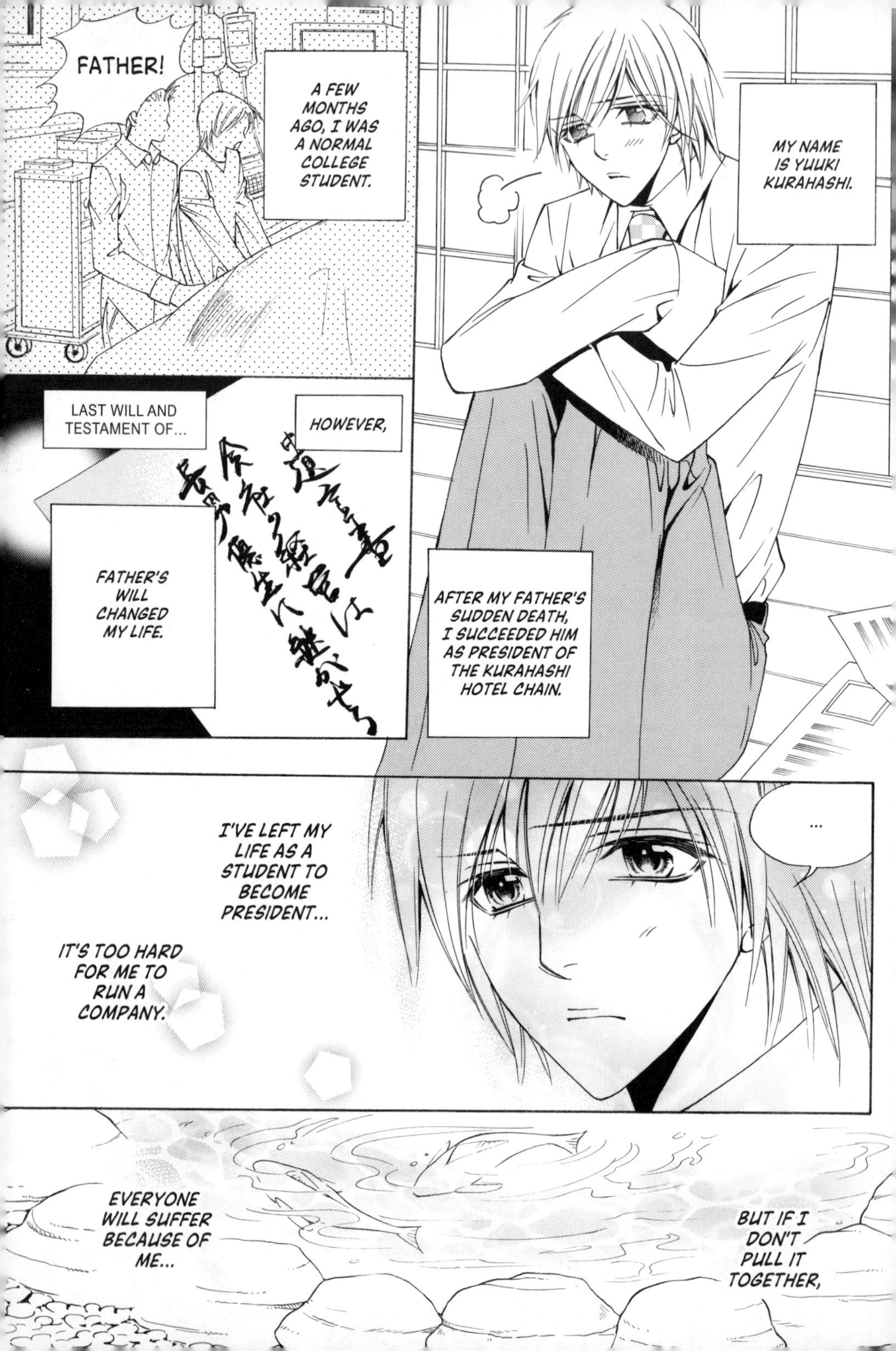
MY NAME IS YUUKI KURAHASHI.
AFTER MY FATHER'S SUDDEN DEATH, I SUCCEEDED HIM AS PRESIDENT OF THE KURAHASHI HOTEL CHAIN.
A FEW MONTHS AGO, I WAS A NORMAL COLLEGE STUDENT.
FATHER!
HOWEVER,
LAST WILL AND TESTAMENT OF...
FATHER'S WILL CHANGED MY LIFE.
...
I'VE LEFT MY LIFE AS A STUDENT TO BECOME PRESIDENT...
IT'S TOO HARD FOR ME TO RUN A COMPANY.
BUT IF I DON'T PULL IT TOGETHER,
EVERYONE WILL SUFFER BECAUSE OF ME...

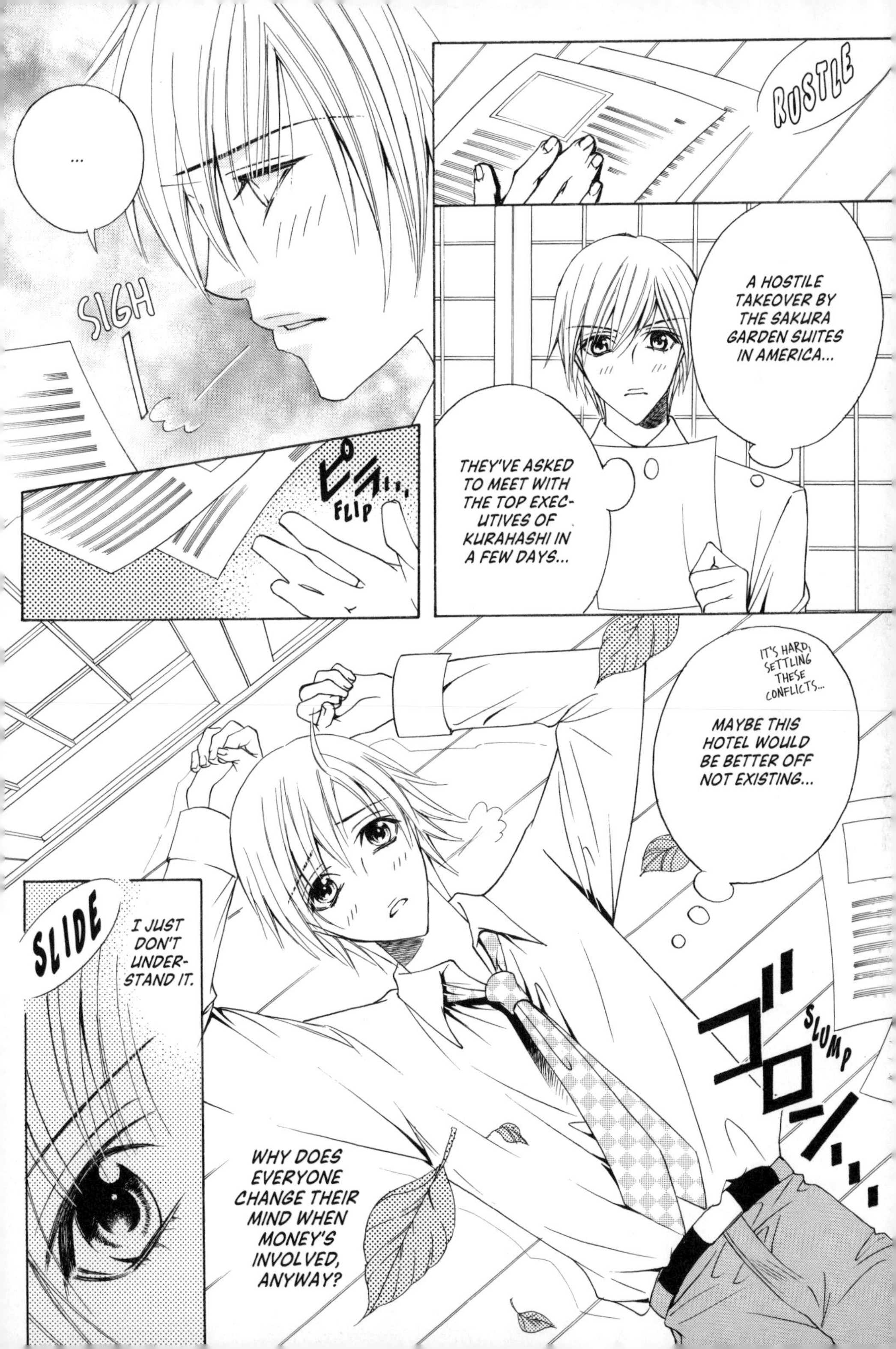
RUSTLE
A HOSTILE TAKEOVER BY THE SAKURA GARDEN SUITES IN AMERICA...
THEY'VE ASKED TO MEET WITH THE TOP EXEC-UTIVES OF KURAHASHI IN A FEW DAYS...
...
SIGH
ピラ...
FLIP
IT'S HARD, SETTLING THESE CONFLICTS...
MAYBE THIS HOTEL WOULD BE BETTER OFF NOT EXISTING...
ゴローン...
SLUMP
SLIDE
I JUST DON'T UNDER-STAND IT.
WHY DOES EVERYONE CHANGE THEIR MIND WHEN MONEY'S INVOLVED, ANYWAY?

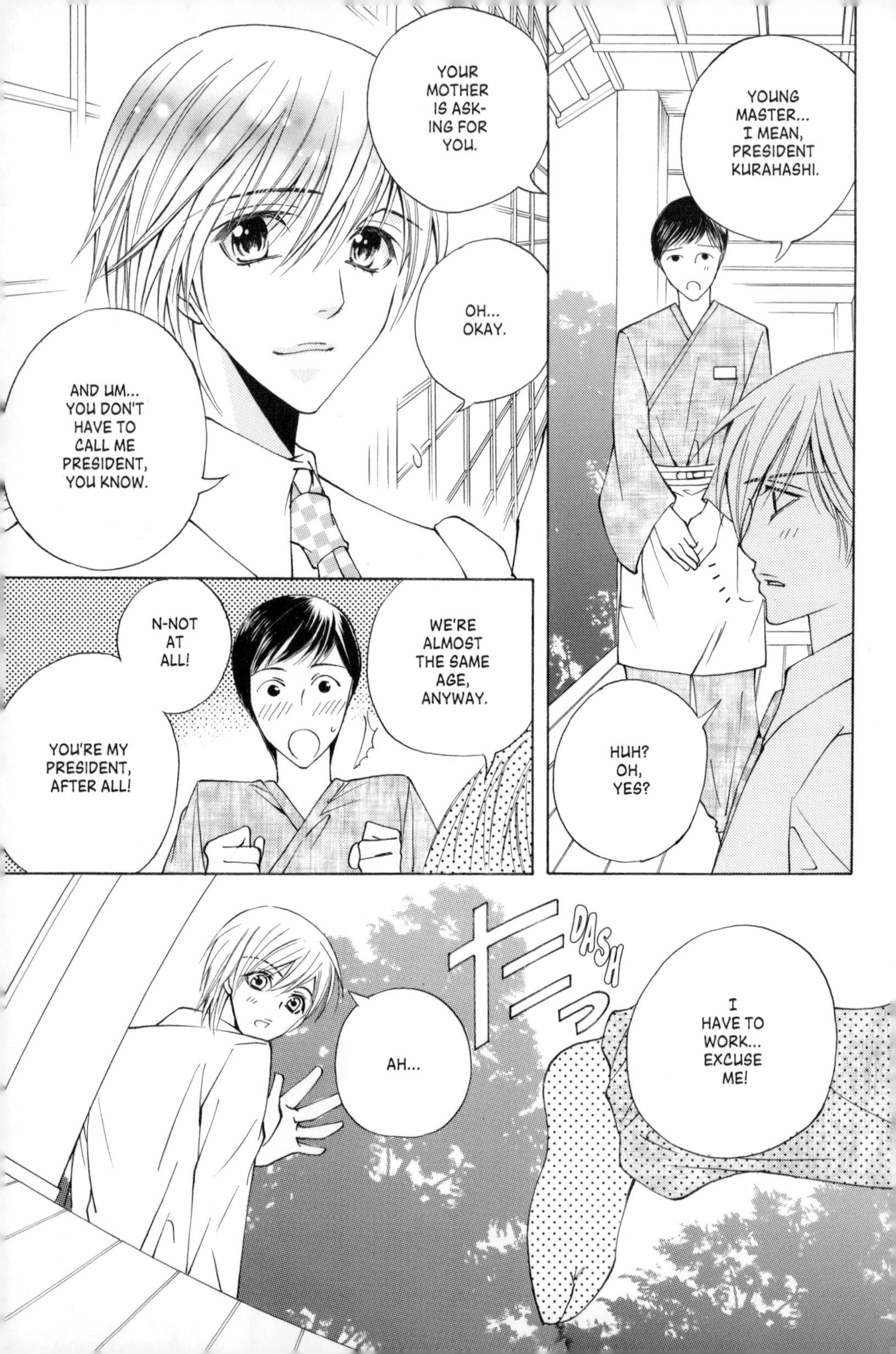

YOUNG MASTER... I MEAN, PRESIDENT KURAHASHI.
HUH? OH, YES?
YOUR MOTHER IS ASKING FOR YOU.
OH... OKAY.
AND UM... YOU DON'T HAVE TO CALL ME PRESIDENT, YOU KNOW.
WE'RE ALMOST THE SAME AGE, ANYWAY.
N-NOT AT ALL!
YOU'RE MY PRESIDENT, AFTER ALL!
DASH
I HAVE TO WORK... EXCUSE ME!
AH...

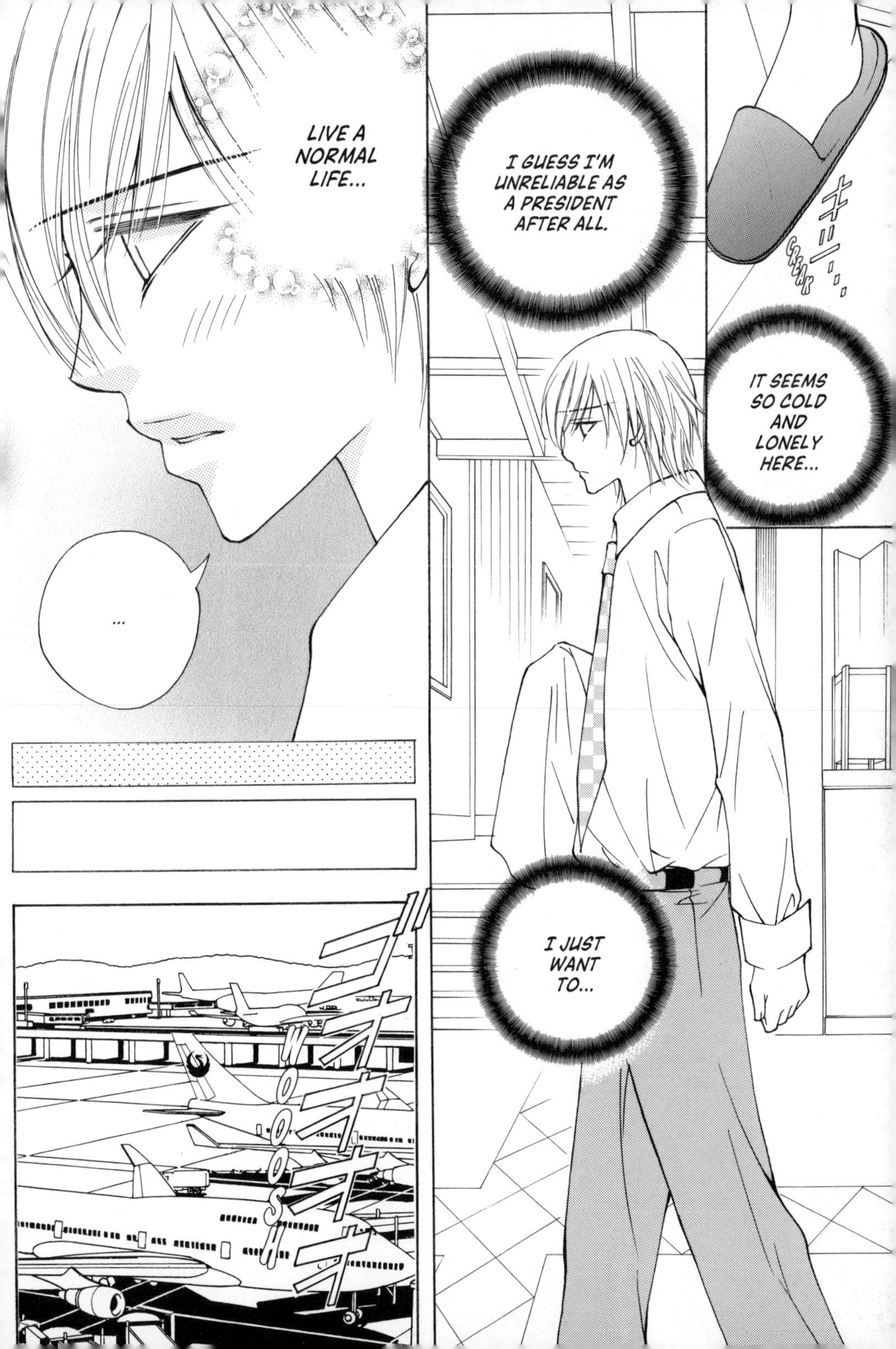
CREAK
I GUESS I'M UNRELIABLE AS A PRESIDENT AFTER ALL.
IT SEEMS SO COLD AND LONELY HERE...
I JUST WANT TO...
LIVE A NORMAL LIFE...
...
WOOOOSH

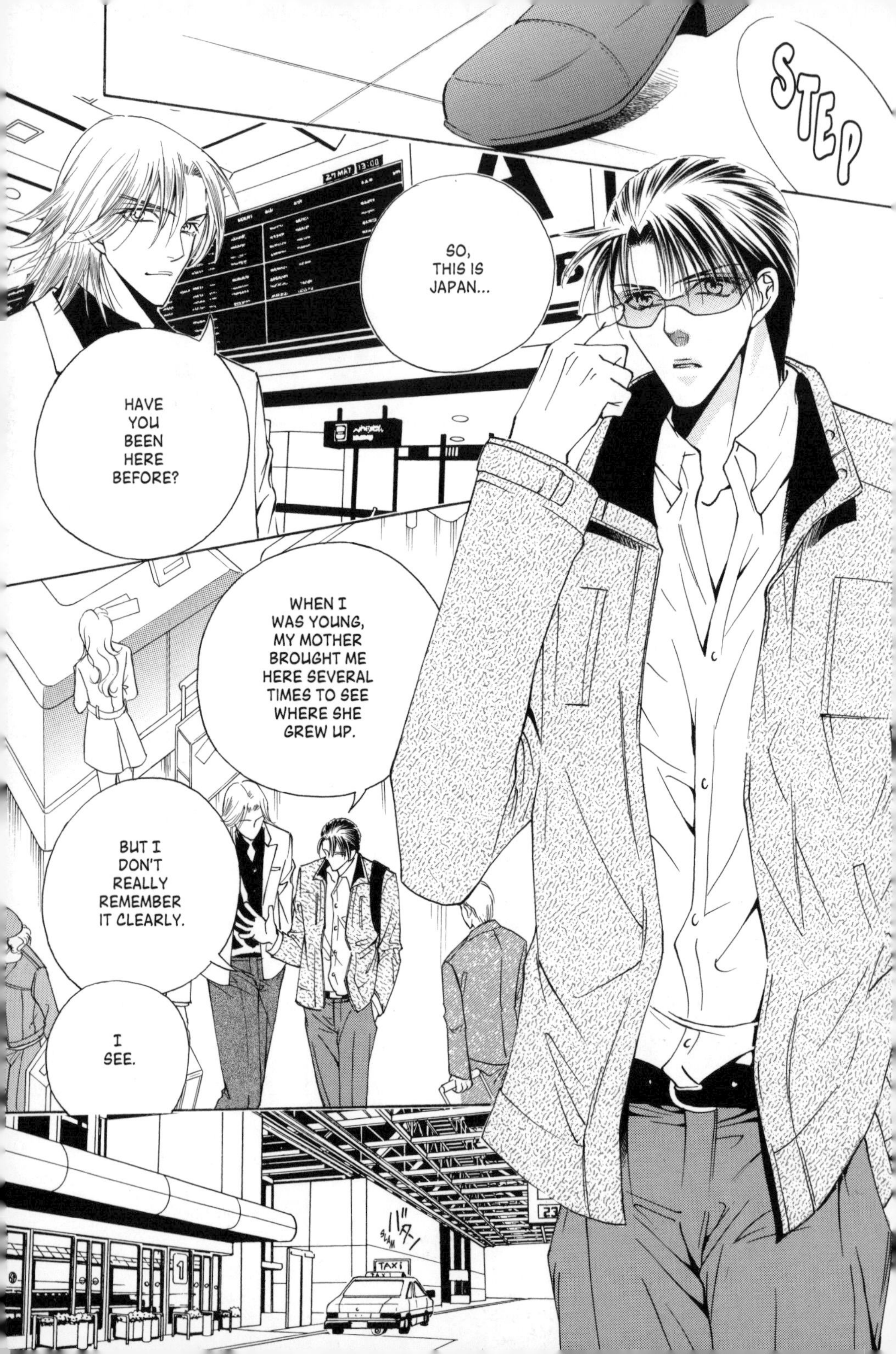
STEP
SO, THIS IS JAPAN...
HAVE YOU BEEN HERE BEFORE?
WHEN I WAS YOUNG, MY MOTHER BROUGHT ME HERE SEVERAL TIMES TO SEE WHERE SHE GREW UP.
BUT I DON'T REALLY REMEMBER IT CLEARLY.
I SEE.
TAXI
SLAM

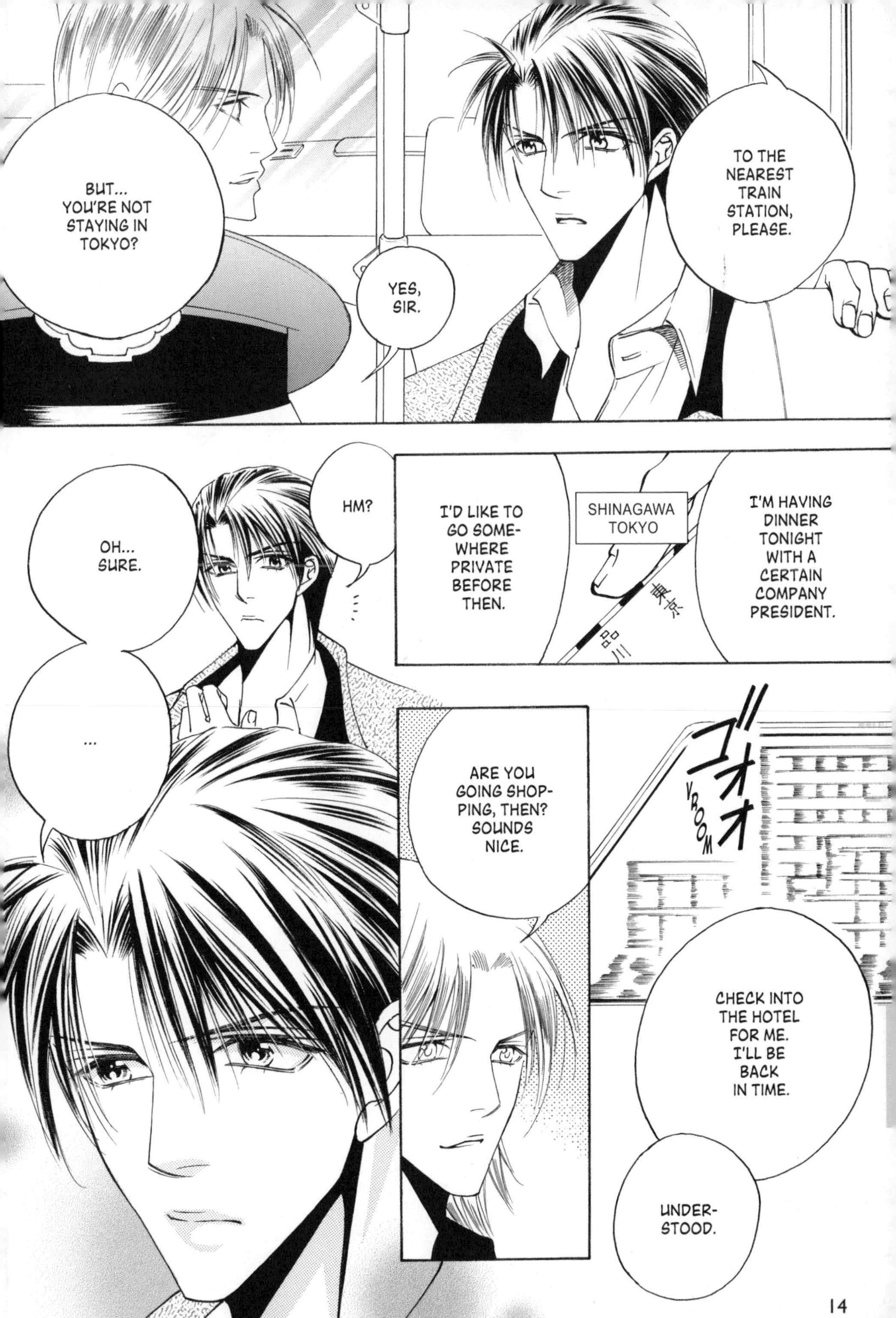
TO THE NEAREST TRAIN STATION, PLEASE.
YES, SIR.
BUT... YOU'RE NOT STAYING IN TOKYO?
I'M HAVING DINNER TONIGHT WITH A CERTAIN COMPANY PRESIDENT.
SHINAGAWA TOKYO
I'D LIKE TO GO SOME-WHERE PRIVATE BEFORE THEN.
VROOM
CHECK INTO THE HOTEL FOR ME. I'LL BE BACK IN TIME.
UNDER-STOOD.
ARE YOU GOING SHOP-PING, THEN? SOUNDS NICE.
HM?
OH... SURE.
...

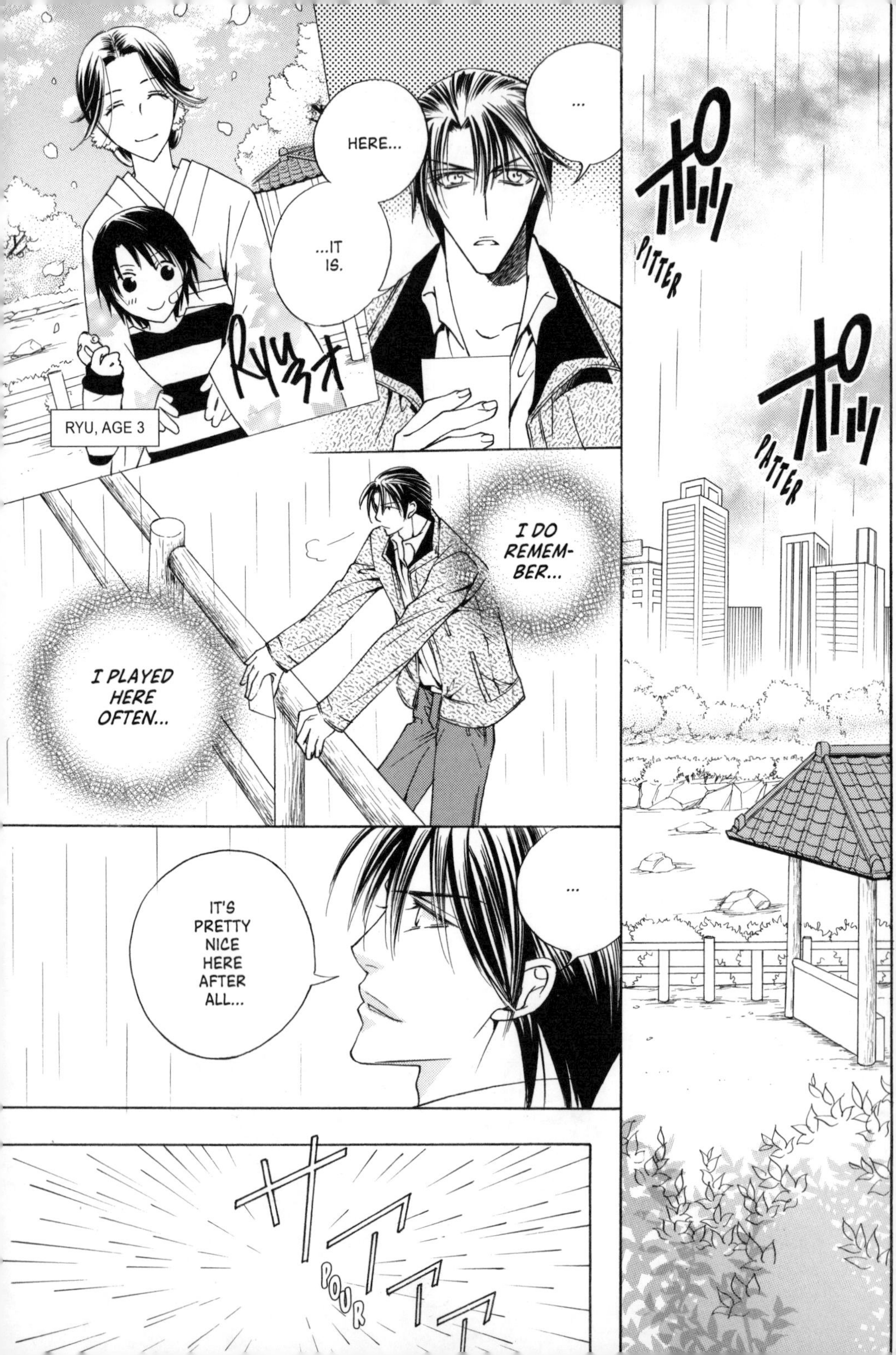

ポツ
PITTER
ポツ
PATTER
...
HERE...
...IT IS.
RYU, AGE 3
I DO REMEM-BER...
I PLAYED HERE OFTEN...
...
IT'S PRETTY NICE HERE AFTER ALL...
サァァァ
POUR

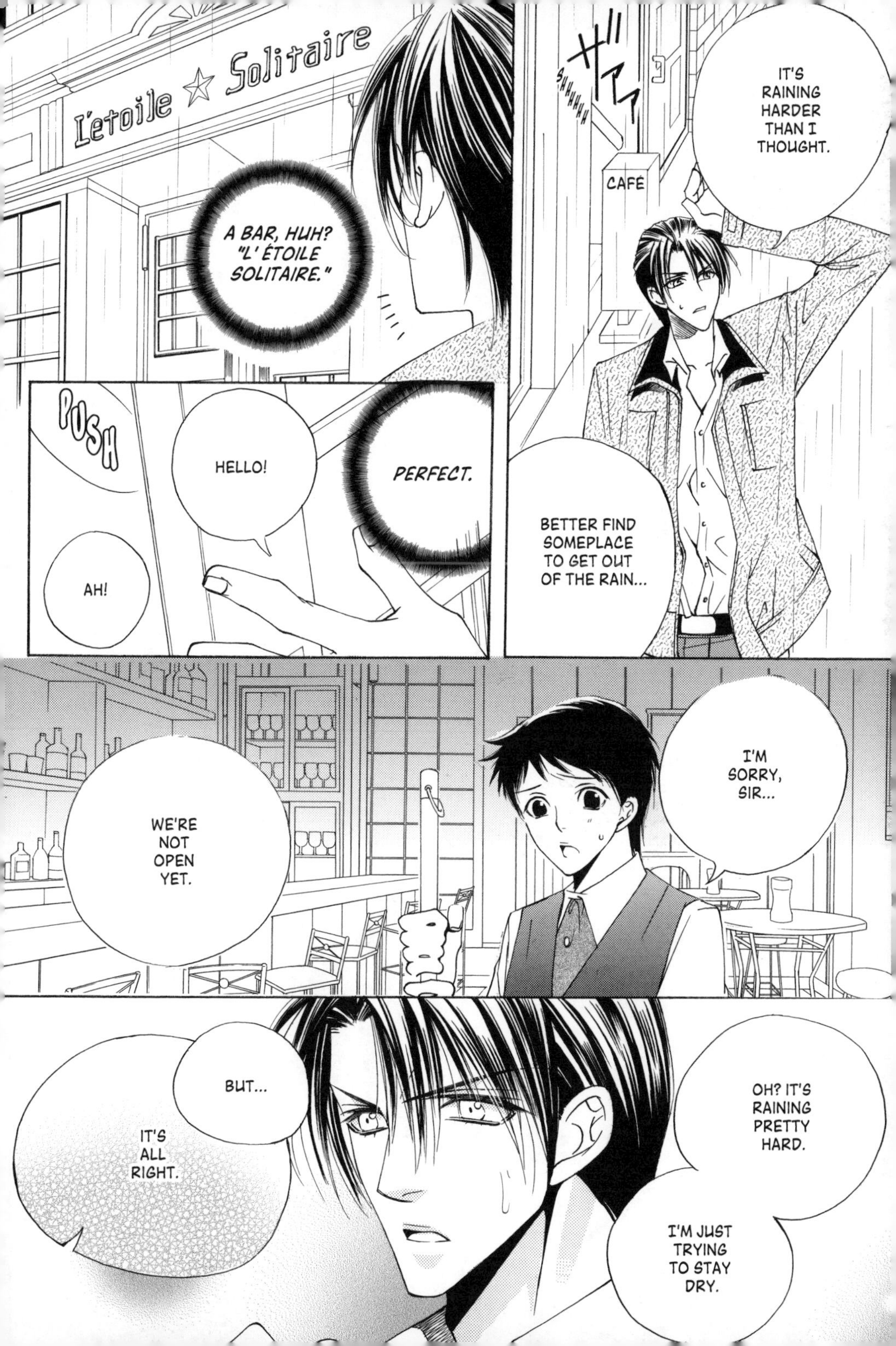
ザアア
SHHHHHH
IT'S RAINING HARDER THAN I THOUGHT.
CAFÉ
BETTER FIND SOMEPLACE TO GET OUT OF THE RAIN...
L'etoile ☆ Solitaire
A BAR, HUH? "L' ÉTOILE SOLITAIRE."
PERFECT.
HELLO!
PUSH
AH!
I'M SORRY, SIR...
WE'RE NOT OPEN YET.
OH? IT'S RAINING PRETTY HARD.
I'M JUST TRYING TO STAY DRY.
BUT...
IT'S ALL RIGHT.

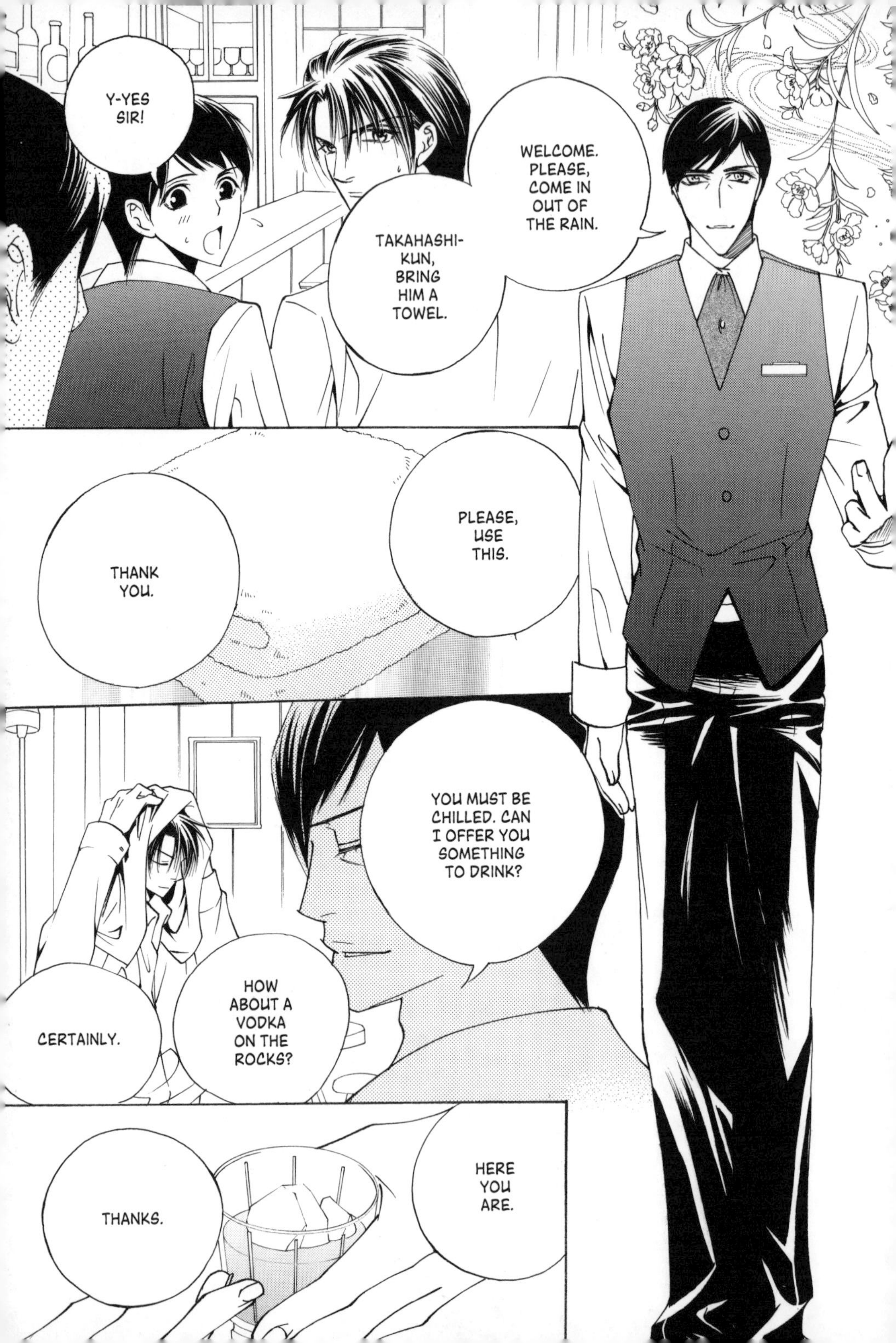
WELCOME. PLEASE, COME IN OUT OF THE RAIN.
TAKAHASHI-KUN, BRING HIM A TOWEL.
Y-YES SIR!
PLEASE, USE THIS.
THANK YOU.
YOU MUST BE CHILLED. CAN I OFFER YOU SOMETHING TO DRINK?
HOW ABOUT A VODKA ON THE ROCKS?
CERTAINLY.
HERE YOU ARE.
THANKS.

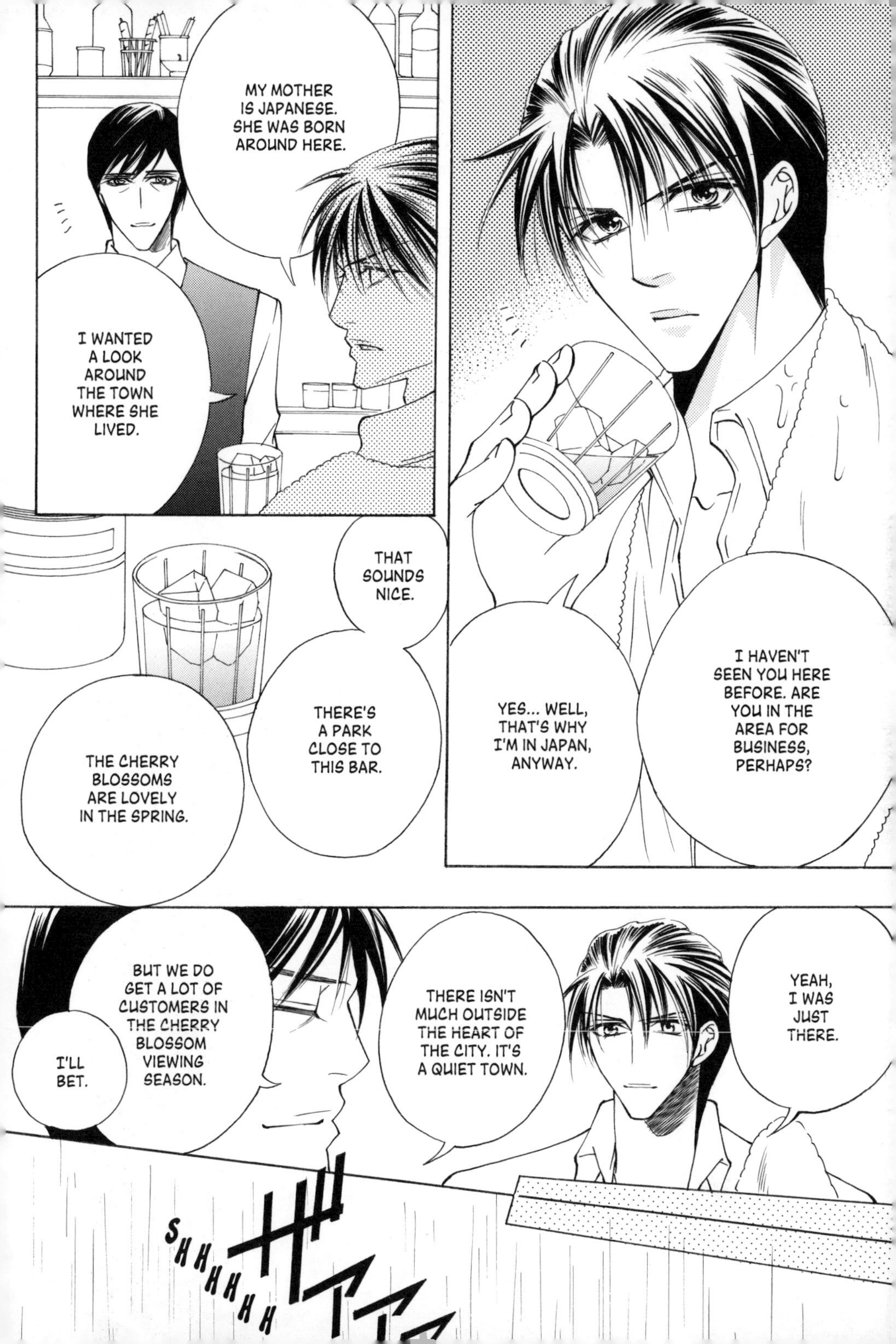
I HAVEN'T SEEN YOU HERE BEFORE. ARE YOU IN THE AREA FOR BUSINESS, PERHAPS?
YES... WELL, THAT'S WHY I'M IN JAPAN, ANYWAY.
MY MOTHER IS JAPANESE. SHE WAS BORN AROUND HERE.
I WANTED A LOOK AROUND THE TOWN WHERE SHE LIVED.
THAT SOUNDS NICE.
THERE'S A PARK CLOSE TO THIS BAR.
THE CHERRY BLOSSOMS ARE LOVELY IN THE SPRING.
YEAH, I WAS JUST THERE.
THERE ISN'T MUCH OUTSIDE THE HEART OF THE CITY. IT'S A QUIET TOWN.
BUT WE DO GET A LOT OF CUSTOMERS IN THE CHERRY BLOSSOM VIEWING SEASON.
I'LL BET.
SHHHHHH

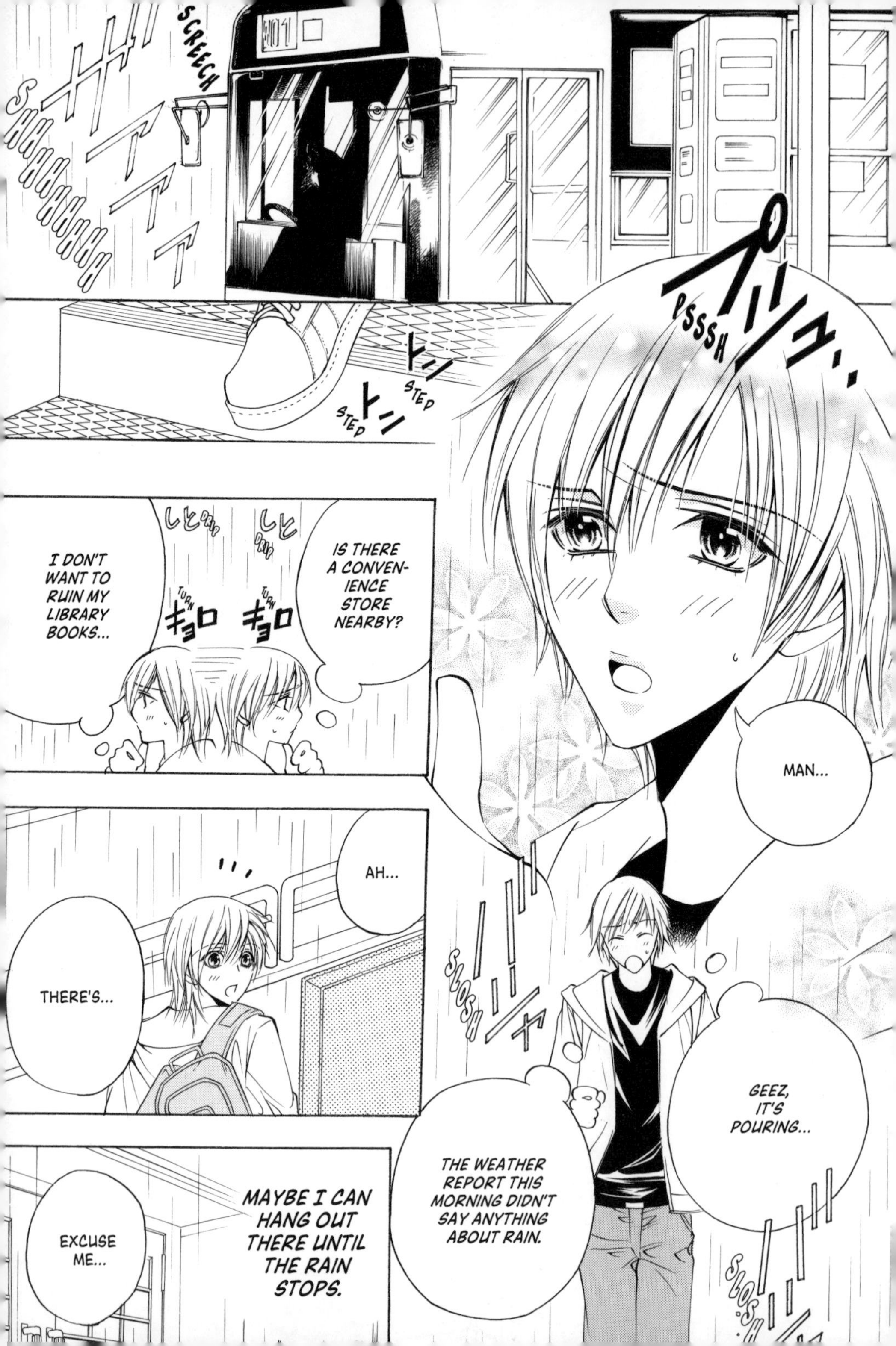
SHAAAAAA
SCREECH
PSSSH
MAN...
GEEZ, IT'S POURING...
THE WEATHER REPORT THIS MORNING DIDN'T SAY ANYTHING ABOUT RAIN.
SLOSH
SLOSH
STEP
STEP
IS THERE A CONVEN-IENCE STORE NEARBY?
DRIP
DRIP
TURN
TURN
I DON'T WANT TO RUIN MY LIBRARY BOOKS...
AH...
THERE'S...
MAYBE I CAN HANG OUT THERE UNTIL THE RAIN STOPS.
EXCUSE ME...

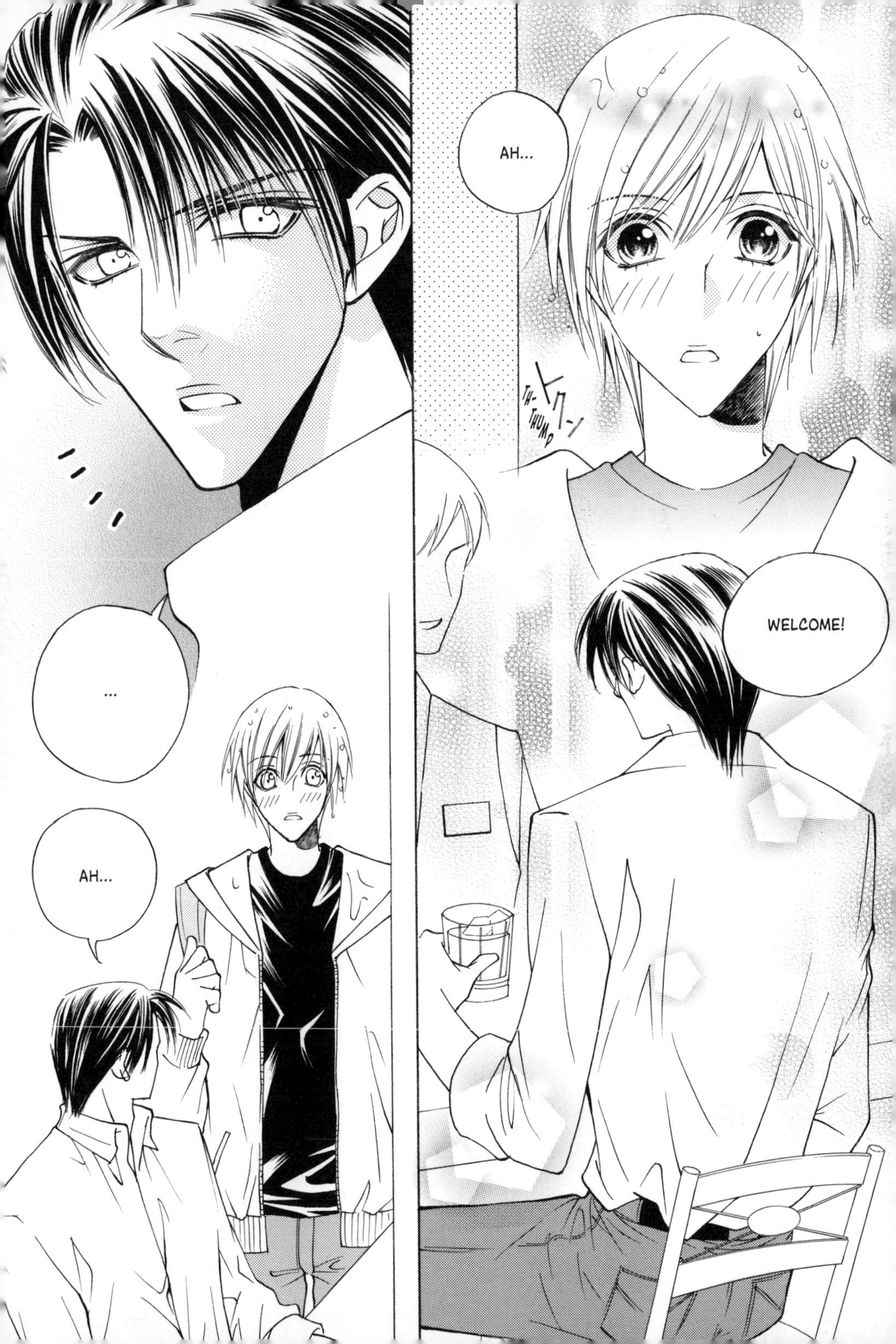
AH...
TH-THUMP
WELCOME!
...
AH...

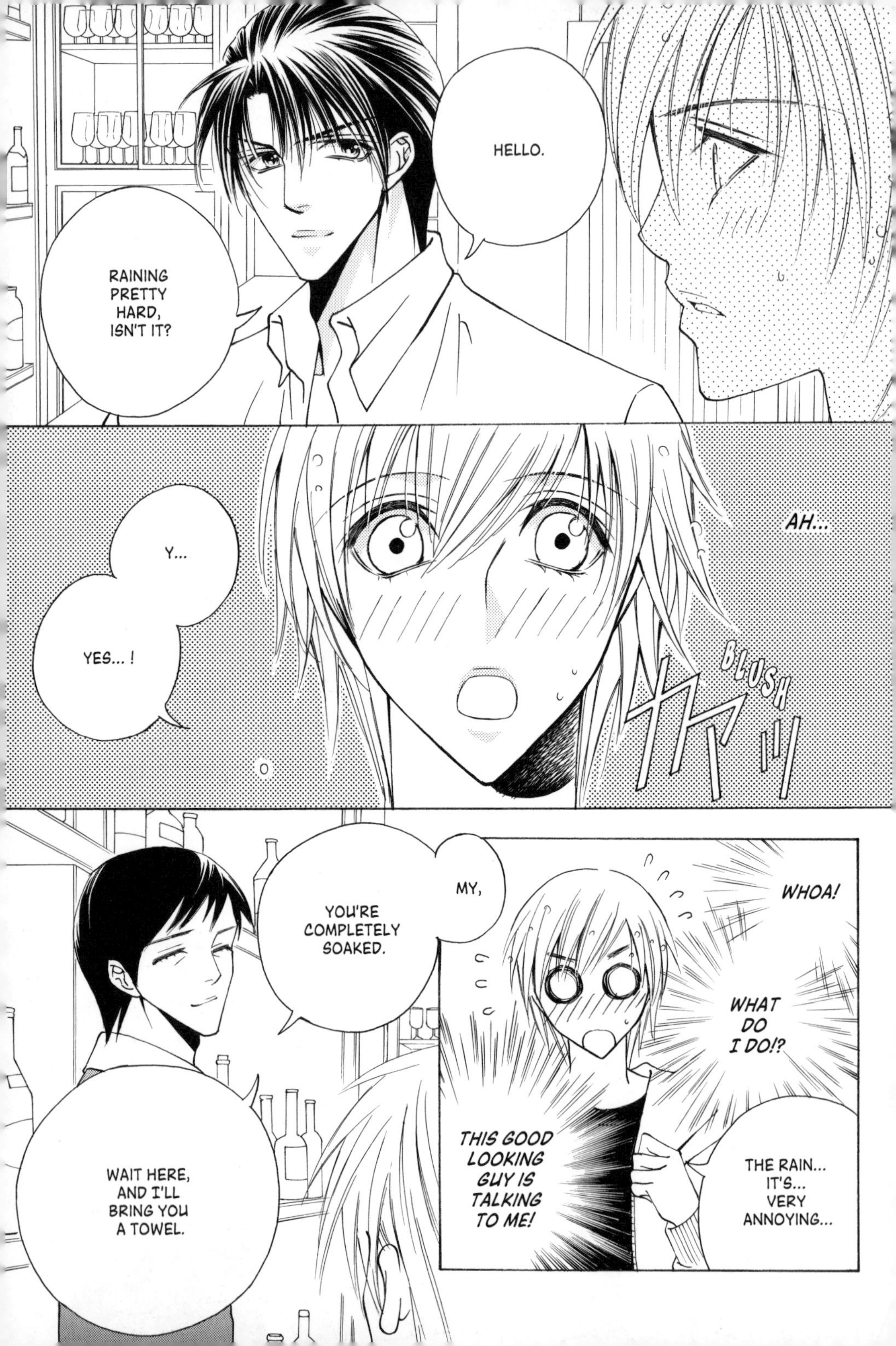
HELLO.
RAINING PRETTY HARD, ISN'T IT?
AH...
BLUSH
Y...
YES...!
WHOA!
WHAT DO I DO!?
THIS GOOD LOOKING GUY IS TALKING TO ME!
THE RAIN... IT'S... VERY ANNOYING...
MY,
YOU'RE COMPLETELY SOAKED.
WAIT HERE, AND I'LL BRING YOU A TOWEL.

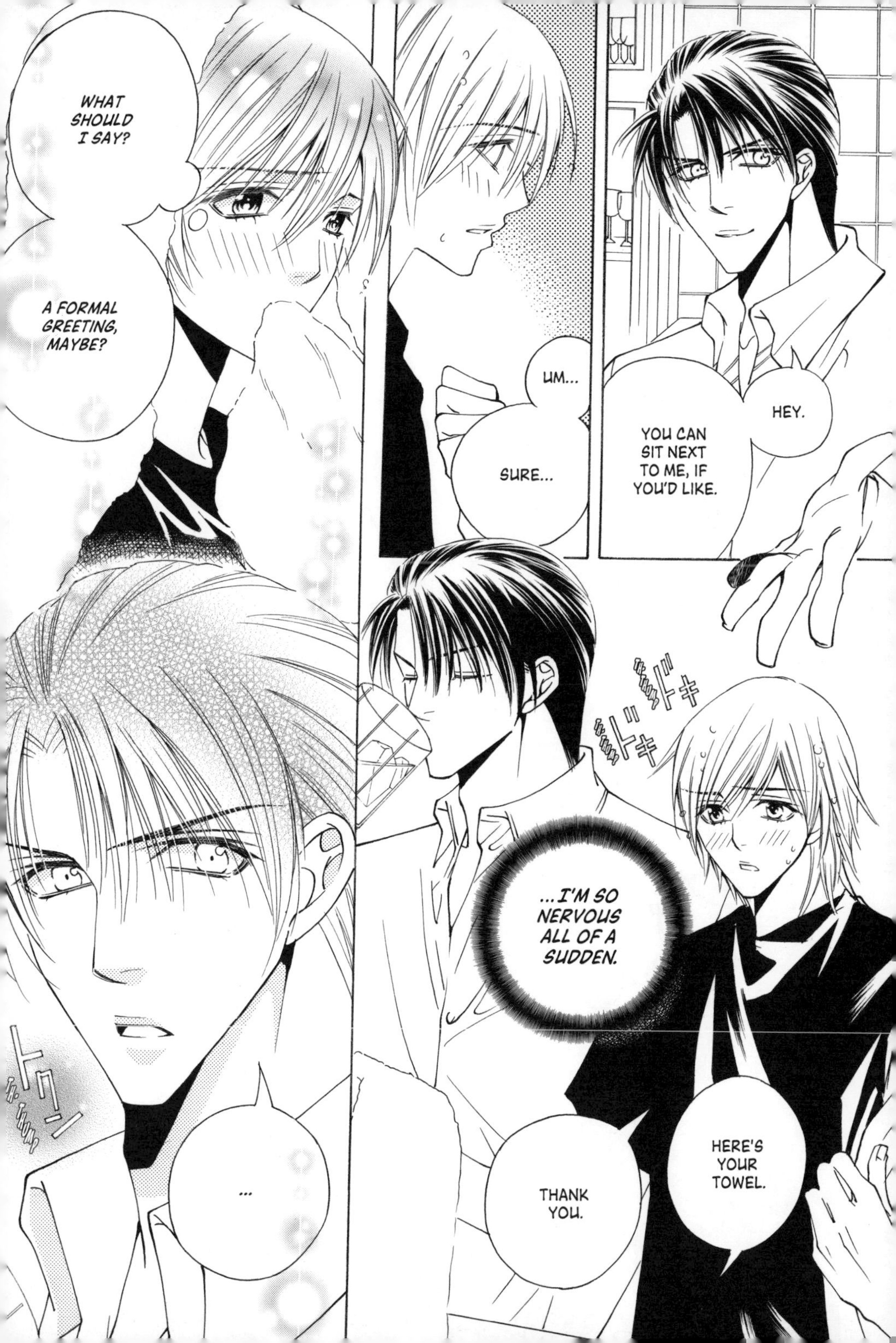
HEY.
YOU CAN SIT NEXT TO ME, IF YOU'D LIKE.
UM...
SURE...
...I'M SO NERVOUS ALL OF A SUDDEN.
HERE'S YOUR TOWEL.
THANK YOU.
WHAT SHOULD I SAY?
A FORMAL GREETING, MAYBE?
...

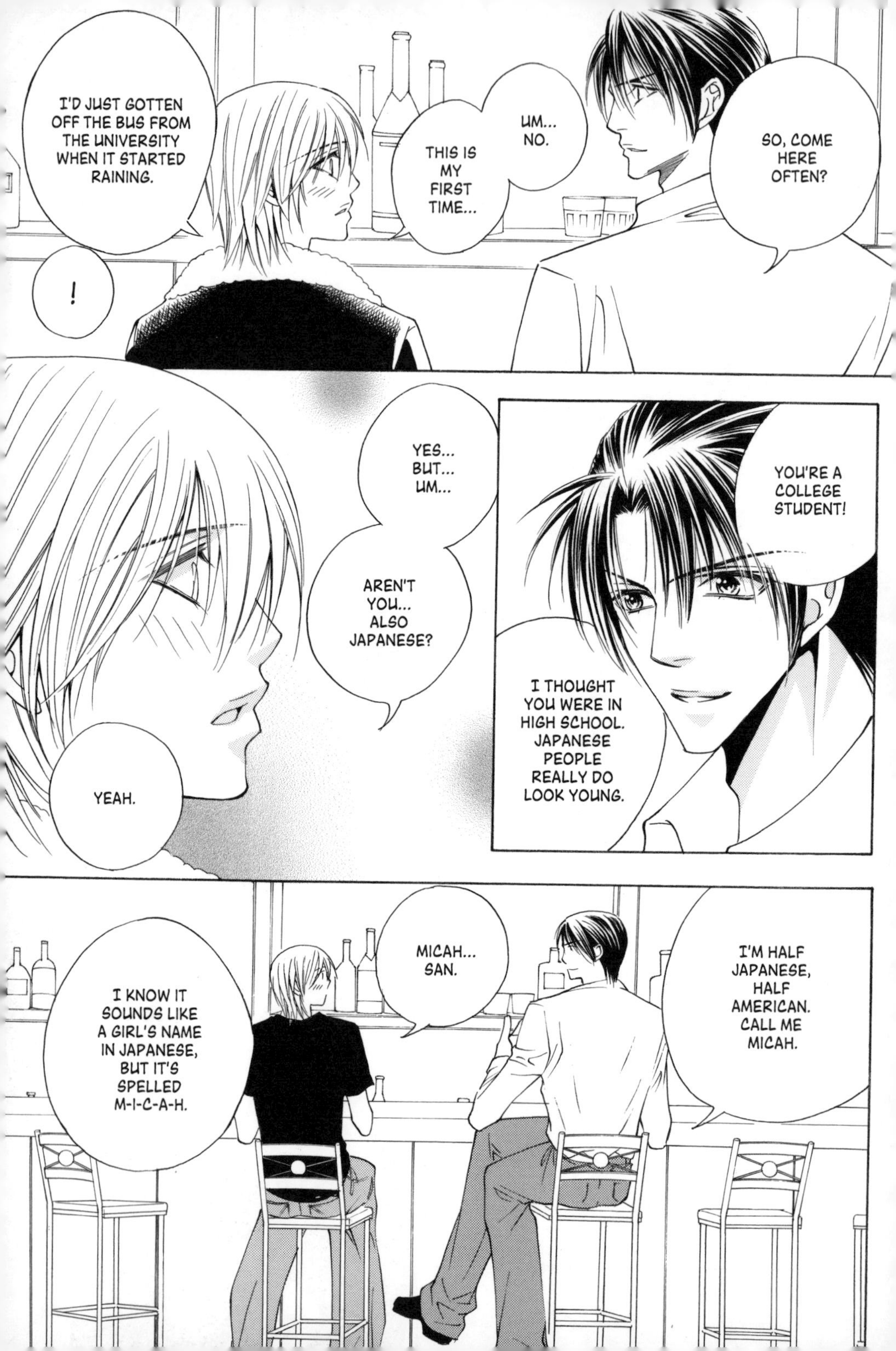
SO, COME HERE OFTEN?
UM... NO.
THIS IS MY FIRST TIME...
I'D JUST GOTTEN OFF THE BUS FROM THE UNIVERSITY WHEN IT STARTED RAINING.
!
YOU'RE A COLLEGE STUDENT!
I THOUGHT YOU WERE IN HIGH SCHOOL. JAPANESE PEOPLE REALLY DO LOOK YOUNG.
YES... BUT... UM...
AREN'T YOU... ALSO JAPANESE?
YEAH.
I'M HALF JAPANESE, HALF AMERICAN. CALL ME MICAH.
MICAH... SAN.
I KNOW IT SOUNDS LIKE A GIRL'S NAME IN JAPANESE, BUT IT'S SPELLED M-I-C-A-H.

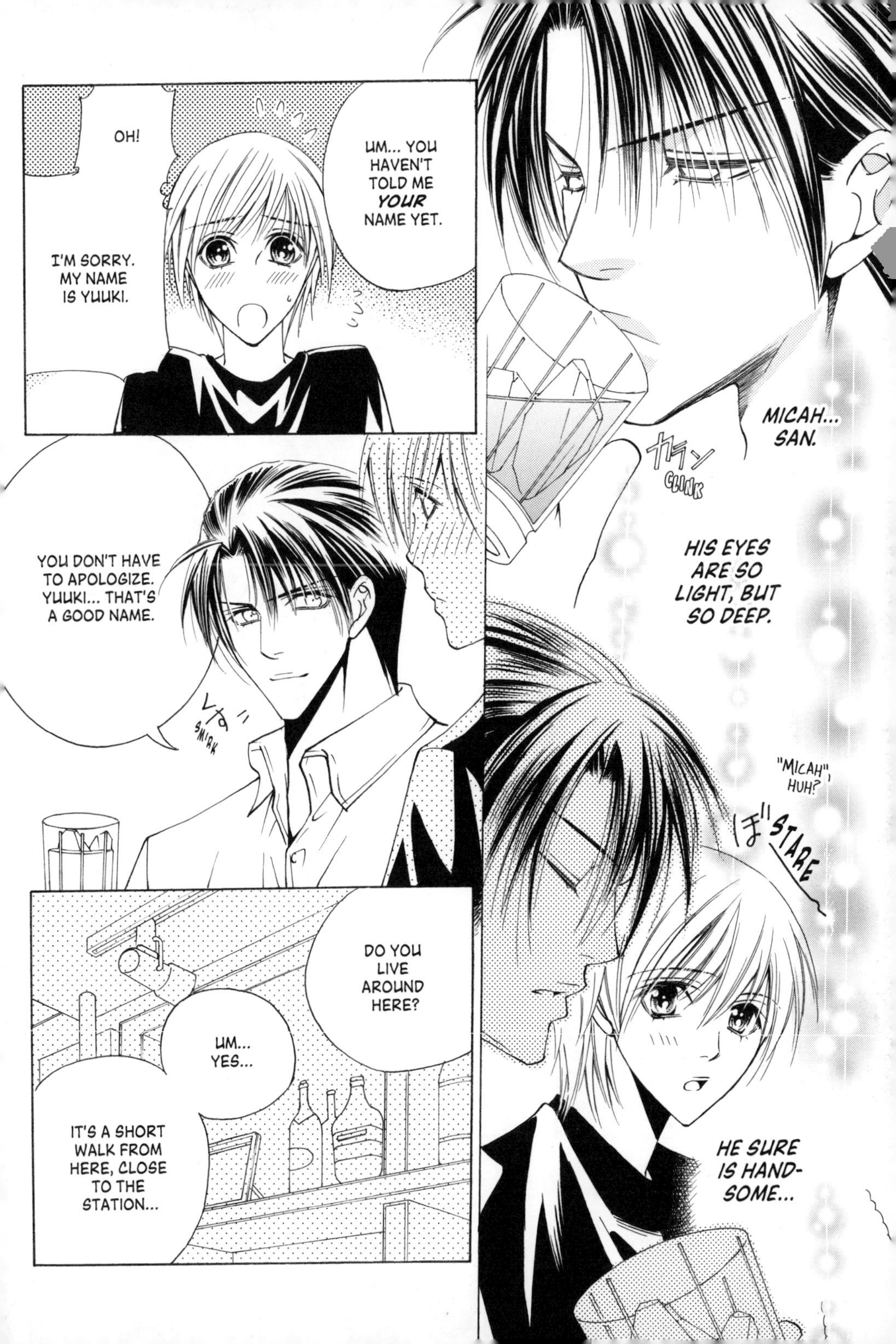
MICAH... SAN.
カラン
CLINK
HIS EYES ARE SO LIGHT, BUT SO DEEP.
"MICAH", HUH?
STARE
HE SURE IS HAND-SOME...
UM... YOU HAVEN'T TOLD ME *YOUR* NAME YET.
OH!
I'M SORRY. MY NAME IS YUUKI.
YOU DON'T HAVE TO APOLOGIZE. YUUKI... THAT'S A GOOD NAME.
SMIRK
DO YOU LIVE AROUND HERE?
UM... YES...
IT'S A SHORT WALK FROM HERE, CLOSE TO THE STATION...

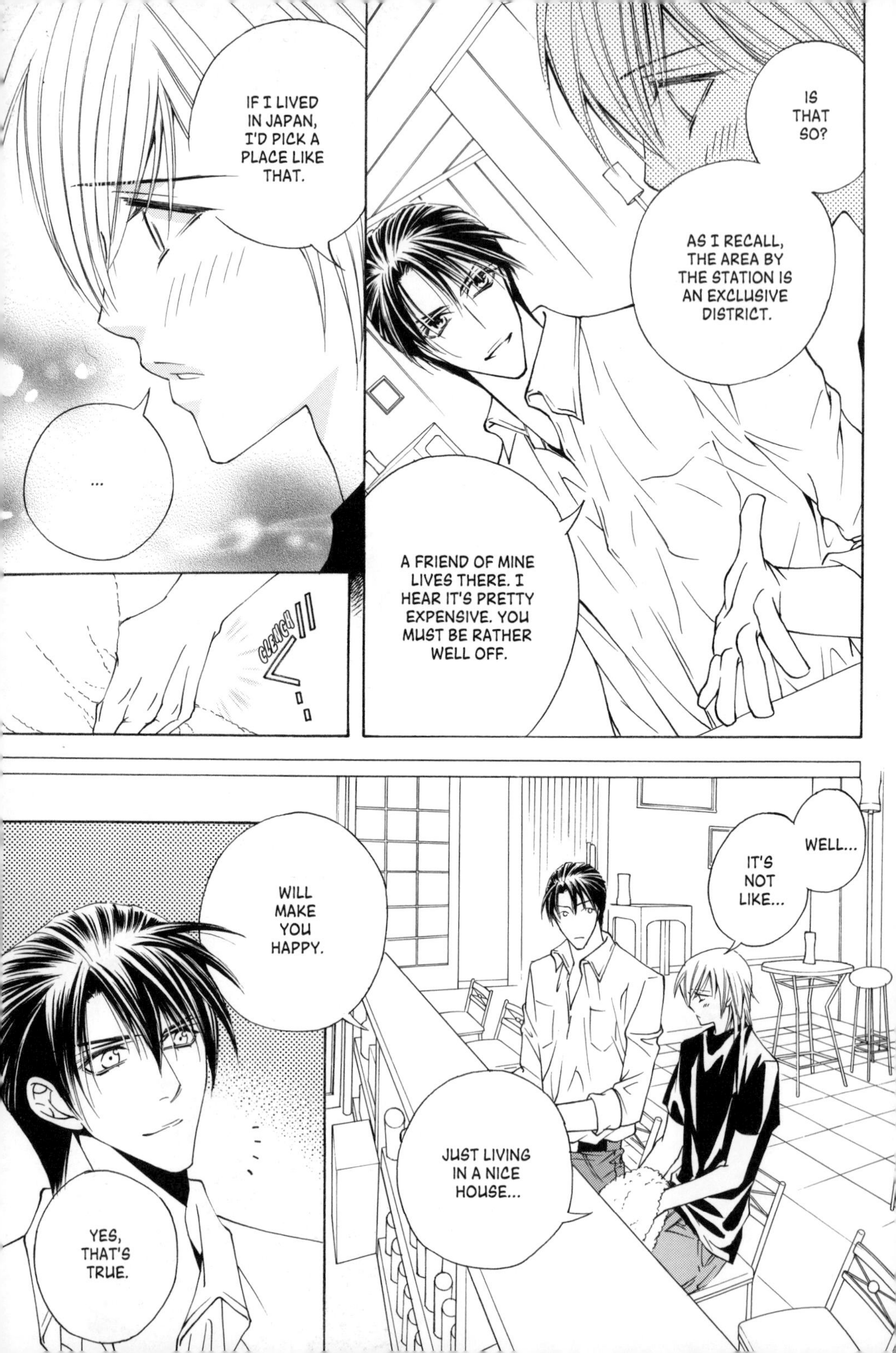
IS THAT SO?
AS I RECALL, THE AREA BY THE STATION IS AN EXCLUSIVE DISTRICT.
A FRIEND OF MINE LIVES THERE. I HEAR IT'S PRETTY EXPENSIVE. YOU MUST BE RATHER WELL OFF.
IF I LIVED IN JAPAN, I'D PICK A PLACE LIKE THAT.
...
CLENCH
WELL...
IT'S NOT LIKE...
JUST LIVING IN A NICE HOUSE...
WILL MAKE YOU HAPPY.
YES, THAT'S TRUE.

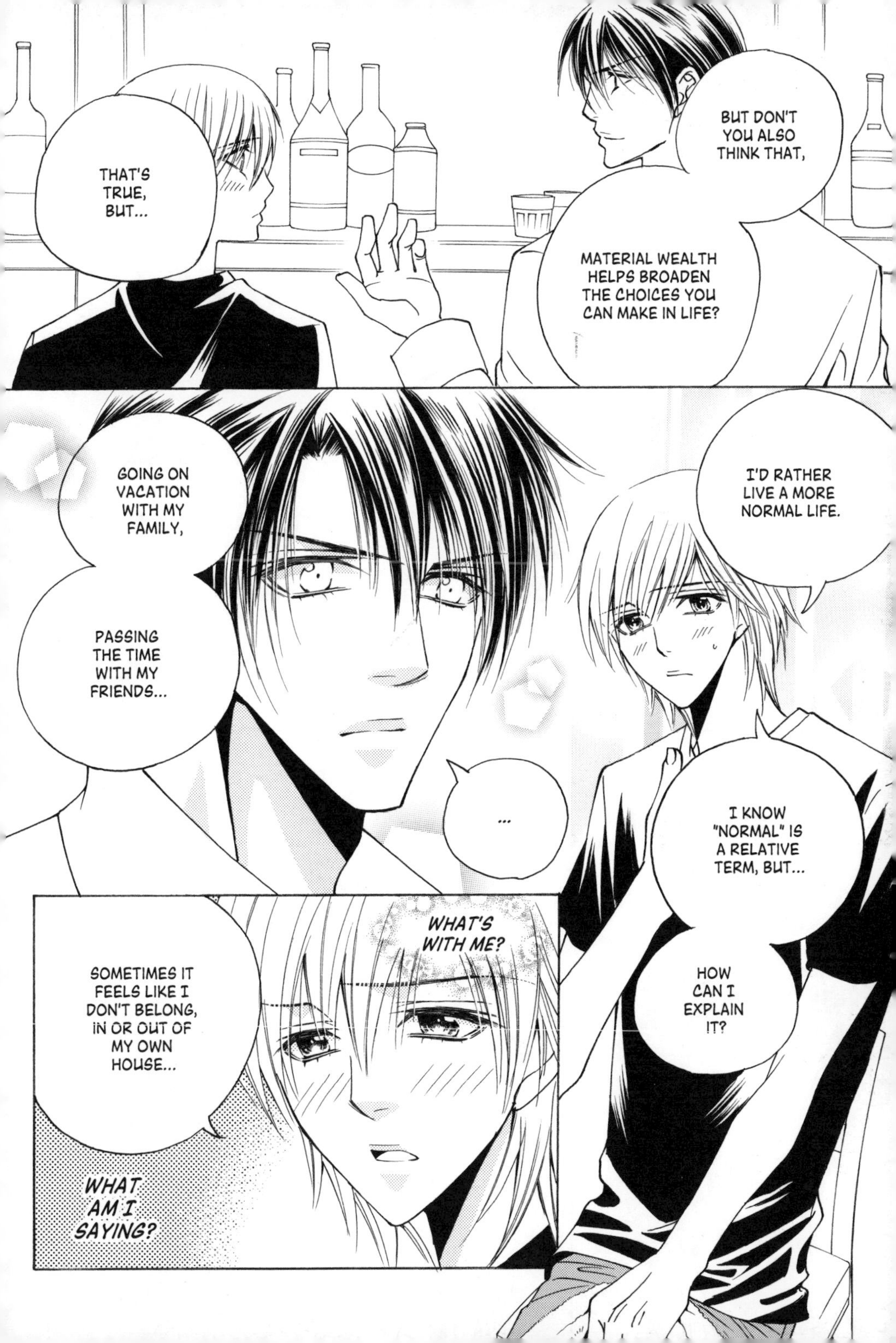
BUT DON'T YOU ALSO THINK THAT,
MATERIAL WEALTH HELPS BROADEN THE CHOICES YOU CAN MAKE IN LIFE?
THAT'S TRUE, BUT...
I'D RATHER LIVE A MORE NORMAL LIFE.
GOING ON VACATION WITH MY FAMILY,
PASSING THE TIME WITH MY FRIENDS...
...
I KNOW "NORMAL" IS A RELATIVE TERM, BUT...
HOW CAN I EXPLAIN IT?
WHAT'S WITH ME?
SOMETIMES IT FEELS LIKE I DON'T BELONG, IN OR OUT OF MY OWN HOUSE...
WHAT AM I SAYING?

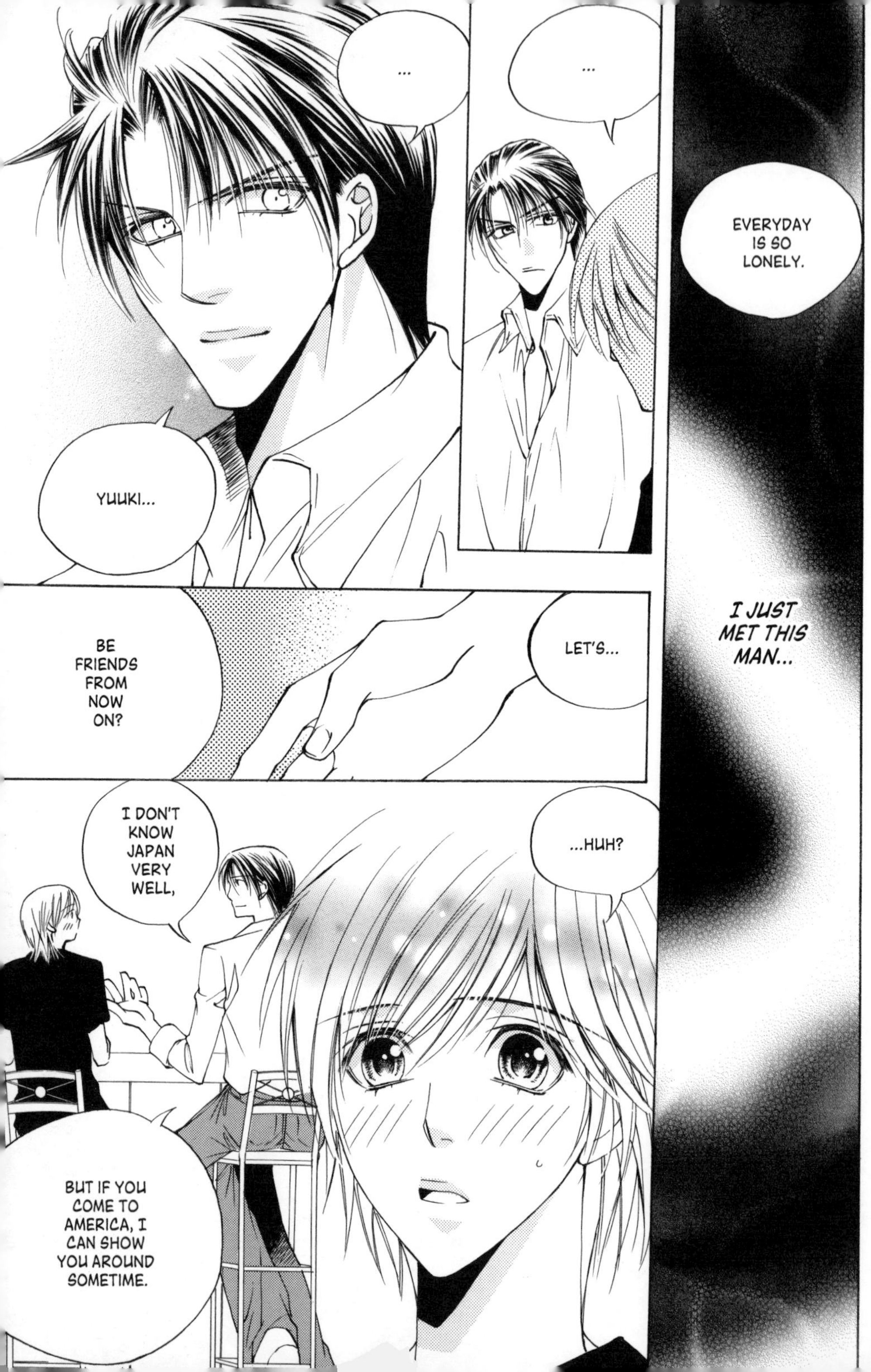
EVERYDAY IS SO LONELY.
I JUST MET THIS MAN...
...
...
YUUKI...
LET'S...
BE FRIENDS FROM NOW ON?
...HUH?
I DON'T KNOW JAPAN VERY WELL,
BUT IF YOU COME TO AMERICA, I CAN SHOW YOU AROUND SOMETIME.

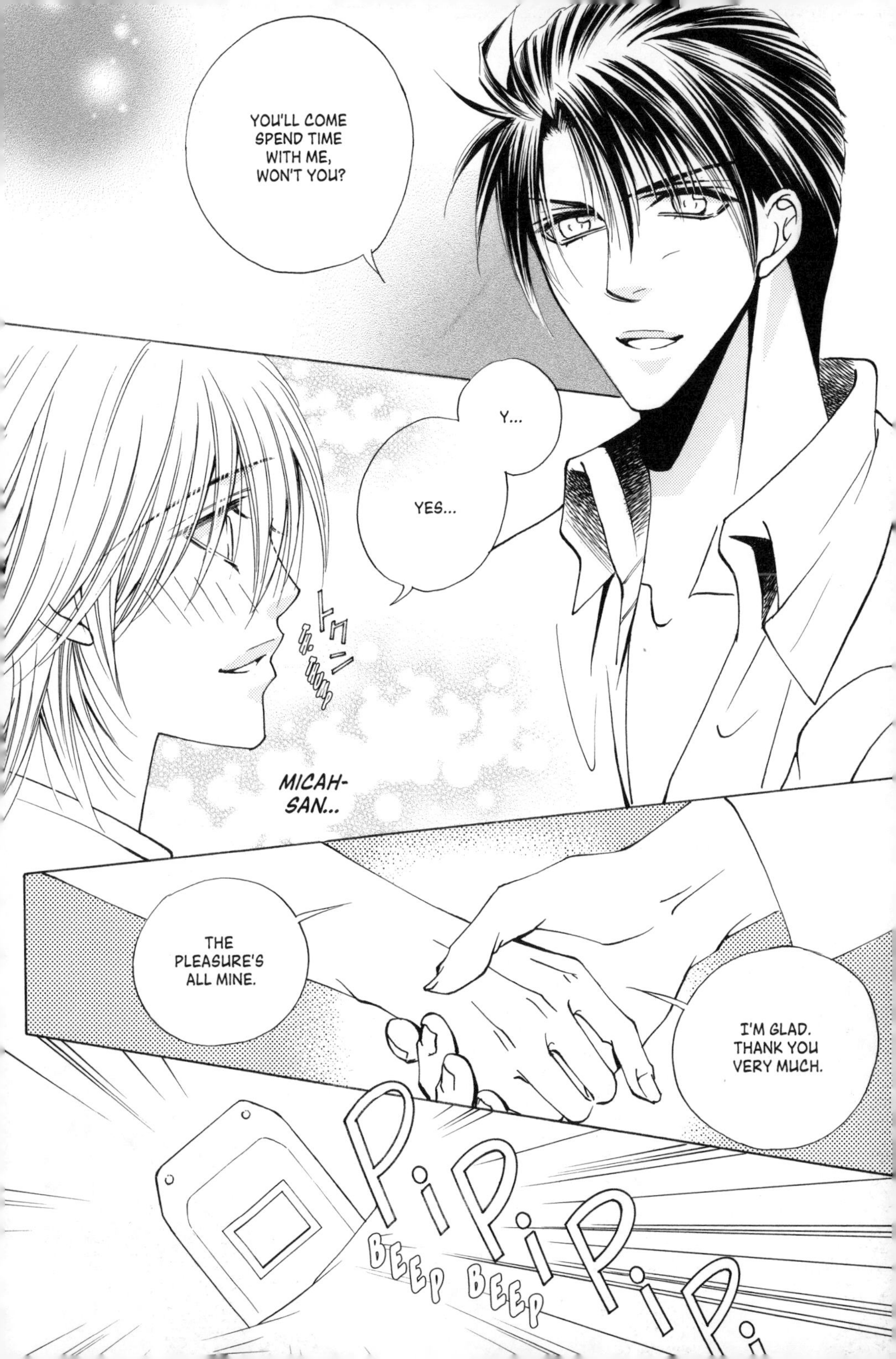
YOU'LL COME SPEND TIME WITH ME, WON'T YOU?
Y...
YES...
トクン
TH-THUMP
MICAH-SAN...
I'M GLAD. THANK YOU VERY MUCH.
THE PLEASURE'S ALL MINE.
PIPIPIPI
BEEP BEEP

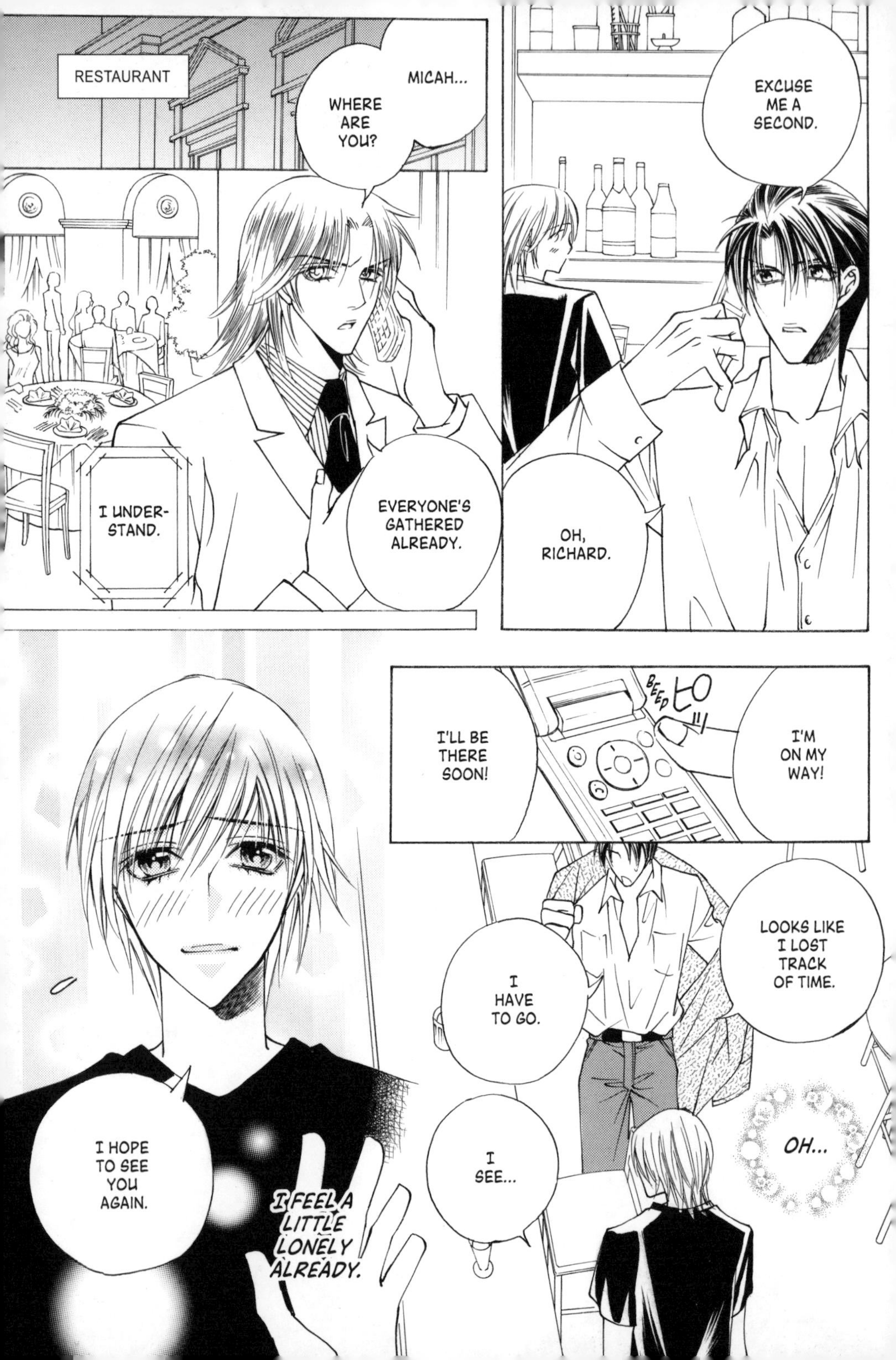
EXCUSE ME A SECOND.
OH, RICHARD.
RESTAURANT
MICAH... WHERE ARE YOU?
EVERYONE'S GATHERED ALREADY.
I UNDERSTAND.
I'M ON MY WAY!
BEEP
I'LL BE THERE SOON!
LOOKS LIKE I LOST TRACK OF TIME.
I HAVE TO GO.
OH...
I SEE...
I HOPE TO SEE YOU AGAIN.
I FEEL A LITTLE LONELY ALREADY.

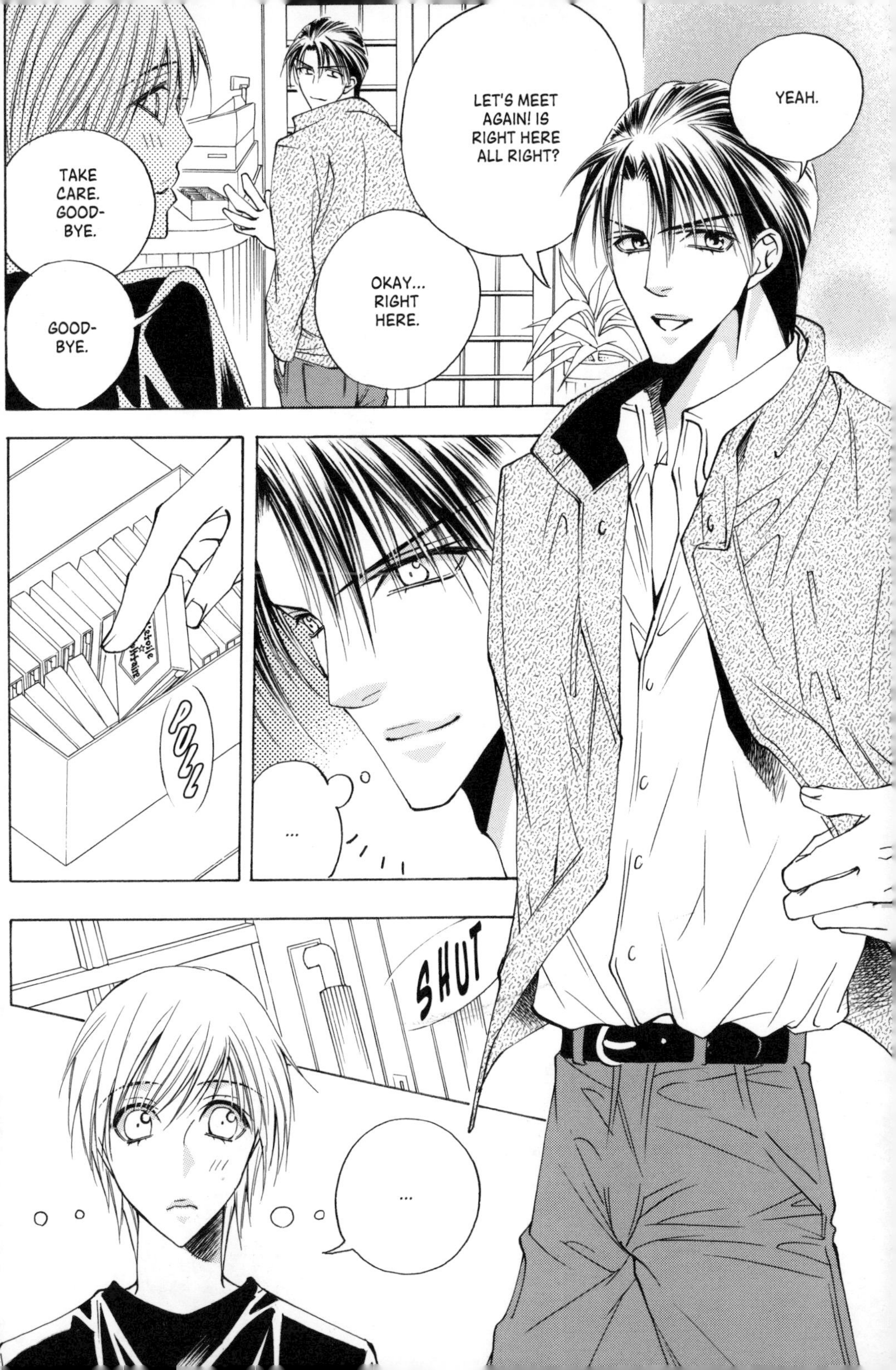
LET'S MEET AGAIN! IS RIGHT HERE ALL RIGHT?
OKAY... RIGHT HERE.
YEAH.
TAKE CARE. GOOD-BYE.
GOOD-BYE.
PULL
...
SHUT
...

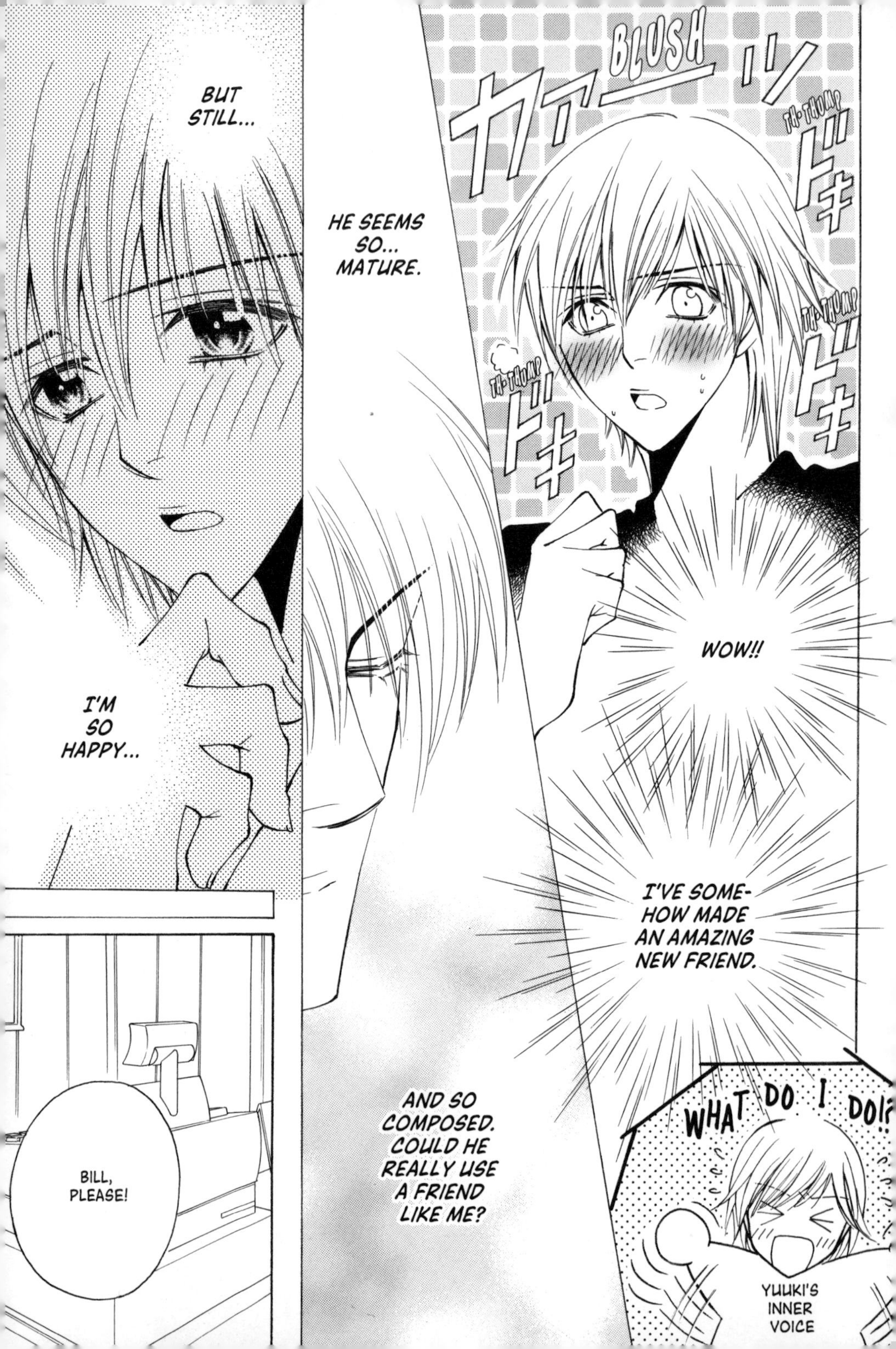
カァーッ
BLUSH
ドキ
TH-THUMP
ドキ
TH-THUMP
ドキ
TH-THUMP
WOW!!
I'VE SOME-HOW MADE AN AMAZING NEW FRIEND.
WHAT DO I DO!?
YUUKI'S INNER VOICE
HE SEEMS SO... MATURE.
AND SO COMPOSED. COULD HE REALLY USE A FRIEND LIKE ME?
BUT STILL...
I'M SO HAPPY...
BILL, PLEASE!

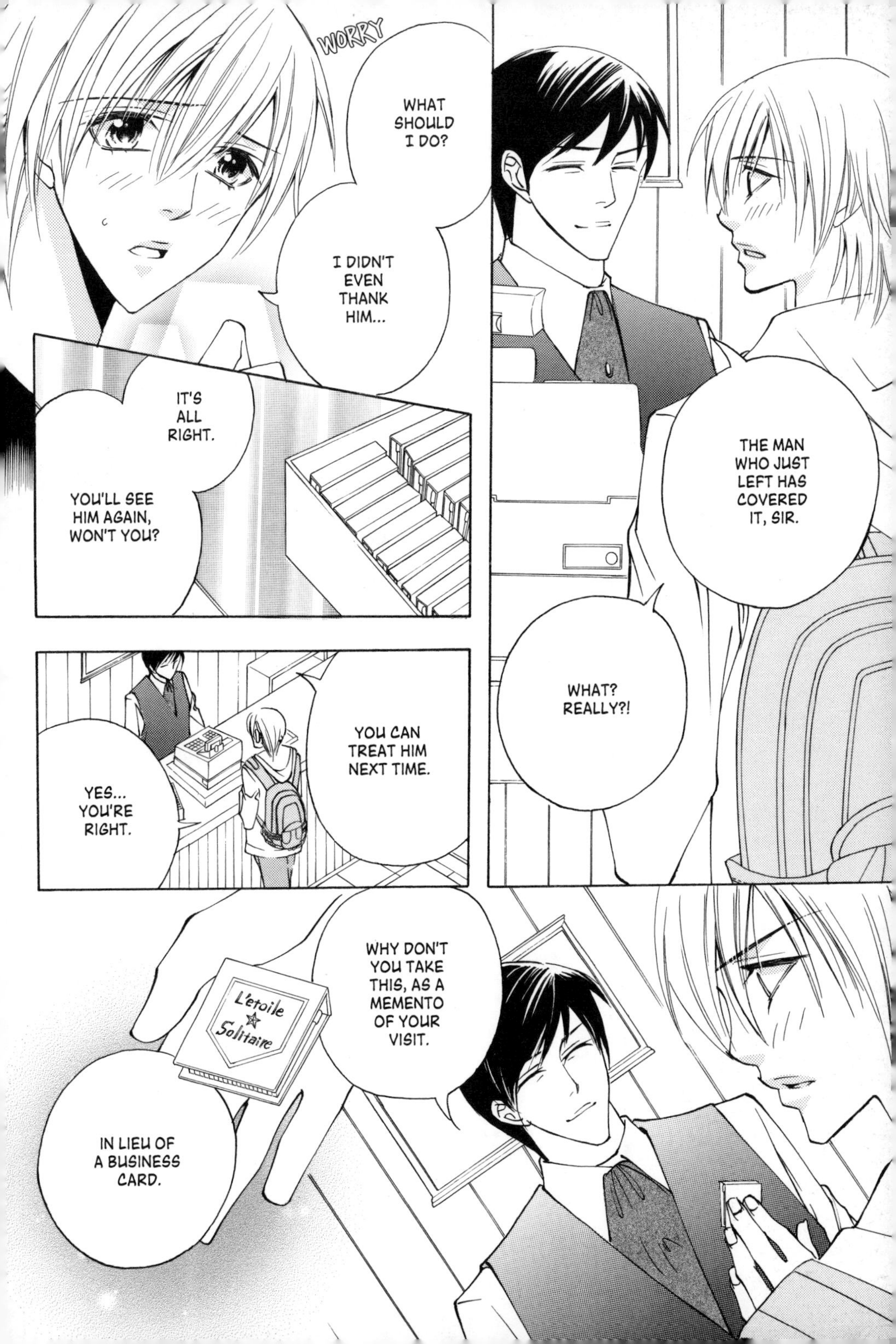
THE MAN WHO JUST LEFT HAS COVERED IT, SIR.
WHAT? REALLY?!
WORRY
WHAT SHOULD I DO?
I DIDN'T EVEN THANK HIM...
IT'S ALL RIGHT.
YOU'LL SEE HIM AGAIN, WON'T YOU?
YOU CAN TREAT HIM NEXT TIME.
YES... YOU'RE RIGHT.
WHY DON'T YOU TAKE THIS, AS A MEMENTO OF YOUR VISIT.
IN LIEU OF A BUSINESS CARD.
L'etoile Solitaire

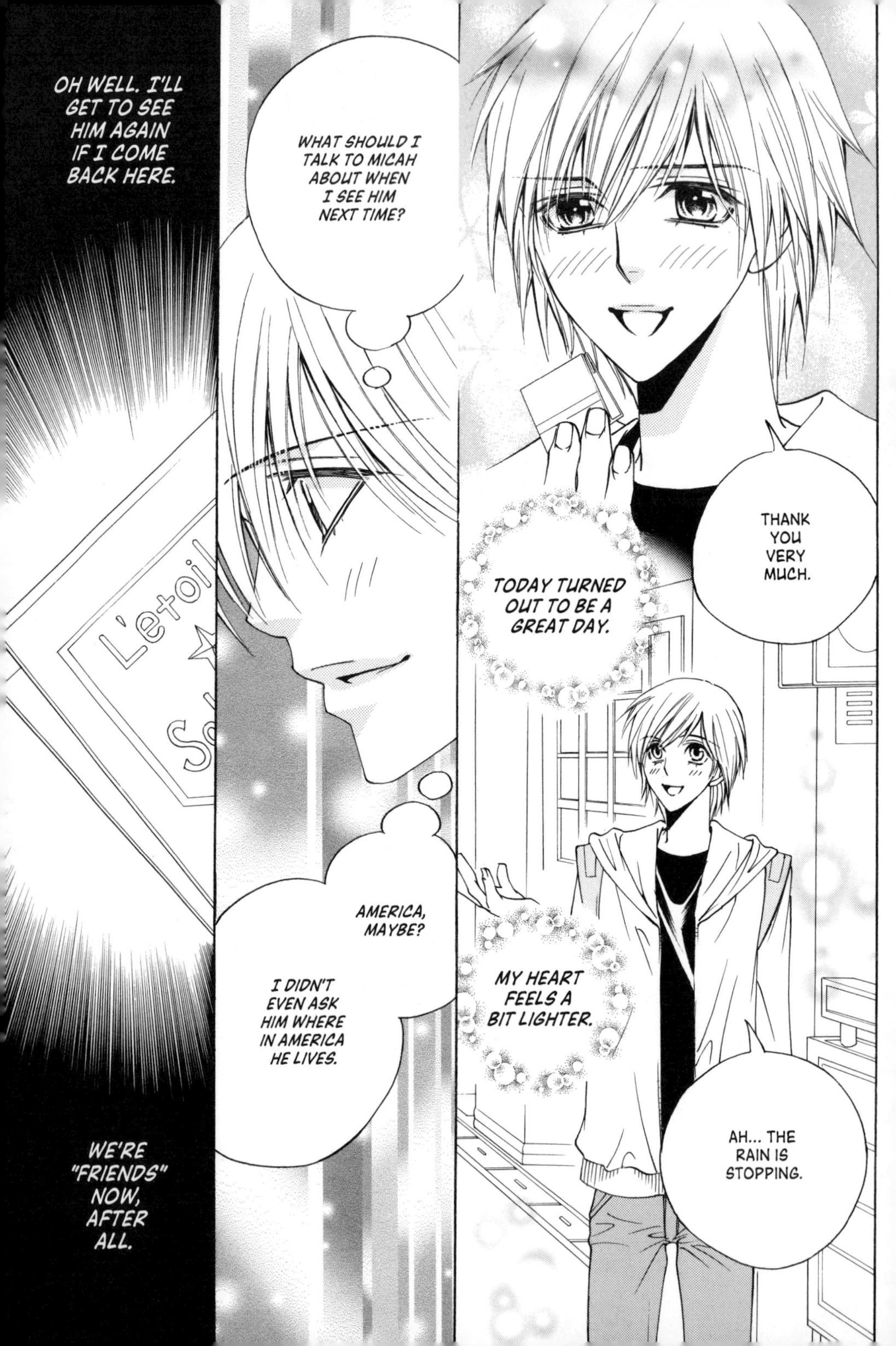
THANK YOU VERY MUCH.
TODAY TURNED OUT TO BE A GREAT DAY.
MY HEART FEELS A BIT LIGHTER.
AH... THE RAIN IS STOPPING.
WHAT SHOULD I TALK TO MICAH ABOUT WHEN I SEE HIM NEXT TIME?
AMERICA, MAYBE?
I DIDN'T EVEN ASK HIM WHERE IN AMERICA HE LIVES.
OH WELL. I'LL GET TO SEE HIM AGAIN IF I COME BACK HERE.
WE'RE "FRIENDS" NOW, AFTER ALL.

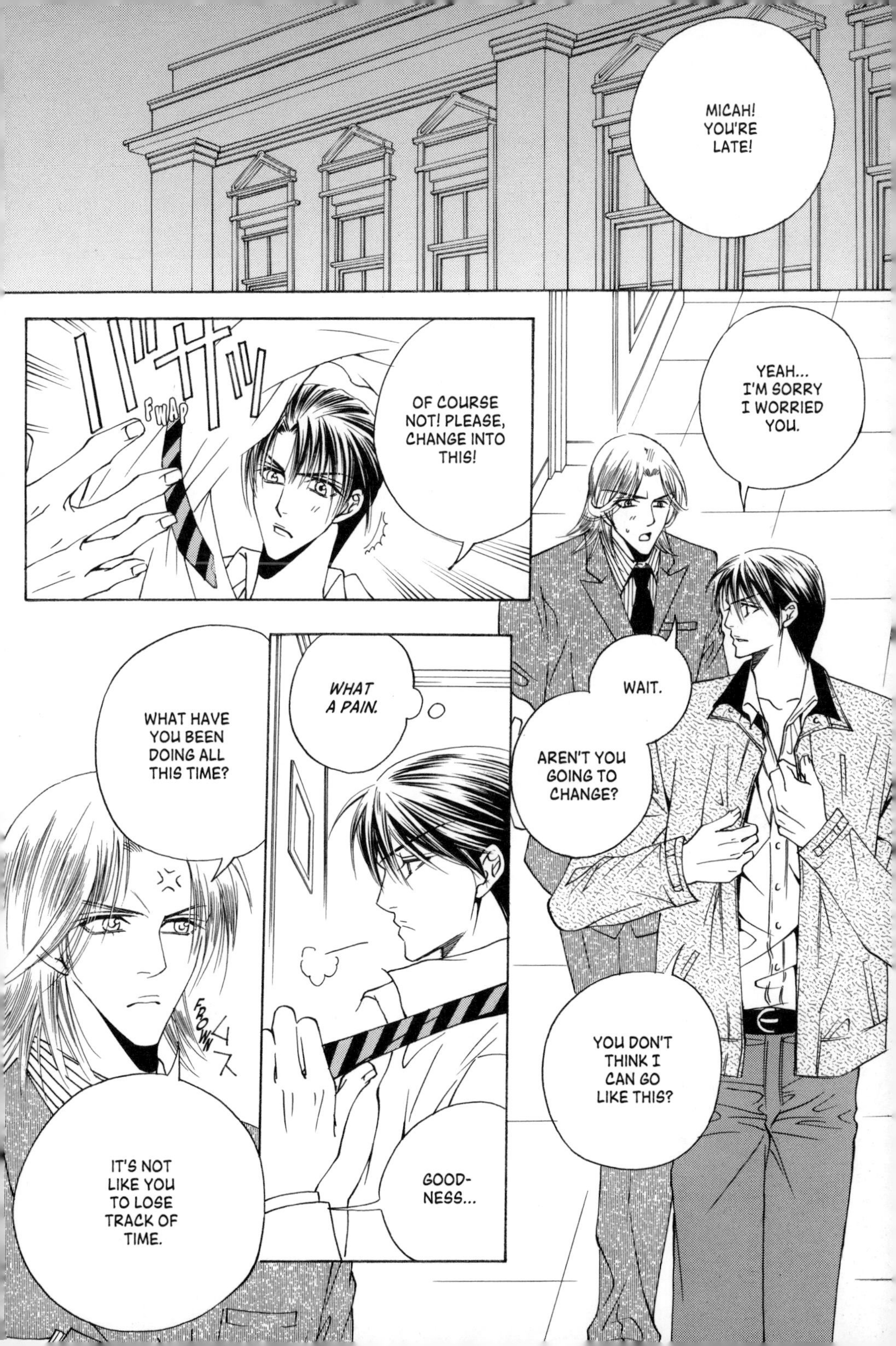
MICAH! YOU'RE LATE!
YEAH... I'M SORRY I WORRIED YOU.
WAIT.
AREN'T YOU GOING TO CHANGE?
YOU DON'T THINK I CAN GO LIKE THIS?
FWAP
OF COURSE NOT! PLEASE, CHANGE INTO THIS!
WHAT A PAIN.
GOOD-NESS...
WHAT HAVE YOU BEEN DOING ALL THIS TIME?
FROWN
IT'S NOT LIKE YOU TO LOSE TRACK OF TIME.

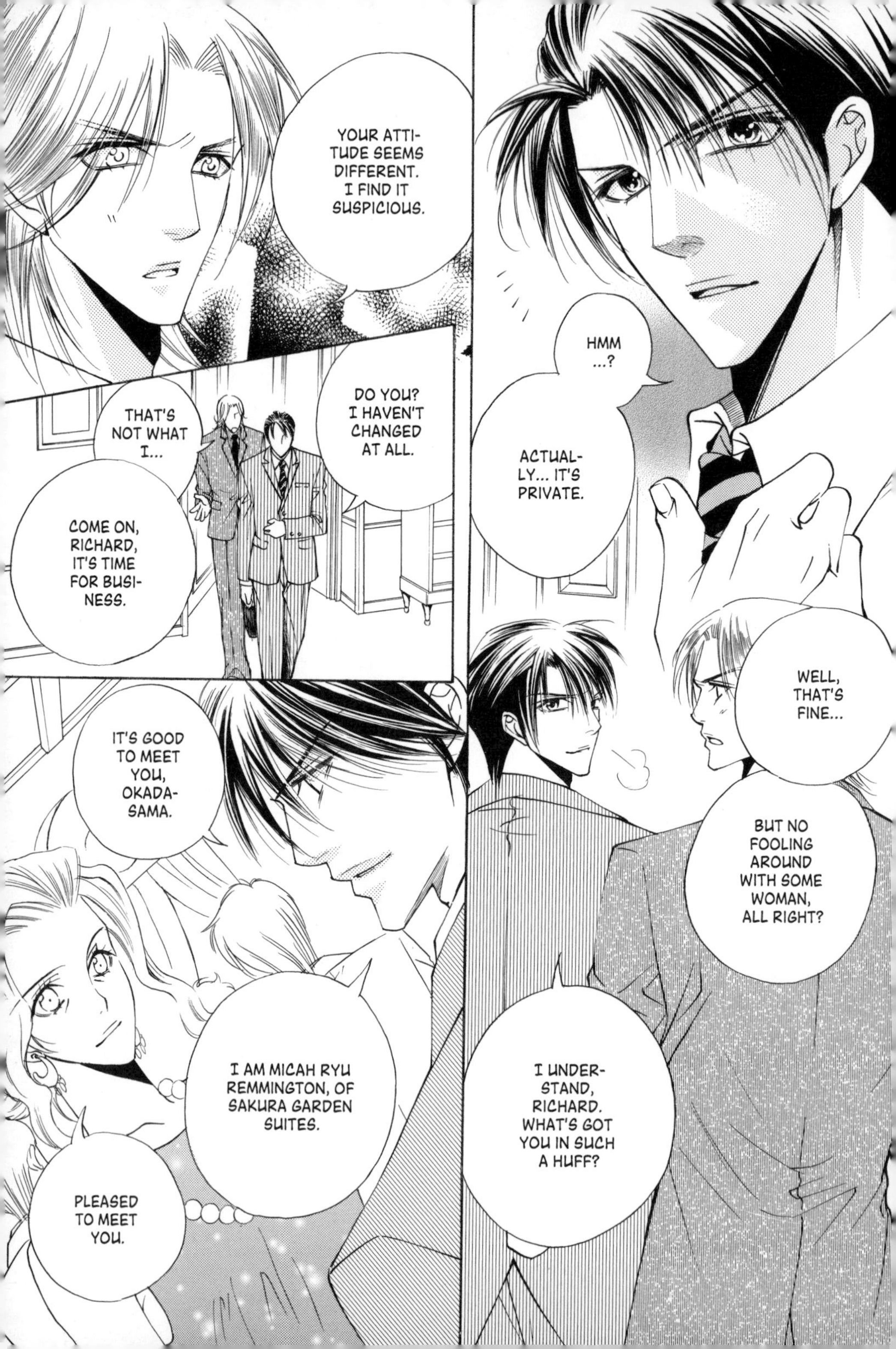
HMM ...?
ACTUALLY... IT'S PRIVATE.
WELL, THAT'S FINE...
BUT NO FOOLING AROUND WITH SOME WOMAN, ALL RIGHT?
I UNDERSTAND, RICHARD. WHAT'S GOT YOU IN SUCH A HUFF?
YOUR ATTITUDE SEEMS DIFFERENT. I FIND IT SUSPICIOUS.
DO YOU? I HAVEN'T CHANGED AT ALL.
THAT'S NOT WHAT I...
COME ON, RICHARD, IT'S TIME FOR BUSINESS.
IT'S GOOD TO MEET YOU, OKADA-SAMA.
I AM MICAH RYU REMMINGTON, OF SAKURA GARDEN SUITES.
PLEASED TO MEET YOU.

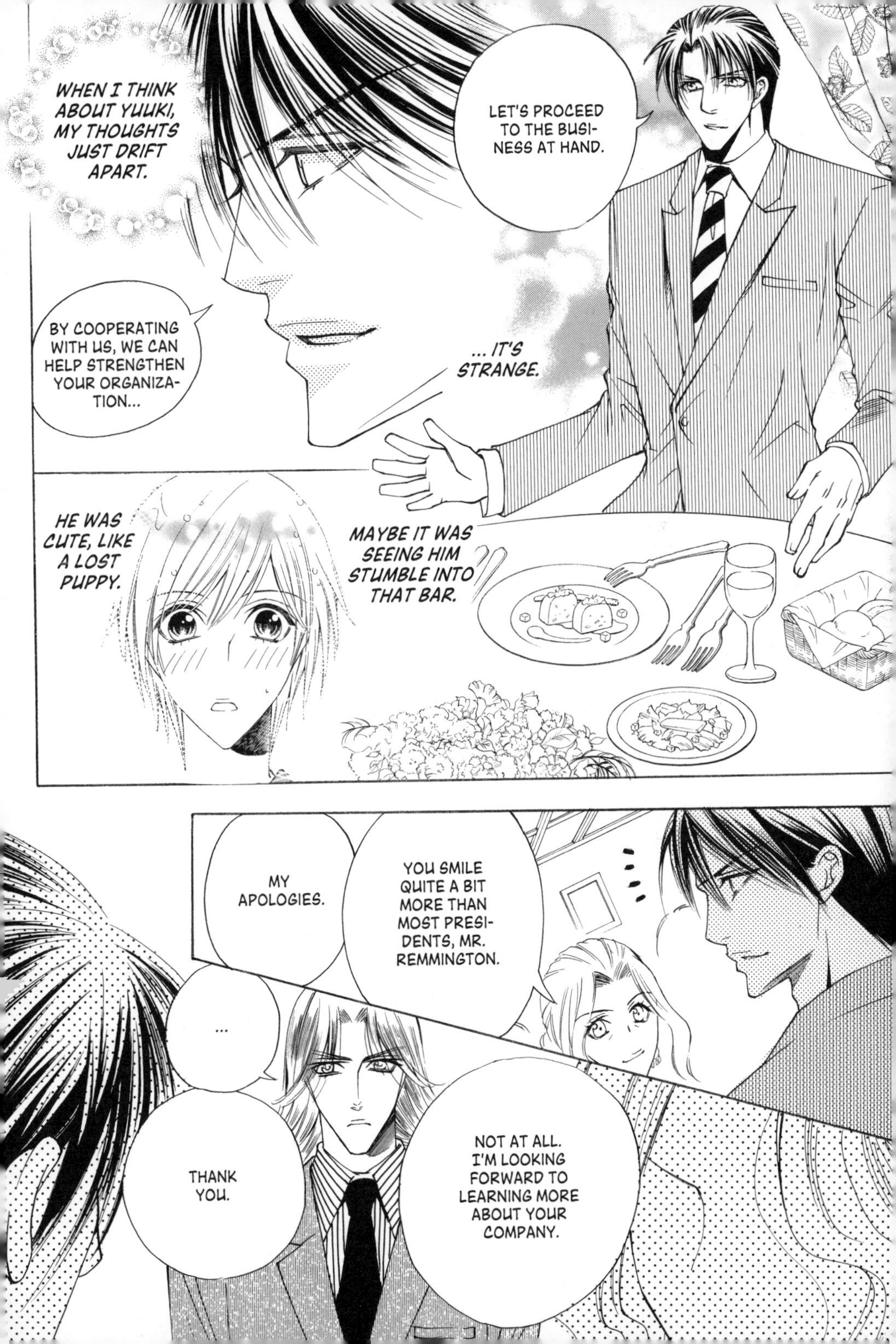
LET'S PROCEED TO THE BUSINESS AT HAND.
WHEN I THINK ABOUT YUUKI, MY THOUGHTS JUST DRIFT APART.
... IT'S STRANGE.
BY COOPERATING WITH US, WE CAN HELP STRENGTHEN YOUR ORGANIZATION...
MAYBE IT WAS SEEING HIM STUMBLE INTO THAT BAR.
HE WAS CUTE, LIKE A LOST PUPPY.
YOU SMILE QUITE A BIT MORE THAN MOST PRESIDENTS, MR. REMMINGTON.
MY APOLOGIES.
...
NOT AT ALL. I'M LOOKING FORWARD TO LEARNING MORE ABOUT YOUR COMPANY.
THANK YOU.

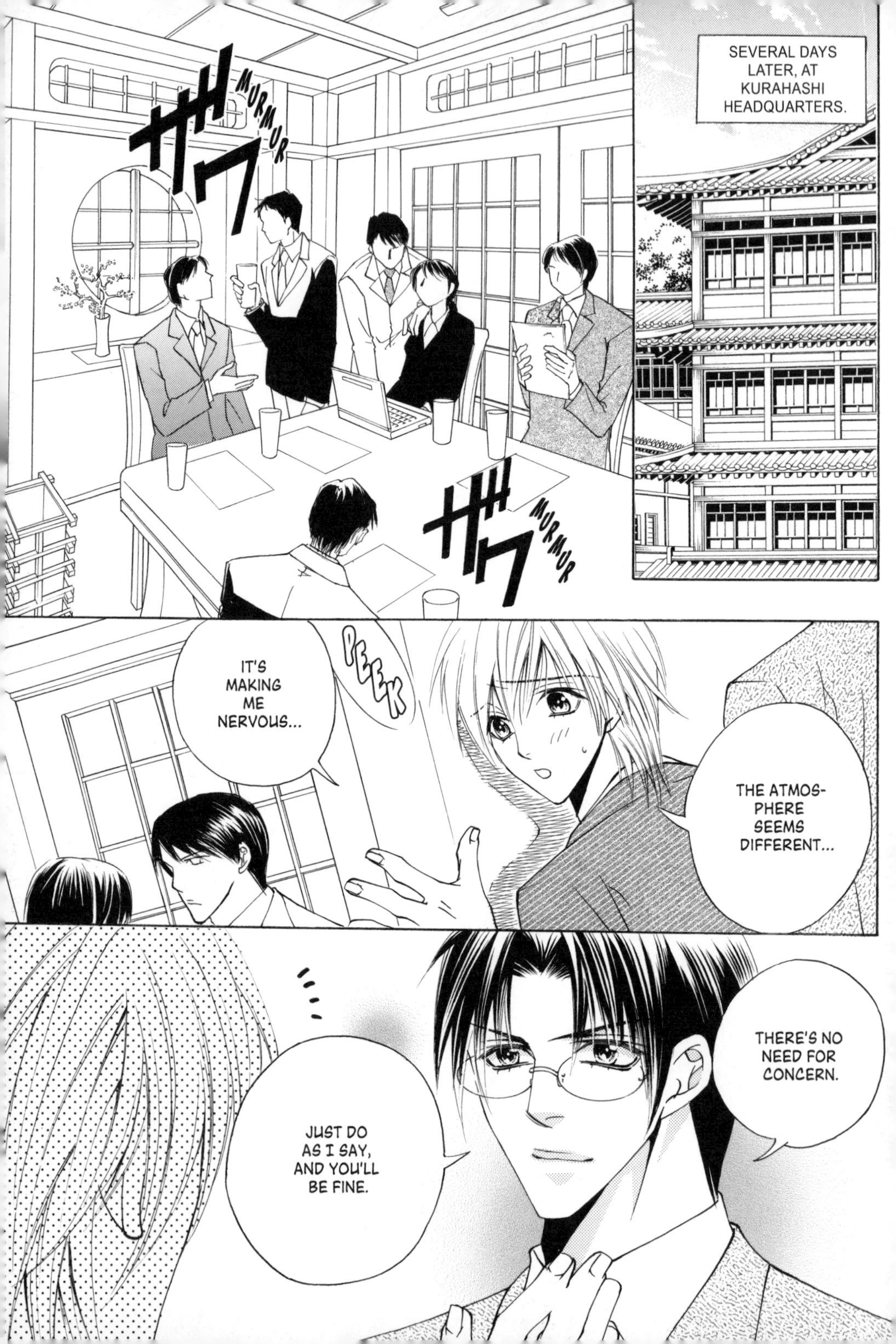
SEVERAL DAYS LATER, AT KURAHASHI HEADQUARTERS.
ザワ MURMUR
ザワ MURMUR
THE ATMOS-PHERE SEEMS DIFFERENT...
PEEK
IT'S MAKING ME NERVOUS...
THERE'S NO NEED FOR CONCERN.
JUST DO AS I SAY, AND YOU'LL BE FINE.
...

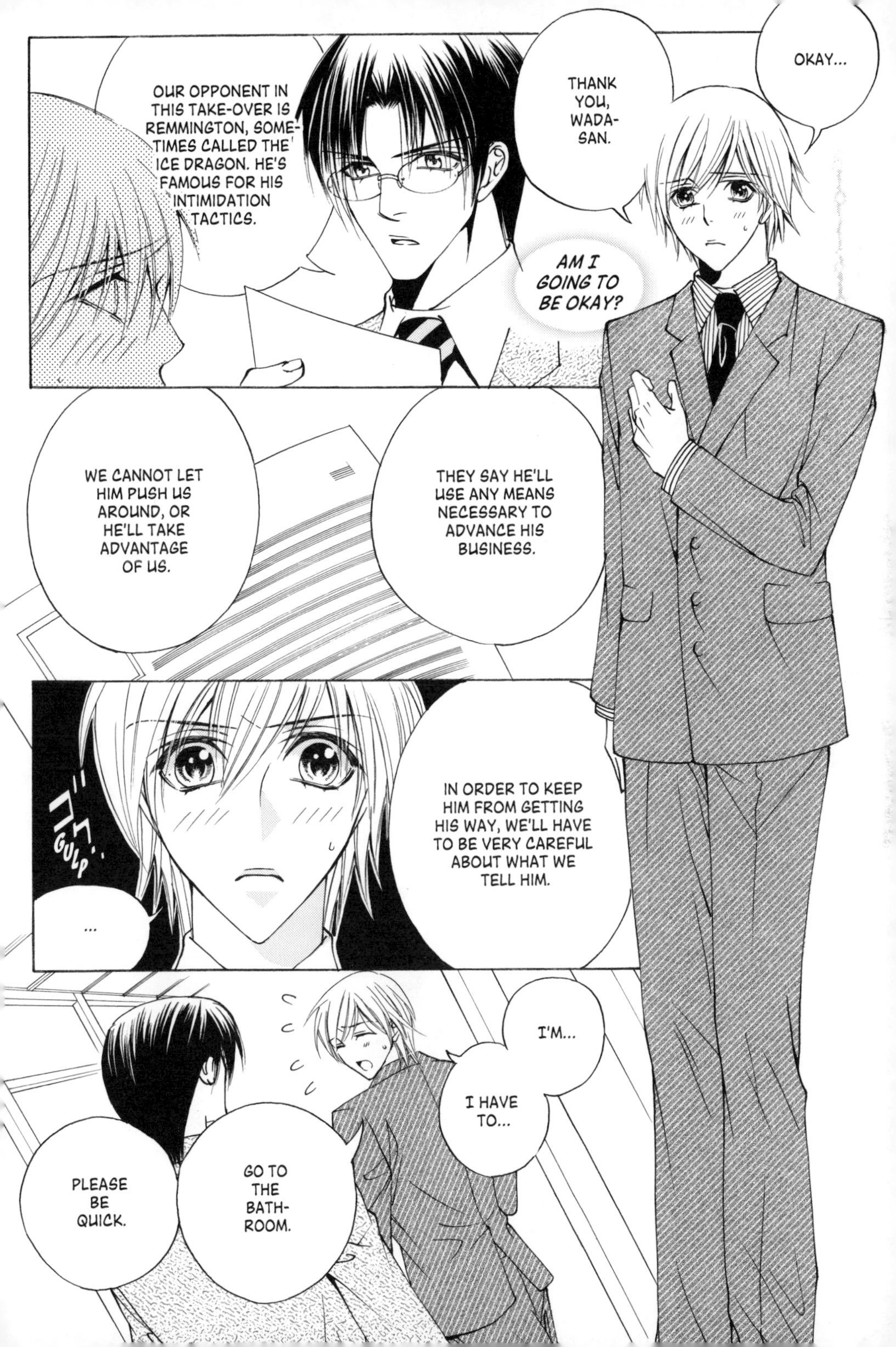
OKAY...
THANK YOU, WADA-SAN.
AM I GOING TO BE OKAY?
OUR OPPONENT IN THIS TAKE-OVER IS REMMINGTON, SOMETIMES CALLED THE ICE DRAGON. HE'S FAMOUS FOR HIS INTIMIDATION TACTICS.
THEY SAY HE'LL USE ANY MEANS NECESSARY TO ADVANCE HIS BUSINESS.
WE CANNOT LET HIM PUSH US AROUND, OR HE'LL TAKE ADVANTAGE OF US.
IN ORDER TO KEEP HIM FROM GETTING HIS WAY, WE'LL HAVE TO BE VERY CAREFUL ABOUT WHAT WE TELL HIM.
GULP
...
I'M...
I HAVE TO...
GO TO THE BATH-ROOM.
PLEASE BE QUICK.

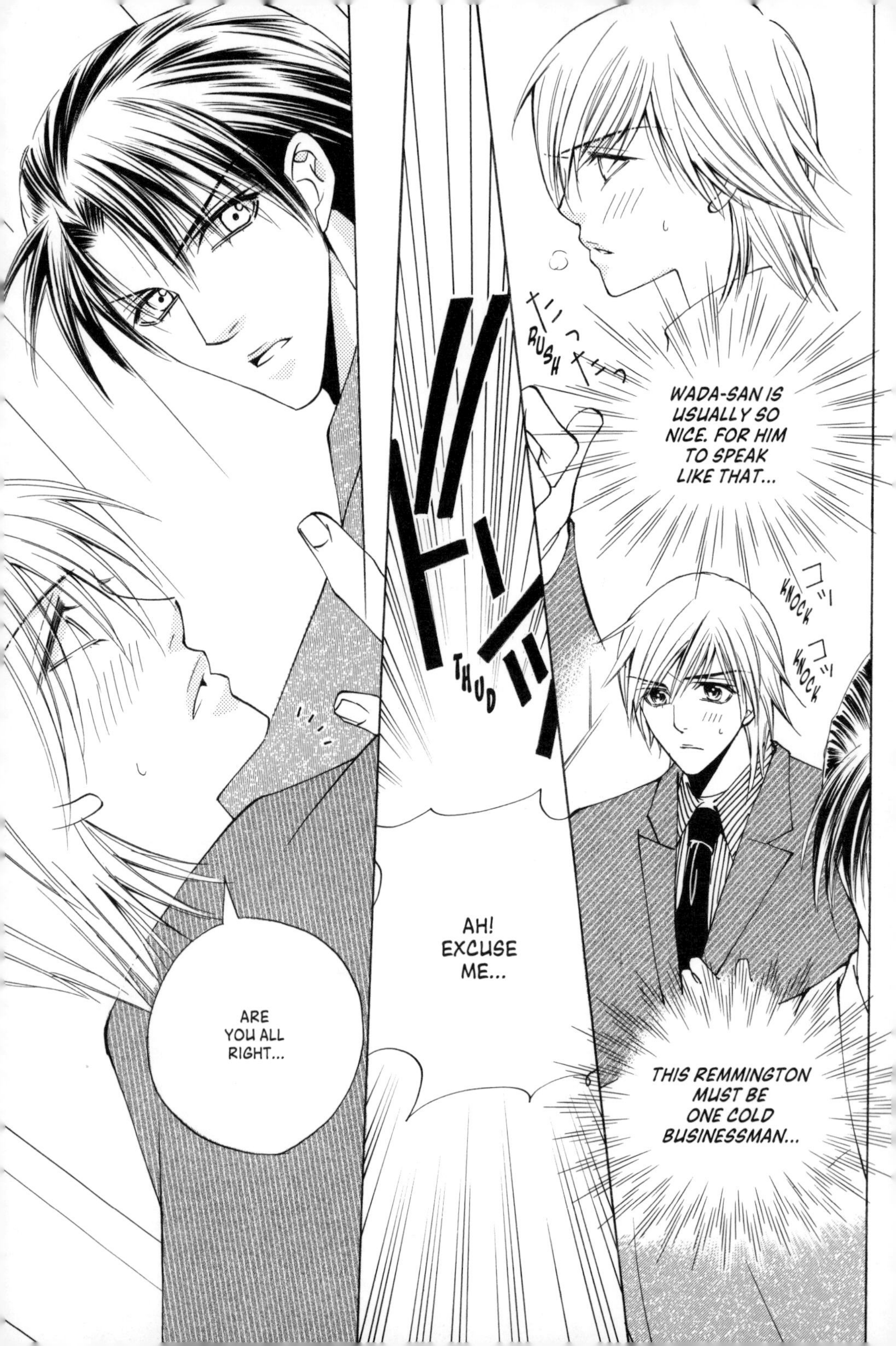
RUSH
WADA-SAN IS USUALLY SO NICE. FOR HIM TO SPEAK LIKE THAT...
KNOCK
KNOCK
THIS REMMINGTON MUST BE ONE COLD BUSINESSMAN...
THUD
AH! EXCUSE ME...
ARE YOU ALL RIGHT...

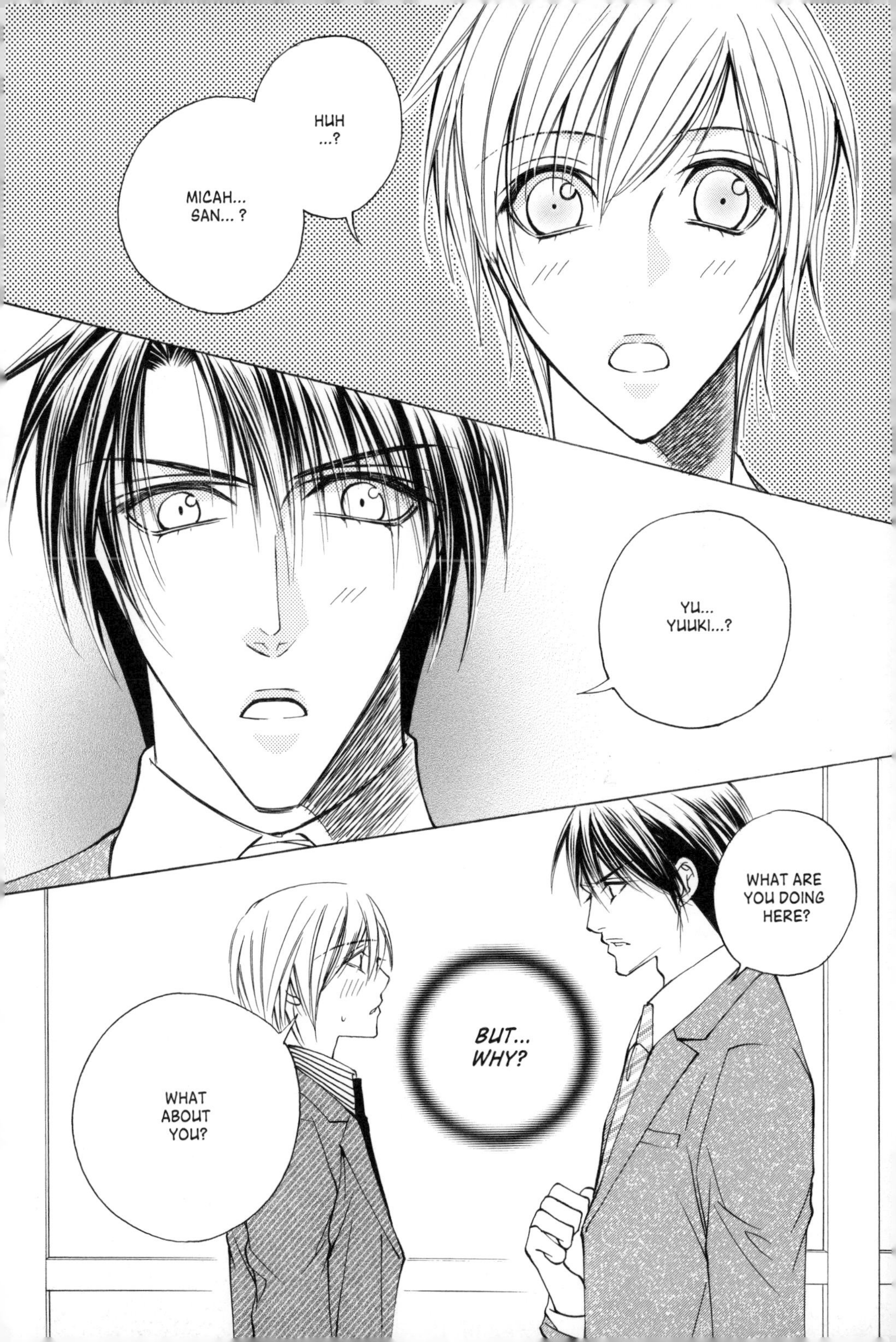
HUH ...?
MICAH... SAN... ?
YU... YUUKI...?
WHAT ARE YOU DOING HERE?
BUT... WHY?
WHAT ABOUT YOU?

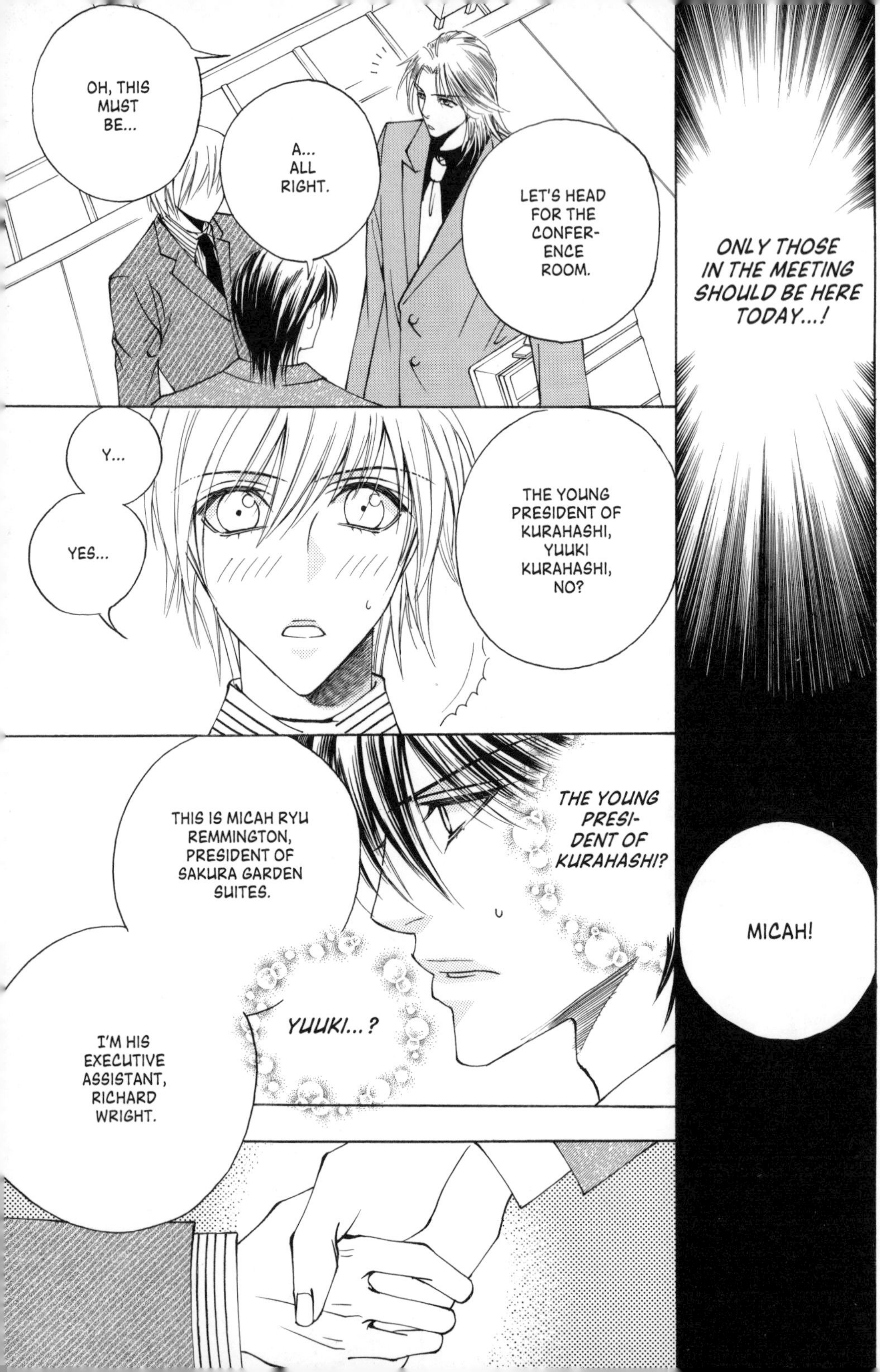
ONLY THOSE IN THE MEETING SHOULD BE HERE TODAY...!
MICAH!
LET'S HEAD FOR THE CONFERENCE ROOM.
A... ALL RIGHT.
OH, THIS MUST BE...
THE YOUNG PRESIDENT OF KURAHASHI, YUUKI KURAHASHI, NO?
Y...
YES...
THE YOUNG PRESIDENT OF KURAHASHI?
THIS IS MICAH RYU REMMINGTON, PRESIDENT OF SAKURA GARDEN SUITES.
YUUKI...?
I'M HIS EXECUTIVE ASSISTANT, RICHARD WRIGHT.

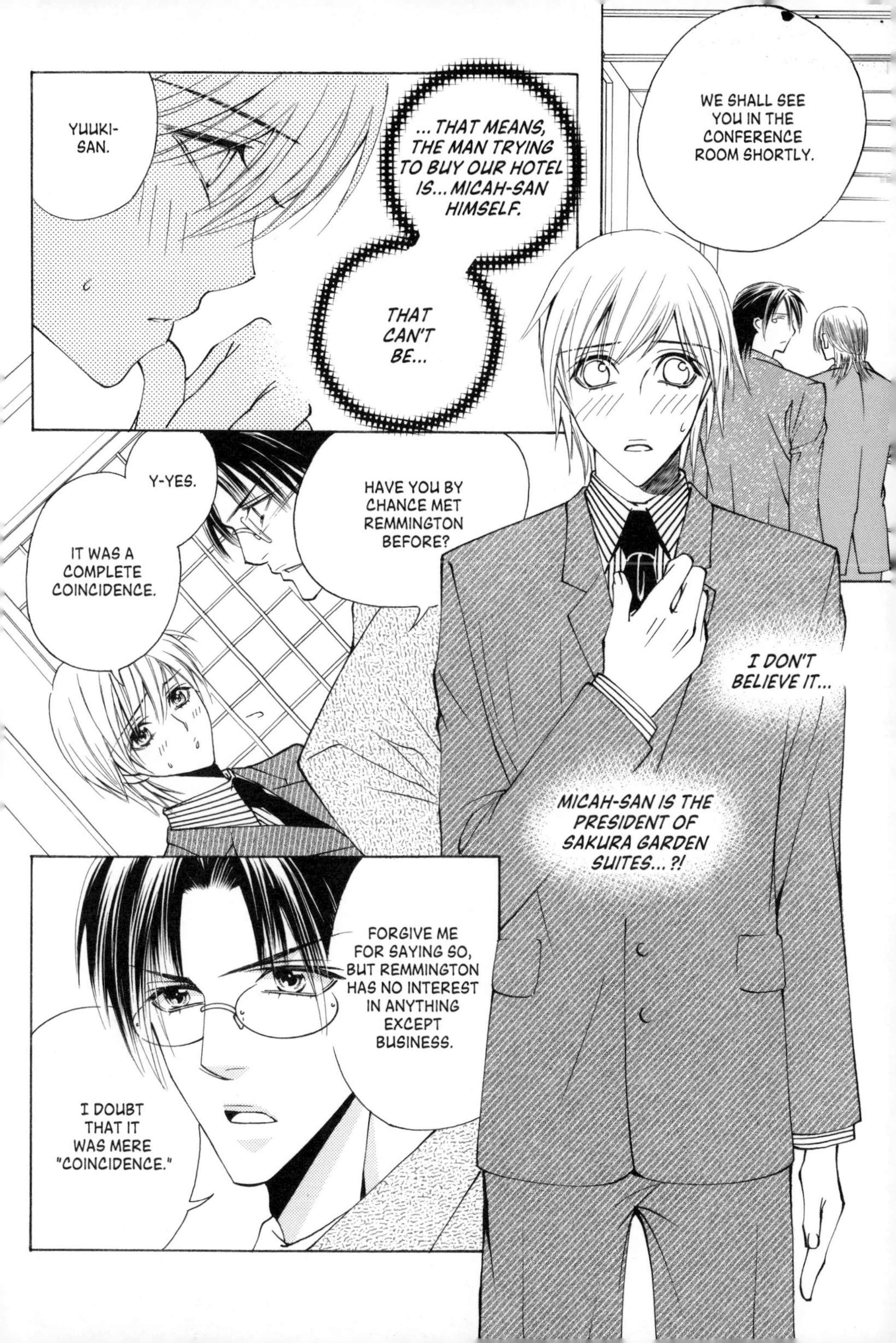
WE SHALL SEE YOU IN THE CONFERENCE ROOM SHORTLY.
I DON'T BELIEVE IT...
MICAH-SAN IS THE PRESIDENT OF SAKURA GARDEN SUITES...?!
...THAT MEANS, THE MAN TRYING TO BUY OUR HOTEL IS... MICAH-SAN HIMSELF.
THAT CAN'T BE...
YUUKI-SAN.
HAVE YOU BY CHANCE MET REMMINGTON BEFORE?
Y-YES.
IT WAS A COMPLETE COINCIDENCE.
FORGIVE ME FOR SAYING SO, BUT REMMINGTON HAS NO INTEREST IN ANYTHING EXCEPT BUSINESS.
I DOUBT THAT IT WAS MERE "COINCIDENCE."

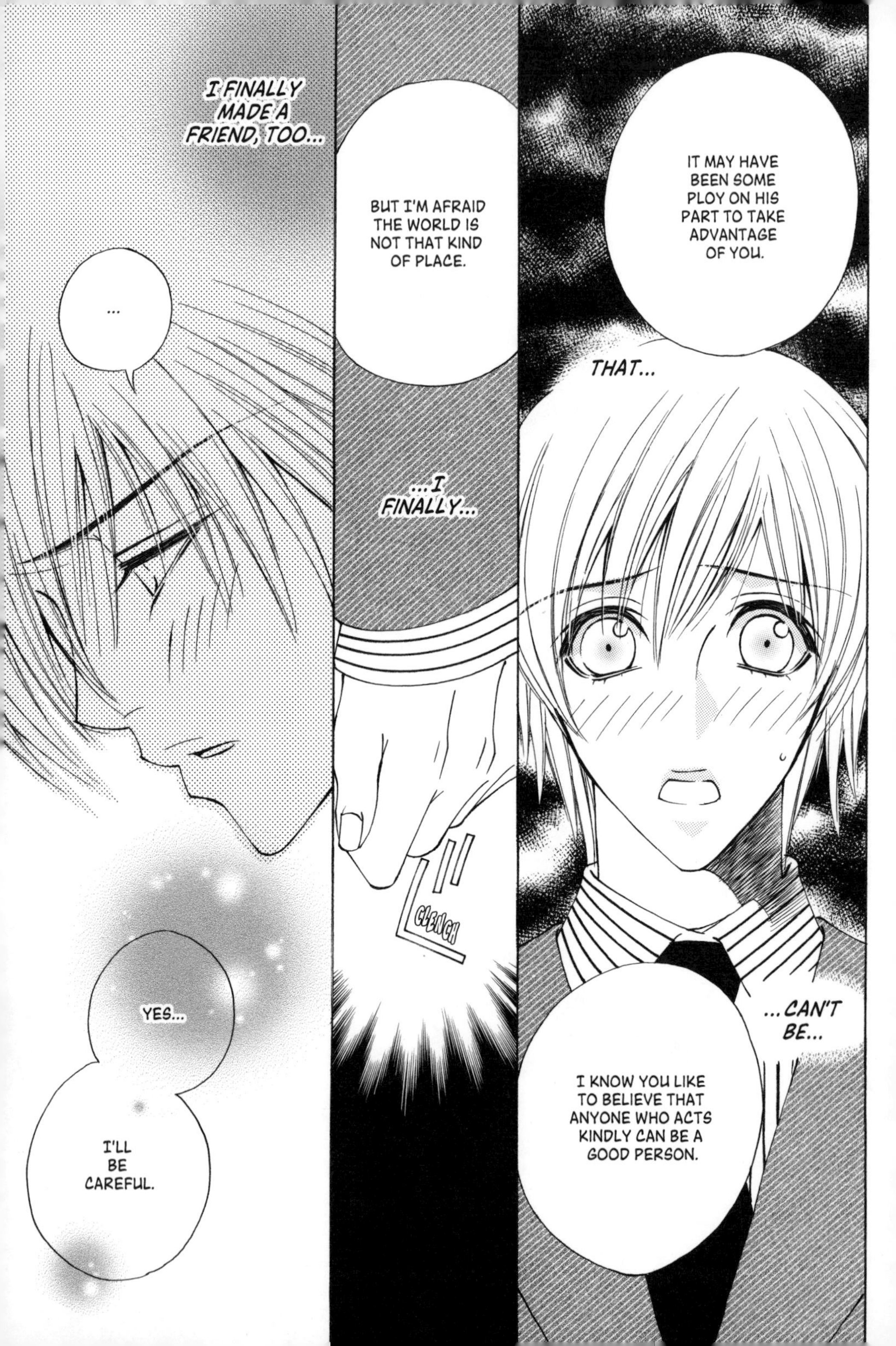
IT MAY HAVE BEEN SOME PLOY ON HIS PART TO TAKE ADVANTAGE OF YOU.
THAT...
...CAN'T BE...
I KNOW YOU LIKE TO BELIEVE THAT ANYONE WHO ACTS KINDLY CAN BE A GOOD PERSON.
BUT I'M AFRAID THE WORLD IS NOT THAT KIND OF PLACE.
...I FINALLY...
CLENCH
I FINALLY MADE A FRIEND, TOO...
...
YES...
I'LL BE CAREFUL.

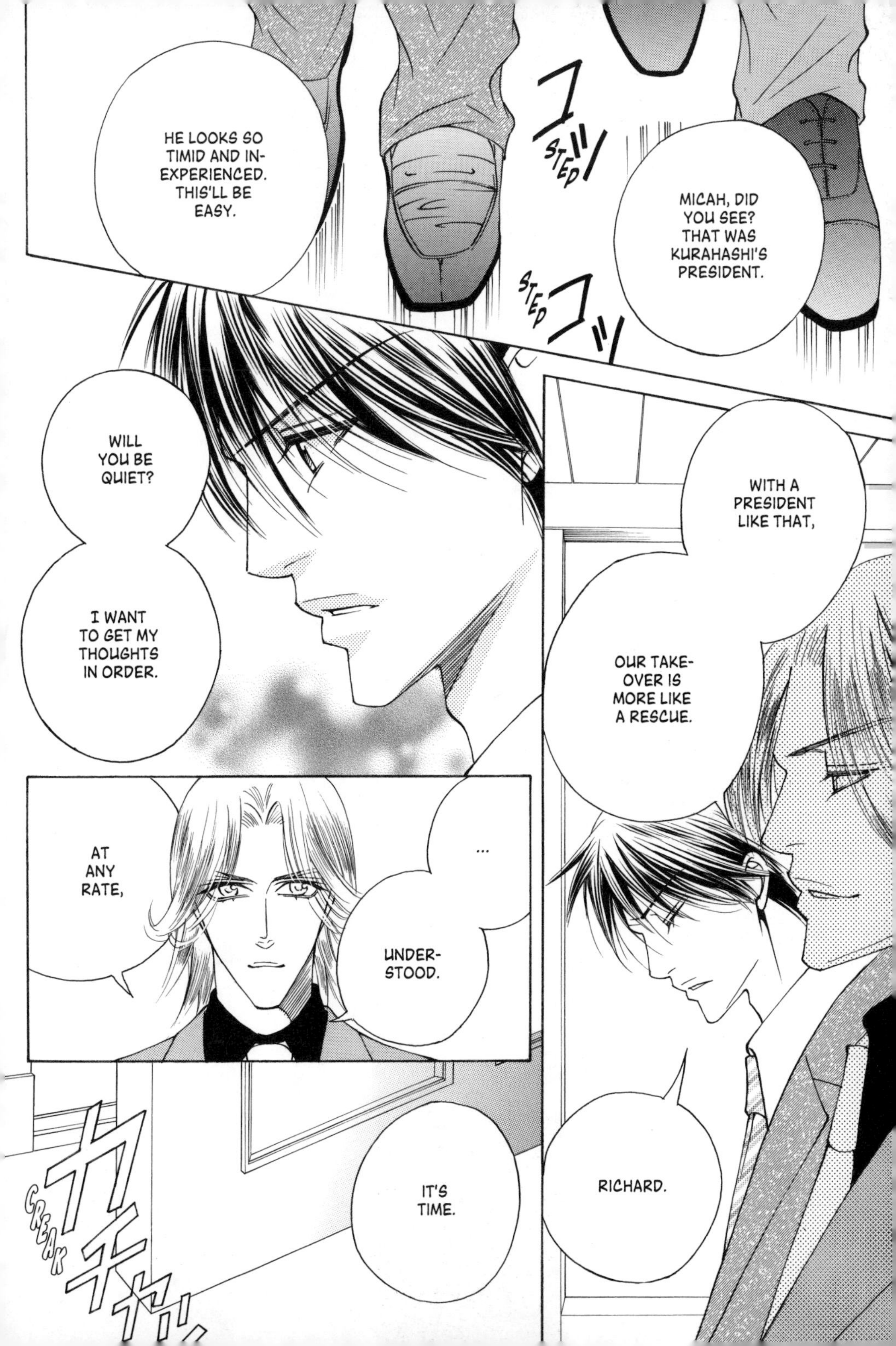
STEP
STEP
MICAH, DID YOU SEE? THAT WAS KURAHASHI'S PRESIDENT.
HE LOOKS SO TIMID AND IN-EXPERIENCED. THIS'LL BE EASY.
WITH A PRESIDENT LIKE THAT,
OUR TAKE-OVER IS MORE LIKE A RESCUE.
RICHARD.
WILL YOU BE QUIET?
I WANT TO GET MY THOUGHTS IN ORDER.
...
UNDER-STOOD.
AT ANY RATE,
IT'S TIME.
CREAK

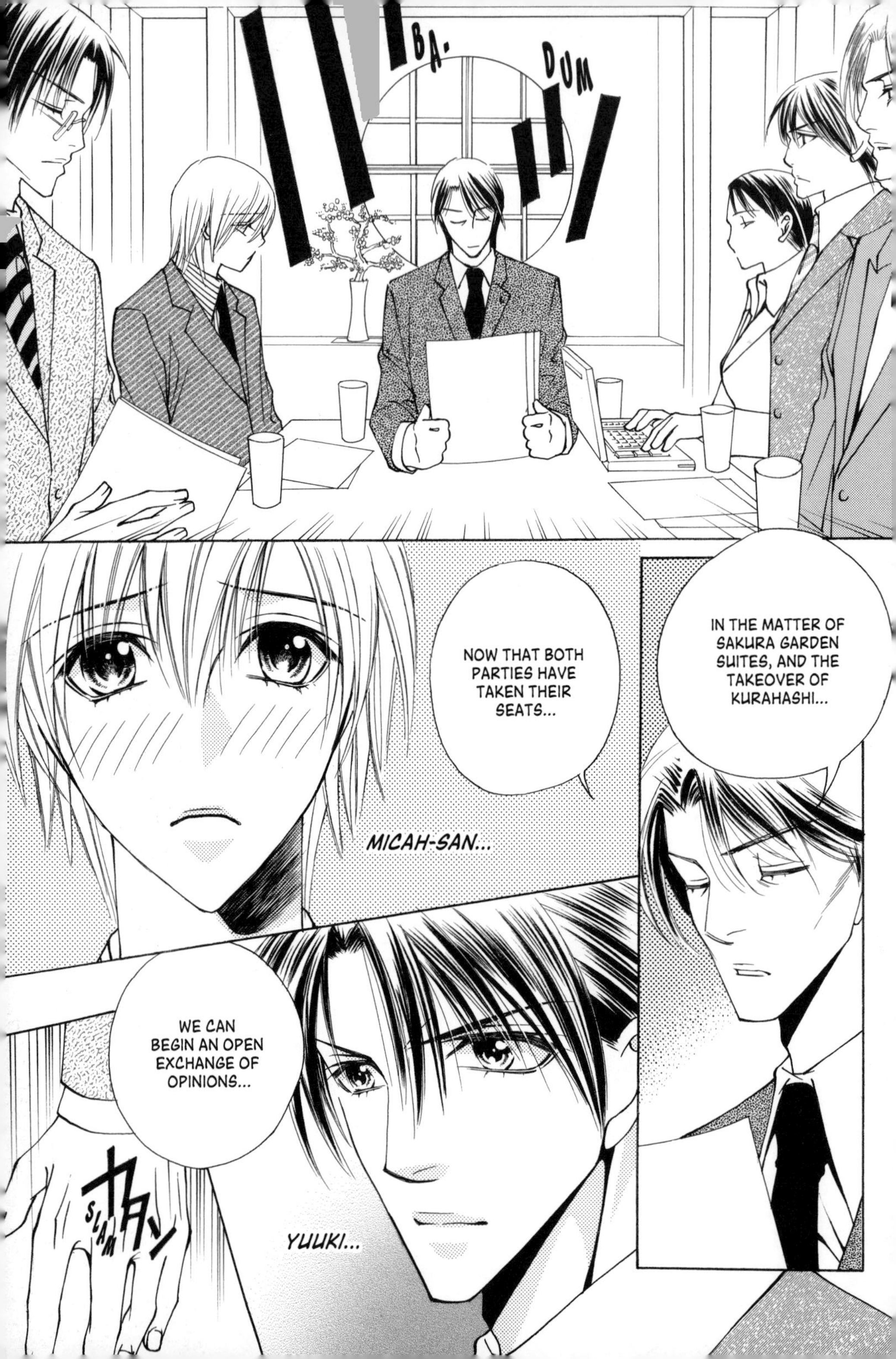
BA-DUM
IN THE MATTER OF SAKURA GARDEN SUITES, AND THE TAKEOVER OF KURAHASHI...
NOW THAT BOTH PARTIES HAVE TAKEN THEIR SEATS...
MICAH-SAN...
WE CAN BEGIN AN OPEN EXCHANGE OF OPINIONS...
YUUKI...
カタン
SLAM

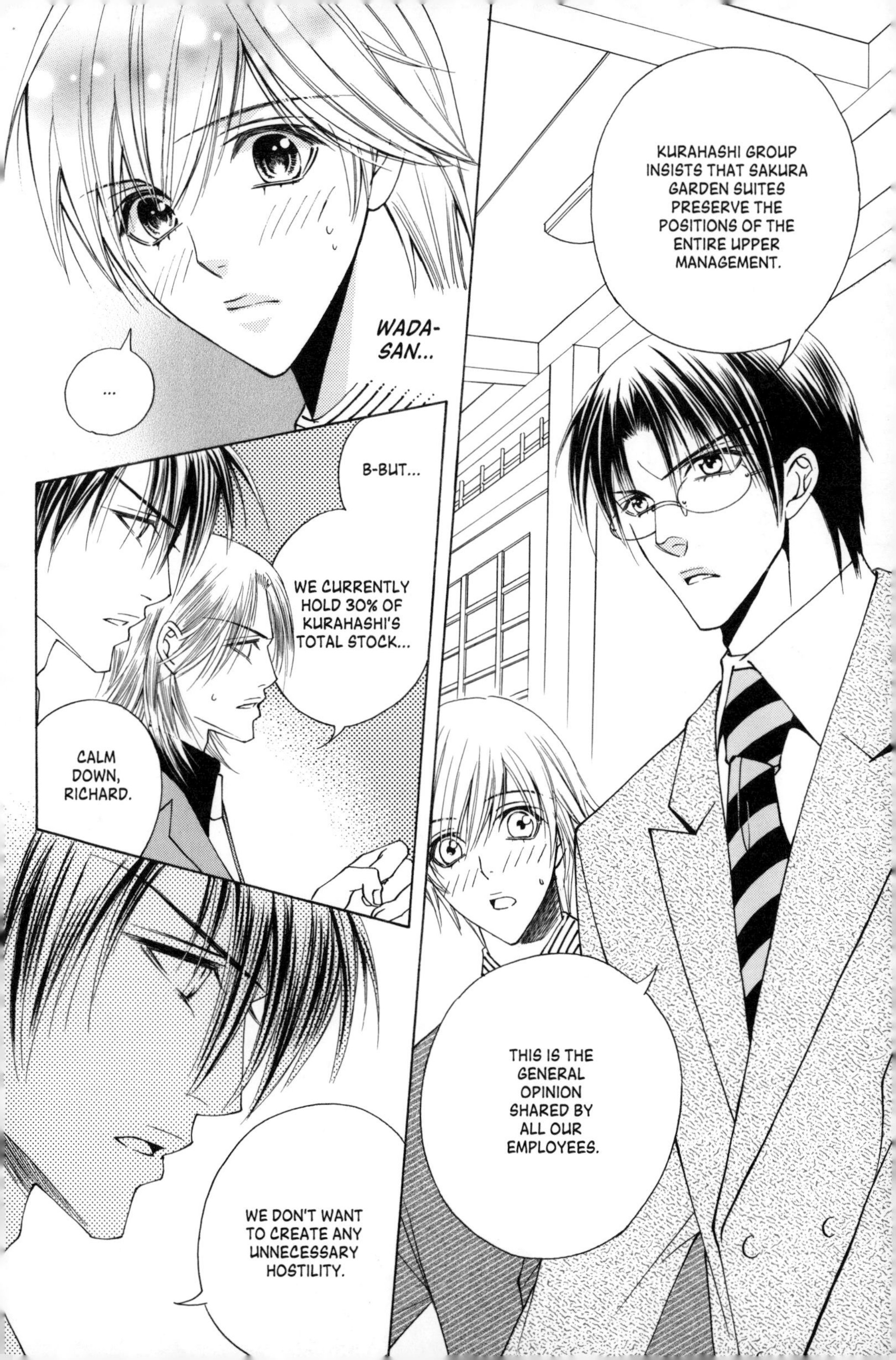
KURAHASHI GROUP INSISTS THAT SAKURA GARDEN SUITES PRESERVE THE POSITIONS OF THE ENTIRE UPPER MANAGEMENT.
THIS IS THE GENERAL OPINION SHARED BY ALL OUR EMPLOYEES.
WADA-SAN...
...
B-BUT...
WE CURRENTLY HOLD 30% OF KURAHASHI'S TOTAL STOCK...
CALM DOWN, RICHARD.
WE DON'T WANT TO CREATE ANY UNNECESSARY HOSTILITY.

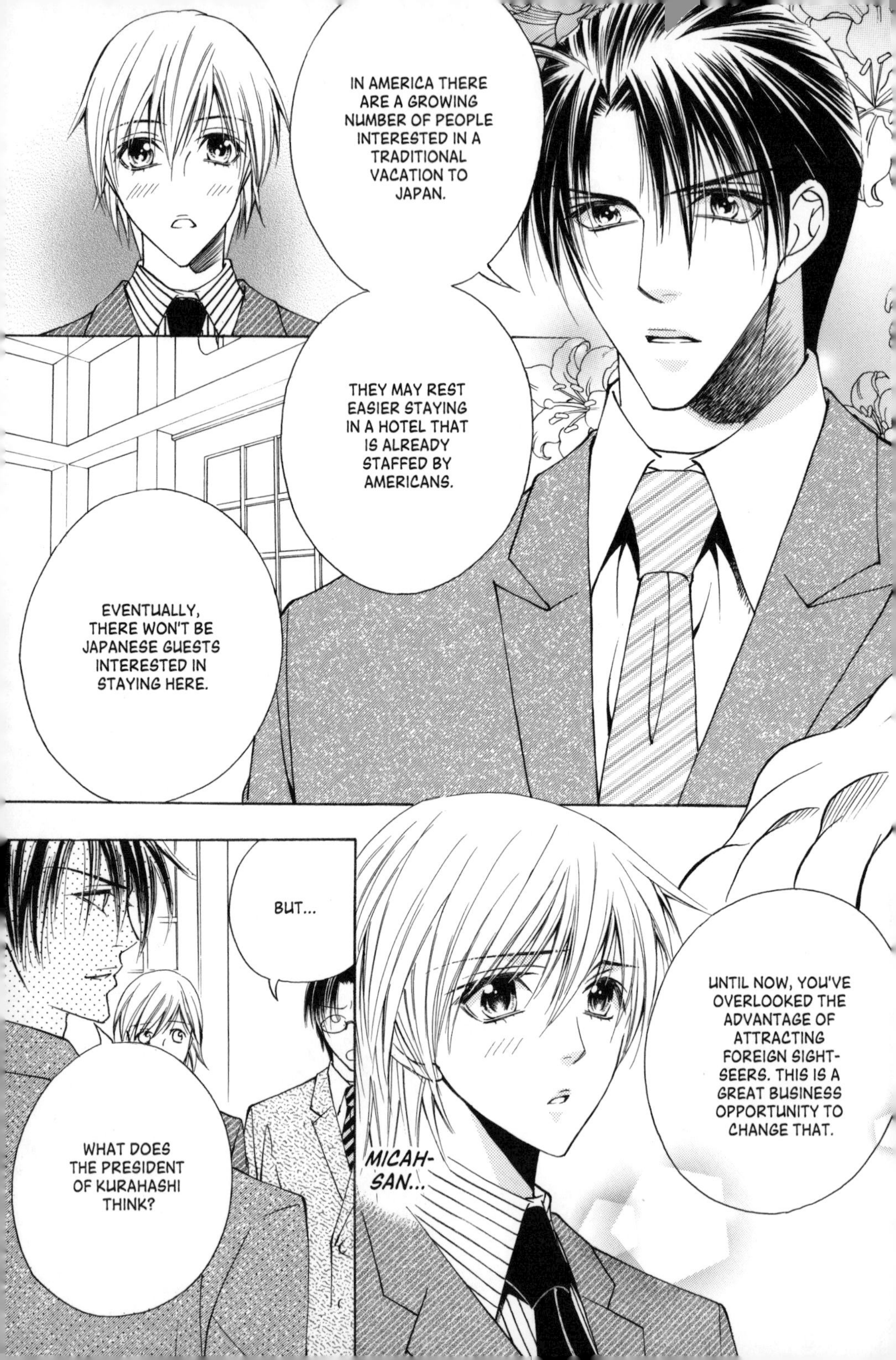
IN AMERICA THERE ARE A GROWING NUMBER OF PEOPLE INTERESTED IN A TRADITIONAL VACATION TO JAPAN.
THEY MAY REST EASIER STAYING IN A HOTEL THAT IS ALREADY STAFFED BY AMERICANS.
EVENTUALLY, THERE WON'T BE JAPANESE GUESTS INTERESTED IN STAYING HERE.
UNTIL NOW, YOU'VE OVERLOOKED THE ADVANTAGE OF ATTRACTING FOREIGN SIGHT-SEERS. THIS IS A GREAT BUSINESS OPPORTUNITY TO CHANGE THAT.
MICAH-SAN...
BUT...
WHAT DOES THE PRESIDENT OF KURAHASHI THINK?

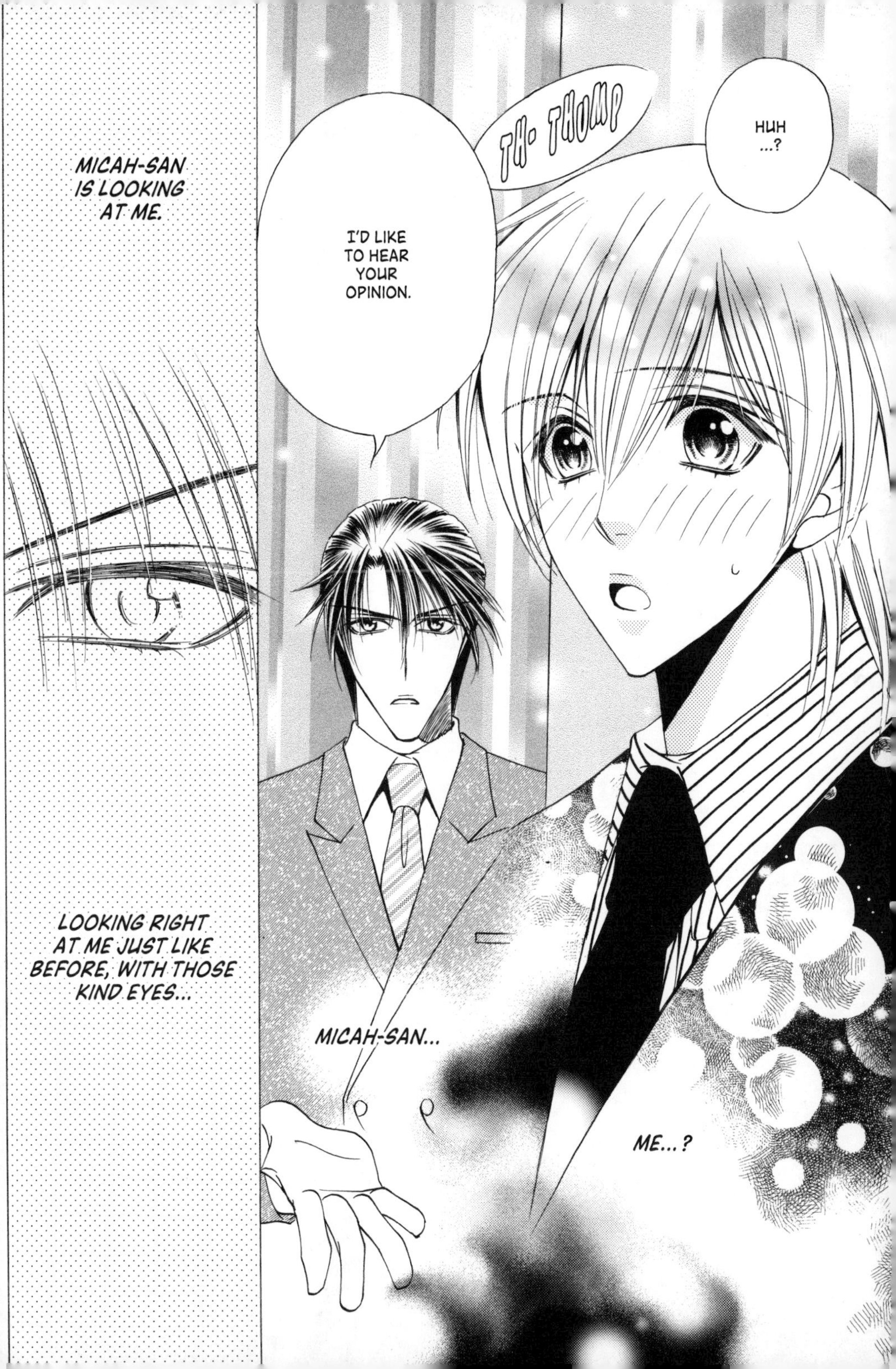
HUH ...?
TH- THOMP
I'D LIKE TO HEAR YOUR OPINION.
ME...?
MICAH-SAN...
MICAH-SAN IS LOOKING AT ME.
LOOKING RIGHT AT ME JUST LIKE BEFORE, WITH THOSE KIND EYES...

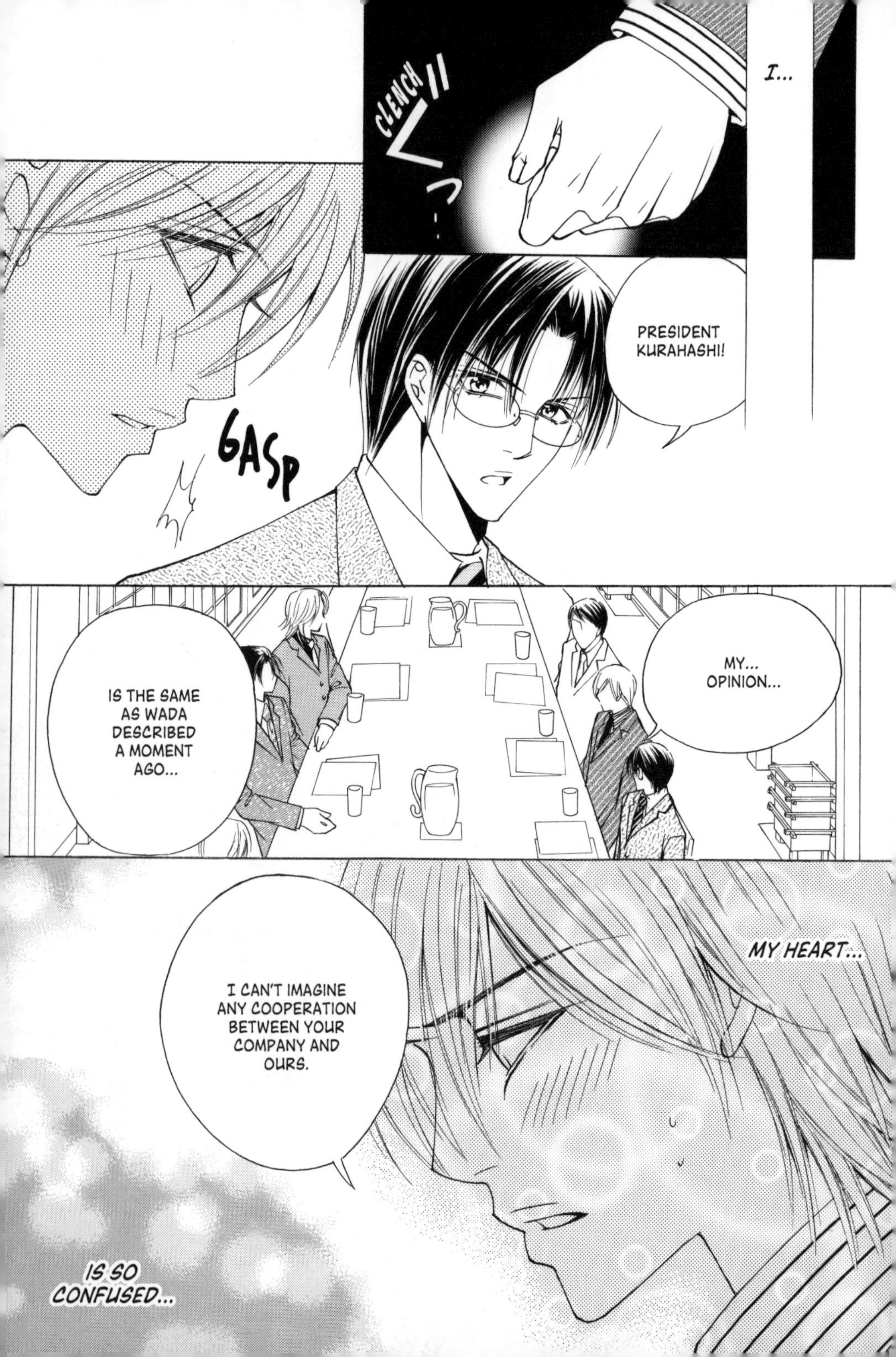
I...
CLENCH
PRESIDENT KURAHASHI!
GASP
MY... OPINION...
IS THE SAME AS WADA DESCRIBED A MOMENT AGO...
MY HEART...
I CAN'T IMAGINE ANY COOPERATION BETWEEN YOUR COMPANY AND OURS.
IS SO CONFUSED...

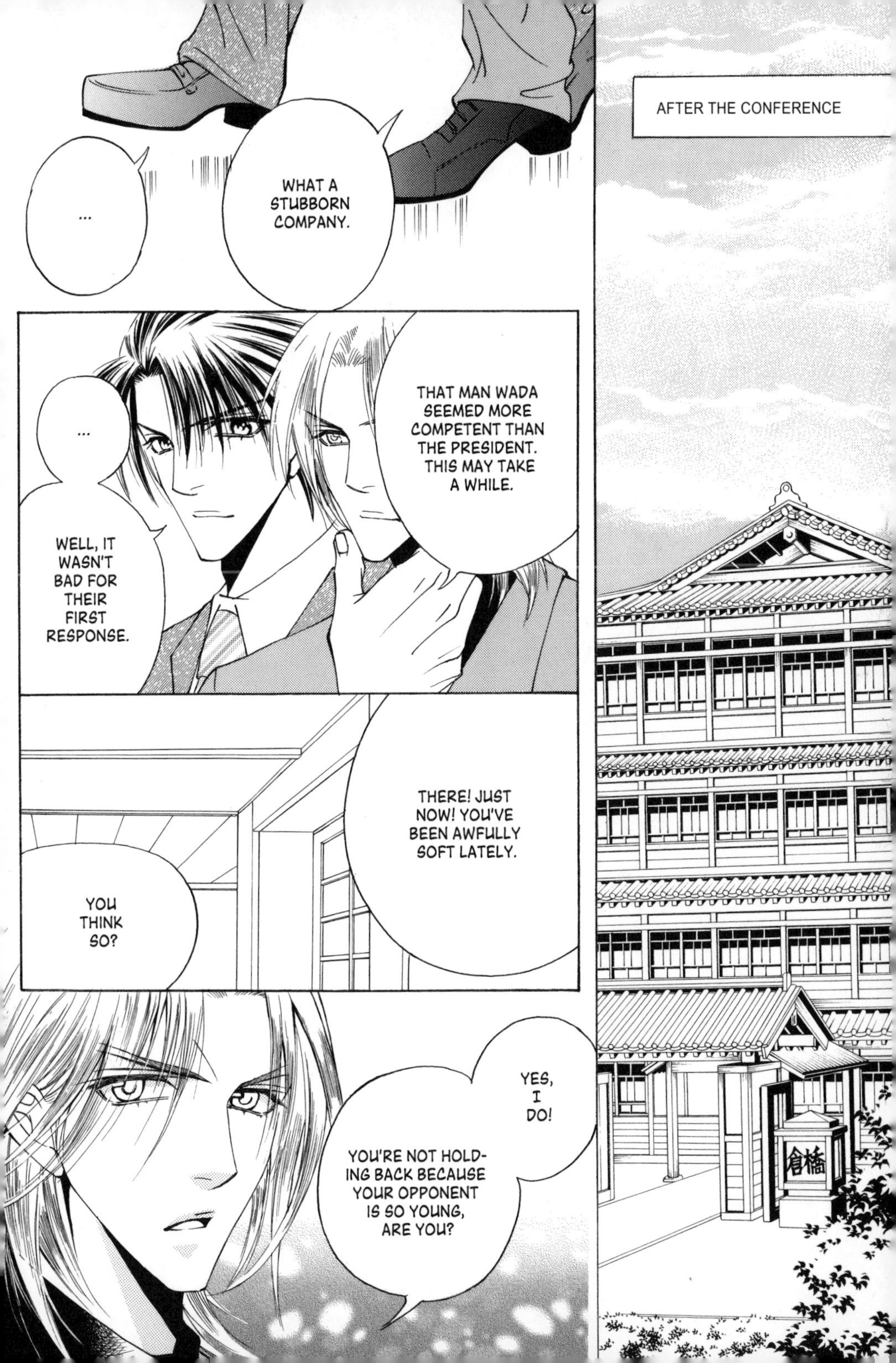
AFTER THE CONFERENCE
WHAT A STUBBORN COMPANY.
...
THAT MAN WADA SEEMED MORE COMPETENT THAN THE PRESIDENT. THIS MAY TAKE A WHILE.
...
WELL, IT WASN'T BAD FOR THEIR FIRST RESPONSE.
THERE! JUST NOW! YOU'VE BEEN AWFULLY SOFT LATELY.
YOU THINK SO?
YES, I DO!
YOU'RE NOT HOLD-ING BACK BECAUSE YOUR OPPONENT IS SO YOUNG, ARE YOU?

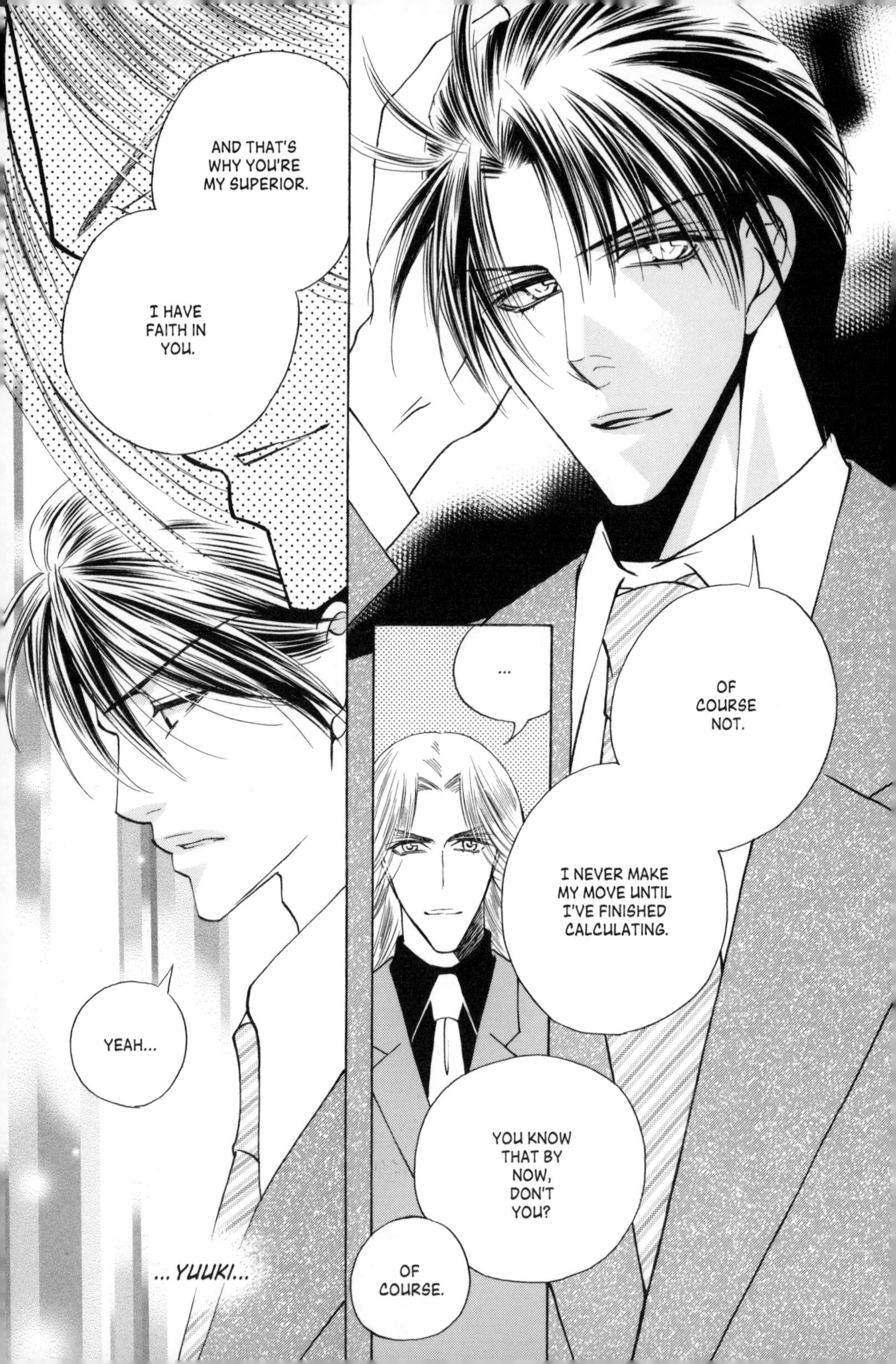
OF COURSE NOT.
I NEVER MAKE MY MOVE UNTIL I'VE FINISHED CALCULATING.
YOU KNOW THAT BY NOW, DON'T YOU?
...
OF COURSE.
AND THAT'S WHY YOU'RE MY SUPERIOR.
I HAVE FAITH IN YOU.
YEAH...
...YUUKI...

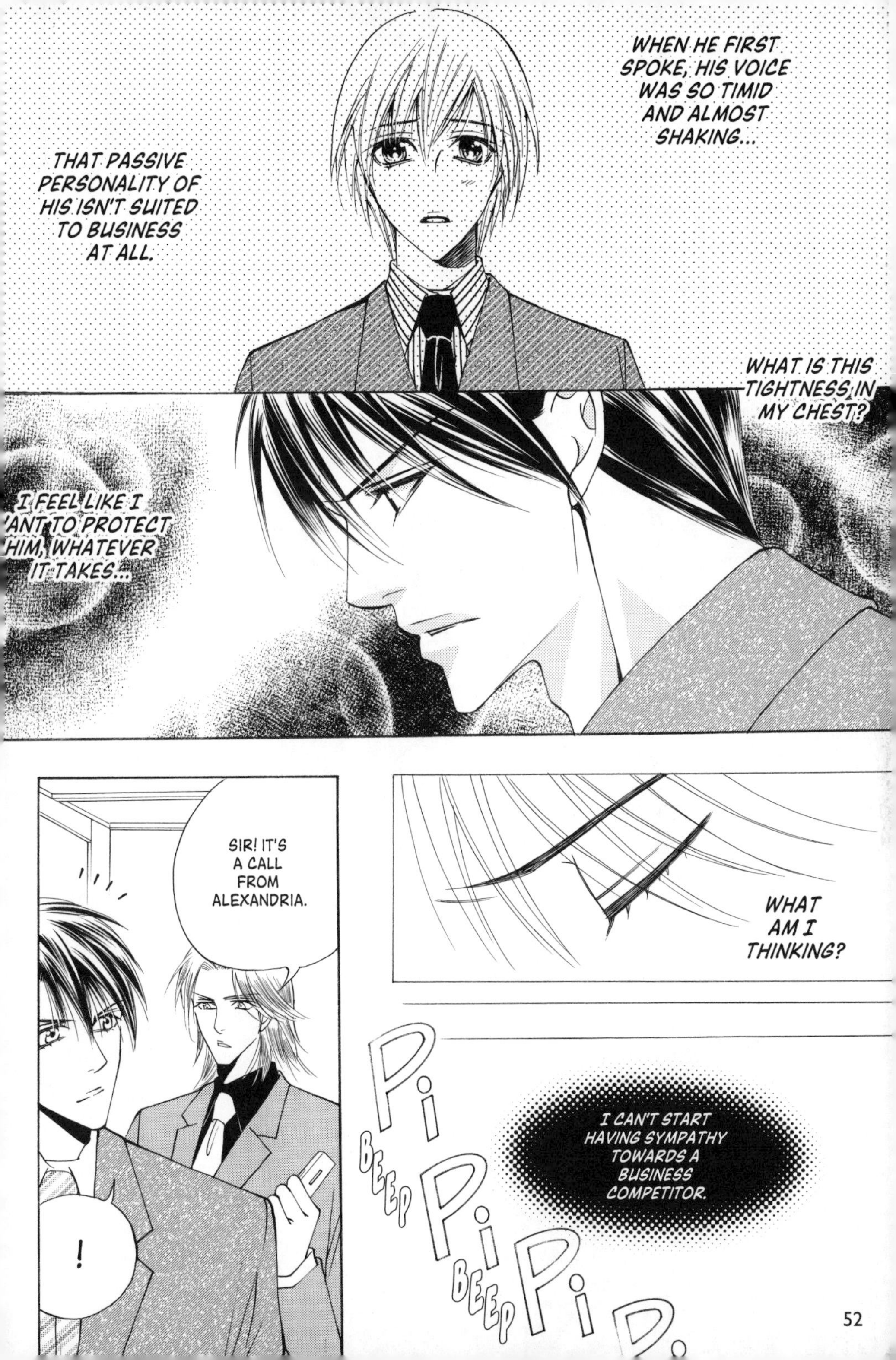
WHEN HE FIRST SPOKE, HIS VOICE WAS SO TIMID AND ALMOST SHAKING...
THAT PASSIVE PERSONALITY OF HIS ISN'T SUITED TO BUSINESS AT ALL.
WHAT IS THIS TIGHTNESS IN MY CHEST?
I FEEL LIKE I ANT TO PROTECT HIM, WHATEVER IT TAKES...
WHAT AM I THINKING?
PI PI PI PI PI
BEEP BEEP
I CAN'T START HAVING SYMPATHY TOWARDS A BUSINESS COMPETITOR.
SIR! IT'S A CALL FROM ALEXANDRIA.
!

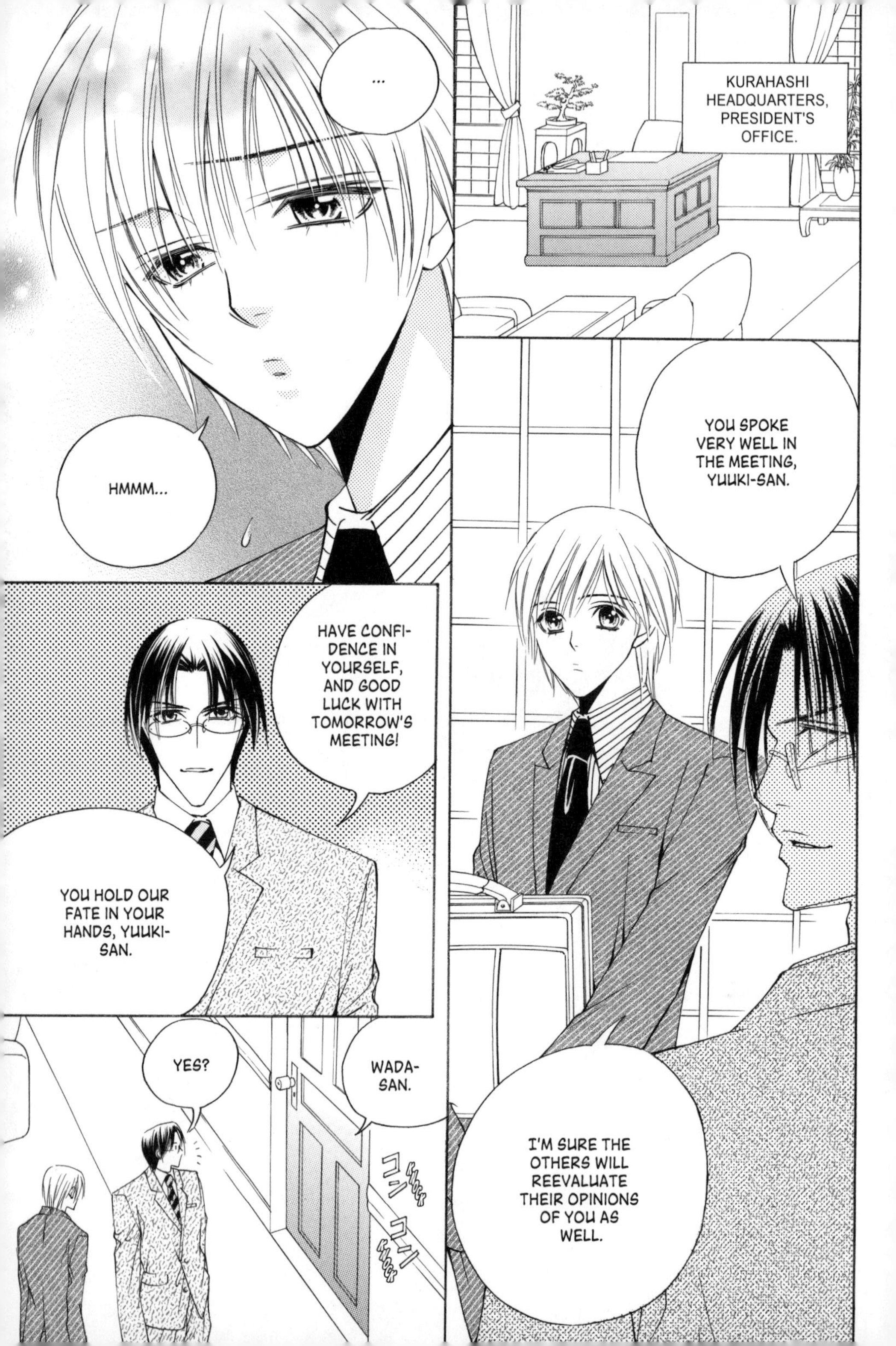
KURAHASHI HEADQUARTERS, PRESIDENT'S OFFICE.
YOU SPOKE VERY WELL IN THE MEETING, YUUKI-SAN.
I'M SURE THE OTHERS WILL REEVALUATE THEIR OPINIONS OF YOU AS WELL.
...
HMMM...
HAVE CONFI-DENCE IN YOURSELF, AND GOOD LUCK WITH TOMORROW'S MEETING!
YOU HOLD OUR FATE IN YOUR HANDS, YUUKI-SAN.
WADA-SAN.
YES?
KNOCK
KNOCK

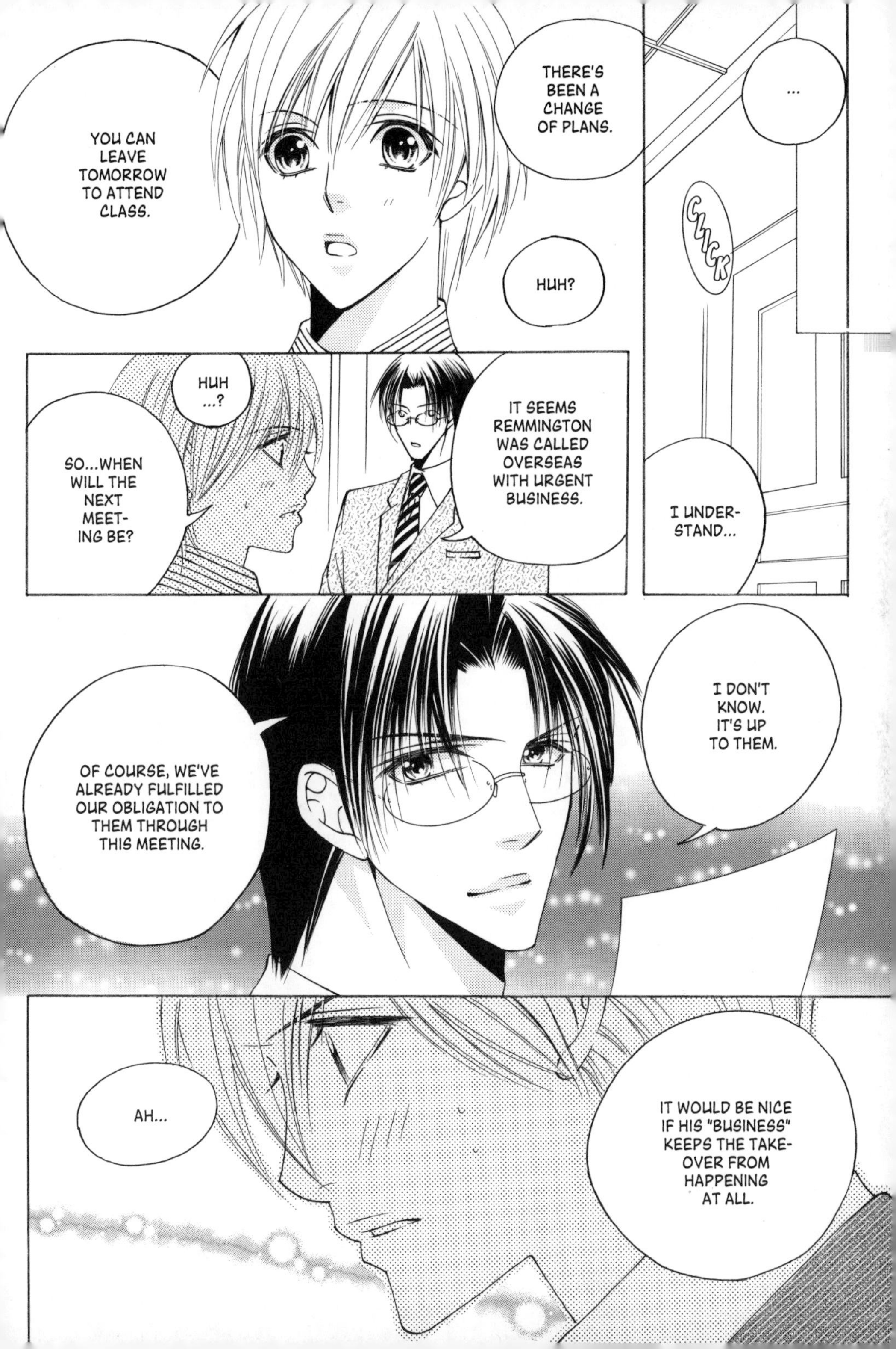
...
CLICK
I UNDER-STAND...
THERE'S BEEN A CHANGE OF PLANS.
YOU CAN LEAVE TOMORROW TO ATTEND CLASS.
HUH?
IT SEEMS REMMINGTON WAS CALLED OVERSEAS WITH URGENT BUSINESS.
HUH ...?
SO...WHEN WILL THE NEXT MEET-ING BE?
I DON'T KNOW. IT'S UP TO THEM.
OF COURSE, WE'VE ALREADY FULFILLED OUR OBLIGATION TO THEM THROUGH THIS MEETING.
IT WOULD BE NICE IF HIS "BUSINESS" KEEPS THE TAKE-OVER FROM HAPPENING AT ALL.
AH...

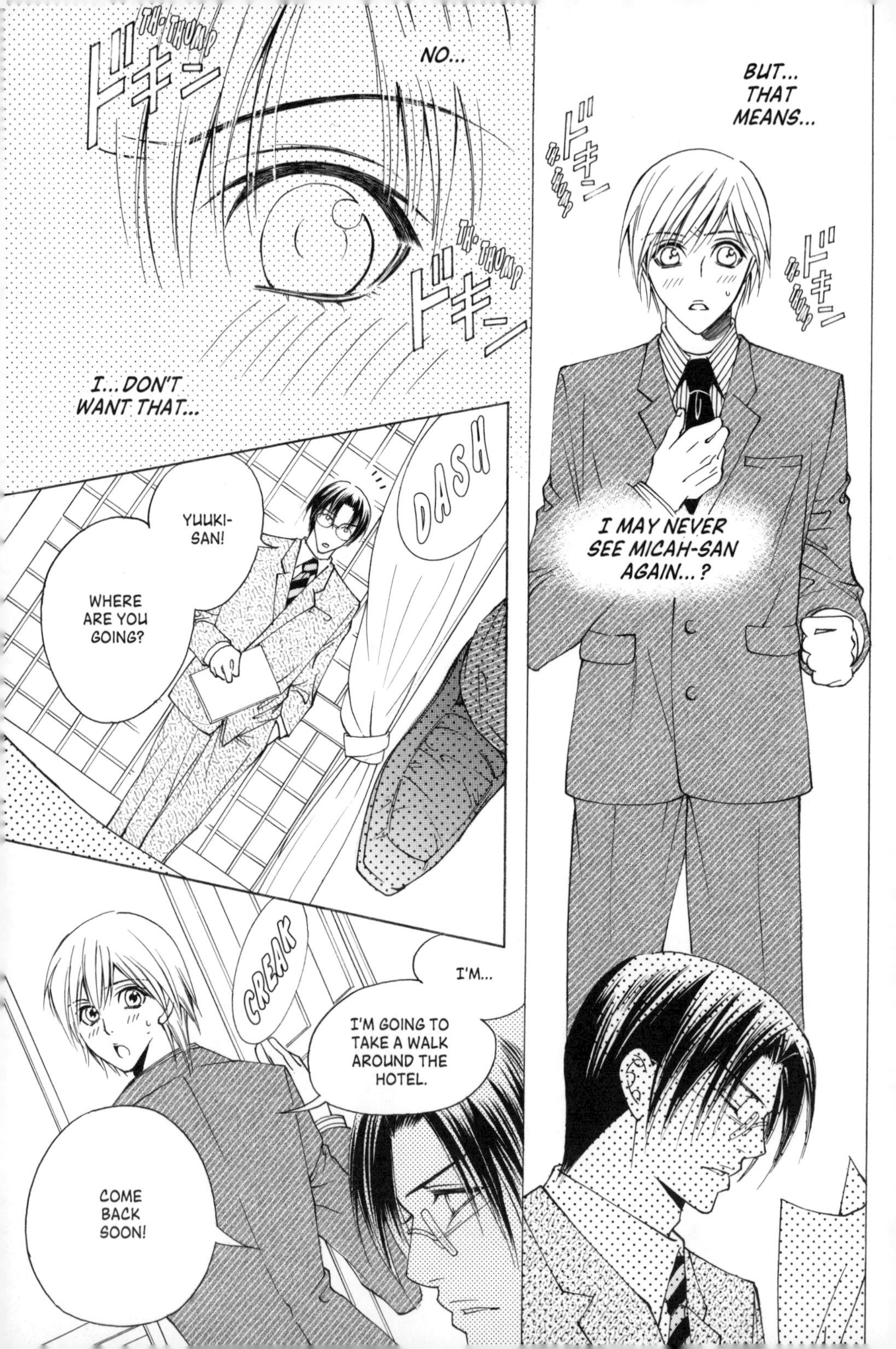
BUT... THAT MEANS...
ドキン
TH-THUMP
ドキン
TH-THUMP
I MAY NEVER SEE MICAH-SAN AGAIN...?
NO...
ドキン
TH-THUMP
ドキン
TH-THUMP
I... DON'T WANT THAT...
DASH
YUUKI-SAN!
WHERE ARE YOU GOING?
CREAK
I'M...
I'M GOING TO TAKE A WALK AROUND THE HOTEL.
COME BACK SOON!

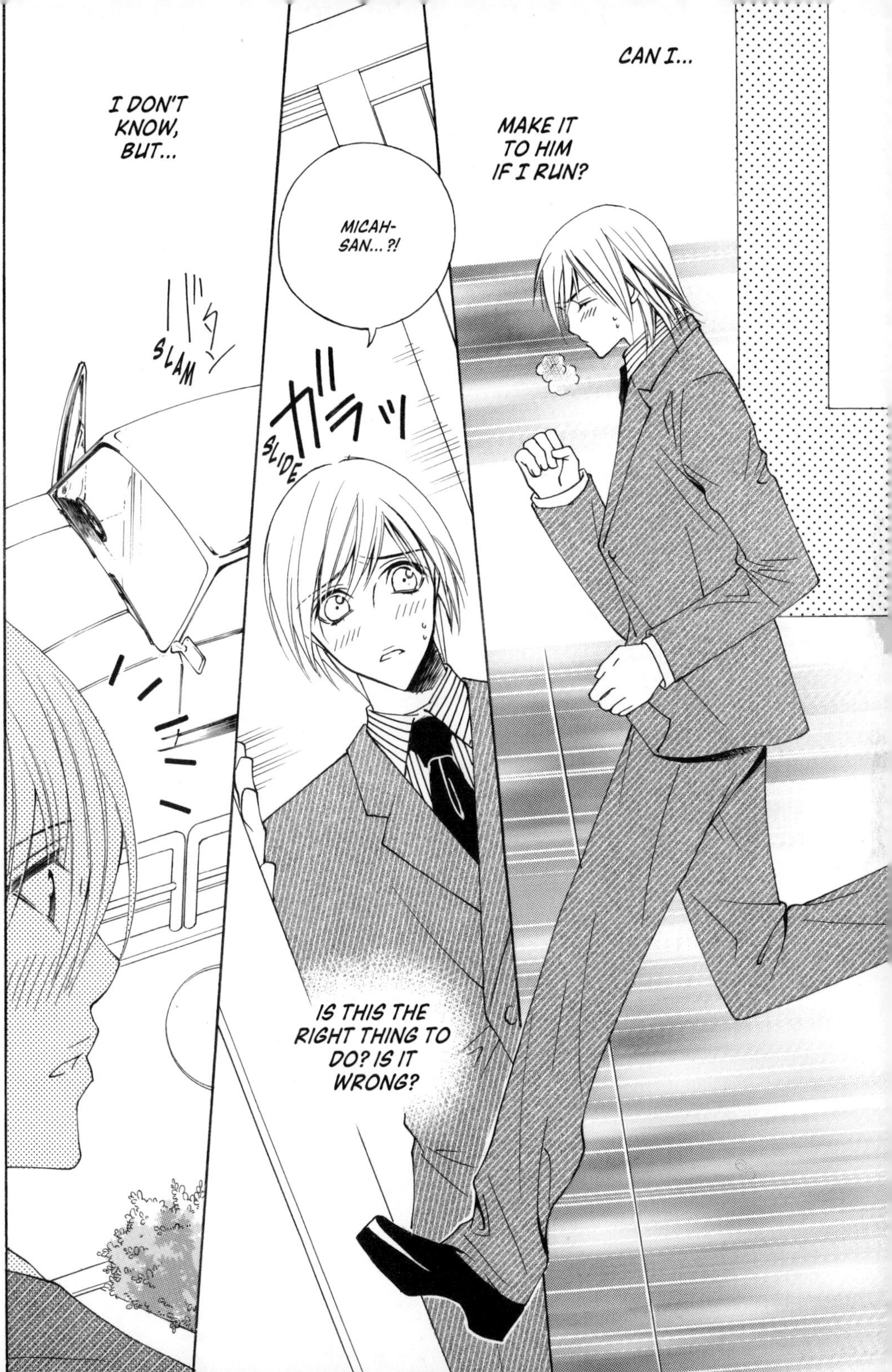
CAN I...
MAKE IT TO HIM IF I RUN?
MICAH-SAN...?!
ガラッ
SLIDE
IS THIS THE RIGHT THING TO DO? IS IT WRONG?
I DON'T KNOW, BUT...
バタン
SLAM

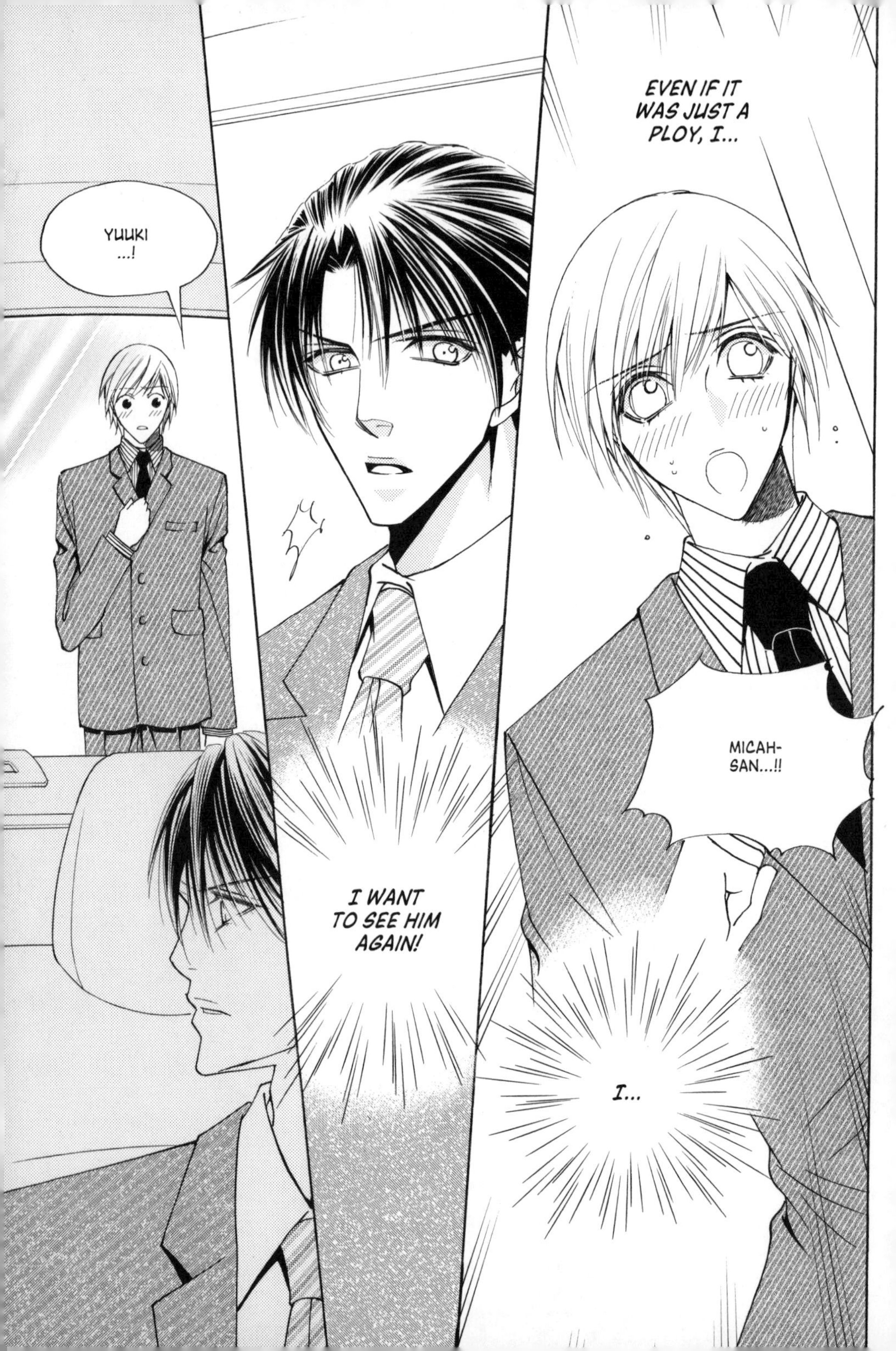
EVEN IF IT WAS JUST A PLOY, I...
MICAH-SAN...!!
I...
I WANT TO SEE HIM AGAIN!
YUUKI ...!

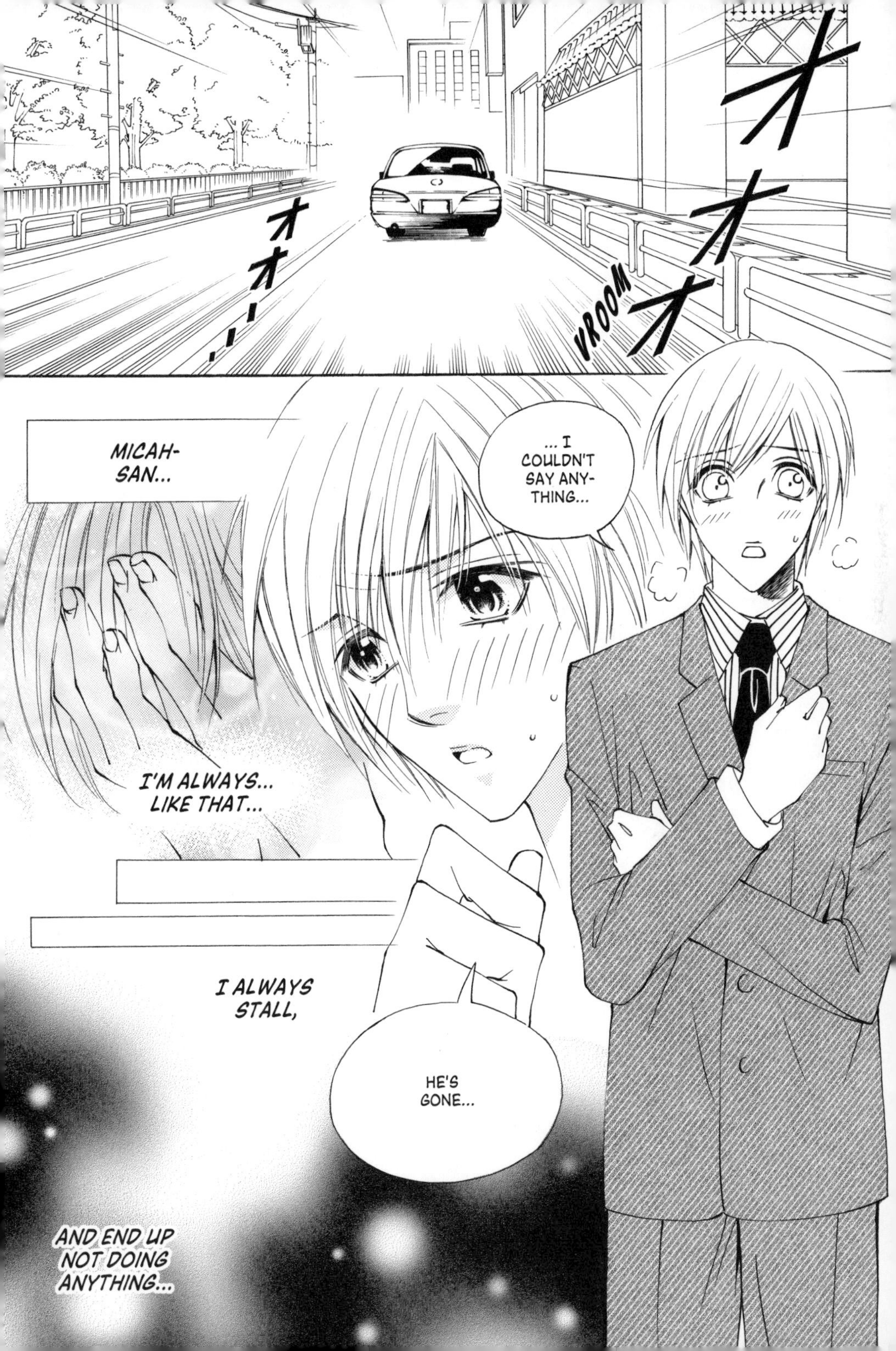

オオオ
VROOM
オオー
... I COULDN'T SAY ANYTHING...
MICAH-SAN...
I'M ALWAYS... LIKE THAT...
I ALWAYS STALL,
HE'S GONE...
AND END UP NOT DOING ANYTHING...

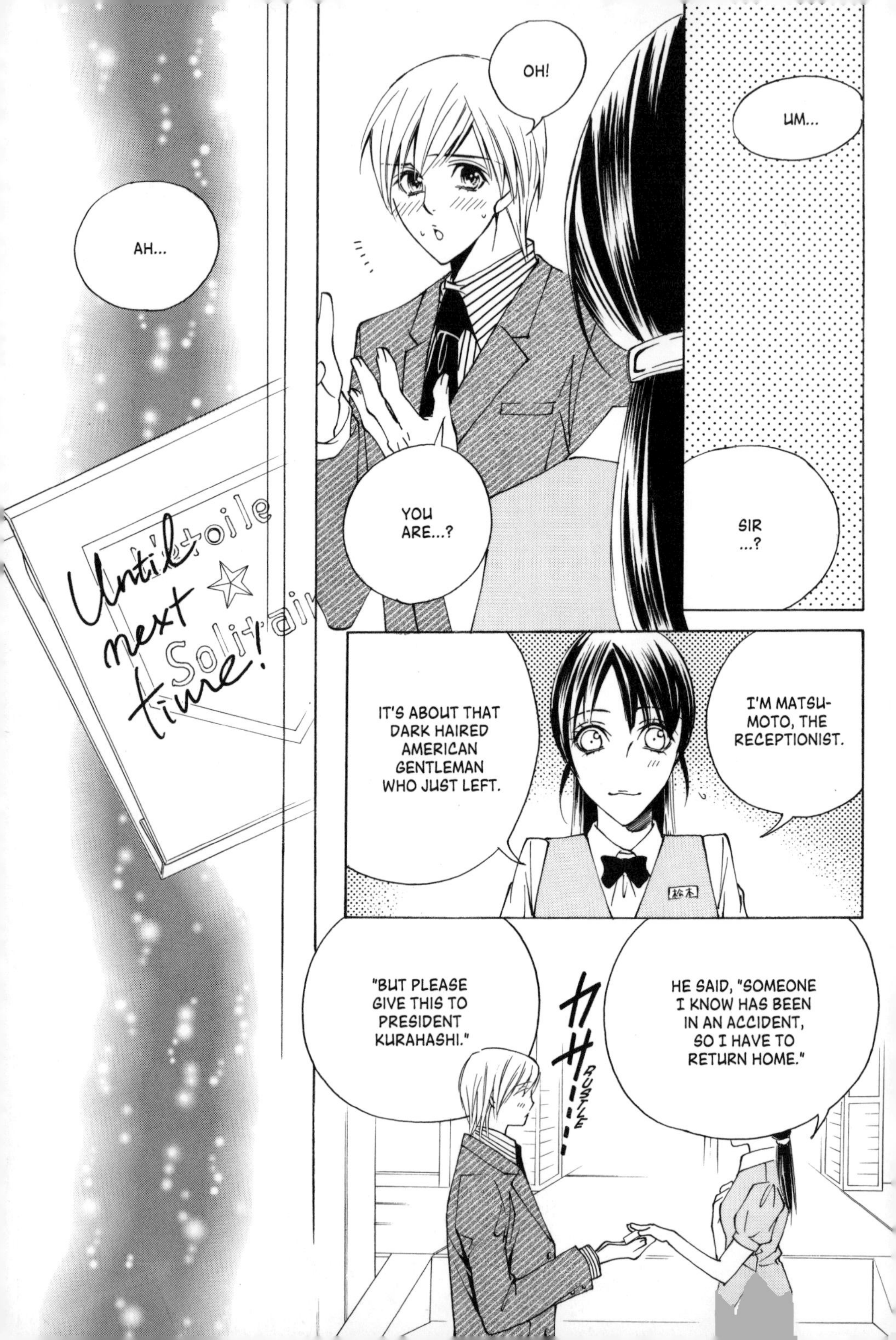
UM...
SIR ...?
OH!
YOU ARE...?
I'M MATSU-MOTO, THE RECEPTIONIST.
IT'S ABOUT THAT DARK HAIRED AMERICAN GENTLEMAN WHO JUST LEFT.
松本
HE SAID, "SOMEONE I KNOW HAS BEEN IN AN ACCIDENT, SO I HAVE TO RETURN HOME."
"BUT PLEASE GIVE THIS TO PRESIDENT KURAHASHI."
カサ
RUSTLE
AH...
L'étoile Solitaire
Until next time!

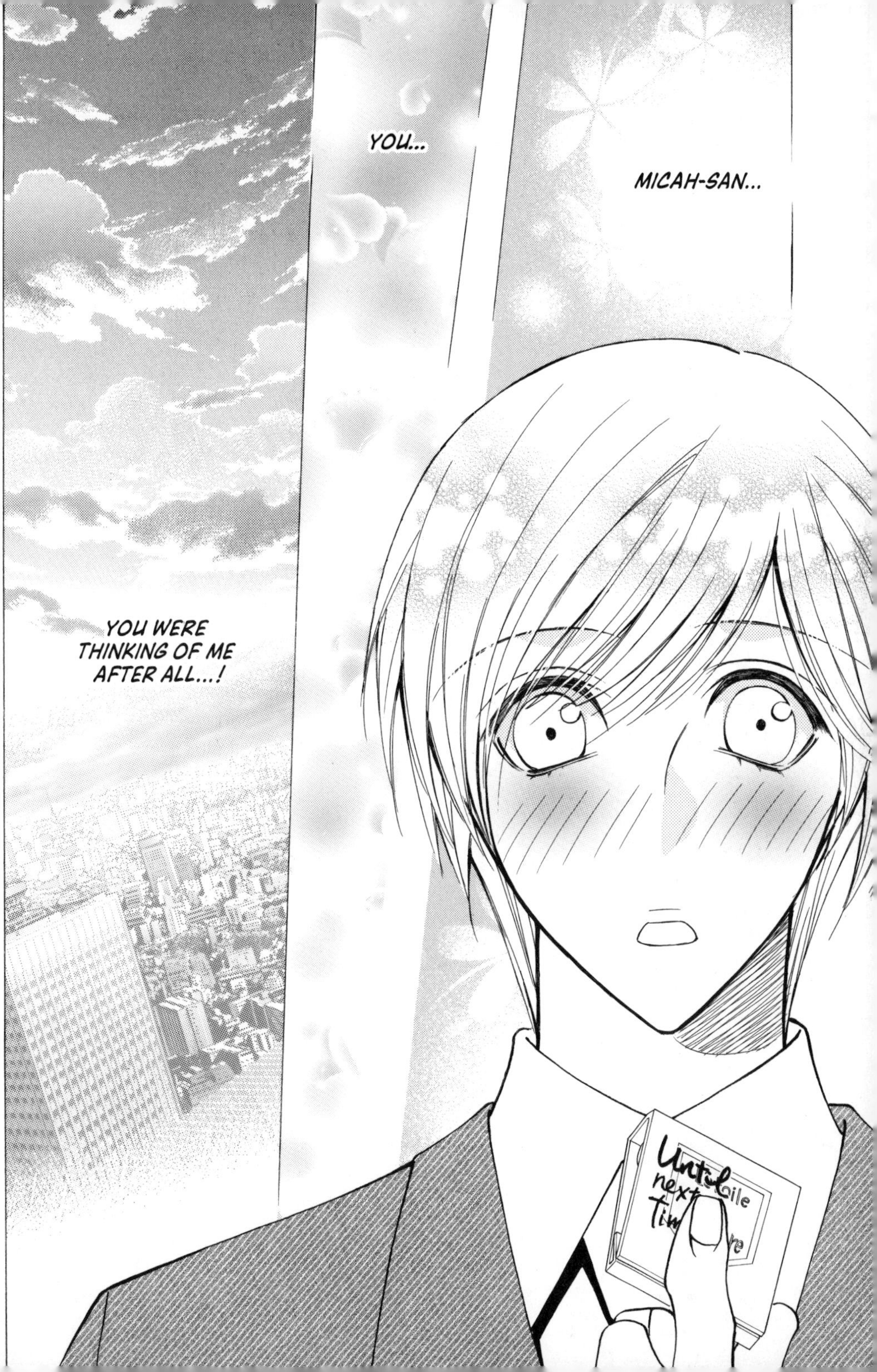
MICAH-SAN...
YOU...
YOU WERE THINKING OF ME AFTER ALL...!

Chapter 2

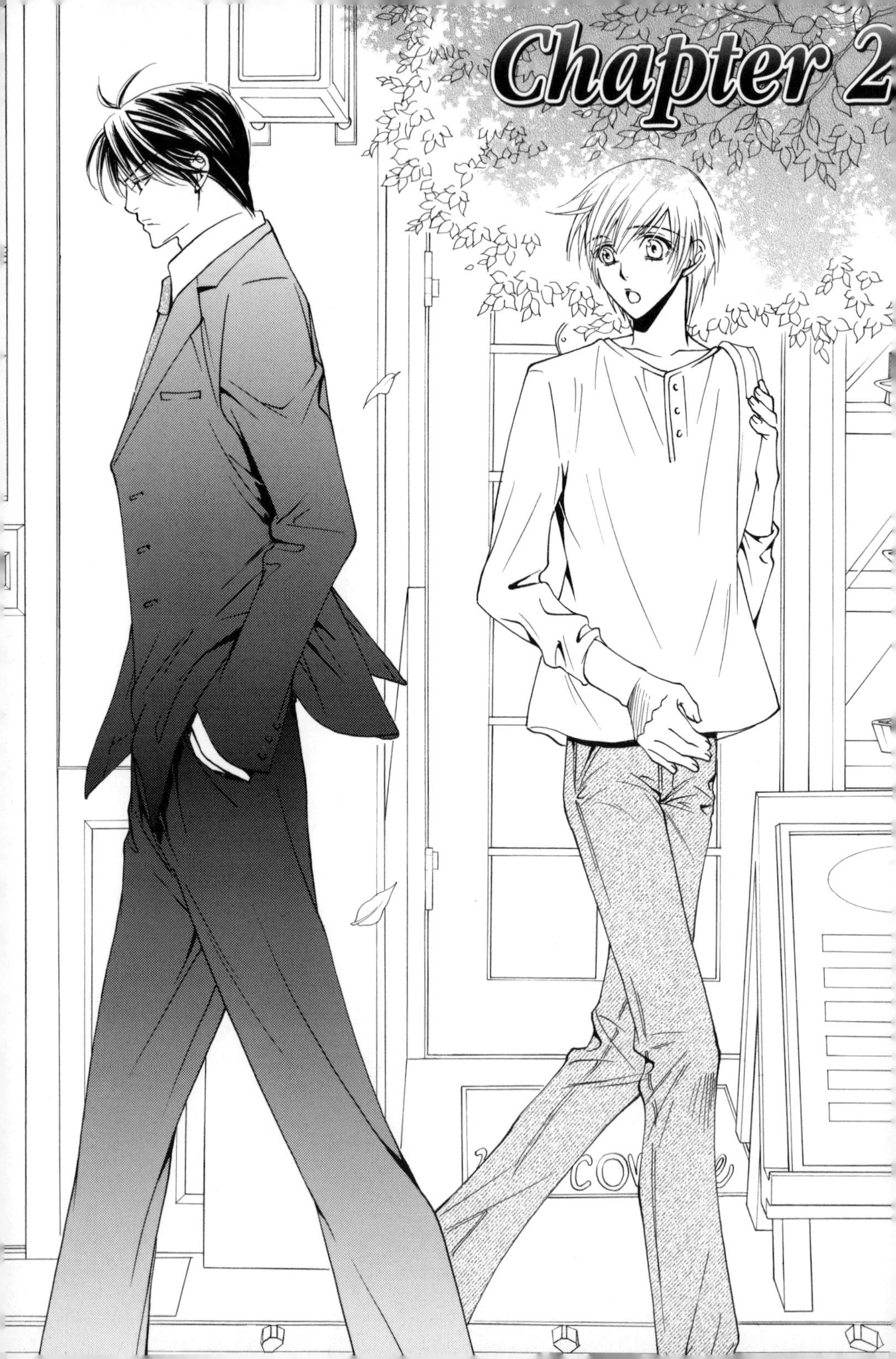

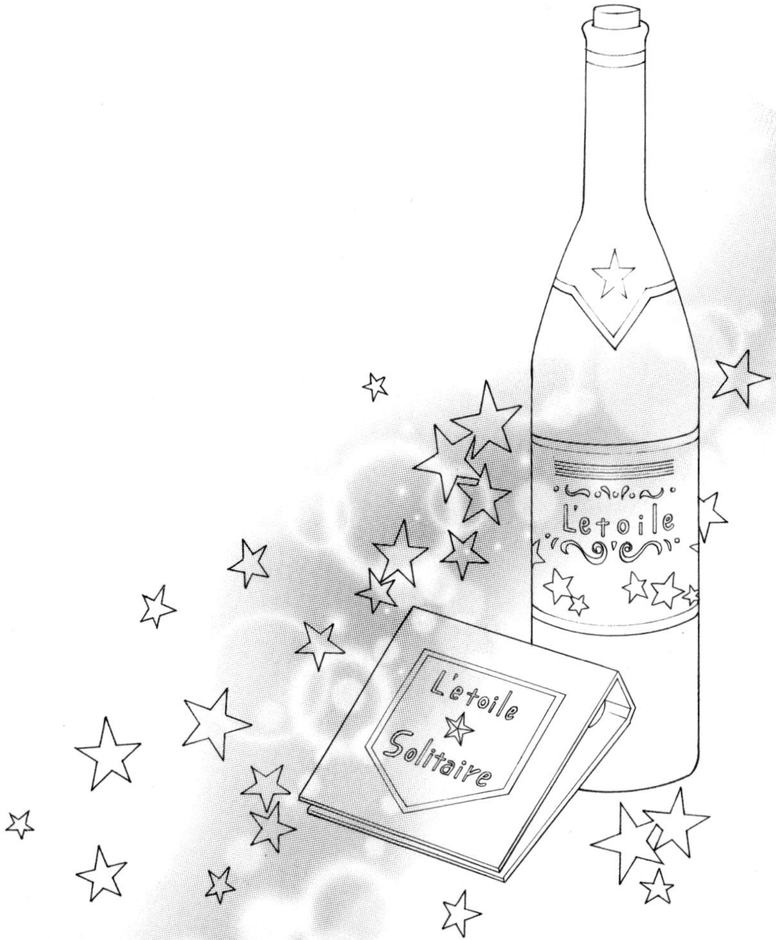
L'etoile
L'etoile Solitaire

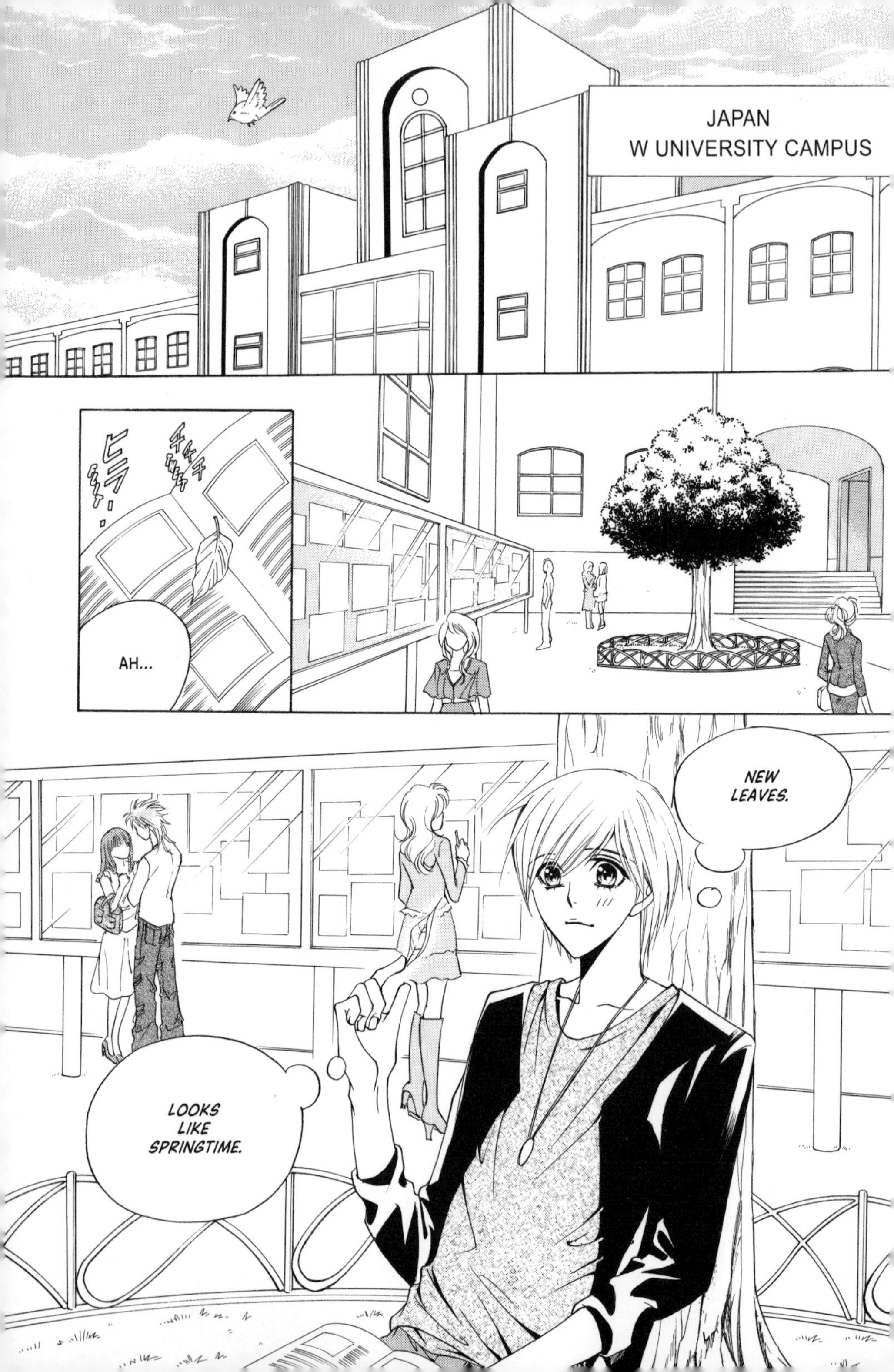
JAPAN
W UNIVERSITY CAMPUS
チチチ
ヒラ
AH...
NEW LEAVES.
LOOKS LIKE SPRINGTIME.

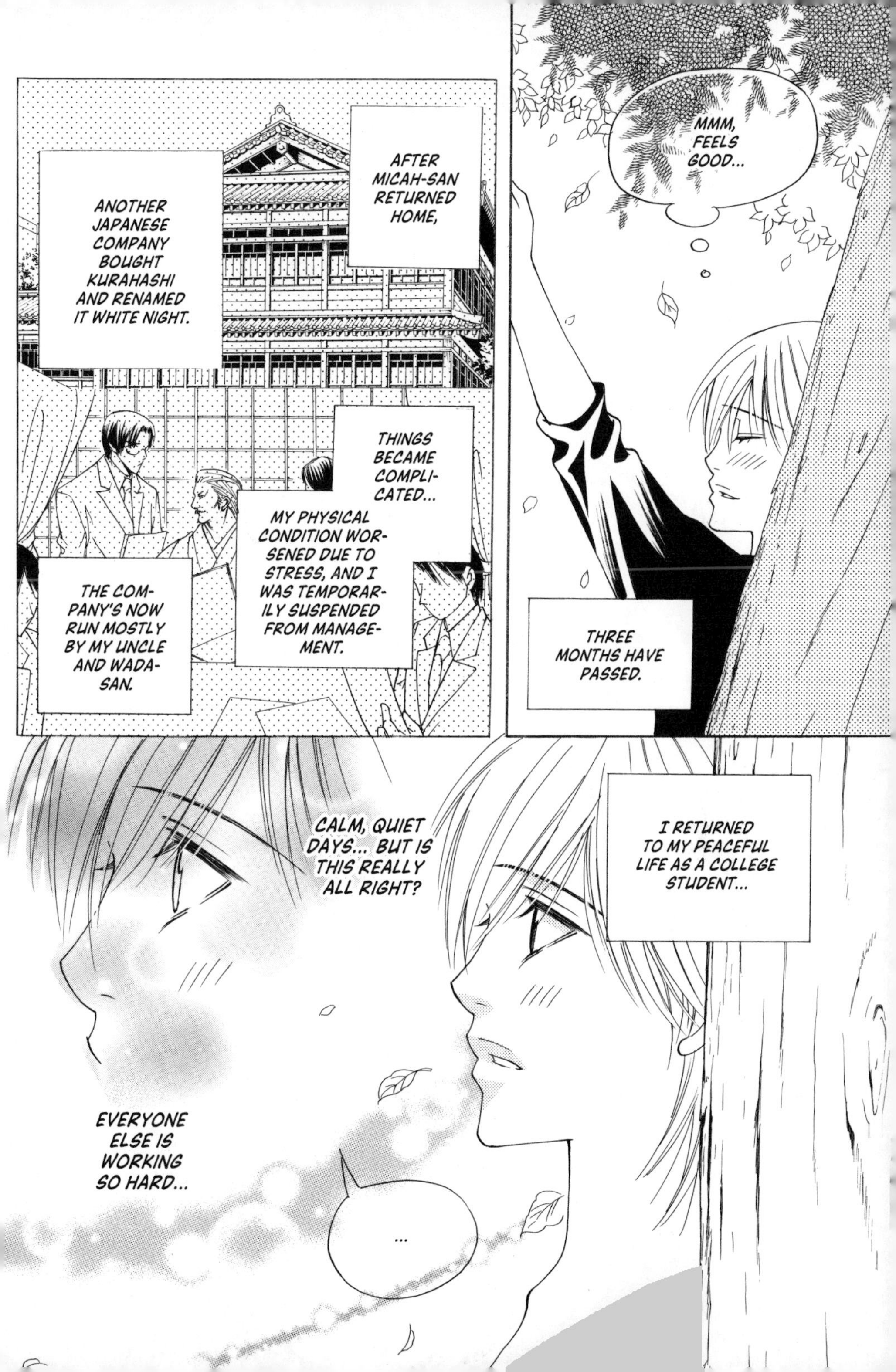
MMM, FEELS GOOD...
THREE MONTHS HAVE PASSED.
AFTER MICAH-SAN RETURNED HOME,
ANOTHER JAPANESE COMPANY BOUGHT KURAHASHI AND RENAMED IT WHITE NIGHT.
THINGS BECAME COMPLICATED...
MY PHYSICAL CONDITION WORSENED DUE TO STRESS, AND I WAS TEMPORARILY SUSPENDED FROM MANAGEMENT.
THE COMPANY'S NOW RUN MOSTLY BY MY UNCLE AND WADA-SAN.
I RETURNED TO MY PEACEFUL LIFE AS A COLLEGE STUDENT...
CALM, QUIET DAYS... BUT IS THIS REALLY ALL RIGHT?
EVERYONE ELSE IS WORKING SO HARD...
...

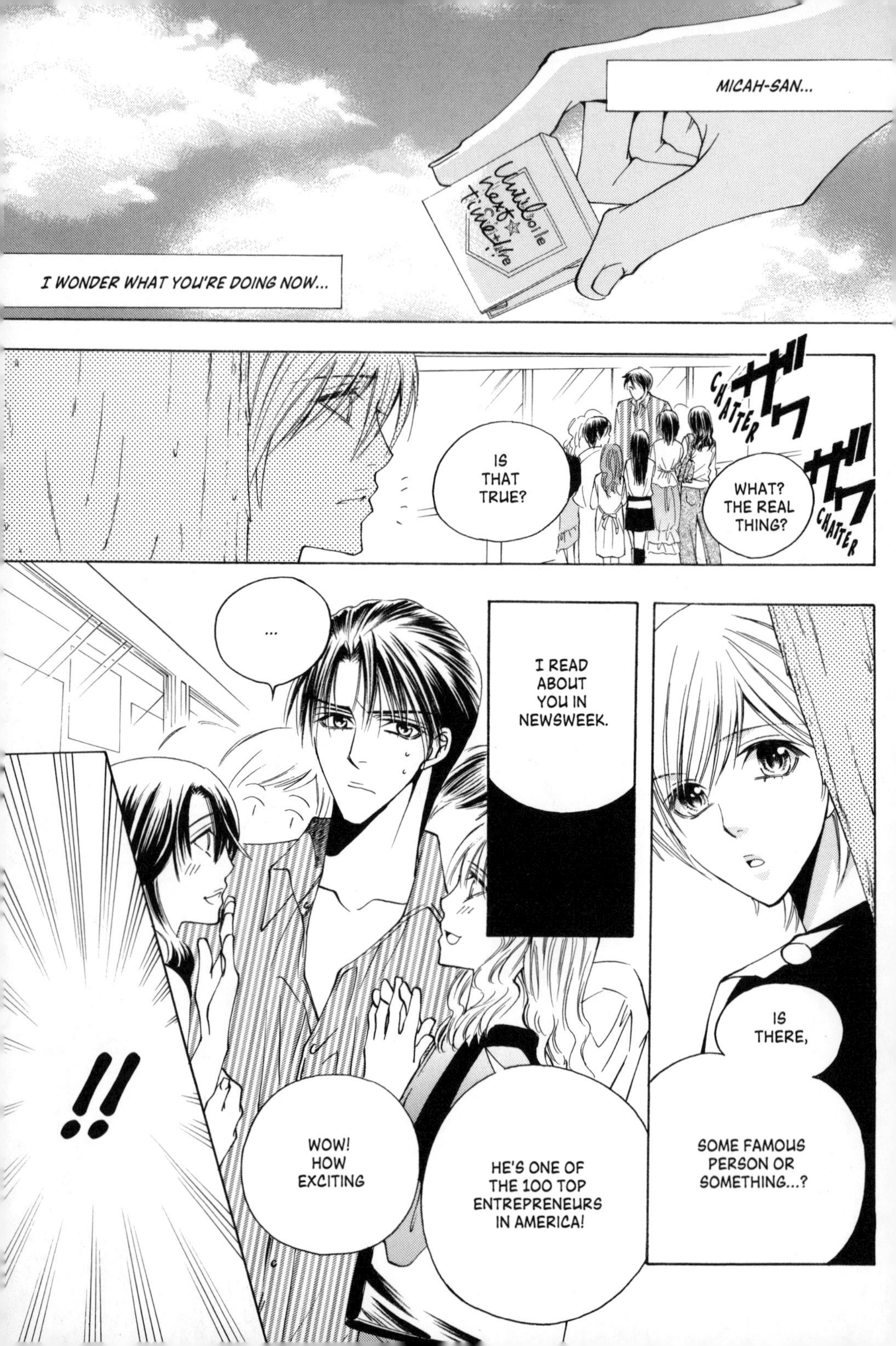
MICAH-SAN...
I WONDER WHAT YOU'RE DOING NOW...
CHATTER
CHATTER
WHAT? THE REAL THING?
IS THAT TRUE?
IS THERE, SOME FAMOUS PERSON OR SOMETHING...?
I READ ABOUT YOU IN NEWSWEEK.
...
HE'S ONE OF THE 100 TOP ENTREPRENEURS IN AMERICA!
WOW! HOW EXCITING
!!

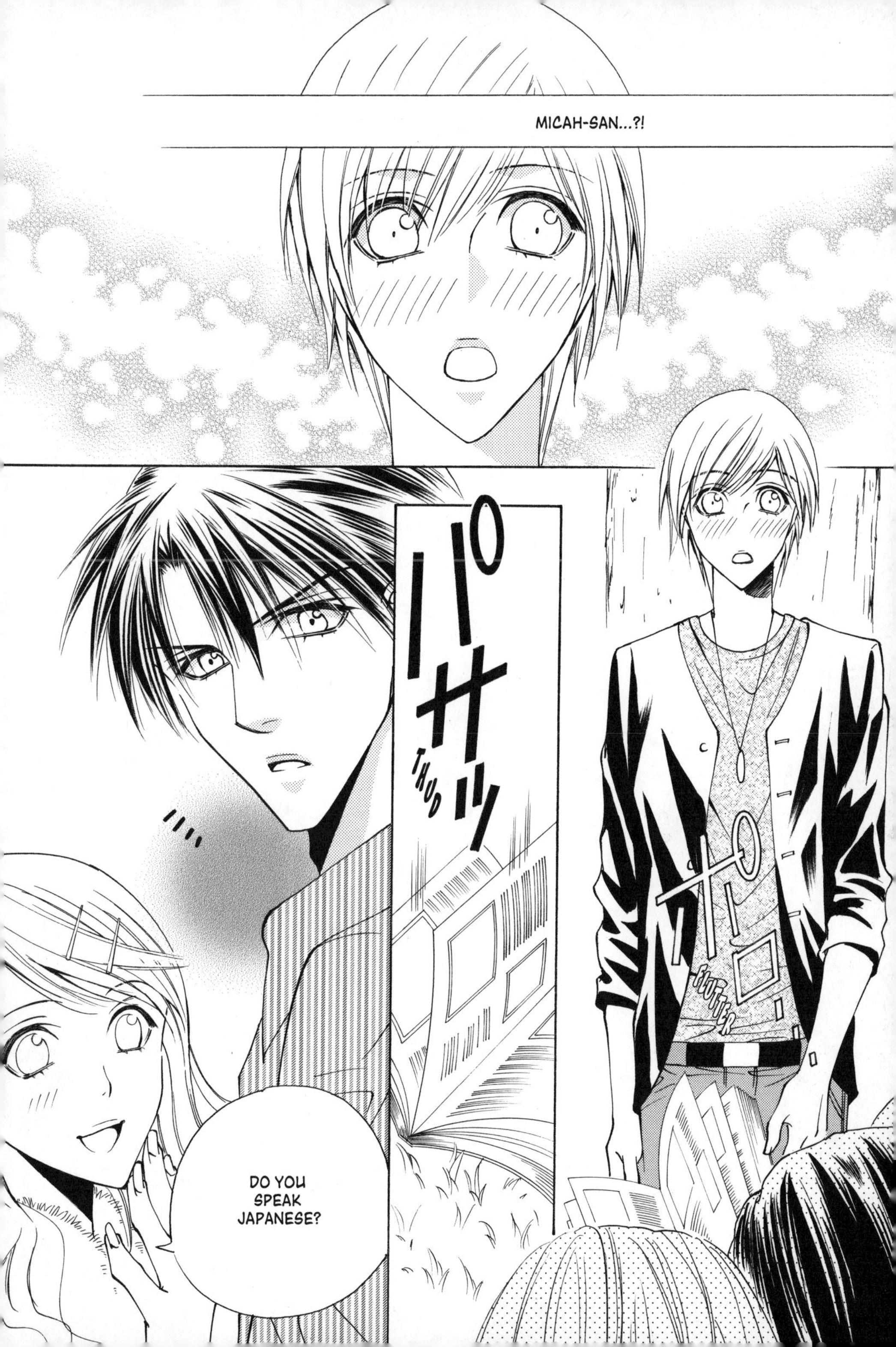
MICAH-SAN...?!
FLUTTER
パサッ
THUD
...
DO YOU SPEAK JAPANESE?

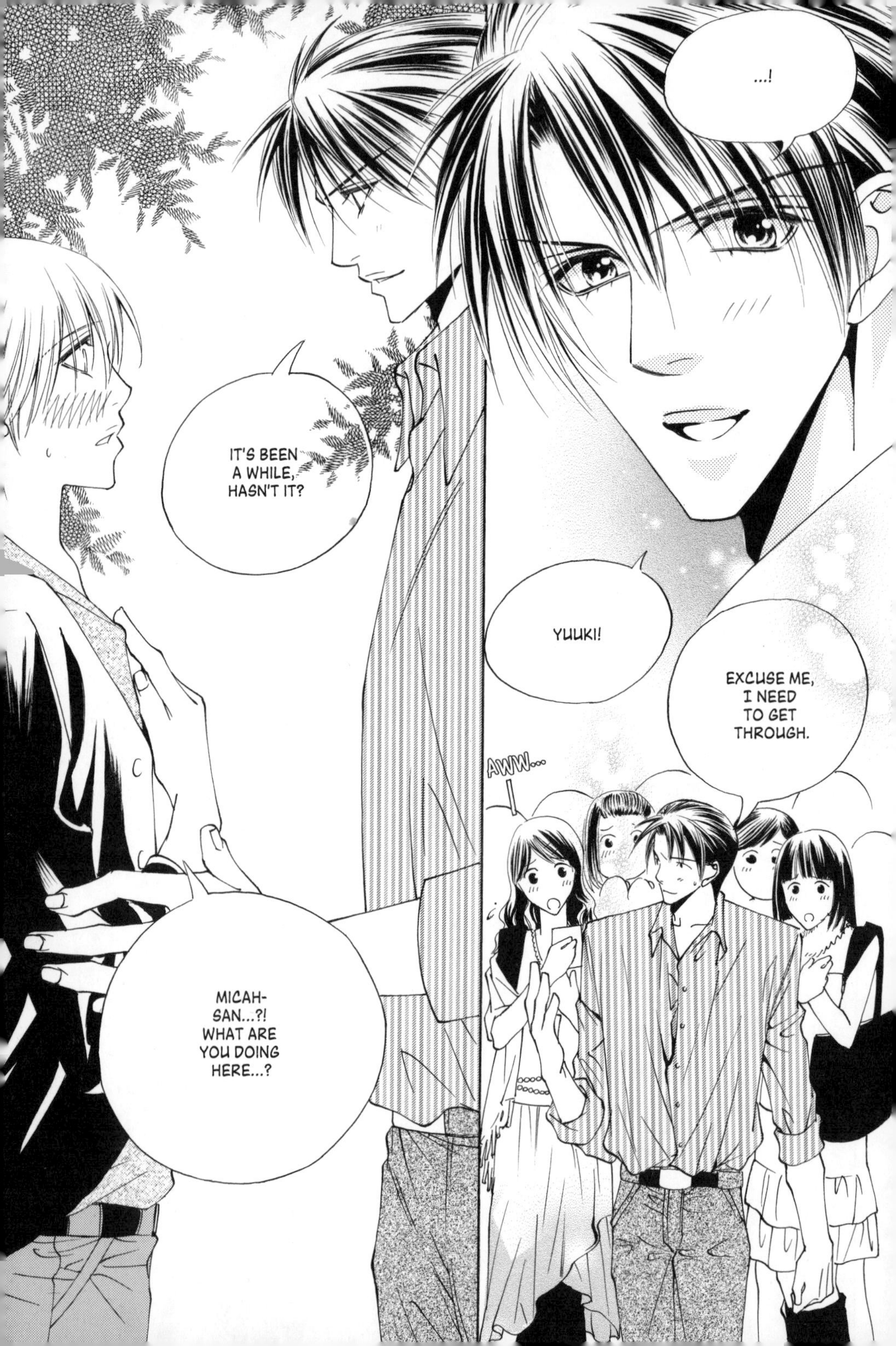
...!
YUUKI!
EXCUSE ME, I NEED TO GET THROUGH.
AWW...
IT'S BEEN A WHILE, HASN'T IT?
MICAH-SAN...?! WHAT ARE YOU DOING HERE...?

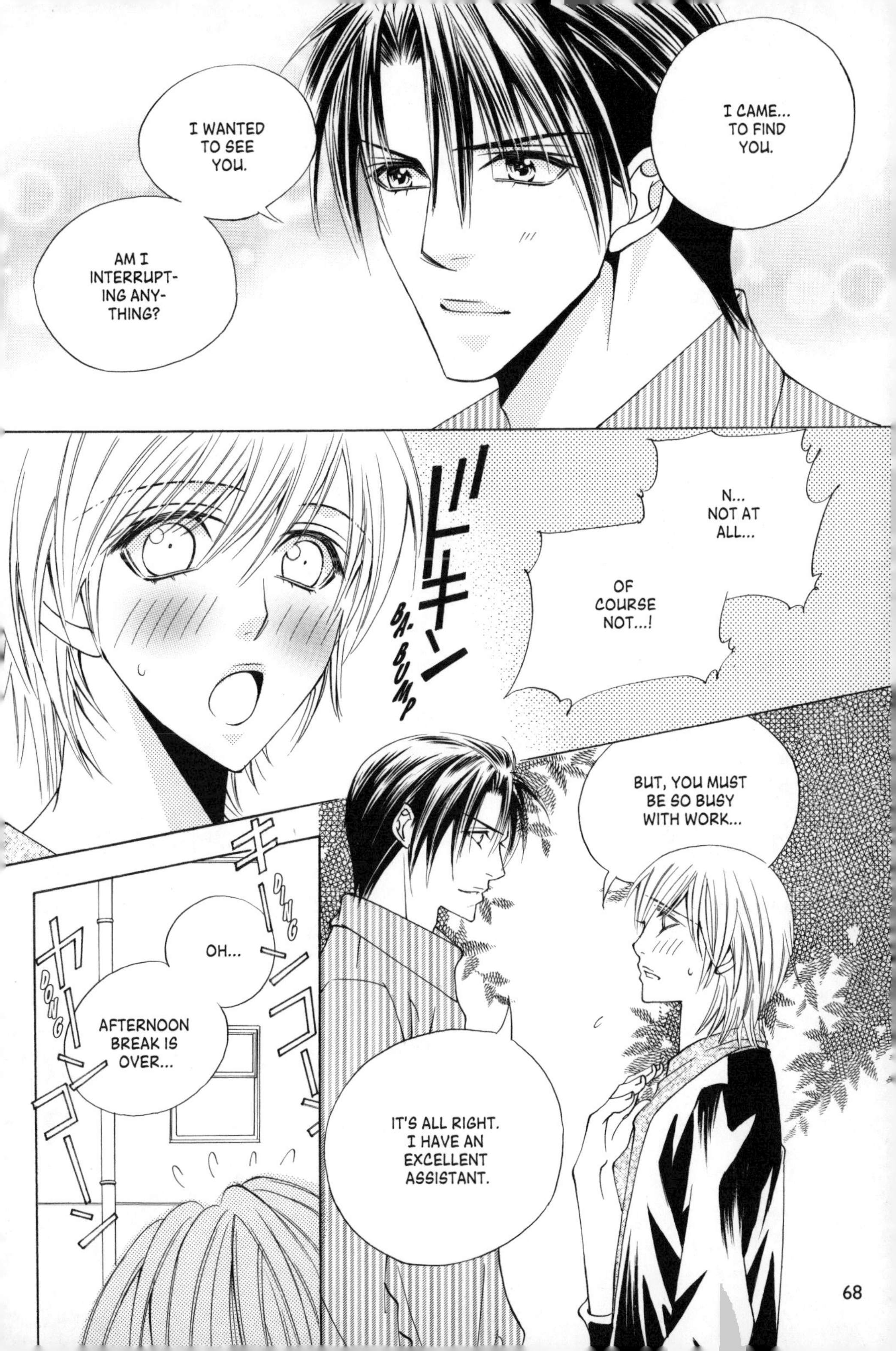
I CAME... TO FIND YOU.
I WANTED TO SEE YOU.
AM I INTERRUPTING ANYTHING?
BA-BUMP
N... NOT AT ALL...
OF COURSE NOT...!
BUT, YOU MUST BE SO BUSY WITH WORK...
IT'S ALL RIGHT. I HAVE AN EXCELLENT ASSISTANT.
DING
DONG
OH...
AFTERNOON BREAK IS OVER...

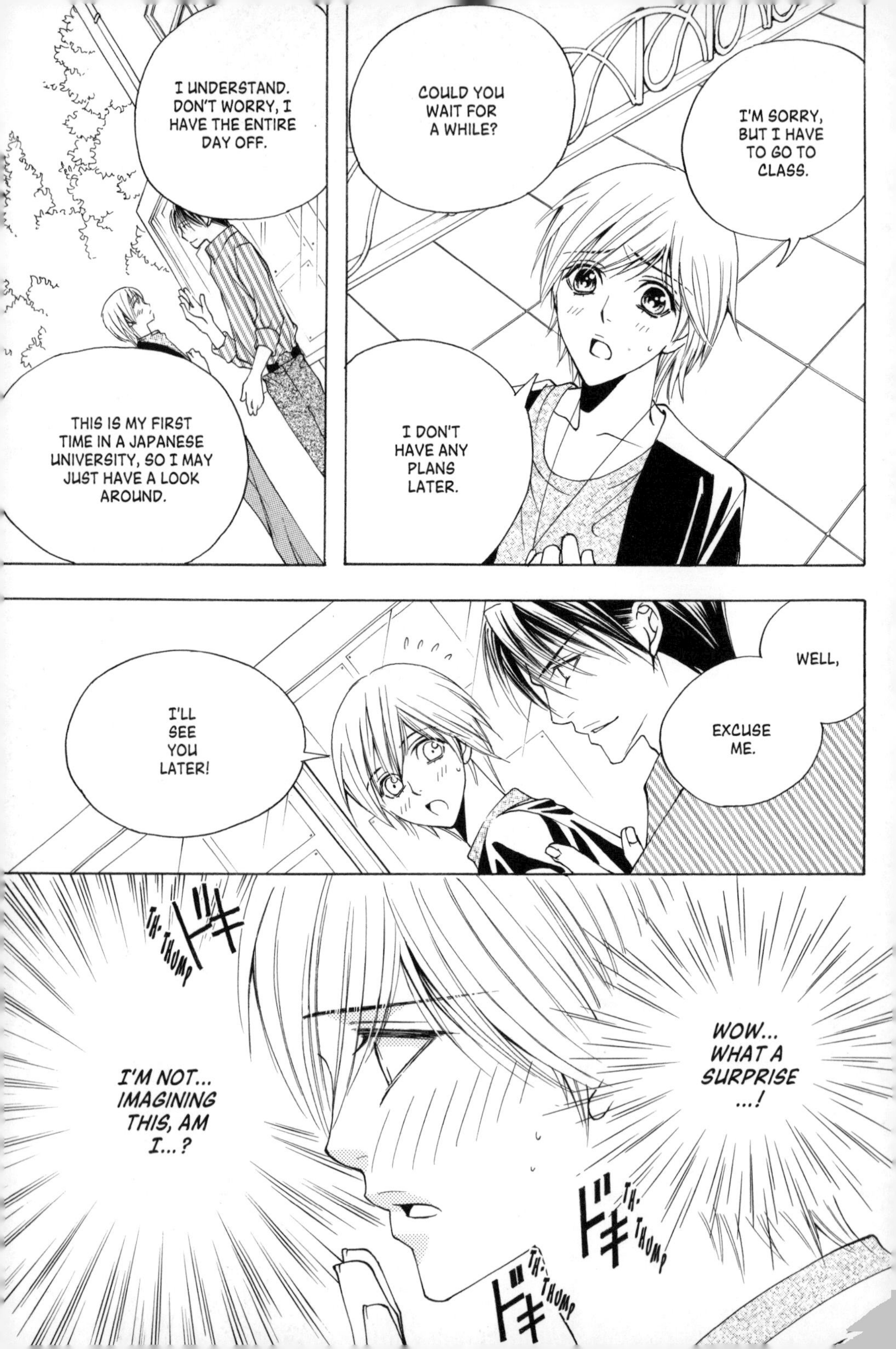
I'M SORRY, BUT I HAVE TO GO TO CLASS.
COULD YOU WAIT FOR A WHILE?
I DON'T HAVE ANY PLANS LATER.
I UNDERSTAND. DON'T WORRY, I HAVE THE ENTIRE DAY OFF.
THIS IS MY FIRST TIME IN A JAPANESE UNIVERSITY, SO I MAY JUST HAVE A LOOK AROUND.
WELL,
EXCUSE ME.
I'LL SEE YOU LATER!
ドキ TH-THOMP
WOW... WHAT A SURPRISE ...!
ドキ TH-THOMP
ドキ TH-THOMP
I'M NOT... IMAGINING THIS, AM I...?

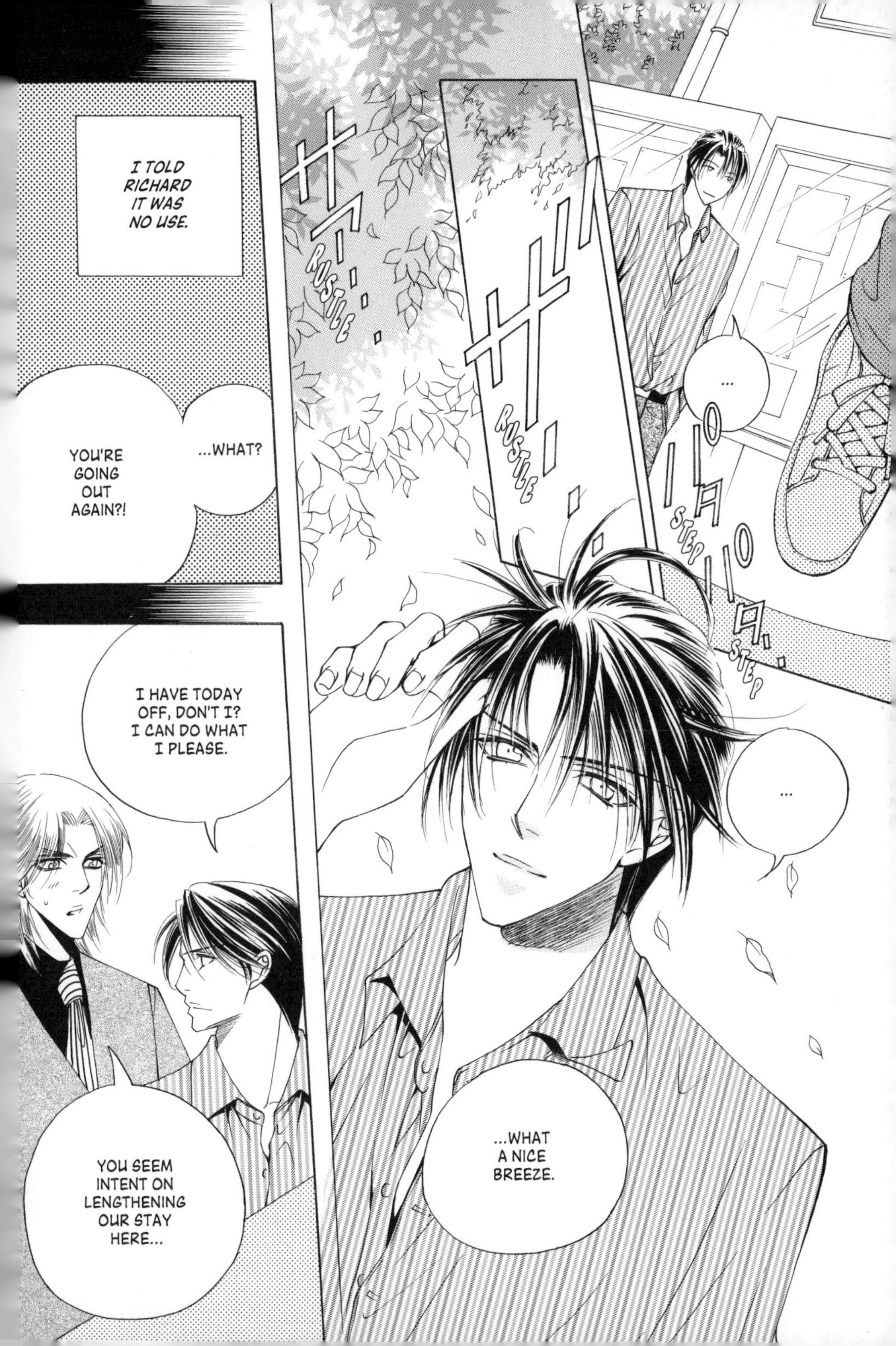

STEP
STEP
...
RUSTLE
RUSTLE
...
...WHAT A NICE BREEZE.
I TOLD RICHARD IT WAS NO USE.
...WHAT?
YOU'RE GOING OUT AGAIN?!
I HAVE TODAY OFF, DON'T I? I CAN DO WHAT I PLEASE.
YOU SEEM INTENT ON LENGTHENING OUR STAY HERE...

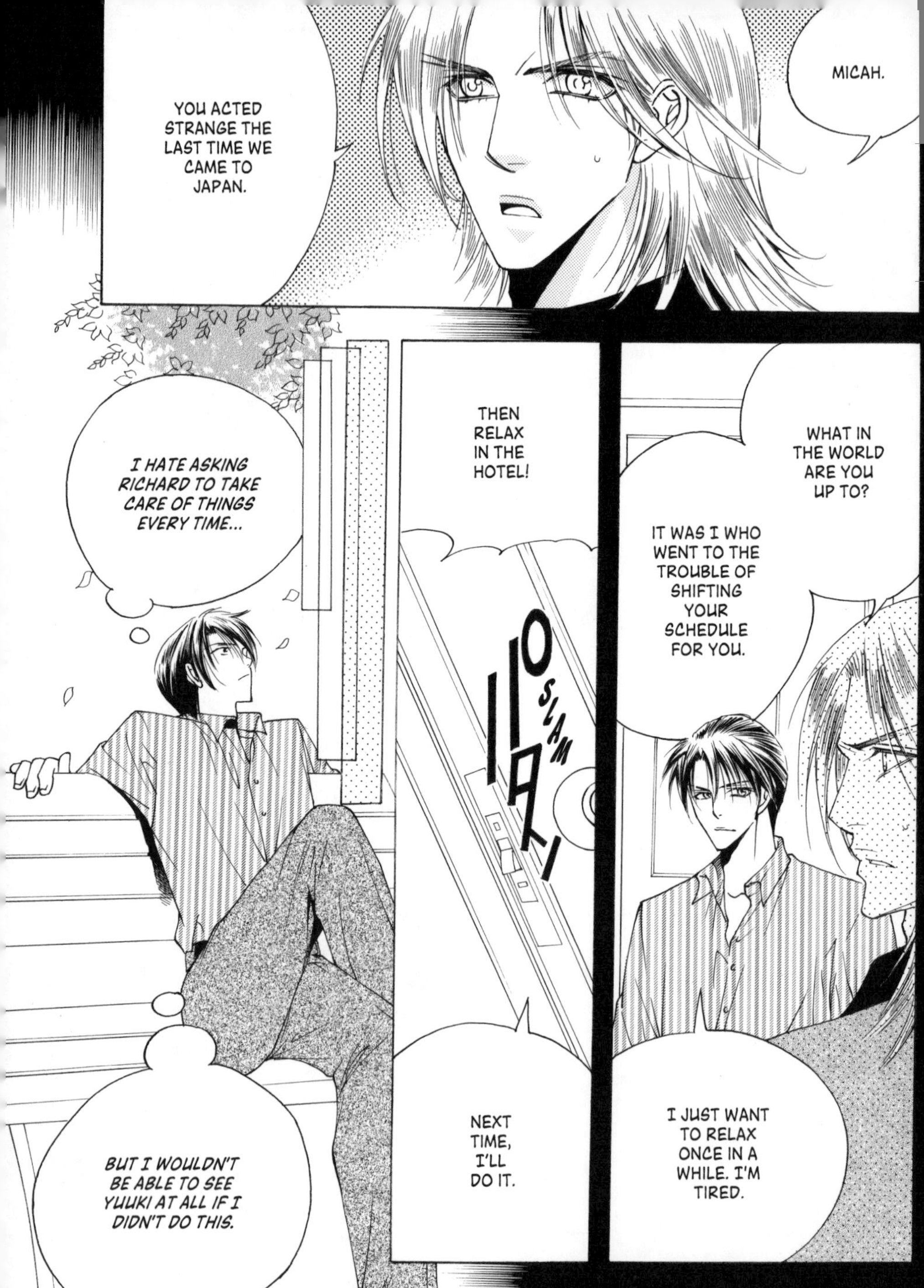
MICAH.
YOU ACTED STRANGE THE LAST TIME WE CAME TO JAPAN.
WHAT IN THE WORLD ARE YOU UP TO?
IT WAS I WHO WENT TO THE TROUBLE OF SHIFTING YOUR SCHEDULE FOR YOU.
I JUST WANT TO RELAX ONCE IN A WHILE. I'M TIRED.
THEN RELAX IN THE HOTEL!
SLAM
NEXT TIME, I'LL DO IT.
I HATE ASKING RICHARD TO TAKE CARE OF THINGS EVERY TIME...
BUT I WOULDN'T BE ABLE TO SEE YUUKI AT ALL IF I DIDN'T DO THIS.

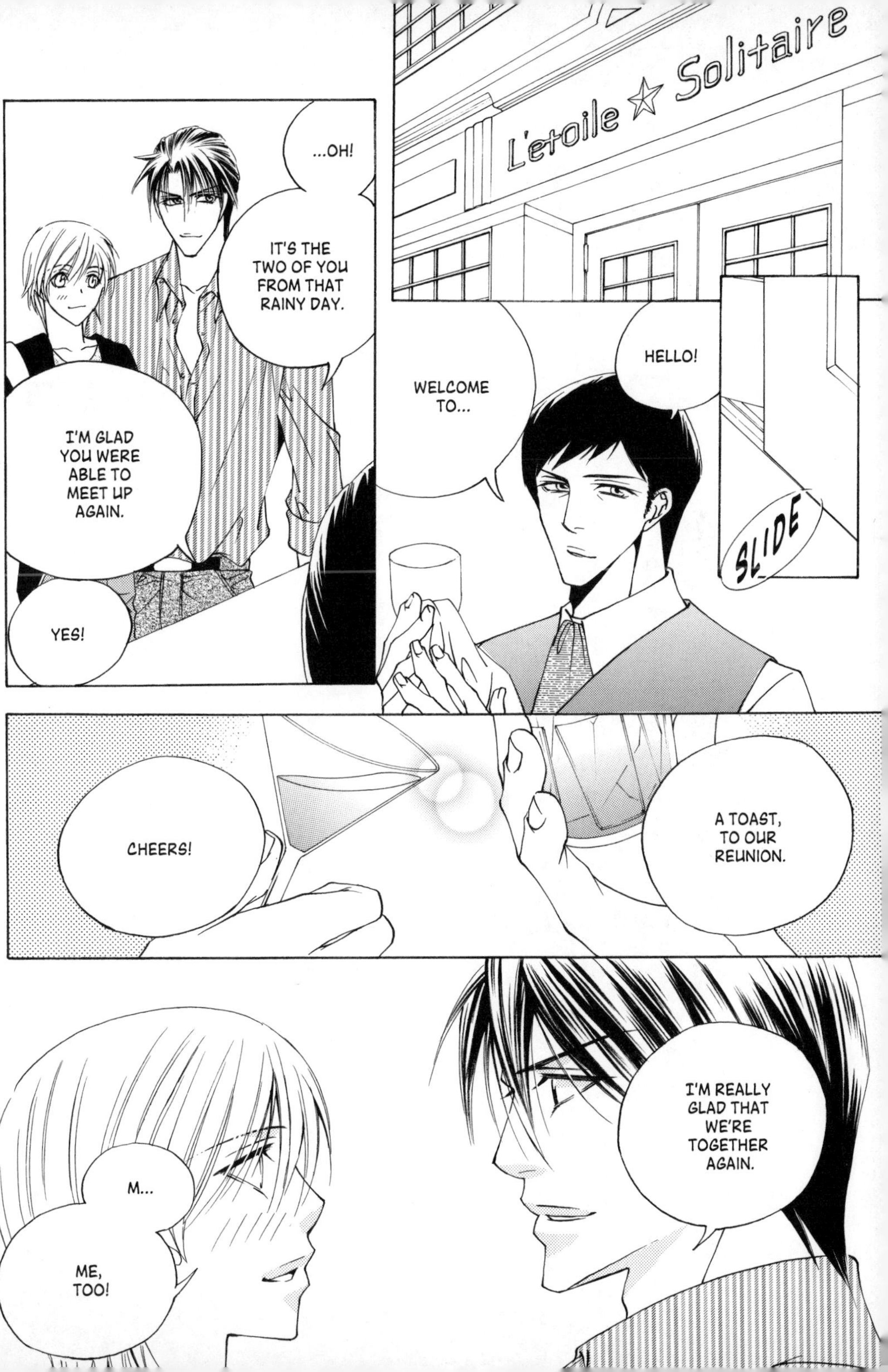
L'etoile ☆ Solitaire
SLIDE
HELLO!
WELCOME TO...
...OH!
IT'S THE TWO OF YOU FROM THAT RAINY DAY.
I'M GLAD YOU WERE ABLE TO MEET UP AGAIN.
YES!
A TOAST, TO OUR REUNION.
CHEERS!
I'M REALLY GLAD THAT WE'RE TOGETHER AGAIN.
M...
ME, TOO!

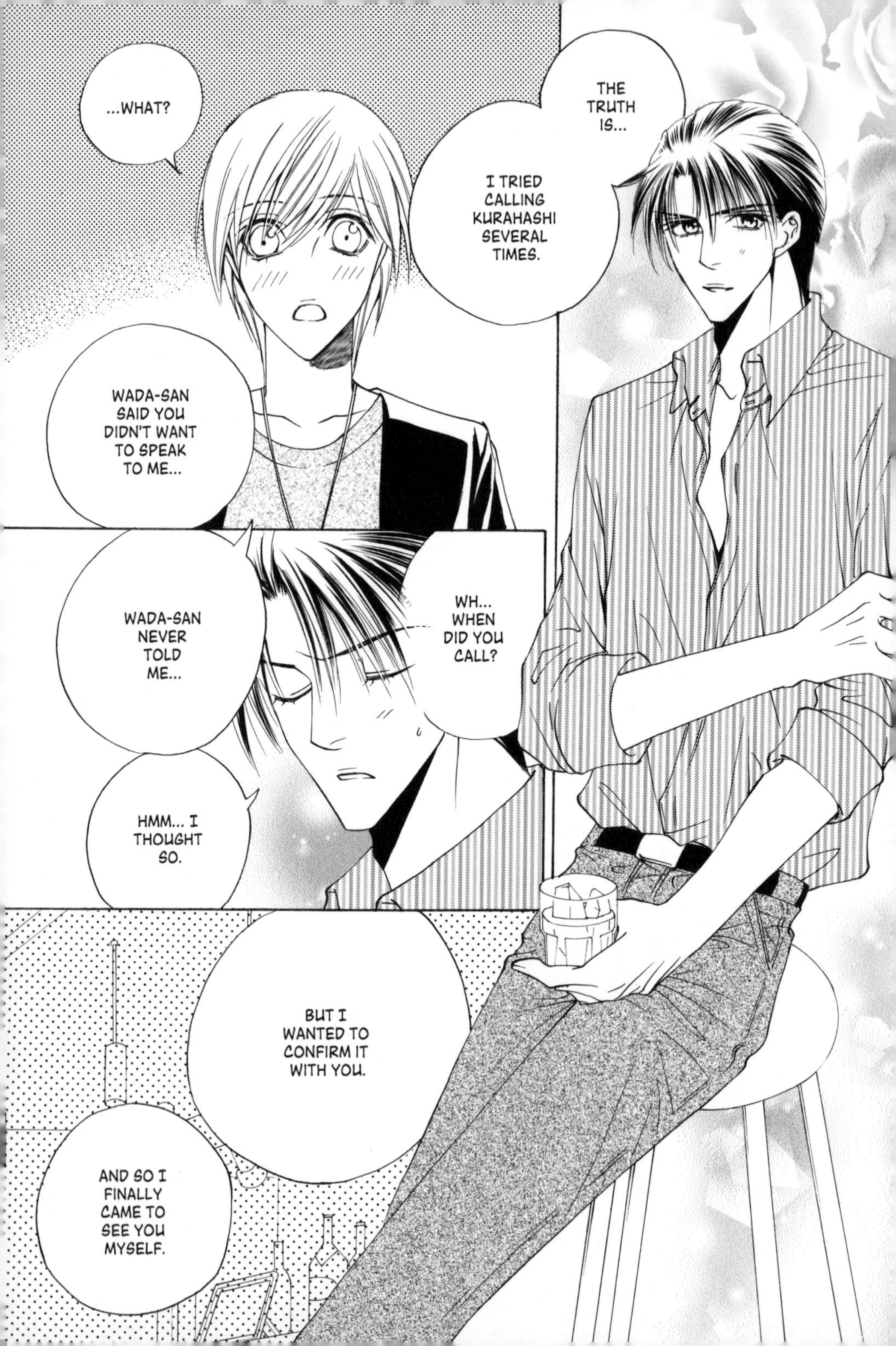
THE TRUTH IS...
I TRIED CALLING KURAHASHI SEVERAL TIMES.
...WHAT?
WADA-SAN SAID YOU DIDN'T WANT TO SPEAK TO ME...
WH... WHEN DID YOU CALL?
WADA-SAN NEVER TOLD ME...
HMM... I THOUGHT SO.
BUT I WANTED TO CONFIRM IT WITH YOU.
AND SO I FINALLY CAME TO SEE YOU MYSELF.

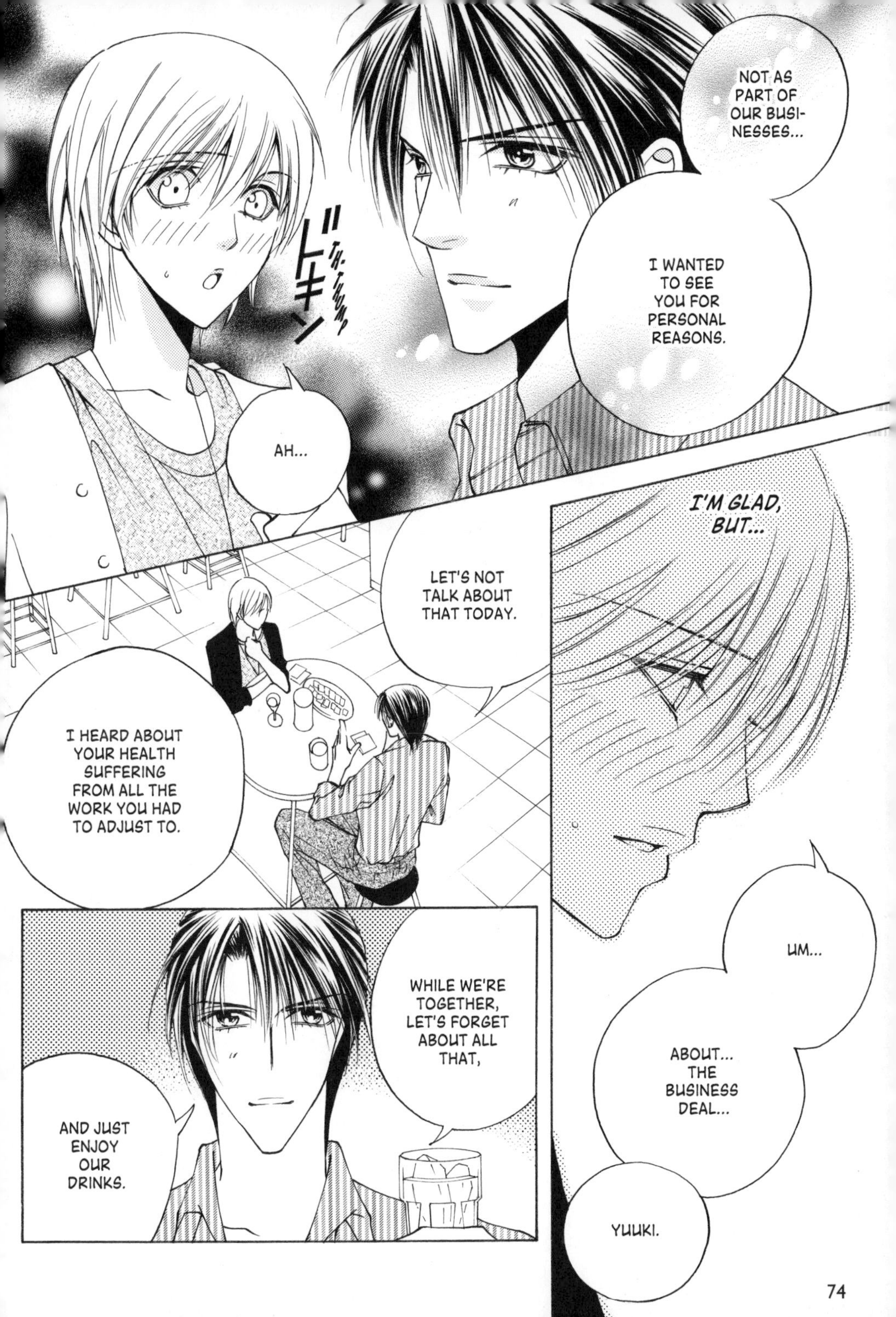
NOT AS PART OF OUR BUSINESSES...
I WANTED TO SEE YOU FOR PERSONAL REASONS.
ドキン
TH-THUMP
AH...
I'M GLAD, BUT...
UM...
ABOUT... THE BUSINESS DEAL...
YUUKI.
LET'S NOT TALK ABOUT THAT TODAY.
I HEARD ABOUT YOUR HEALTH SUFFERING FROM ALL THE WORK YOU HAD TO ADJUST TO.
WHILE WE'RE TOGETHER, LET'S FORGET ABOUT ALL THAT,
AND JUST ENJOY OUR DRINKS.

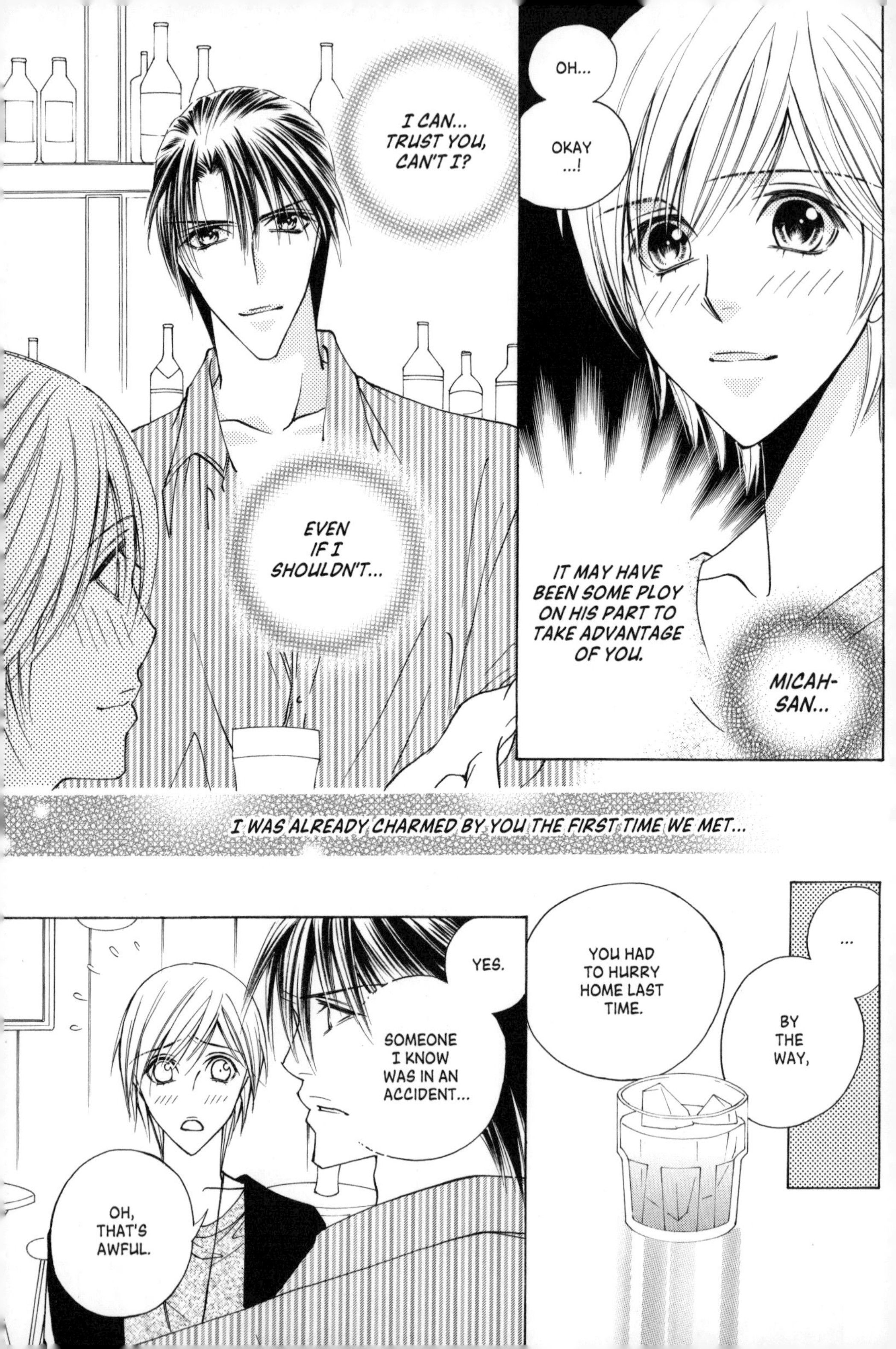

OH...
OKAY ...!
IT MAY HAVE BEEN SOME PLOY ON HIS PART TO TAKE ADVANTAGE OF YOU.
MICAH-SAN...
I CAN... TRUST YOU, CAN'T I?
EVEN IF I SHOULDN'T...
I WAS ALREADY CHARMED BY YOU THE FIRST TIME WE MET...
...
BY THE WAY,
YOU HAD TO HURRY HOME LAST TIME.
YES.
SOMEONE I KNOW WAS IN AN ACCIDENT...
OH, THAT'S AWFUL.

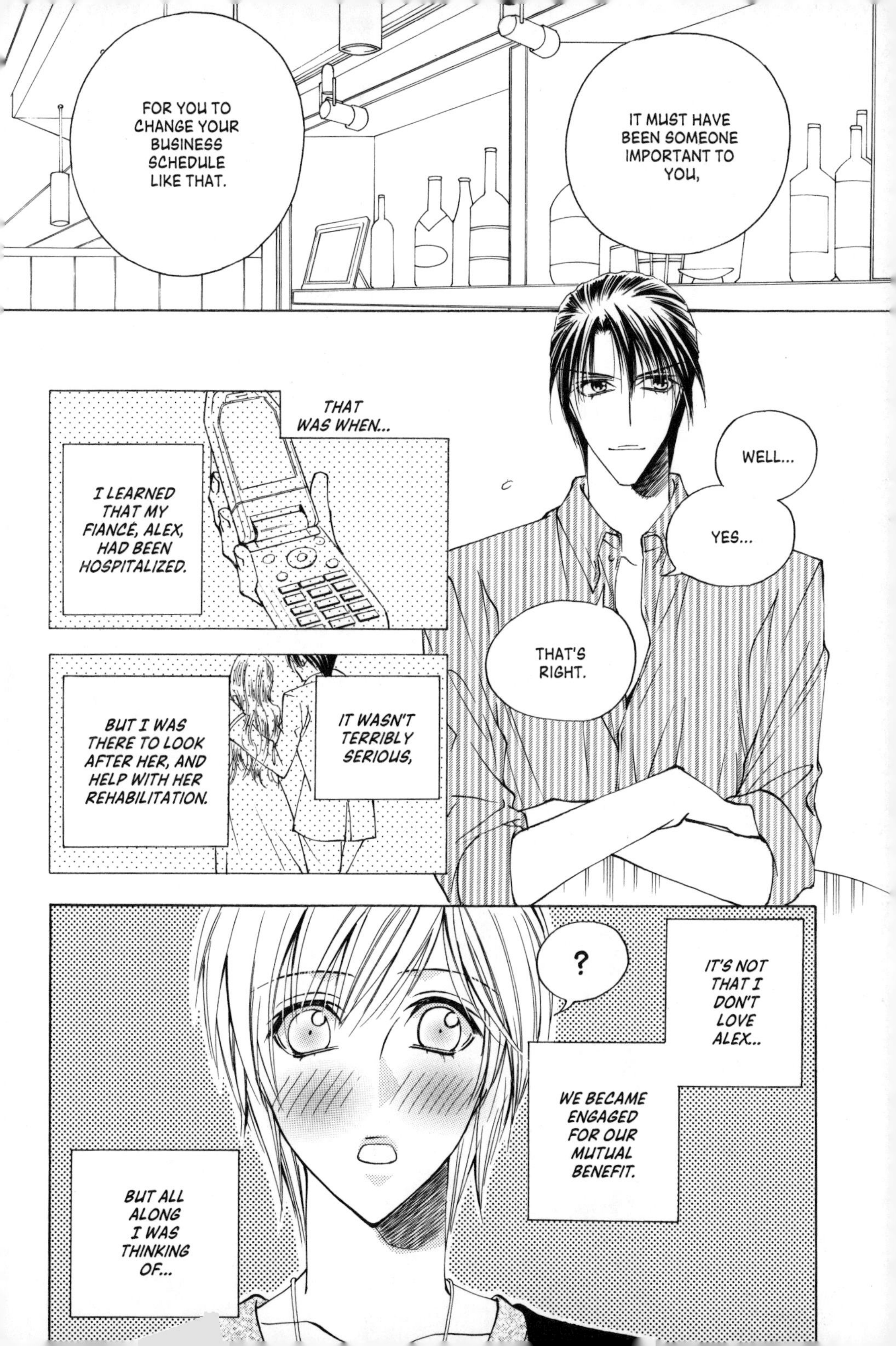

IT MUST HAVE BEEN SOMEONE IMPORTANT TO YOU,
FOR YOU TO CHANGE YOUR BUSINESS SCHEDULE LIKE THAT.
WELL...
YES...
THAT'S RIGHT.
THAT WAS WHEN...
I LEARNED THAT MY FIANCÉ, ALEX, HAD BEEN HOSPITALIZED.
IT WASN'T TERRIBLY SERIOUS,
BUT I WAS THERE TO LOOK AFTER HER, AND HELP WITH HER REHABILITATION.
IT'S NOT THAT I DON'T LOVE ALEX...
?
WE BECAME ENGAGED FOR OUR MUTUAL BENEFIT.
BUT ALL ALONG I WAS THINKING OF...

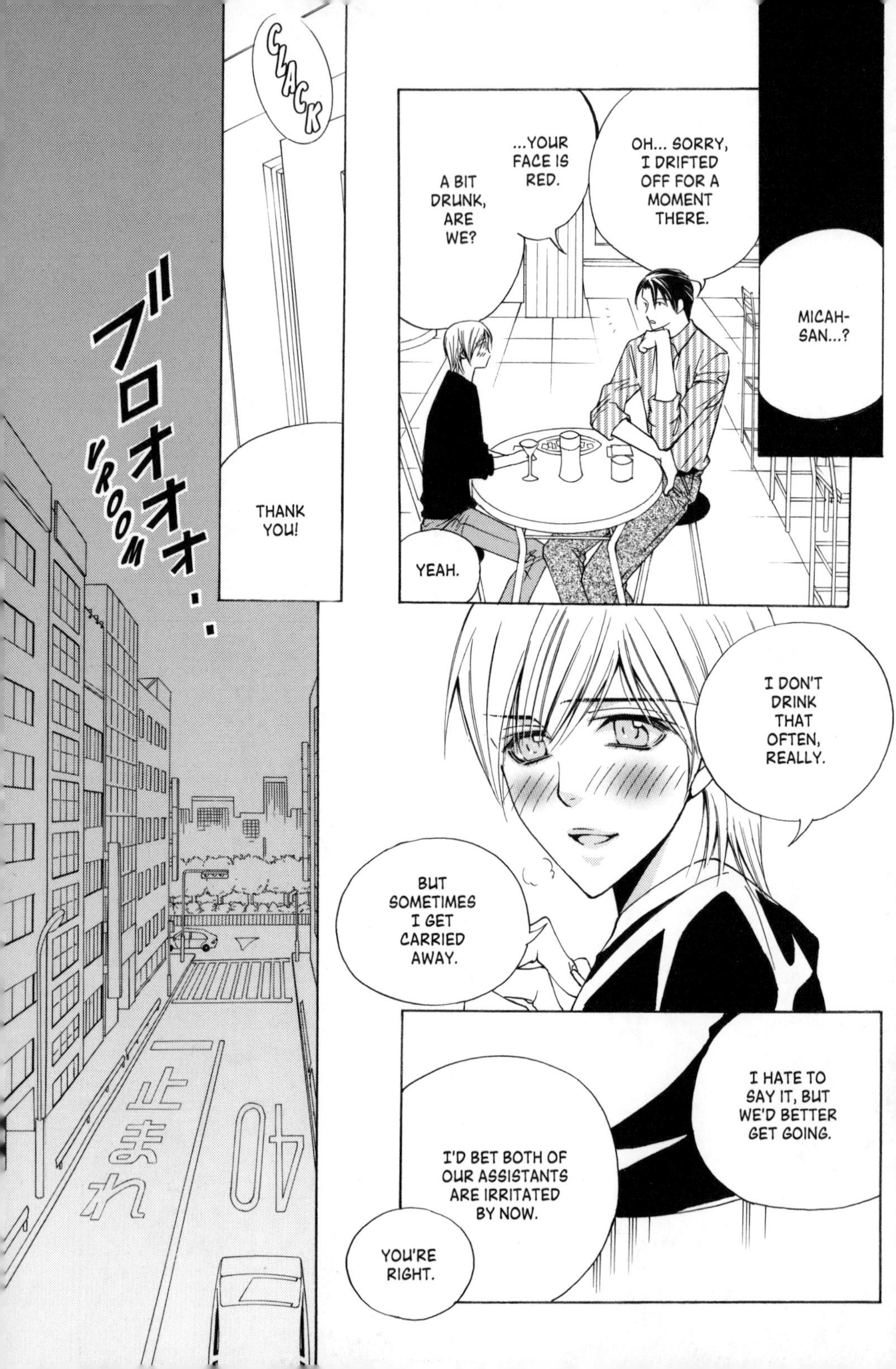
MICAH-SAN...?
OH... SORRY, I DRIFTED OFF FOR A MOMENT THERE.
...YOUR FACE IS RED.
A BIT DRUNK, ARE WE?
YEAH.
CLACK
THANK YOU!
I DON'T DRINK THAT OFTEN, REALLY.
BUT SOMETIMES I GET CARRIED AWAY.
I HATE TO SAY IT, BUT WE'D BETTER GET GOING.
I'D BET BOTH OF OUR ASSISTANTS ARE IRRITATED BY NOW.
YOU'RE RIGHT.
ブロオオオ・・
VROOM
止まれ
40

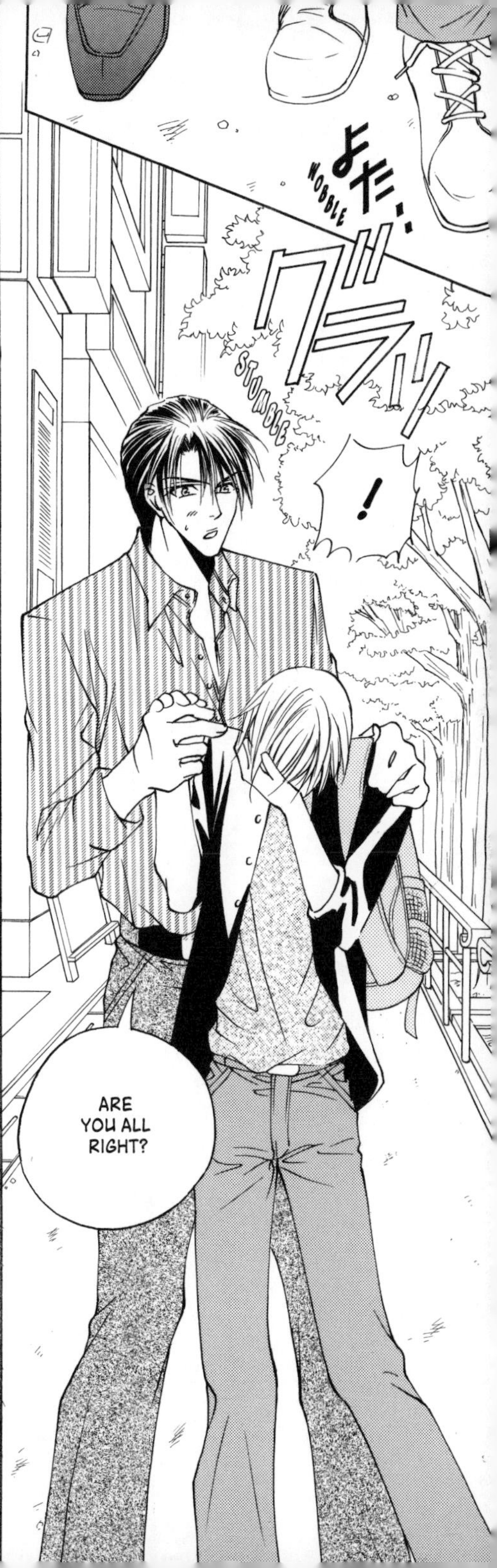
よた…
WOBBLE
グラッ
STUMBLE
!
ARE YOU ALL RIGHT?

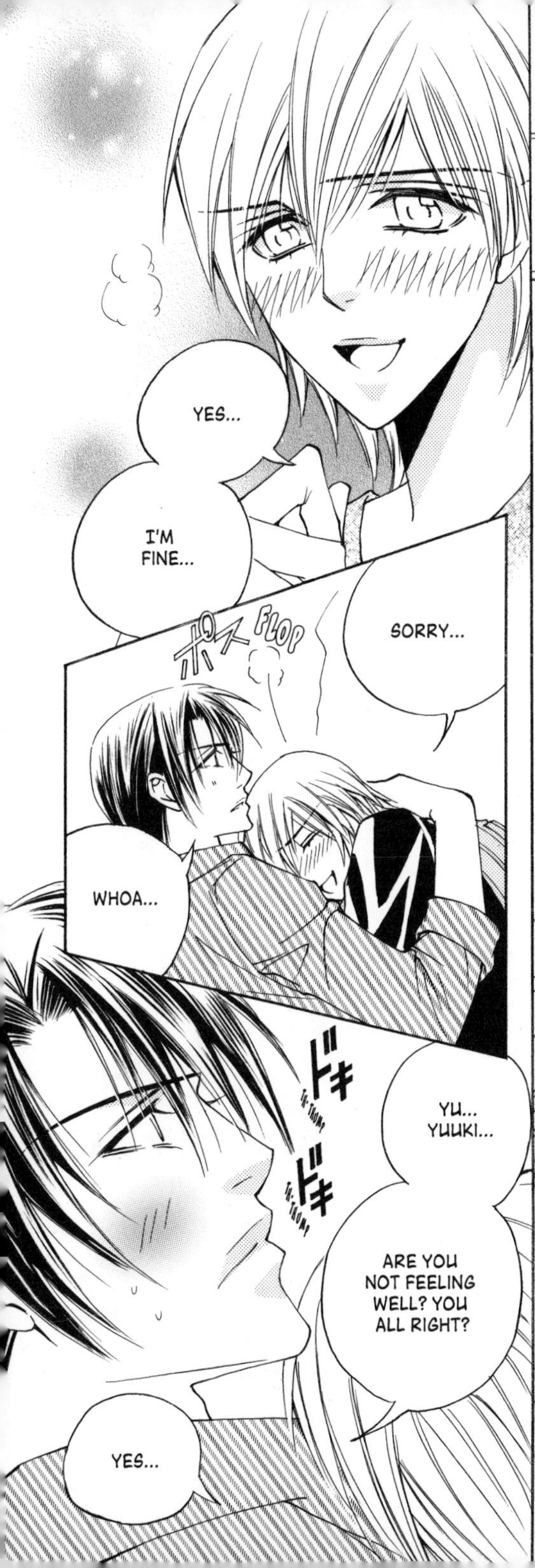
YES...
I'M FINE...
SORRY...
ポス
FLOP
WHOA...
ドキ
ドキ
YU... YUUKI...
ARE YOU NOT FEELING WELL? YOU ALL RIGHT?
YES...

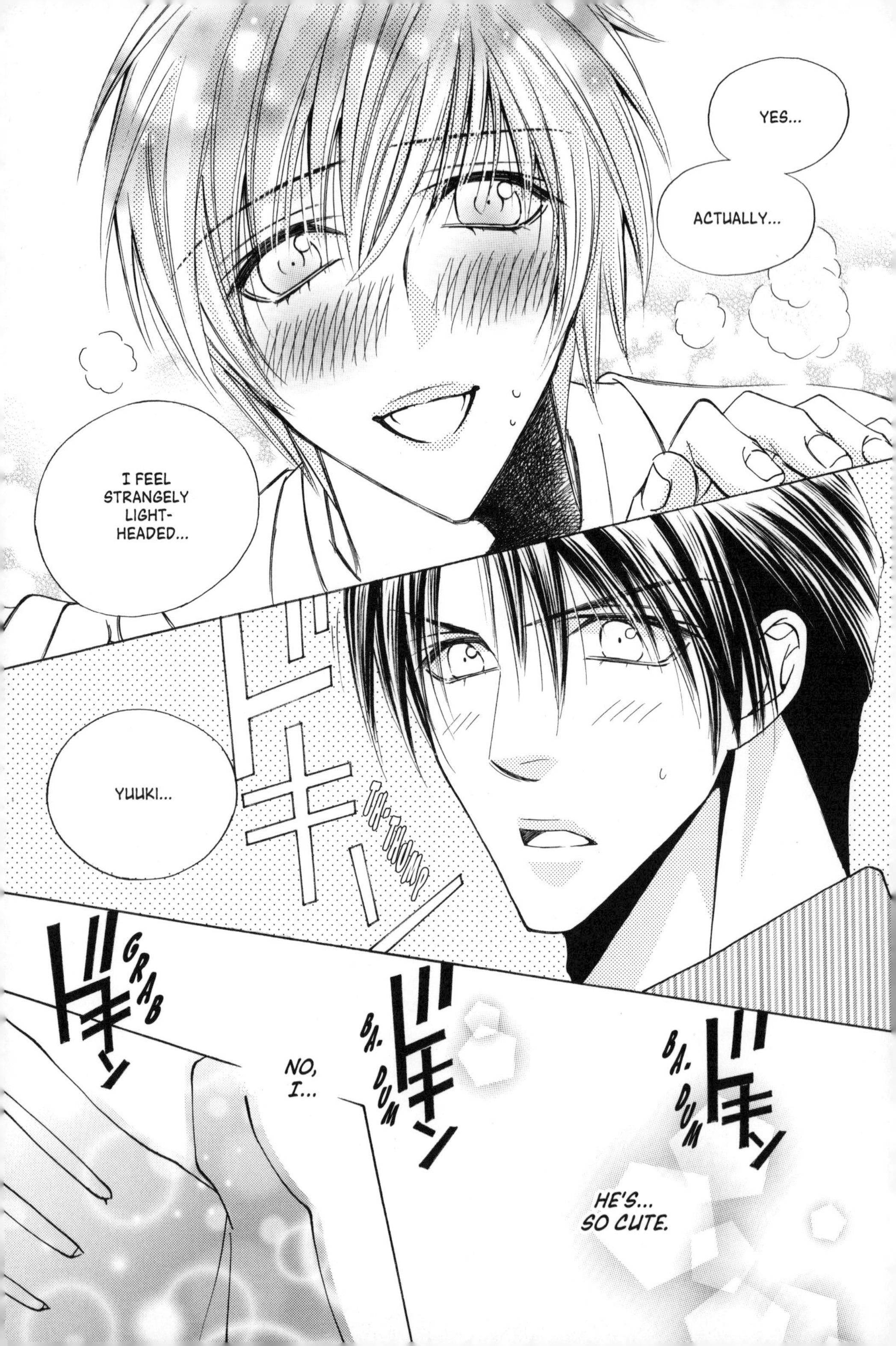
YES...
ACTUALLY...
I FEEL STRANGELY LIGHT-HEADED...
TH-THUMP
YUUKI...
BA-DUM
BA-DUM
NO, I...
GRAB
HE'S... SO CUTE.

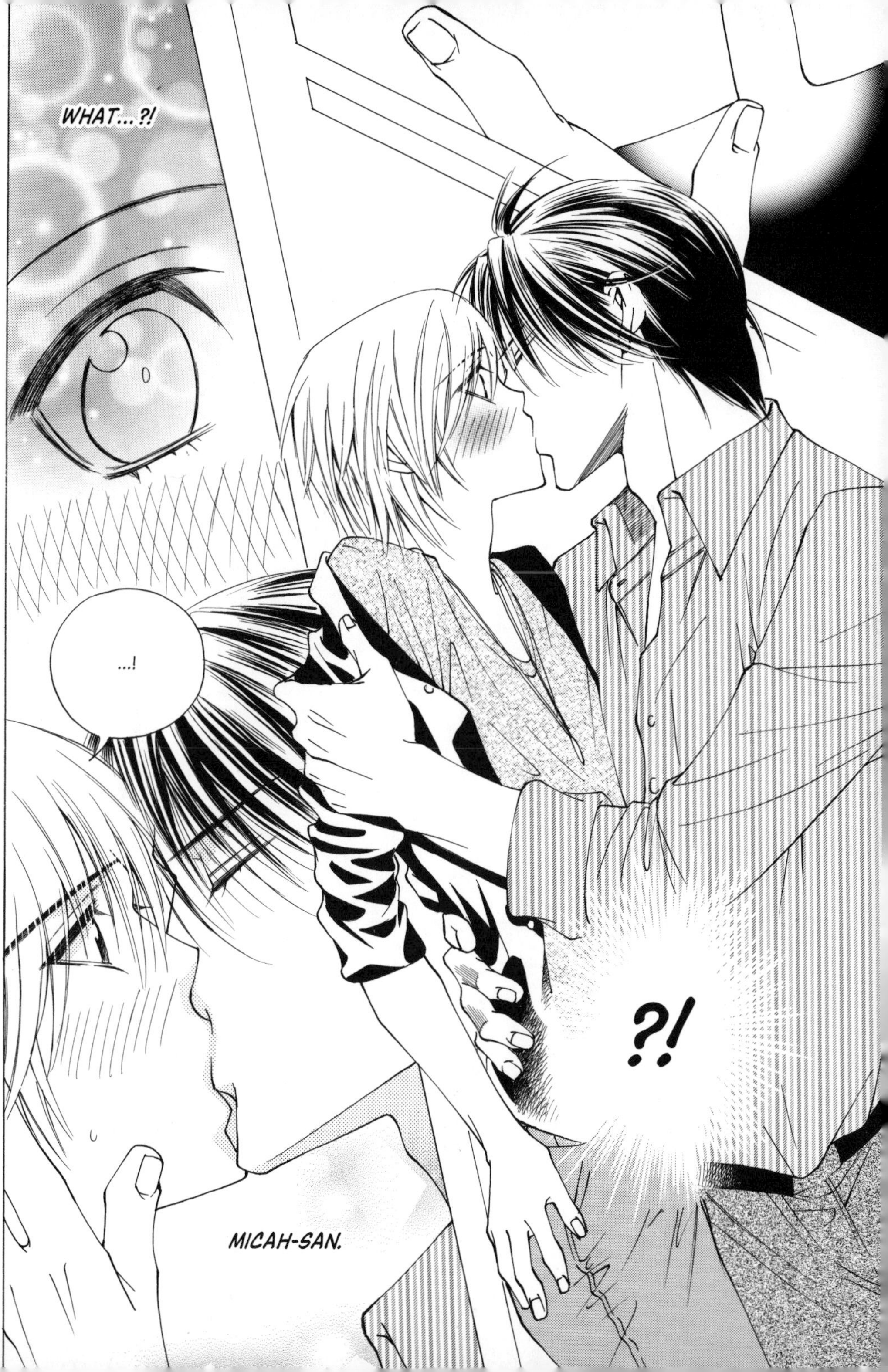
?!
WHAT...?!
...!
MICAH-SAN.

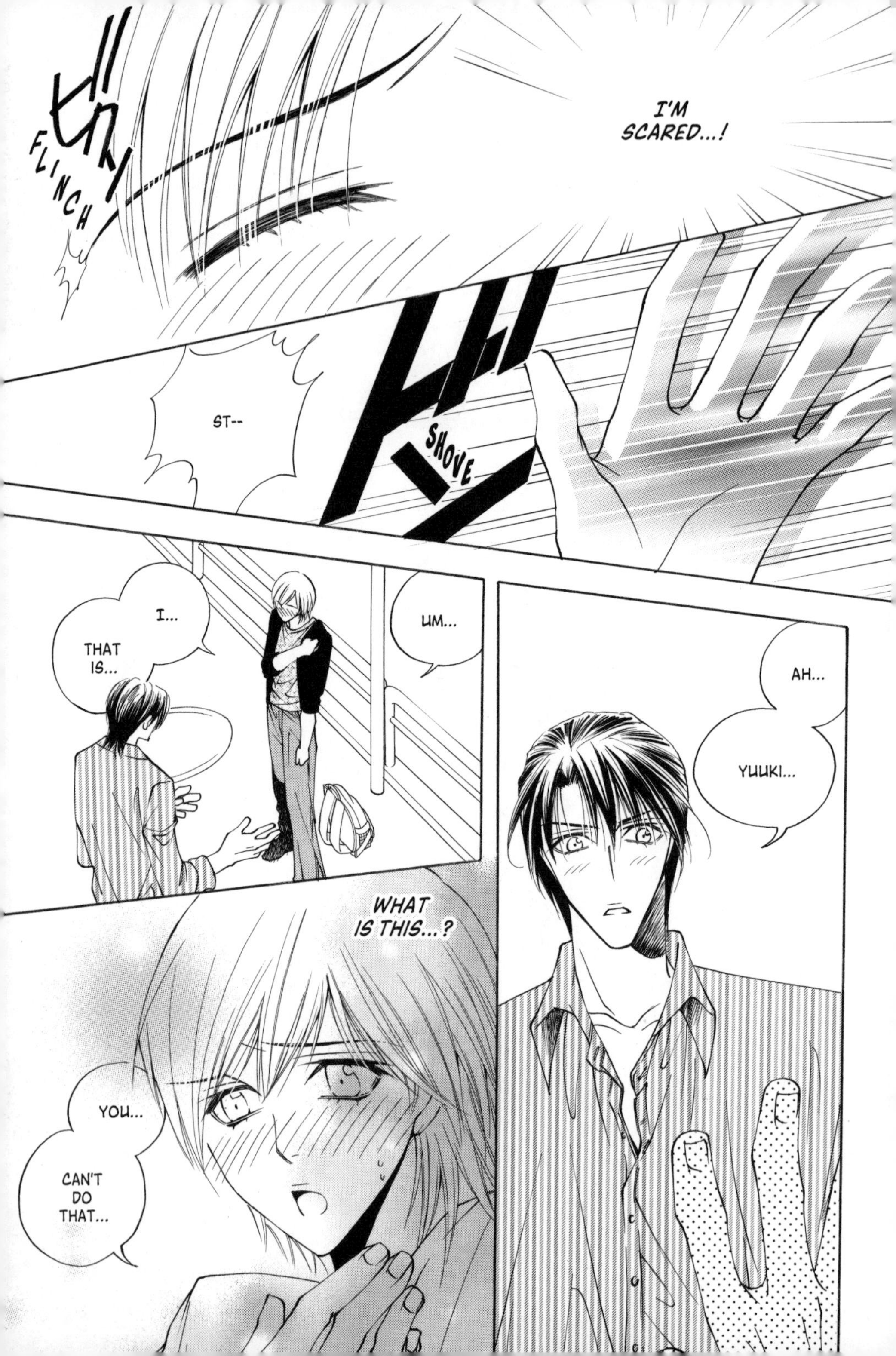

I'M SCARED...!
FLINCH
SHOVE
ST--
AH...
YUUKI...
UM...
I...
THAT IS...
WHAT IS THIS...?
YOU...
CAN'T DO THAT...

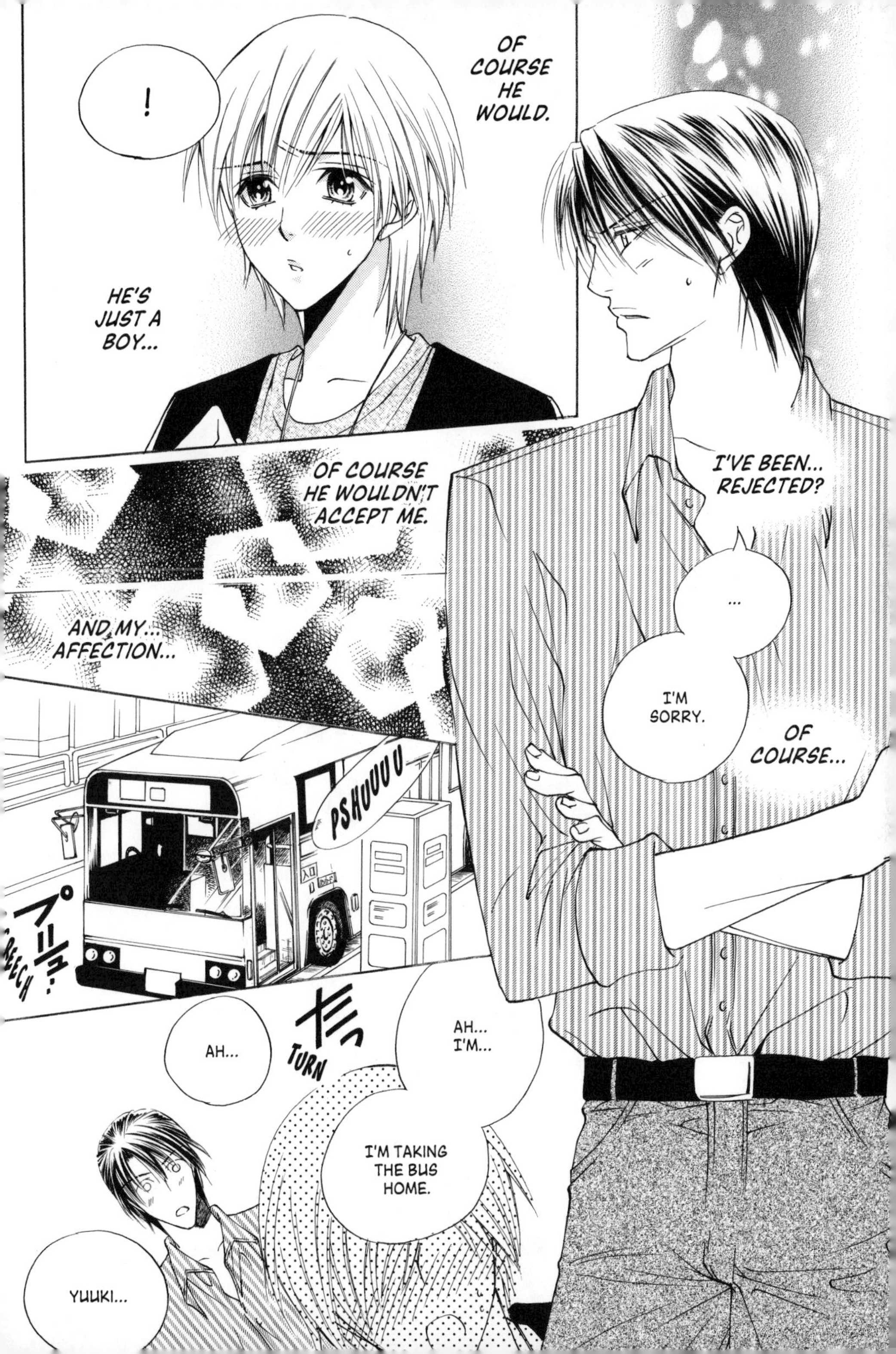
I'VE BEEN... REJECTED?
...
I'M SORRY.
OF COURSE...
!
OF COURSE HE WOULD.
HE'S JUST A BOY...
OF COURSE HE WOULDN'T ACCEPT ME.
AND MY... AFFECTION...
PSHUUUU
TURN
AH... I'M...
I'M TAKING THE BUS HOME.
AH...
YUUKI...

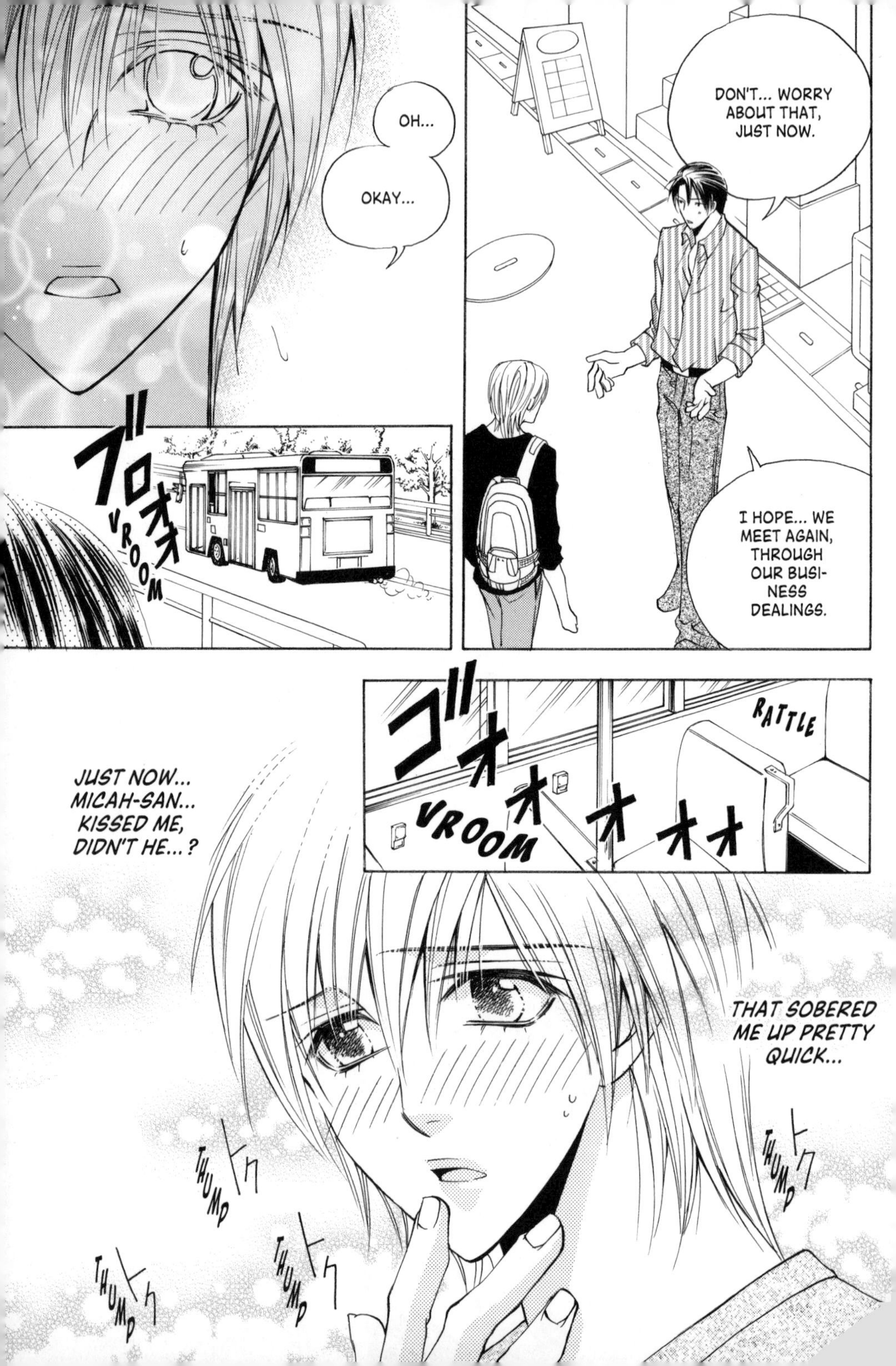
DON'T... WORRY ABOUT THAT, JUST NOW.
I HOPE... WE MEET AGAIN, THROUGH OUR BUSI-NESS DEALINGS.
OH...
OKAY...
ブロオオ
VROOM
ゴオオオオオ
VROOM
RATTLE
JUST NOW... MICAH-SAN... KISSED ME, DIDN'T HE...?
THAT SOBERED ME UP PRETTY QUICK...
トク
THUMP
トク
THUMP
トク
THUMP
トク
THUMP

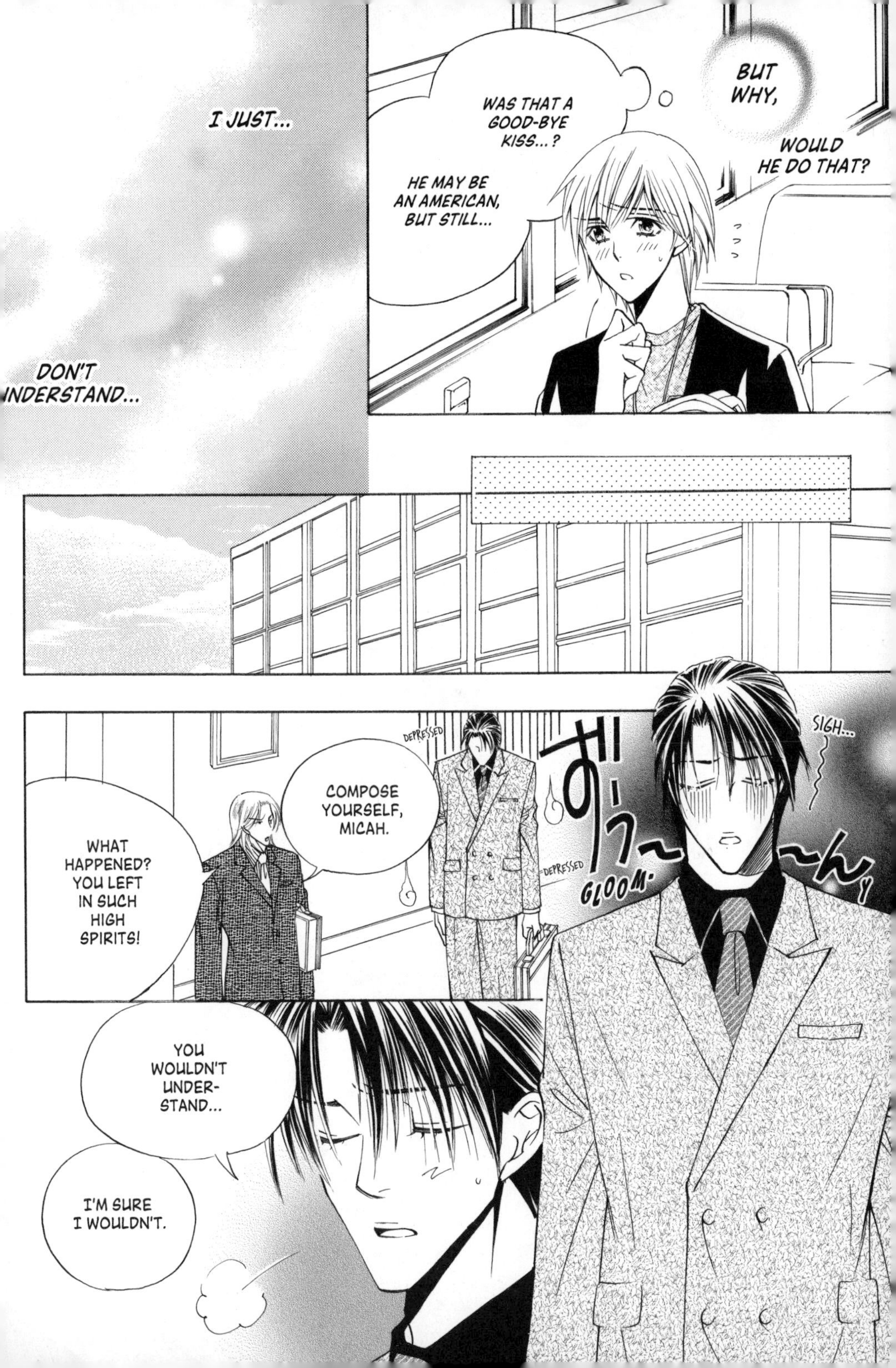
BUT WHY,
WOULD HE DO THAT?
WAS THAT A GOOD-BYE KISS...?
HE MAY BE AN AMERICAN, BUT STILL...
I JUST...
DON'T UNDERSTAND...
SIGH...
ずぅ~~ん
GLOOM
DEPRESSED
DEPRESSED
COMPOSE YOURSELF, MICAH.
WHAT HAPPENED? YOU LEFT IN SUCH HIGH SPIRITS!
YOU WOULDN'T UNDER-STAND...
I'M SURE I WOULDN'T.

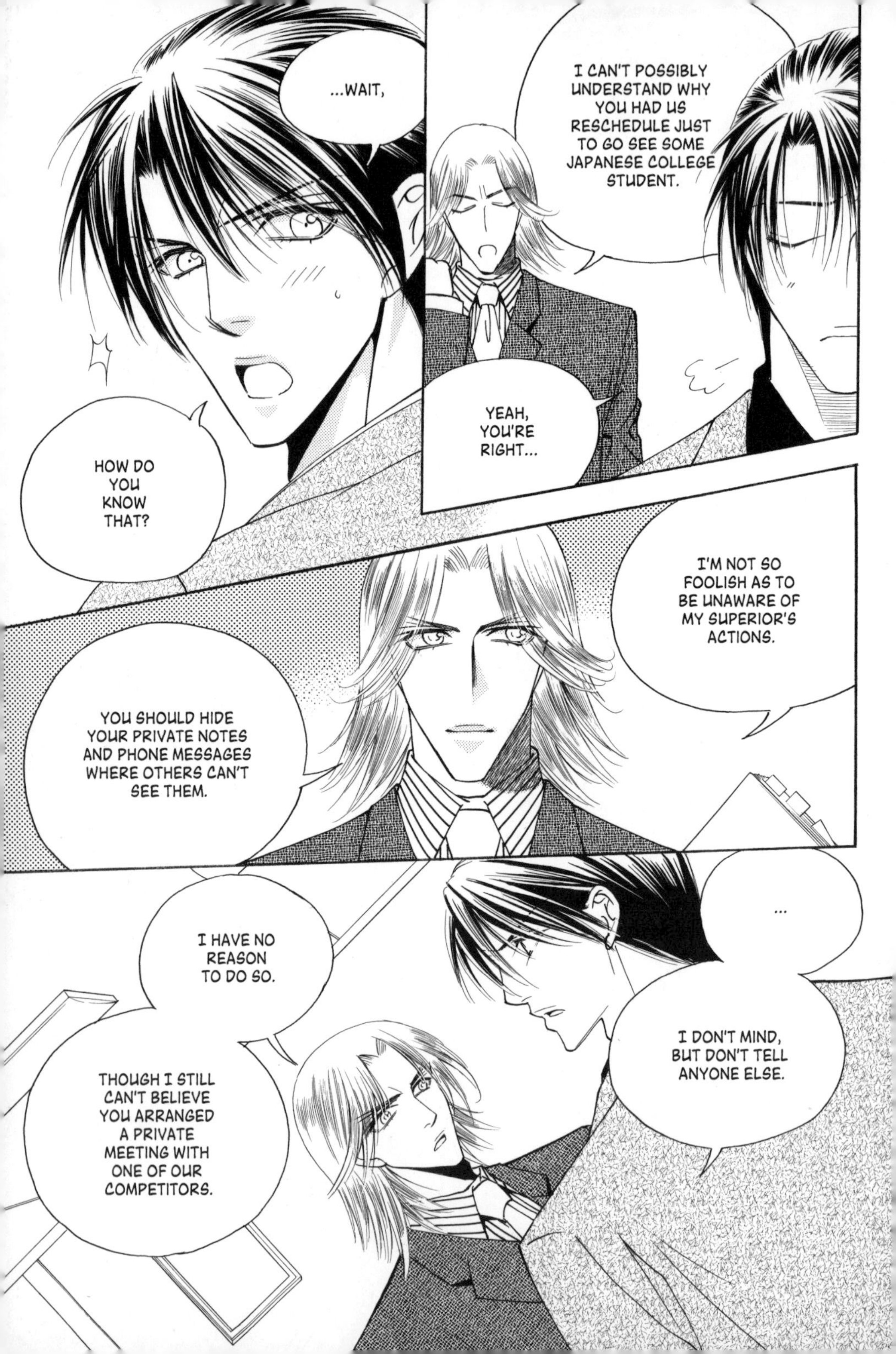
I CAN'T POSSIBLY UNDERSTAND WHY YOU HAD US RESCHEDULE JUST TO GO SEE SOME JAPANESE COLLEGE STUDENT.
YEAH, YOU'RE RIGHT...
...WAIT,
HOW DO YOU KNOW THAT?
I'M NOT SO FOOLISH AS TO BE UNAWARE OF MY SUPERIOR'S ACTIONS.
YOU SHOULD HIDE YOUR PRIVATE NOTES AND PHONE MESSAGES WHERE OTHERS CAN'T SEE THEM.
...
I DON'T MIND, BUT DON'T TELL ANYONE ELSE.
I HAVE NO REASON TO DO SO.
THOUGH I STILL CAN'T BELIEVE YOU ARRANGED A PRIVATE MEETING WITH ONE OF OUR COMPETITORS.

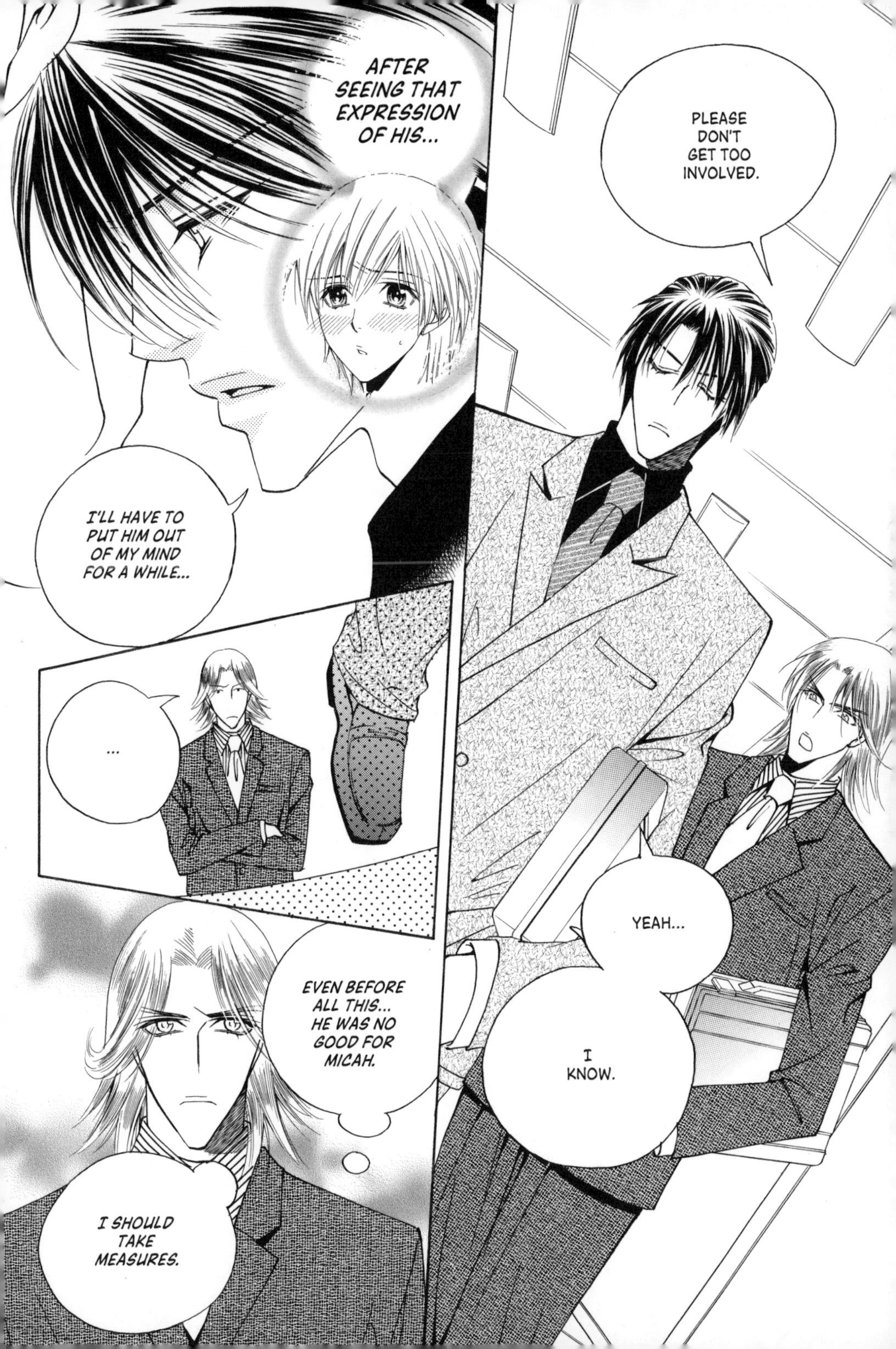
PLEASE DON'T GET TOO INVOLVED.
YEAH...
I KNOW.
AFTER SEEING THAT EXPRESSION OF HIS...
I'LL HAVE TO PUT HIM OUT OF MY MIND FOR A WHILE...
...
EVEN BEFORE ALL THIS... HE WAS NO GOOD FOR MICAH.
I SHOULD TAKE MEASURES.

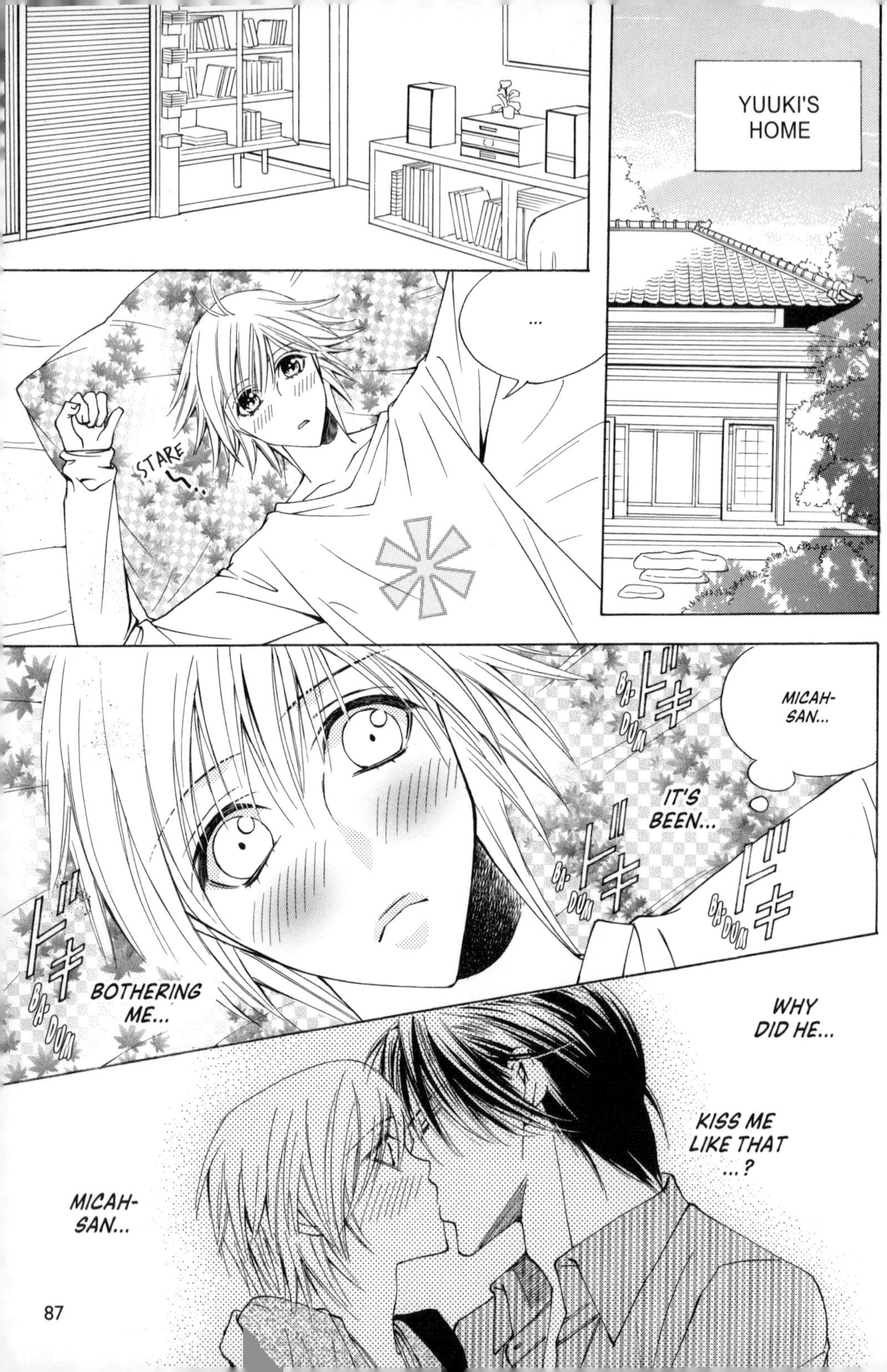
YUUKI'S HOME
...
STARE
MICAH-SAN...
ドキ BA-DUM
IT'S BEEN...
ドキ BA-DUM
ドキ BA-DUM
ドキ BA-DUM
BOTHERING ME...
WHY DID HE...
KISS ME LIKE THAT ...?
MICAH-SAN...

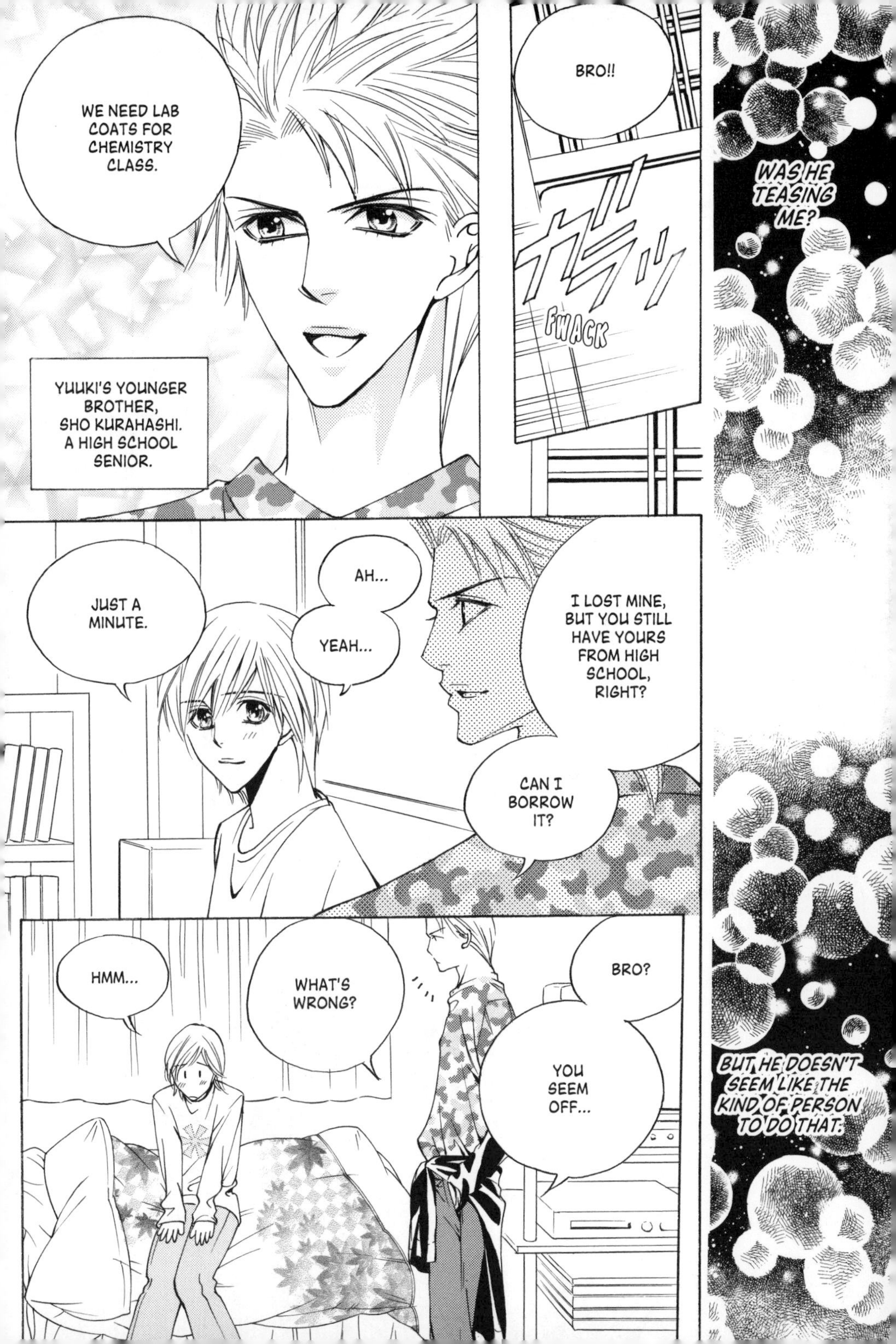
WAS HE TEASING ME?
BUT HE DOESN'T SEEM LIKE THE KIND OF PERSON TO DO THAT.
BRO!!
FWACK
WE NEED LAB COATS FOR CHEMISTRY CLASS.
YUUKI'S YOUNGER BROTHER, SHO KURAHASHI. A HIGH SCHOOL SENIOR.
I LOST MINE, BUT YOU STILL HAVE YOURS FROM HIGH SCHOOL, RIGHT?
CAN I BORROW IT?
AH...
YEAH...
JUST A MINUTE.
BRO?
YOU SEEM OFF...
WHAT'S WRONG?
HMM...

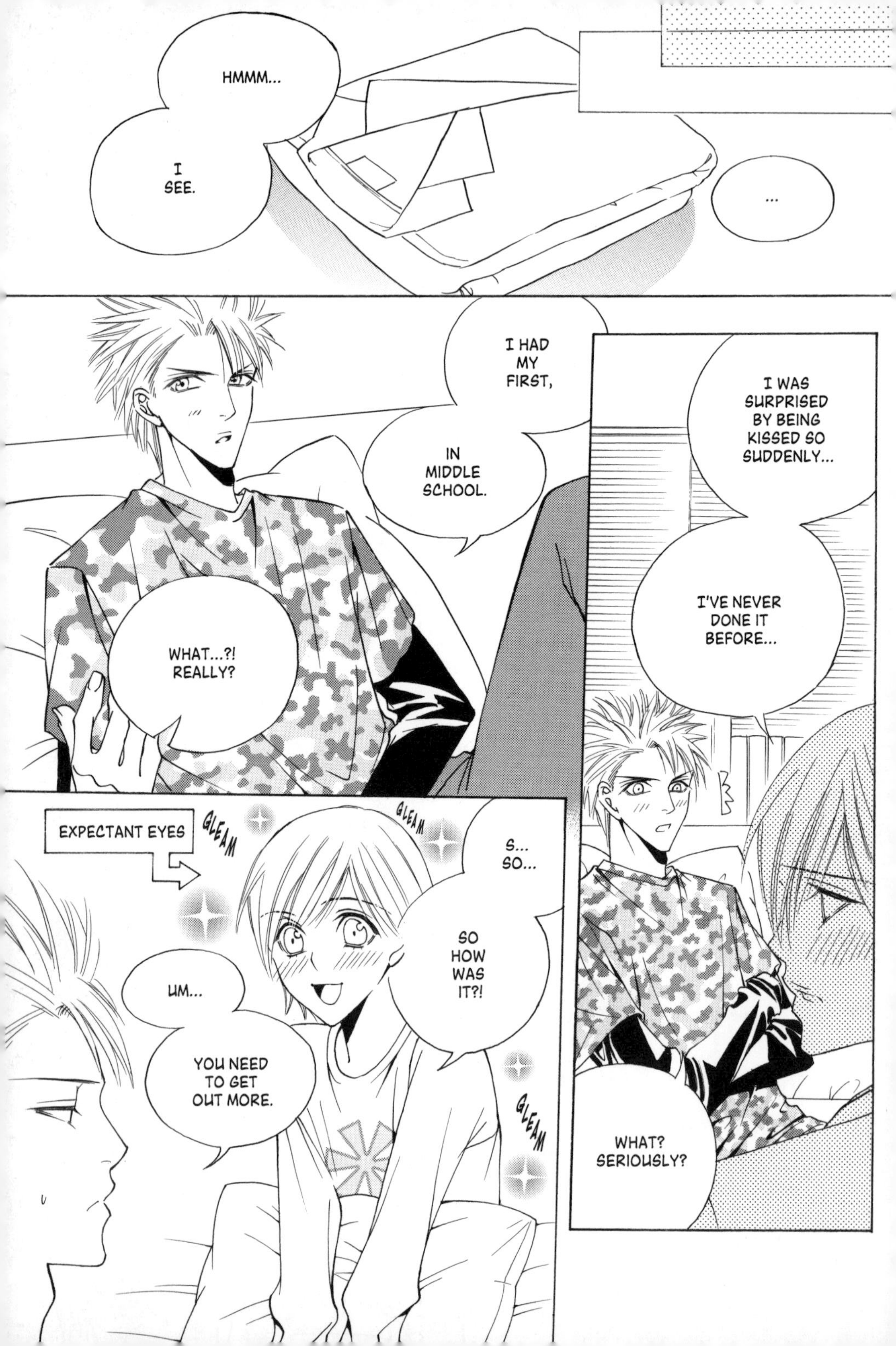
...
HMMM...
I SEE.
I WAS SURPRISED BY BEING KISSED SO SUDDENLY...
I'VE NEVER DONE IT BEFORE...
WHAT? SERIOUSLY?
I HAD MY FIRST,
IN MIDDLE SCHOOL.
WHAT...?! REALLY?
S... SO...
SO HOW WAS IT?!
GLEAM
GLEAM
GLEAM
EXPECTANT EYES
UM...
YOU NEED TO GET OUT MORE.

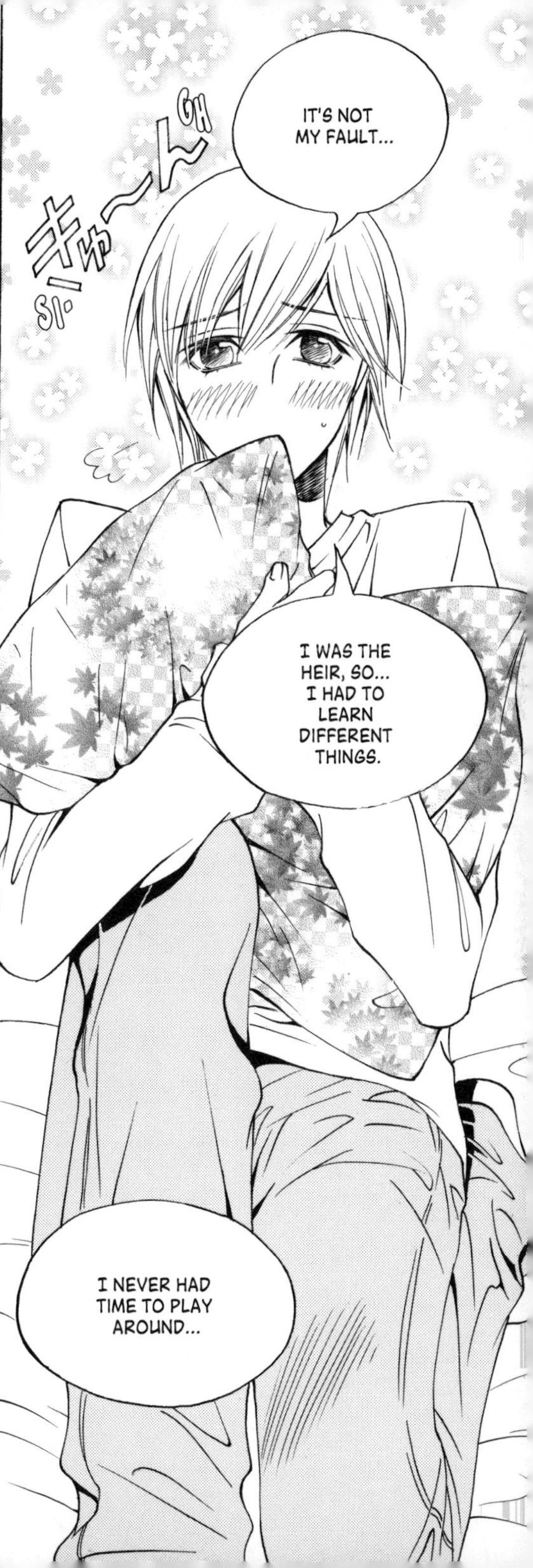
IT'S NOT MY FAULT...
I WAS THE HEIR, SO... I HAD TO LEARN DIFFERENT THINGS.
I NEVER HAD TIME TO PLAY AROUND...
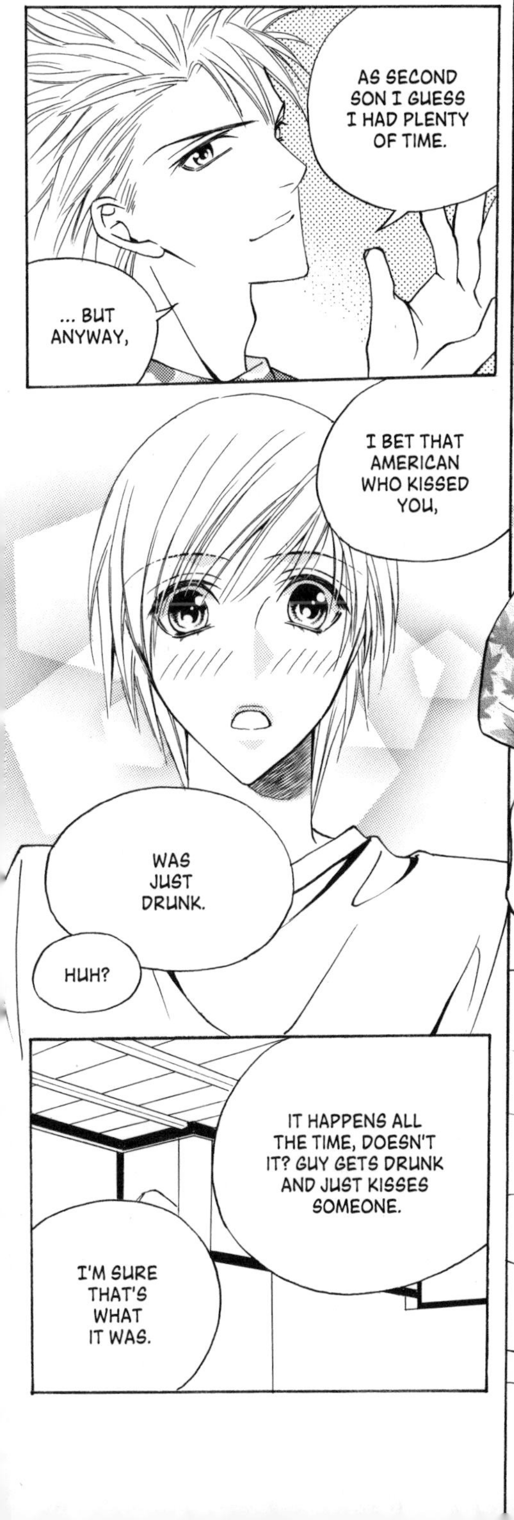
AS SECOND SON I GUESS I HAD PLENTY OF TIME.
... BUT ANYWAY,
I BET THAT AMERICAN WHO KISSED YOU,
WAS JUST DRUNK.
HUH?
IT HAPPENS ALL THE TIME, DOESN'T IT? GUY GETS DRUNK AND JUST KISSES SOMEONE.
I'M SURE THAT'S WHAT IT WAS.

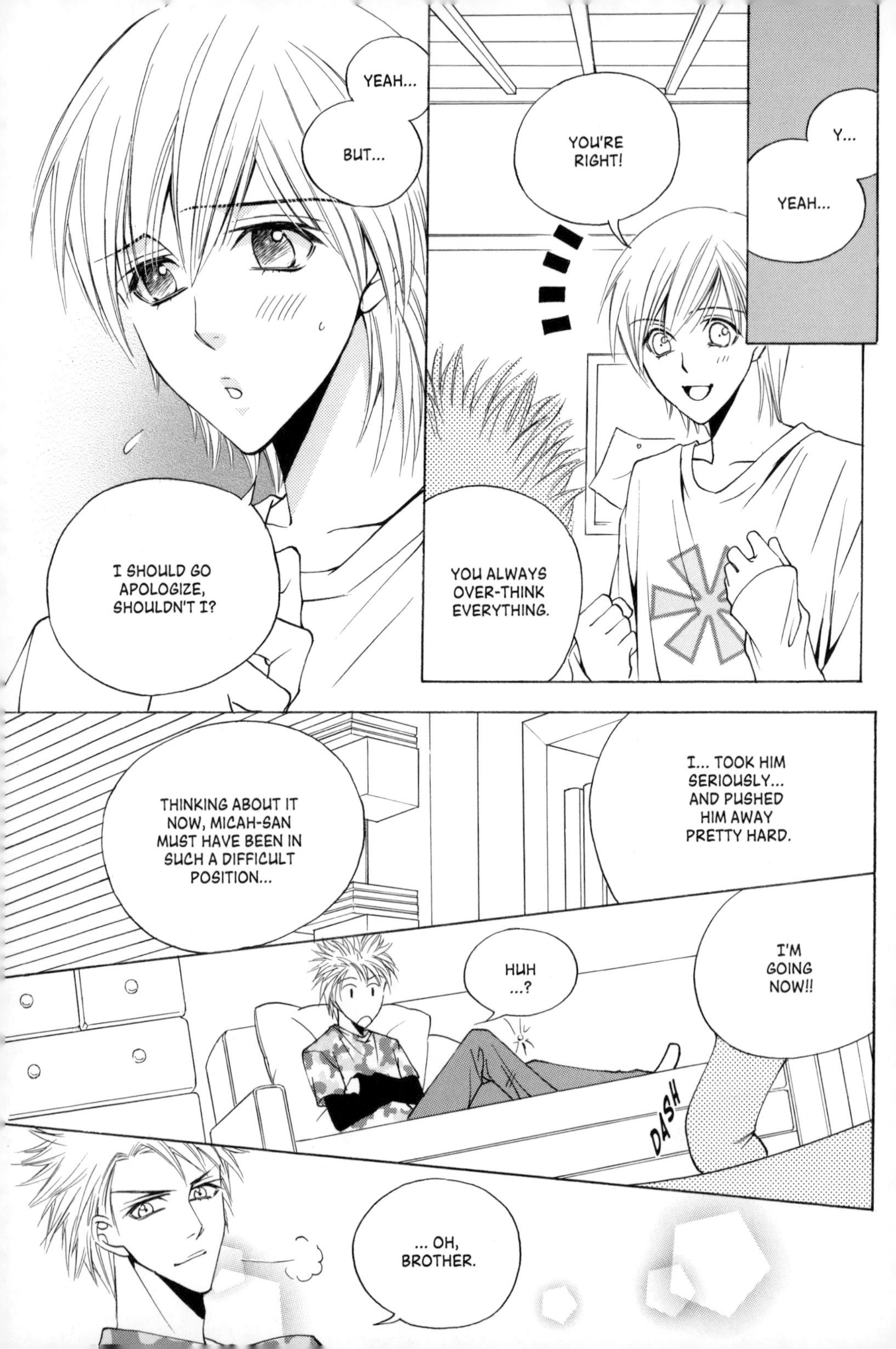
Y...
YEAH...
YOU'RE RIGHT!
YOU ALWAYS OVER-THINK EVERYTHING.
YEAH...
BUT...
I SHOULD GO APOLOGIZE, SHOULDN'T I?
I... TOOK HIM SERIOUSLY... AND PUSHED HIM AWAY PRETTY HARD.
THINKING ABOUT IT NOW, MICAH-SAN MUST HAVE BEEN IN SUCH A DIFFICULT POSITION...
I'M GOING NOW!!
DASH
HUH ...?
... OH, BROTHER.

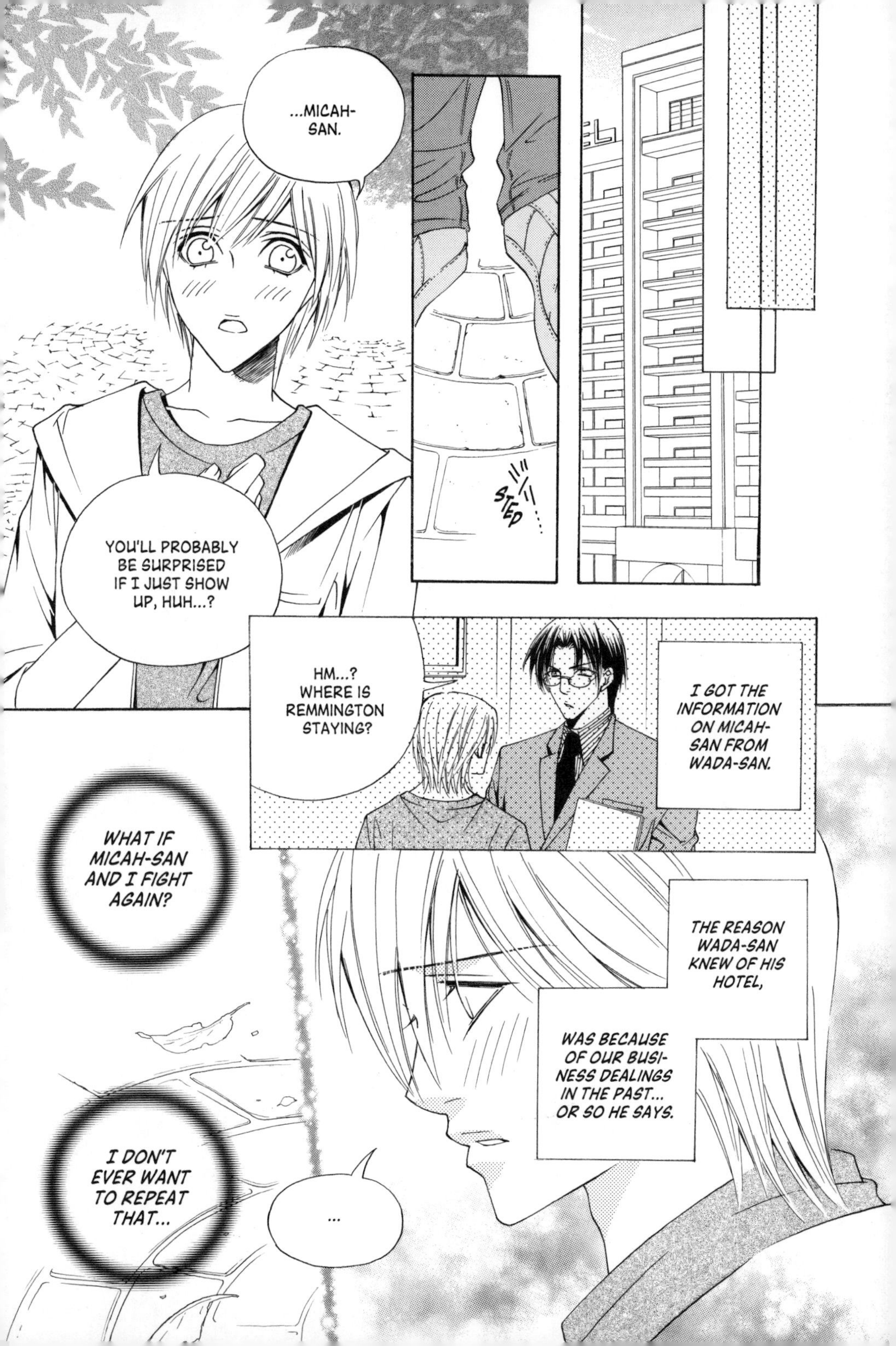
STEP
...MICAH-SAN.
YOU'LL PROBABLY BE SURPRISED IF I JUST SHOW UP, HUH...?
I GOT THE INFORMATION ON MICAH-SAN FROM WADA-SAN.
HM...? WHERE IS REMMINGTON STAYING?
THE REASON WADA-SAN KNEW OF HIS HOTEL,
WAS BECAUSE OF OUR BUSINESS DEALINGS IN THE PAST... OR SO HE SAYS.
...
WHAT IF MICAH-SAN AND I FIGHT AGAIN?
I DON'T EVER WANT TO REPEAT THAT...

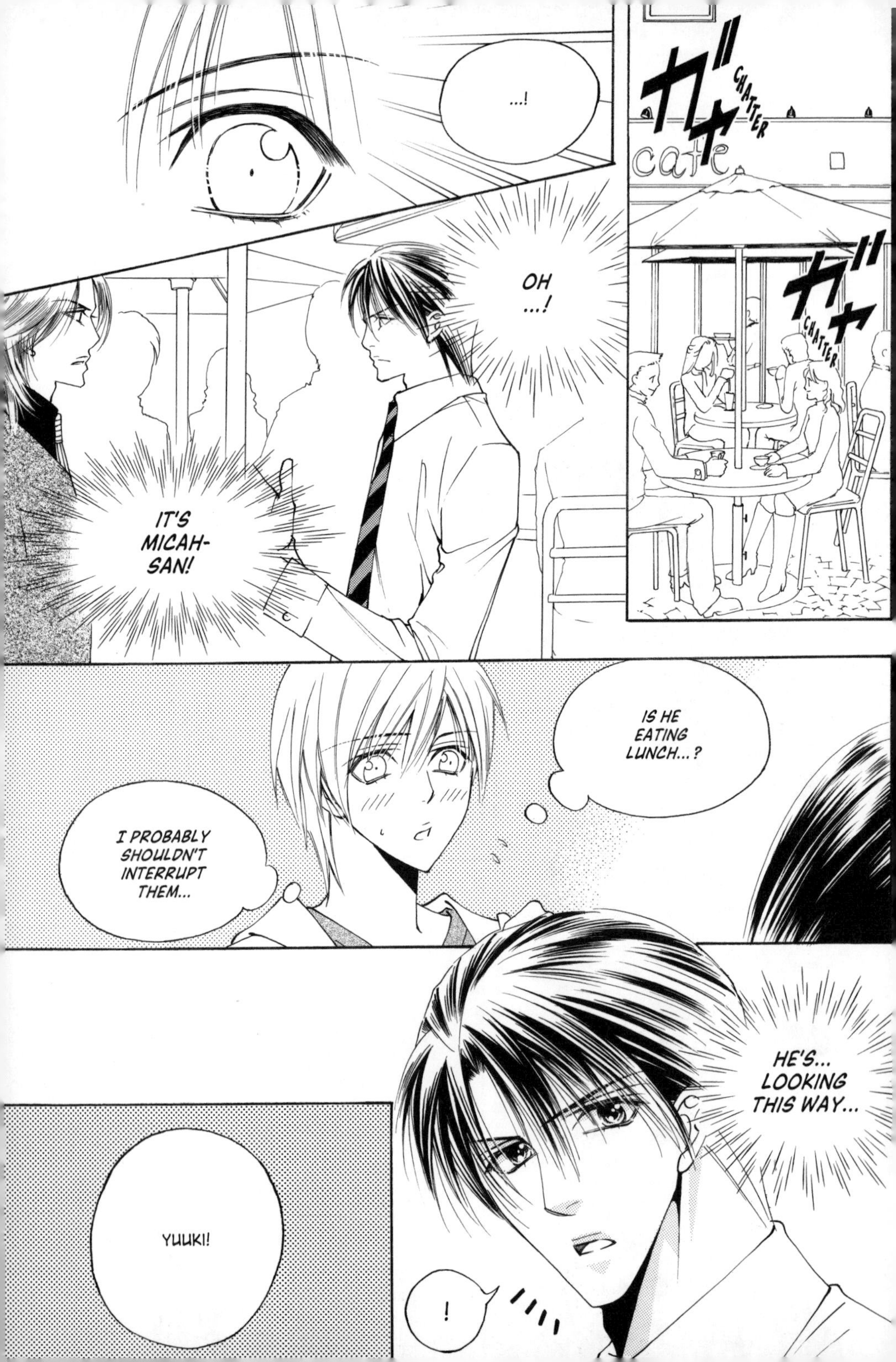
ガヤ
CHATTER
ガヤ
CHATTER
...!
OH ...!
IT'S MICAH-SAN!
IS HE EATING LUNCH...?
I PROBABLY SHOULDN'T INTERRUPT THEM...
HE'S... LOOKING THIS WAY...
!
YUUKI!

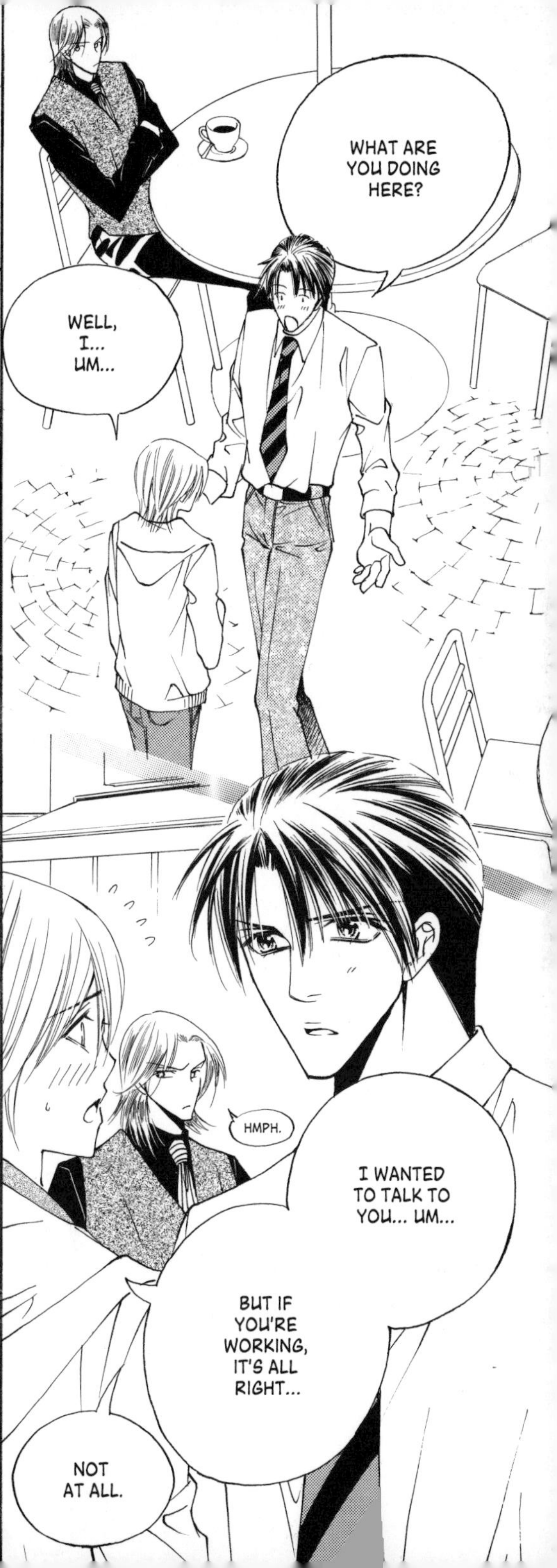
WHAT ARE YOU DOING HERE?
WELL, I... UM...
HMPH.
I WANTED TO TALK TO YOU... UM...
BUT IF YOU'RE WORKING, IT'S ALL RIGHT...
NOT AT ALL.

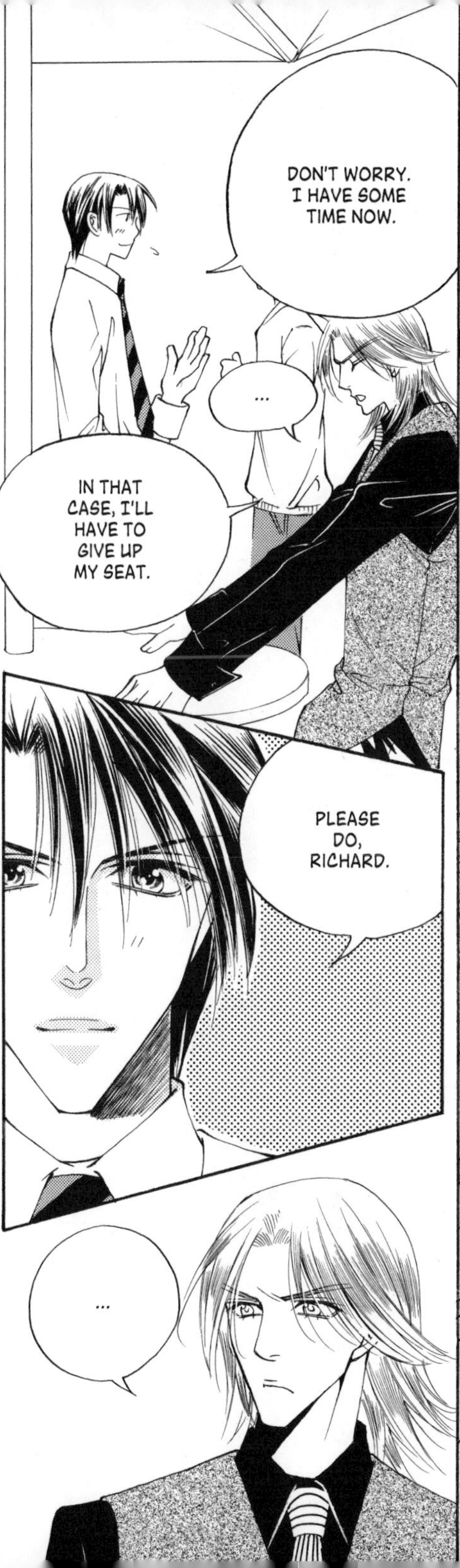
DON'T WORRY. I HAVE SOME TIME NOW.
...
IN THAT CASE, I'LL HAVE TO GIVE UP MY SEAT.
PLEASE DO, RICHARD.
...

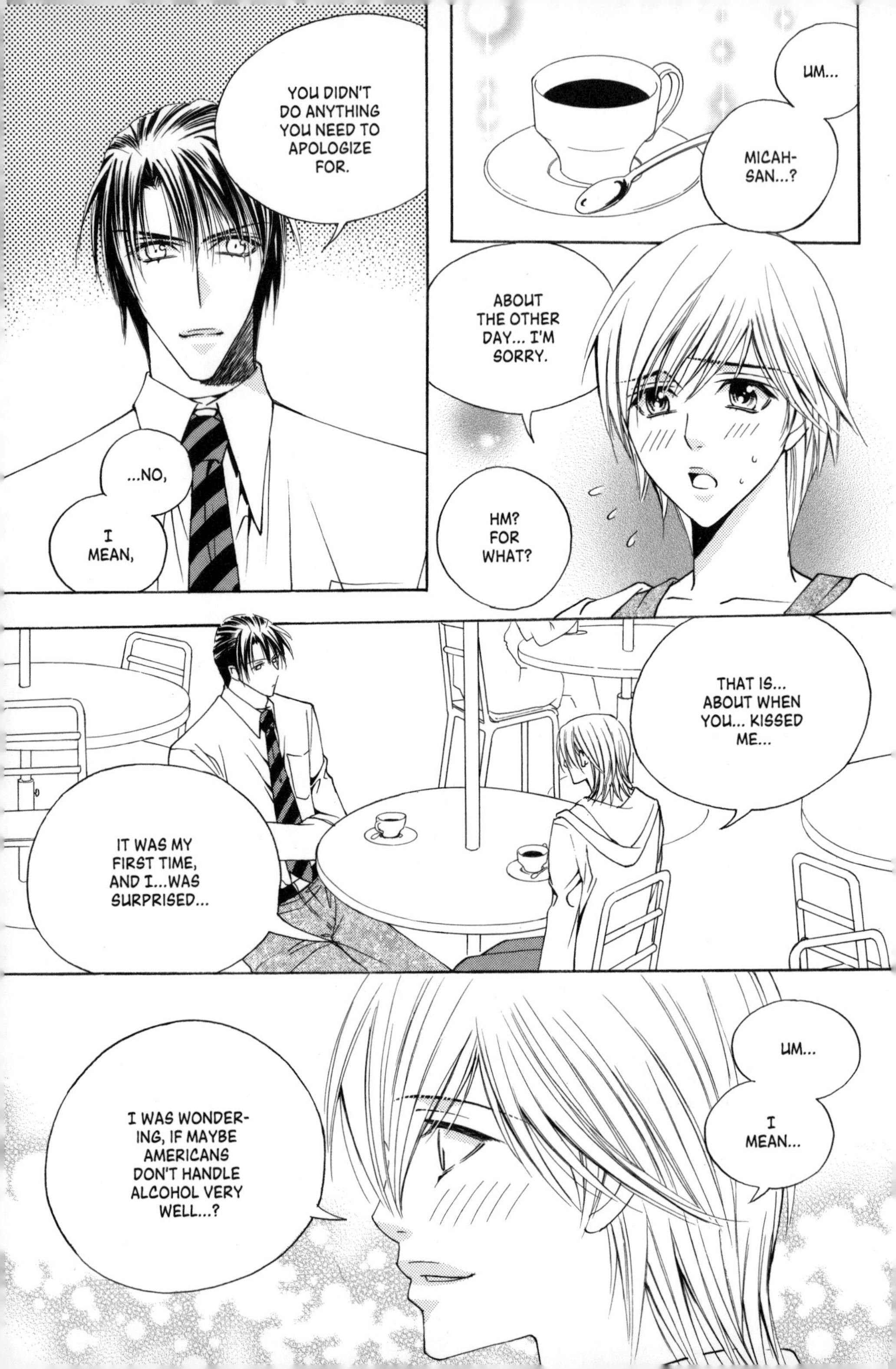
UM...
MICAH-SAN...?
ABOUT THE OTHER DAY... I'M SORRY.
HM? FOR WHAT?
YOU DIDN'T DO ANYTHING YOU NEED TO APOLOGIZE FOR.
...NO,
I MEAN,
THAT IS... ABOUT WHEN YOU... KISSED ME...
IT WAS MY FIRST TIME, AND I...WAS SURPRISED...
UM...
I MEAN...
I WAS WONDER-ING, IF MAYBE AMERICANS DON'T HANDLE ALCOHOL VERY WELL...?

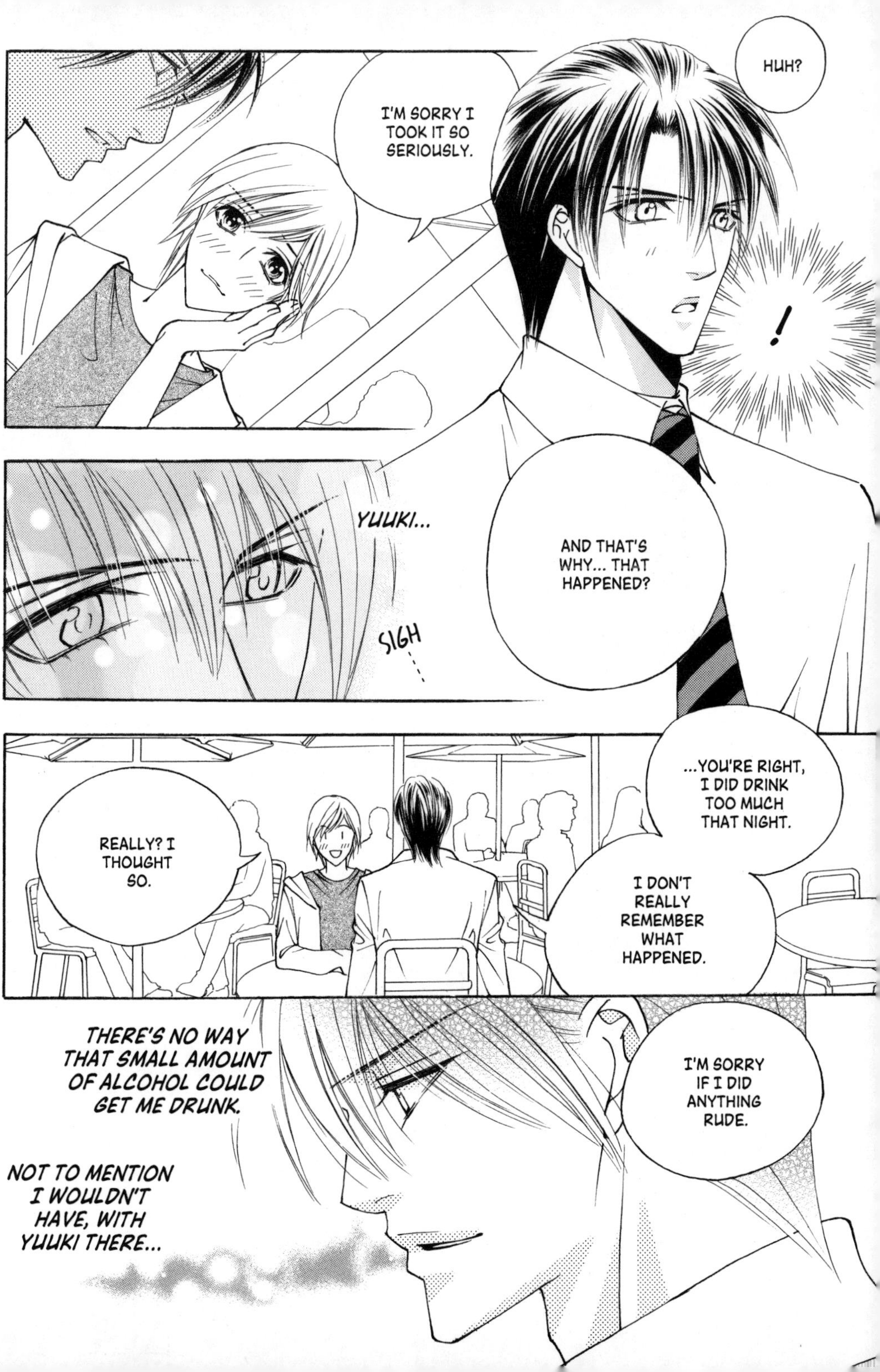
HUH?
!
AND THAT'S WHY... THAT HAPPENED?
I'M SORRY I TOOK IT SO SERIOUSLY.
YUUKI...
SIGH
...YOU'RE RIGHT, I DID DRINK TOO MUCH THAT NIGHT.
I DON'T REALLY REMEMBER WHAT HAPPENED.
REALLY? I THOUGHT SO.
I'M SORRY IF I DID ANYTHING RUDE.
THERE'S NO WAY THAT SMALL AMOUNT OF ALCOHOL COULD GET ME DRUNK.
NOT TO MENTION I WOULDN'T HAVE, WITH YUUKI THERE...

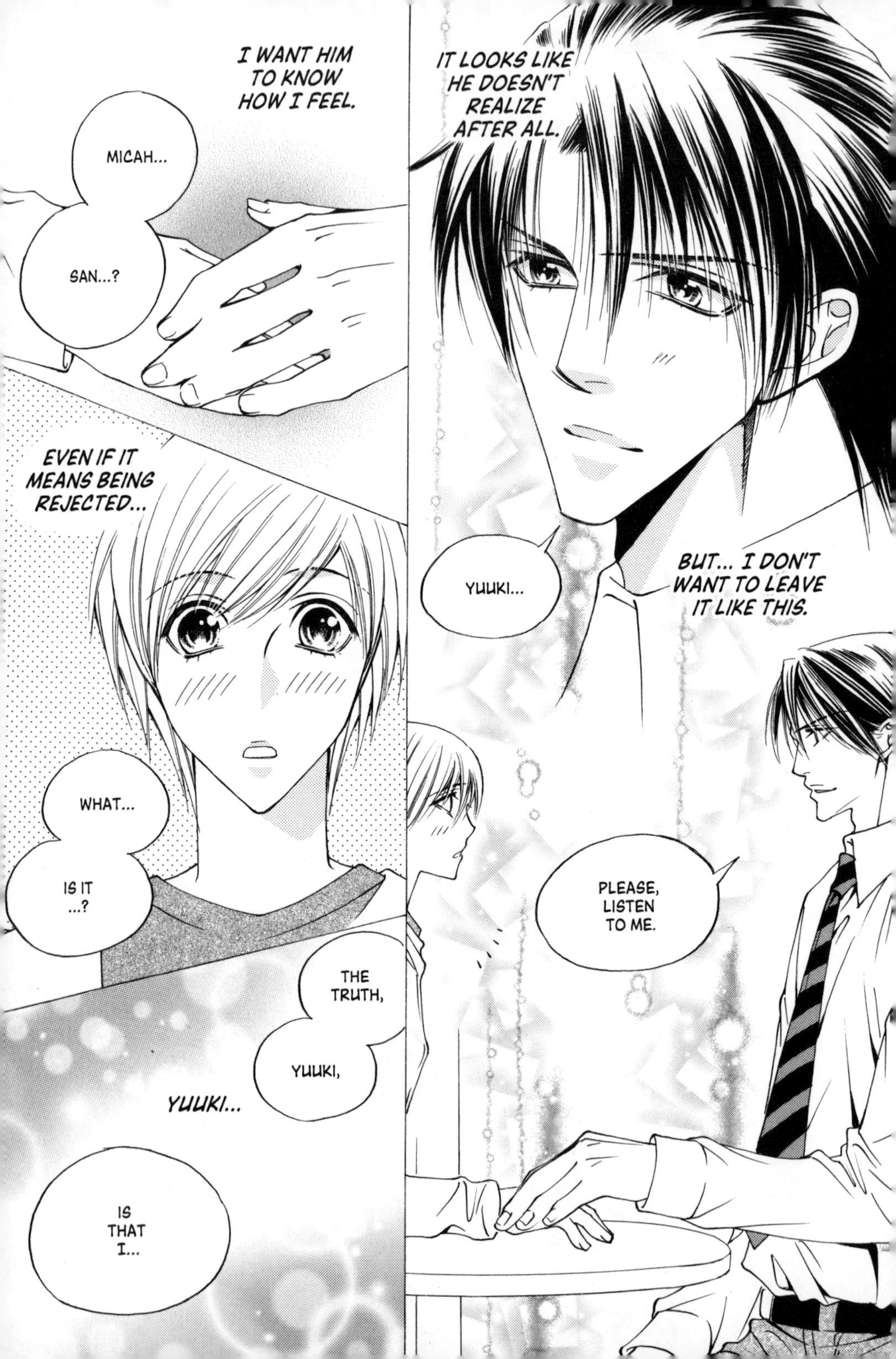
IT LOOKS LIKE HE DOESN'T REALIZE AFTER ALL.
YUUKI...
BUT... I DON'T WANT TO LEAVE IT LIKE THIS.
PLEASE, LISTEN TO ME.
I WANT HIM TO KNOW HOW I FEEL.
MICAH...
SAN...?
EVEN IF IT MEANS BEING REJECTED...
WHAT...
IS IT ...?
THE TRUTH,
YUUKI,
YUUKI...
IS THAT I...

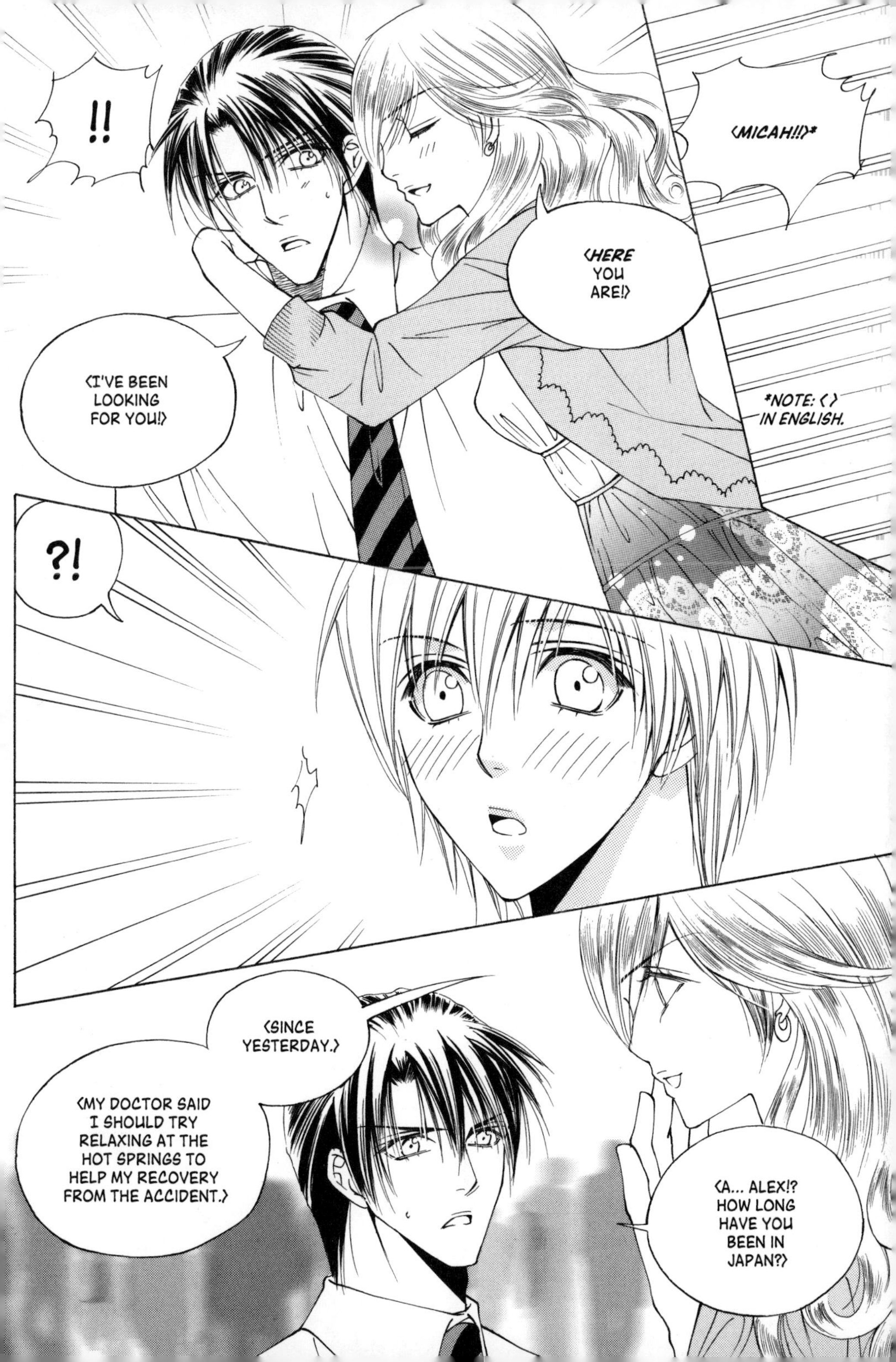
<MICAH!!>*
<HERE YOU ARE!>
!!
<I'VE BEEN LOOKING FOR YOU!>
*NOTE: < > IN ENGLISH.
?!
<A... ALEX!? HOW LONG HAVE YOU BEEN IN JAPAN?>
<SINCE YESTERDAY.>
<MY DOCTOR SAID I SHOULD TRY RELAXING AT THE HOT SPRINGS TO HELP MY RECOVERY FROM THE ACCIDENT.>

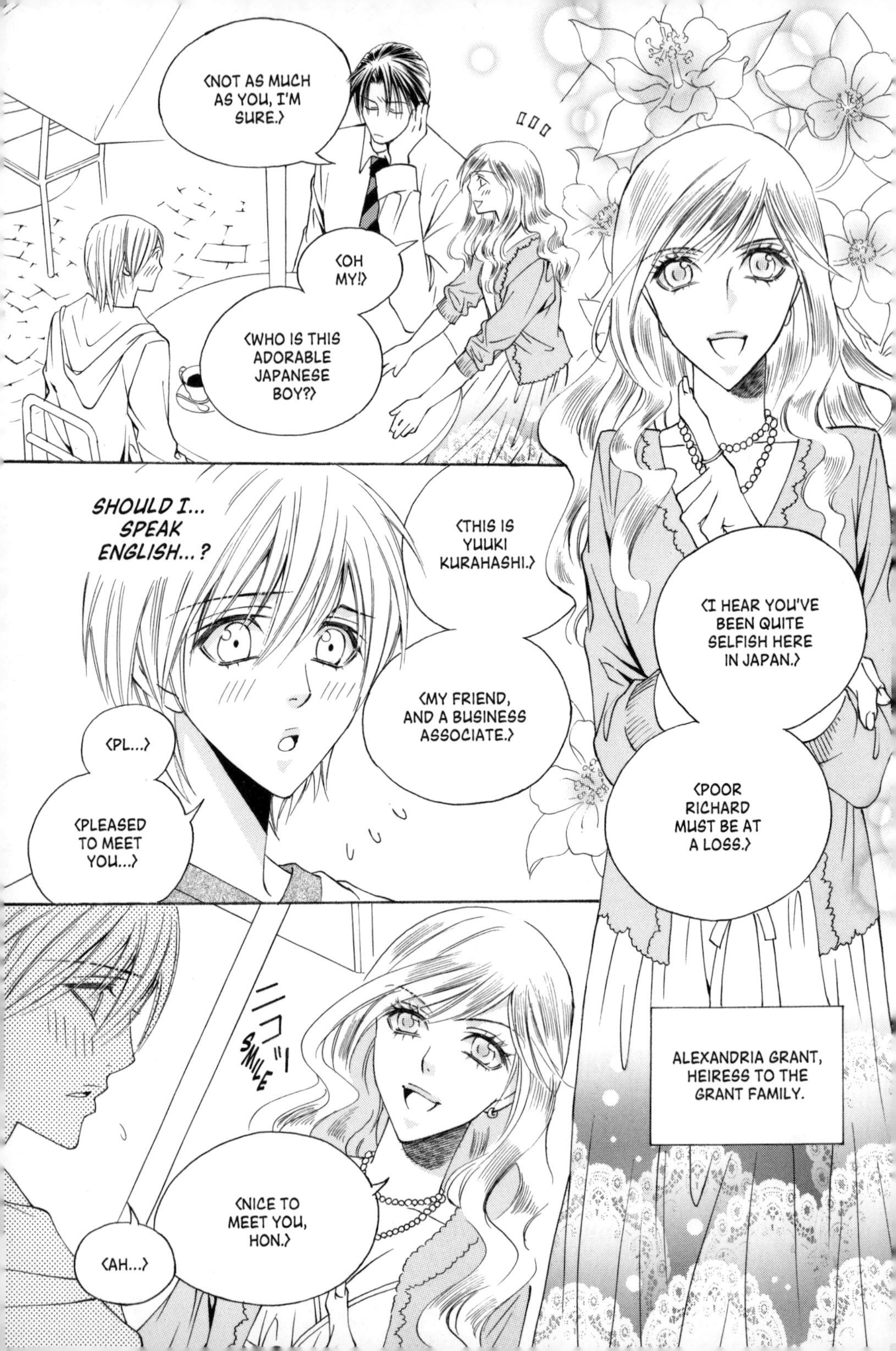

⟨I HEAR YOU'VE BEEN QUITE SELFISH HERE IN JAPAN.⟩
⟨POOR RICHARD MUST BE AT A LOSS.⟩
ALEXANDRIA GRANT, HEIRESS TO THE GRANT FAMILY.
⟨NOT AS MUCH AS YOU, I'M SURE.⟩
⟨OH MY!⟩
⟨WHO IS THIS ADORABLE JAPANESE BOY?⟩
⟨THIS IS YUUKI KURAHASHI.⟩
⟨MY FRIEND, AND A BUSINESS ASSOCIATE.⟩
SHOULD I... SPEAK ENGLISH...?
⟨PL...⟩
⟨PLEASED TO MEET YOU...⟩
SMILE
⟨NICE TO MEET YOU, HON.⟩
⟨AH...⟩

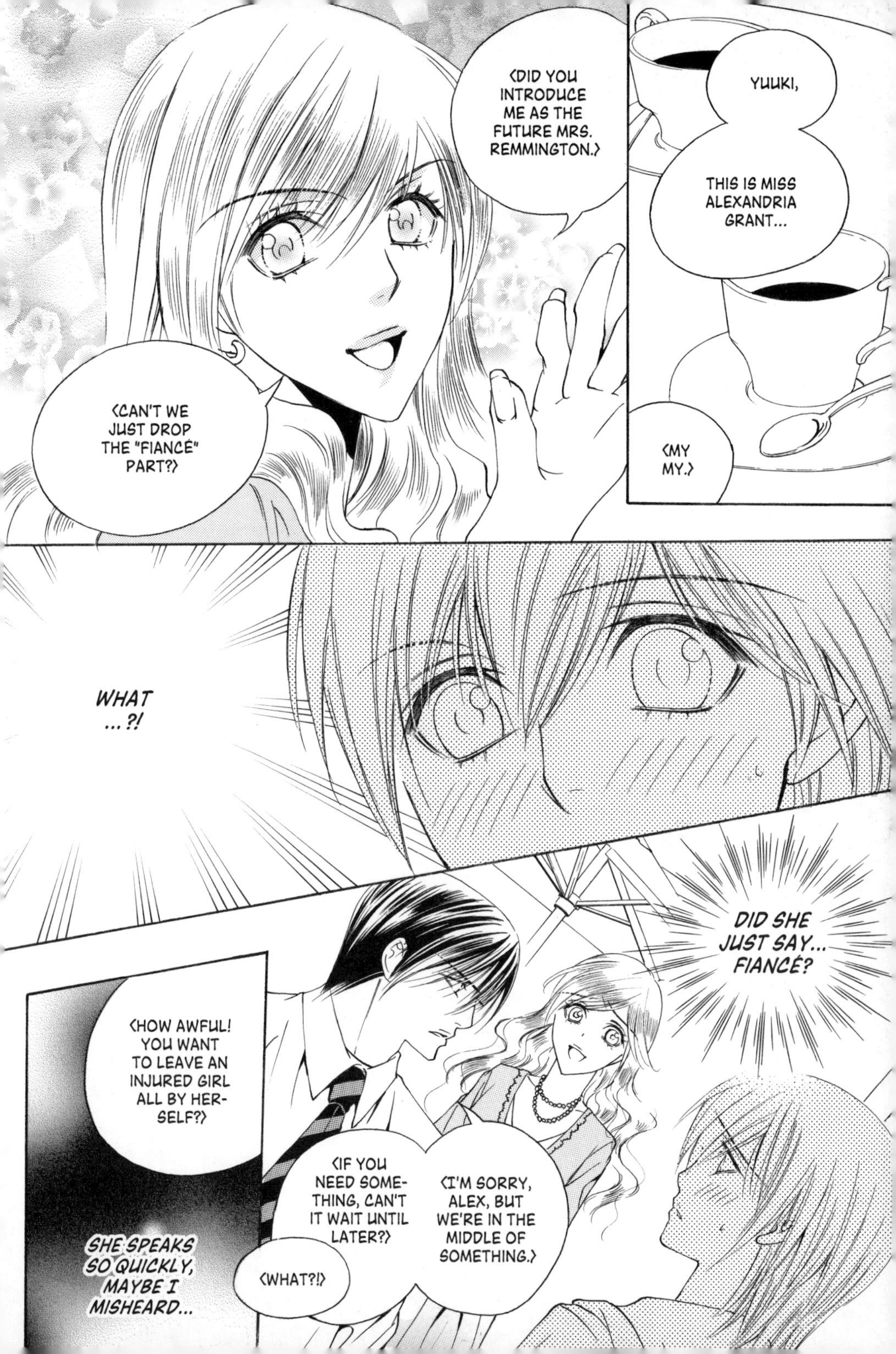
YUUKI,
THIS IS MISS ALEXANDRIA GRANT...
‹MY MY.›
‹DID YOU INTRODUCE ME AS THE FUTURE MRS. REMMINGTON.›
‹CAN'T WE JUST DROP THE "FIANCÉ" PART?›
WHAT ...?!
DID SHE JUST SAY... FIANCÉ?
‹I'M SORRY, ALEX, BUT WE'RE IN THE MIDDLE OF SOMETHING.›
‹IF YOU NEED SOME-THING, CAN'T IT WAIT UNTIL LATER?›
‹WHAT?!›
‹HOW AWFUL! YOU WANT TO LEAVE AN INJURED GIRL ALL BY HER-SELF?›
SHE SPEAKS SO QUICKLY, MAYBE I MISHEARD...

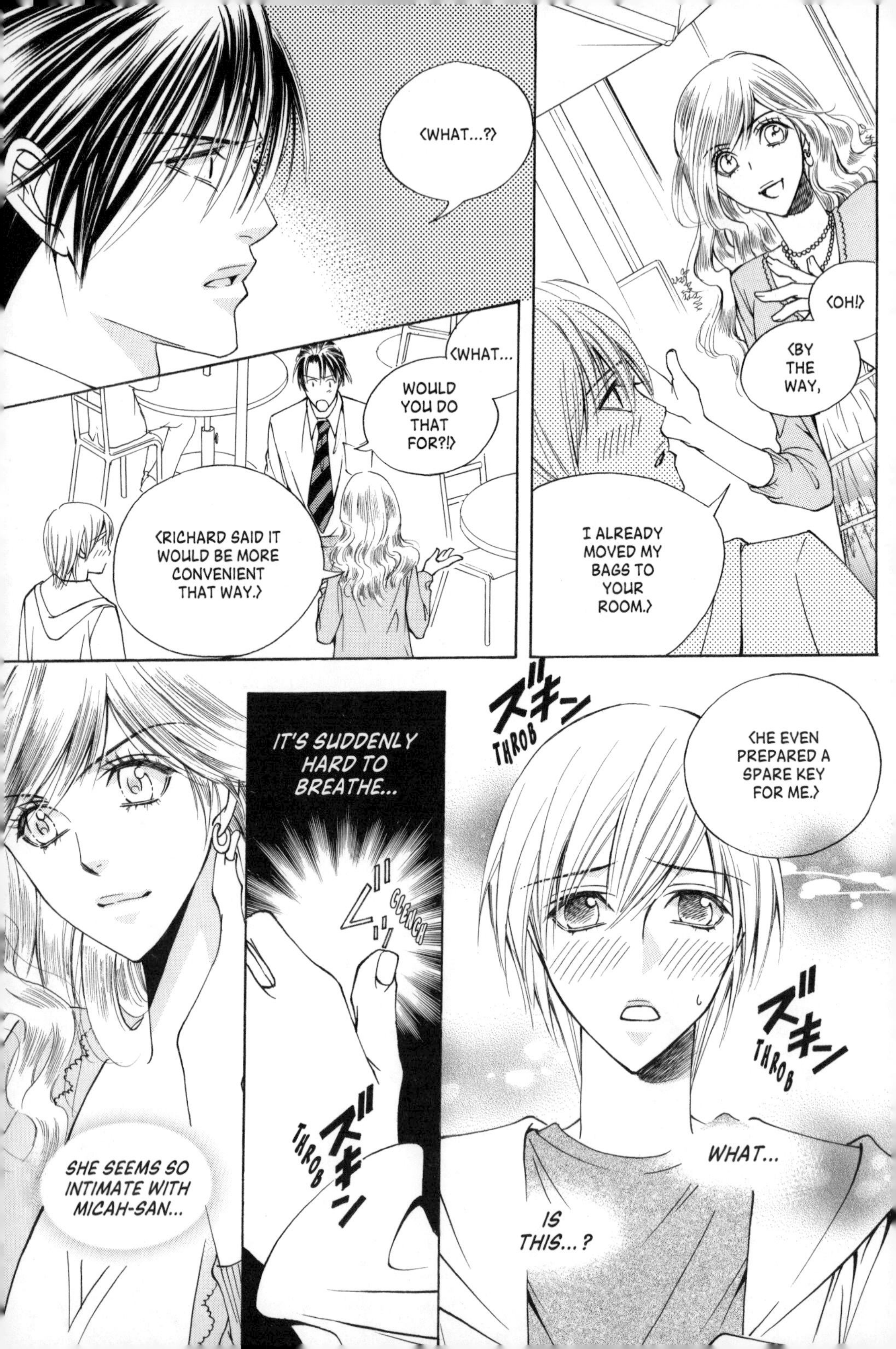
<OH!>
<BY THE WAY,
I ALREADY MOVED MY BAGS TO YOUR ROOM.>
<WHAT...?>
<WHAT...
WOULD YOU DO THAT FOR?!>
<RICHARD SAID IT WOULD BE MORE CONVENIENT THAT WAY.>
THROB
<HE EVEN PREPARED A SPARE KEY FOR ME.>
THROB
WHAT...
IS THIS...?
IT'S SUDDENLY HARD TO BREATHE...
CLENCH
THROB
SHE SEEMS SO INTIMATE WITH MICAH-SAN...

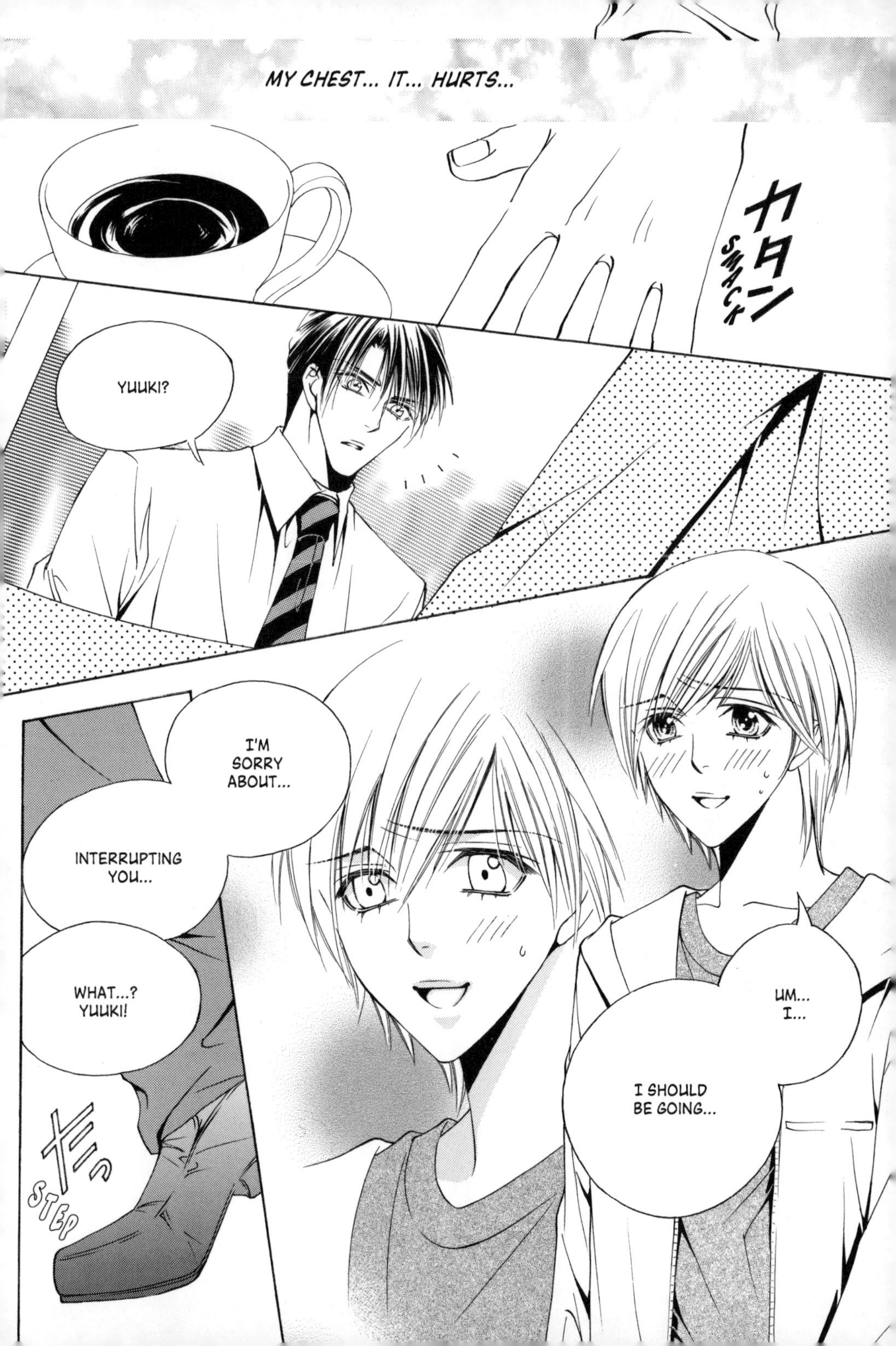
MY CHEST... IT... HURTS...
カタン
SMACK
YUUKI?
I'M SORRY ABOUT...
INTERRUPTING YOU...
UM... I...
I SHOULD BE GOING...
WHAT...? YUUKI!
ダッ
STEP

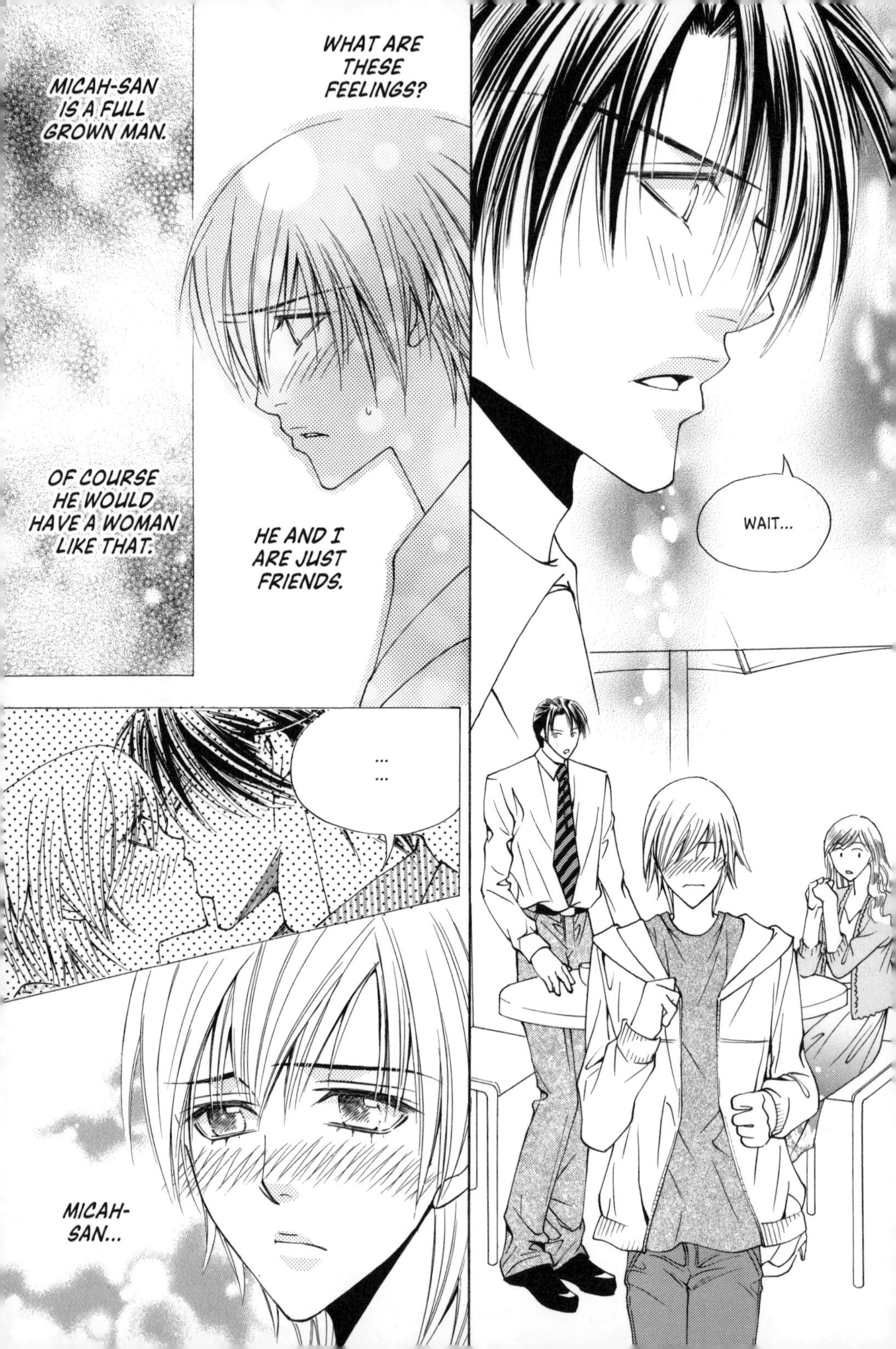
WAIT...
WHAT ARE THESE FEELINGS?
MICAH-SAN IS A FULL GROWN MAN.
OF COURSE HE WOULD HAVE A WOMAN LIKE THAT.
HE AND I ARE JUST FRIENDS.
... ...
MICAH-SAN...

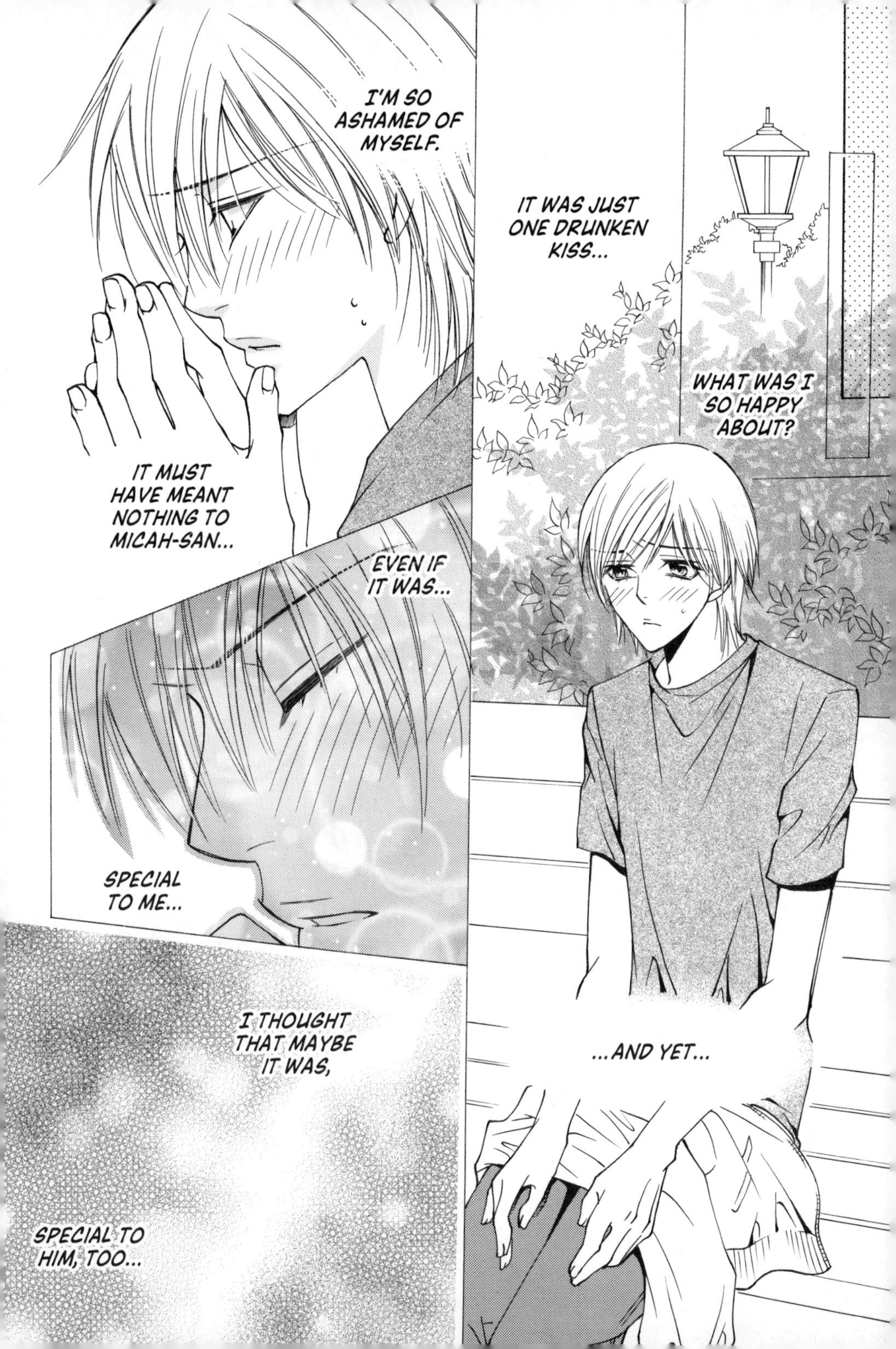
IT WAS JUST ONE DRUNKEN KISS...
WHAT WAS I SO HAPPY ABOUT?
...AND YET...
I'M SO ASHAMED OF MYSELF.
IT MUST HAVE MEANT NOTHING TO MICAH-SAN...
EVEN IF IT WAS...
SPECIAL TO ME...
I THOUGHT THAT MAYBE IT WAS,
SPECIAL TO HIM, TOO...

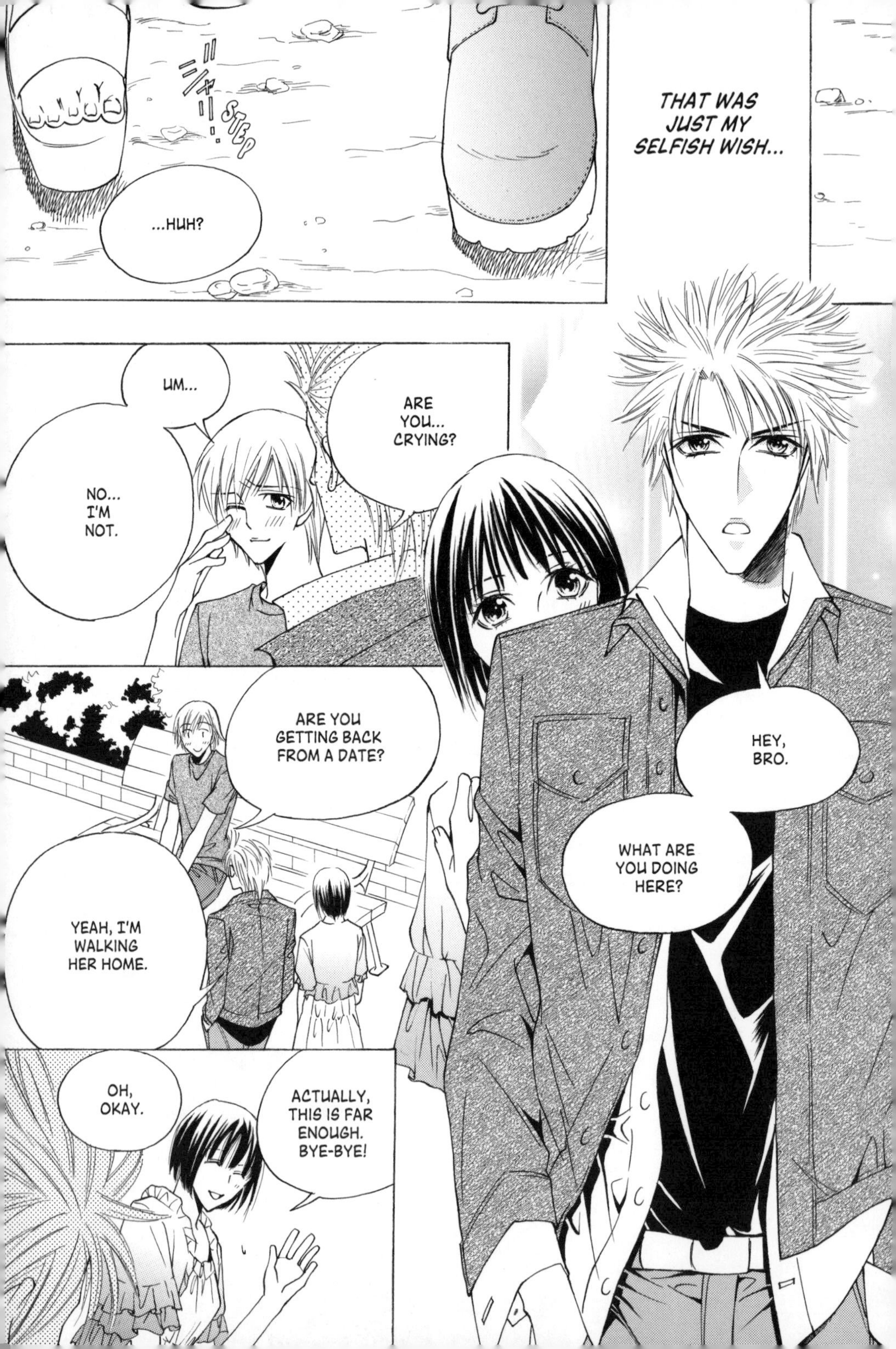
THAT WAS JUST MY SELFISH WISH...
STEP
...HUH?
HEY, BRO.
WHAT ARE YOU DOING HERE?
ARE YOU... CRYING?
UM...
NO... I'M NOT.
ARE YOU GETTING BACK FROM A DATE?
YEAH, I'M WALKING HER HOME.
ACTUALLY, THIS IS FAR ENOUGH. BYE-BYE!
OH, OKAY.

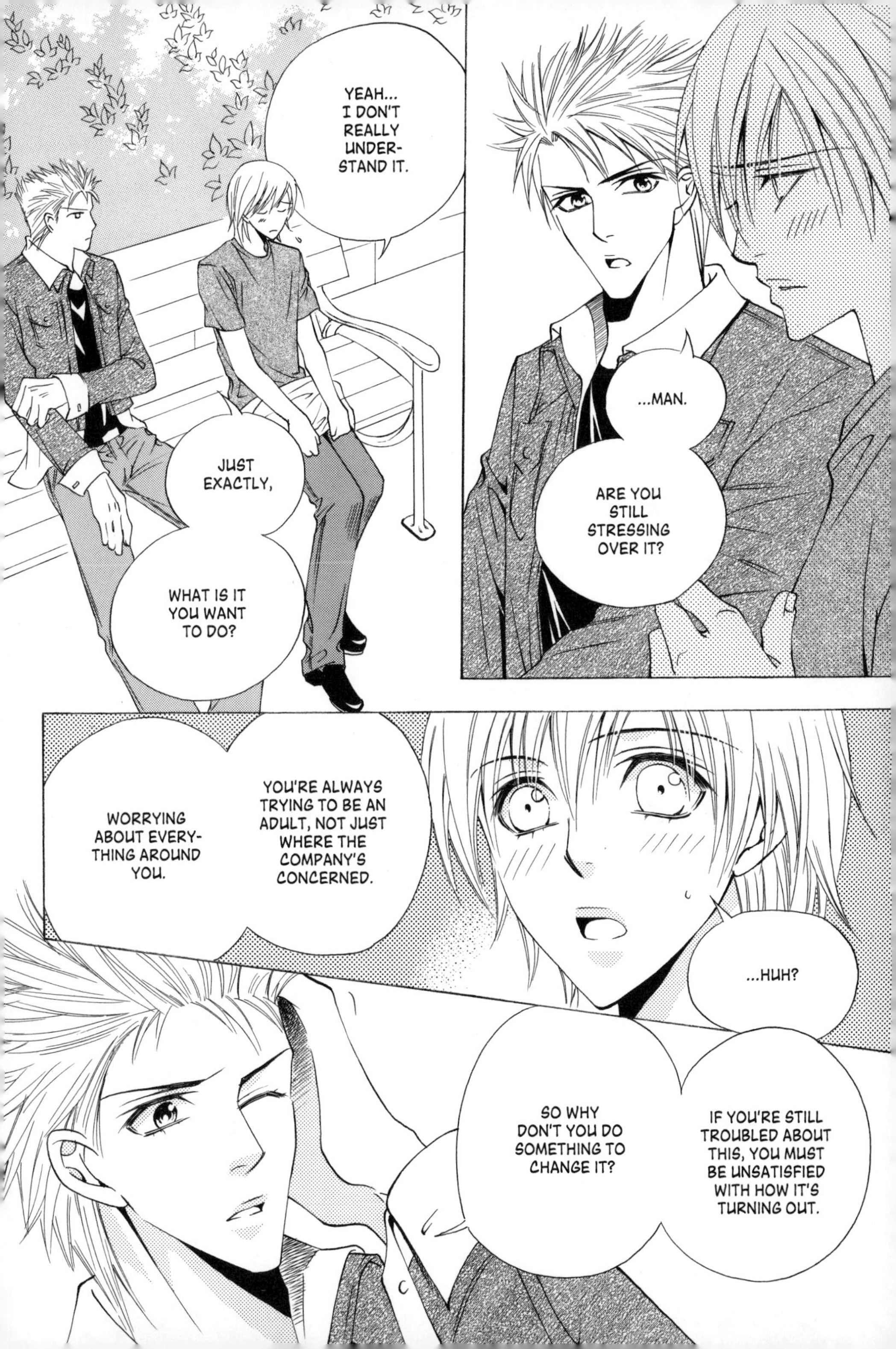
...MAN.
ARE YOU STILL STRESSING OVER IT?
YEAH... I DON'T REALLY UNDER-STAND IT.
JUST EXACTLY,
WHAT IS IT YOU WANT TO DO?
YOU'RE ALWAYS TRYING TO BE AN ADULT, NOT JUST WHERE THE COMPANY'S CONCERNED.
WORRYING ABOUT EVERY-THING AROUND YOU.
...HUH?
IF YOU'RE STILL TROUBLED ABOUT THIS, YOU MUST BE UNSATISFIED WITH HOW IT'S TURNING OUT.
SO WHY DON'T YOU DO SOMETHING TO CHANGE IT?

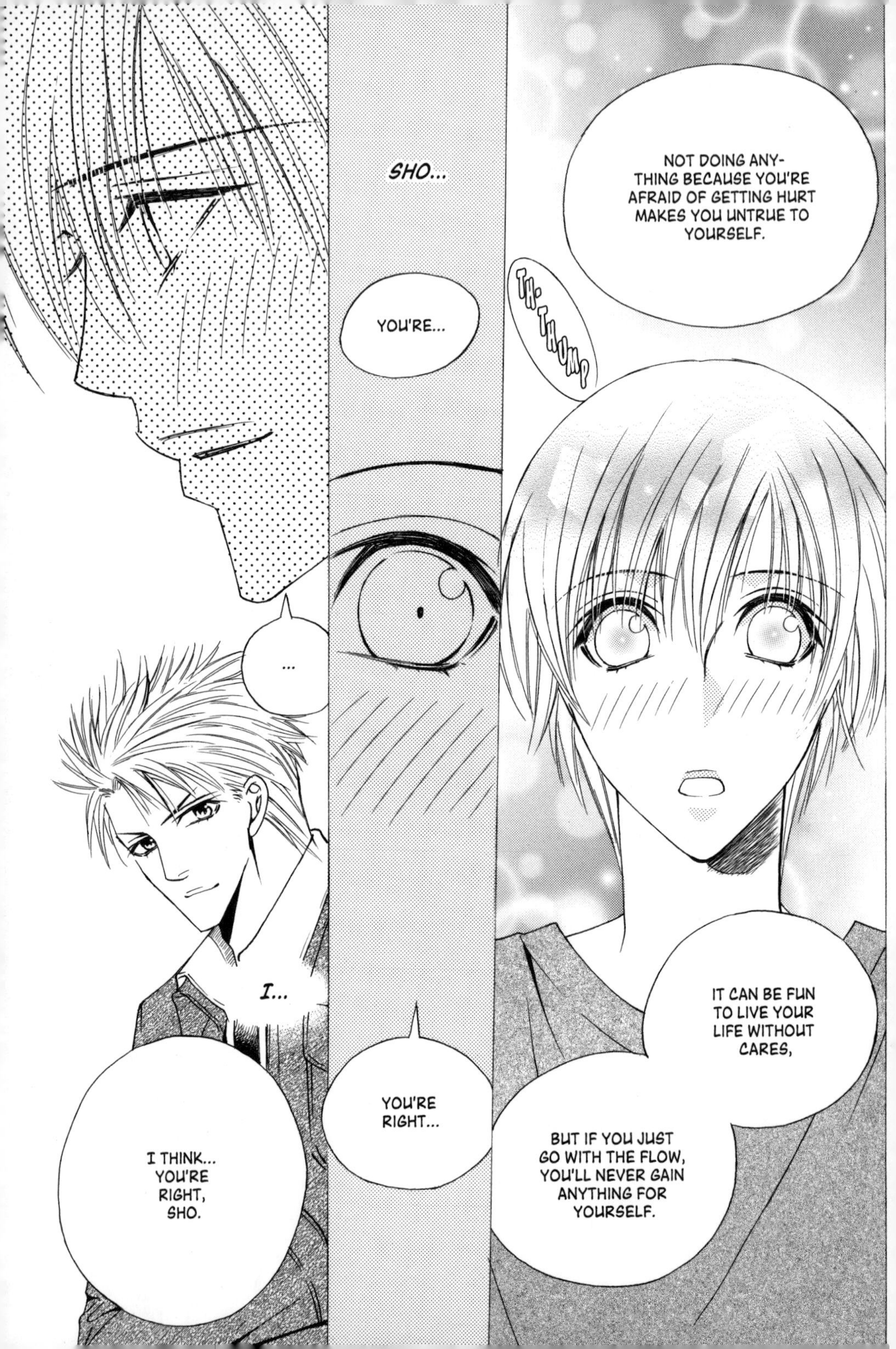
NOT DOING ANY-THING BECAUSE YOU'RE AFRAID OF GETTING HURT MAKES YOU UNTRUE TO YOURSELF.
TH-THUMP
IT CAN BE FUN TO LIVE YOUR LIFE WITHOUT CARES,
BUT IF YOU JUST GO WITH THE FLOW, YOU'LL NEVER GAIN ANYTHING FOR YOURSELF.
SHO...
YOU'RE...
YOU'RE RIGHT...
...
I...
I THINK... YOU'RE RIGHT, SHO.

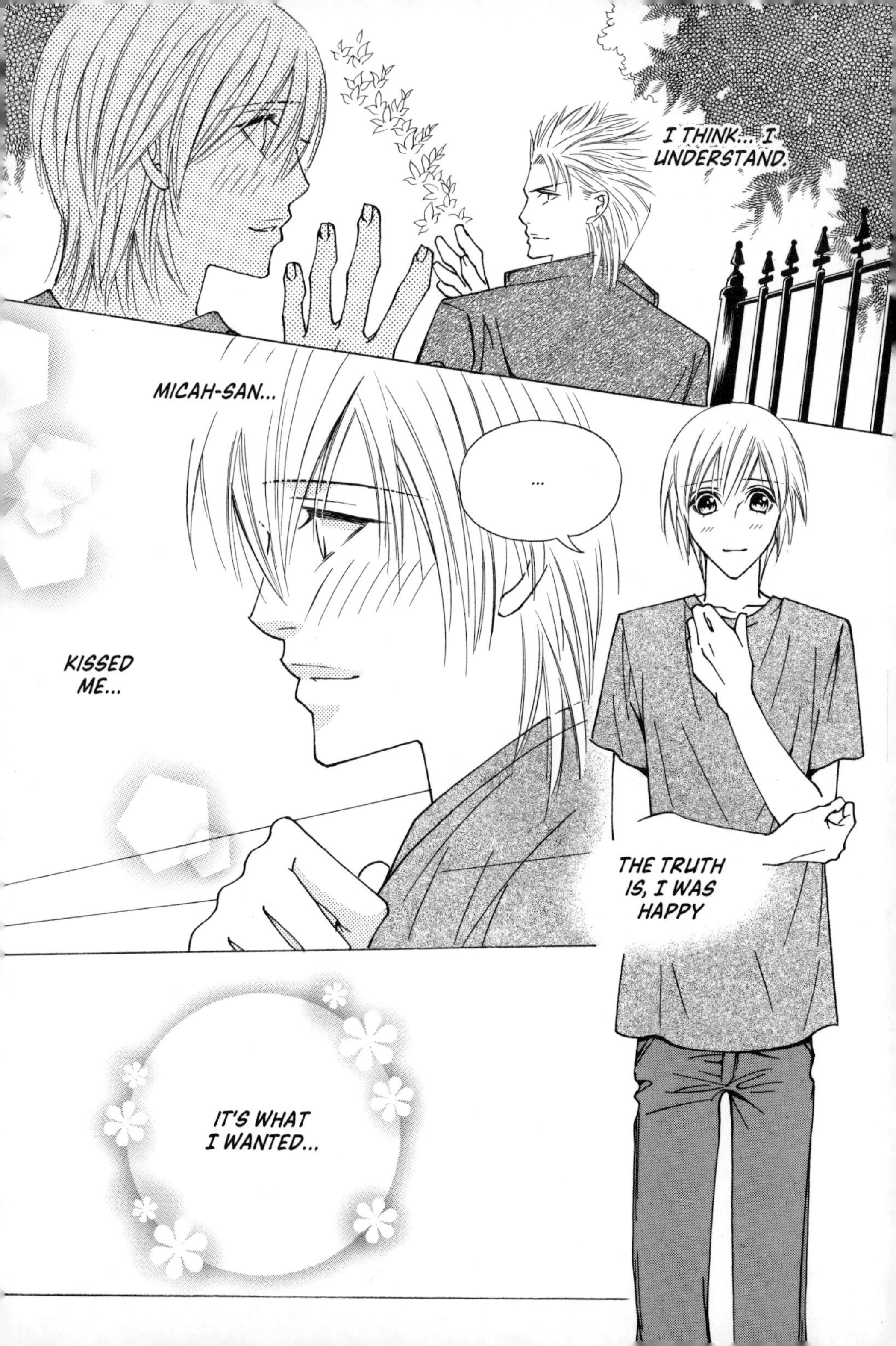
I THINK... I UNDERSTAND.
...
MICAH-SAN...
KISSED ME...
THE TRUTH IS, I WAS HAPPY
IT'S WHAT I WANTED...

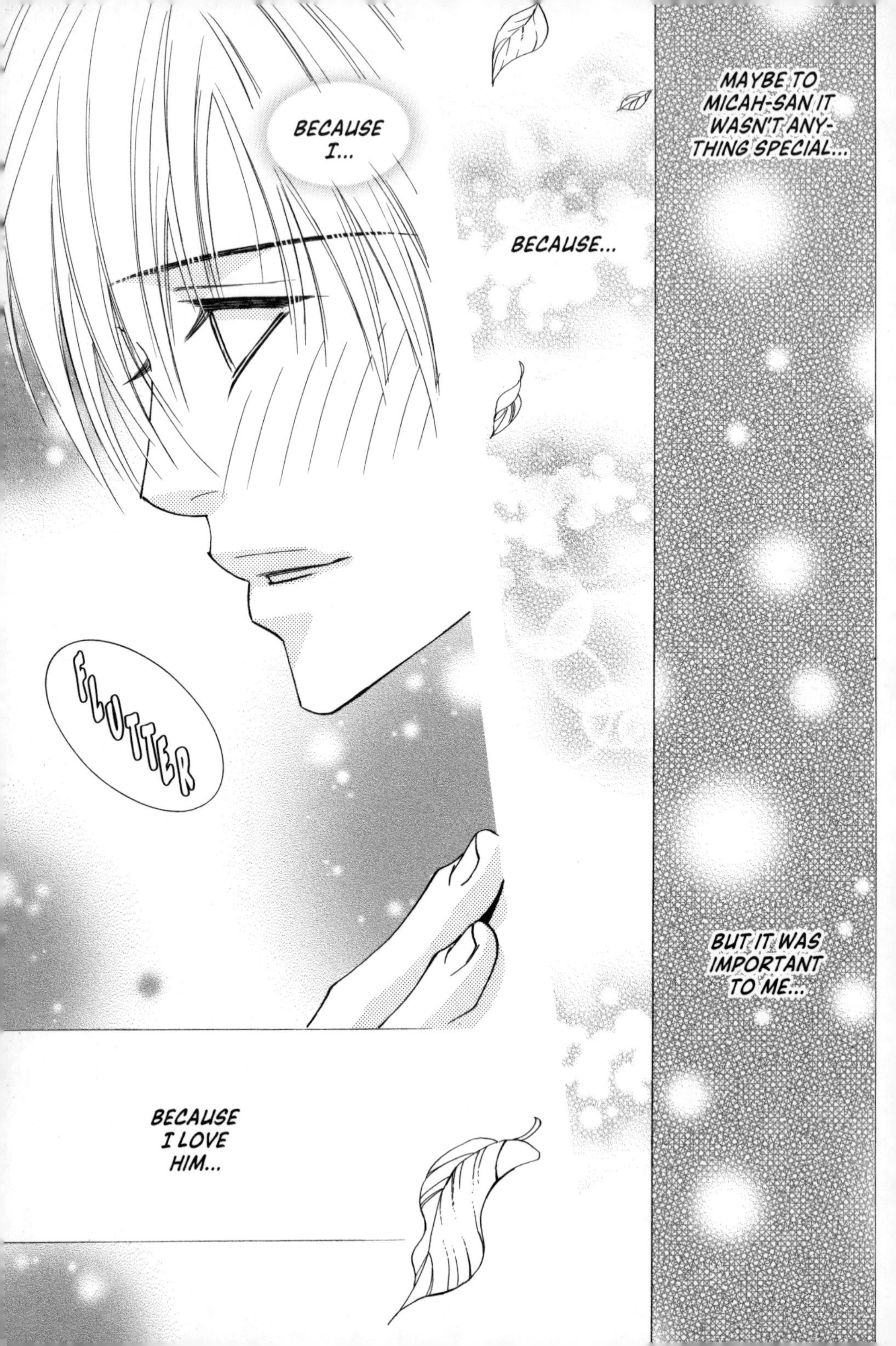
MAYBE TO MICAH-SAN IT WASN'T ANYTHING SPECIAL...
BUT IT WAS IMPORTANT TO ME...
BECAUSE I...
BECAUSE...
FLUTTER
BECAUSE I LOVE HIM...

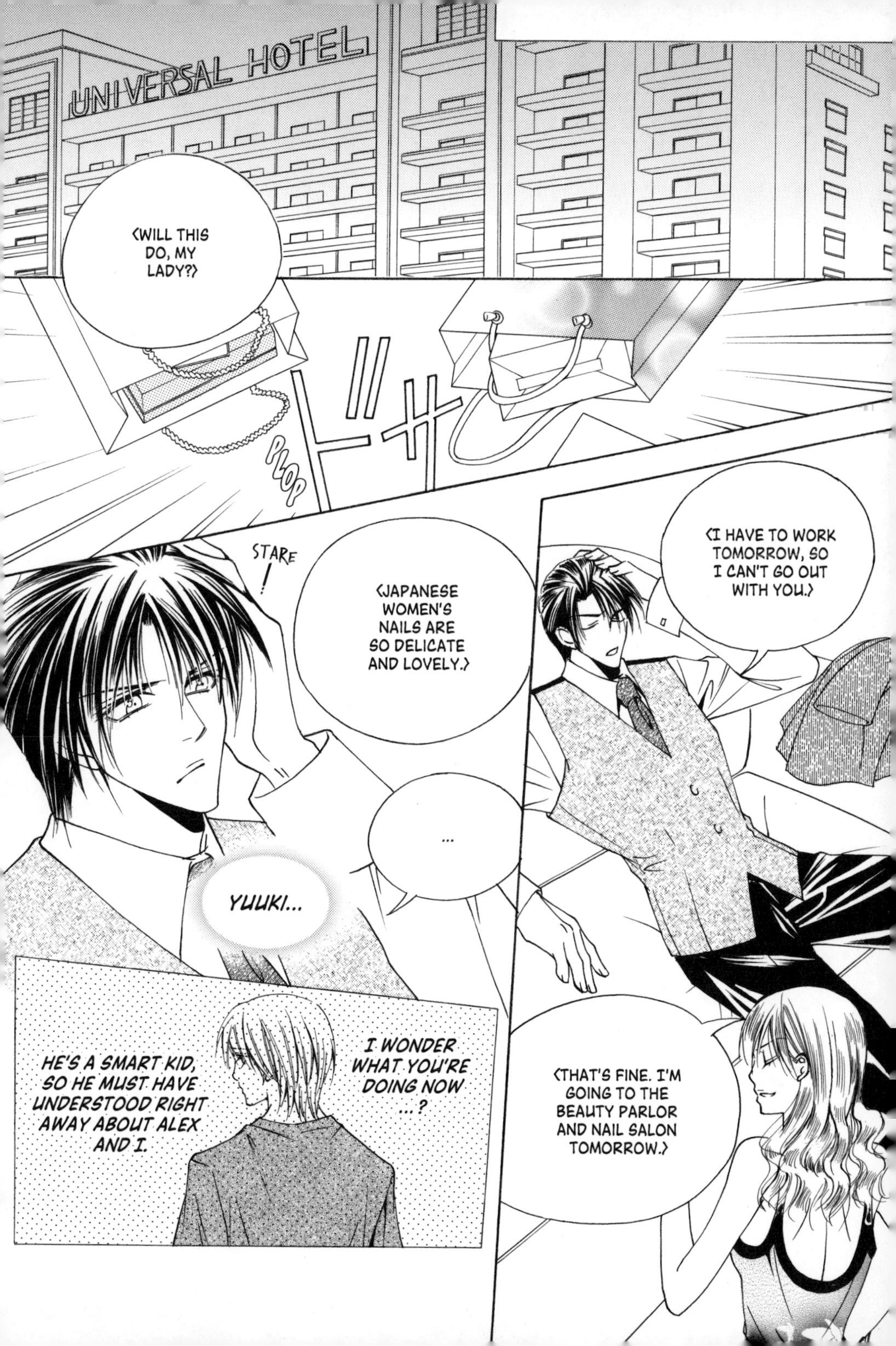
UNIVERSAL HOTEL
‹WILL THIS DO, MY LADY?›
PLOP
‹I HAVE TO WORK TOMORROW, SO I CAN'T GO OUT WITH YOU.›
‹THAT'S FINE. I'M GOING TO THE BEAUTY PARLOR AND NAIL SALON TOMORROW.›
‹JAPANESE WOMEN'S NAILS ARE SO DELICATE AND LOVELY.›
STARE
!
...
YUUKI...
I WONDER WHAT YOU'RE DOING NOW ...?
HE'S A SMART KID, SO HE MUST HAVE UNDERSTOOD RIGHT AWAY ABOUT ALEX AND I.

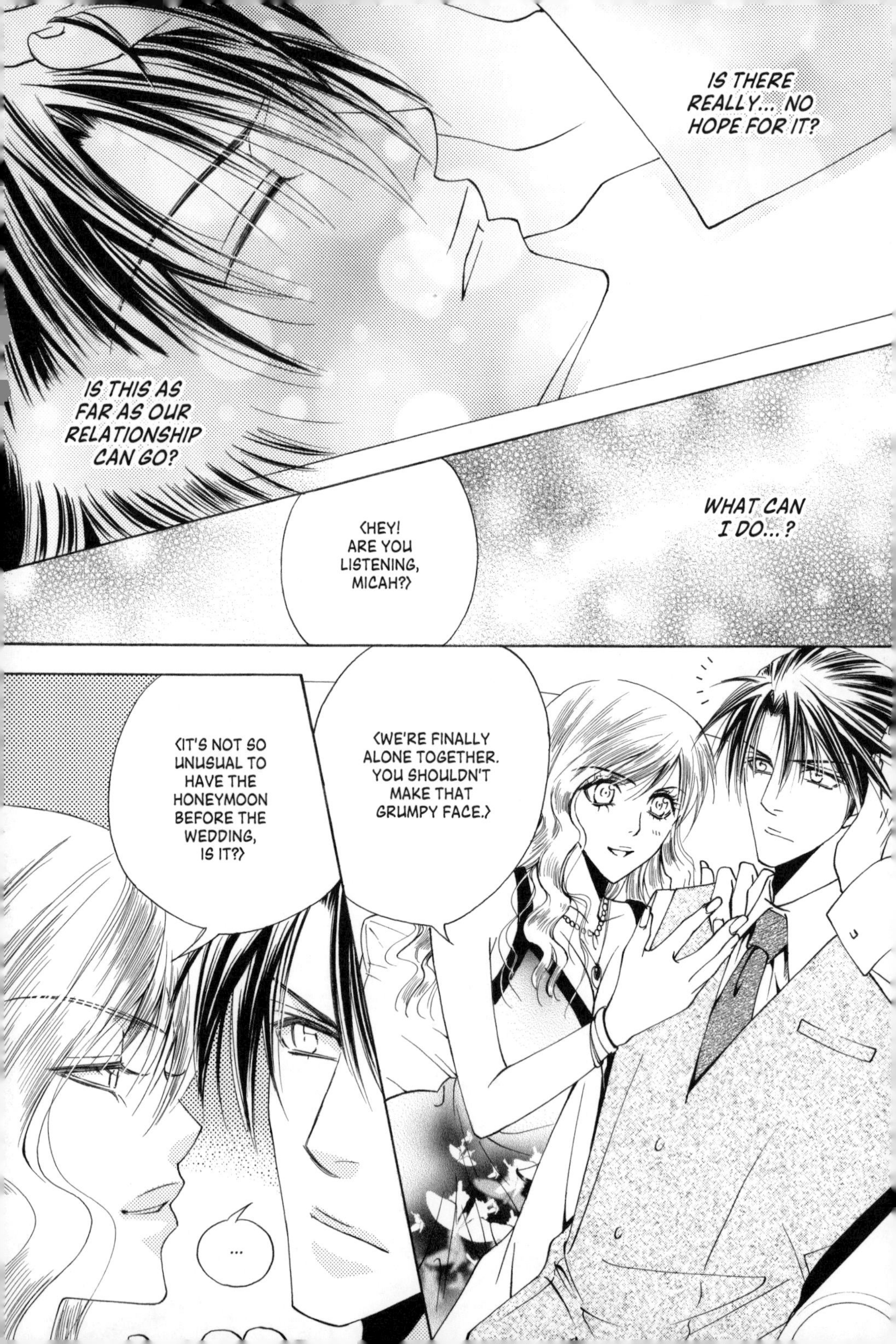
IS THERE REALLY... NO HOPE FOR IT?
IS THIS AS FAR AS OUR RELATIONSHIP CAN GO?
WHAT CAN I DO...?
<HEY! ARE YOU LISTENING, MICAH?>
<WE'RE FINALLY ALONE TOGETHER. YOU SHOULDN'T MAKE THAT GRUMPY FACE.>
<IT'S NOT SO UNUSUAL TO HAVE THE HONEYMOON BEFORE THE WEDDING, IS IT?>
...

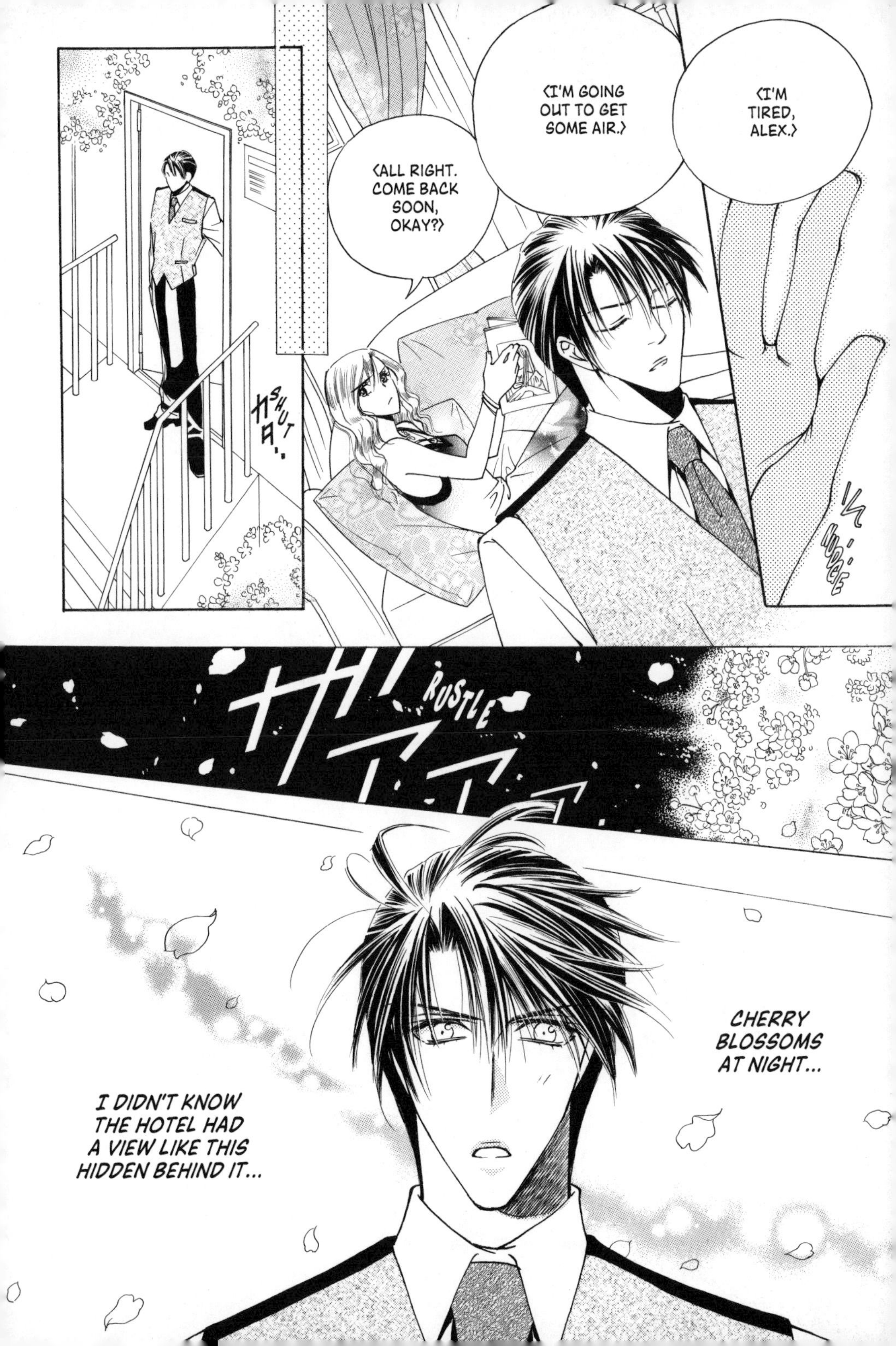
<I'M TIRED, ALEX.>
<I'M GOING OUT TO GET SOME AIR.>
<ALL RIGHT. COME BACK SOON, OKAY?>
NUDGE
SHUT
RUSTLE
CHERRY BLOSSOMS AT NIGHT...
I DIDN'T KNOW THE HOTEL HAD A VIEW LIKE THIS HIDDEN BEHIND IT...

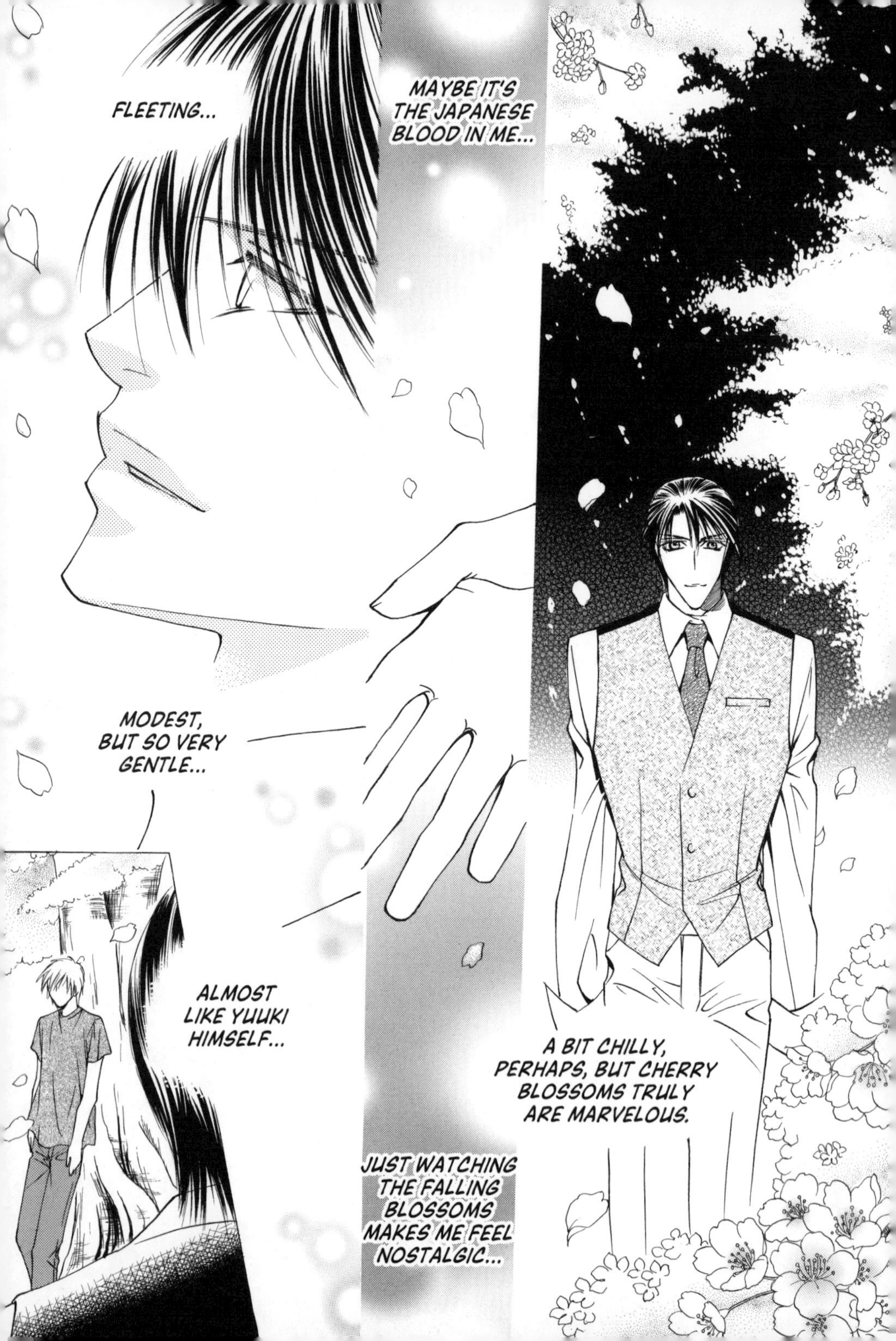

A BIT CHILLY, PERHAPS, BUT CHERRY BLOSSOMS TRULY ARE MARVELOUS.
JUST WATCHING THE FALLING BLOSSOMS MAKES ME FEEL NOSTALGIC...
MAYBE IT'S THE JAPANESE BLOOD IN ME...
FLEETING...
MODEST, BUT SO VERY GENTLE...
ALMOST LIKE YUUKI HIMSELF...

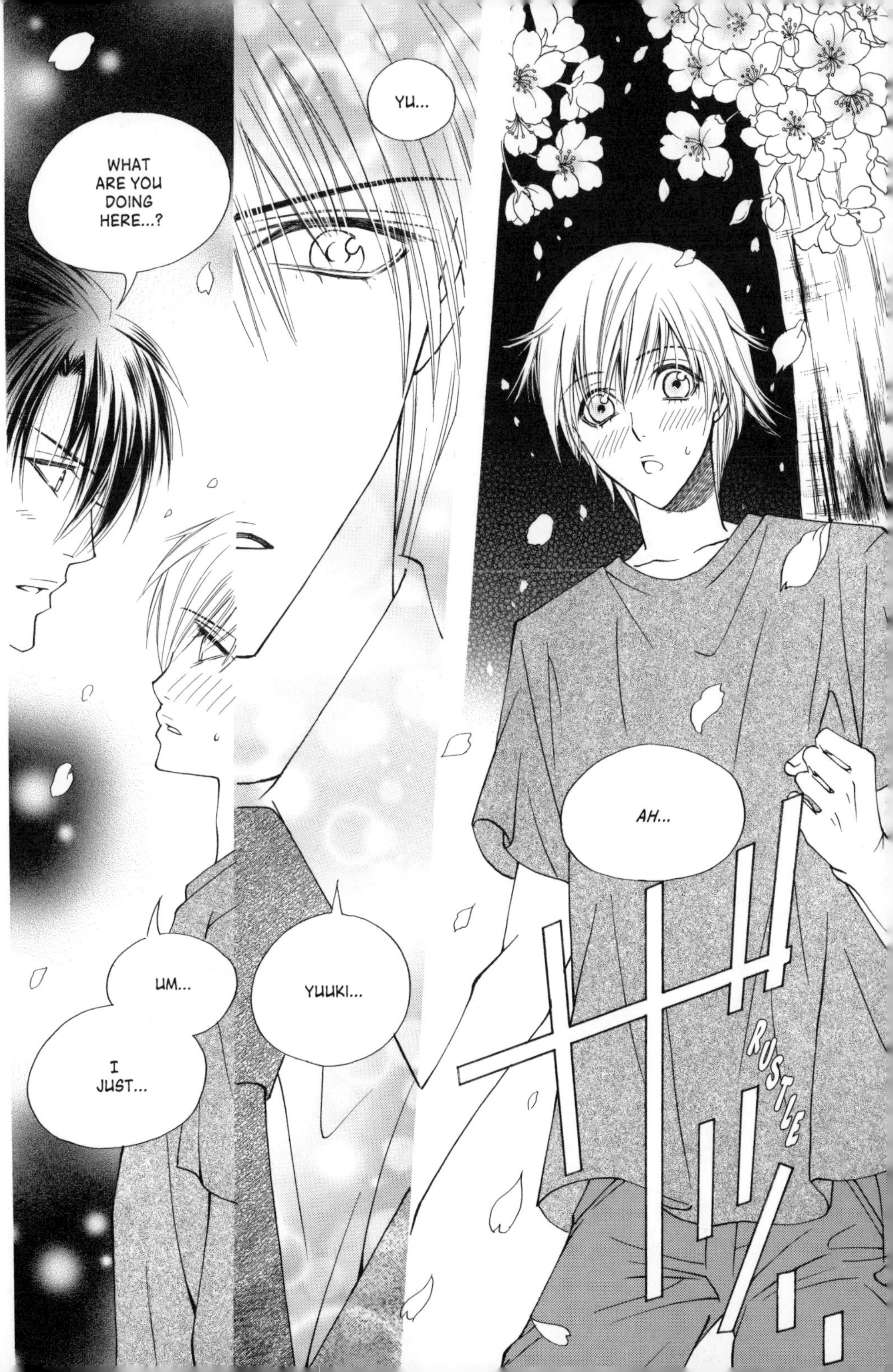
AH...
RUSTLE
YU...
WHAT ARE YOU DOING HERE...?
YUUKI...
UM...
I JUST...

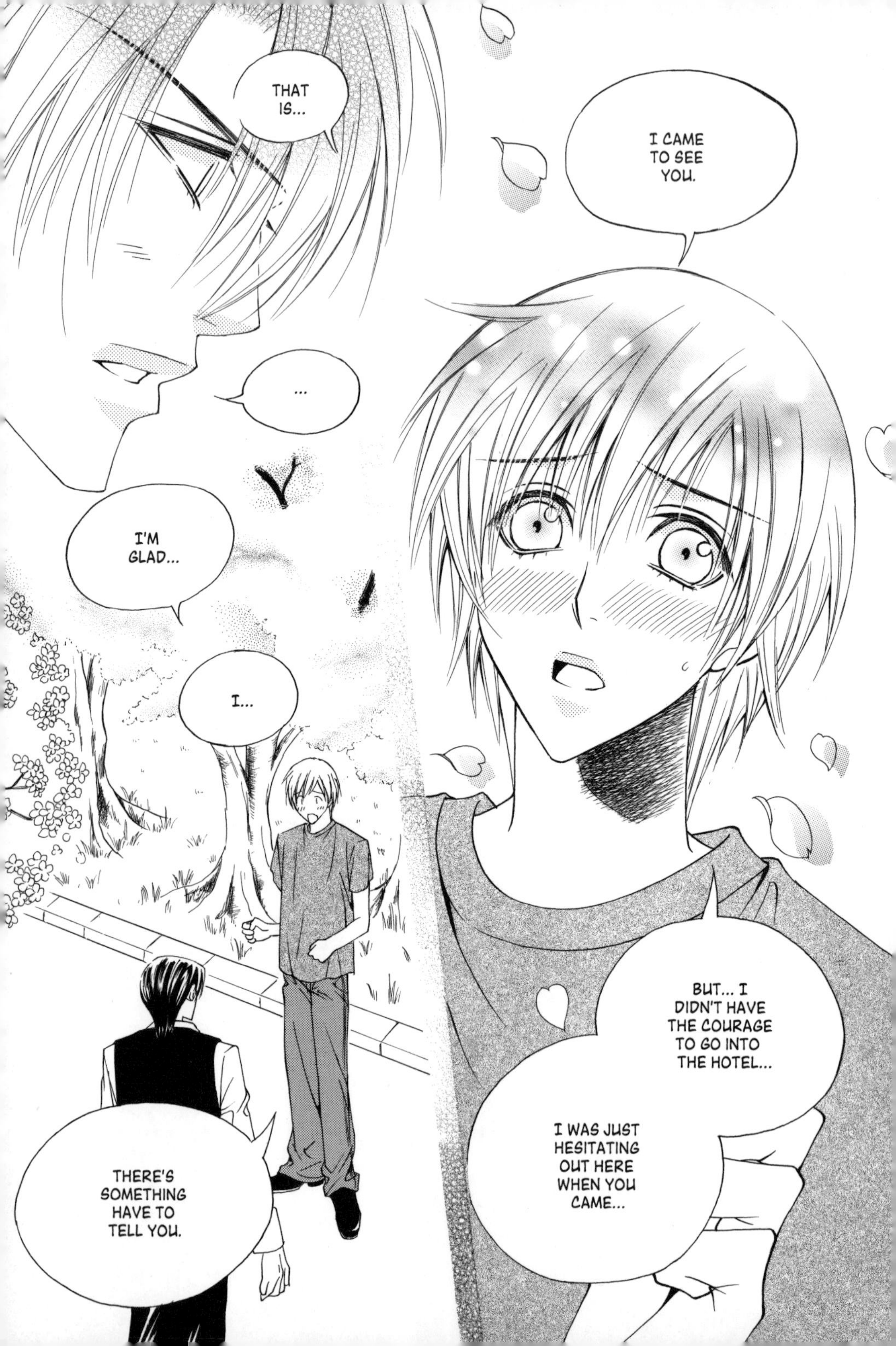
I CAME TO SEE YOU.
BUT... I DIDN'T HAVE THE COURAGE TO GO INTO THE HOTEL...
I WAS JUST HESITATING OUT HERE WHEN YOU CAME...
THAT IS...
...
I'M GLAD...
I...
THERE'S SOMETHING HAVE TO TELL YOU.

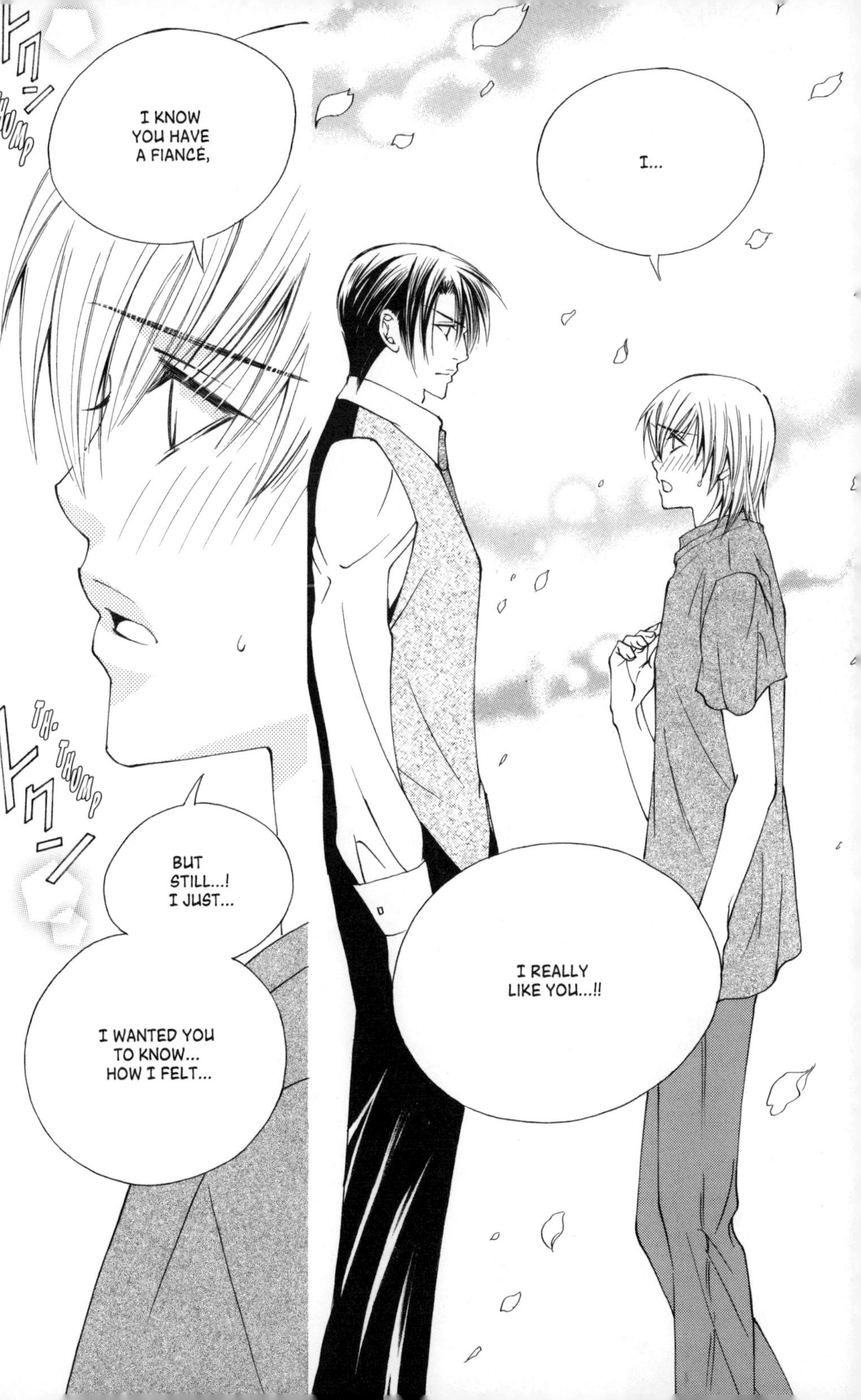
I...
I REALLY LIKE YOU...!!
TH-THUMP
I KNOW YOU HAVE A FIANCÉ,
BUT STILL...! I JUST...
I WANTED YOU TO KNOW... HOW I FELT...
TH-THUMP

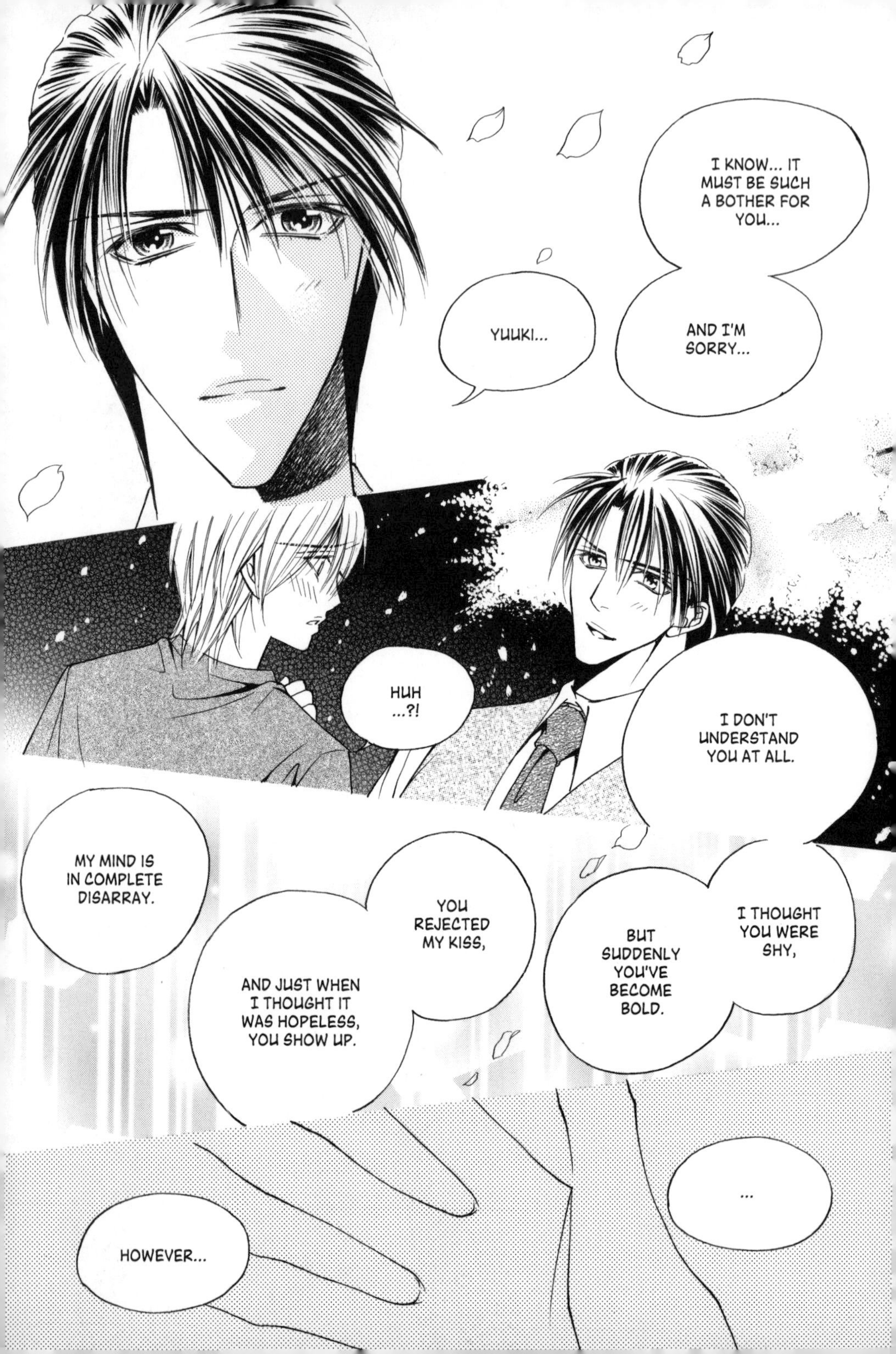
I KNOW... IT MUST BE SUCH A BOTHER FOR YOU...
AND I'M SORRY...
YUUKI...
HUH ...?!
I DON'T UNDERSTAND YOU AT ALL.
I THOUGHT YOU WERE SHY,
BUT SUDDENLY YOU'VE BECOME BOLD.
YOU REJECTED MY KISS,
AND JUST WHEN I THOUGHT IT WAS HOPELESS, YOU SHOW UP.
MY MIND IS IN COMPLETE DISARRAY.
...
HOWEVER...

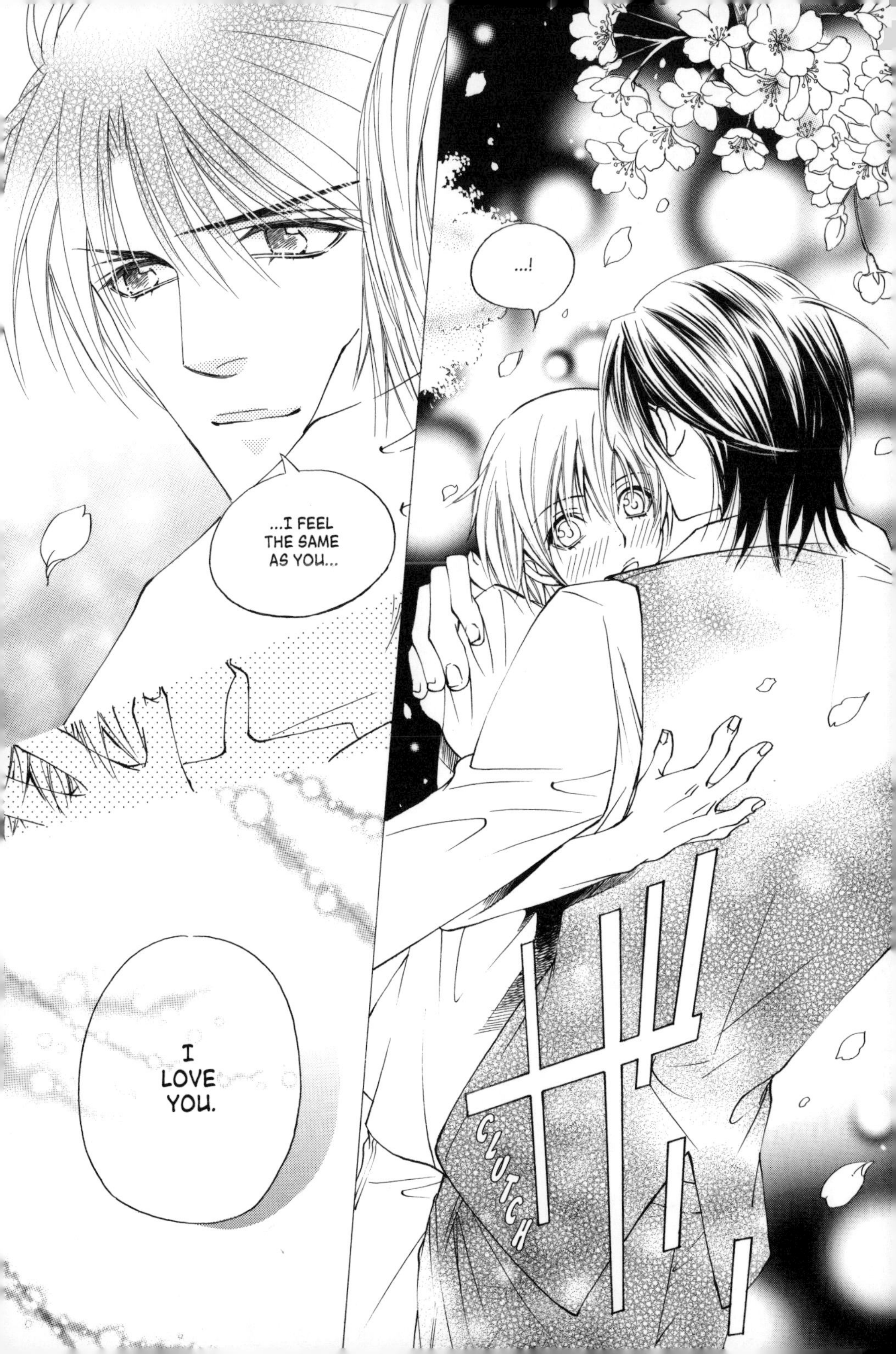
...!
CLUTCH
...I FEEL THE SAME AS YOU...
I LOVE YOU.

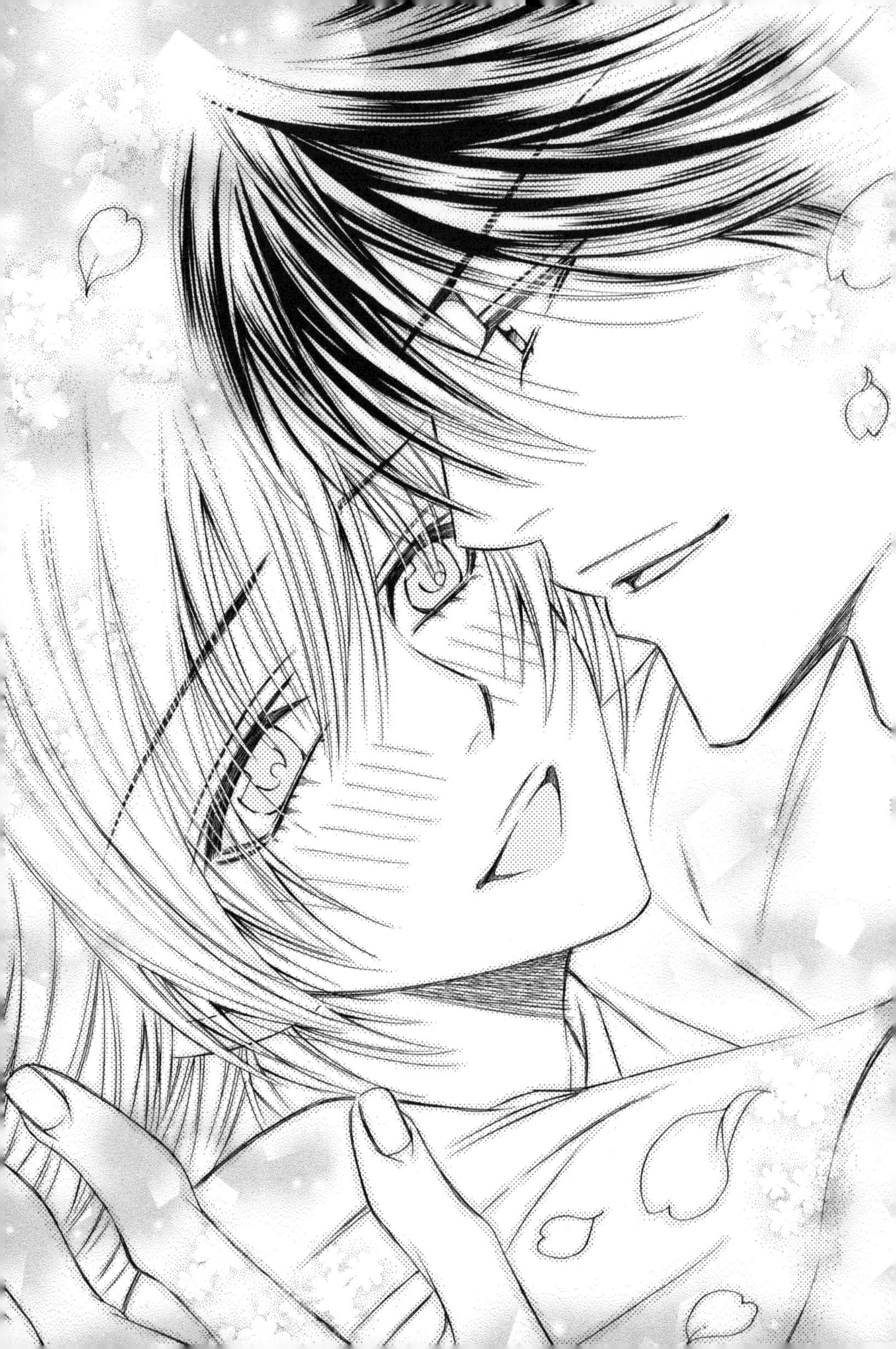

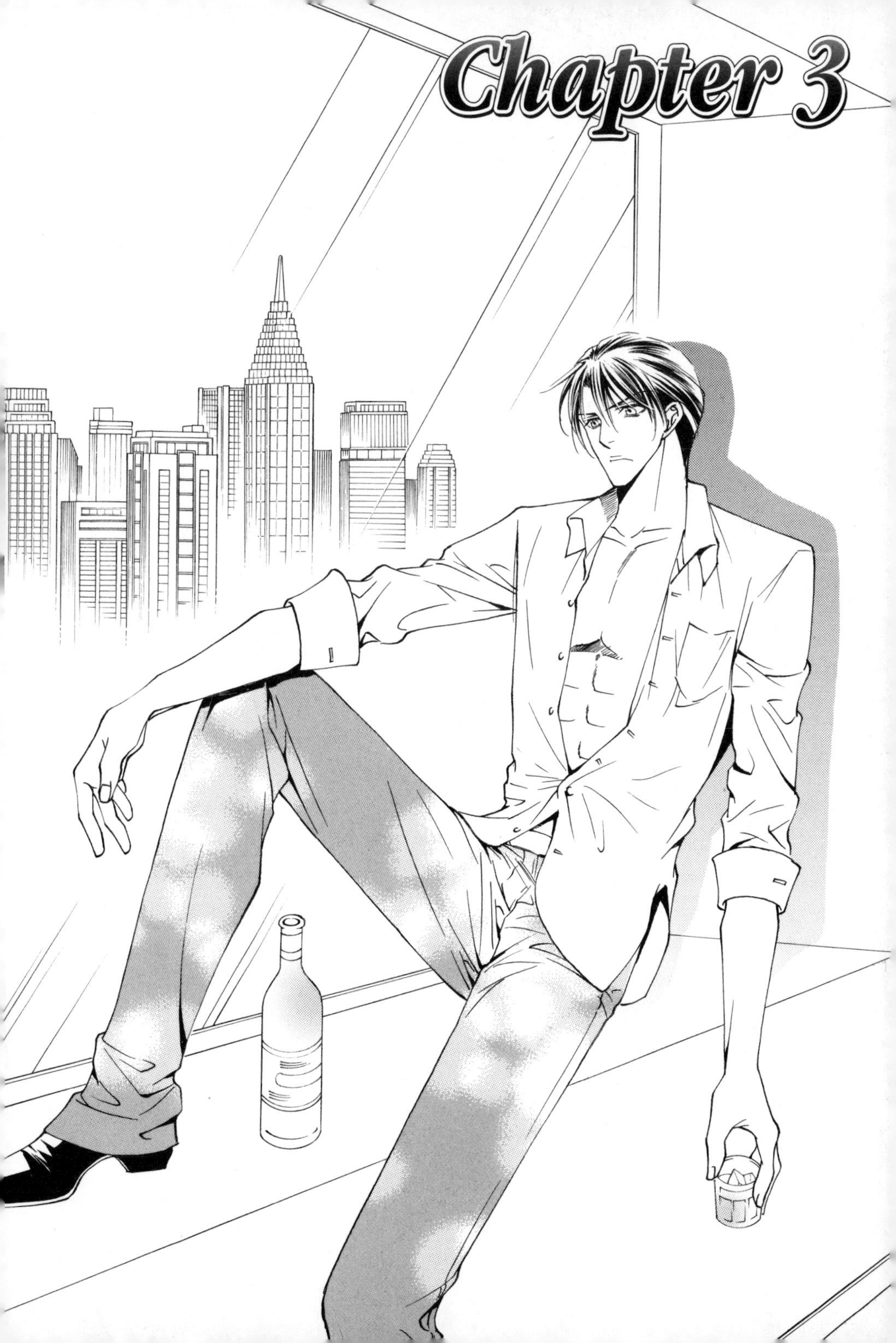
Chapter 3

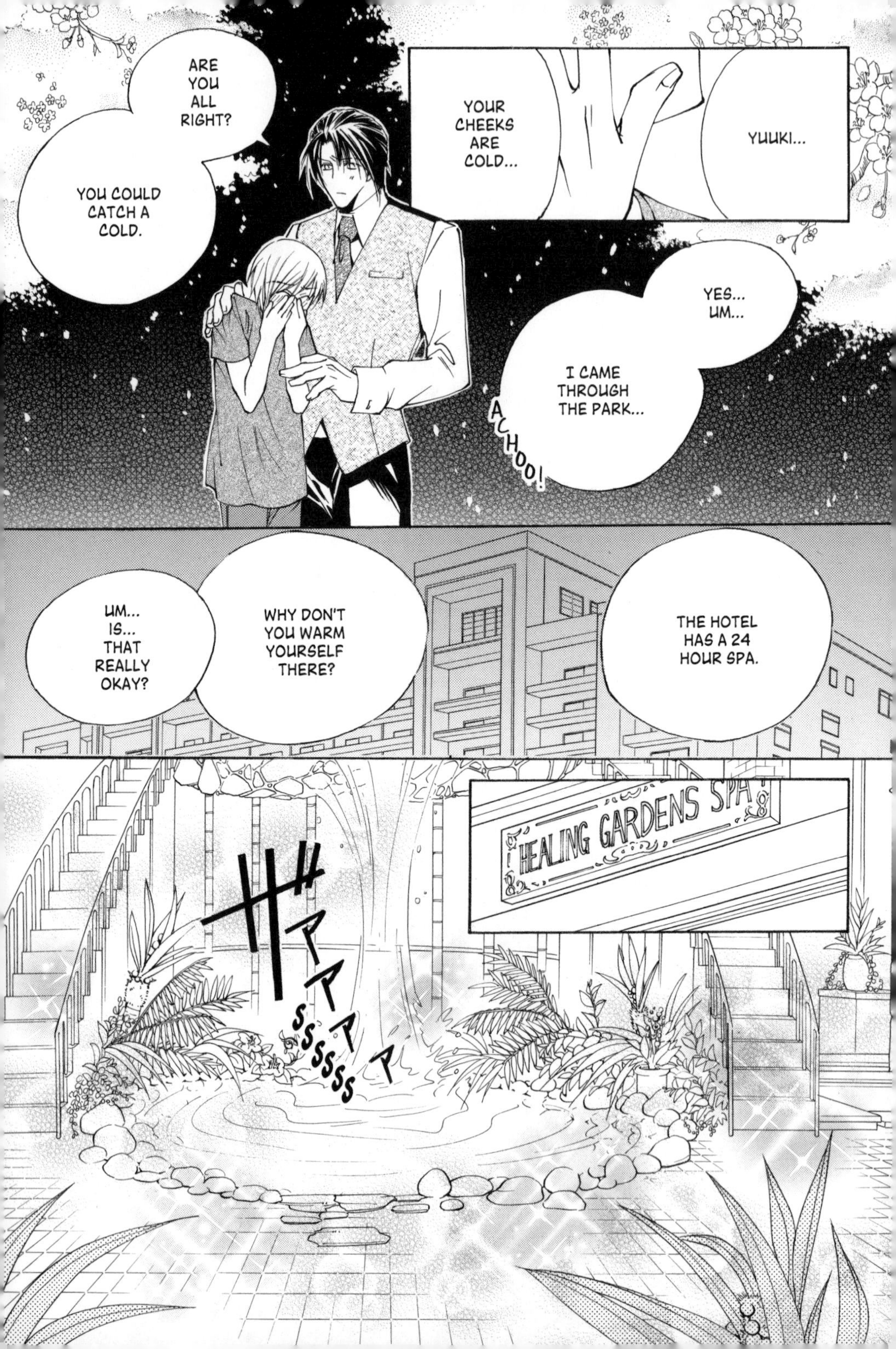
YUUKI...
YOUR CHEEKS ARE COLD...
ARE YOU ALL RIGHT?
YOU COULD CATCH A COLD.
YES... UM...
I CAME THROUGH THE PARK...
ACHOO!
THE HOTEL HAS A 24 HOUR SPA.
WHY DON'T YOU WARM YOURSELF THERE?
UM... IS... THAT REALLY OKAY?
HEALING GARDENS SPA
HPPPPP
SSSSSS

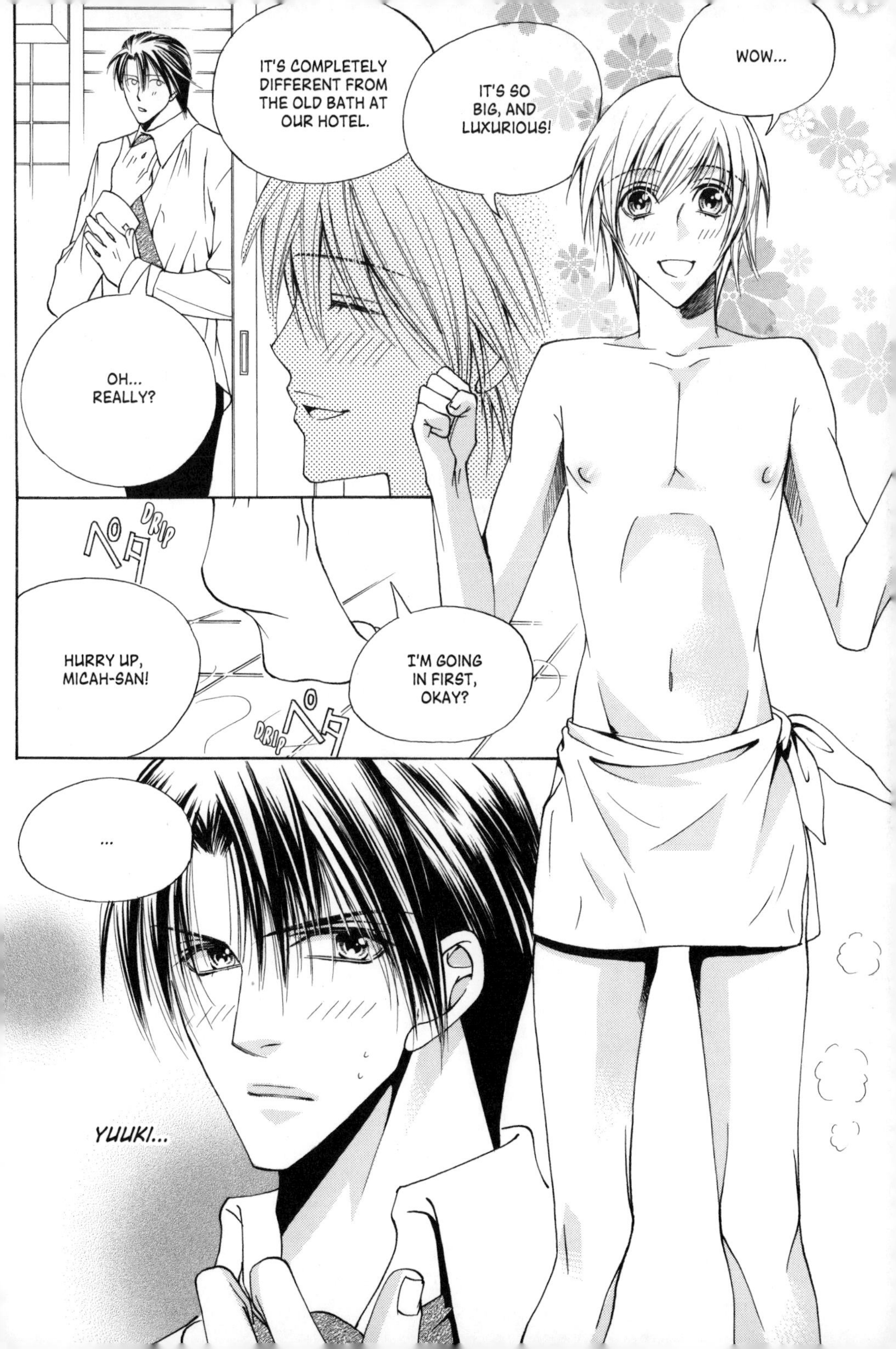
WOW...
IT'S SO BIG, AND LUXURIOUS!
IT'S COMPLETELY DIFFERENT FROM THE OLD BATH AT OUR HOTEL.
OH... REALLY?
ペタ DRIP
I'M GOING IN FIRST, OKAY?
HURRY UP, MICAH-SAN!
ペタ DRIP
...
YUUKI...

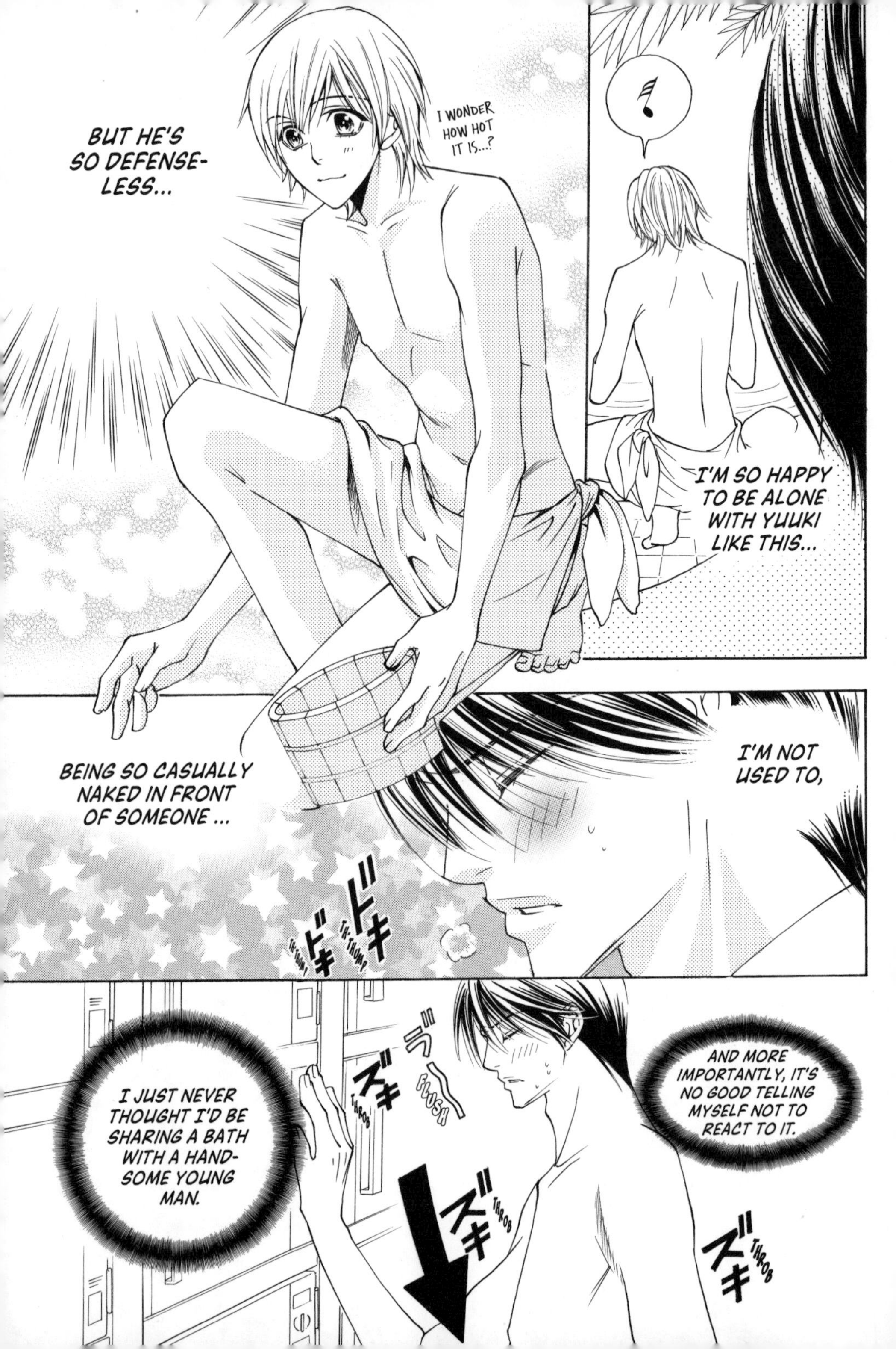
I'M SO HAPPY TO BE ALONE WITH YUUKI LIKE THIS...
I WONDER HOW HOT IT IS...?
BUT HE'S SO DEFENSE-LESS...
I'M NOT USED TO,
BEING SO CASUALLY NAKED IN FRONT OF SOMEONE ...
TH-THOMP
TH-THOMP
AND MORE IMPORTANTLY, IT'S NO GOOD TELLING MYSELF NOT TO REACT TO IT.
FLUSH
THROB
I JUST NEVER THOUGHT I'D BE SHARING A BATH WITH A HAND-SOME YOUNG MAN.
THROB
THROB

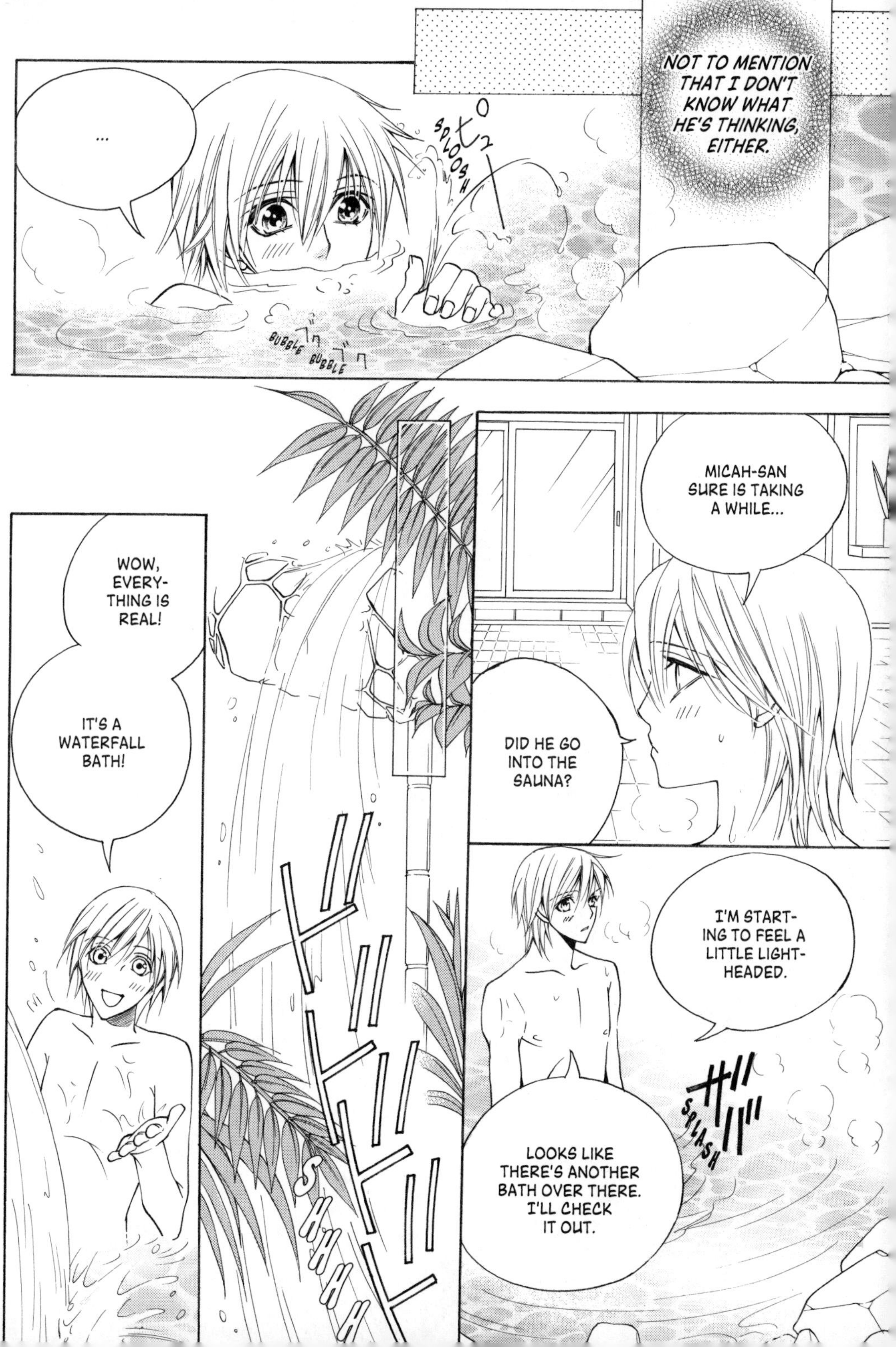

NOT TO MENTION THAT I DON'T KNOW WHAT HE'S THINKING, EITHER.
...
SPLOOSH
BUBBLE BUBBLE
MICAH-SAN SURE IS TAKING A WHILE...
DID HE GO INTO THE SAUNA?
I'M STARTING TO FEEL A LITTLE LIGHT-HEADED.
LOOKS LIKE THERE'S ANOTHER BATH OVER THERE. I'LL CHECK IT OUT.
SPLASH
WOW, EVERYTHING IS REAL!
IT'S A WATERFALL BATH!
SHHHHH

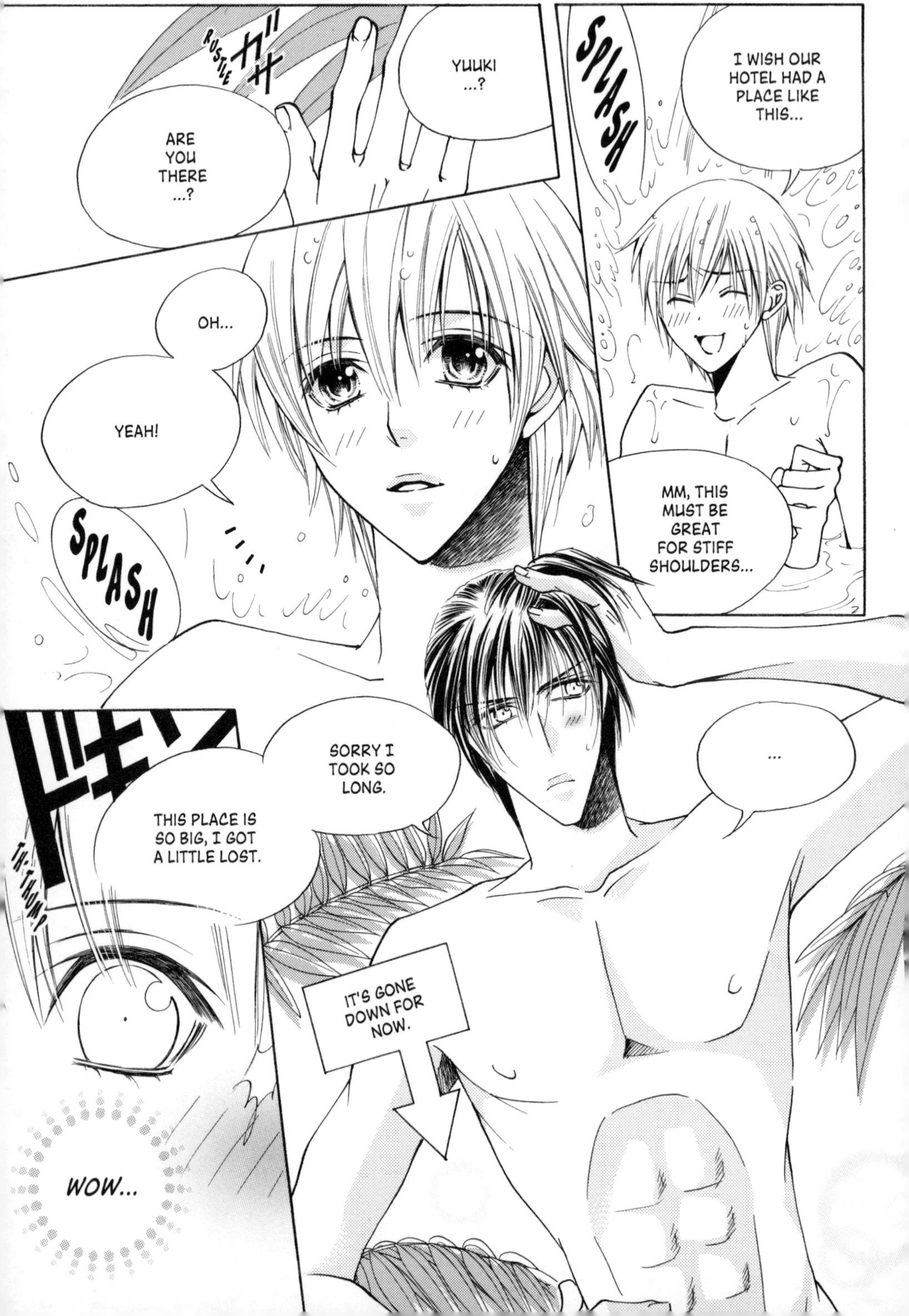
SPLASH
I WISH OUR HOTEL HAD A PLACE LIKE THIS...
MM, THIS MUST BE GREAT FOR STIFF SHOULDERS...
YUUKI ...?
RUSTLE
ARE YOU THERE ...?
OH...
YEAH!
SPLASH
...
SORRY I TOOK SO LONG.
THIS PLACE IS SO BIG, I GOT A LITTLE LOST.
IT'S GONE DOWN FOR NOW.
TH-THOMP
WOW...

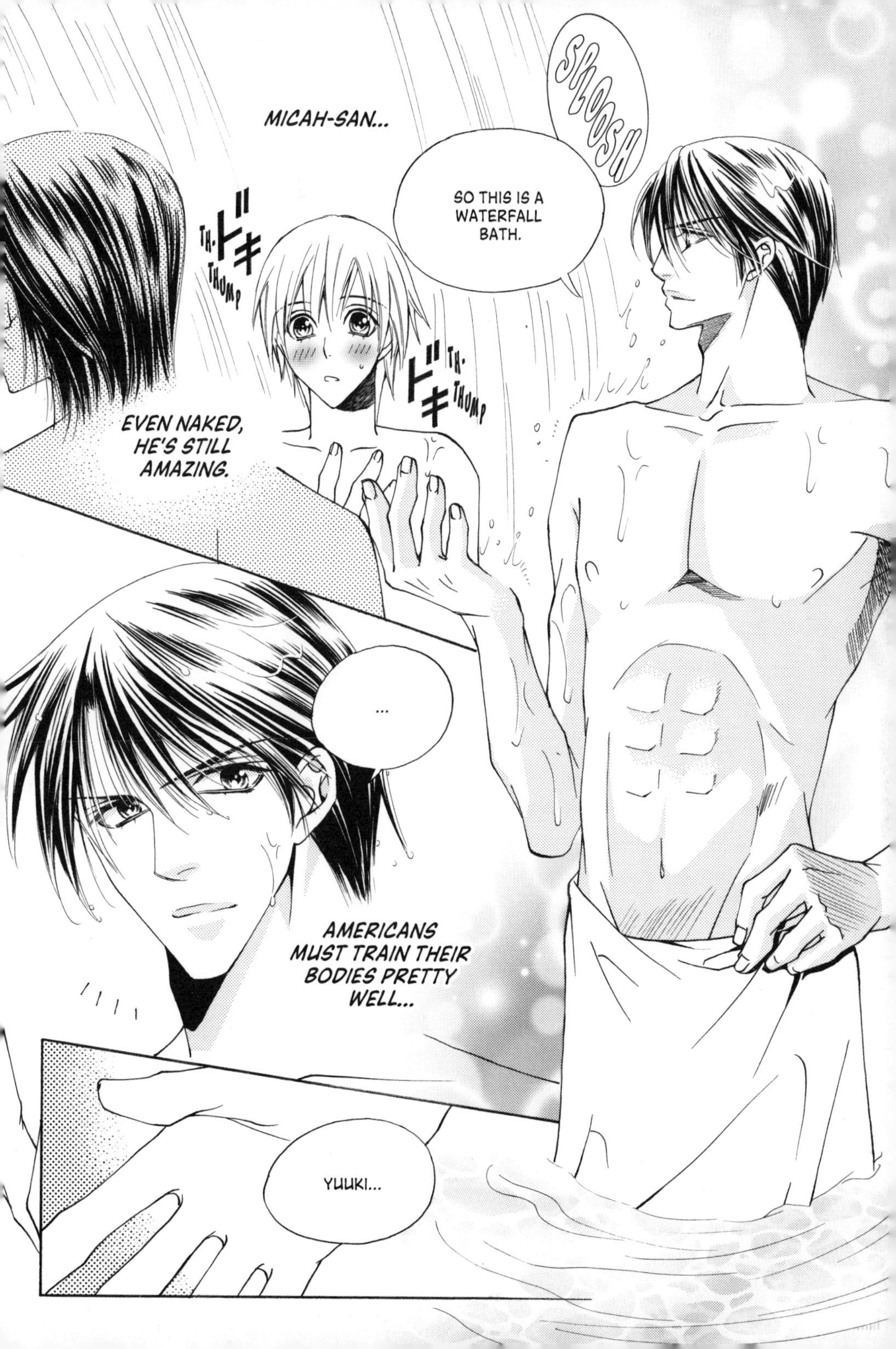
SPLOOSH
SO THIS IS A WATERFALL BATH.
MICAH-SAN...
ドキ TH-THUMP
ドキ TH-THUMP
EVEN NAKED, HE'S STILL AMAZING.
...
AMERICANS MUST TRAIN THEIR BODIES PRETTY WELL...
YUUKI...

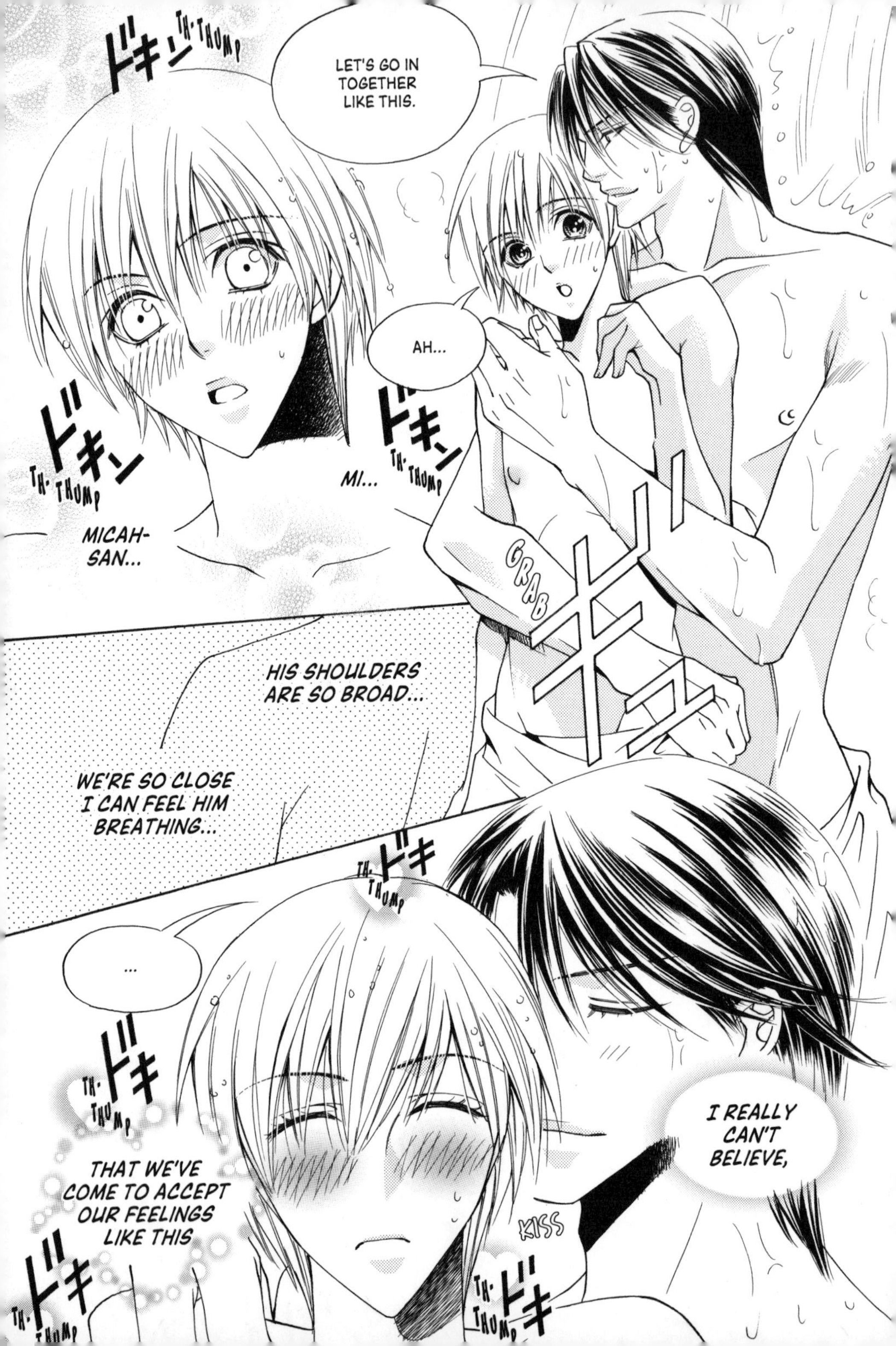
LET'S GO IN TOGETHER LIKE THIS.
AH...
GRAB
ギュ
ドキン
TH-THUMP
MI...
ドキン
TH-THUMP
ドキン
TH-THUMP
MICAH-SAN...
HIS SHOULDERS ARE SO BROAD...
WE'RE SO CLOSE I CAN FEEL HIM BREATHING...
ドキ
TH-THUMP
...
I REALLY CAN'T BELIEVE,
THAT WE'VE COME TO ACCEPT OUR FEELINGS LIKE THIS
KISS
ドキ
TH-THUMP
ドキ
TH-THUMP
ドキ
TH-THUMP

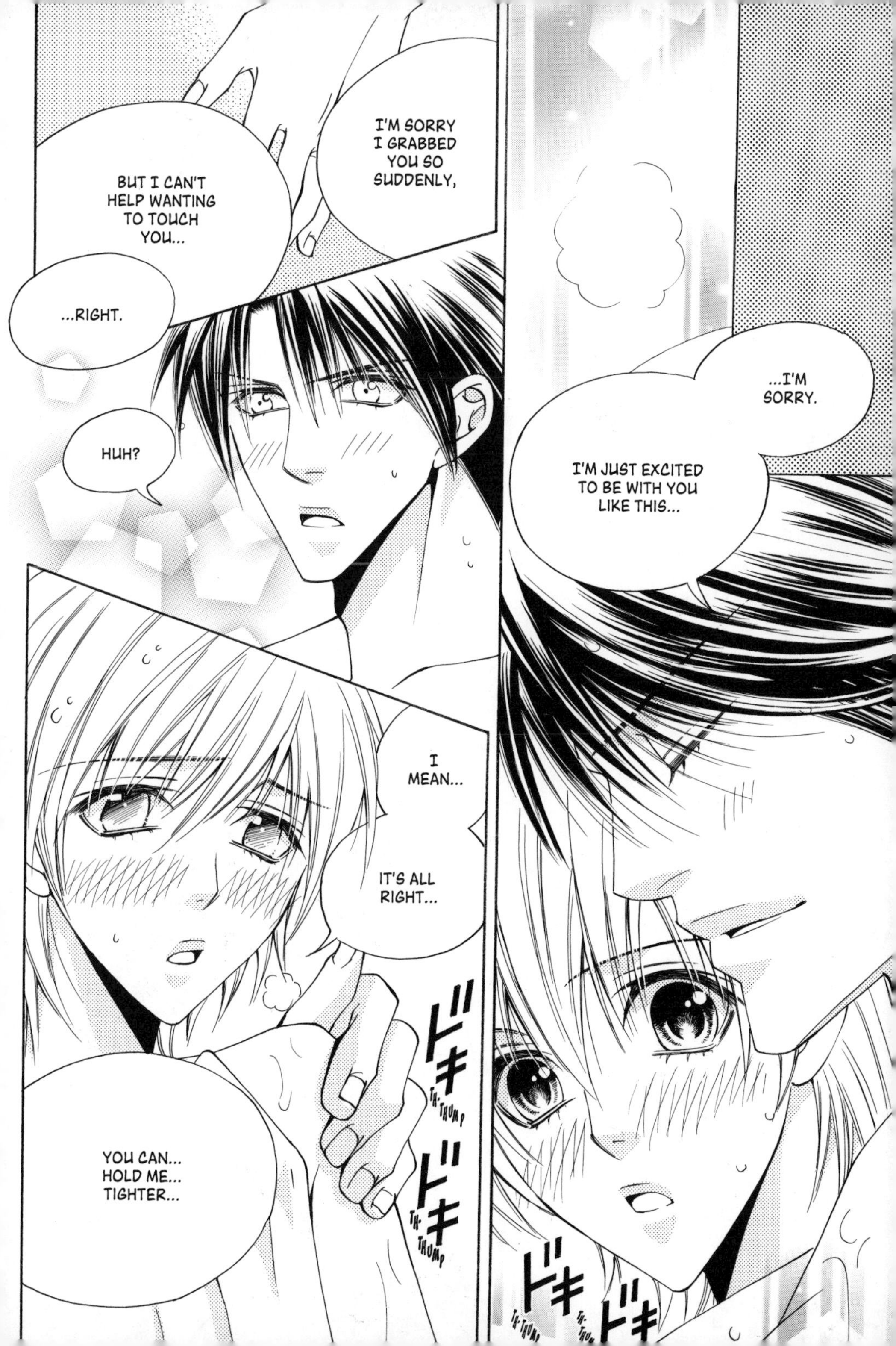
...I'M SORRY.
I'M JUST EXCITED TO BE WITH YOU LIKE THIS...
ドキ TH-THUMP
ドキ TH-THUMP
I'M SORRY I GRABBED YOU SO SUDDENLY,
BUT I CAN'T HELP WANTING TO TOUCH YOU...
...RIGHT.
HUH?
I MEAN...
IT'S ALL RIGHT...
ドキ TH-THUMP
ドキ TH-THUMP
YOU CAN... HOLD ME... TIGHTER...

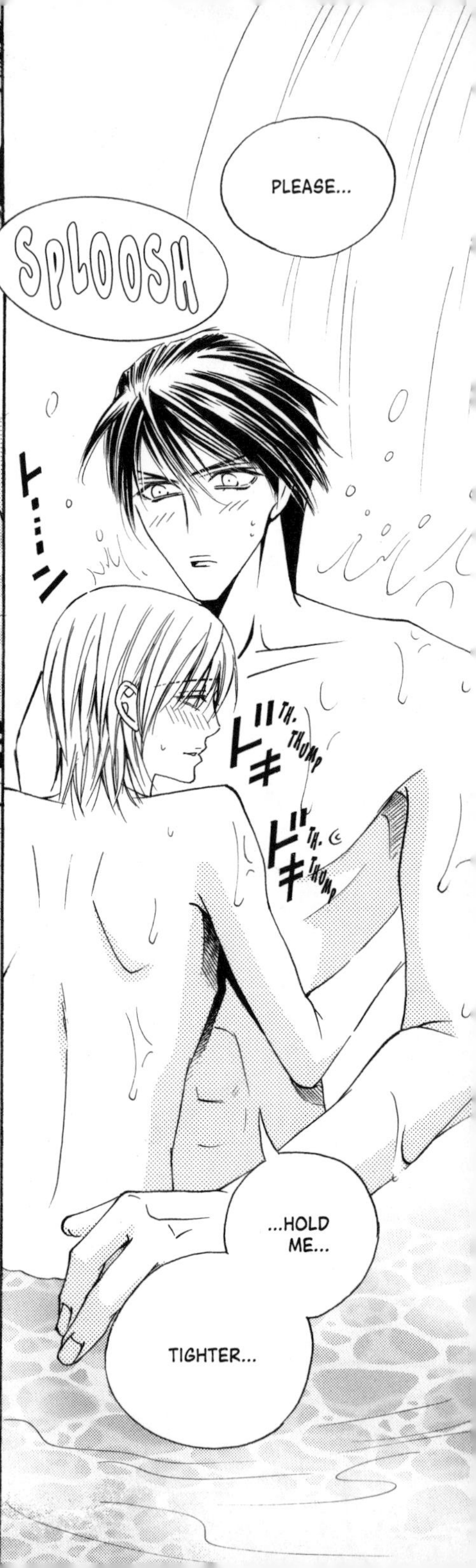
PLEASE...
SPLOOSH
ドキ TH. THUMP
ドキ TH. THUMP
...HOLD ME...
TIGHTER...

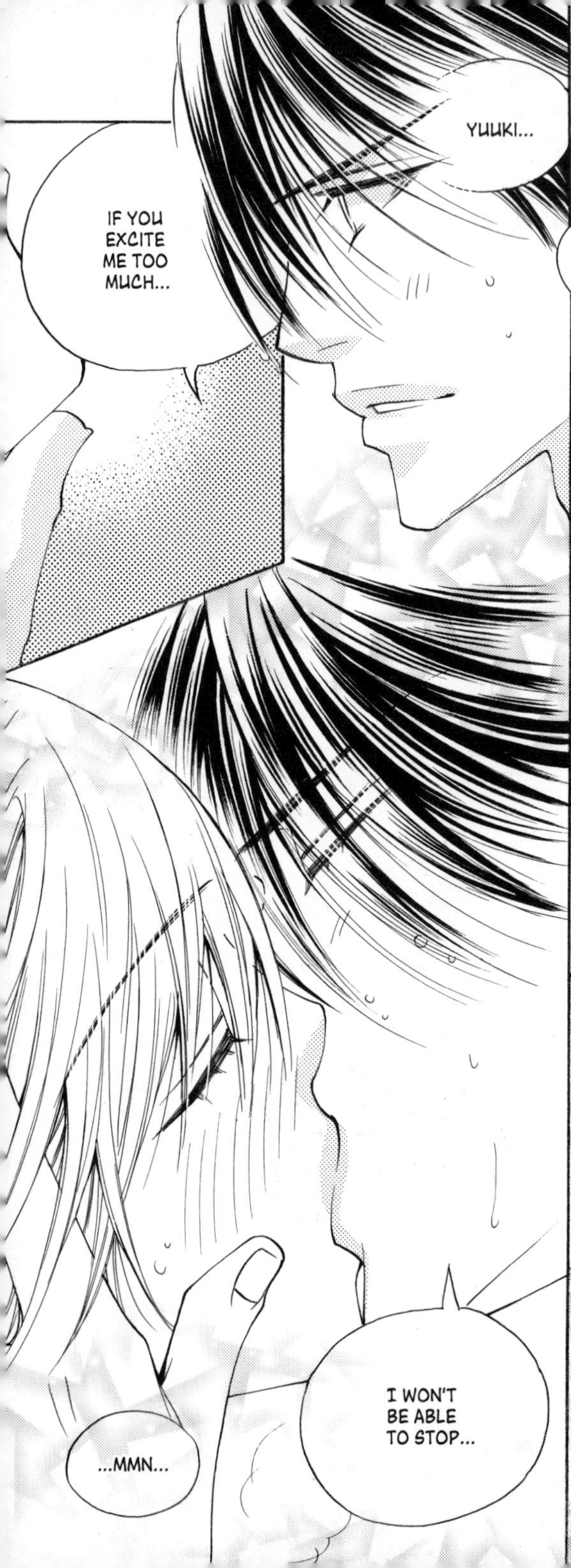
YUUKI...
IF YOU EXCITE ME TOO MUCH...
I WON'T BE ABLE TO STOP...
...MMN...

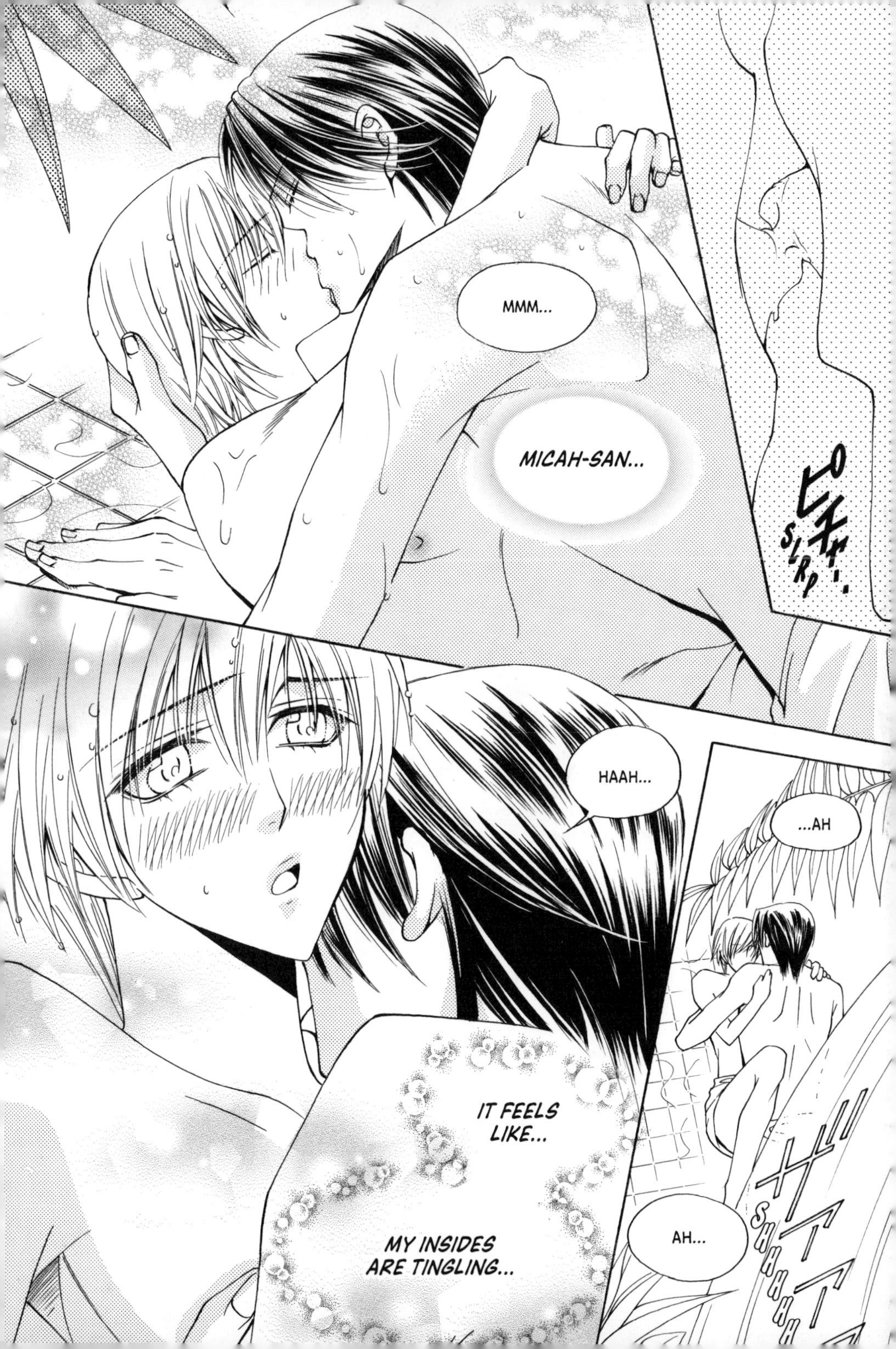
SLRP
MMM...
MICAH-SAN...
...AH
AH...
SHHHHHH
HAAH...
IT FEELS LIKE...
MY INSIDES ARE TINGLING...

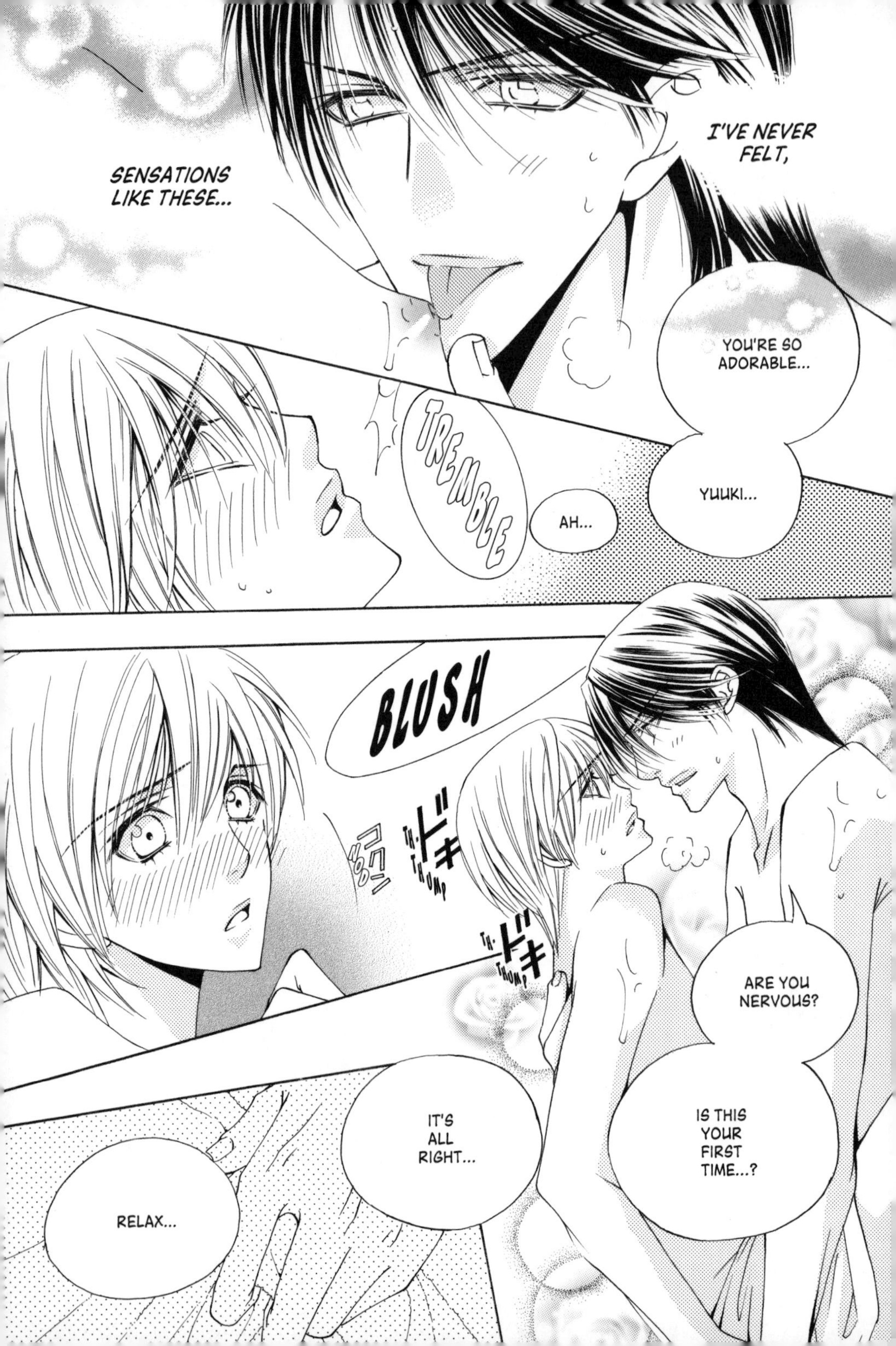
I'VE NEVER FELT,
SENSATIONS LIKE THESE...
YOU'RE SO ADORABLE...
YUUKI...
AH...
TREMBLE
TH-THUMP ドキ
TH-THUMP ドキ
ARE YOU NERVOUS?
IS THIS YOUR FIRST TIME...?
BLUSH
IT'S ALL RIGHT...
RELAX...

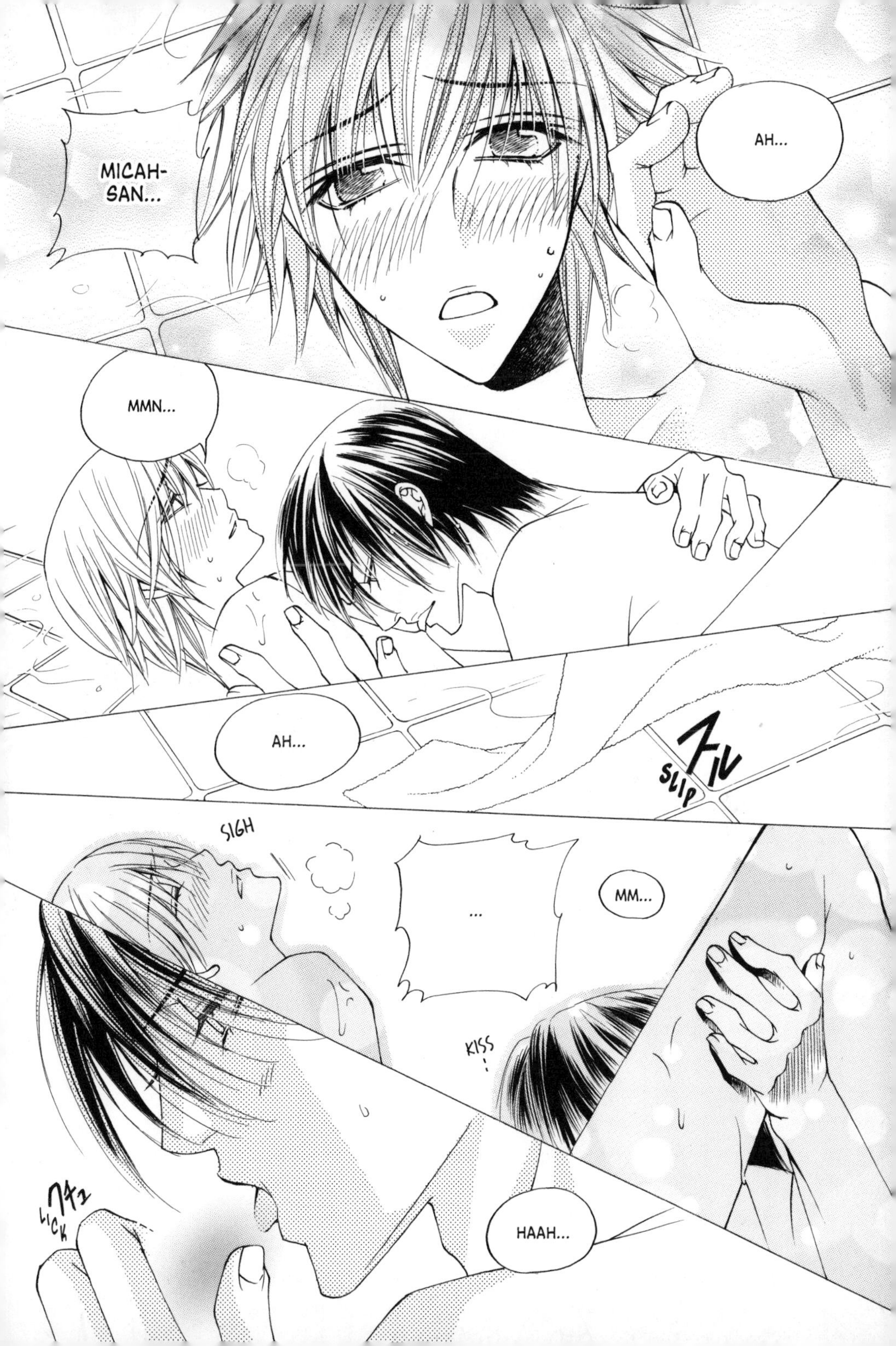
AH...
MICAH-SAN...
MMN...
SLIP
AH...
MM...
KISS
...
SIGH
HAAH...
LICK

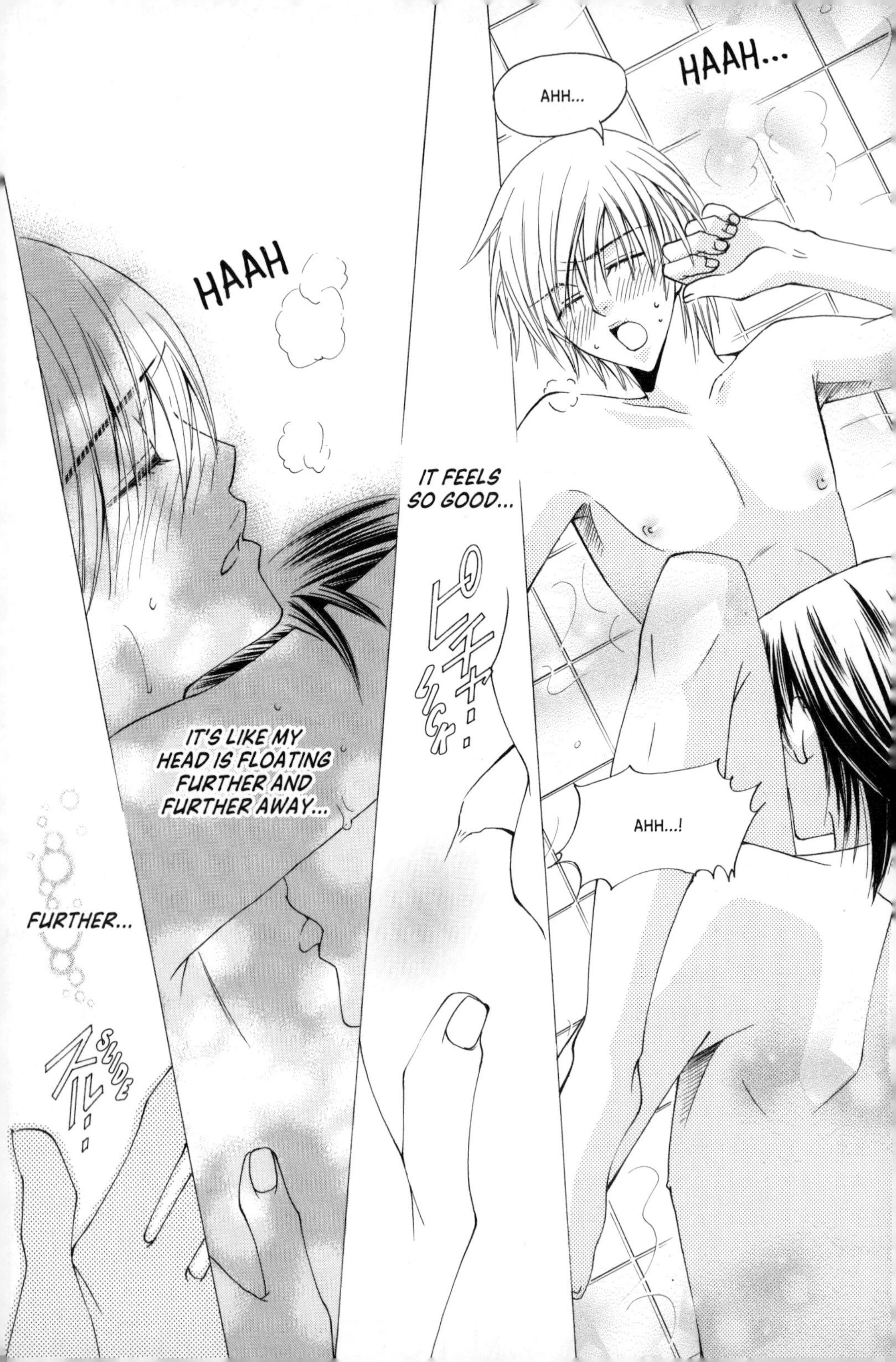

HAAH...
AHH...
AHH...!
IT FEELS SO GOOD...
LICK
HAAH
IT'S LIKE MY HEAD IS FLOATING FURTHER AND FURTHER AWAY...
FURTHER...
SLIDE

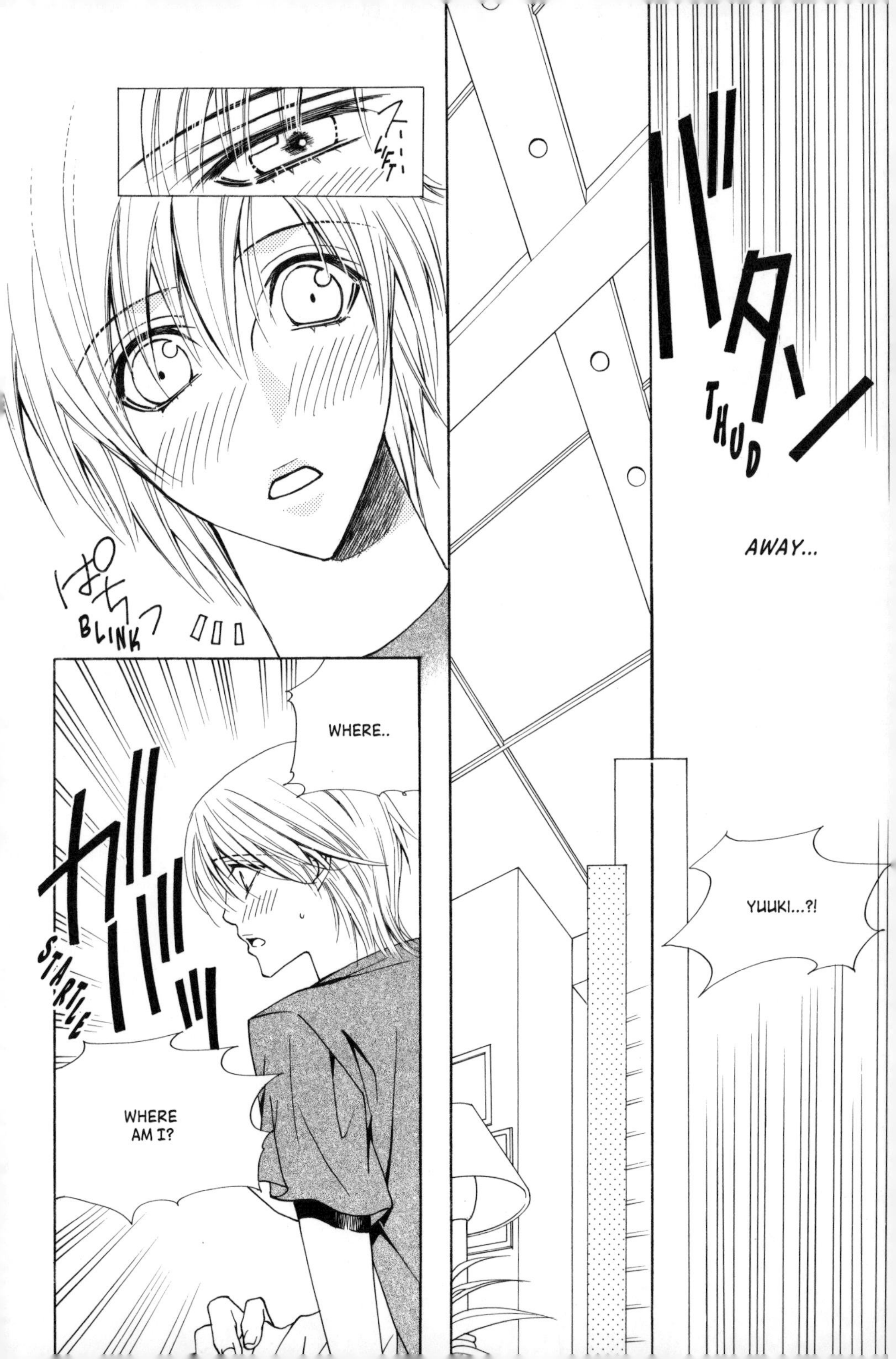
バタン
THUD
AWAY...
YUUKI...?!
LIFT
ぱちっ
BLINK
WHERE..
STARTLE
WHERE AM I?

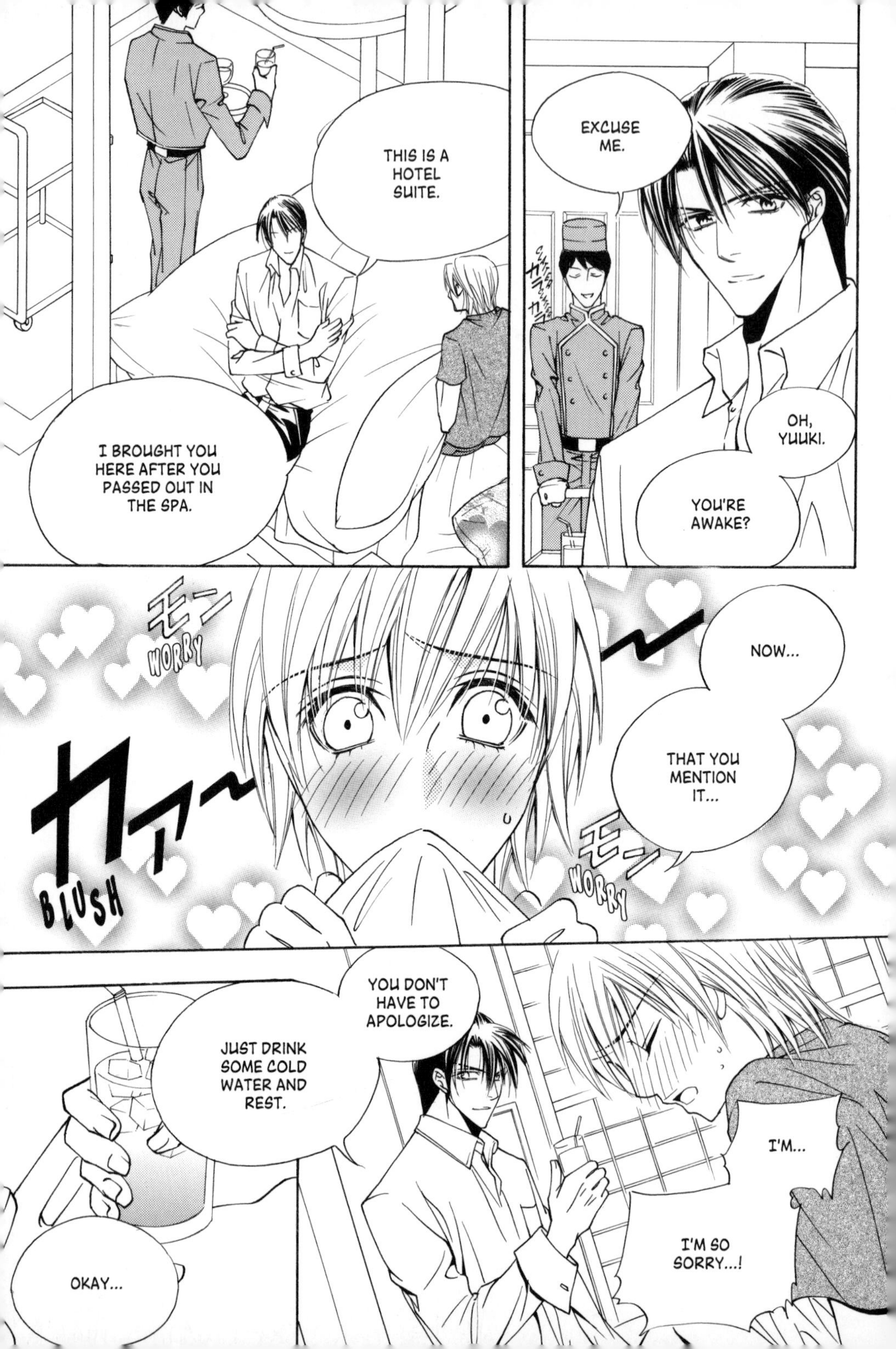

EXCUSE ME.
OH, YUUKI.
YOU'RE AWAKE?
THIS IS A HOTEL SUITE.
I BROUGHT YOU HERE AFTER YOU PASSED OUT IN THE SPA.
NOW...
THAT YOU MENTION IT...
モ~ン WORRY
カァ~ BLUSH
モ~ン WORRY
I'M...
I'M SO SORRY...!
YOU DON'T HAVE TO APOLOGIZE.
JUST DRINK SOME COLD WATER AND REST.
OKAY...

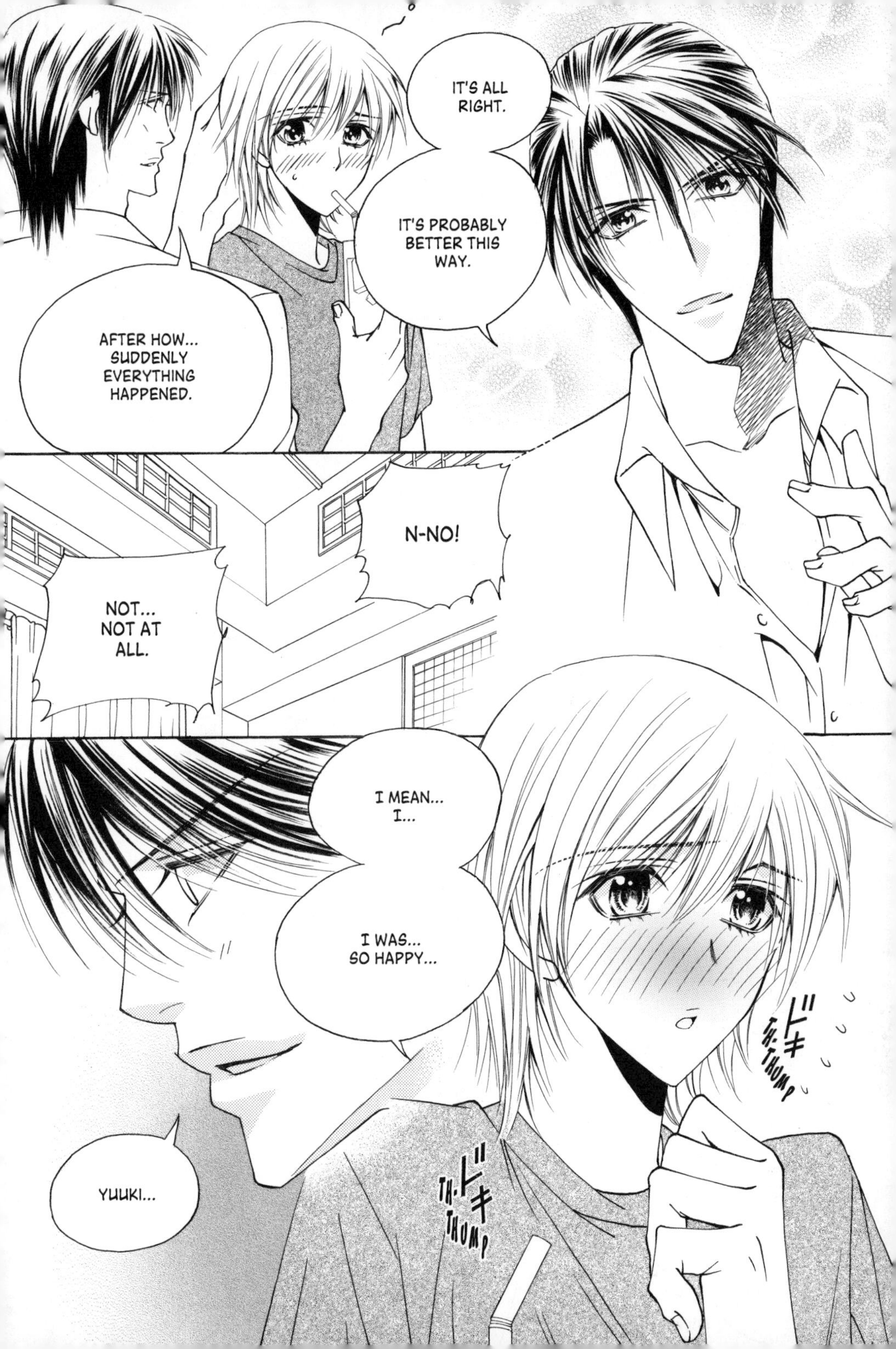
IT'S ALL RIGHT.
IT'S PROBABLY BETTER THIS WAY.
AFTER HOW... SUDDENLY EVERYTHING HAPPENED.
N-NO!
NOT... NOT AT ALL.
I MEAN... I...
I WAS... SO HAPPY...
ドキ
TH-THUMP
ドキ
TH-THUMP
YUUKI...

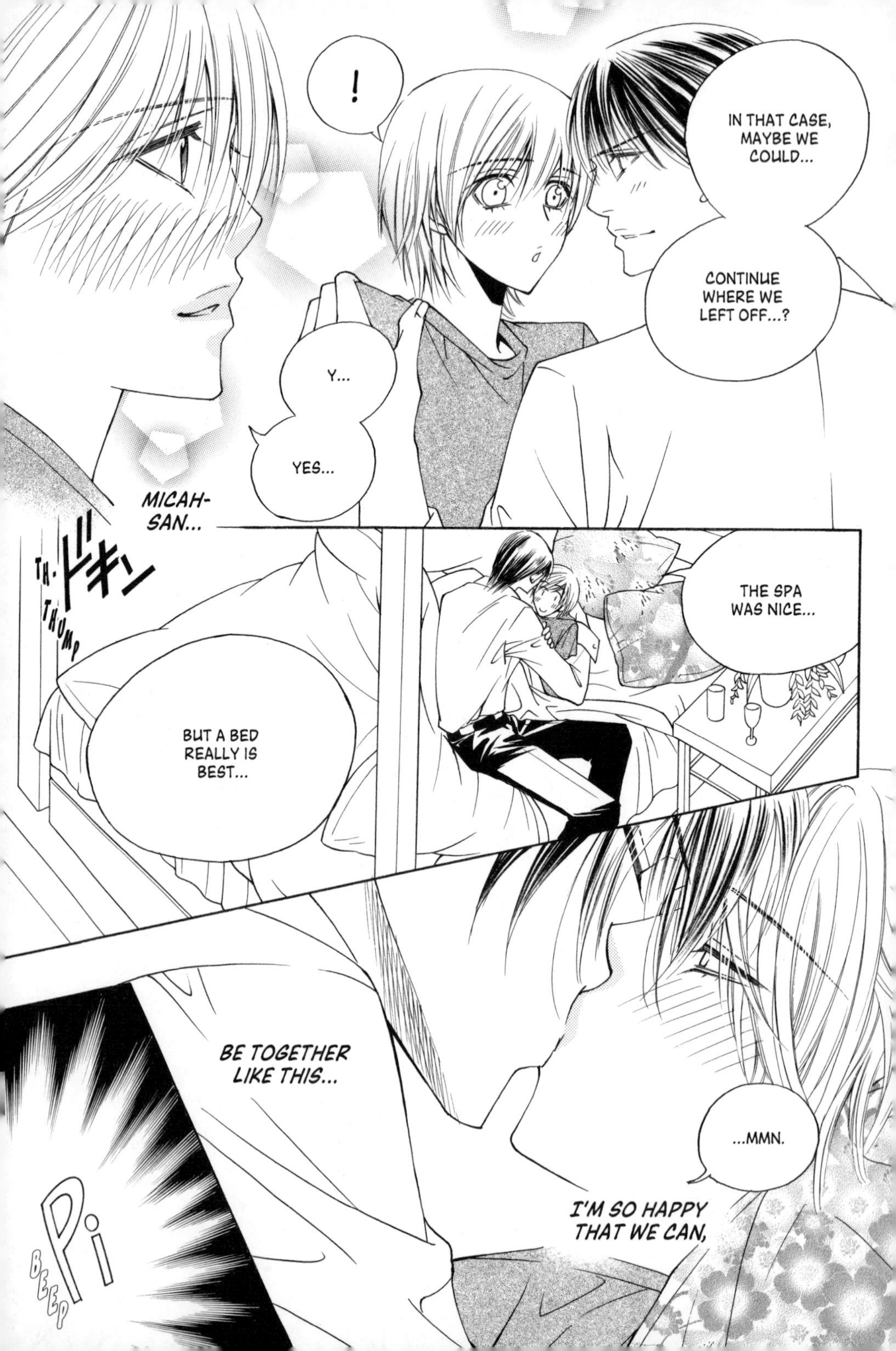
IN THAT CASE, MAYBE WE COULD...
CONTINUE WHERE WE LEFT OFF...?
!
Y...
YES...
MICAH-SAN...
TH-THUMP
ドキン
THE SPA WAS NICE...
BUT A BED REALLY IS BEST...
...MMN.
I'M SO HAPPY THAT WE CAN,
BE TOGETHER LIKE THIS...
BEEP
Pi

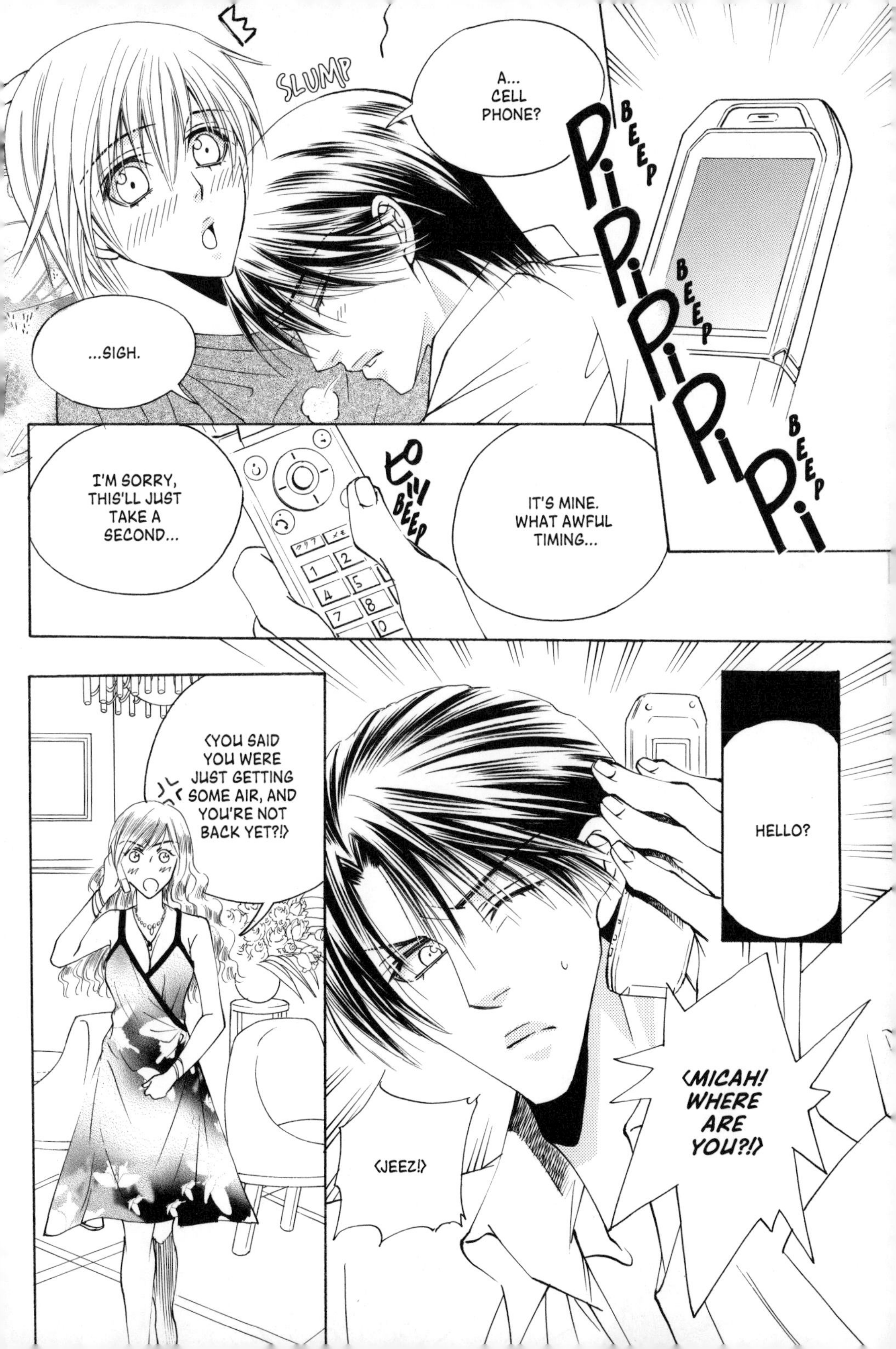
PiPiPiPiPi
BEEP
BEEP
BEEP
A... CELL PHONE?
SLUMP
...SIGH.
IT'S MINE. WHAT AWFUL TIMING...
BEEP
I'M SORRY, THIS'LL JUST TAKE A SECOND...
HELLO?
‹MICAH! WHERE ARE YOU?!›
‹JEEZ!›
‹YOU SAID YOU WERE JUST GETTING SOME AIR, AND YOU'RE NOT BACK YET?!›

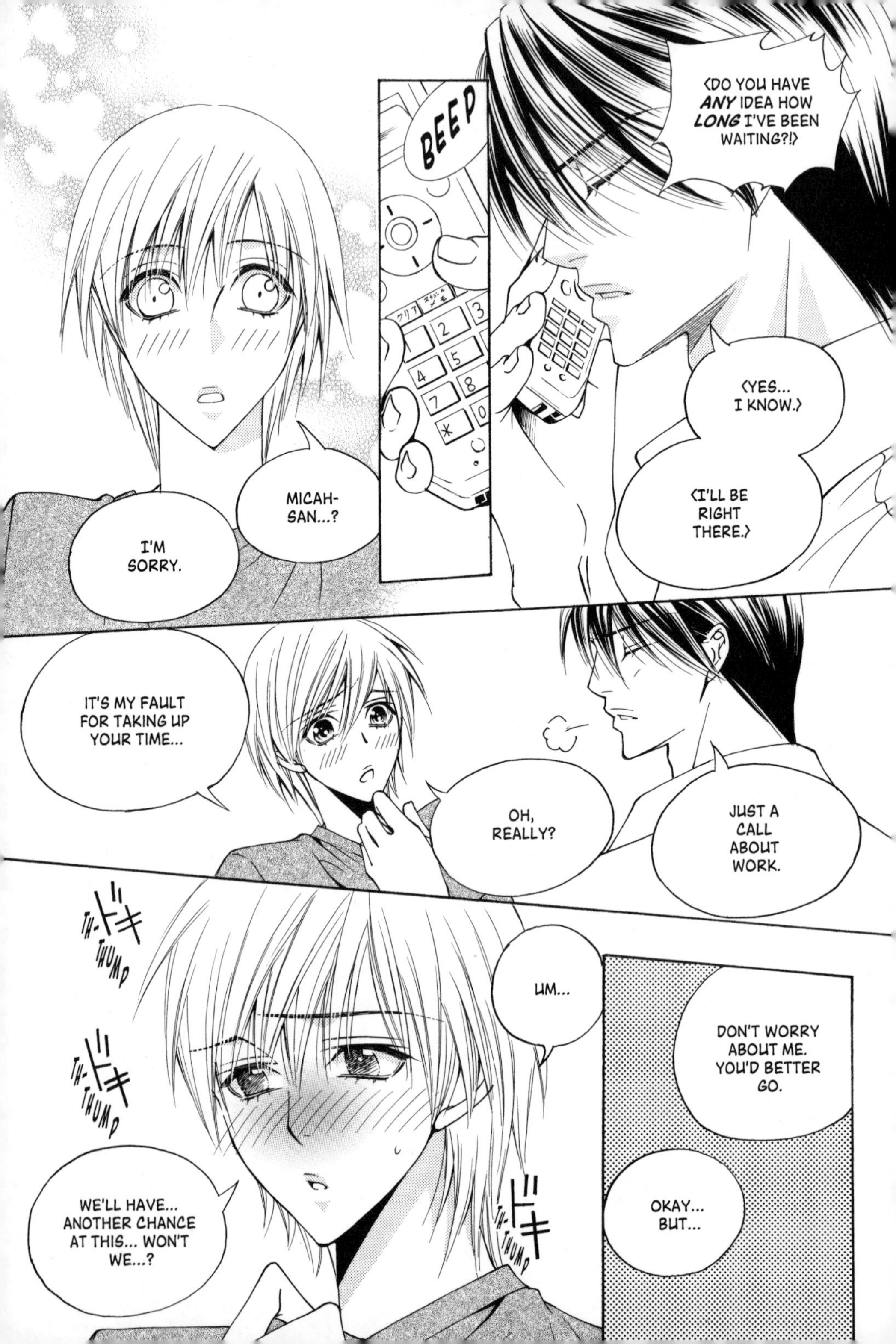
<DO YOU HAVE ANY IDEA HOW LONG I'VE BEEN WAITING?!>
<YES... I KNOW.>
<I'LL BE RIGHT THERE.>
BEEP
MICAH-SAN...?
I'M SORRY.
JUST A CALL ABOUT WORK.
OH, REALLY?
IT'S MY FAULT FOR TAKING UP YOUR TIME...
DON'T WORRY ABOUT ME. YOU'D BETTER GO.
OKAY... BUT...
UM...
ドキ TH-THUMP
ドキ TH-THUMP
ドキ TH-THUMP
WE'LL HAVE... ANOTHER CHANCE AT THIS... WON'T WE...?

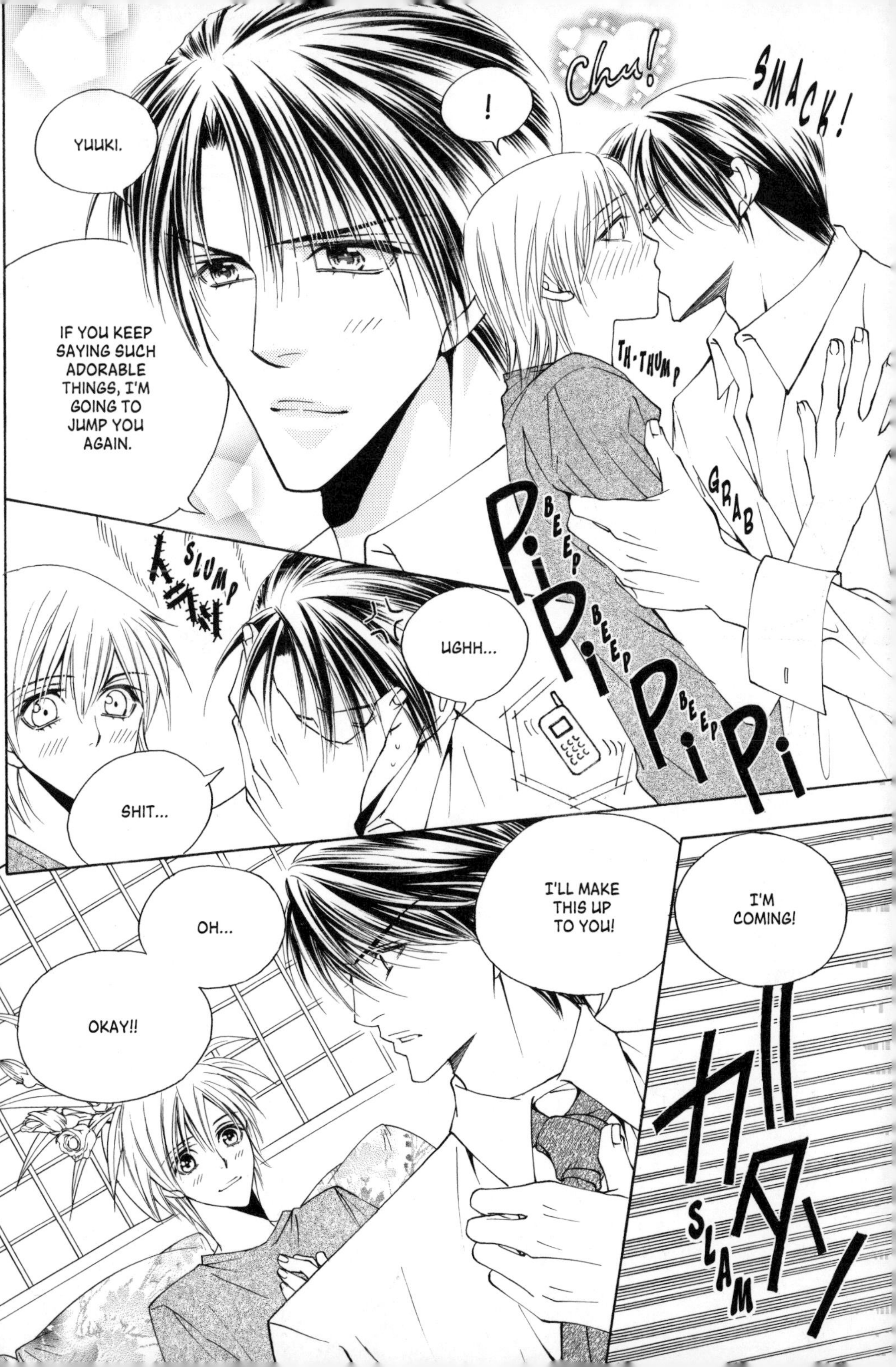
Chu!
SMACK!
TH-THUMP
GRAB
!
YUUKI.
IF YOU KEEP SAYING SUCH ADORABLE THINGS, I'M GOING TO JUMP YOU AGAIN.
PiPiPiPiPi
BEEP BEEP BEEP
UGHH...
SLUMP
SHIT...
SLAM
I'M COMING!
I'LL MAKE THIS UP TO YOU!
OH...
OKAY!!

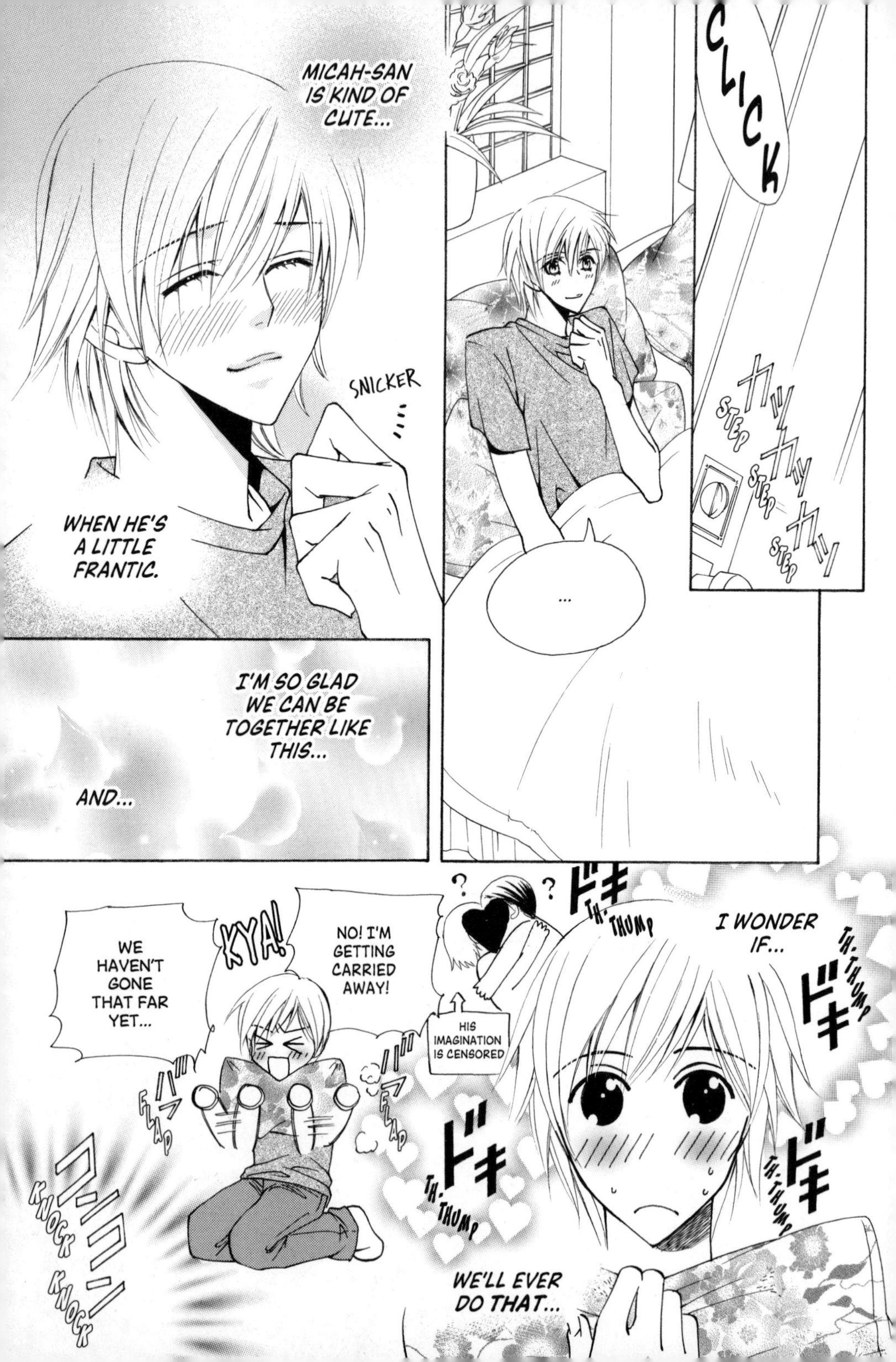
CLICK
STEP
STEP
STEP
...
MICAH-SAN IS KIND OF CUTE...
SNICKER
WHEN HE'S A LITTLE FRANTIC.
I'M SO GLAD WE CAN BE TOGETHER LIKE THIS...
AND...
I WONDER IF...
TH-THUMP
TH-THUMP
TH-THUMP
TH-THUMP
WE'LL EVER DO THAT...
HIS IMAGINATION IS CENSORED
NO! I'M GETTING CARRIED AWAY!
KYA!
WE HAVEN'T GONE THAT FAR YET...
FLAP
FLAP
KNOCK KNOCK

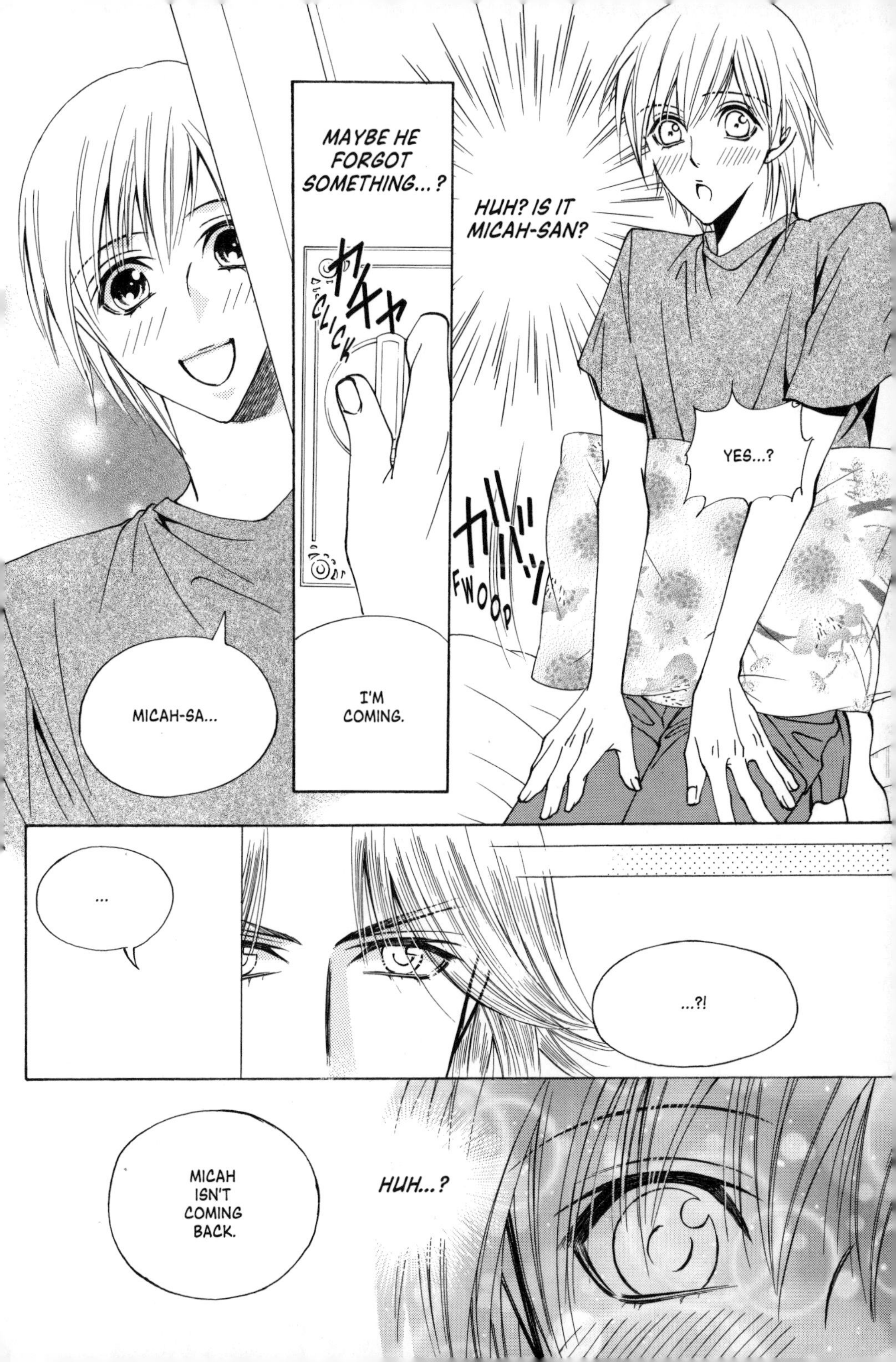
HUH? IS IT MICAH-SAN?
YES...?
FWOOP
MAYBE HE FORGOT SOMETHING...?
CLICK
I'M COMING.
MICAH-SA...
...?!
...
HUH...?
MICAH ISN'T COMING BACK.

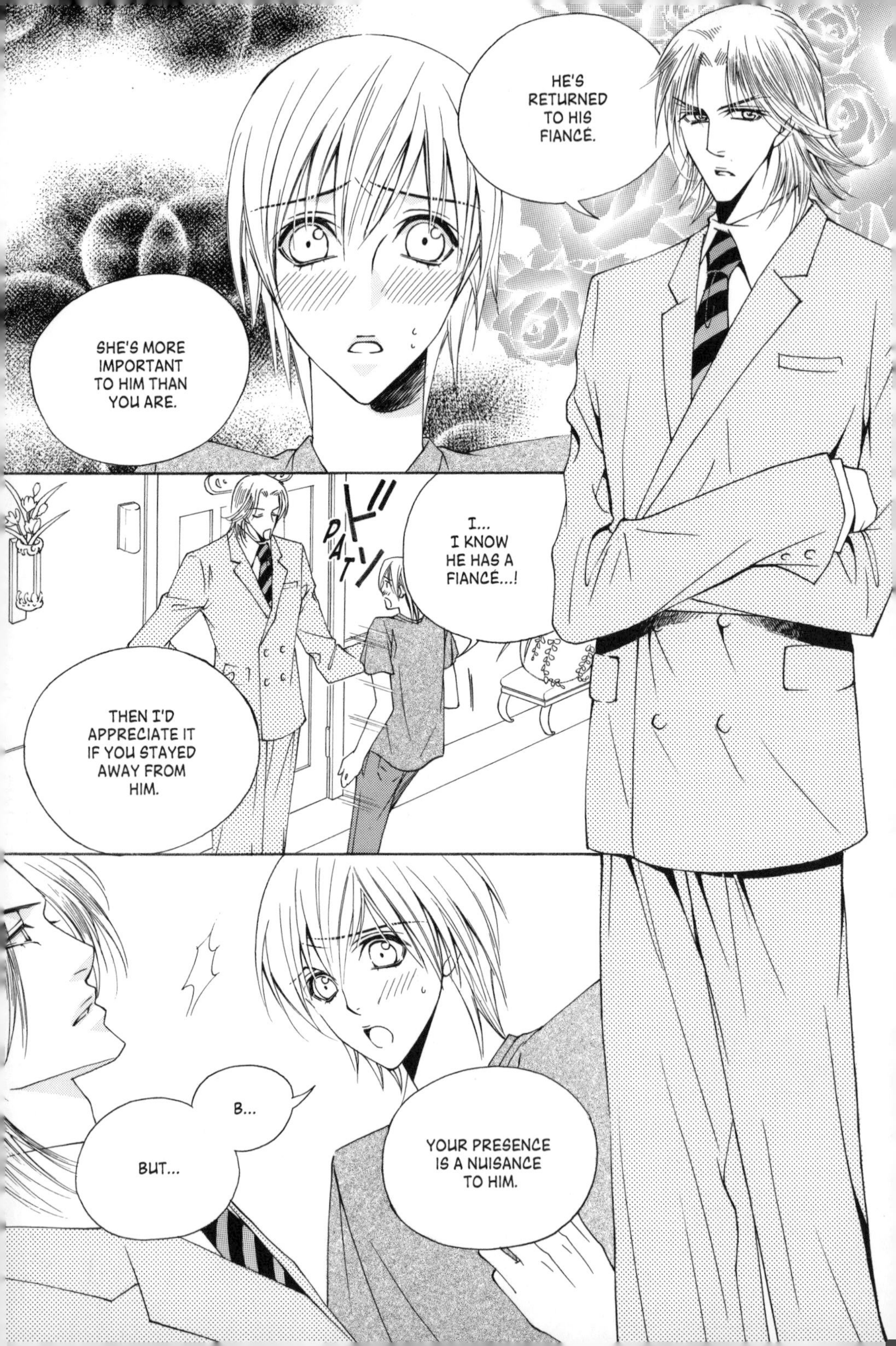
HE'S RETURNED TO HIS FIANCÉ.
SHE'S MORE IMPORTANT TO HIM THAN YOU ARE.
I... I KNOW HE HAS A FIANCÉ...!
ドッ
DAT
THEN I'D APPRECIATE IT IF YOU STAYED AWAY FROM HIM.
YOUR PRESENCE IS A NUISANCE TO HIM.
B...
BUT...

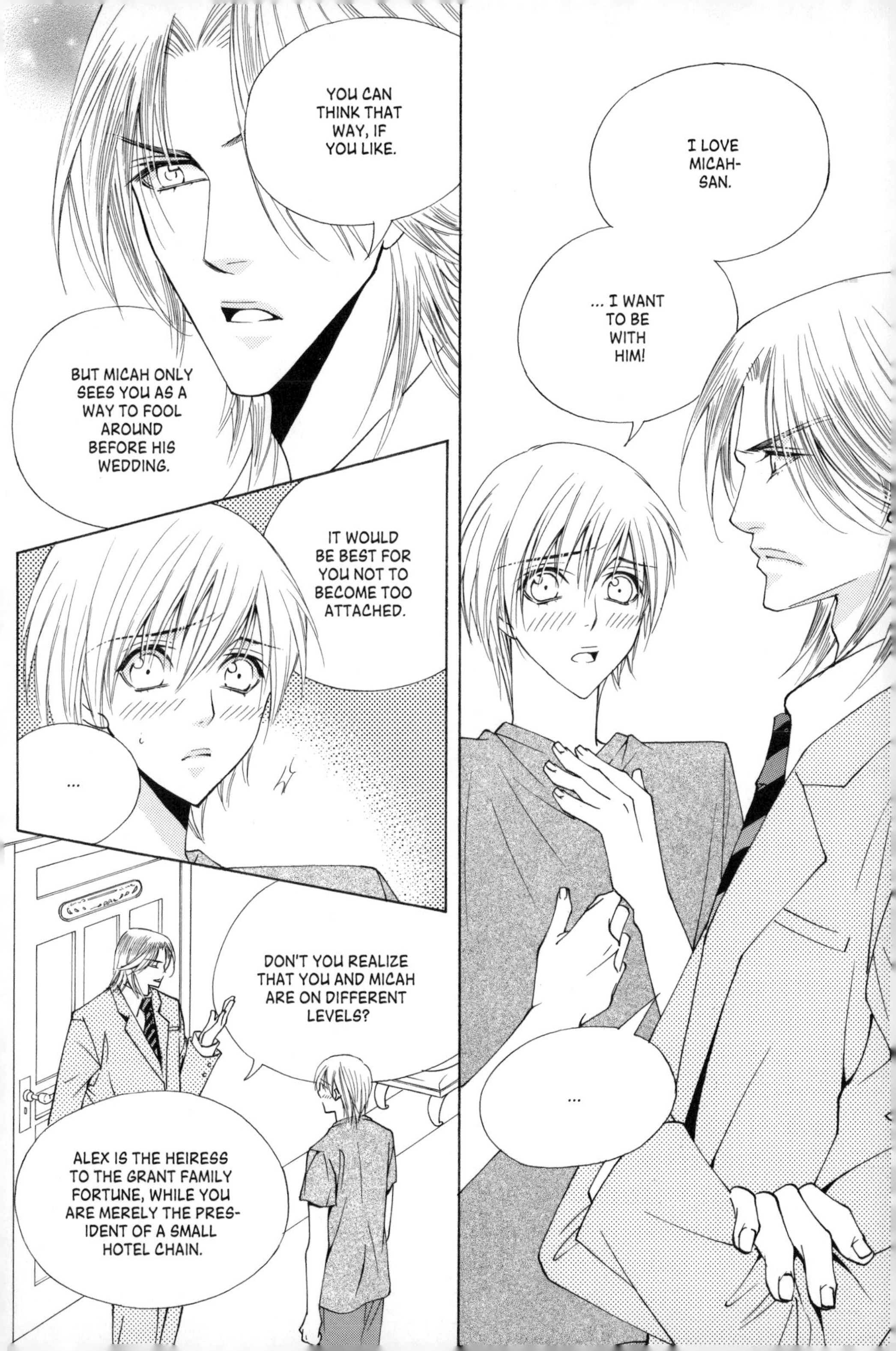
I LOVE MICAH-SAN.
... I WANT TO BE WITH HIM!
...
YOU CAN THINK THAT WAY, IF YOU LIKE.
BUT MICAH ONLY SEES YOU AS A WAY TO FOOL AROUND BEFORE HIS WEDDING.
IT WOULD BE BEST FOR YOU NOT TO BECOME TOO ATTACHED.
...
DON'T YOU REALIZE THAT YOU AND MICAH ARE ON DIFFERENT LEVELS?
ALEX IS THE HEIRESS TO THE GRANT FAMILY FORTUNE, WHILE YOU ARE MERELY THE PRES-IDENT OF A SMALL HOTEL CHAIN.

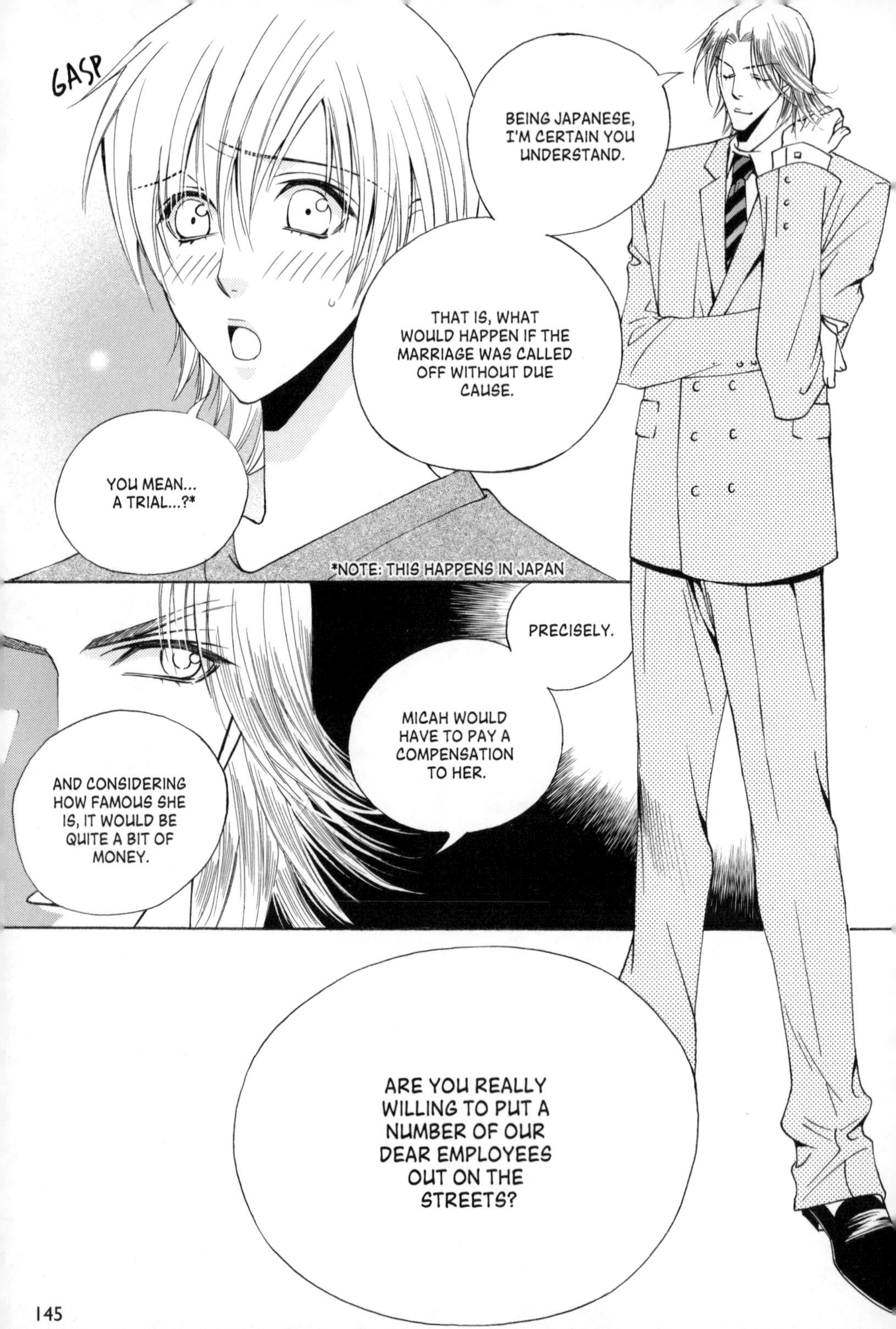
BEING JAPANESE, I'M CERTAIN YOU UNDERSTAND.
THAT IS, WHAT WOULD HAPPEN IF THE MARRIAGE WAS CALLED OFF WITHOUT DUE CAUSE.
GASP
YOU MEAN... A TRIAL...?*
*NOTE: THIS HAPPENS IN JAPAN
PRECISELY.
MICAH WOULD HAVE TO PAY A COMPENSATION TO HER.
AND CONSIDERING HOW FAMOUS SHE IS, IT WOULD BE QUITE A BIT OF MONEY.
ARE YOU REALLY WILLING TO PUT A NUMBER OF OUR DEAR EMPLOYEES OUT ON THE STREETS?

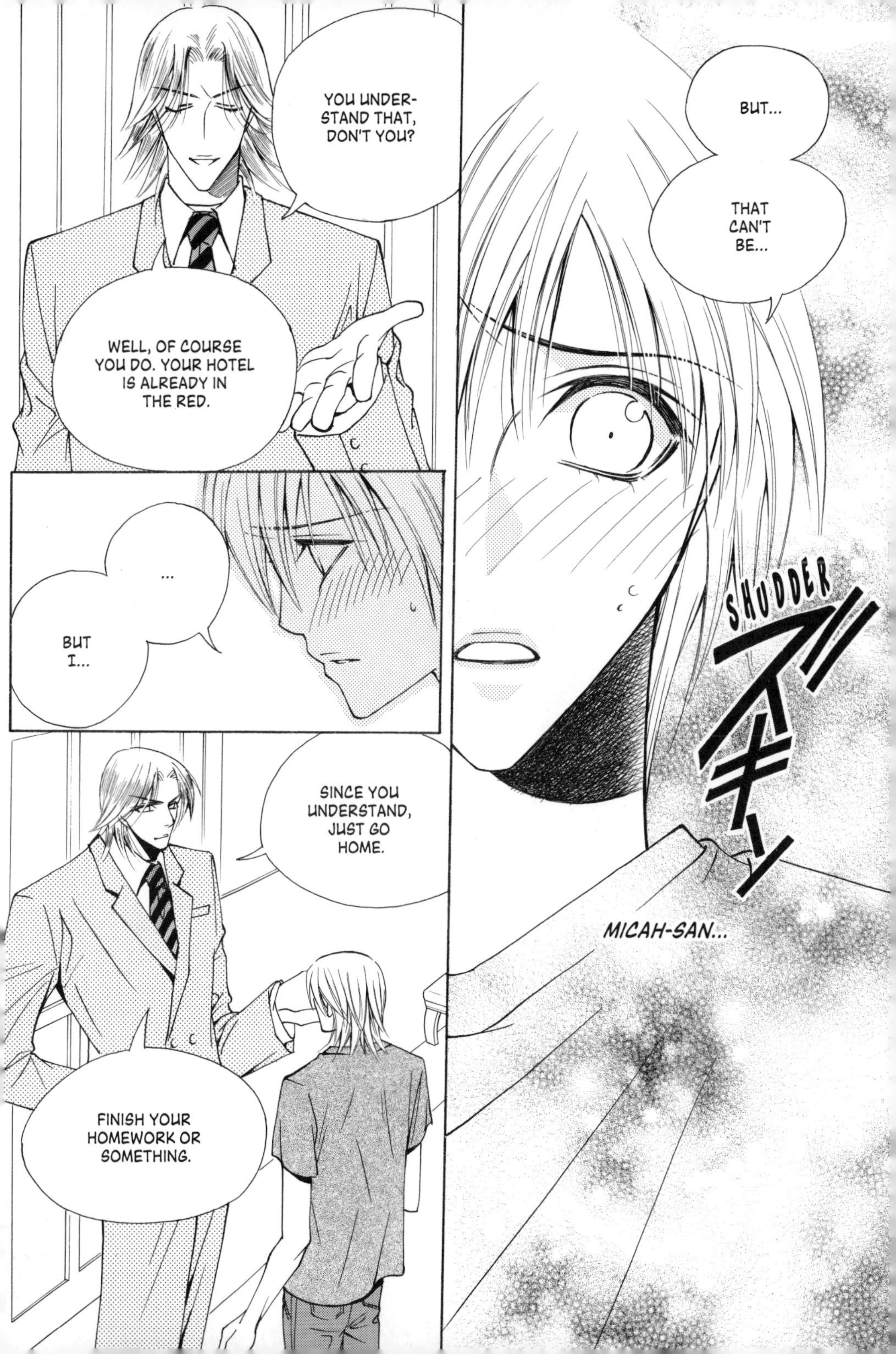
BUT...
THAT CAN'T BE...
SHUDDER
MICAH-SAN...
YOU UNDERSTAND THAT, DON'T YOU?
WELL, OF COURSE YOU DO. YOUR HOTEL IS ALREADY IN THE RED.
...
BUT I...
SINCE YOU UNDERSTAND, JUST GO HOME.
FINISH YOUR HOMEWORK OR SOMETHING.

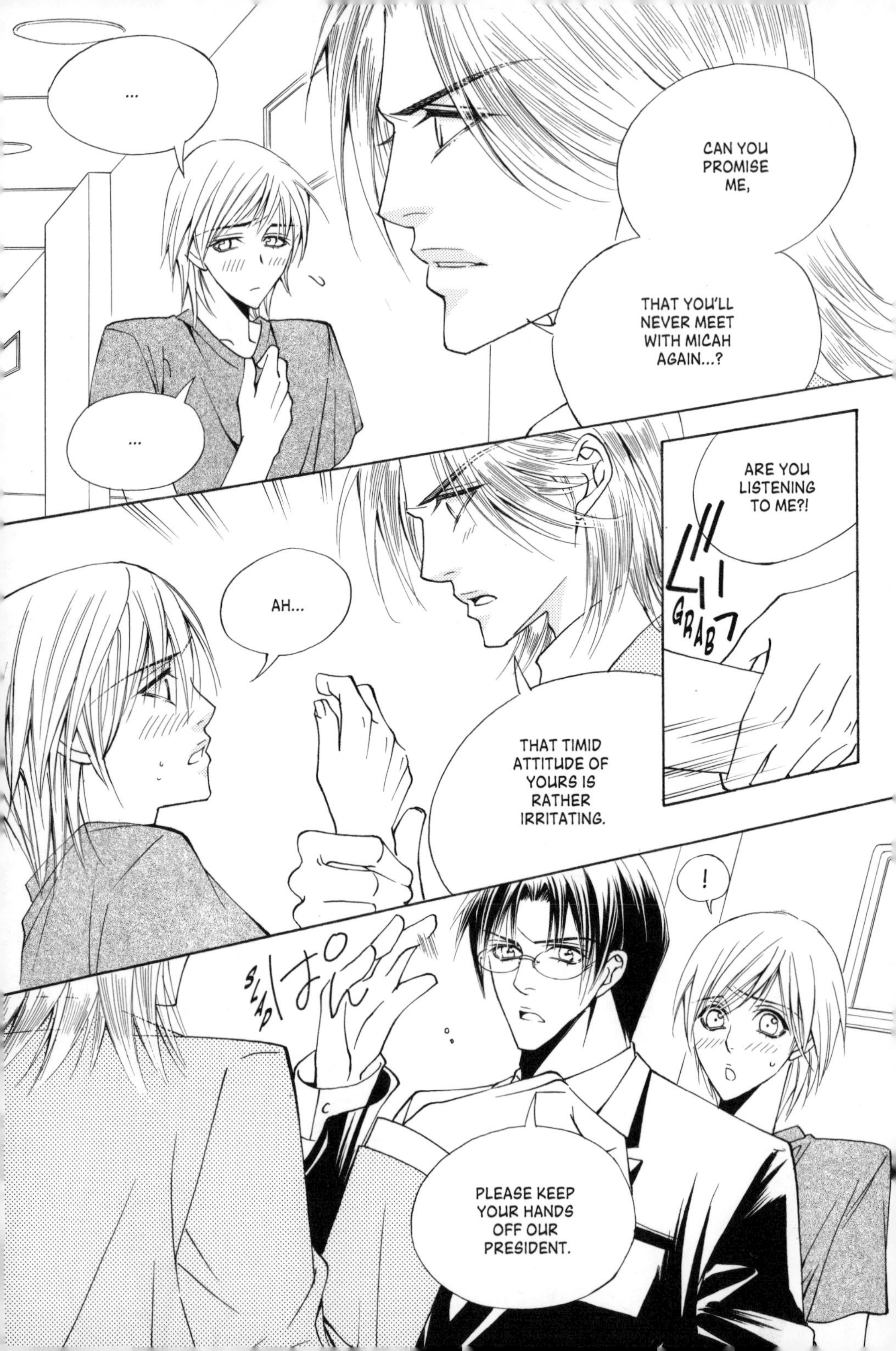
CAN YOU PROMISE ME,
THAT YOU'LL NEVER MEET WITH MICAH AGAIN...?
...
...
ARE YOU LISTENING TO ME?!
GRAB
AH...
THAT TIMID ATTITUDE OF YOURS IS RATHER IRRITATING.
!
SLAP
PLEASE KEEP YOUR HANDS OFF OUR PRESIDENT.

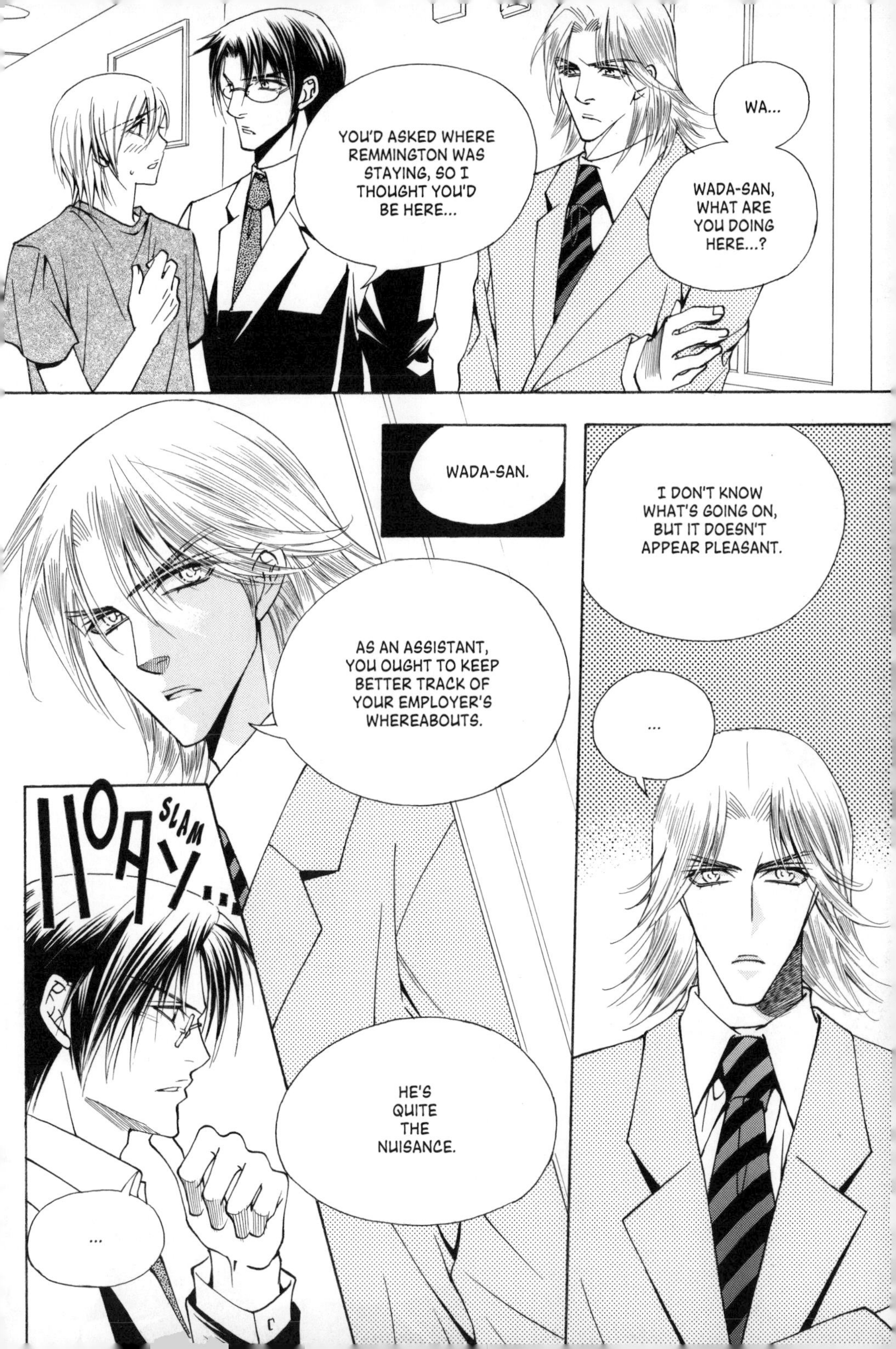
WA...
WADA-SAN, WHAT ARE YOU DOING HERE...?
YOU'D ASKED WHERE REMMINGTON WAS STAYING, SO I THOUGHT YOU'D BE HERE...
I DON'T KNOW WHAT'S GOING ON, BUT IT DOESN'T APPEAR PLEASANT.
...
WADA-SAN.
AS AN ASSISTANT, YOU OUGHT TO KEEP BETTER TRACK OF YOUR EMPLOYER'S WHEREABOUTS.
SLAM
HE'S QUITE THE NUISANCE.
...

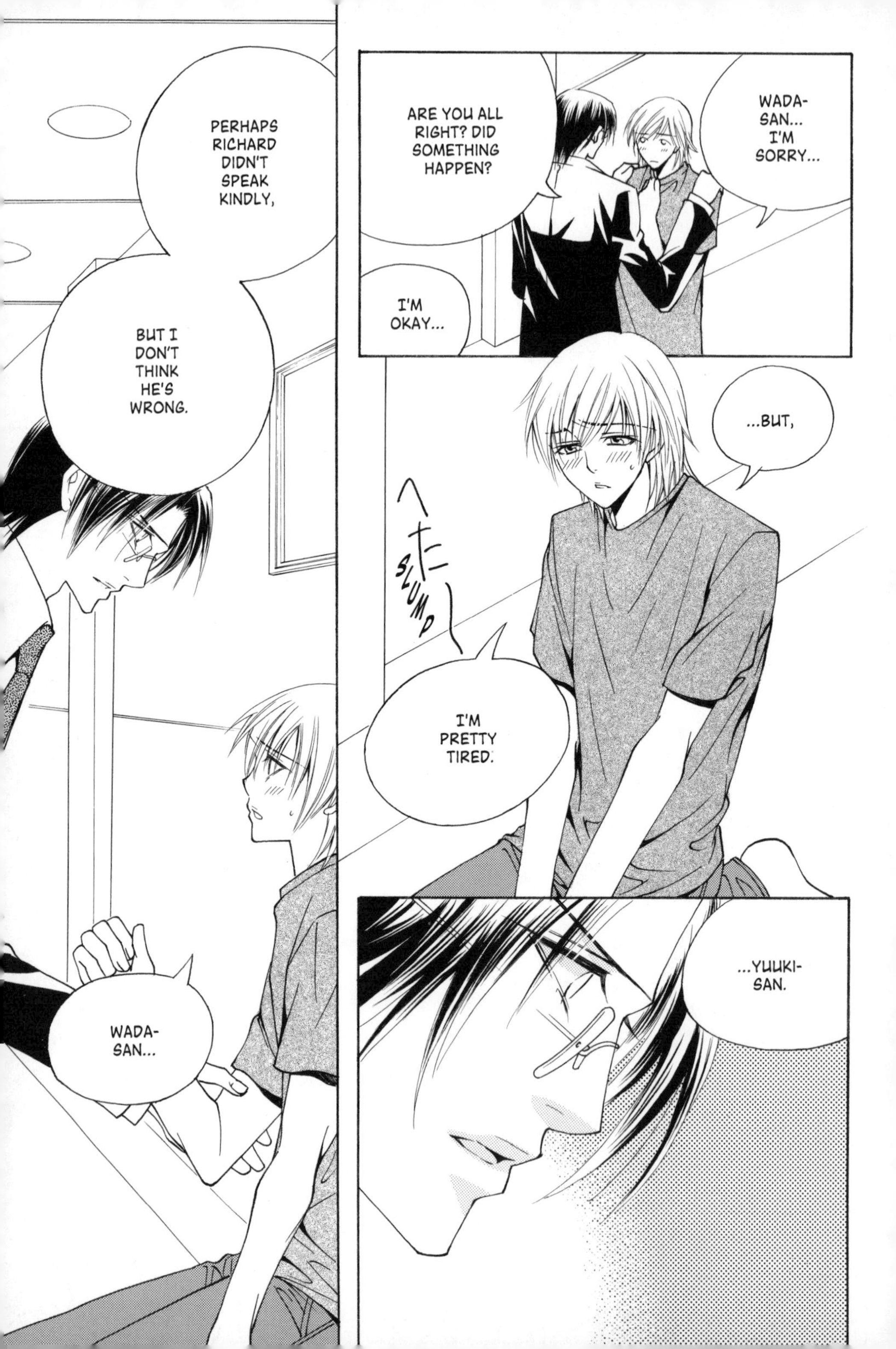
WADA-SAN... I'M SORRY...
ARE YOU ALL RIGHT? DID SOMETHING HAPPEN?
I'M OKAY...
...BUT,
へたー
SLUMP
I'M PRETTY TIRED.
...YUUKI-SAN.
PERHAPS RICHARD DIDN'T SPEAK KINDLY,
BUT I DON'T THINK HE'S WRONG.
WADA-SAN...

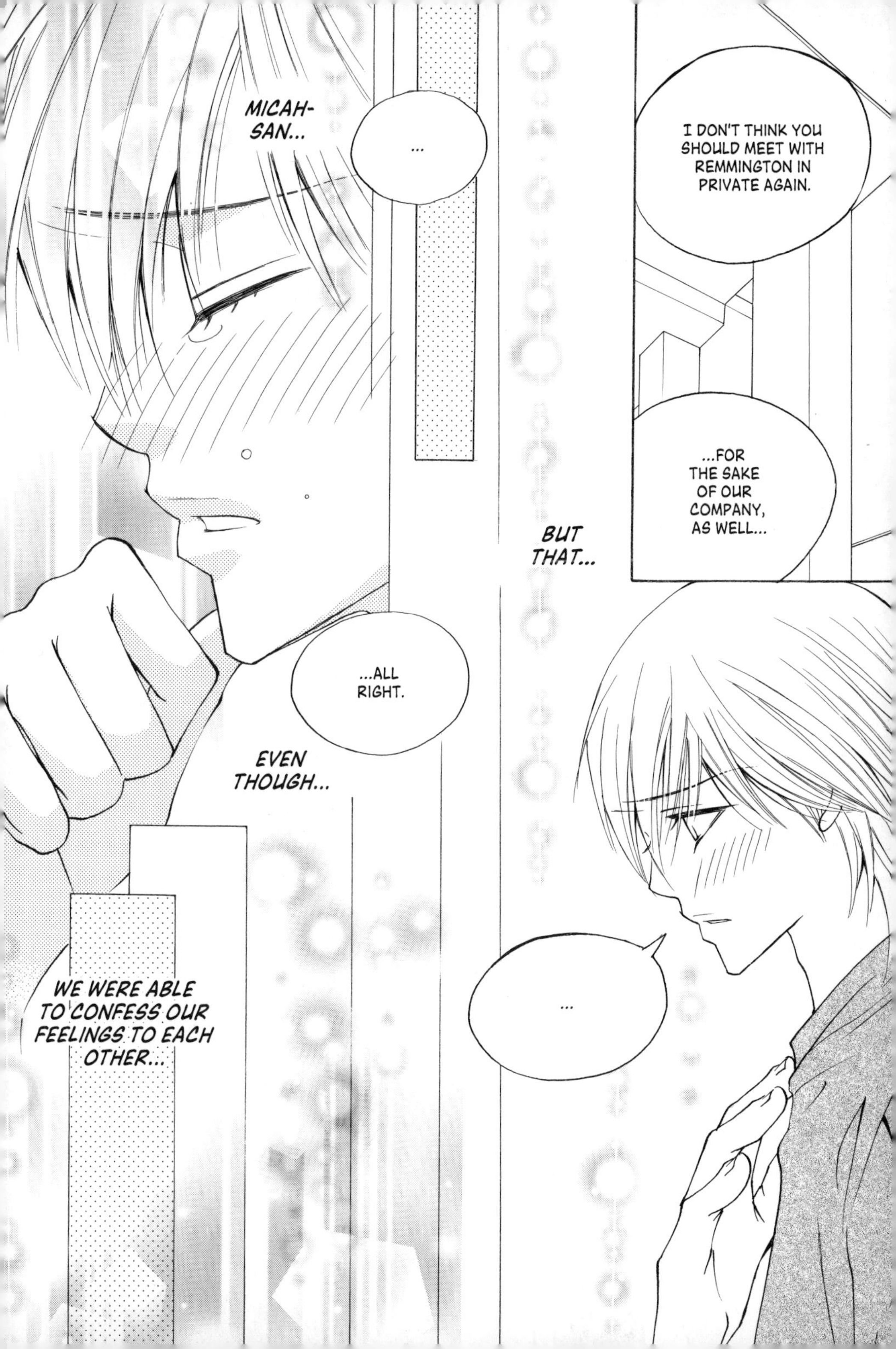
I DON'T THINK YOU SHOULD MEET WITH REMMINGTON IN PRIVATE AGAIN.
...FOR THE SAKE OF OUR COMPANY, AS WELL...
BUT THAT...
...
MICAH-SAN...
...
...ALL RIGHT.
EVEN THOUGH...
WE WERE ABLE TO CONFESS OUR FEELINGS TO EACH OTHER...

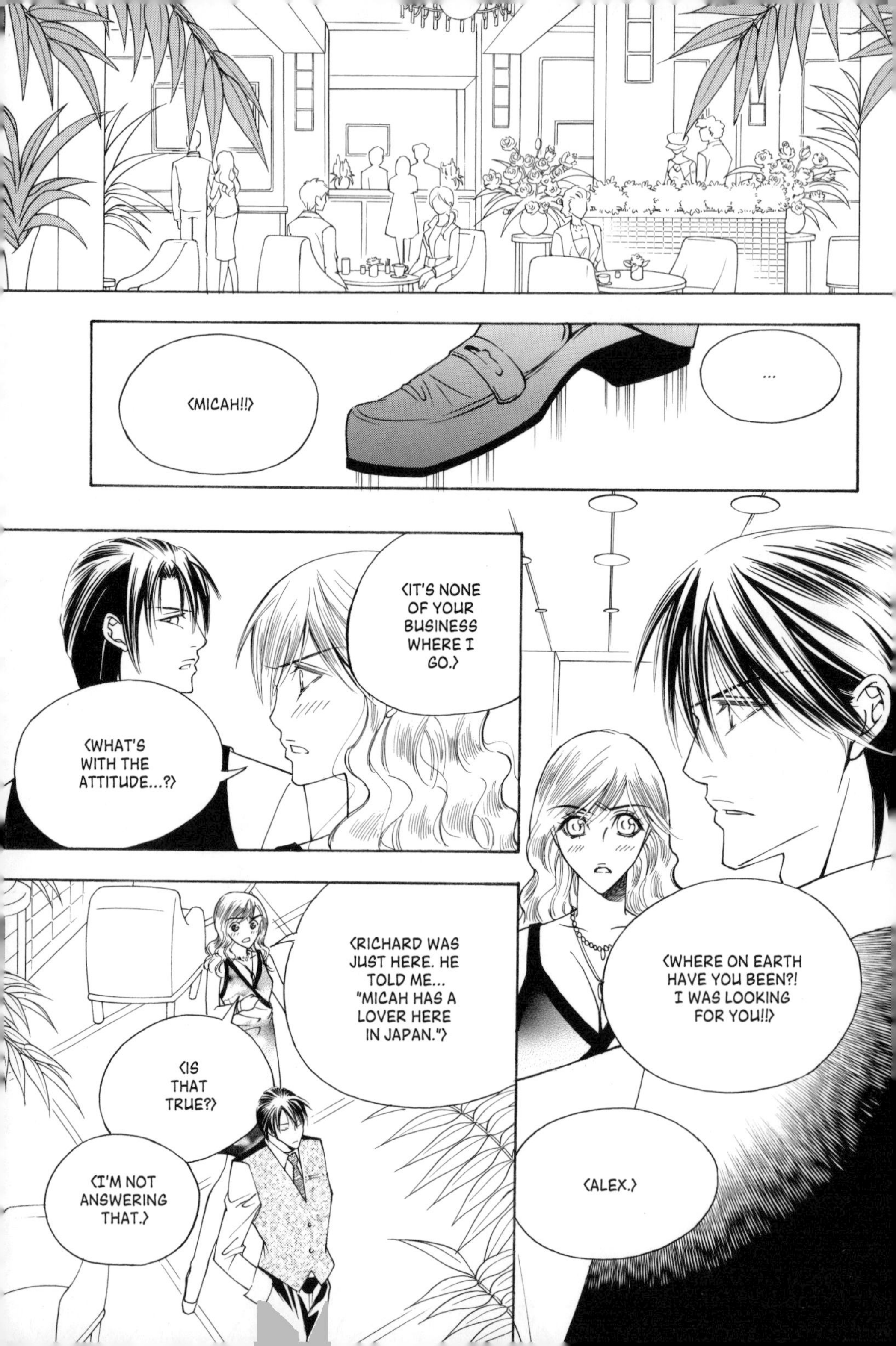
...
<MICAH!!>
<WHERE ON EARTH HAVE YOU BEEN?! I WAS LOOKING FOR YOU!!>
<ALEX.>
<IT'S NONE OF YOUR BUSINESS WHERE I GO.>
<WHAT'S WITH THE ATTITUDE...?>
<RICHARD WAS JUST HERE. HE TOLD ME... "MICAH HAS A LOVER HERE IN JAPAN.">
<IS THAT TRUE?>
<I'M NOT ANSWERING THAT.>

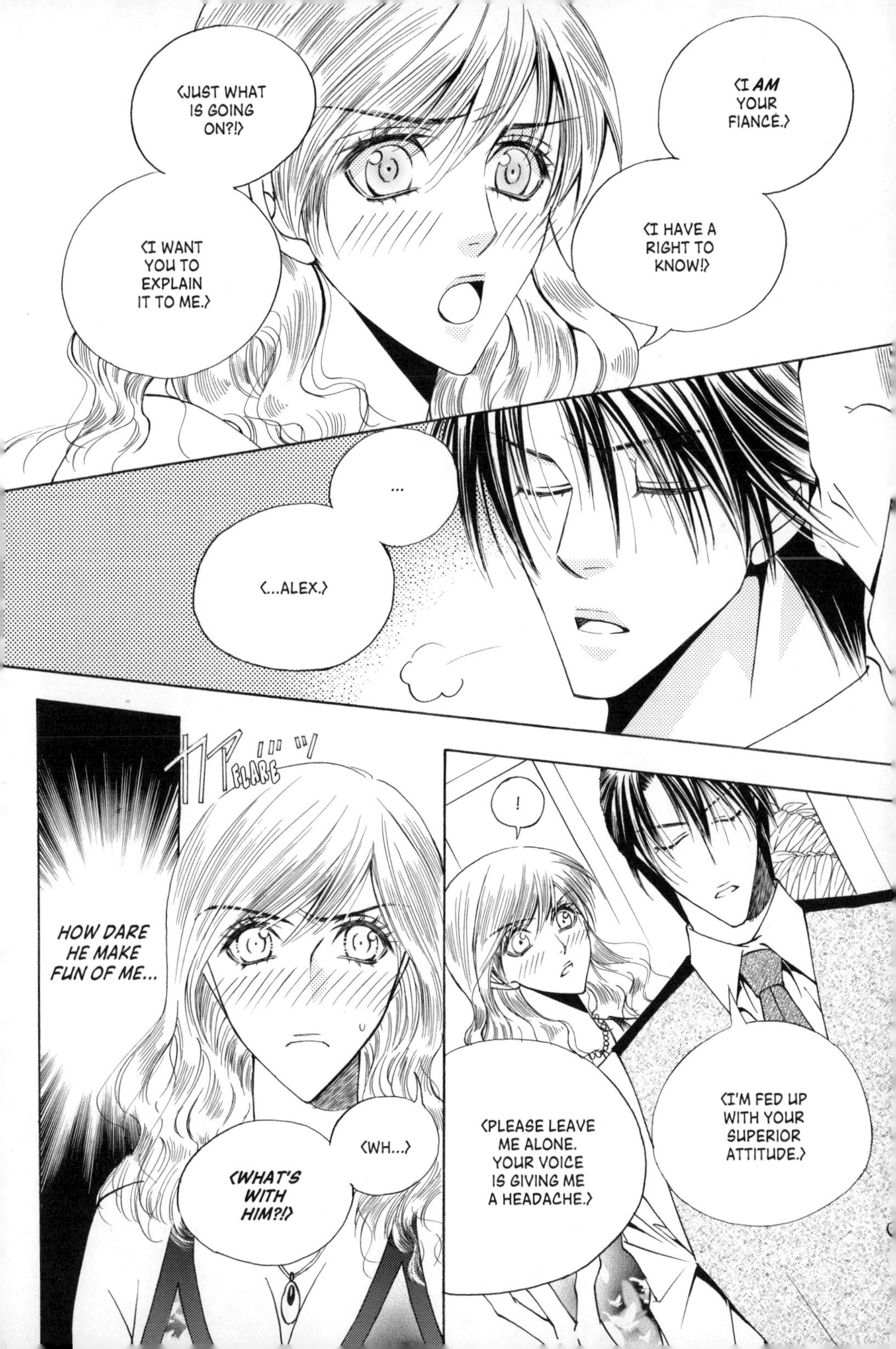
<I AM YOUR FIANCÉ.>
<I HAVE A RIGHT TO KNOW!>
<JUST WHAT IS GOING ON?!>
<I WANT YOU TO EXPLAIN IT TO ME.>
...
<...ALEX.>
!
<I'M FED UP WITH YOUR SUPERIOR ATTITUDE.>
<PLEASE LEAVE ME ALONE. YOUR VOICE IS GIVING ME A HEADACHE.>
FLARE
HOW DARE HE MAKE FUN OF ME...
<WH...>
<WHAT'S WITH HIM?!>

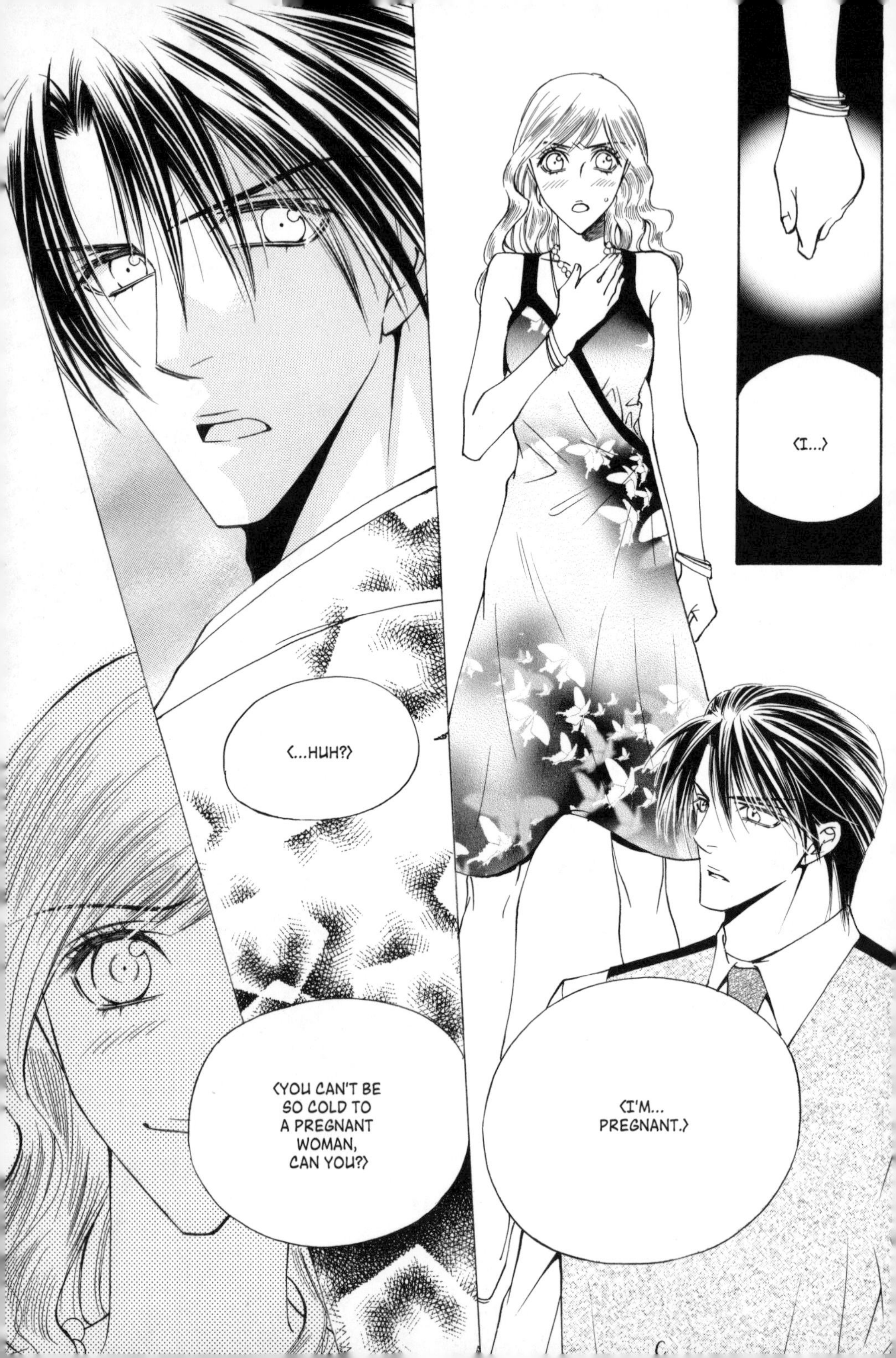
〈I...〉
〈I'M... PREGNANT.〉
〈...HUH?〉
〈YOU CAN'T BE SO COLD TO A PREGNANT WOMAN, CAN YOU?〉

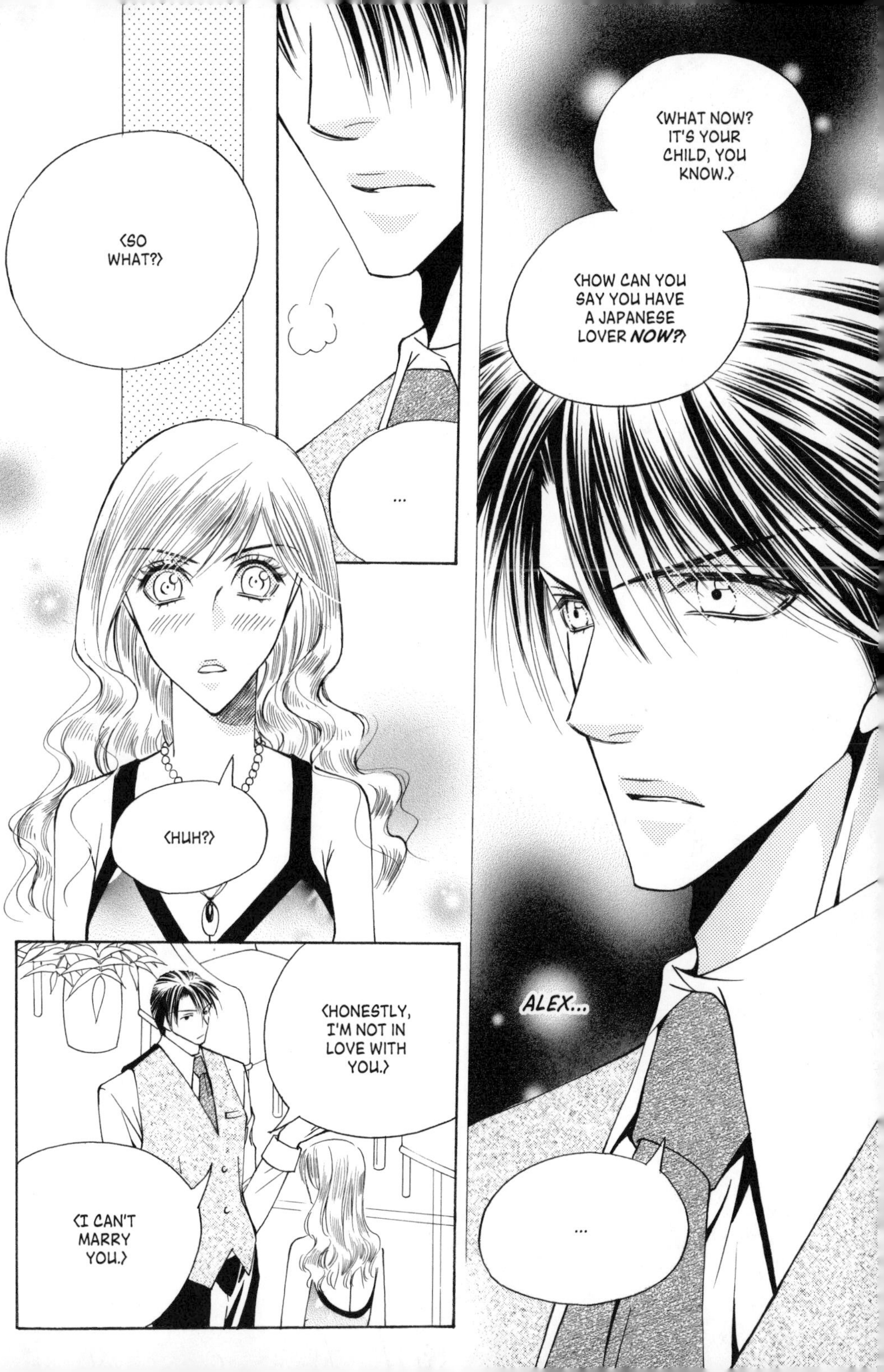
‹WHAT NOW? IT'S YOUR CHILD, YOU KNOW.›
‹HOW CAN YOU SAY YOU HAVE A JAPANESE LOVER *NOW?!*›
ALEX...
...
...
‹SO WHAT?›
‹HUH?›
‹HONESTLY, I'M NOT IN LOVE WITH YOU.›
‹I CAN'T MARRY YOU.›

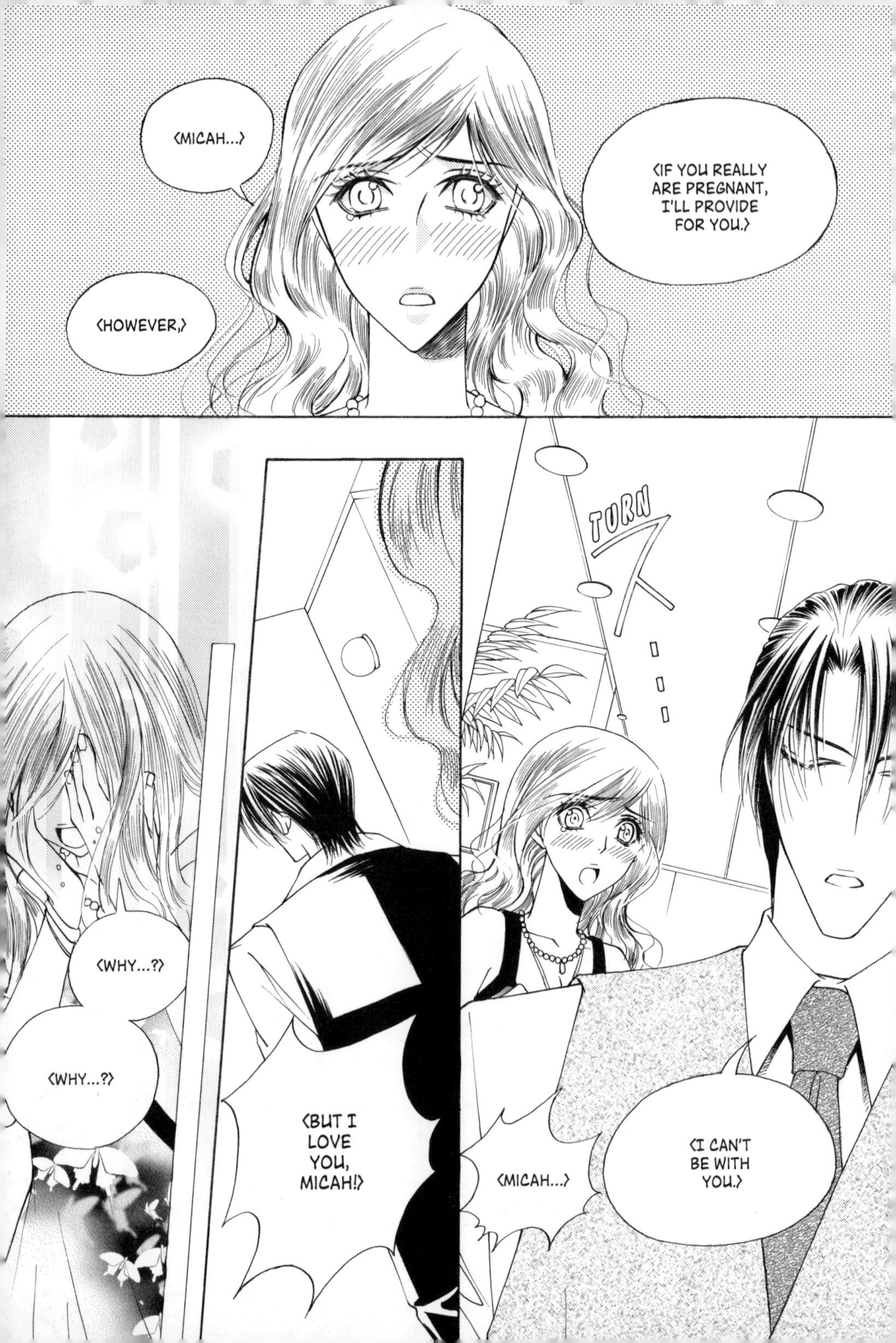
<IF YOU REALLY ARE PREGNANT, I'LL PROVIDE FOR YOU.>
<MICAH...>
<HOWEVER,>
TURN
<I CAN'T BE WITH YOU.>
<MICAH...>
<BUT I LOVE YOU, MICAH!>
<WHY...?>
<WHY...?>

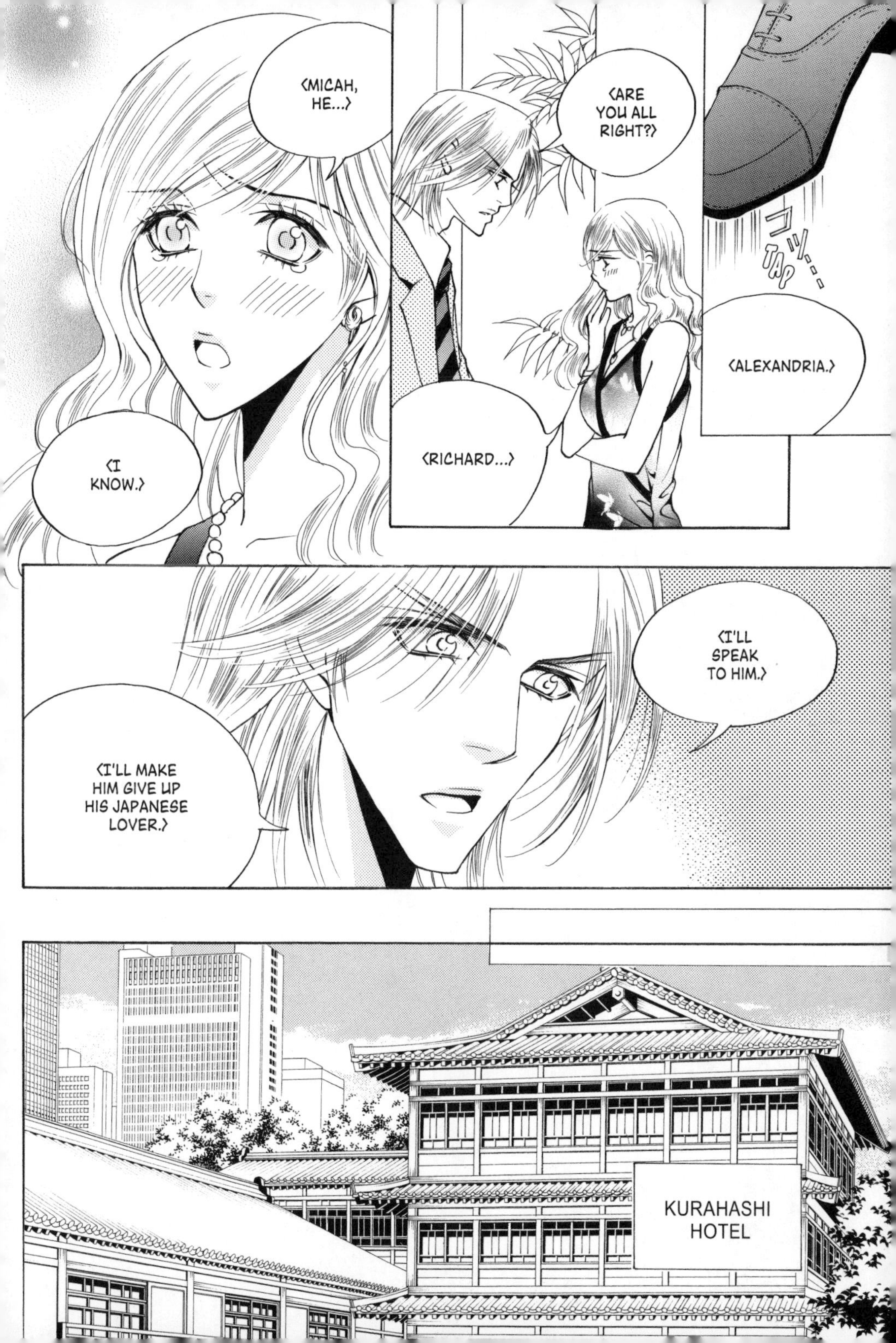
TAP
<ALEXANDRIA.>
<ARE YOU ALL RIGHT?>
<RICHARD...>
<MICAH, HE...>
<I KNOW.>
<I'LL SPEAK TO HIM.>
<I'LL MAKE HIM GIVE UP HIS JAPANESE LOVER.>
KURAHASHI HOTEL

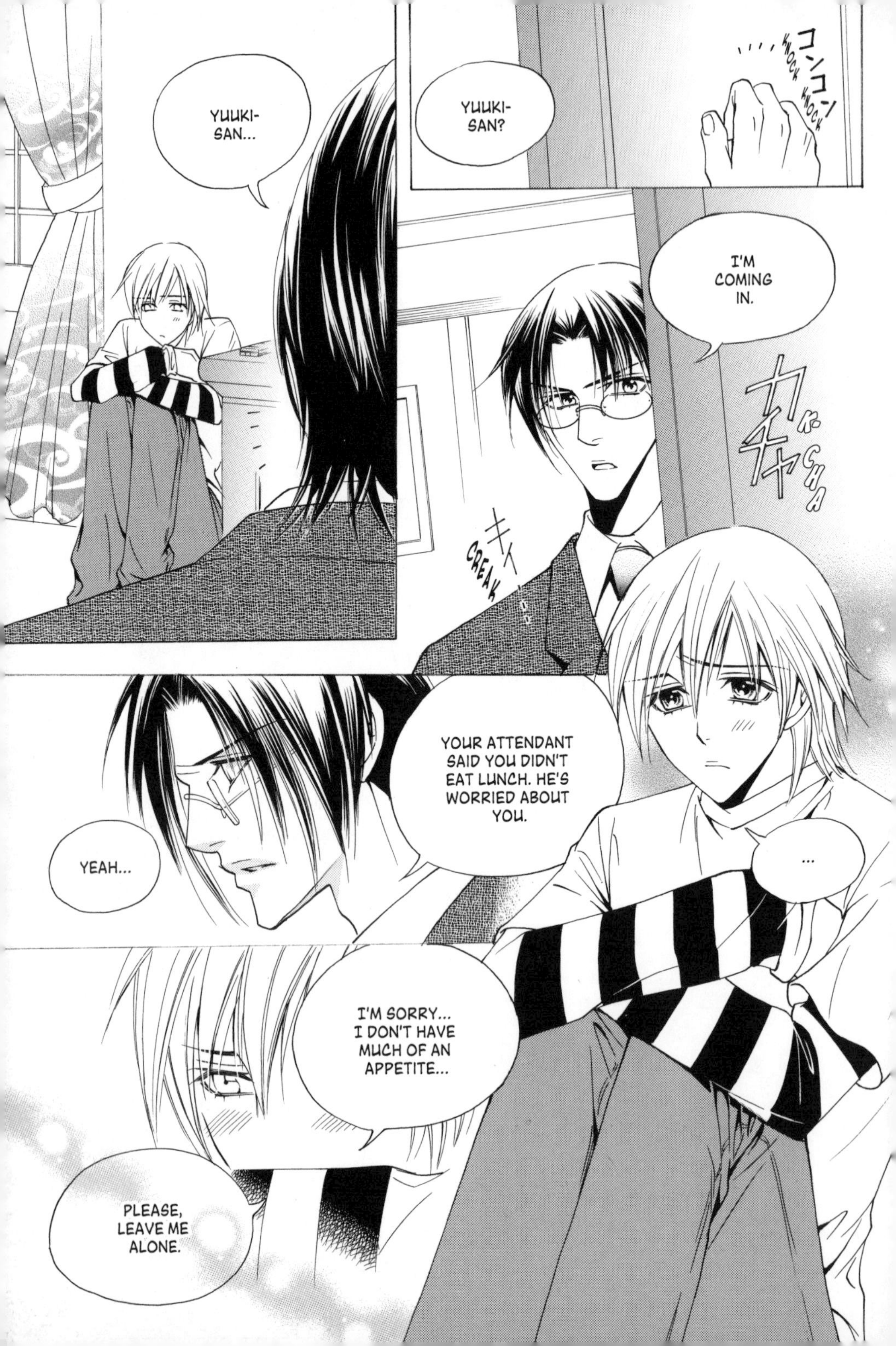
コンコン
KNOCK KNOCK
YUUKI-SAN?
I'M COMING IN.
カチャ
KA-CHA
キィ
CREAK
YUUKI-SAN...
...
YOUR ATTENDANT SAID YOU DIDN'T EAT LUNCH. HE'S WORRIED ABOUT YOU.
YEAH...
I'M SORRY... I DON'T HAVE MUCH OF AN APPETITE...
PLEASE, LEAVE ME ALONE.

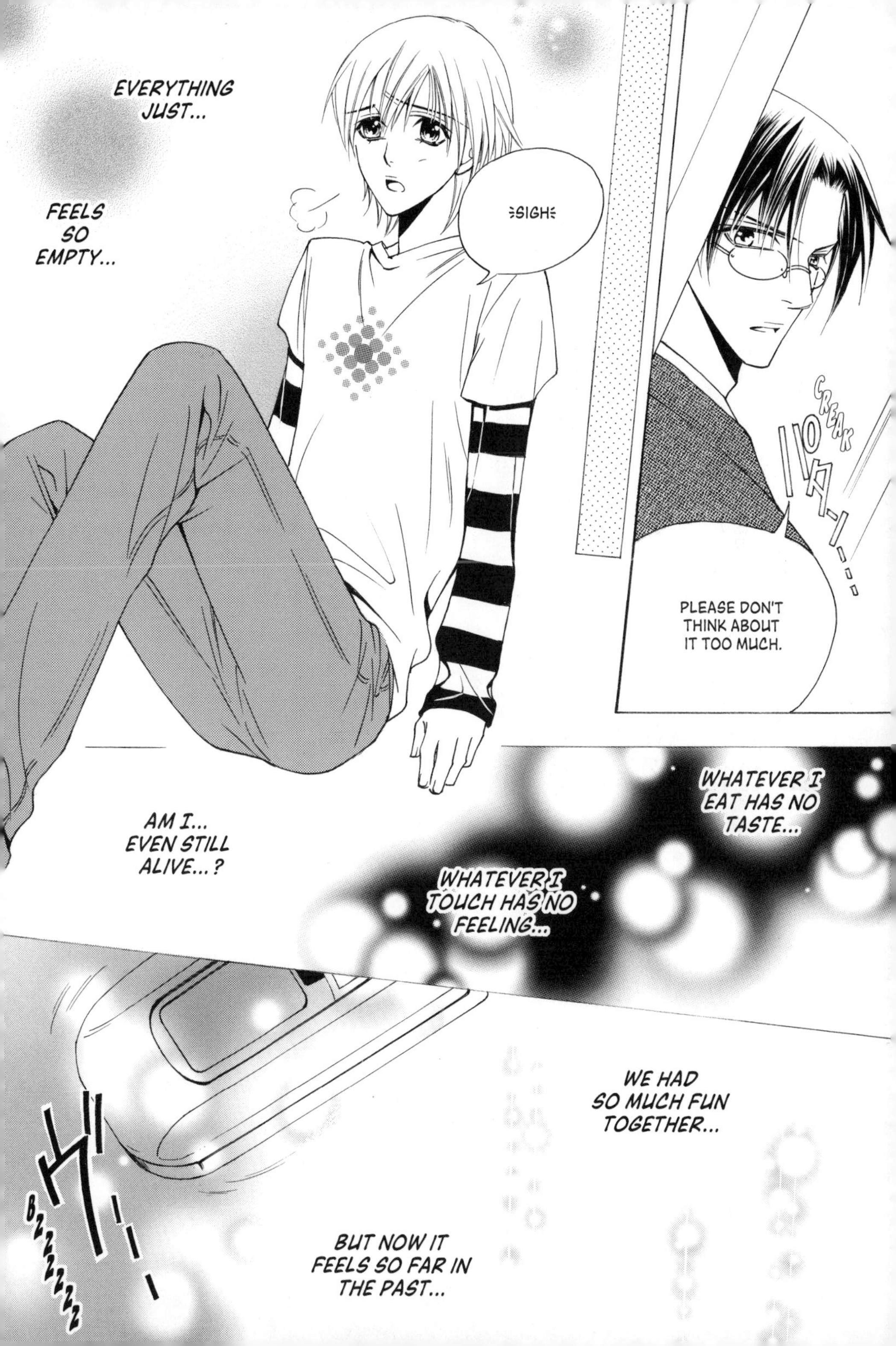
CREAK
PLEASE DON'T THINK ABOUT IT TOO MUCH.
EVERYTHING JUST...
FEELS SO EMPTY...
SIGH
AM I... EVEN STILL ALIVE...?
WHATEVER I EAT HAS NO TASTE...
WHATEVER I TOUCH HAS NO FEELING...
WE HAD SO MUCH FUN TOGETHER...
BZZZZZZZ
BUT NOW IT FEELS SO FAR IN THE PAST...

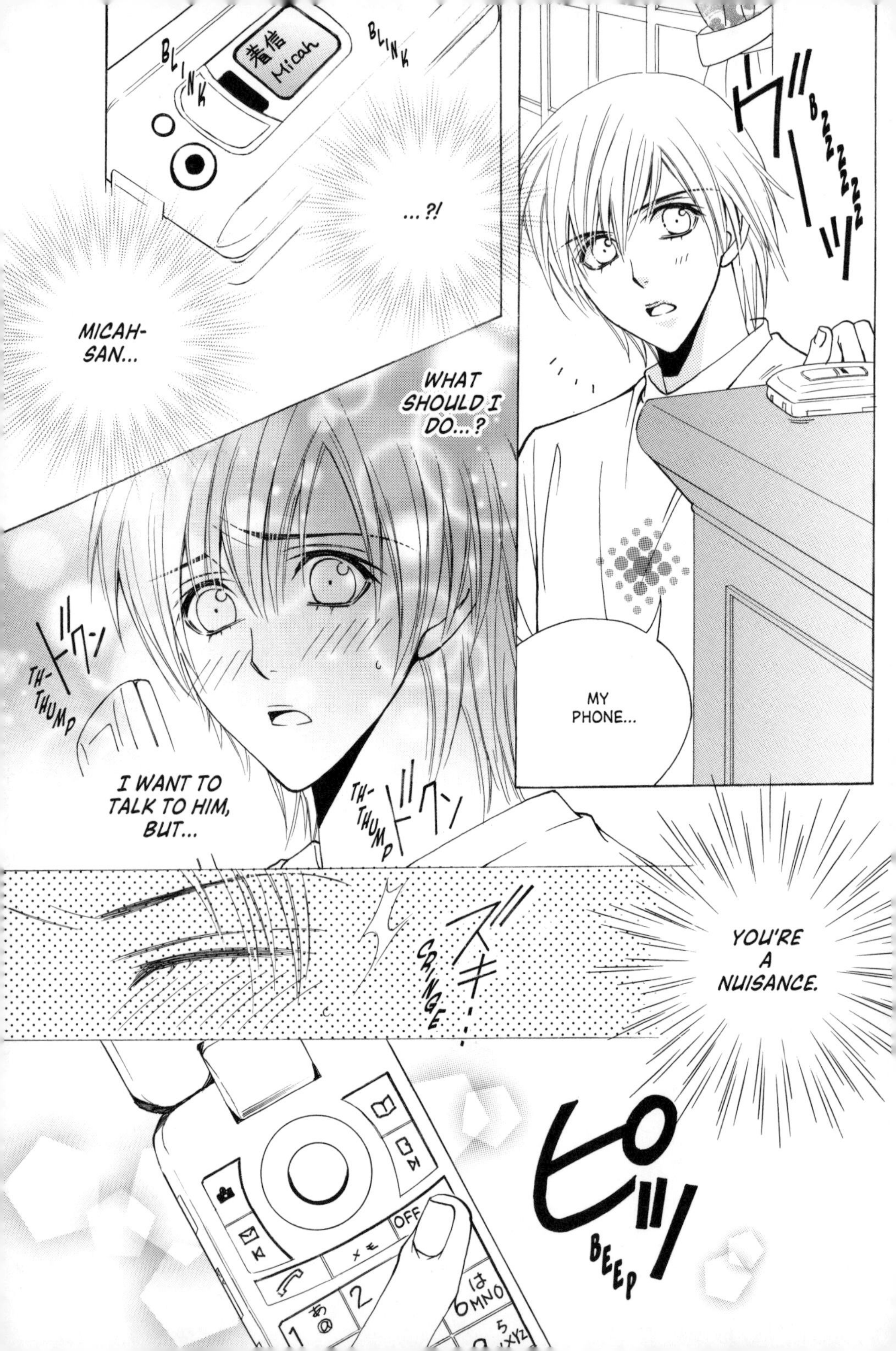
BZZZZZZZ
MY PHONE...
BLINK
着信
Micah
BLINK
...?!
MICAH-SAN...
WHAT SHOULD I DO...?
TH-THUMP
TH-THUMP
I WANT TO TALK TO HIM, BUT...
YOU'RE A NUISANCE.
CRINGE
BEEP

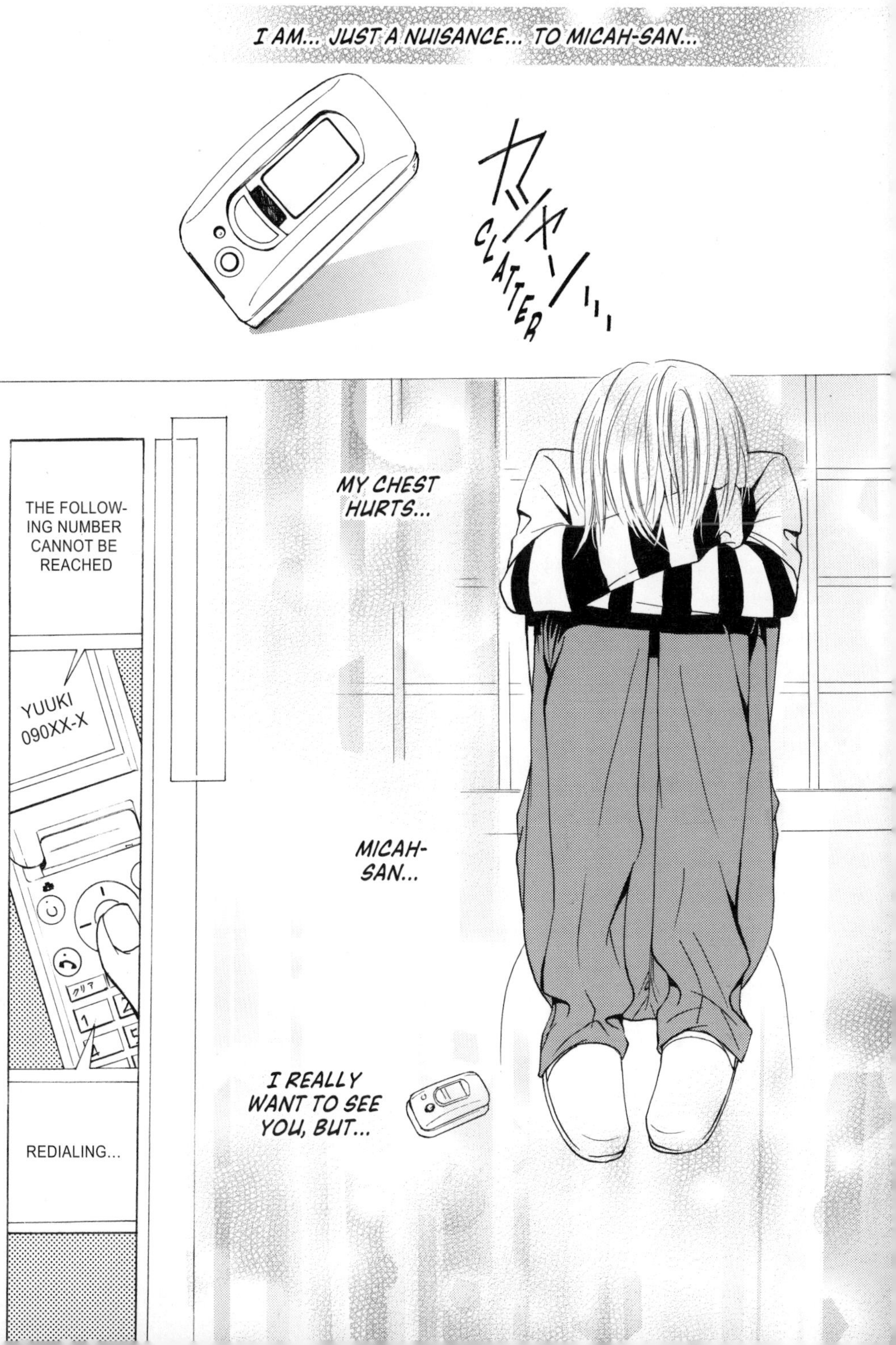
I AM... JUST A NUISANCE... TO MICAH-SAN...
CLATTER
MY CHEST HURTS...
MICAH-SAN...
I REALLY WANT TO SEE YOU, BUT...
THE FOLLOWING NUMBER CANNOT BE REACHED
YUUKI 090XX-X
REDIALING...

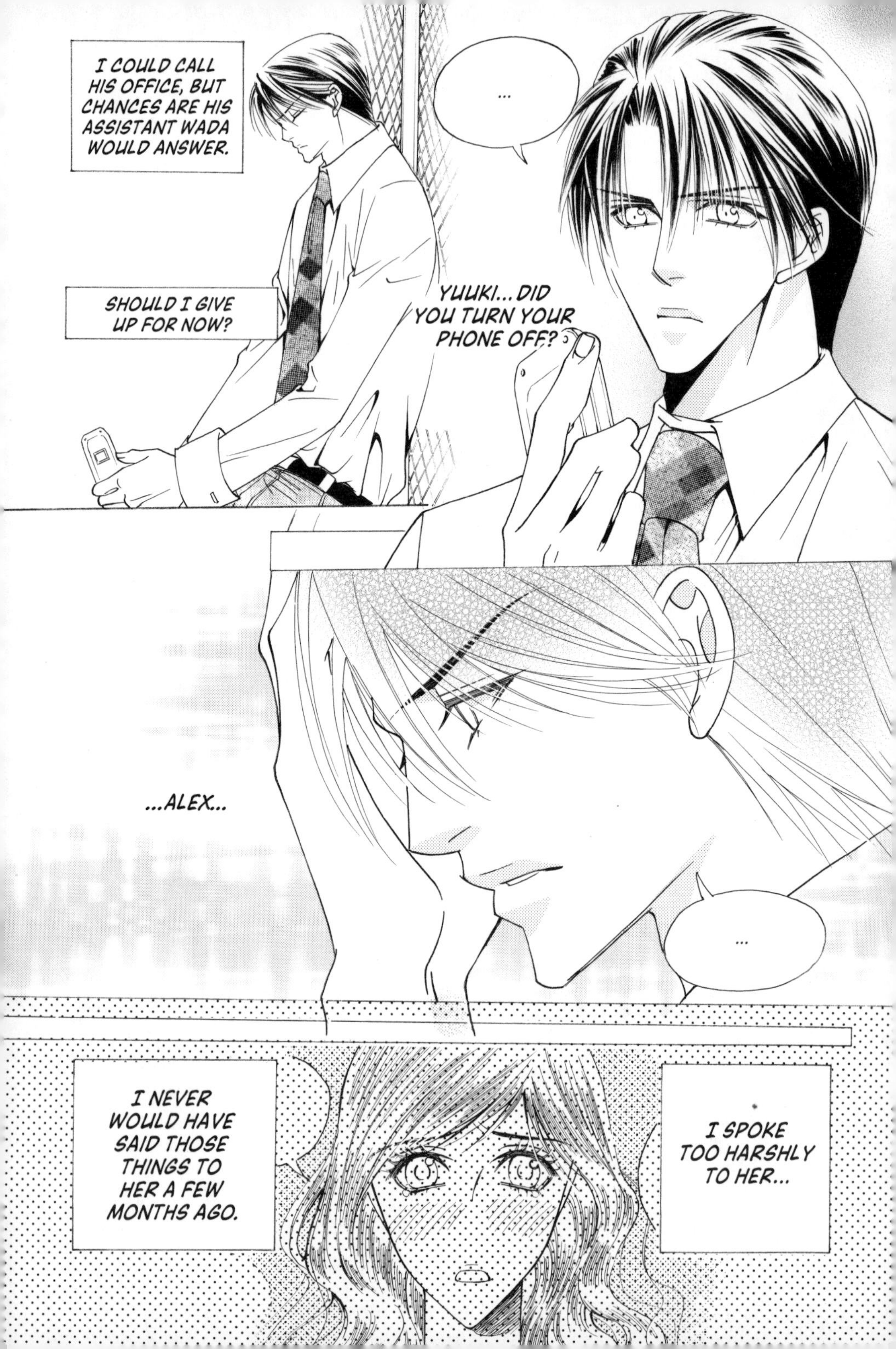
...
YUUKI... DID YOU TURN YOUR PHONE OFF?
I COULD CALL HIS OFFICE, BUT CHANCES ARE HIS ASSISTANT WADA WOULD ANSWER.
SHOULD I GIVE UP FOR NOW?
...ALEX...
...
I SPOKE TOO HARSHLY TO HER...
I NEVER WOULD HAVE SAID THOSE THINGS TO HER A FEW MONTHS AGO.

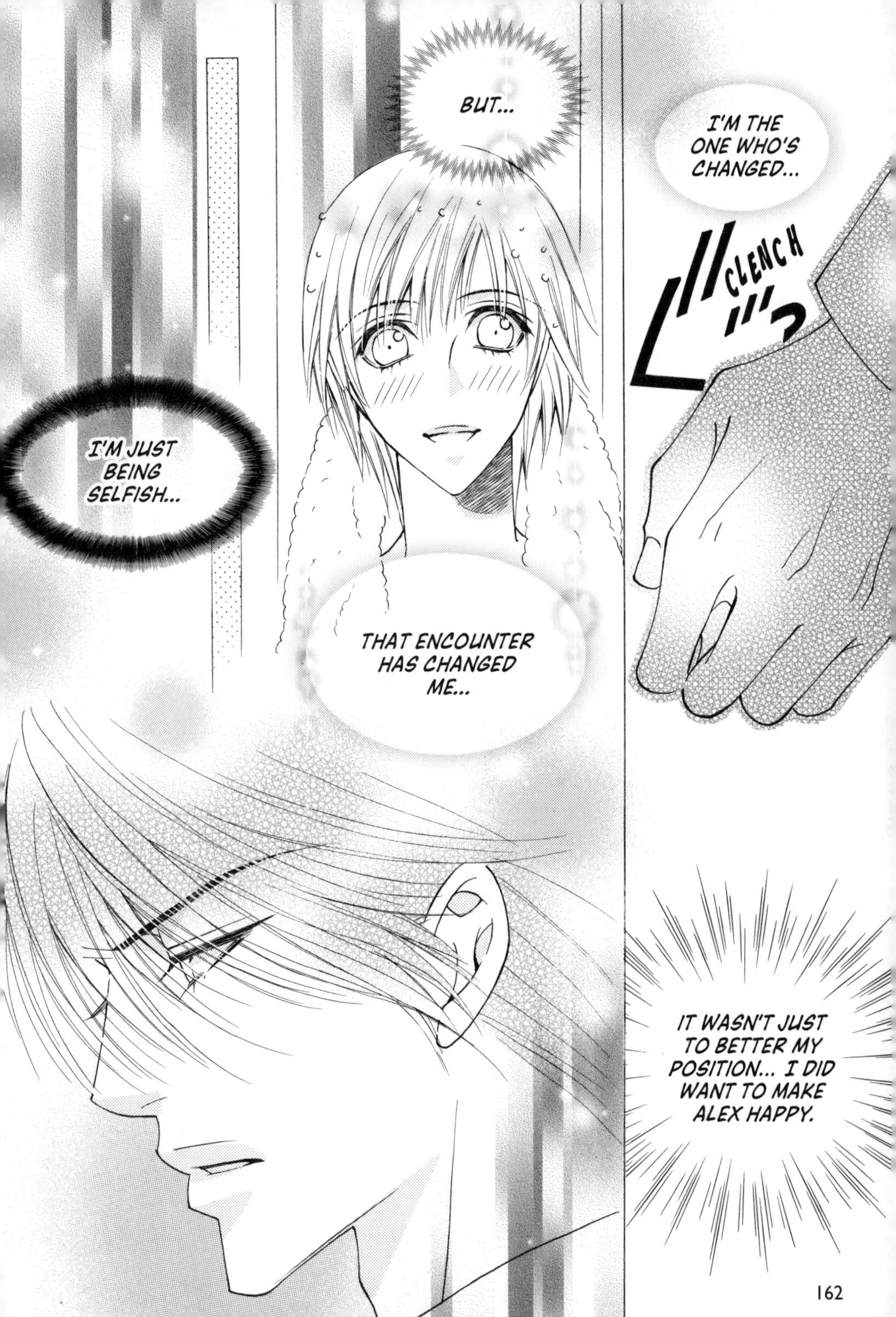
I'M THE ONE WHO'S CHANGED...
CLENCH
BUT...
I'M JUST BEING SELFISH...
THAT ENCOUNTER HAS CHANGED ME...
IT WASN'T JUST TO BETTER MY POSITION... I DID WANT TO MAKE ALEX HAPPY.

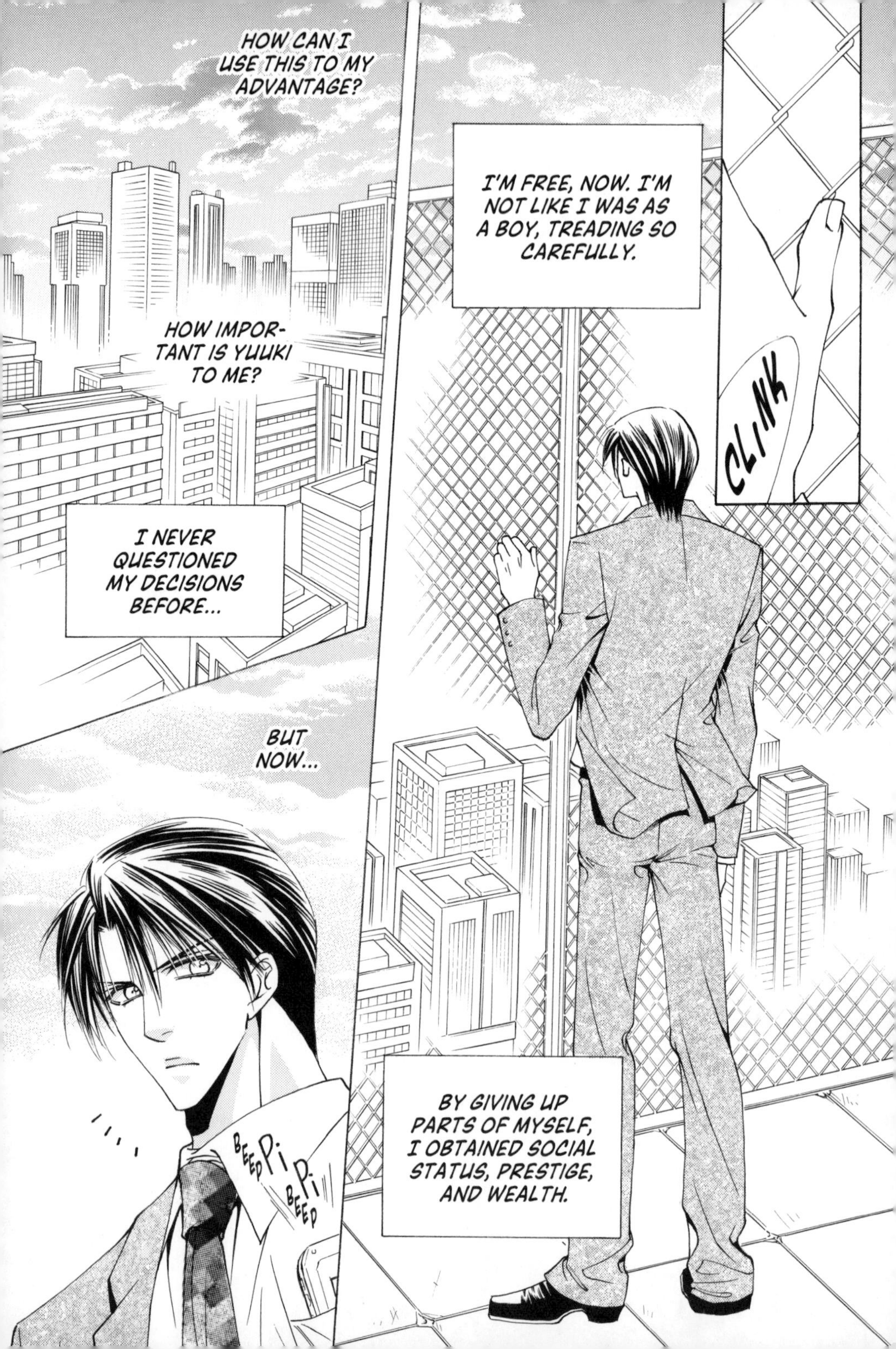
CLINK
I'M FREE, NOW. I'M NOT LIKE I WAS AS A BOY, TREADING SO CAREFULLY.
BY GIVING UP PARTS OF MYSELF, I OBTAINED SOCIAL STATUS, PRESTIGE, AND WEALTH.
HOW CAN I USE THIS TO MY ADVANTAGE?
HOW IMPORTANT IS YUUKI TO ME?
I NEVER QUESTIONED MY DECISIONS BEFORE...
BUT NOW...
BEEP Pi
Pi BEEP

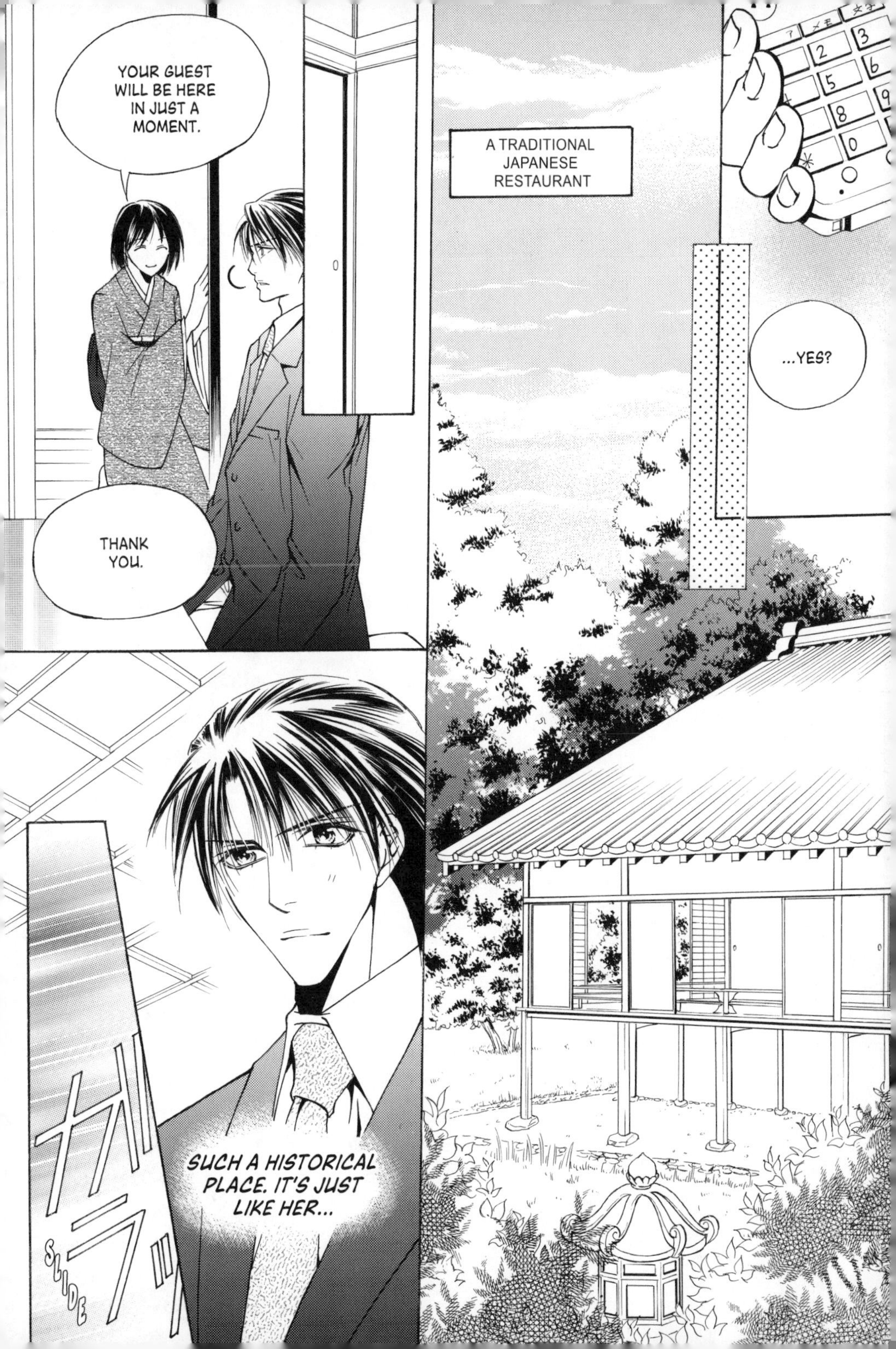
...YES?
A TRADITIONAL JAPANESE RESTAURANT
YOUR GUEST WILL BE HERE IN JUST A MOMENT.
THANK YOU.
SLIDE
SUCH A HISTORICAL PLACE. IT'S JUST LIKE HER...

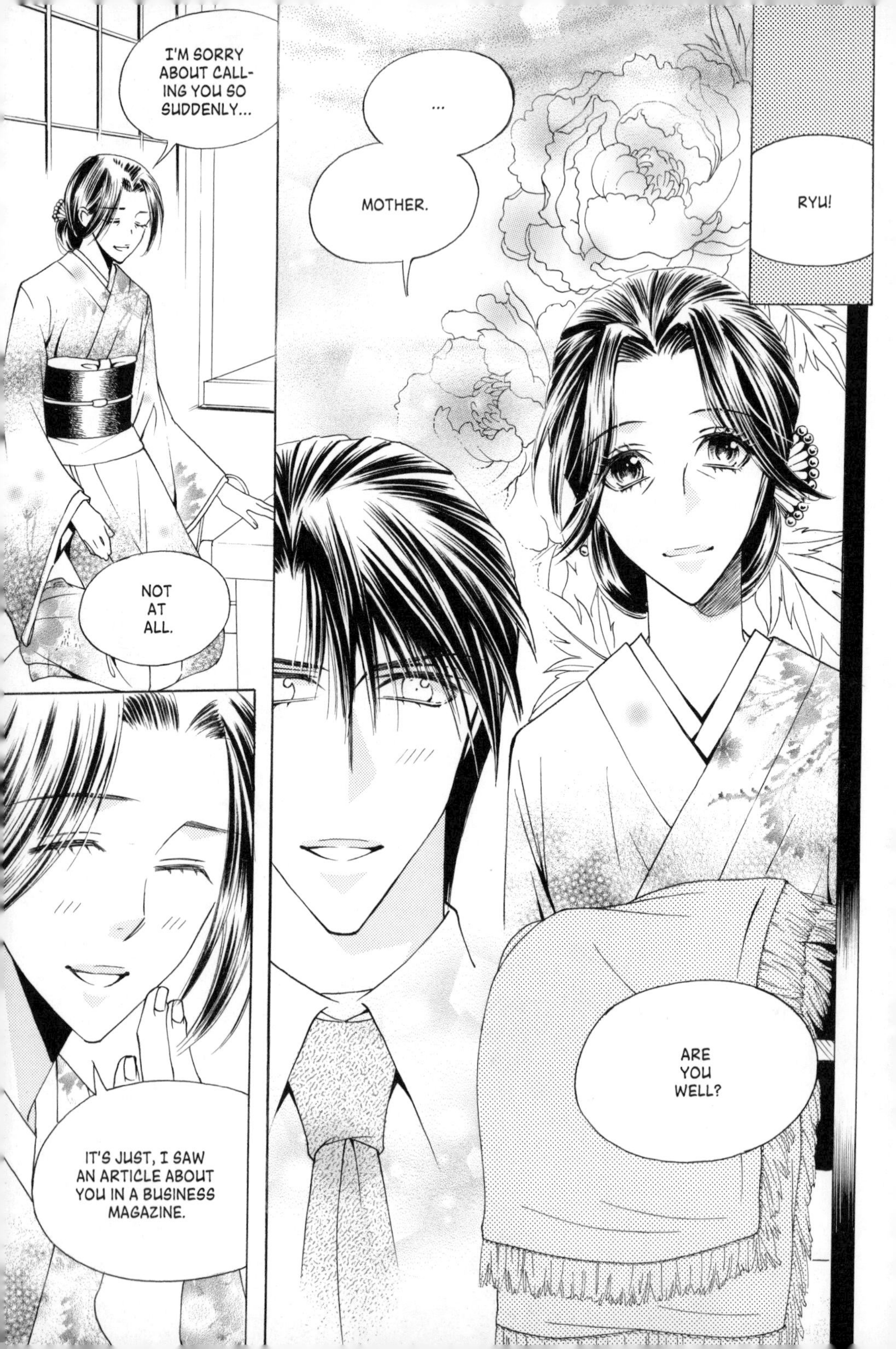
RYU!
...
MOTHER.
ARE YOU WELL?
I'M SORRY ABOUT CALLING YOU SO SUDDENLY...
NOT AT ALL.
IT'S JUST, I SAW AN ARTICLE ABOUT YOU IN A BUSINESS MAGAZINE.

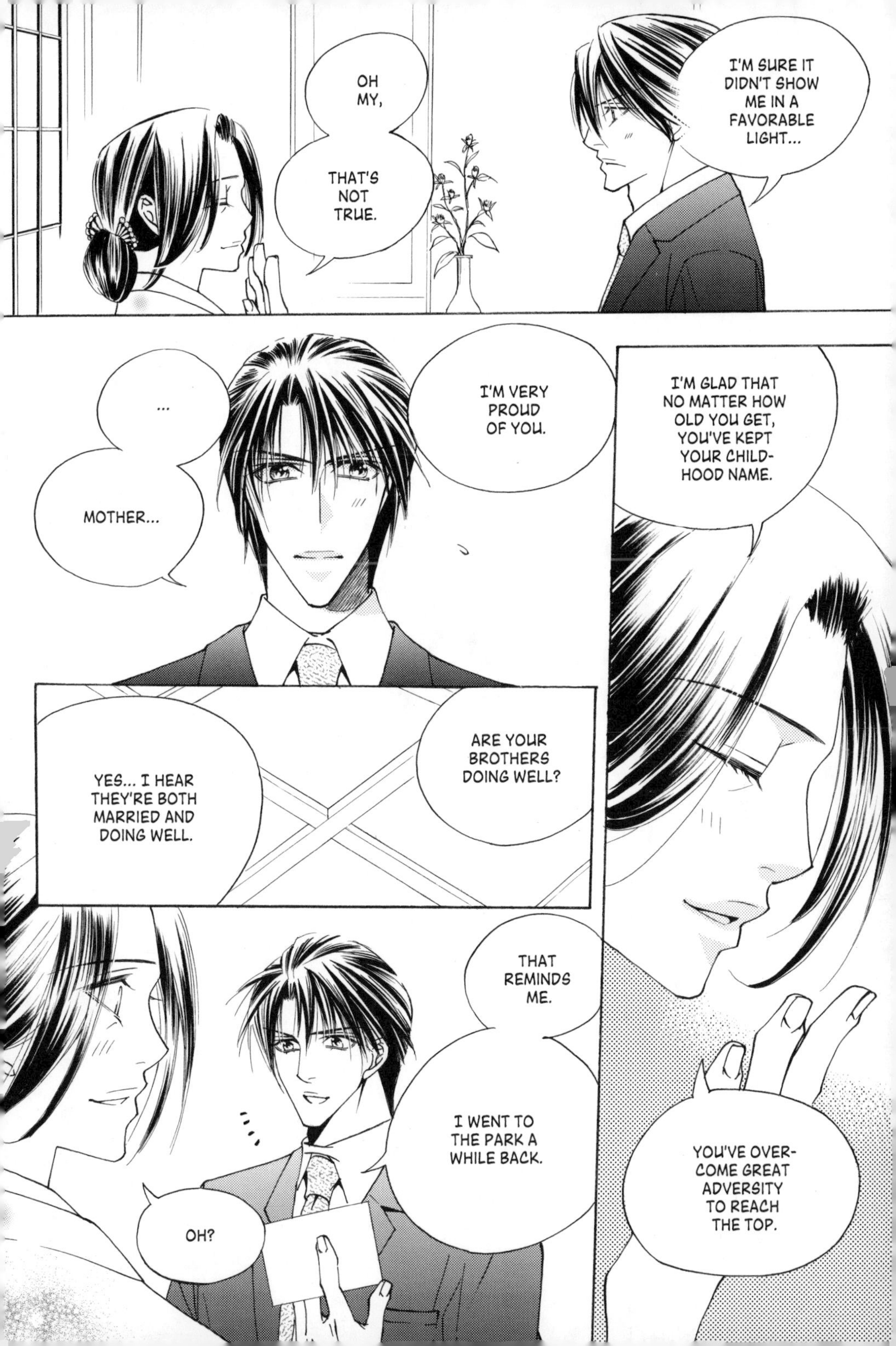
I'M SURE IT DIDN'T SHOW ME IN A FAVORABLE LIGHT...
OH MY,
THAT'S NOT TRUE.
I'M GLAD THAT NO MATTER HOW OLD YOU GET, YOU'VE KEPT YOUR CHILDHOOD NAME.
YOU'VE OVERCOME GREAT ADVERSITY TO REACH THE TOP.
I'M VERY PROUD OF YOU.
...
MOTHER...
ARE YOUR BROTHERS DOING WELL?
YES... I HEAR THEY'RE BOTH MARRIED AND DOING WELL.
THAT REMINDS ME.
I WENT TO THE PARK A WHILE BACK.
OH?

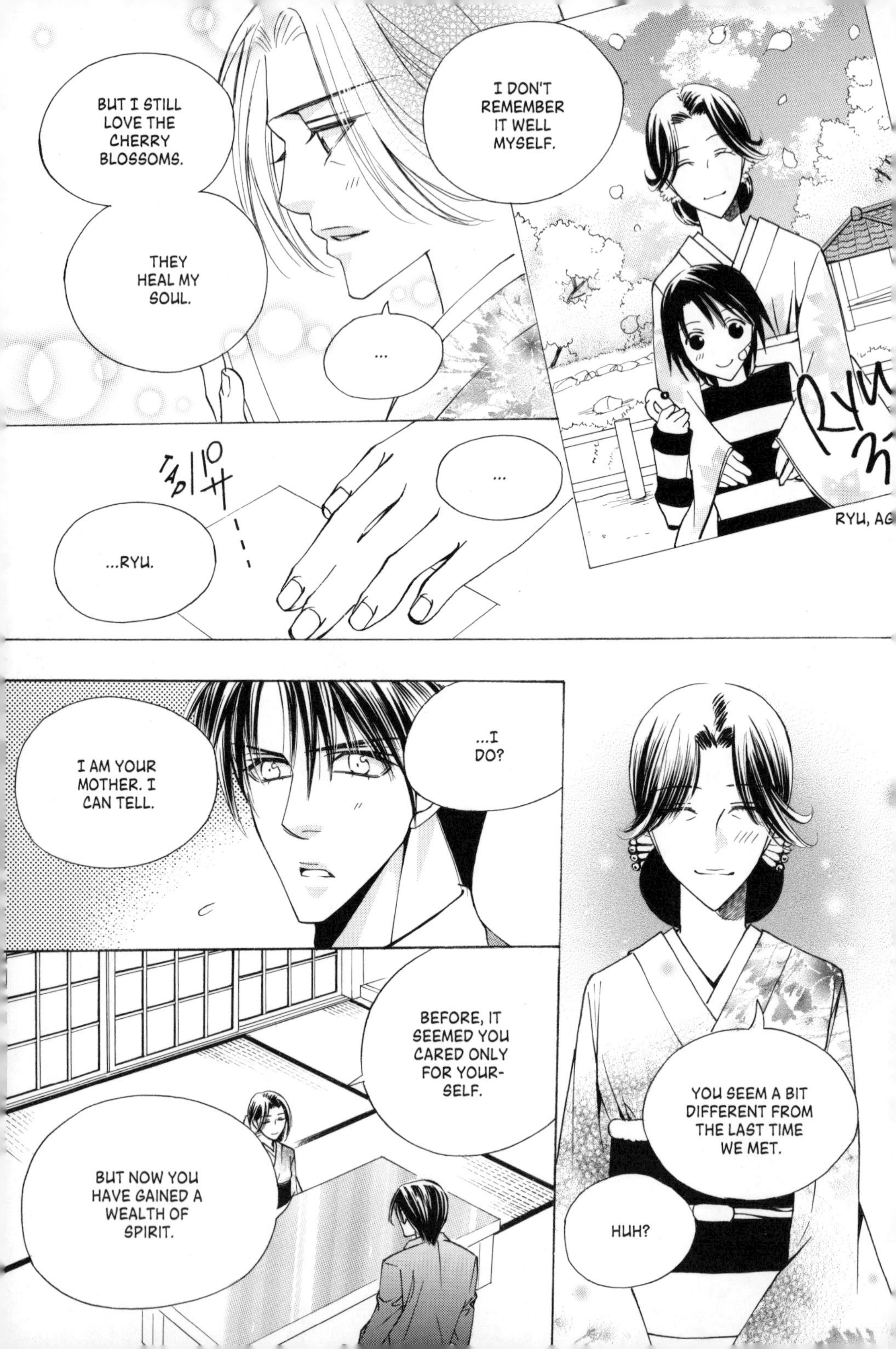
RYU
RYU, AG
I DON'T REMEMBER IT WELL MYSELF.
BUT I STILL LOVE THE CHERRY BLOSSOMS.
THEY HEAL MY SOUL.
...
...
TAP
...RYU.
YOU SEEM A BIT DIFFERENT FROM THE LAST TIME WE MET.
HUH?
...I DO?
I AM YOUR MOTHER. I CAN TELL.
BEFORE, IT SEEMED YOU CARED ONLY FOR YOUR-SELF.
BUT NOW YOU HAVE GAINED A WEALTH OF SPIRIT.

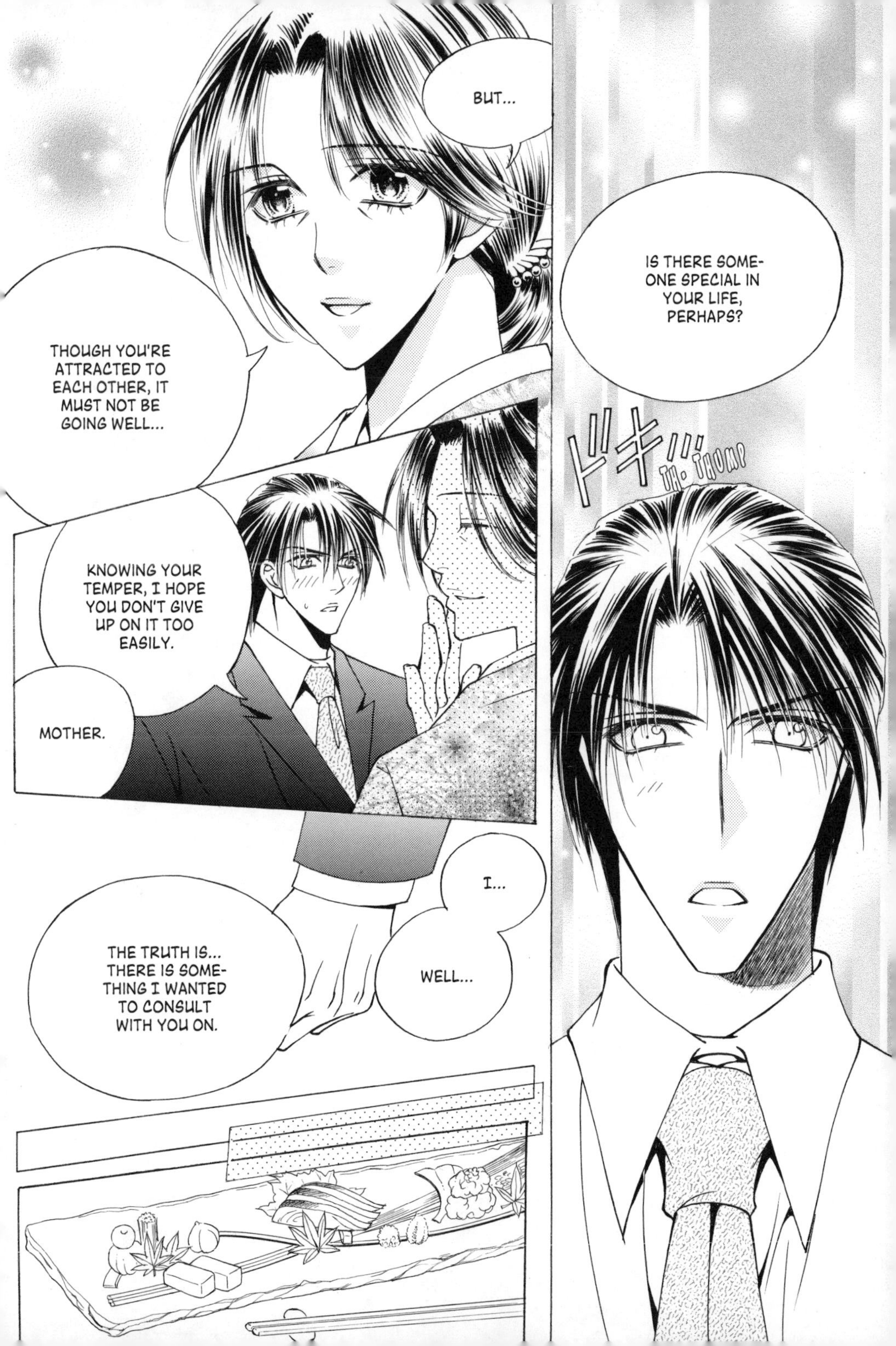
IS THERE SOME-ONE SPECIAL IN YOUR LIFE, PERHAPS?
ドキッ
TH- THUMP
BUT...
THOUGH YOU'RE ATTRACTED TO EACH OTHER, IT MUST NOT BE GOING WELL...
KNOWING YOUR TEMPER, I HOPE YOU DON'T GIVE UP ON IT TOO EASILY.
MOTHER.
I...
WELL...
THE TRUTH IS... THERE IS SOME-THING I WANTED TO CONSULT WITH YOU ON.

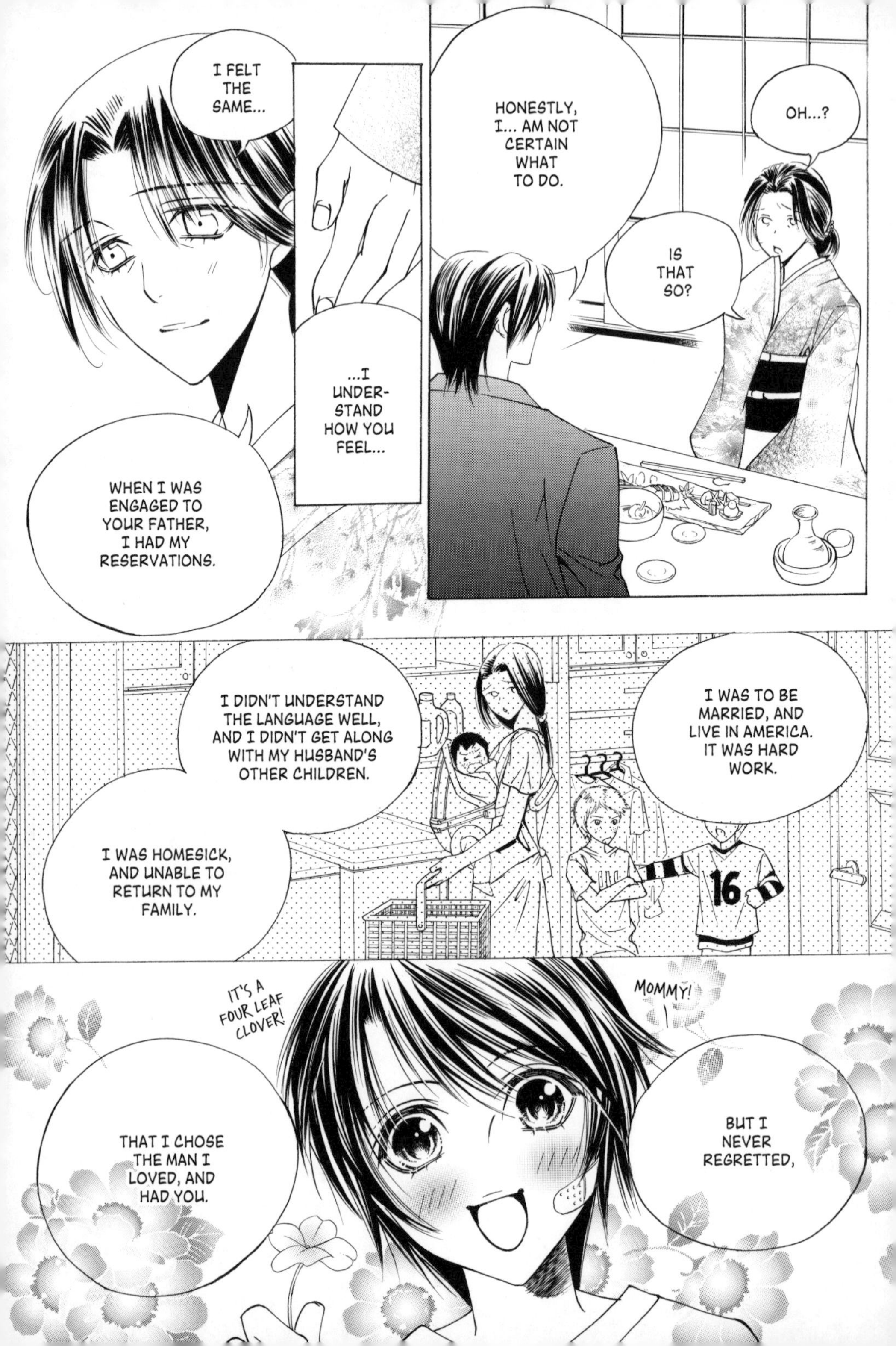
HONESTLY, I... AM NOT CERTAIN WHAT TO DO.
OH...?
IS THAT SO?
...I UNDER-STAND HOW YOU FEEL...
I FELT THE SAME...
WHEN I WAS ENGAGED TO YOUR FATHER, I HAD MY RESERVATIONS.
I WAS TO BE MARRIED, AND LIVE IN AMERICA. IT WAS HARD WORK.
I DIDN'T UNDERSTAND THE LANGUAGE WELL, AND I DIDN'T GET ALONG WITH MY HUSBAND'S OTHER CHILDREN.
I WAS HOMESICK, AND UNABLE TO RETURN TO MY FAMILY.
MOMMY!
IT'S A FOUR LEAF CLOVER!
BUT I NEVER REGRETTED,
THAT I CHOSE THE MAN I LOVED, AND HAD YOU.

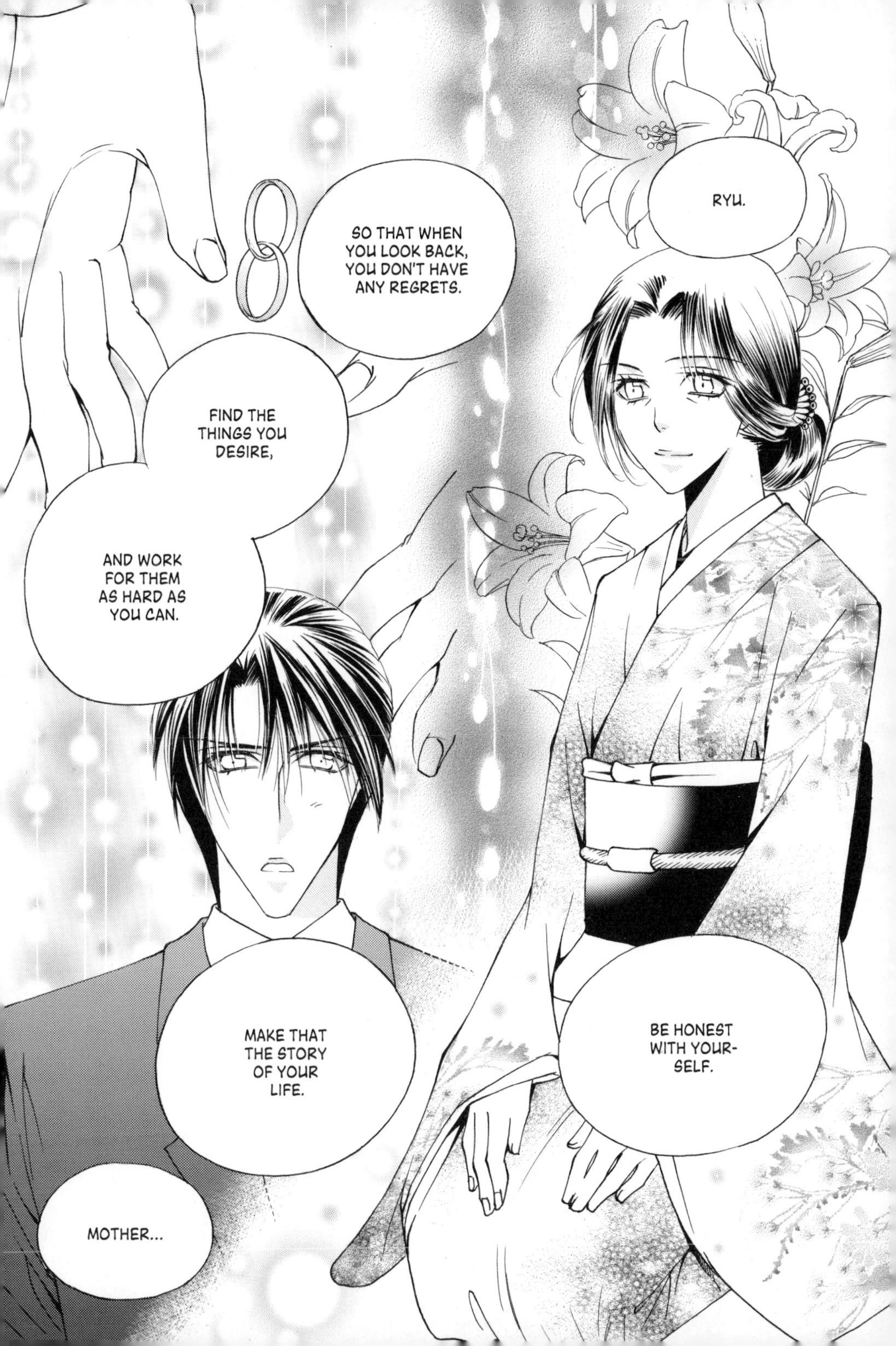
RYU.
SO THAT WHEN YOU LOOK BACK, YOU DON'T HAVE ANY REGRETS.
FIND THE THINGS YOU DESIRE,
AND WORK FOR THEM AS HARD AS YOU CAN.
BE HONEST WITH YOUR-SELF.
MAKE THAT THE STORY OF YOUR LIFE.
MOTHER...

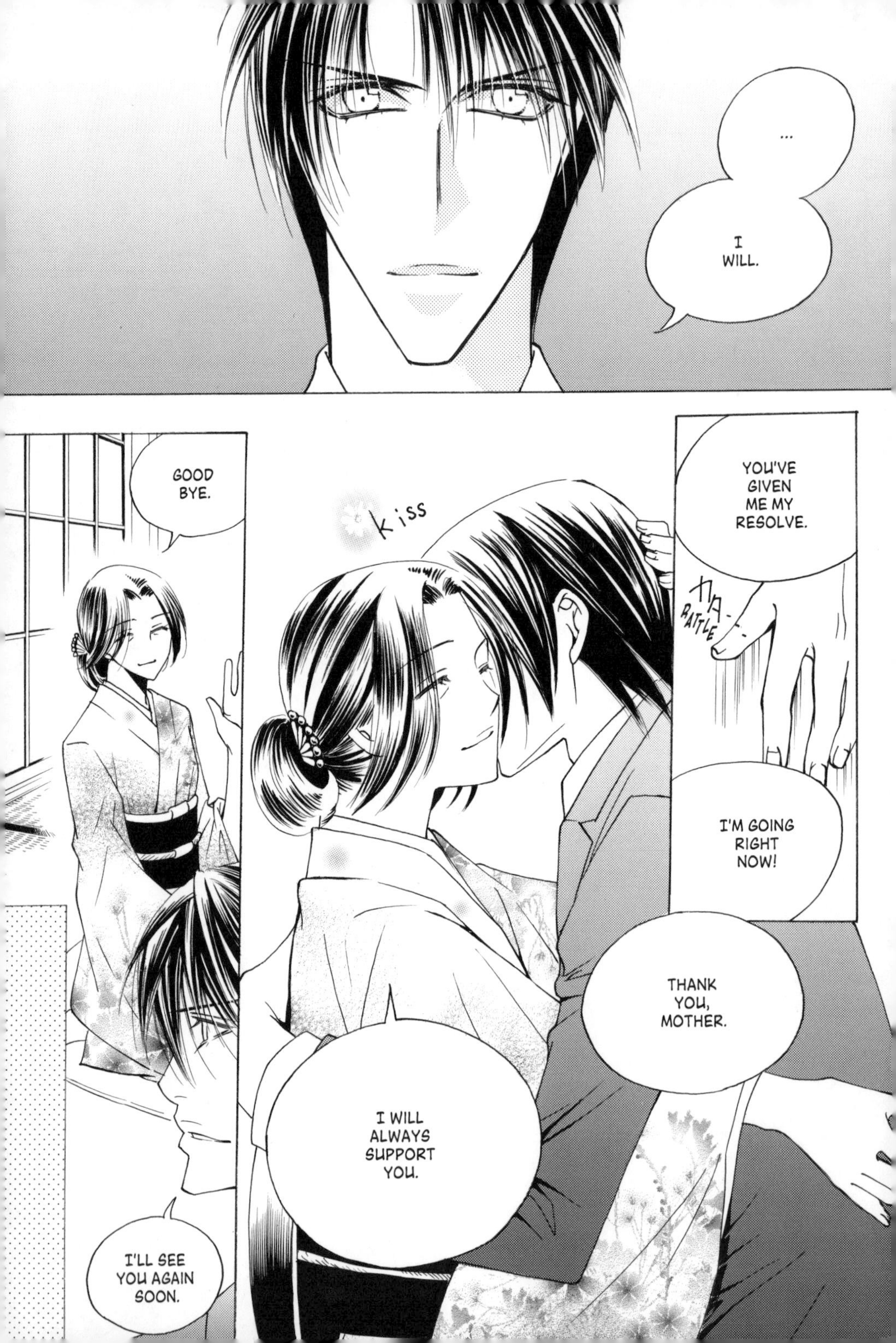
...
I WILL.
YOU'VE GIVEN ME MY RESOLVE.
RATTLE
I'M GOING RIGHT NOW!
kiss
THANK YOU, MOTHER.
I WILL ALWAYS SUPPORT YOU.
GOOD BYE.
I'LL SEE YOU AGAIN SOON.

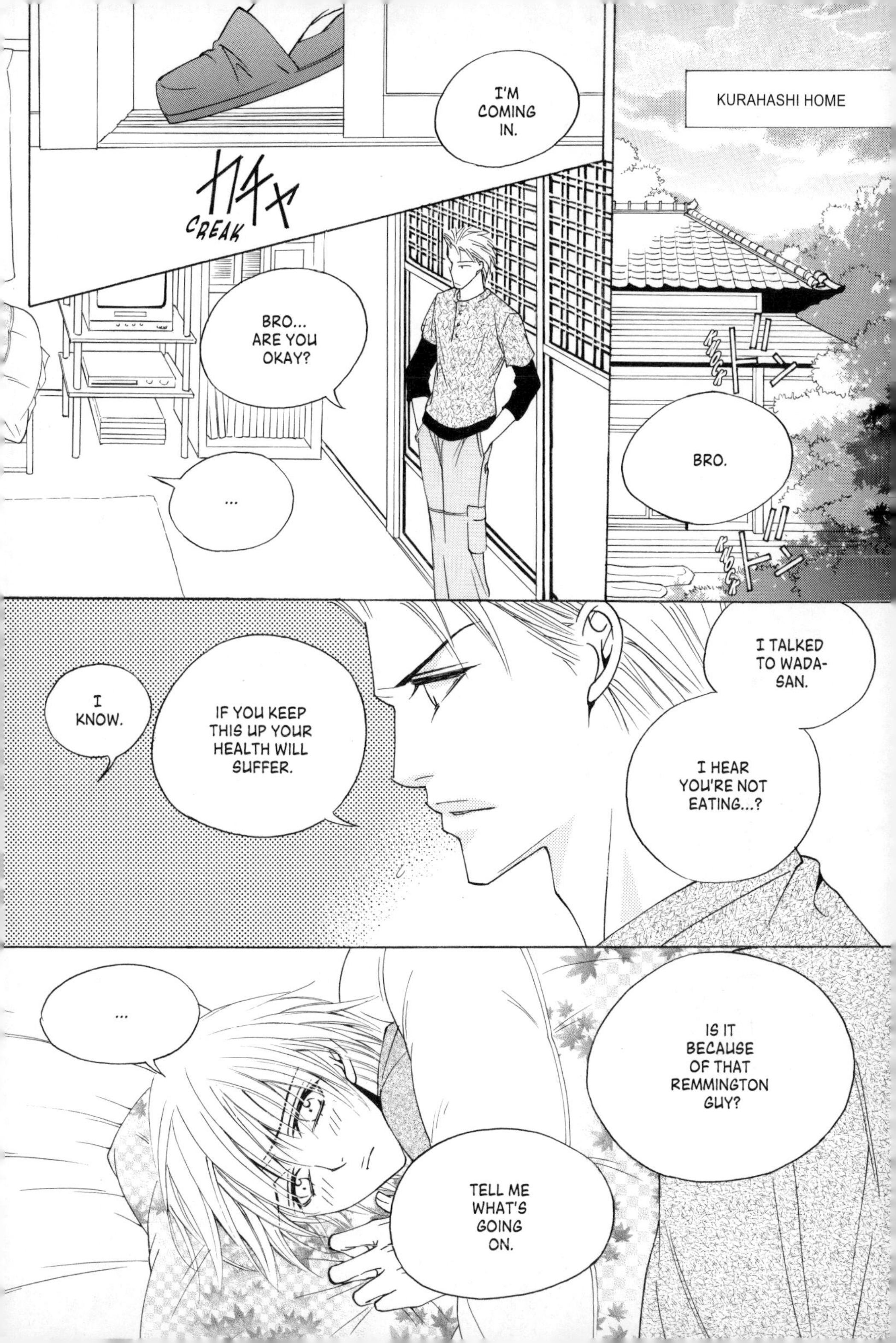
KURAHASHI HOME
KNOCK
BRO.
KNOCK
I'M COMING IN.
カチャ
CREAK
BRO... ARE YOU OKAY?
...
I TALKED TO WADA-SAN.
I HEAR YOU'RE NOT EATING...?
IF YOU KEEP THIS UP YOUR HEALTH WILL SUFFER.
I KNOW.
IS IT BECAUSE OF THAT REMMINGTON GUY?
...
TELL ME WHAT'S GOING ON.

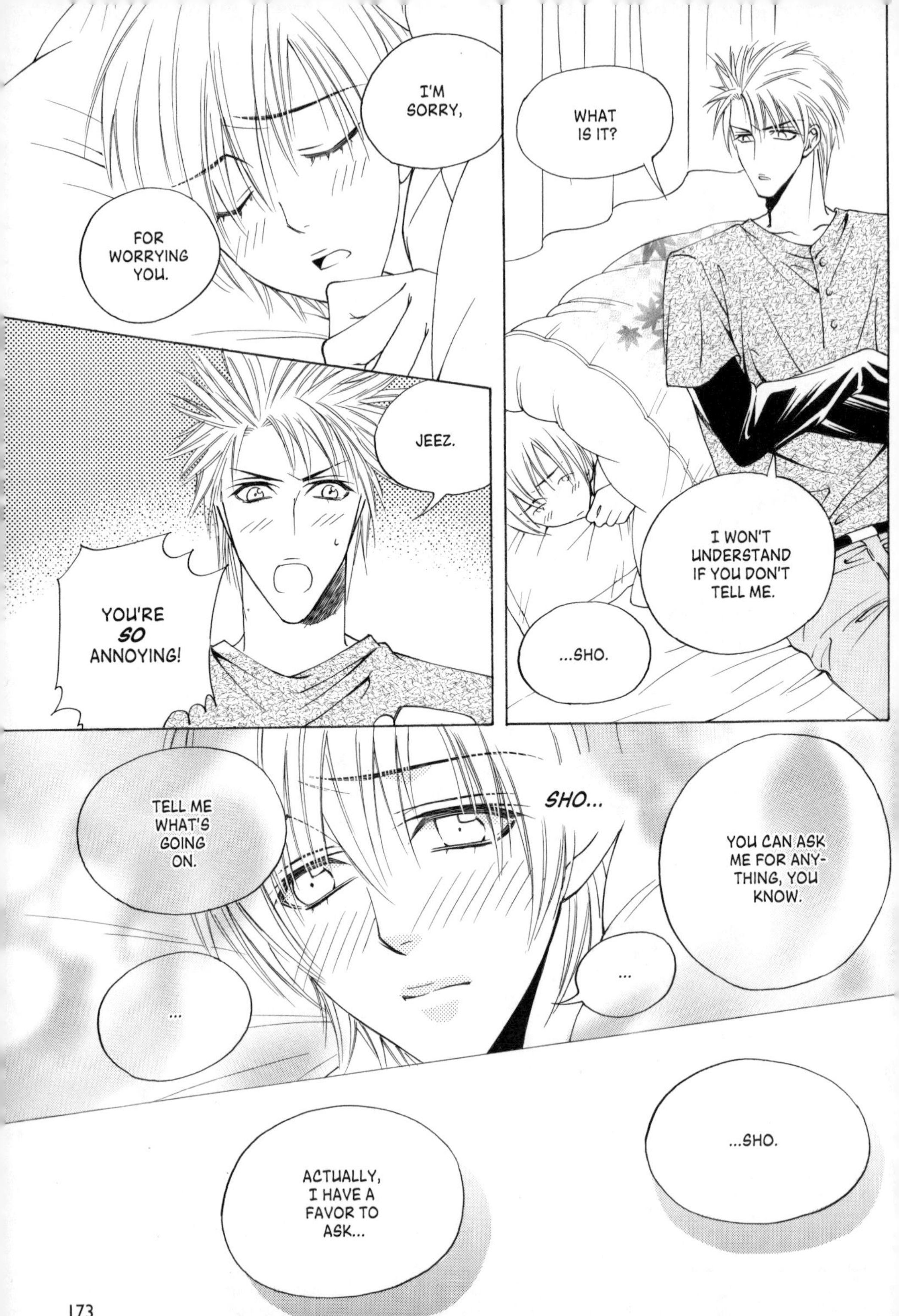
WHAT IS IT?
I WON'T UNDERSTAND IF YOU DON'T TELL ME.
...SHO.
I'M SORRY,
FOR WORRYING YOU.
JEEZ.
YOU'RE *SO* ANNOYING!
SHO...
YOU CAN ASK ME FOR ANYTHING, YOU KNOW.
TELL ME WHAT'S GOING ON.
...
...
...SHO.
ACTUALLY, I HAVE A FAVOR TO ASK...

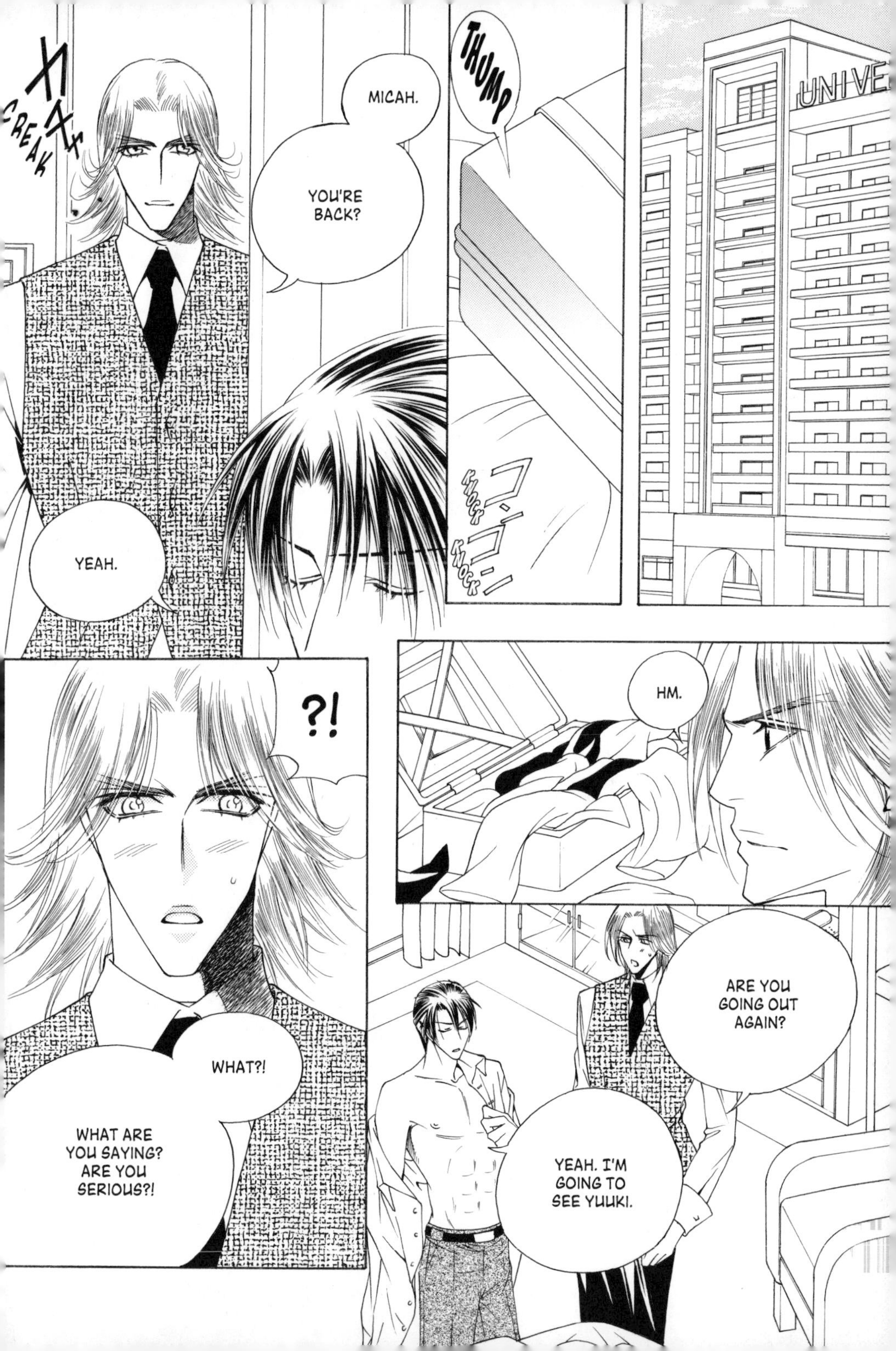
UNIVE
THUMP
KNOCK
KNOCK
MICAH.
YOU'RE BACK?
CREAK
YEAH.
HM.
ARE YOU GOING OUT AGAIN?
YEAH. I'M GOING TO SEE YUUKI.
?!
WHAT?!
WHAT ARE YOU SAYING? ARE YOU SERIOUS?!

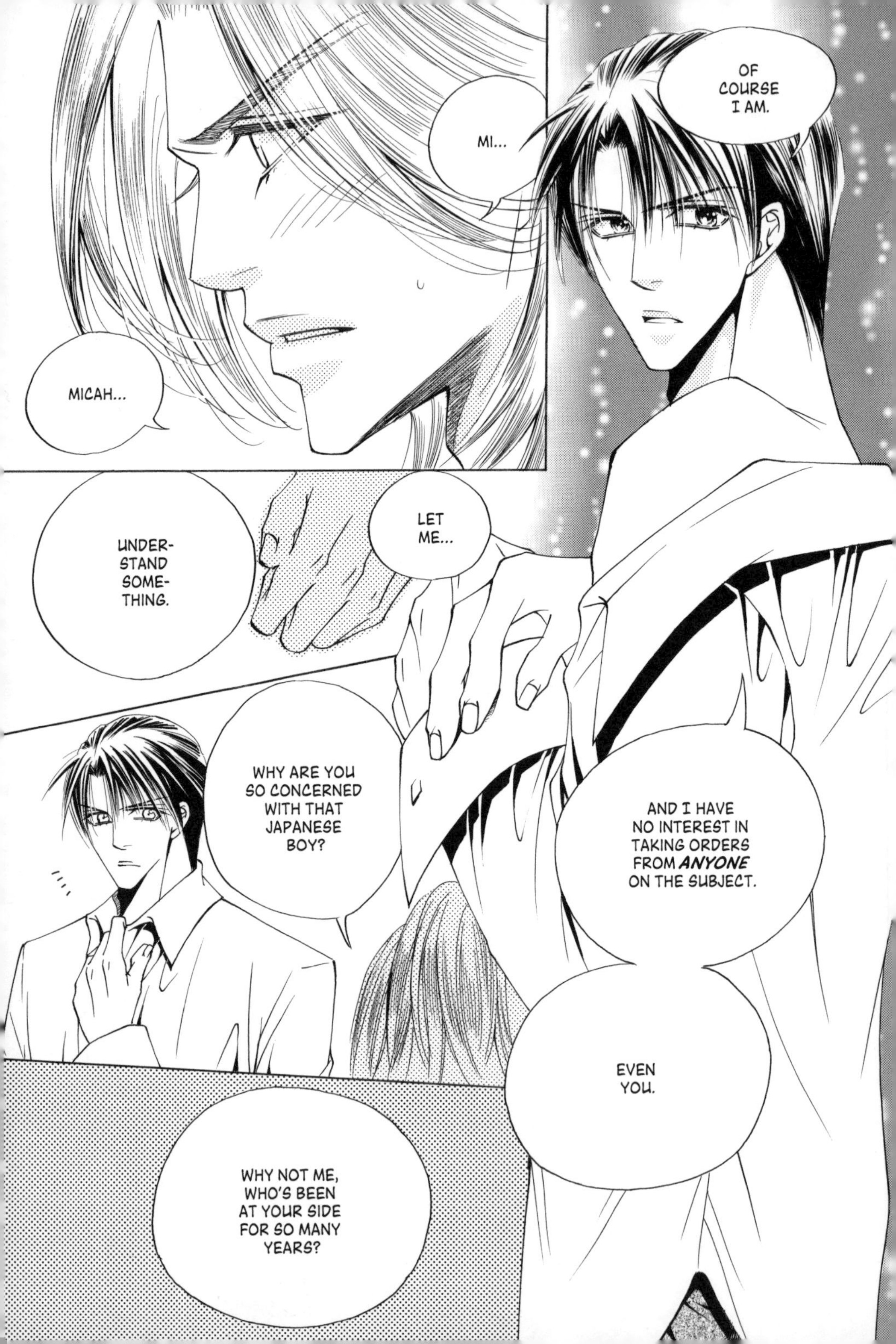

OF COURSE I AM.
MI...
MICAH...
LET ME...
UNDER-STAND SOME-THING.
WHY ARE YOU SO CONCERNED WITH THAT JAPANESE BOY?
WHY NOT ME, WHO'S BEEN AT YOUR SIDE FOR SO MANY YEARS?
AND I HAVE NO INTEREST IN TAKING ORDERS FROM ***ANYONE*** ON THE SUBJECT.
EVEN YOU.

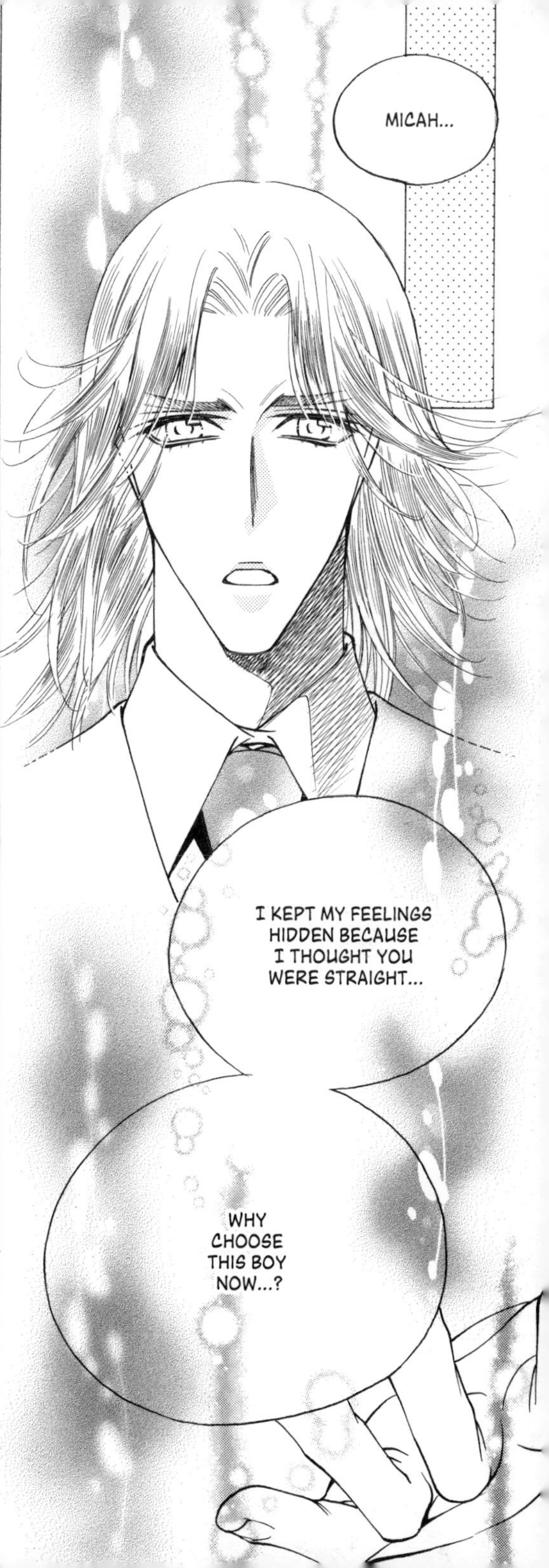
MICAH...
I KEPT MY FEELINGS HIDDEN BECAUSE I THOUGHT YOU WERE STRAIGHT...
WHY CHOOSE THIS BOY NOW...?
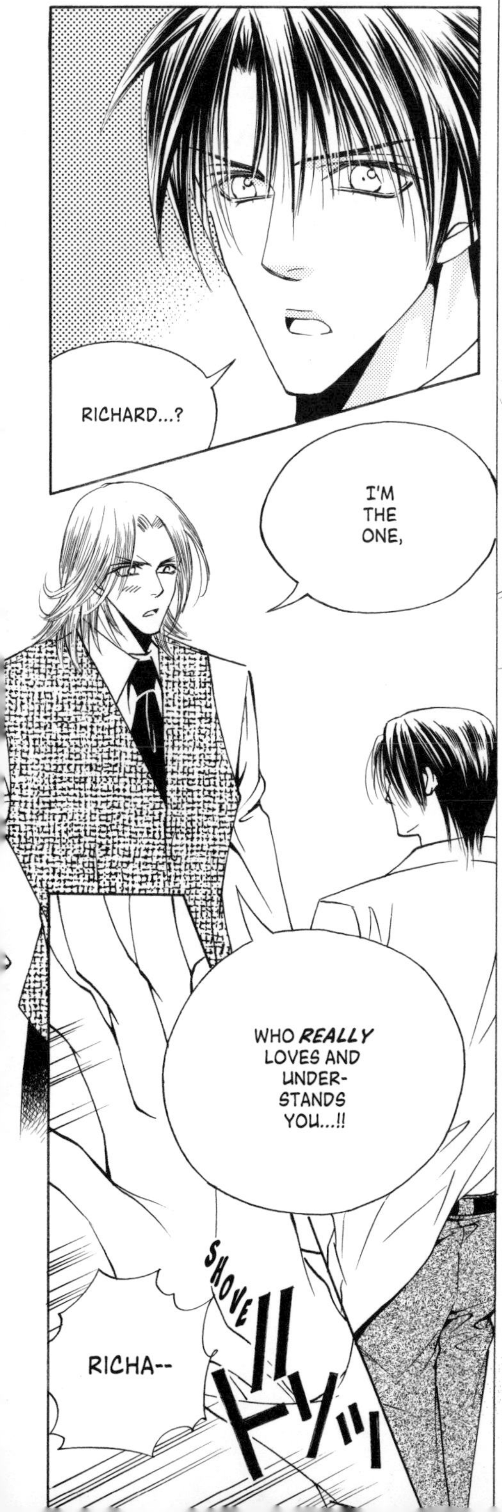
RICHARD...?
I'M THE ONE,
WHO *REALLY* LOVES AND UNDER-STANDS YOU...!!
SHOVE
RICHA--

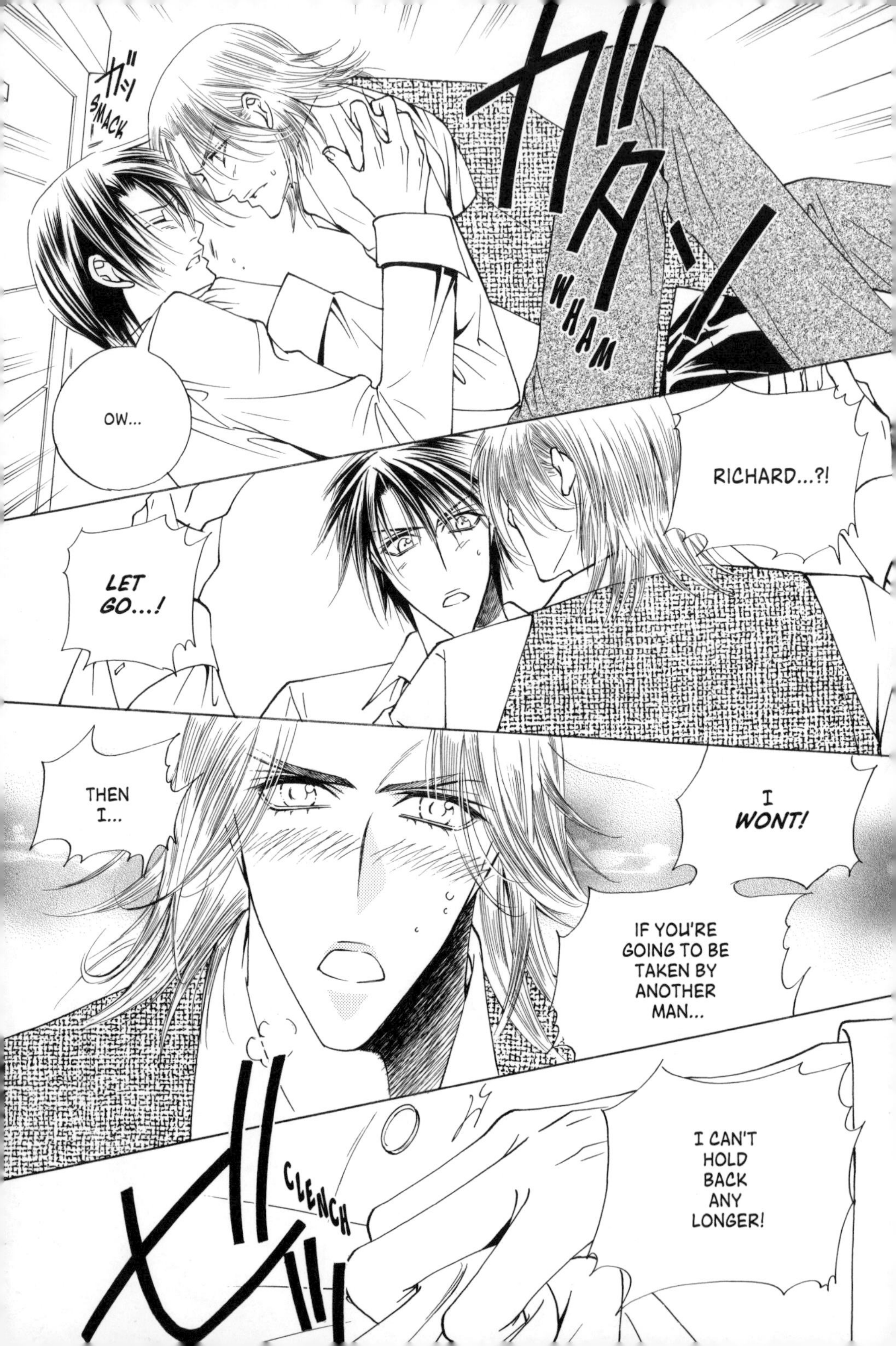
WHAM
ガッ
SMACK
OW...
RICHARD...?!
LET GO...!
I WONT!
IF YOU'RE GOING TO BE TAKEN BY ANOTHER MAN...
THEN I...
I CAN'T HOLD BACK ANY LONGER!
CLENCH

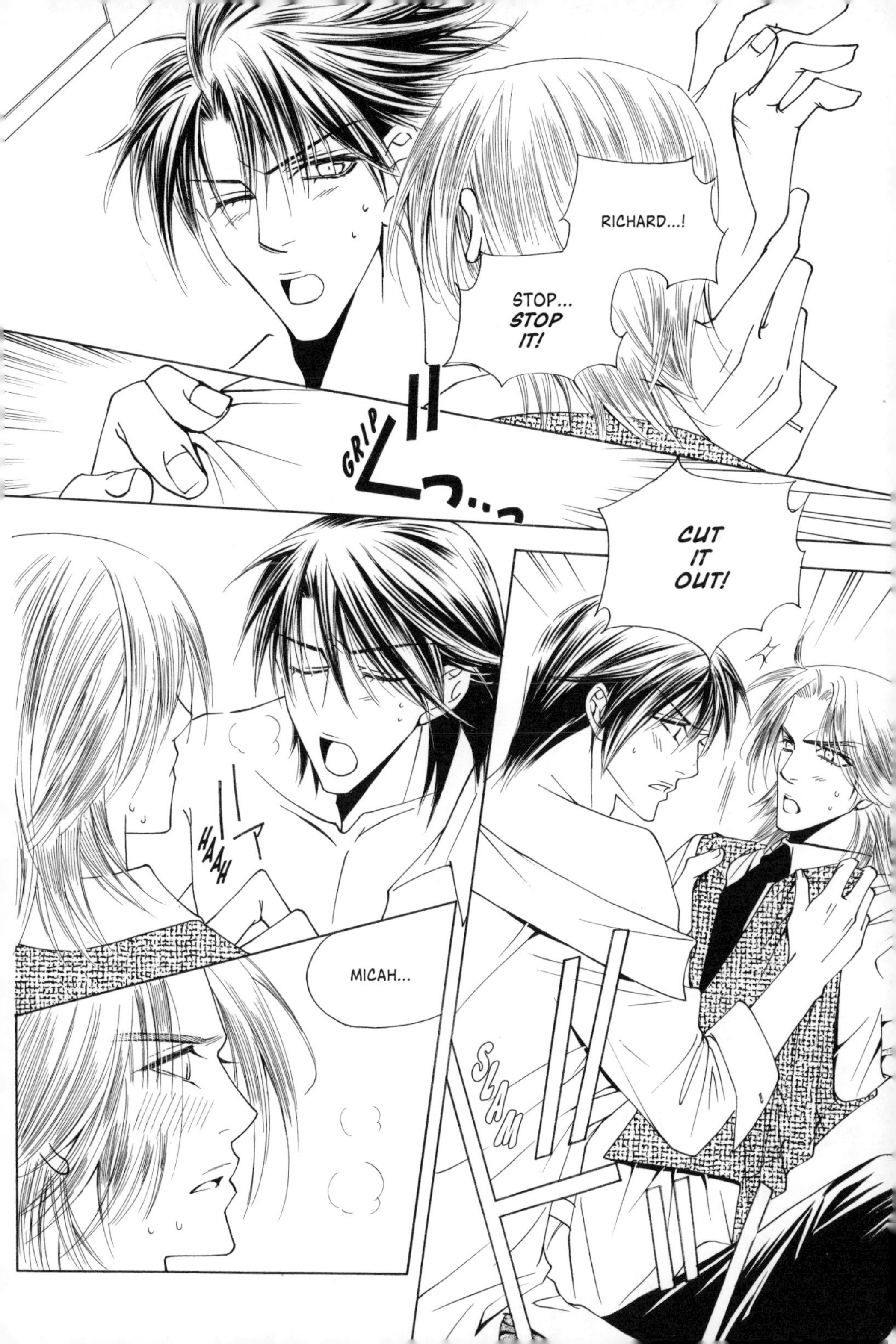
RICHARD...!
STOP... STOP IT!
GRIP
CUT IT OUT!
SLAM
HAAH
MICAH...

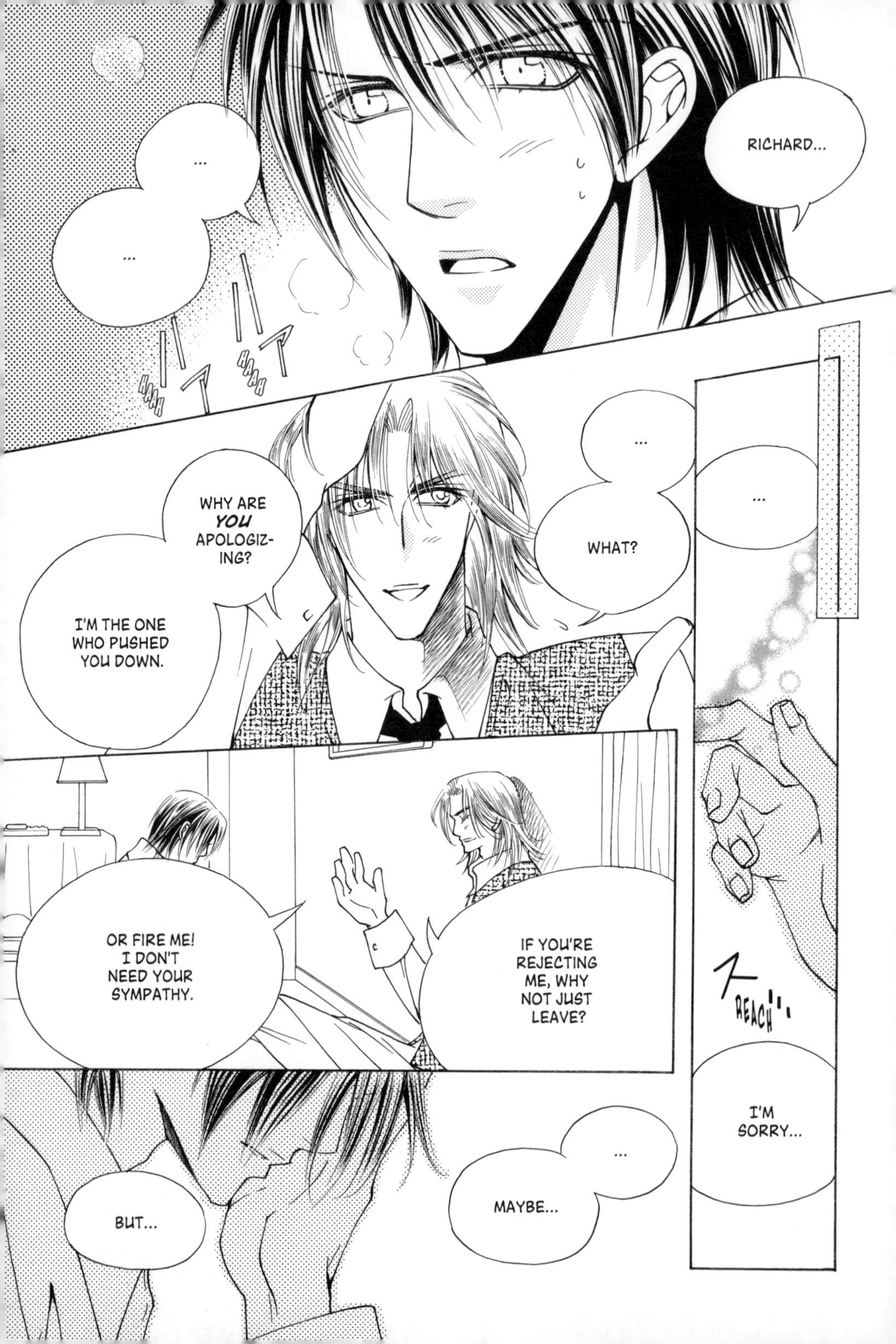
RICHARD...
...
...
HAAH
HAAH
...
REACH
I'M SORRY...
...
WHAT?
WHY ARE YOU APOLOGIZING?
I'M THE ONE WHO PUSHED YOU DOWN.
IF YOU'RE REJECTING ME, WHY NOT JUST LEAVE?
OR FIRE ME! I DON'T NEED YOUR SYMPATHY.
...
MAYBE...
BUT...

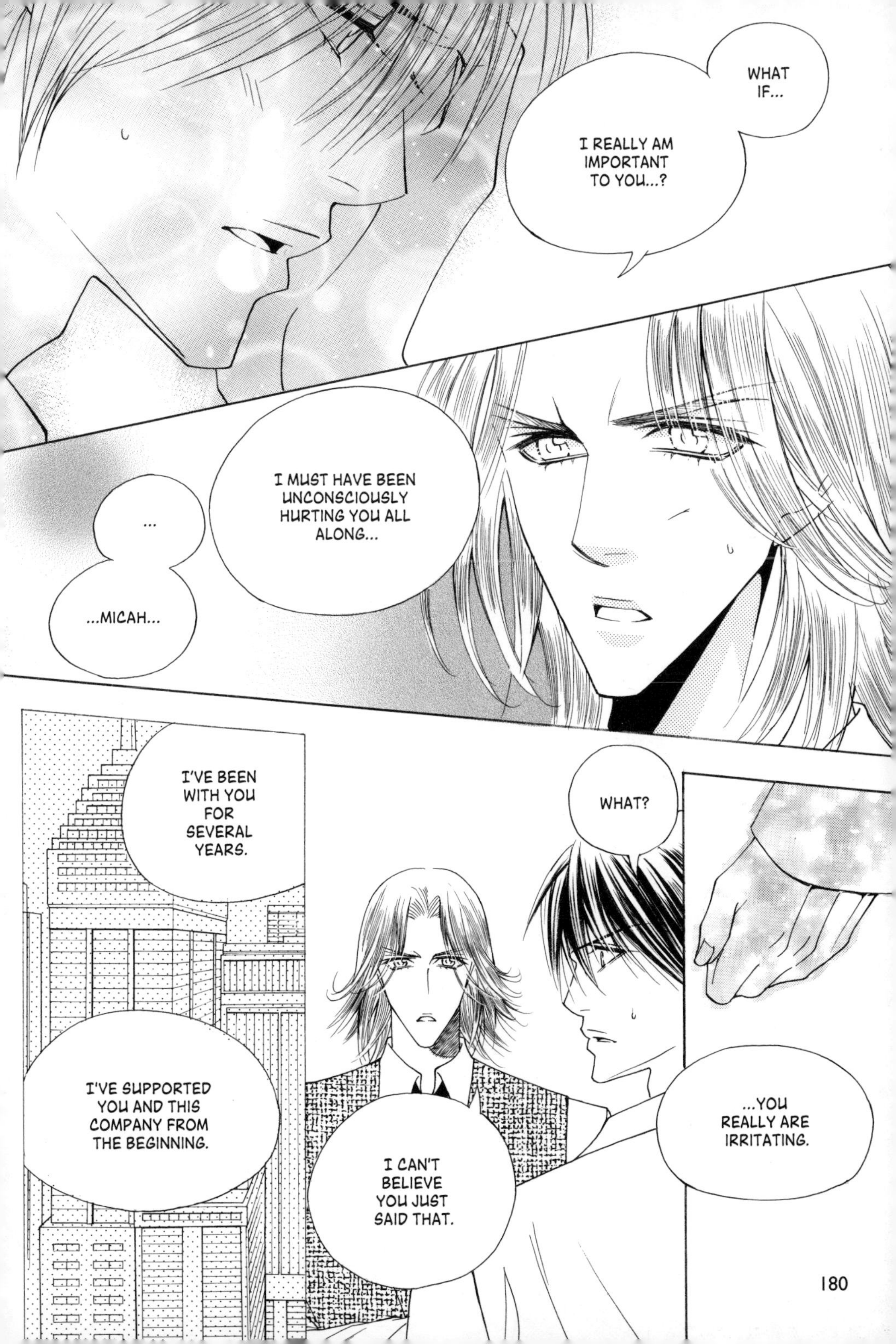
WHAT IF...
I REALLY AM IMPORTANT TO YOU...?
I MUST HAVE BEEN UNCONSCIOUSLY HURTING YOU ALL ALONG...
...
...MICAH...
WHAT?
...YOU REALLY ARE IRRITATING.
I CAN'T BELIEVE YOU JUST SAID THAT.
I'VE BEEN WITH YOU FOR SEVERAL YEARS.
I'VE SUPPORTED YOU AND THIS COMPANY FROM THE BEGINNING.

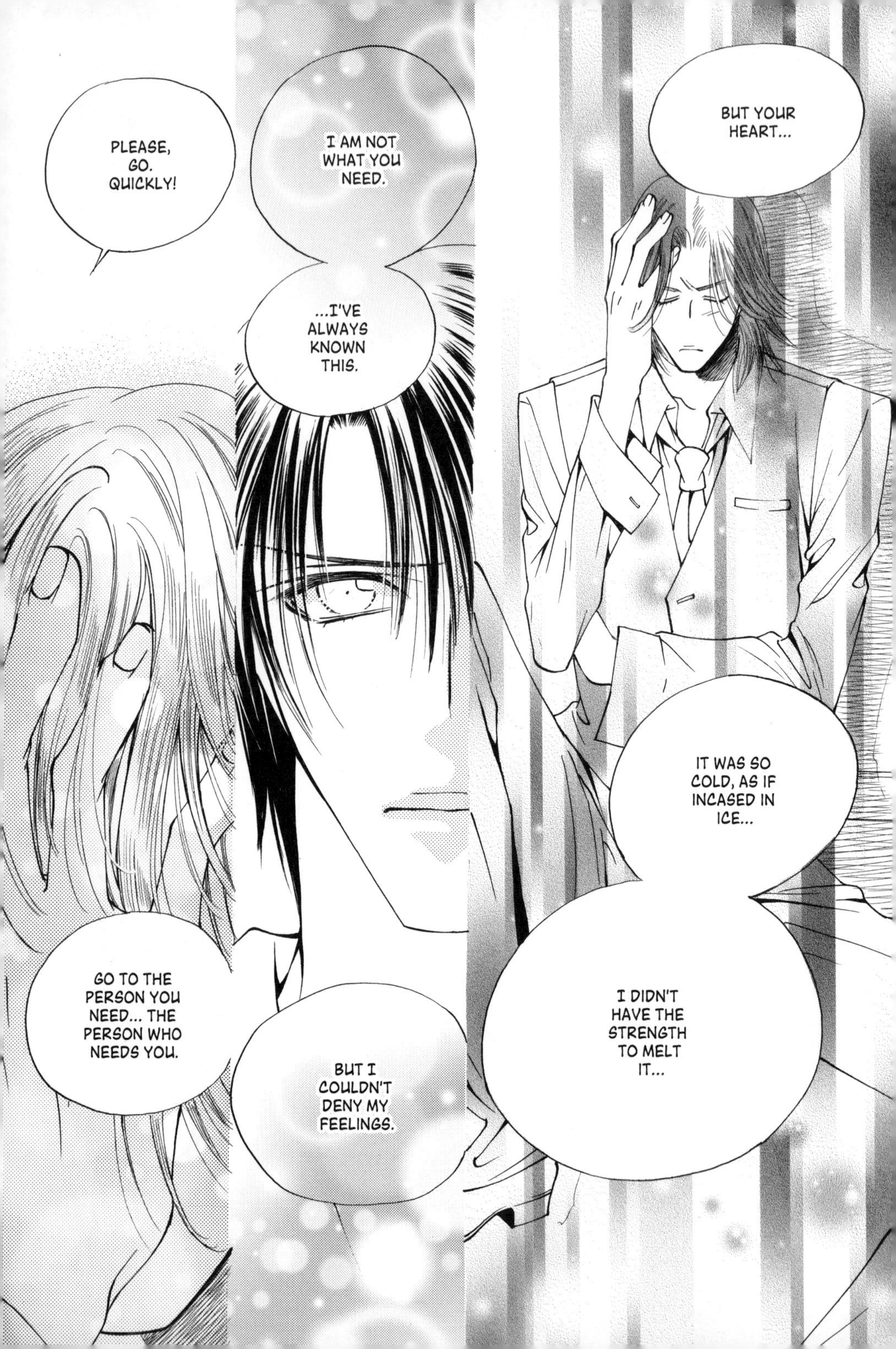
BUT YOUR HEART...
IT WAS SO COLD, AS IF INCASED IN ICE...
I DIDN'T HAVE THE STRENGTH TO MELT IT...
I AM NOT WHAT YOU NEED.
...I'VE ALWAYS KNOWN THIS.
BUT I COULDN'T DENY MY FEELINGS.
PLEASE, GO. QUICKLY!
GO TO THE PERSON YOU NEED... THE PERSON WHO NEEDS YOU.

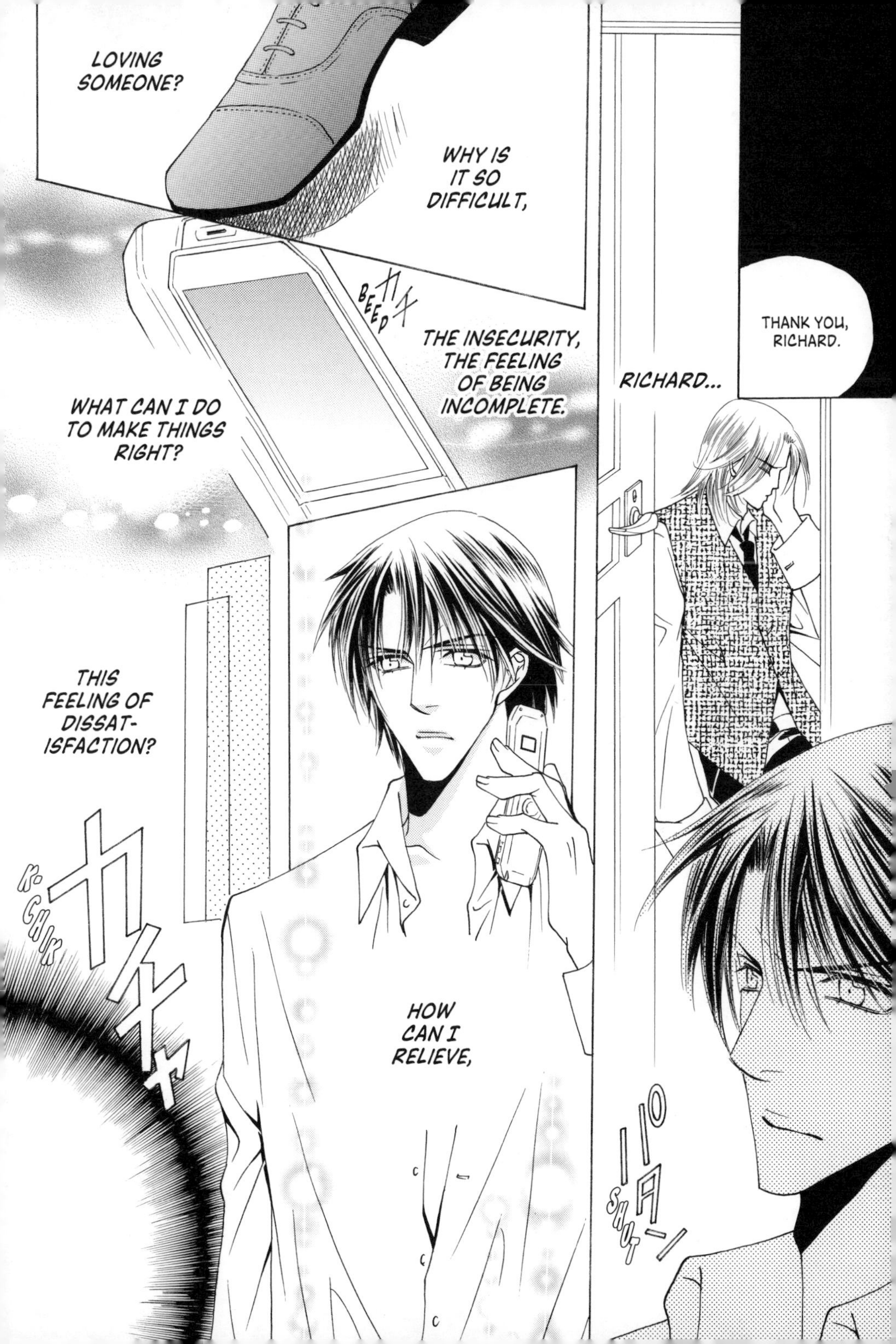
THANK YOU, RICHARD.
RICHARD...
SHUT
LOVING SOMEONE?
WHY IS IT SO DIFFICULT,
BEEP
THE INSECURITY, THE FEELING OF BEING INCOMPLETE.
WHAT CAN I DO TO MAKE THINGS RIGHT?
HOW CAN I RELIEVE,
THIS FEELING OF DISSAT-ISFACTION?
K-CHIK

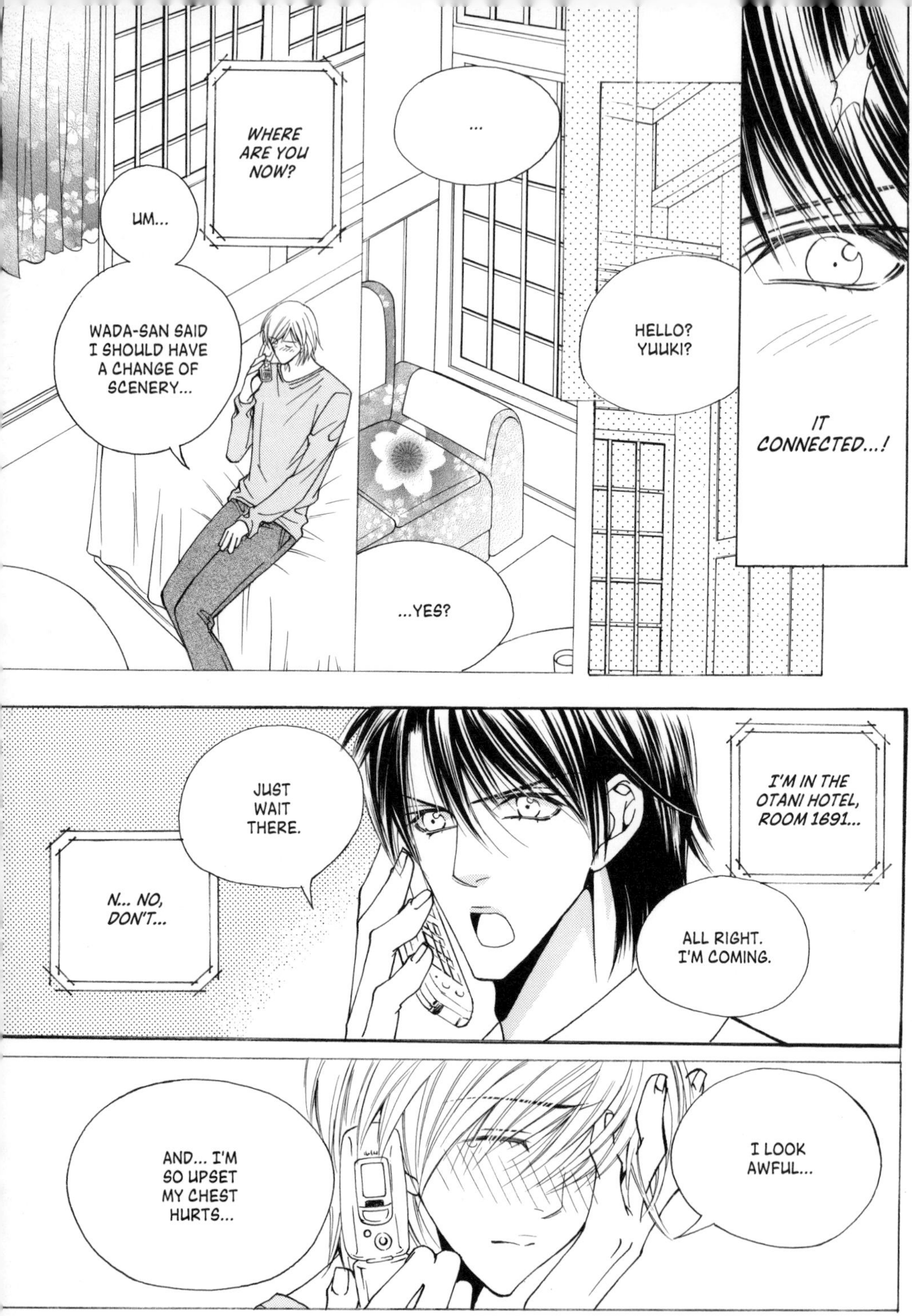
IT CONNECTED...!
HELLO? YUUKI?
...
...YES?
WHERE ARE YOU NOW?
UM...
WADA-SAN SAID I SHOULD HAVE A CHANGE OF SCENERY...
I'M IN THE OTANI HOTEL, ROOM 1691...
ALL RIGHT. I'M COMING.
JUST WAIT THERE.
N... NO, DON'T...
I LOOK AWFUL...
AND... I'M SO UPSET MY CHEST HURTS...

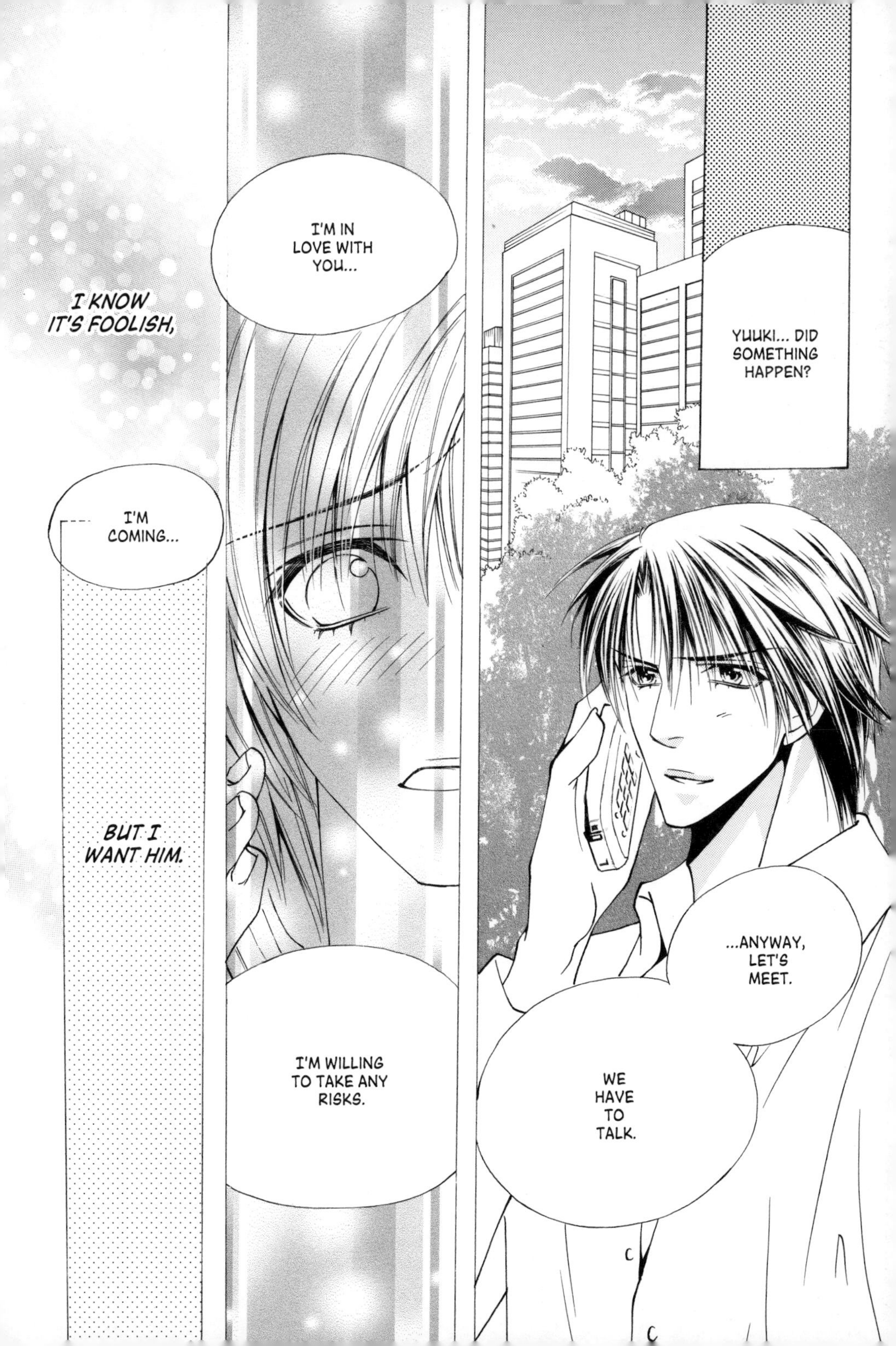
YUUKI... DID SOMETHING HAPPEN?
...ANYWAY, LET'S MEET.
WE HAVE TO TALK.
I'M IN LOVE WITH YOU...
I'M WILLING TO TAKE ANY RISKS.
I KNOW IT'S FOOLISH,
I'M COMING...
BUT I WANT HIM.

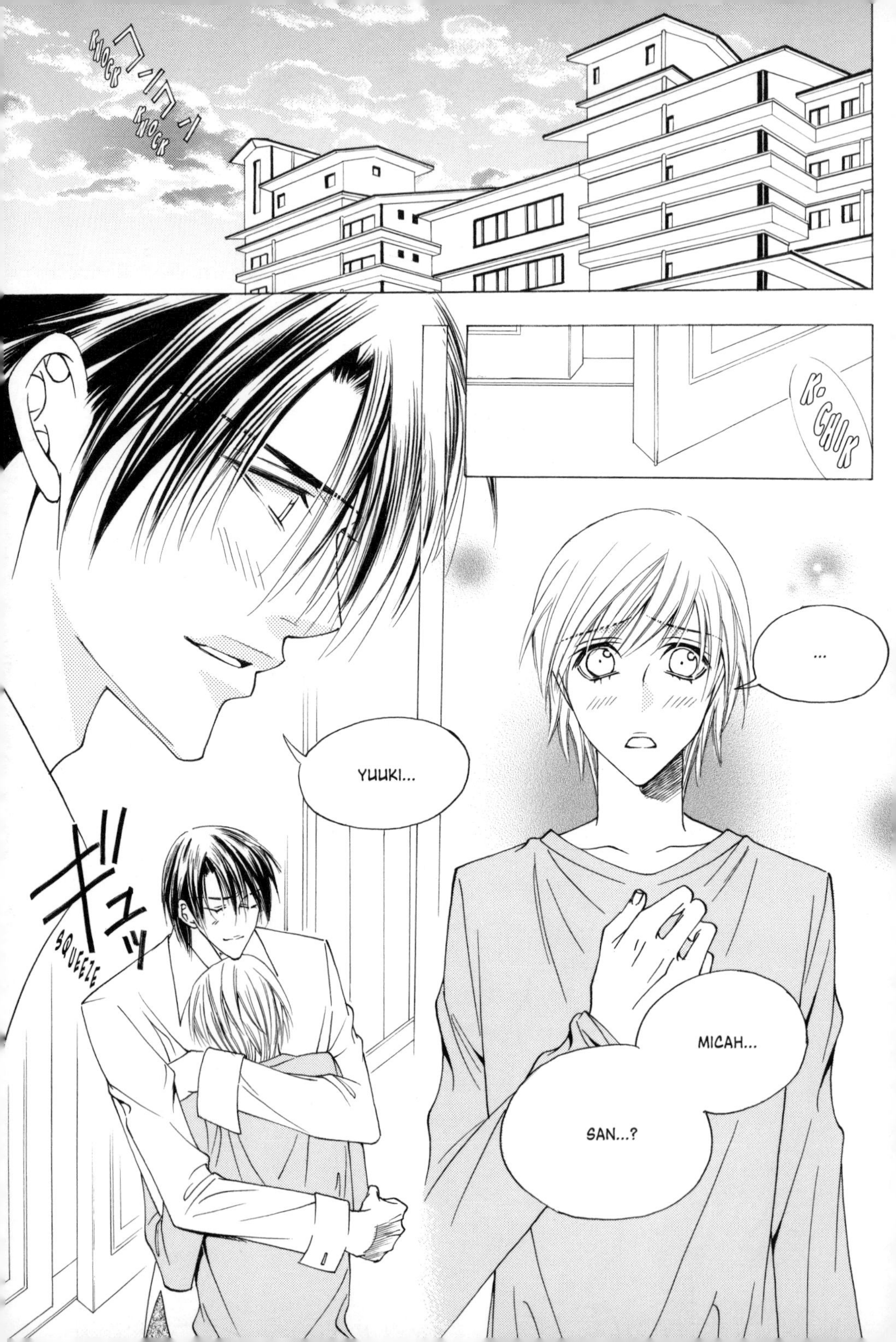
KNOCK KNOCK
K-CHIK
...
YUUKI...
MICAH...
SAN...?
ギュッ
SQUEEZE

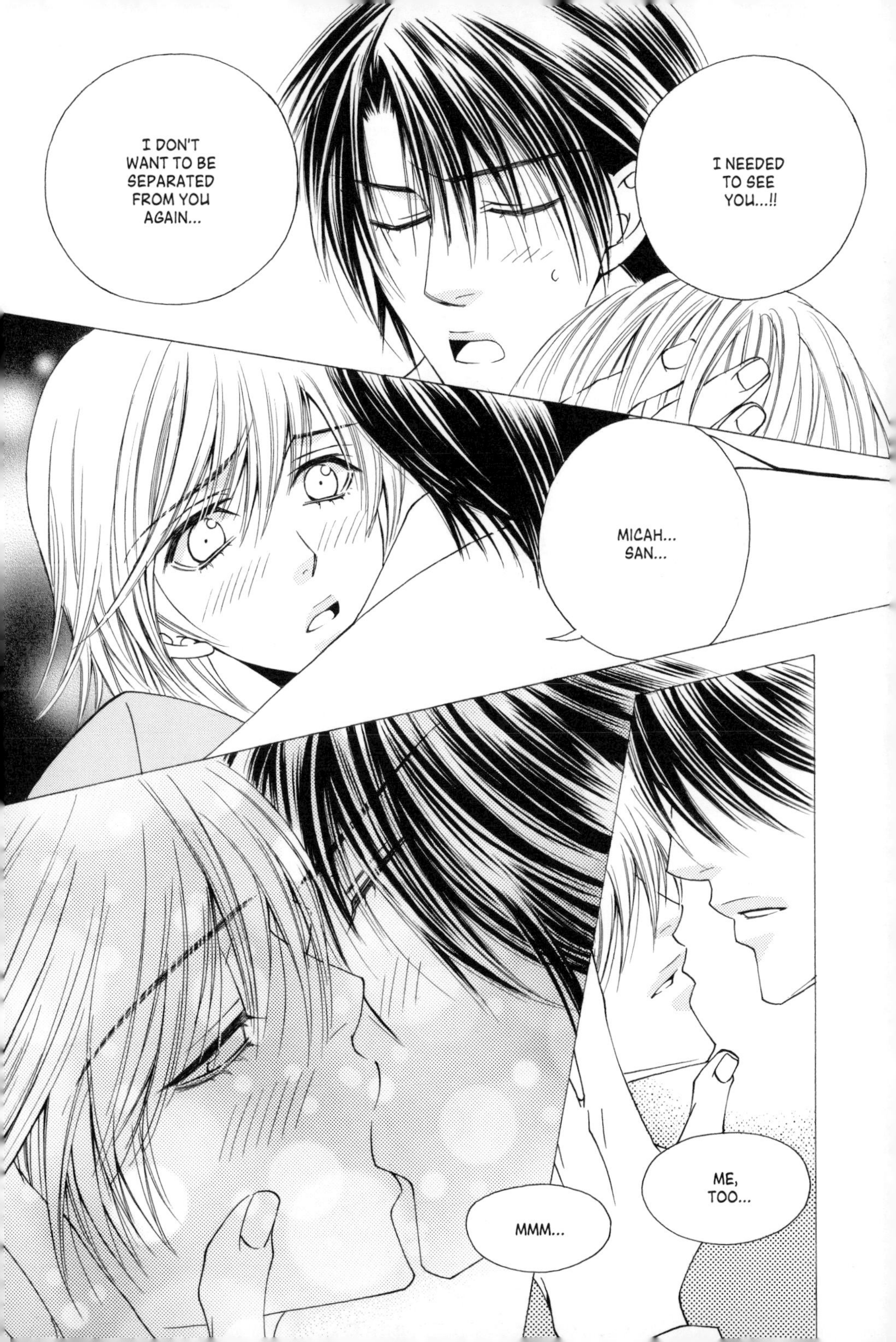
I NEEDED TO SEE YOU...!!
I DON'T WANT TO BE SEPARATED FROM YOU AGAIN...
MICAH... SAN...
ME, TOO...
MMM...

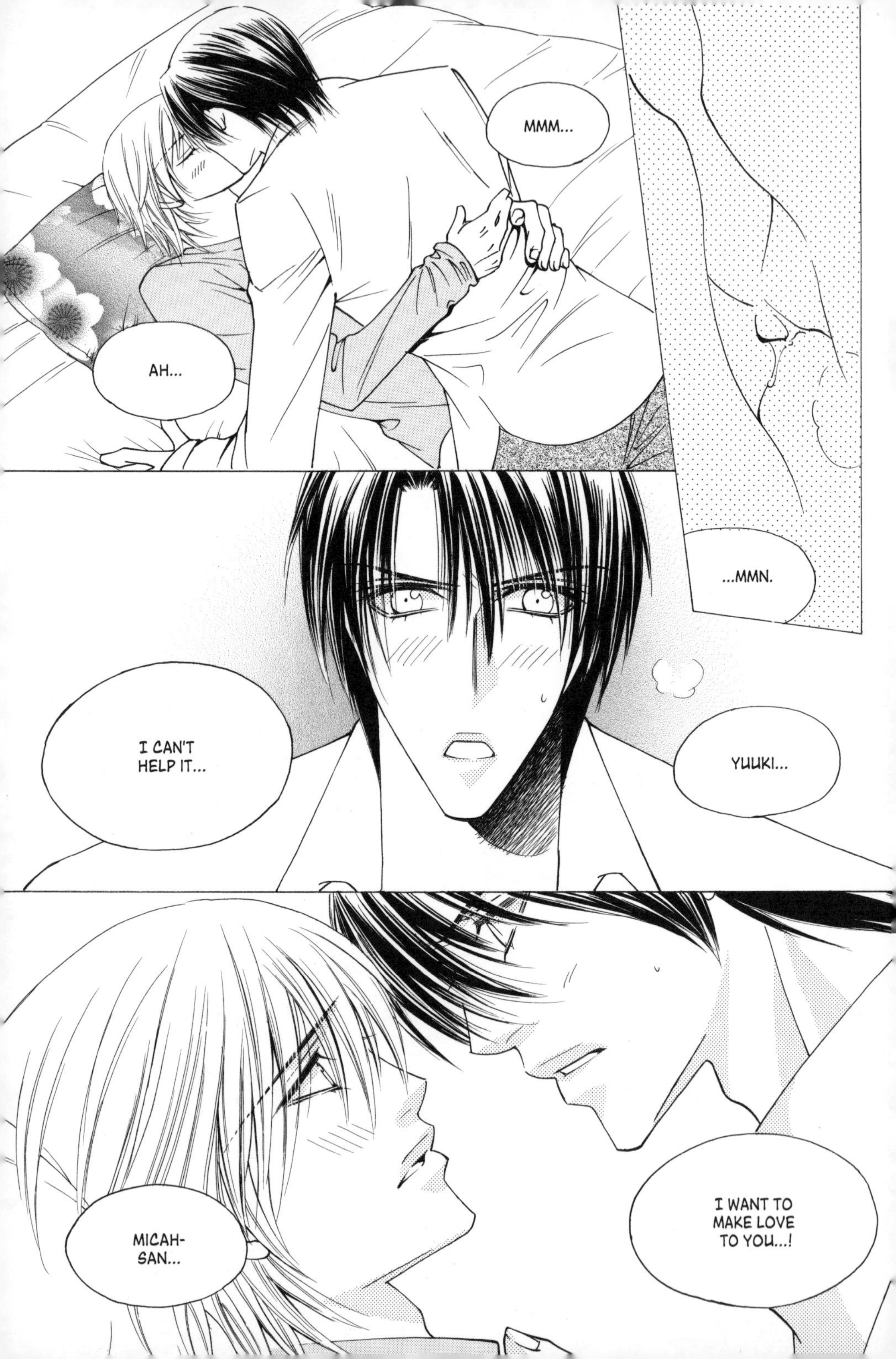
MMM...
AH...
...MMN.
YUUKI...
I CAN'T HELP IT...
I WANT TO MAKE LOVE TO YOU...!
MICAH-SAN...

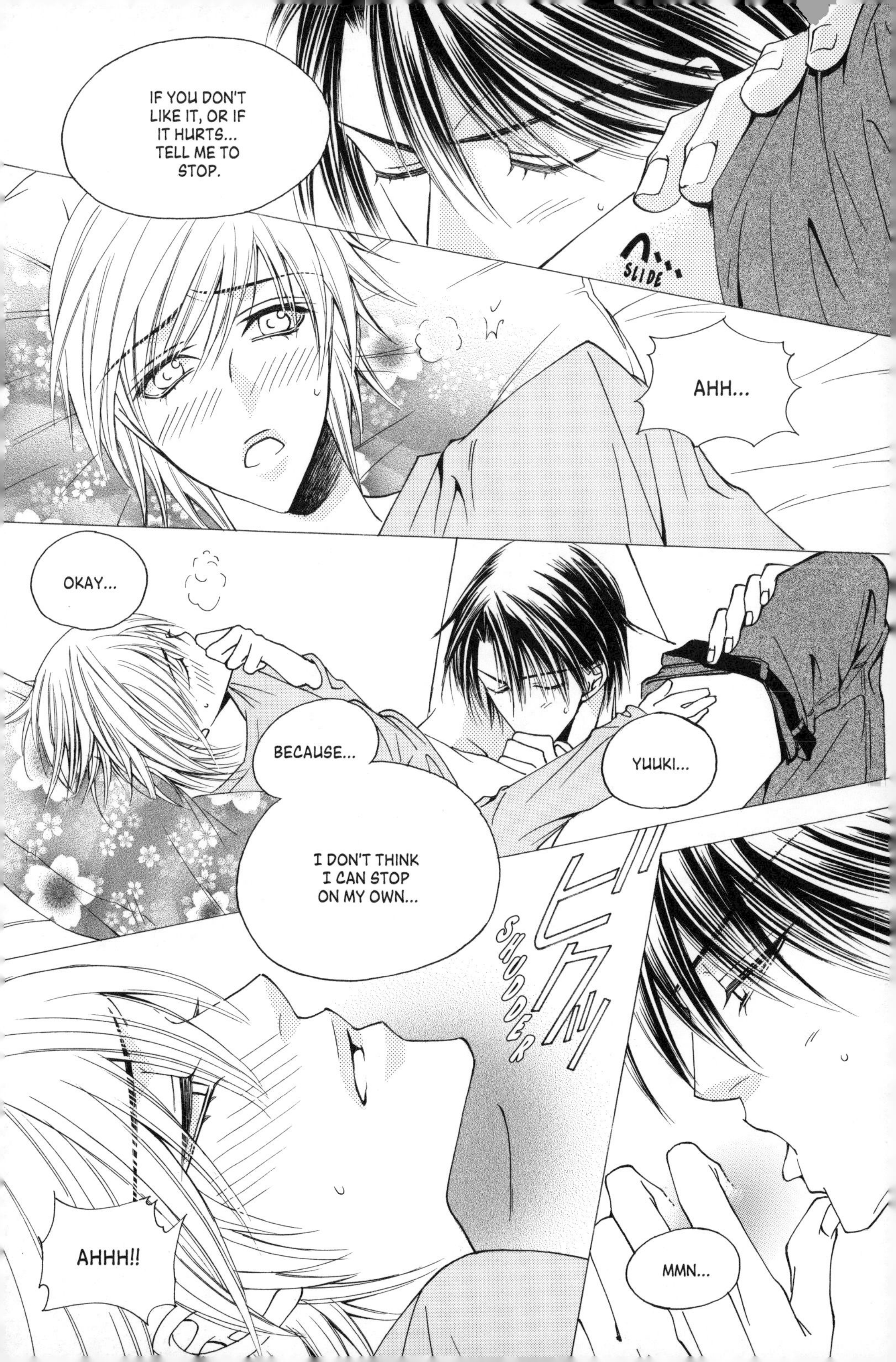
IF YOU DON'T LIKE IT, OR IF IT HURTS... TELL ME TO STOP.
SLIDE
AHH...
YUUKI...
OKAY...
BECAUSE...
I DON'T THINK I CAN STOP ON MY OWN...
MMN...
SHUDDER
AHHH!!

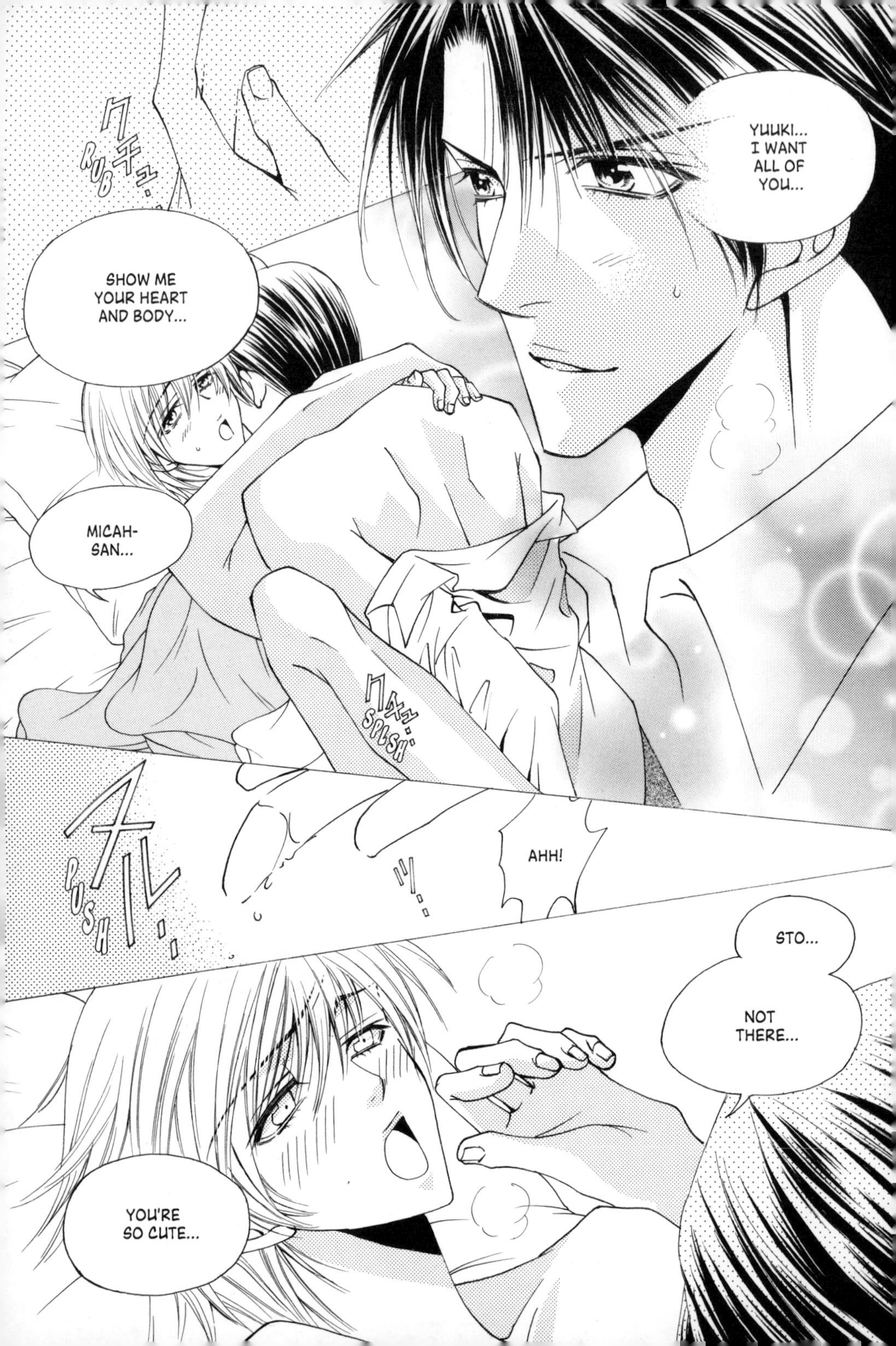
YUUKI... I WANT ALL OF YOU...
クチュ
RUB
SHOW ME YOUR HEART AND BODY...
MICAH-SAN...
クチュ
SPLSH
AHH!
ツ
グル
PUSH
STO...
NOT THERE...
YOU'RE SO CUTE...

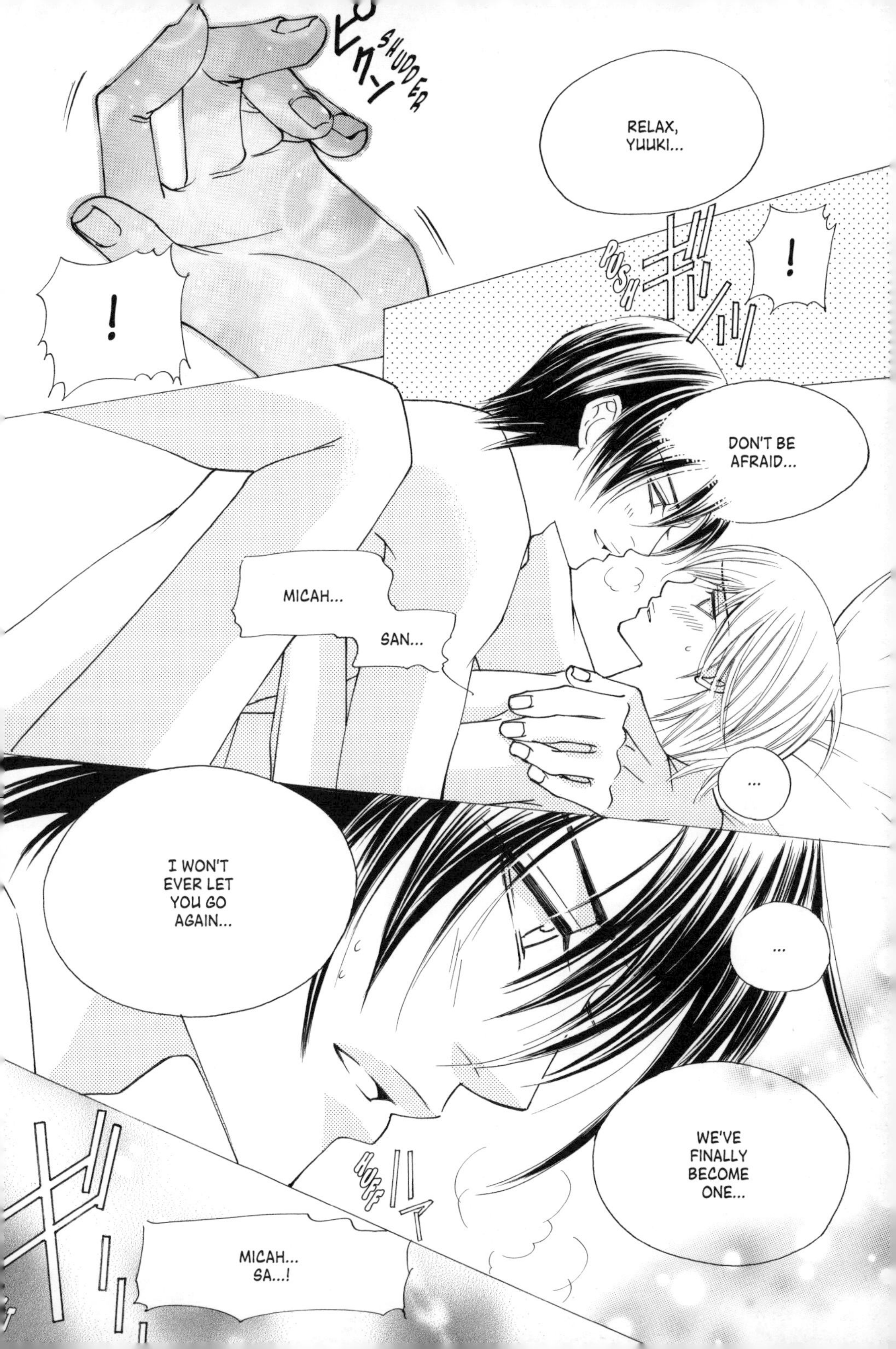
RELAX, YUUKI...
PUSH
!
SHUDDER
!
DON'T BE AFRAID...
MICAH...
SAN...
...
...
I WON'T EVER LET YOU GO AGAIN...
WE'VE FINALLY BECOME ONE...
HUFF
MICAH... SA...!

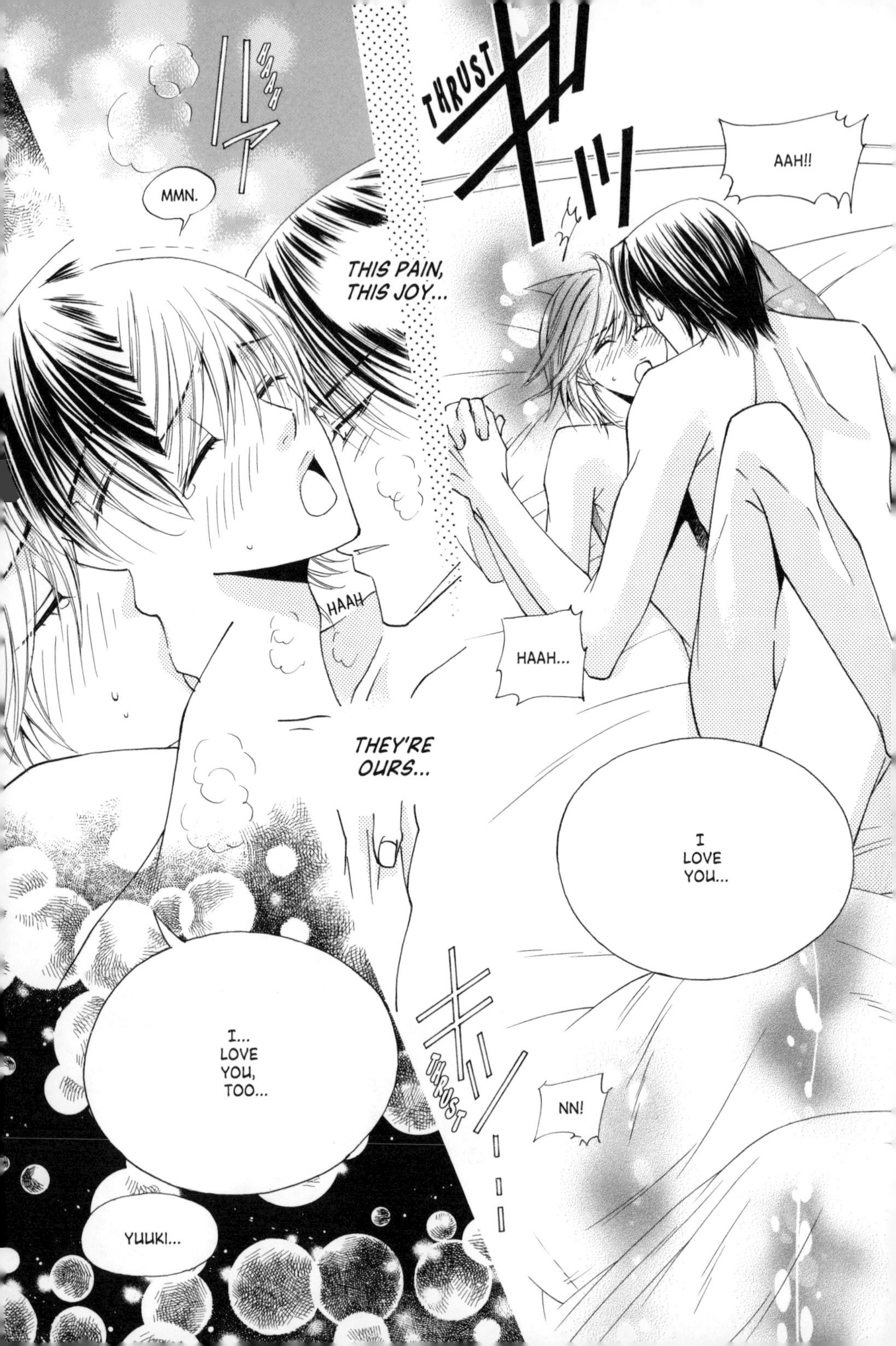
THRUST
AAH!!
HAAH...
I LOVE YOU...
THRUST
NN!
HAAAH
MMN.
THIS PAIN, THIS JOY...
HAAH
THEY'RE OURS...
I... LOVE YOU, TOO...
YUUKI...

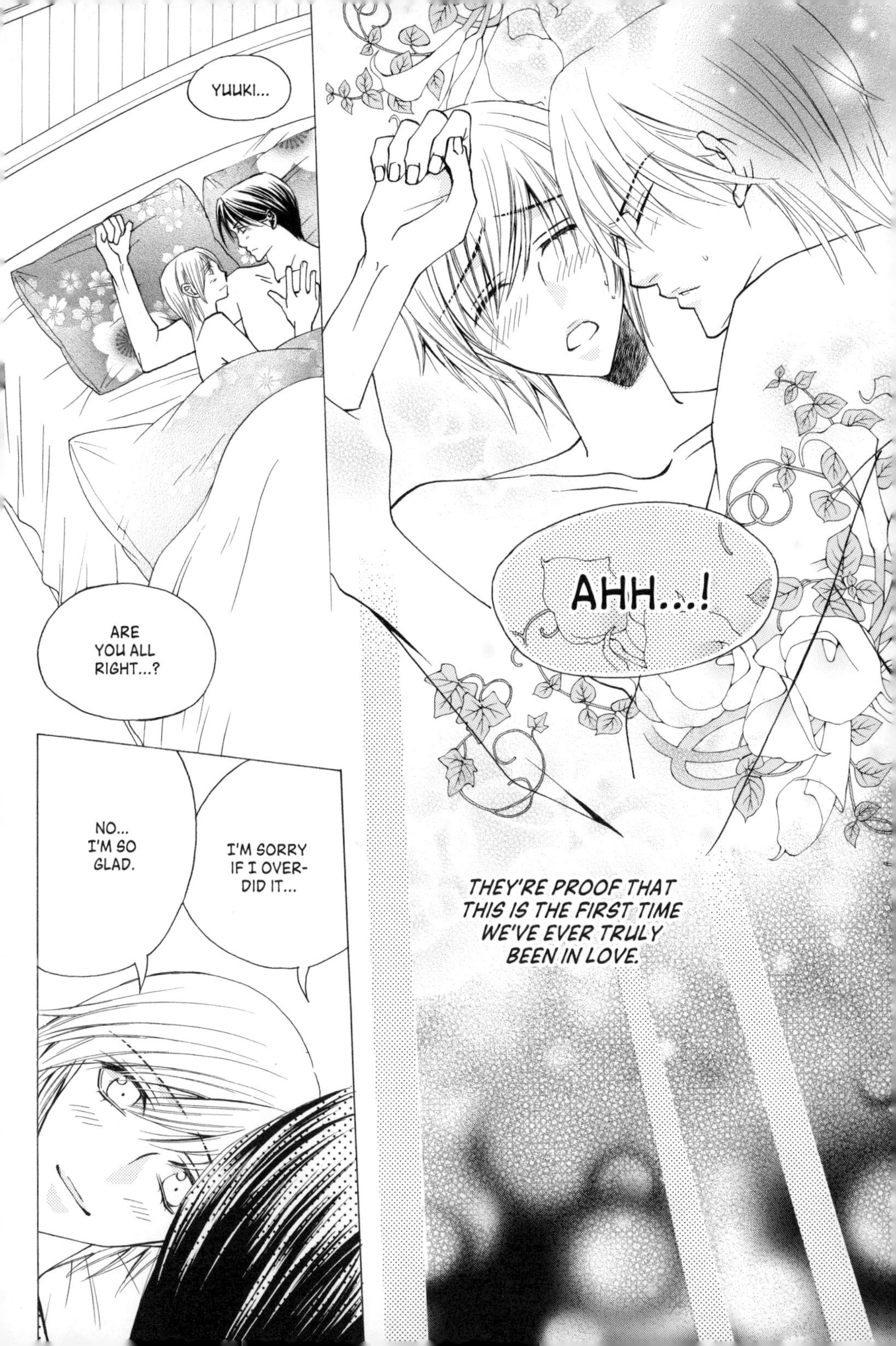
AHH...!
THEY'RE PROOF THAT THIS IS THE FIRST TIME WE'VE EVER TRULY BEEN IN LOVE.
YUUKI...
ARE YOU ALL RIGHT...?
I'M SORRY IF I OVER-DID IT...
NO... I'M SO GLAD.

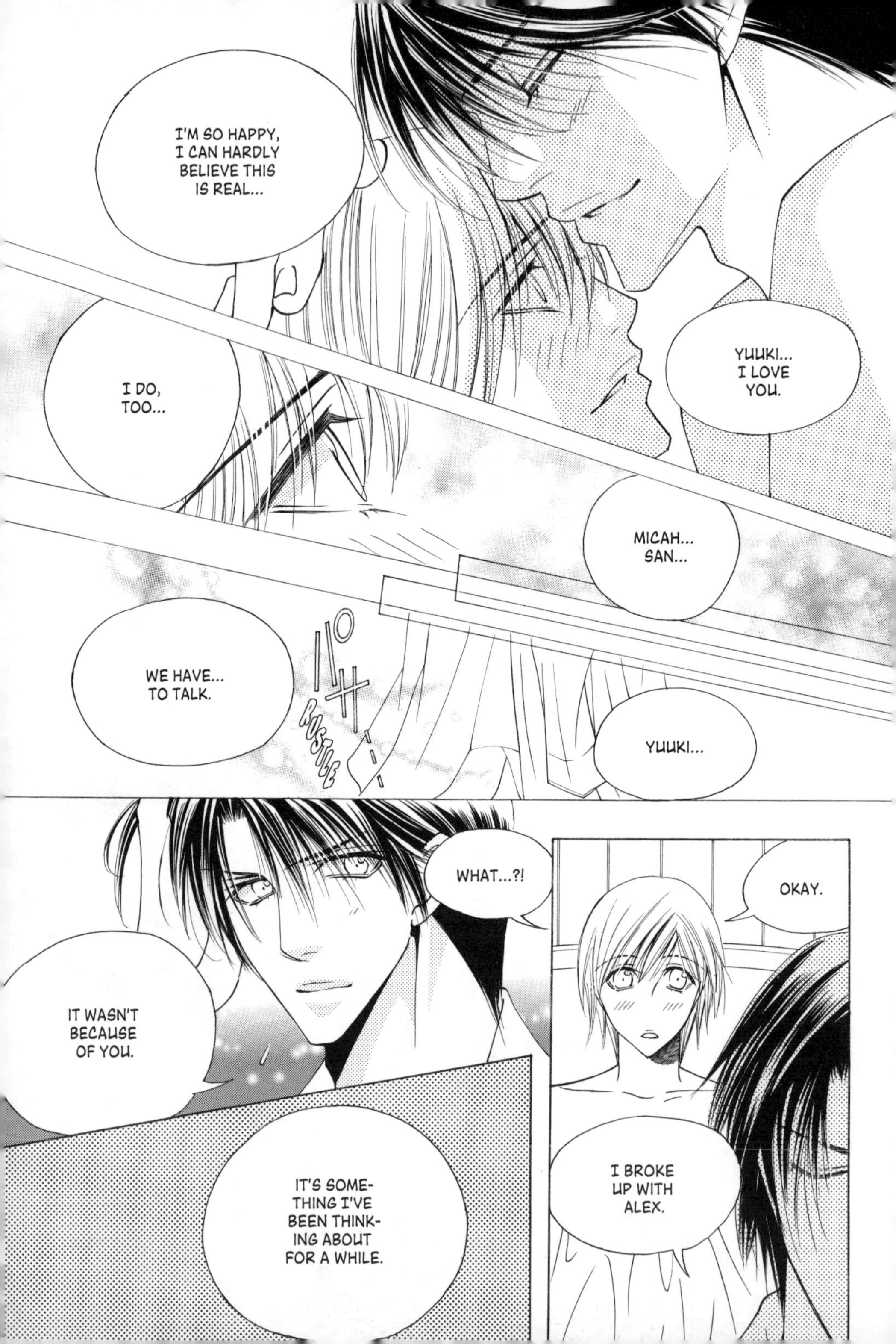
I'M SO HAPPY, I CAN HARDLY BELIEVE THIS IS REAL...
YUUKI... I LOVE YOU.
I DO, TOO...
MICAH... SAN...
YUUKI...
WE HAVE... TO TALK.
RUSTLE
OKAY.
I BROKE UP WITH ALEX.
WHAT...?!
IT WASN'T BECAUSE OF YOU.
IT'S SOME-THING I'VE BEEN THINK-ING ABOUT FOR A WHILE.

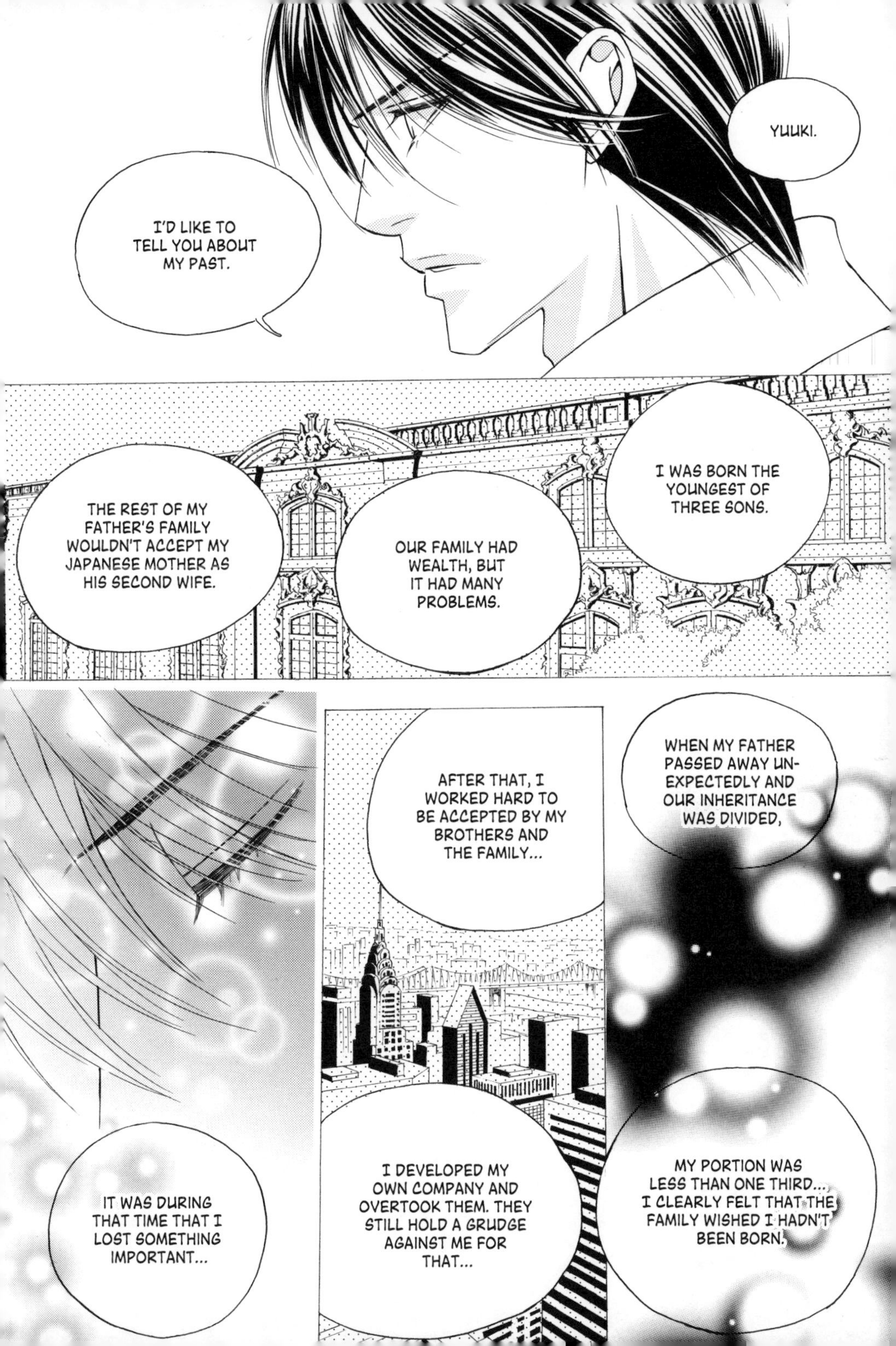
YUUKI.
I'D LIKE TO TELL YOU ABOUT MY PAST.
I WAS BORN THE YOUNGEST OF THREE SONS.
OUR FAMILY HAD WEALTH, BUT IT HAD MANY PROBLEMS.
THE REST OF MY FATHER'S FAMILY WOULDN'T ACCEPT MY JAPANESE MOTHER AS HIS SECOND WIFE.
WHEN MY FATHER PASSED AWAY UN-EXPECTEDLY AND OUR INHERITANCE WAS DIVIDED,
MY PORTION WAS LESS THAN ONE THIRD... I CLEARLY FELT THAT THE FAMILY WISHED I HADN'T BEEN BORN.
AFTER THAT, I WORKED HARD TO BE ACCEPTED BY MY BROTHERS AND THE FAMILY...
I DEVELOPED MY OWN COMPANY AND OVERTOOK THEM. THEY STILL HOLD A GRUDGE AGAINST ME FOR THAT...
IT WAS DURING THAT TIME THAT I LOST SOMETHING IMPORTANT...

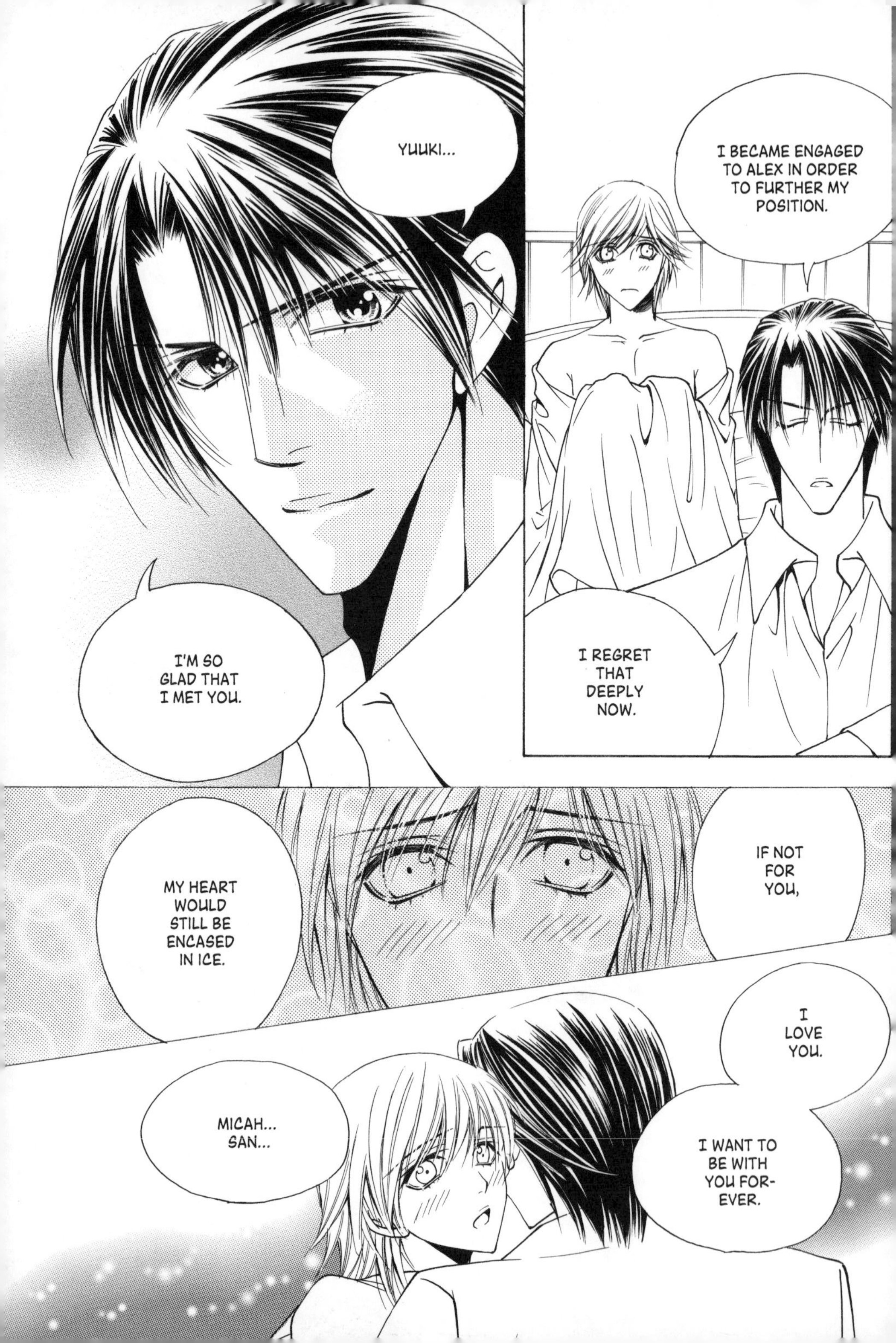
I BECAME ENGAGED TO ALEX IN ORDER TO FURTHER MY POSITION.
I REGRET THAT DEEPLY NOW.
YUUKI...
I'M SO GLAD THAT I MET YOU.
IF NOT FOR YOU,
MY HEART WOULD STILL BE ENCASED IN ICE.
I LOVE YOU.
I WANT TO BE WITH YOU FOR-EVER.
MICAH... SAN...

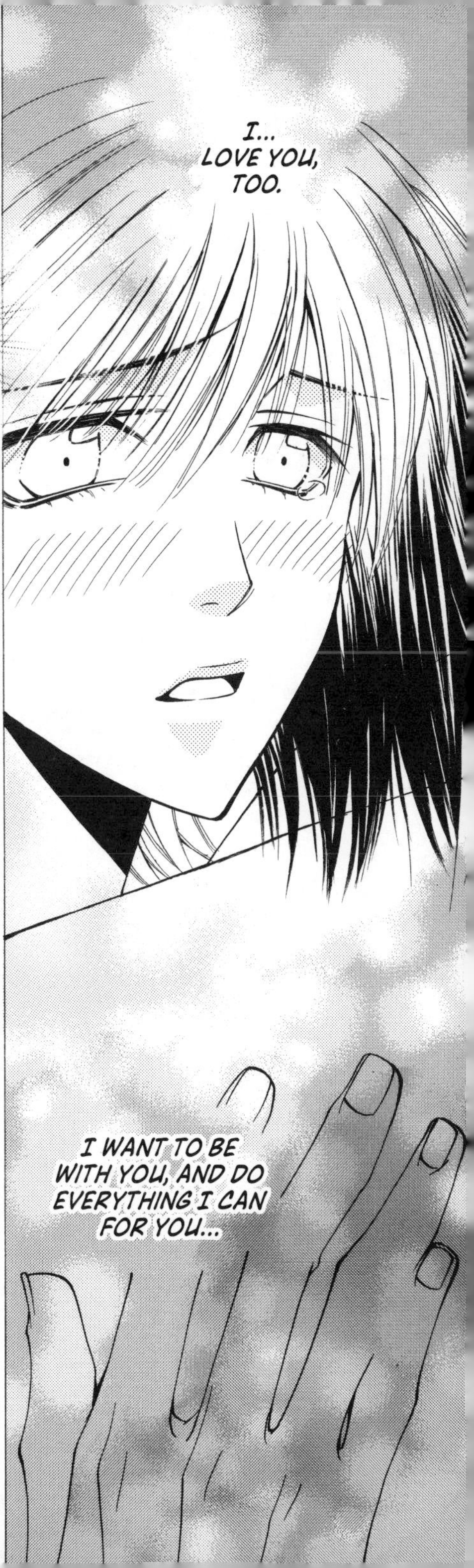
I...
LOVE YOU,
TOO.
I WANT TO BE WITH YOU, AND DO EVERYTHING I CAN FOR YOU...
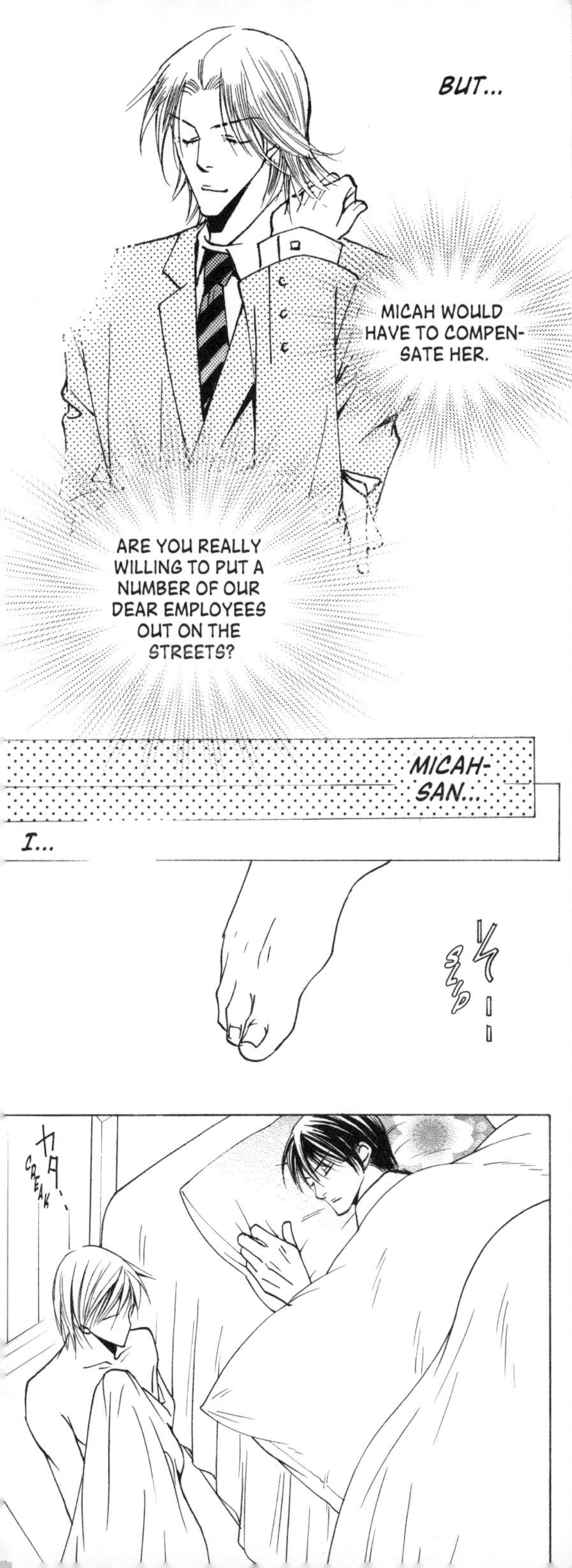
BUT...
MICAH WOULD HAVE TO COMPEN-SATE HER.
ARE YOU REALLY WILLING TO PUT A NUMBER OF OUR DEAR EMPLOYEES OUT ON THE STREETS?
MICAH-SAN...
I...
SLIP
CREAK

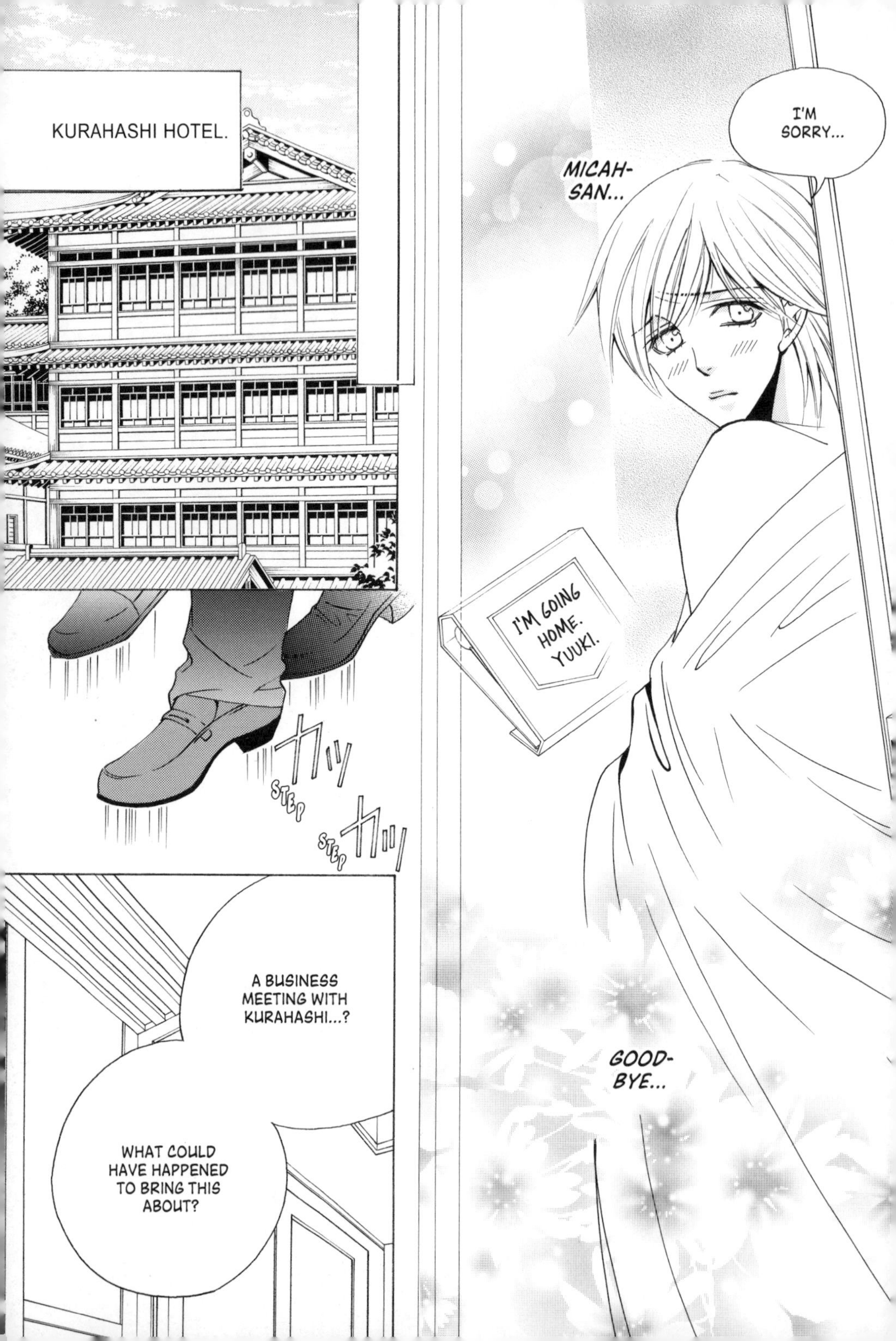

I'M SORRY...
MICAH-SAN...
I'M GOING HOME. YUUKI.
GOOD-BYE...
KURAHASHI HOTEL.
カッ
STEP
カッ
STEP
A BUSINESS MEETING WITH KURAHASHI...?
WHAT COULD HAVE HAPPENED TO BRING THIS ABOUT?

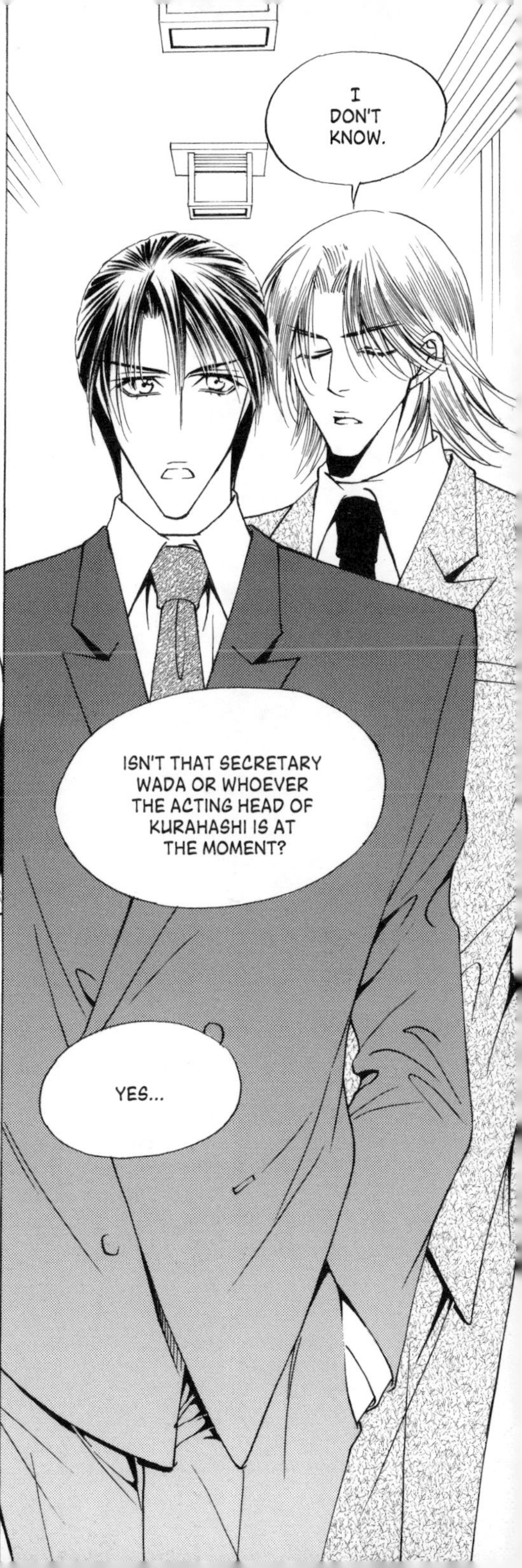
I DON'T KNOW.
ISN'T THAT SECRETARY WADA OR WHOEVER THE ACTING HEAD OF KURAHASHI IS AT THE MOMENT?
YES...

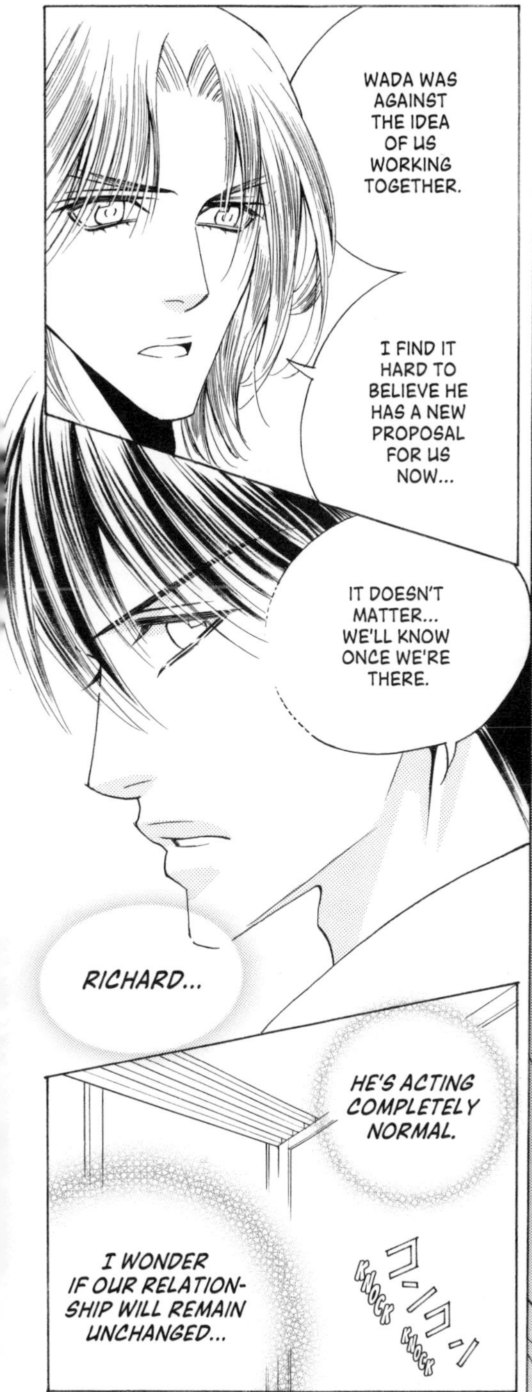
WADA WAS AGAINST THE IDEA OF US WORKING TOGETHER.
I FIND IT HARD TO BELIEVE HE HAS A NEW PROPOSAL FOR US NOW...
IT DOESN'T MATTER... WE'LL KNOW ONCE WE'RE THERE.
RICHARD...
HE'S ACTING COMPLETELY NORMAL.
KNOCK KNOCK
I WONDER IF OUR RELATION-SHIP WILL REMAIN UNCHANGED...

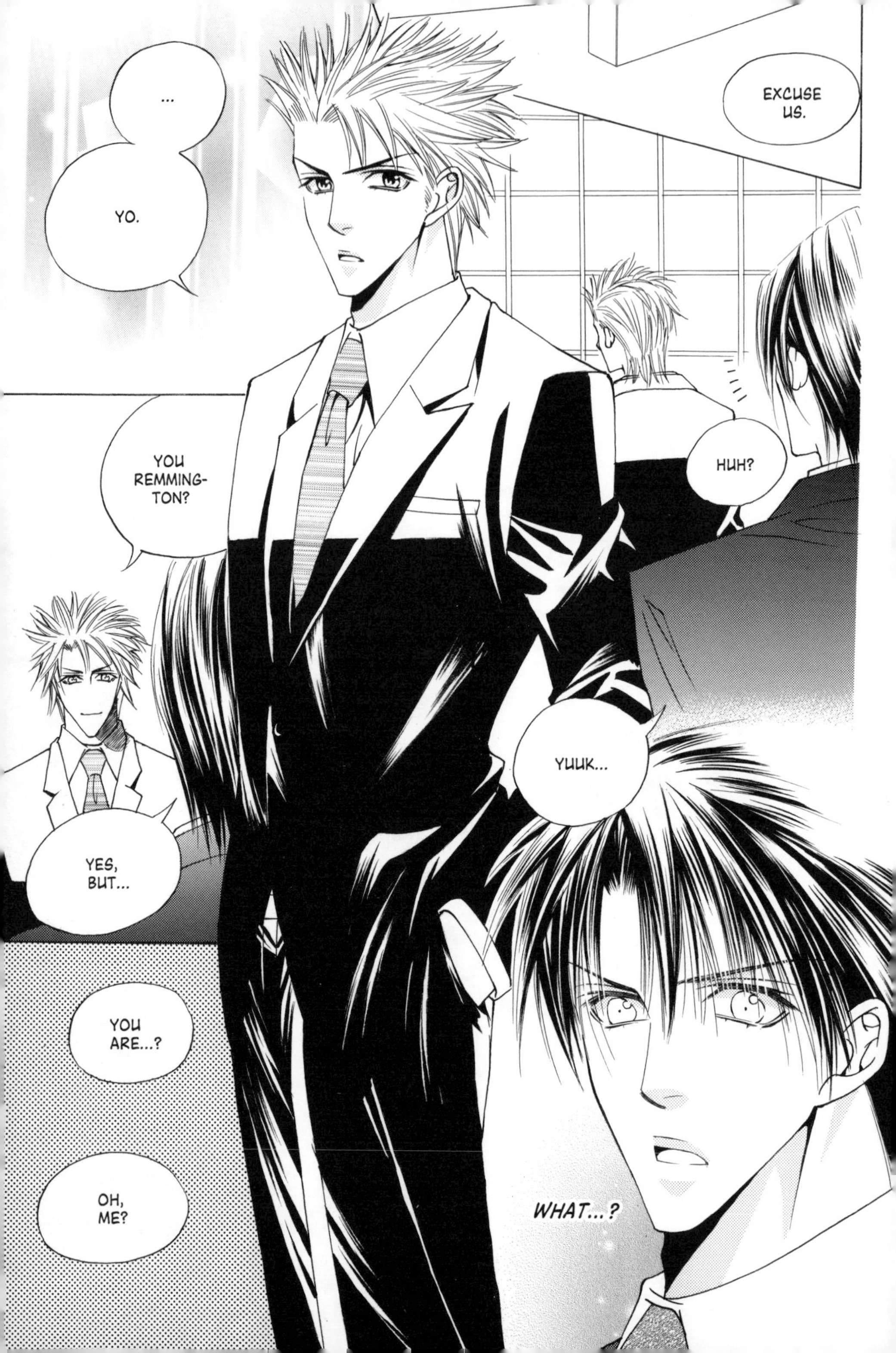

EXCUSE US.
...
YO.
HUH?
YOU REMMING-TON?
YUUK...
WHAT...?
YES, BUT...
YOU ARE...?
OH, ME?

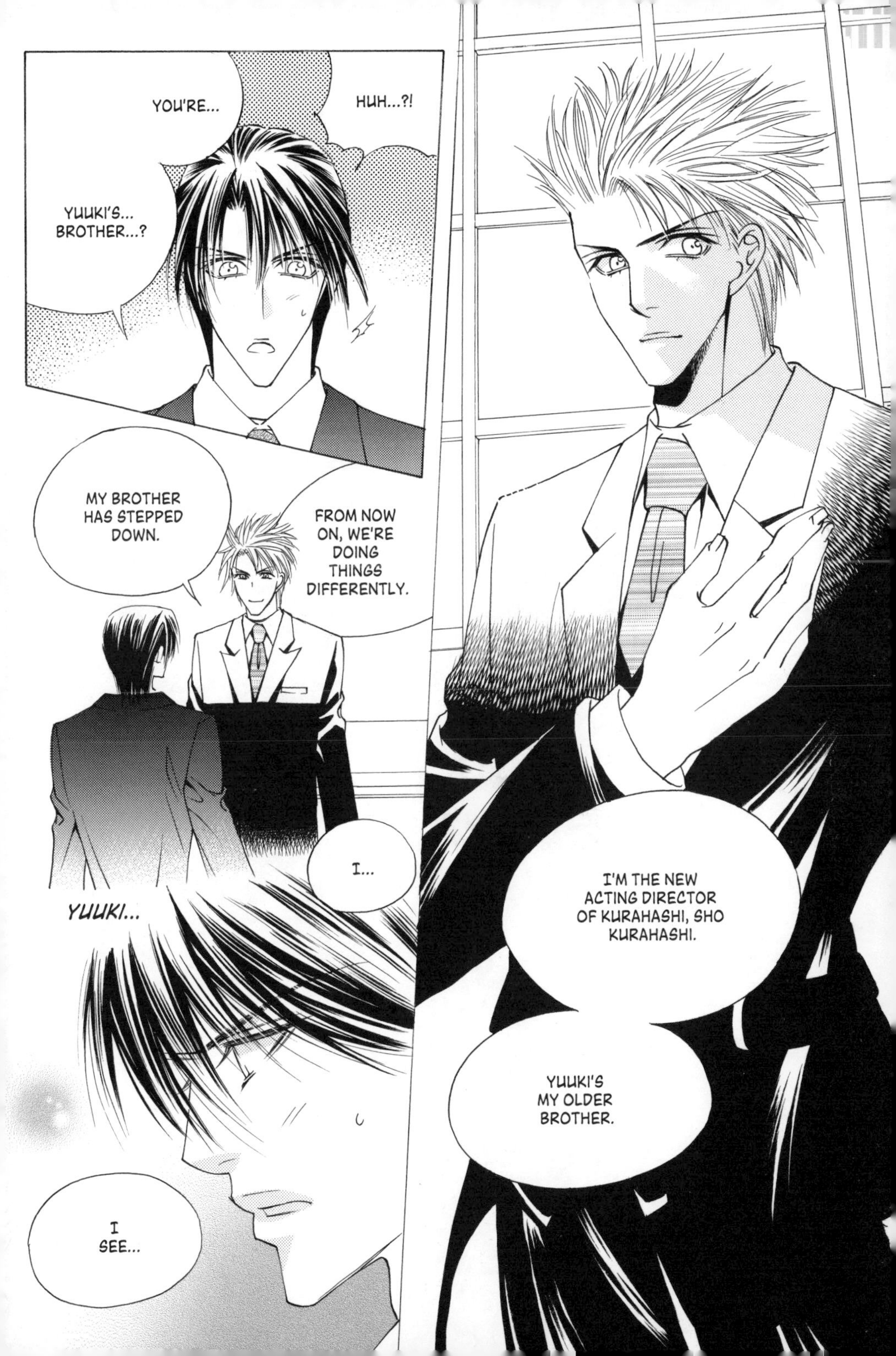
I'M THE NEW ACTING DIRECTOR OF KURAHASHI, SHO KURAHASHI.
YUUKI'S MY OLDER BROTHER.
HUH...?!
YOU'RE...
YUUKI'S... BROTHER...?
MY BROTHER HAS STEPPED DOWN.
FROM NOW ON, WE'RE DOING THINGS DIFFERENTLY.
I...
YUUKI...
I SEE...

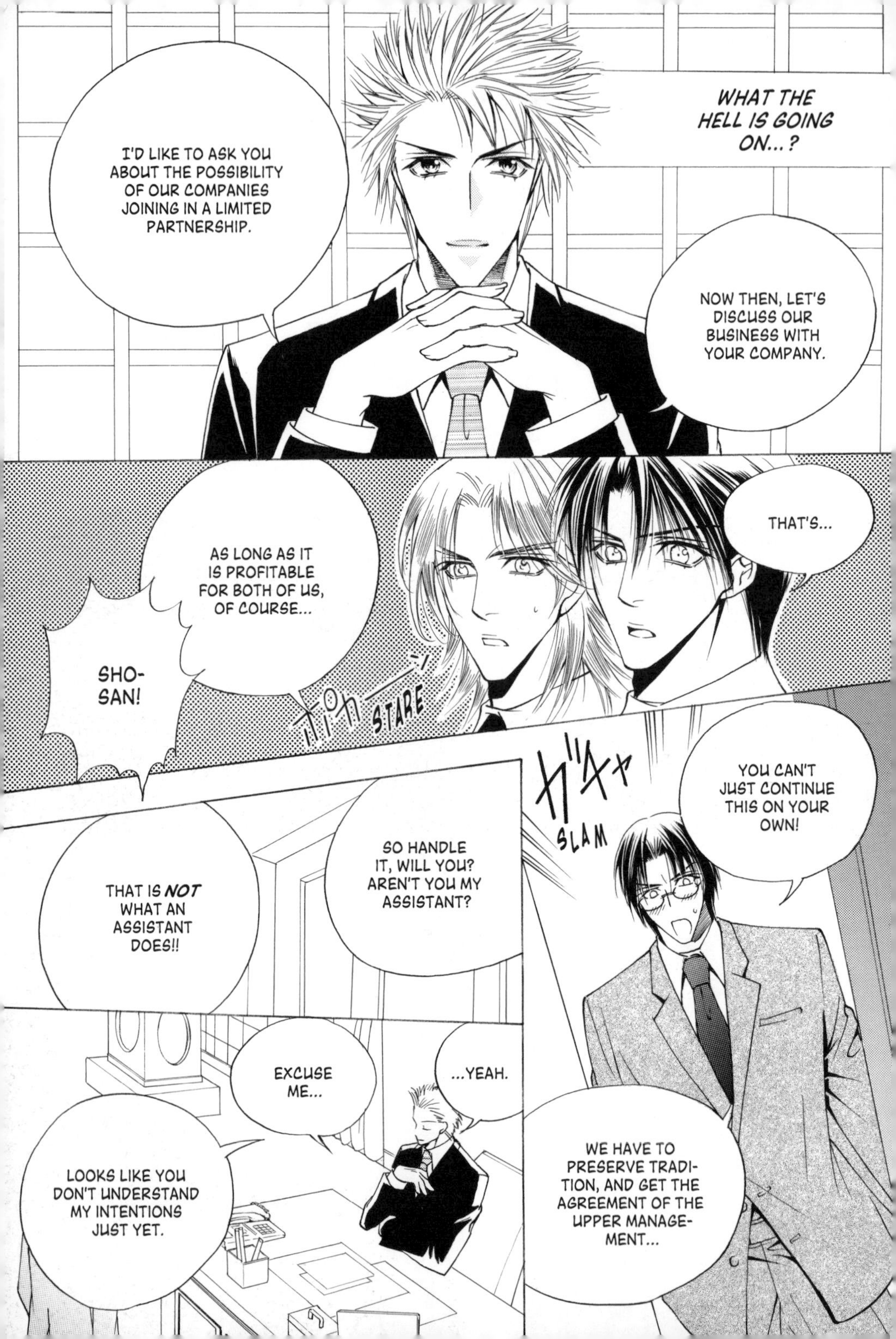
WHAT THE HELL IS GOING ON...?
NOW THEN, LET'S DISCUSS OUR BUSINESS WITH YOUR COMPANY.
I'D LIKE TO ASK YOU ABOUT THE POSSIBILITY OF OUR COMPANIES JOINING IN A LIMITED PARTNERSHIP.
THAT'S...
AS LONG AS IT IS PROFITABLE FOR BOTH OF US, OF COURSE...
STARE
SHO-SAN!
SLAM
YOU CAN'T JUST CONTINUE THIS ON YOUR OWN!
WE HAVE TO PRESERVE TRADITION, AND GET THE AGREEMENT OF THE UPPER MANAGEMENT...
SO HANDLE IT, WILL YOU? AREN'T YOU MY ASSISTANT?
THAT IS **NOT** WHAT AN ASSISTANT DOES!!
...YEAH.
EXCUSE ME...
LOOKS LIKE YOU DON'T UNDERSTAND MY INTENTIONS JUST YET.

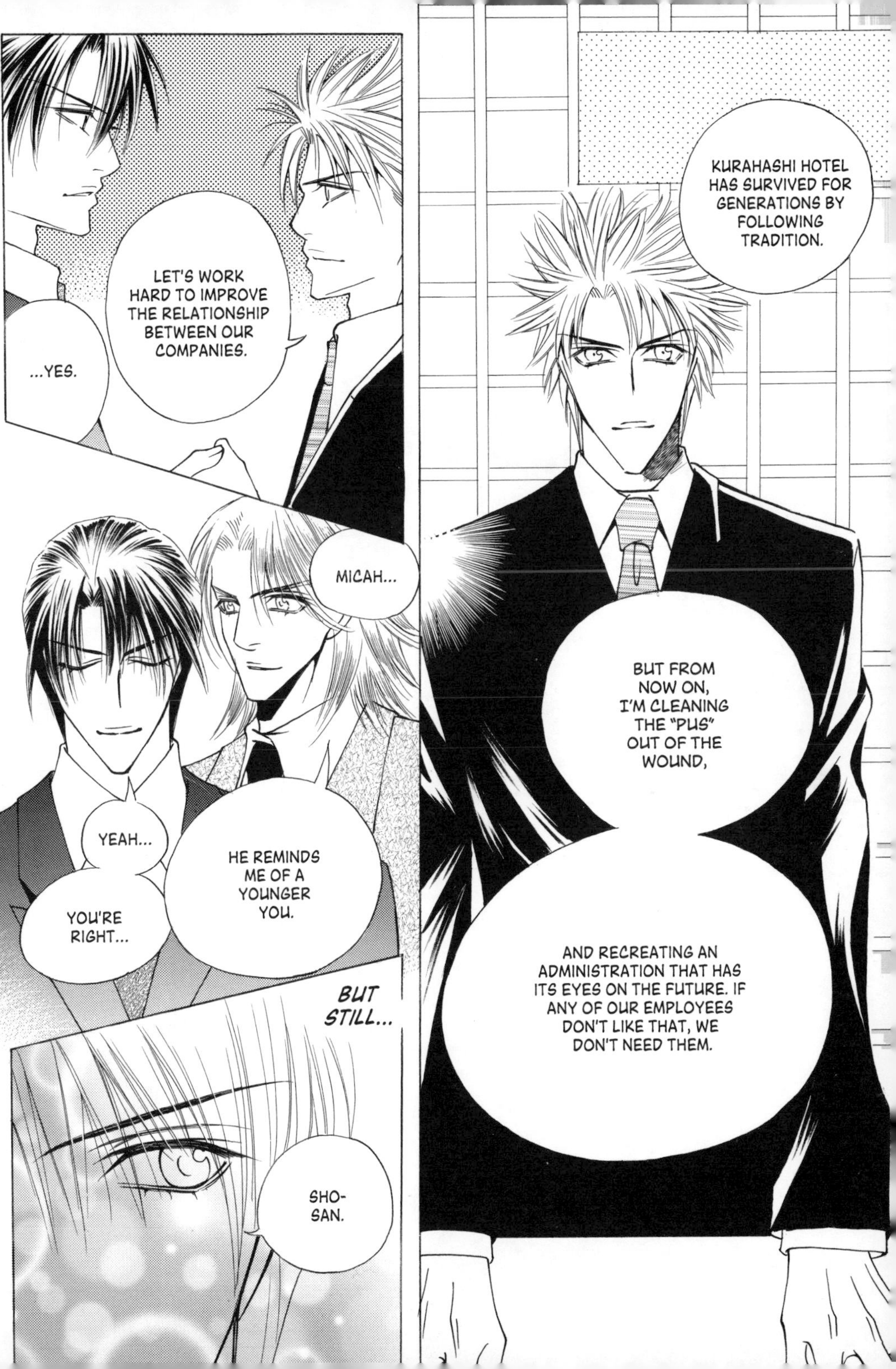
KURAHASHI HOTEL HAS SURVIVED FOR GENERATIONS BY FOLLOWING TRADITION.
BUT FROM NOW ON, I'M CLEANING THE "PUS" OUT OF THE WOUND,
AND RECREATING AN ADMINISTRATION THAT HAS ITS EYES ON THE FUTURE. IF ANY OF OUR EMPLOYEES DON'T LIKE THAT, WE DON'T NEED THEM.
LET'S WORK HARD TO IMPROVE THE RELATIONSHIP BETWEEN OUR COMPANIES.
...YES.
MICAH...
HE REMINDS ME OF A YOUNGER YOU.
YEAH...
YOU'RE RIGHT...
BUT STILL...
SHO-SAN.

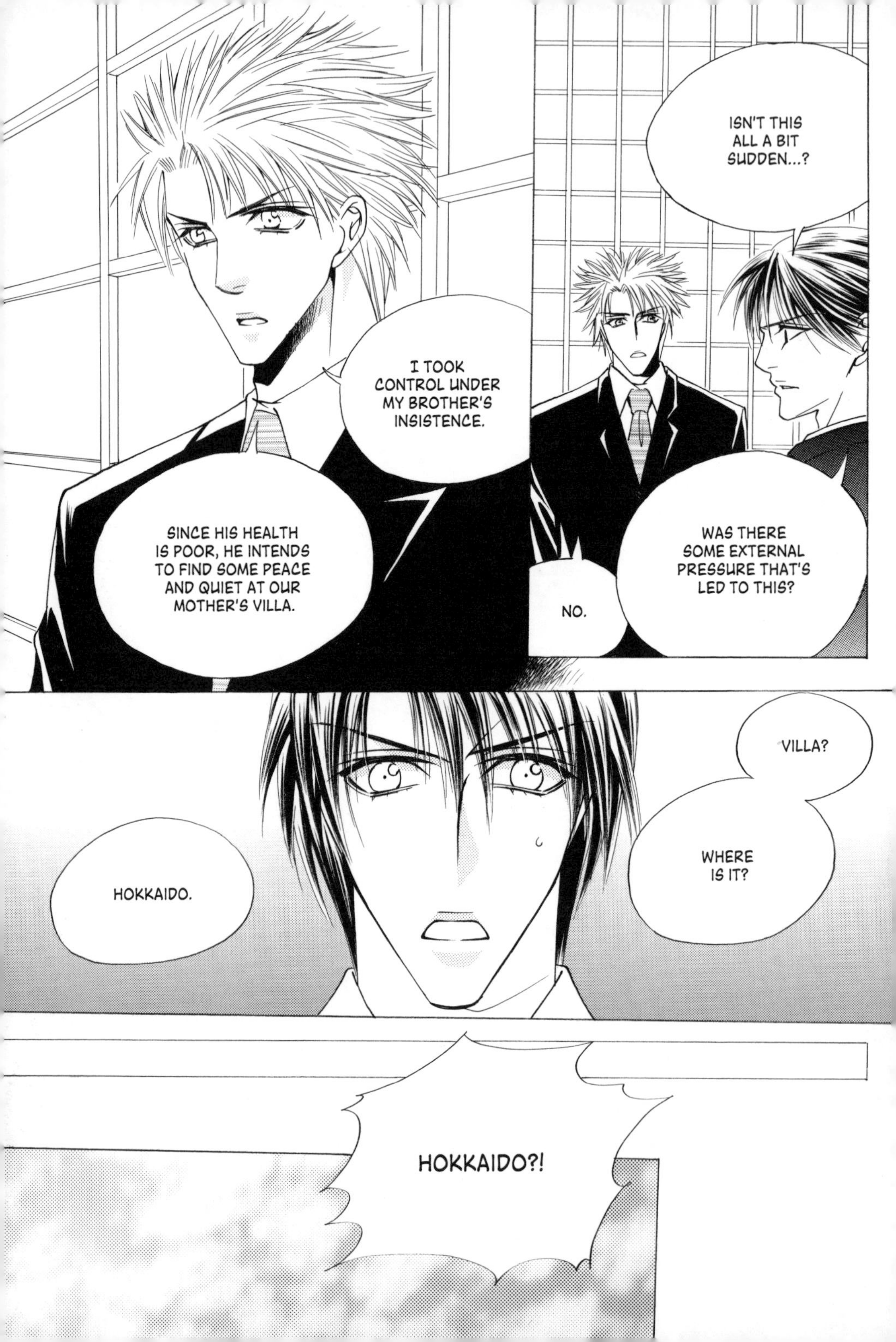
ISN'T THIS ALL A BIT SUDDEN...?
WAS THERE SOME EXTERNAL PRESSURE THAT'S LED TO THIS?
NO.
I TOOK CONTROL UNDER MY BROTHER'S INSISTENCE.
SINCE HIS HEALTH IS POOR, HE INTENDS TO FIND SOME PEACE AND QUIET AT OUR MOTHER'S VILLA.
VILLA?
WHERE IS IT?
HOKKAIDO.
HOKKAIDO?!

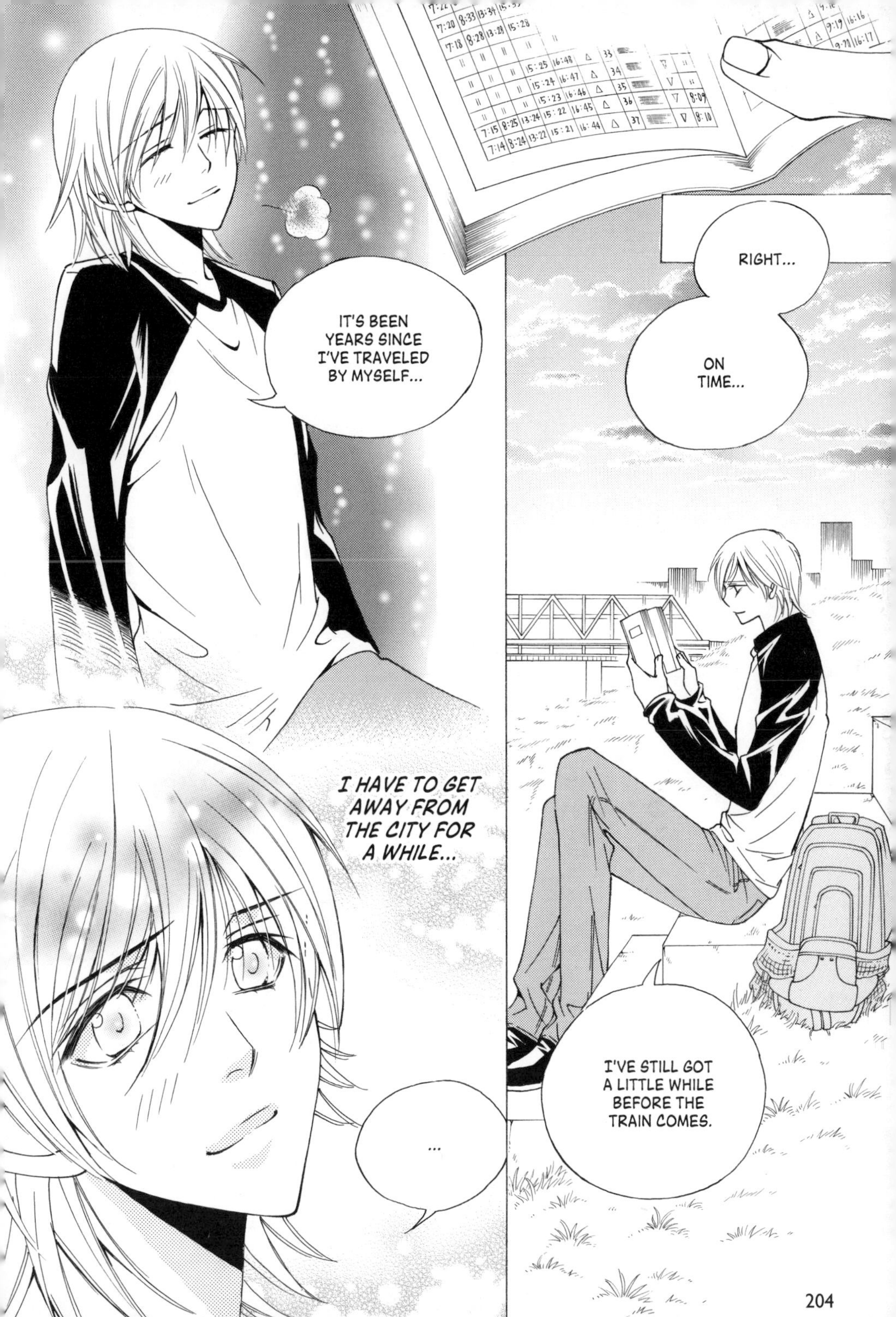
RIGHT... ON TIME...
I'VE STILL GOT A LITTLE WHILE BEFORE THE TRAIN COMES.
IT'S BEEN YEARS SINCE I'VE TRAVELED BY MYSELF...
I HAVE TO GET AWAY FROM THE CITY FOR A WHILE...
...

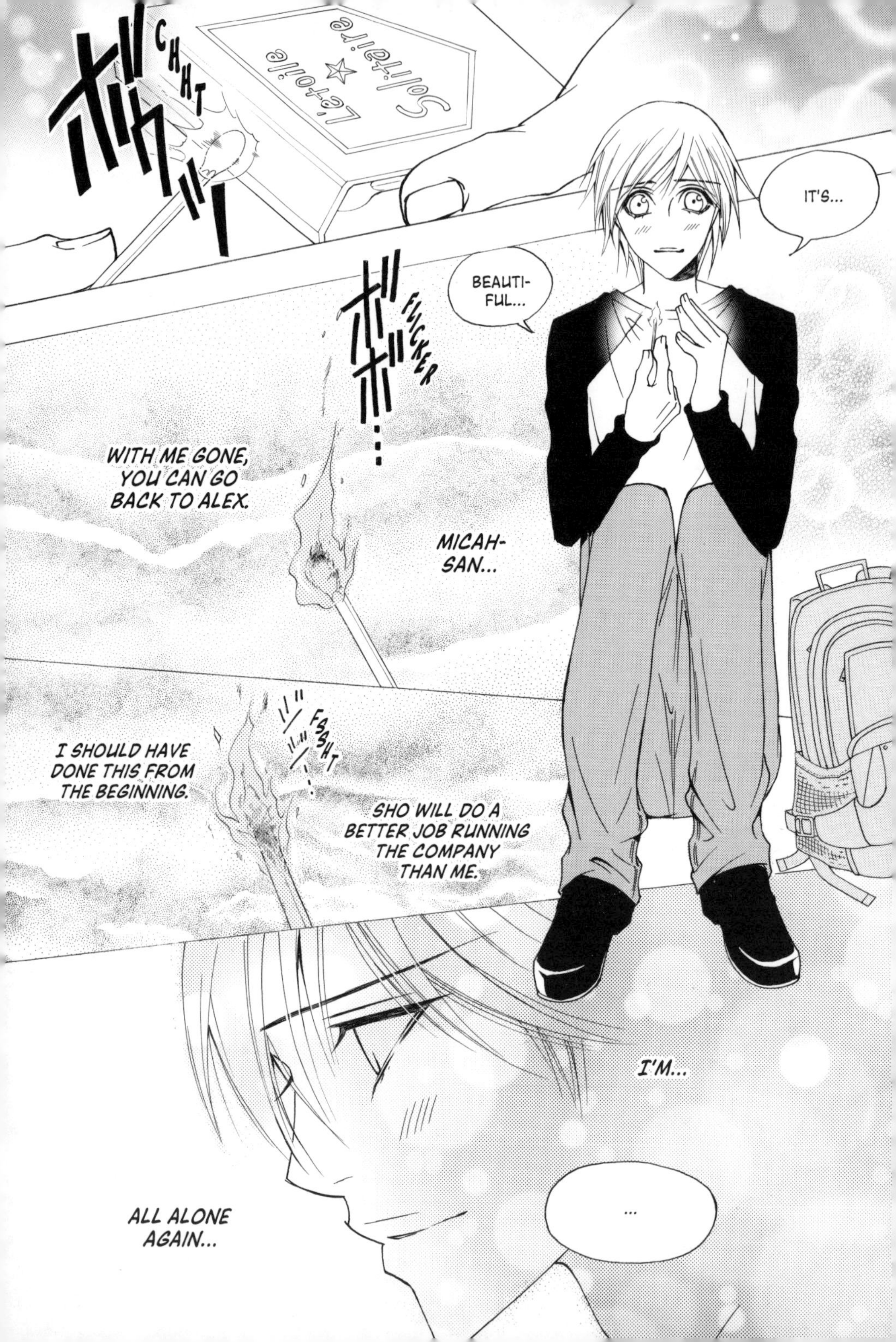

L'etoile
Solitaire
CHHT
IT'S...
BEAUTI-FUL...
FLICKER
MICAH-SAN...
WITH ME GONE, YOU CAN GO BACK TO ALEX.
FSSHT
SHO WILL DO A BETTER JOB RUNNING THE COMPANY THAN ME.
I SHOULD HAVE DONE THIS FROM THE BEGINNING.
I'M...
...
ALL ALONE AGAIN...

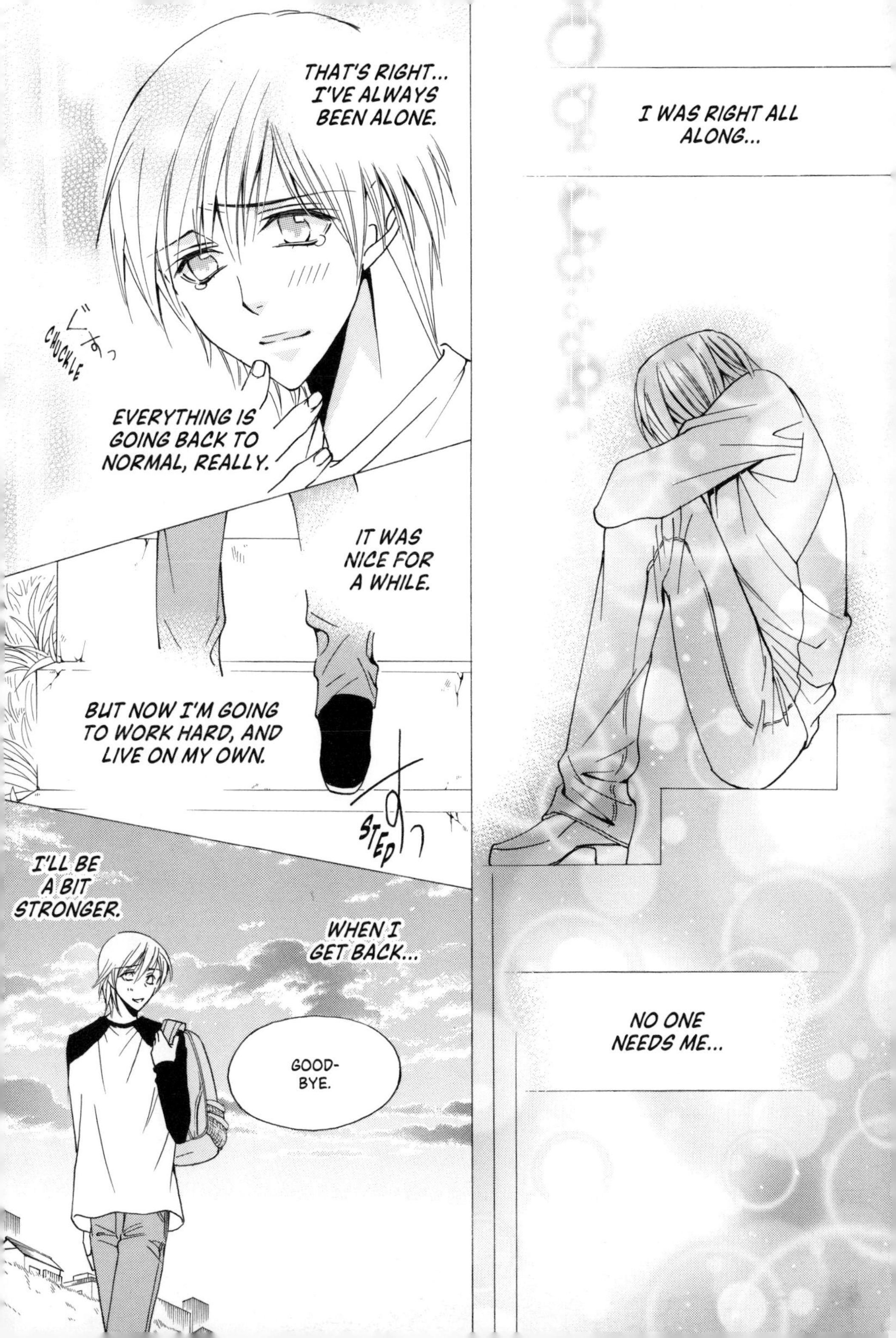
I WAS RIGHT ALL ALONG...
NO ONE NEEDS ME...
THAT'S RIGHT... I'VE ALWAYS BEEN ALONE.
ぐすっ
CHUCKLE
EVERYTHING IS GOING BACK TO NORMAL, REALLY.
IT WAS NICE FOR A WHILE.
BUT NOW I'M GOING TO WORK HARD, AND LIVE ON MY OWN.
STEP
I'LL BE A BIT STRONGER.
WHEN I GET BACK...
GOOD-BYE.

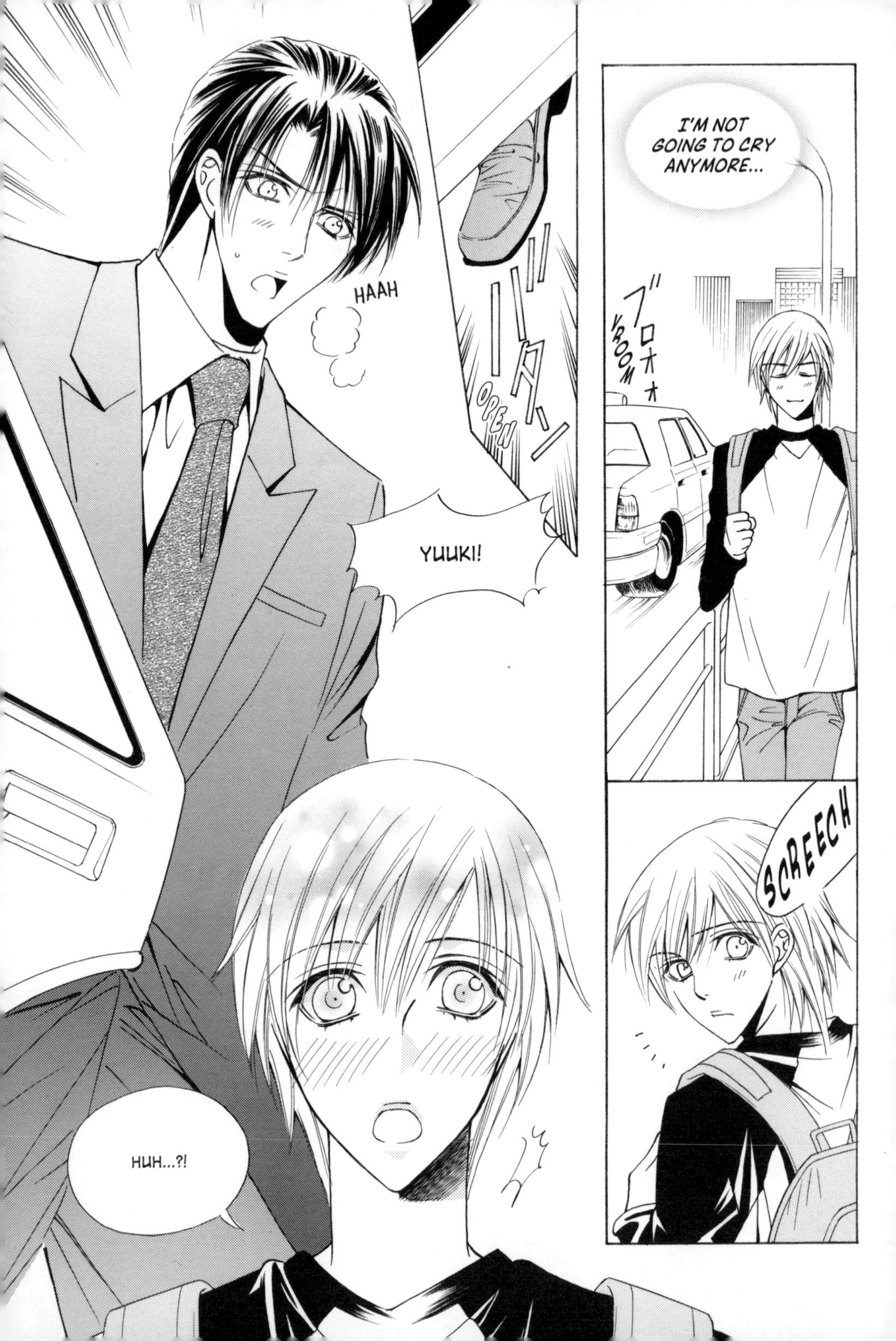
I'M NOT GOING TO CRY ANYMORE...
VROOM
SCREECH
OPEN
HAAH
YUUKI!
HUH...?!

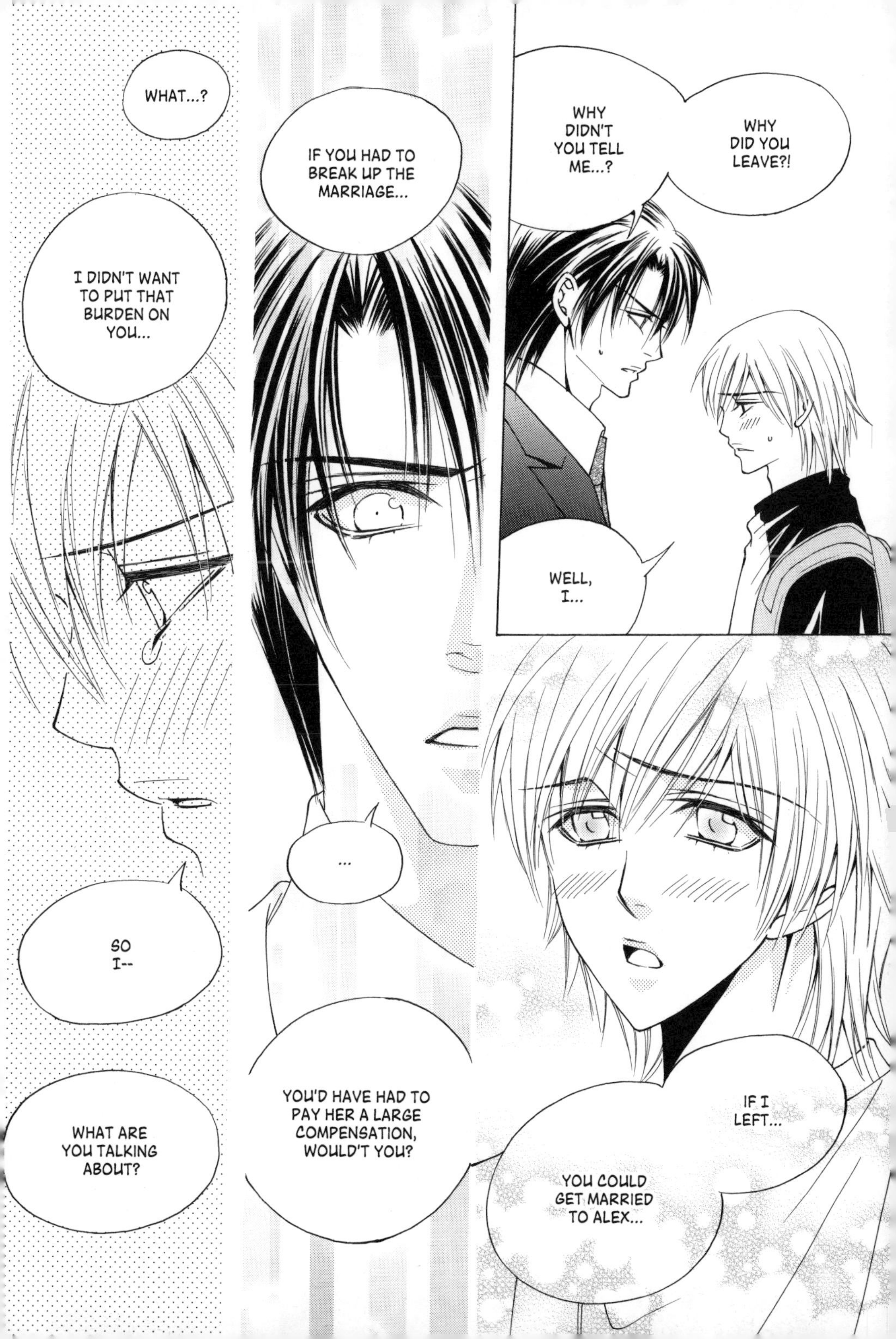
WHY DID YOU LEAVE?!
WHY DIDN'T YOU TELL ME...?
WELL, I...
IF I LEFT...
YOU COULD GET MARRIED TO ALEX...
IF YOU HAD TO BREAK UP THE MARRIAGE...
...
YOU'D HAVE HAD TO PAY HER A LARGE COMPENSATION, WOULD'T YOU?
WHAT...?
I DIDN'T WANT TO PUT THAT BURDEN ON YOU...
SO I--
WHAT ARE YOU TALKING ABOUT?

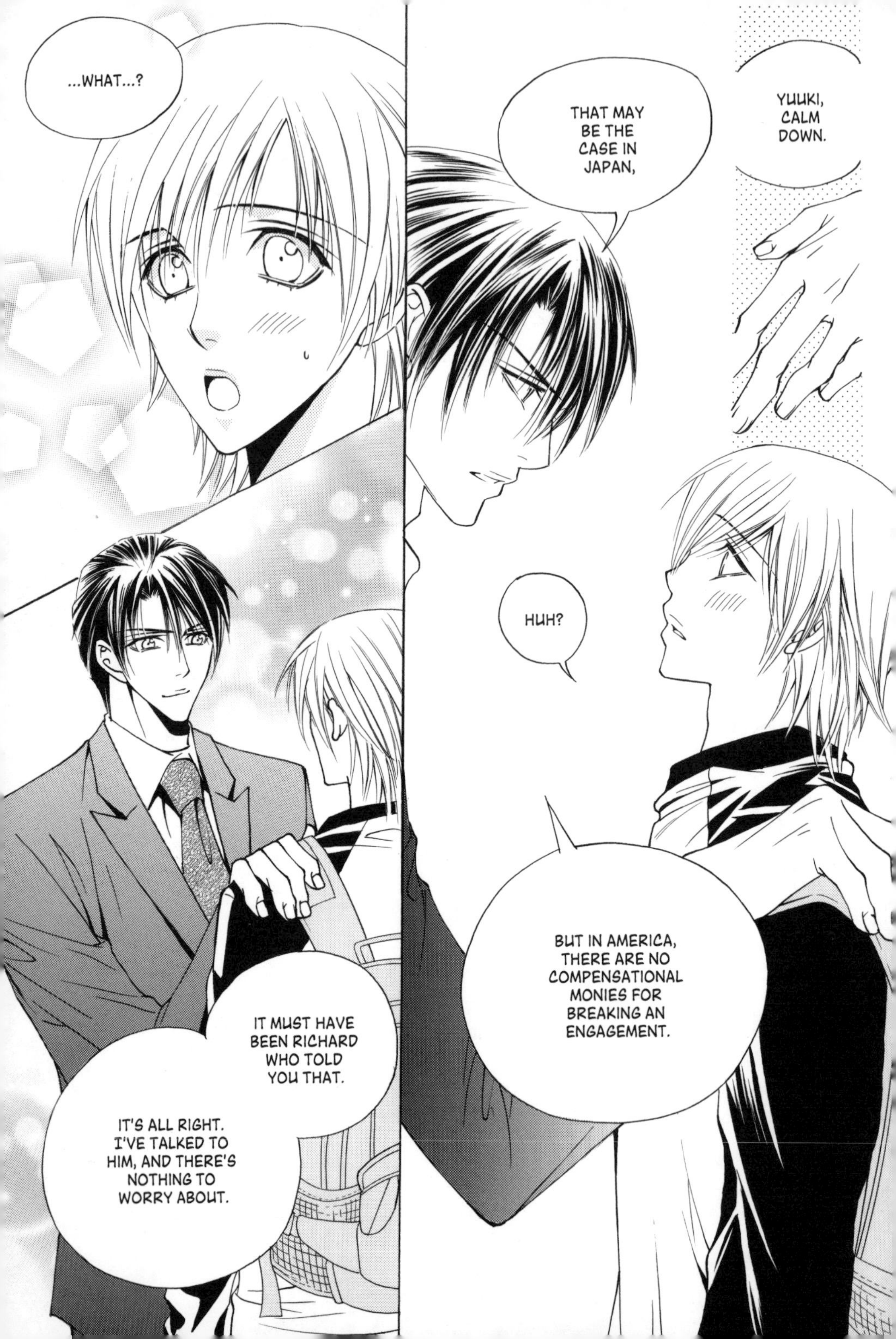
YUUKI, CALM DOWN.
THAT MAY BE THE CASE IN JAPAN,
HUH?
BUT IN AMERICA, THERE ARE NO COMPENSATIONAL MONIES FOR BREAKING AN ENGAGEMENT.
...WHAT...?
IT MUST HAVE BEEN RICHARD WHO TOLD YOU THAT.
IT'S ALL RIGHT. I'VE TALKED TO HIM, AND THERE'S NOTHING TO WORRY ABOUT.

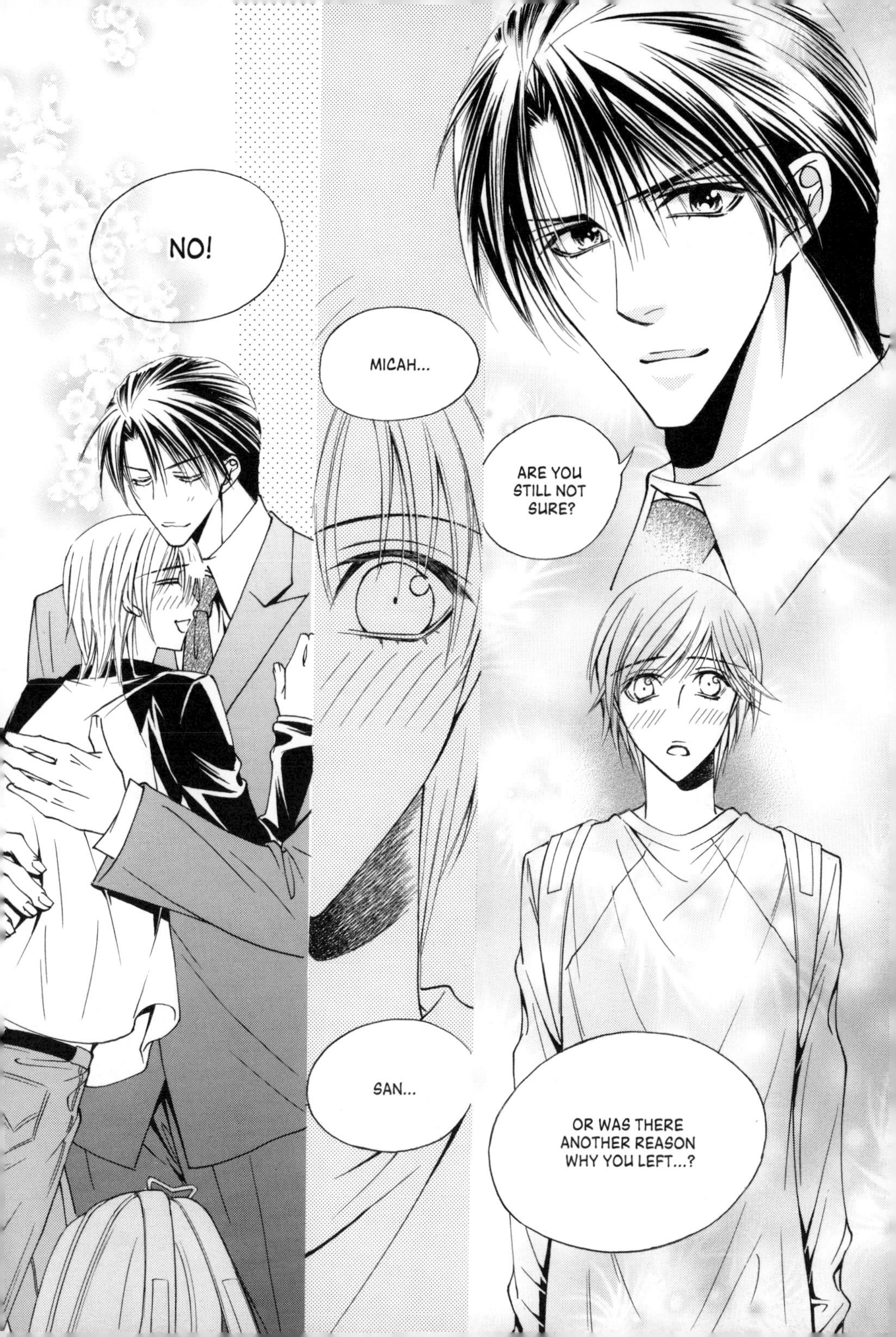
ARE YOU STILL NOT SURE?
OR WAS THERE ANOTHER REASON WHY YOU LEFT...?
MICAH...
SAN...
NO!

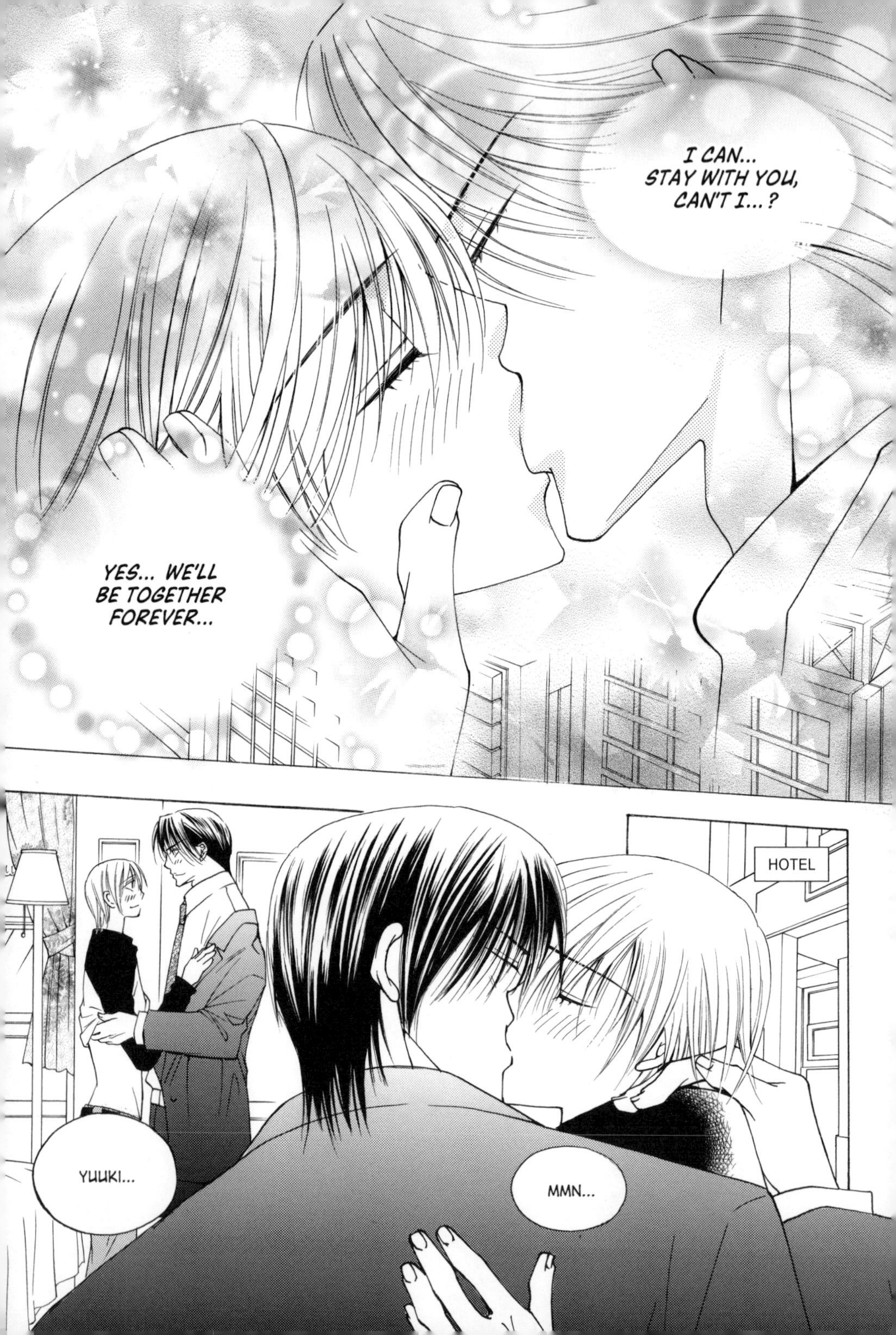
I CAN... STAY WITH YOU, CAN'T I...?
YES... WE'LL BE TOGETHER FOREVER...
HOTEL
MMN...
YUUKI...

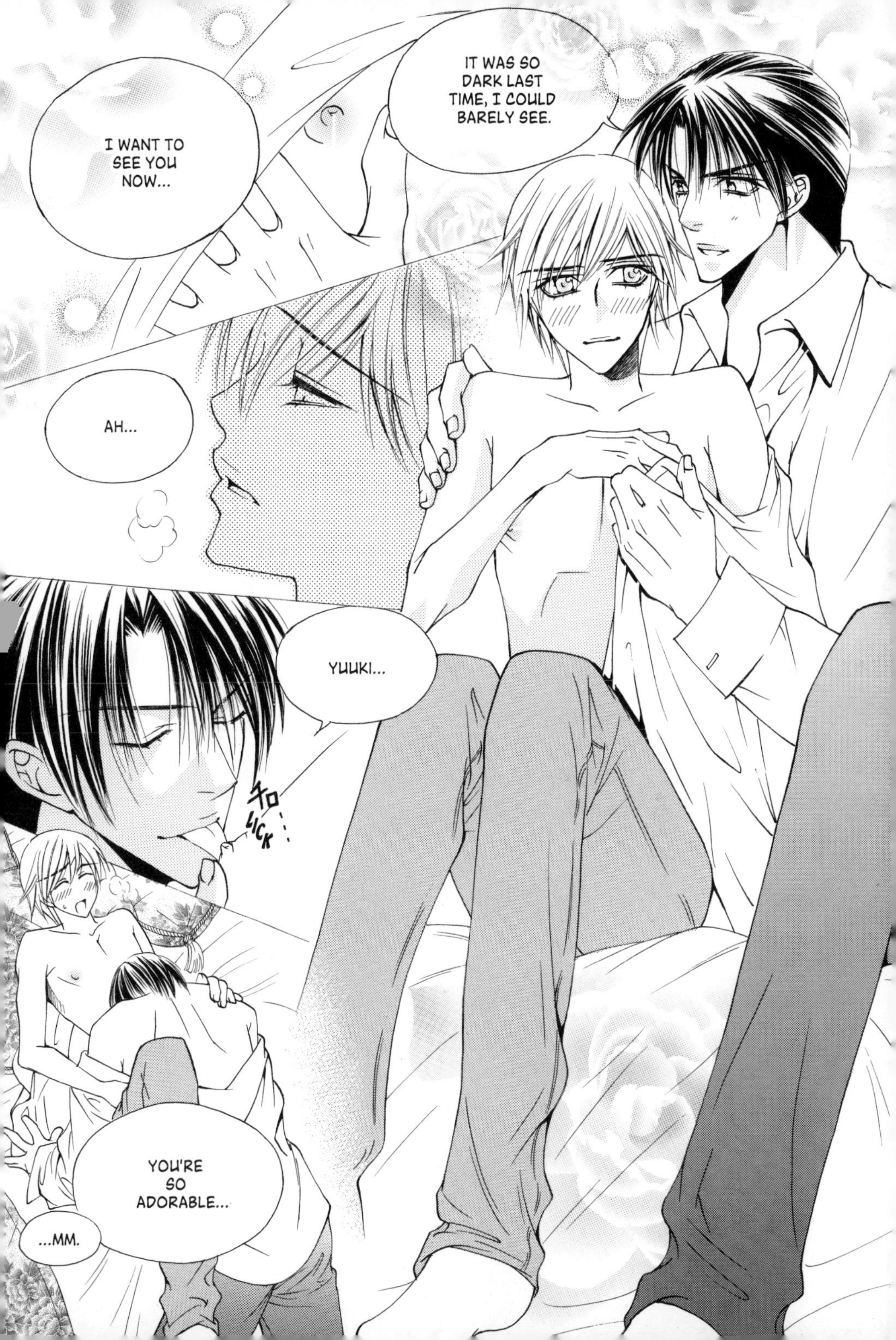
IT WAS SO DARK LAST TIME, I COULD BARELY SEE.
I WANT TO SEE YOU NOW...
AH...
YUUKI...
チロ LICK
YOU'RE SO ADORABLE...
...MM.

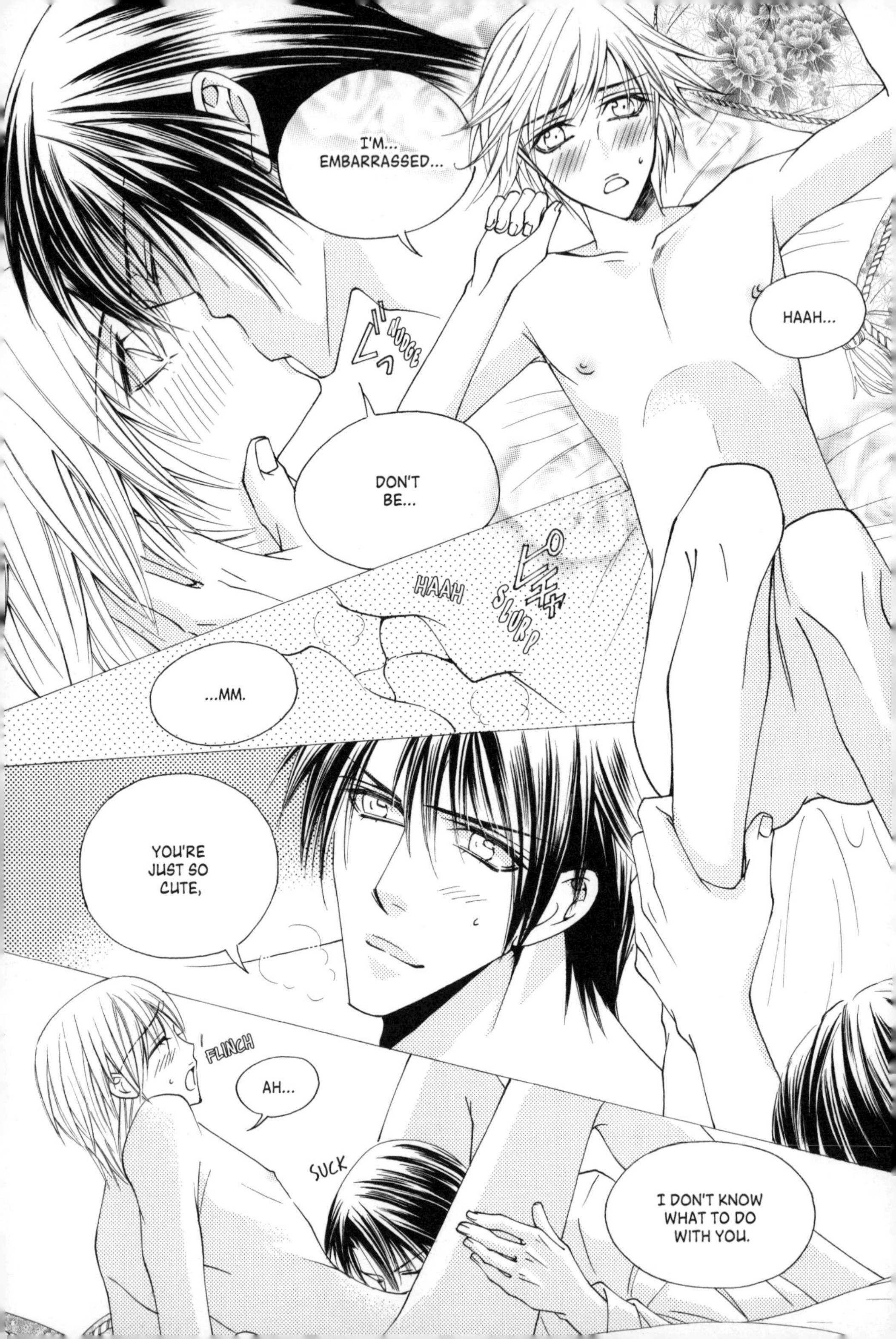
HAAH...
I'M... EMBARRASSED...
NUDGE
DON'T BE...
SLURP
HAAH
...MM.
YOU'RE JUST SO CUTE,
FLINCH
AH...
SUCK
I DON'T KNOW WHAT TO DO WITH YOU.

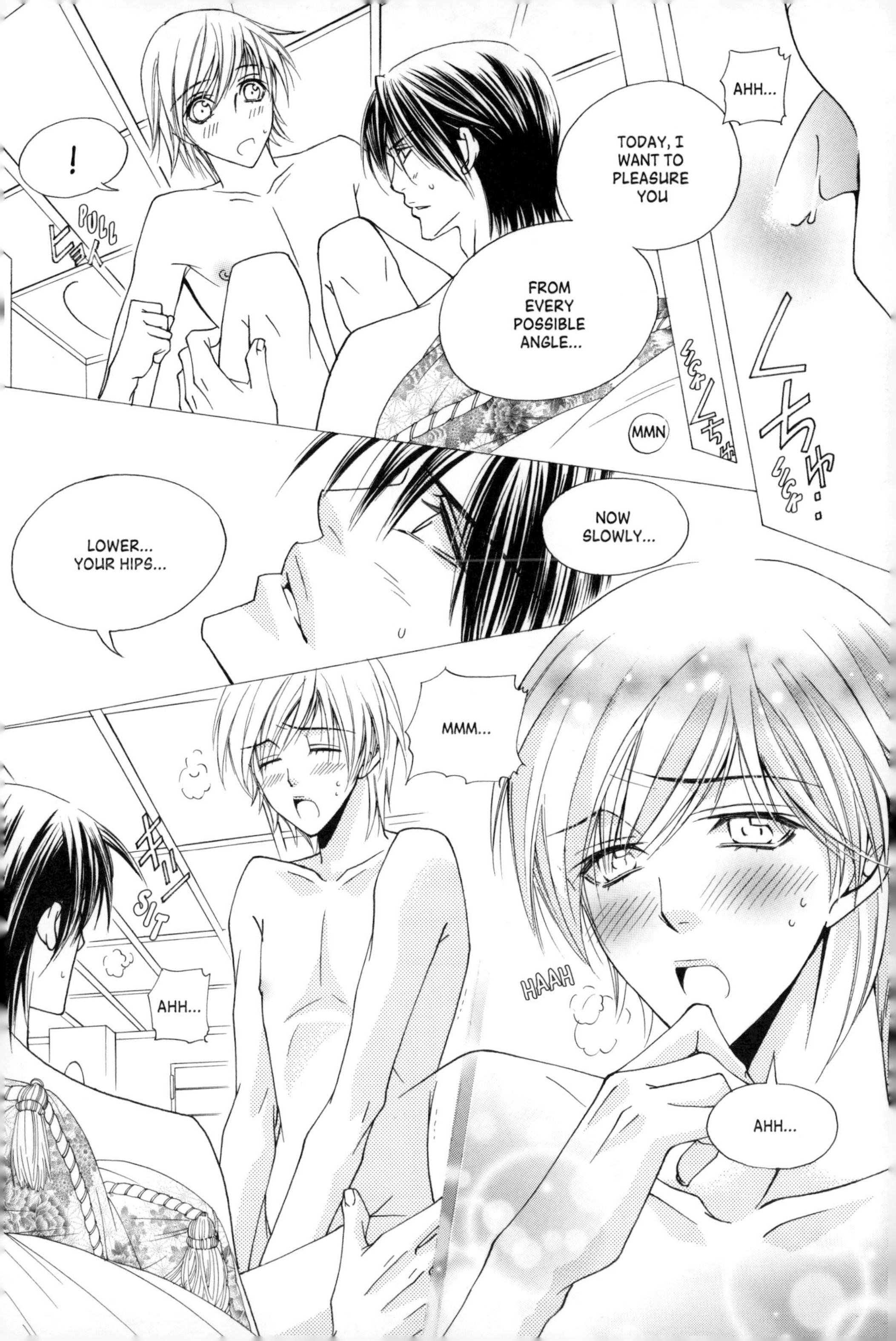
AHH...
LICK
LICK
MMN
TODAY, I WANT TO PLEASURE YOU
FROM EVERY POSSIBLE ANGLE...
!
PULL
NOW SLOWLY...
LOWER... YOUR HIPS...
MMM...
HAAH
AHH...
SIT
AHH...

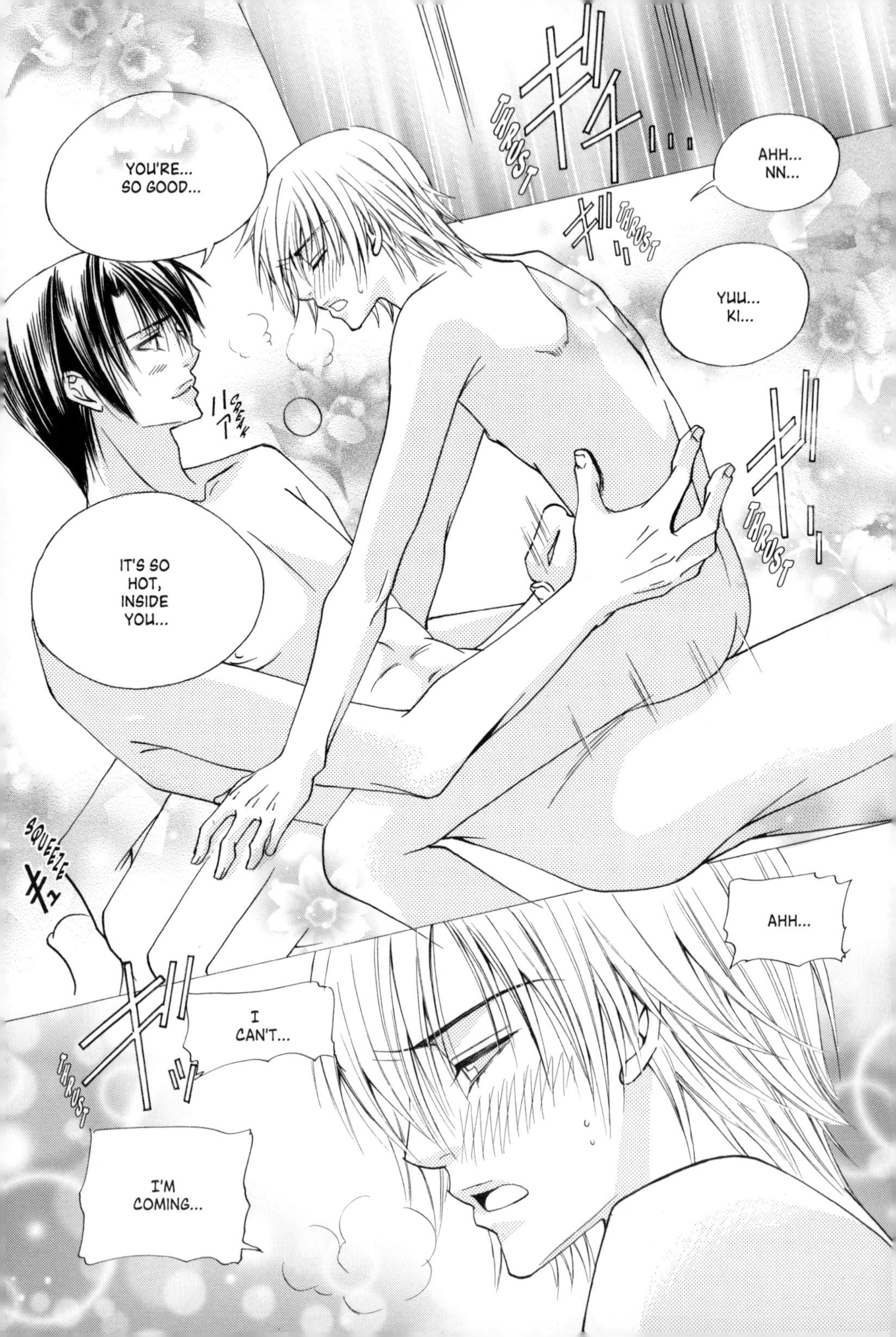
THRUST
AHH... NN...
THRUST
YUU... KI...
YOU'RE... SO GOOD...
CREAK
THRUST
IT'S SO HOT, INSIDE YOU...
SQUEEZE
AHH...
THRUST
I CAN'T...
I'M COMING...

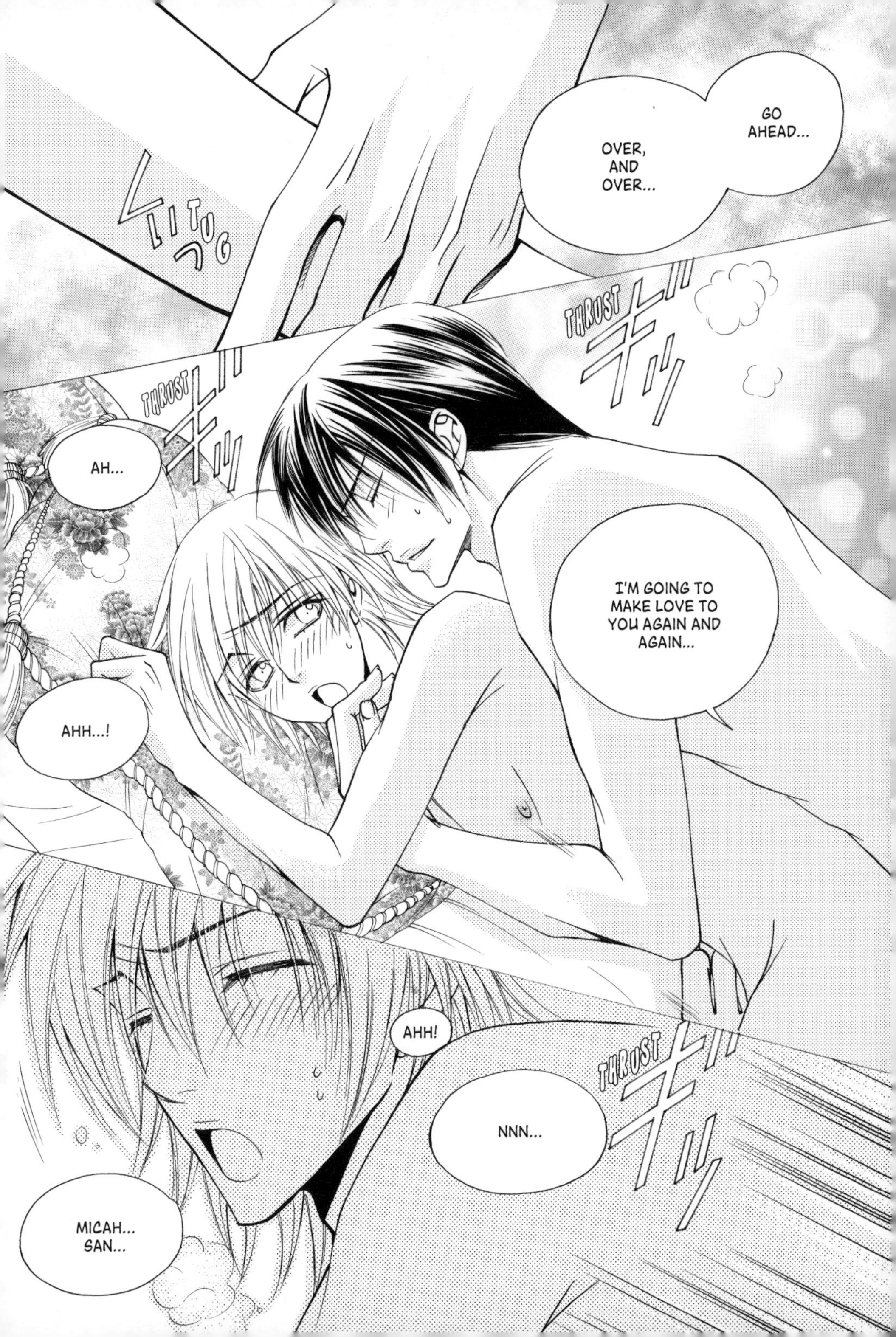
GO AHEAD...
OVER, AND OVER...
TUG
THRUST
I'M GOING TO MAKE LOVE TO YOU AGAIN AND AGAIN...
THRUST
AH...
AHH...!
THRUST
AHH!
NNN...
MICAH... SAN...

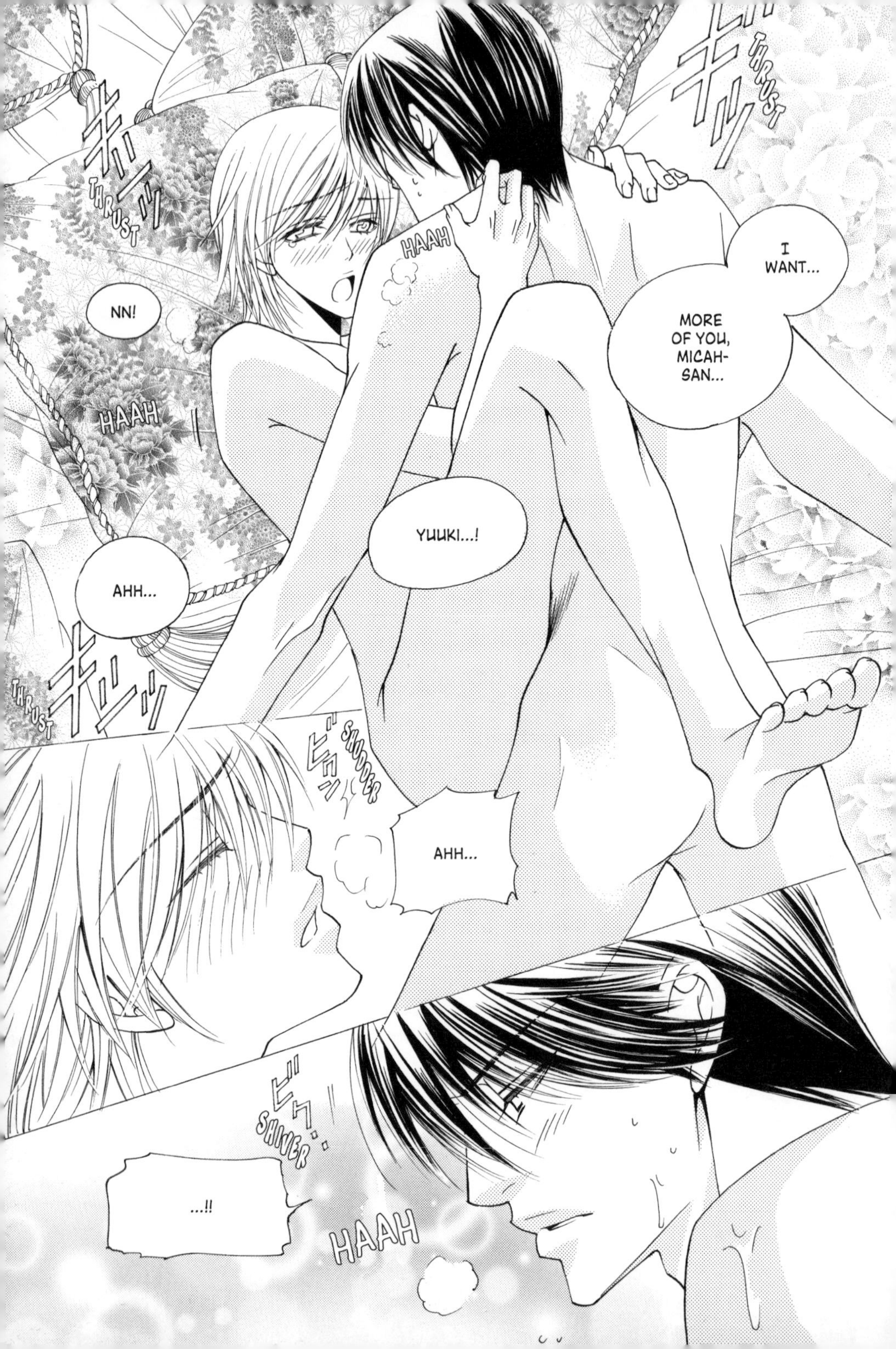
THRUST
I WANT...
MORE OF YOU, MICAH-SAN...
HAAH
THRUST
NN!
HAAH
YUUKI...!
AHH...
THRUST
SHUDDER
AHH...
SHIVER
...!!
HAAH

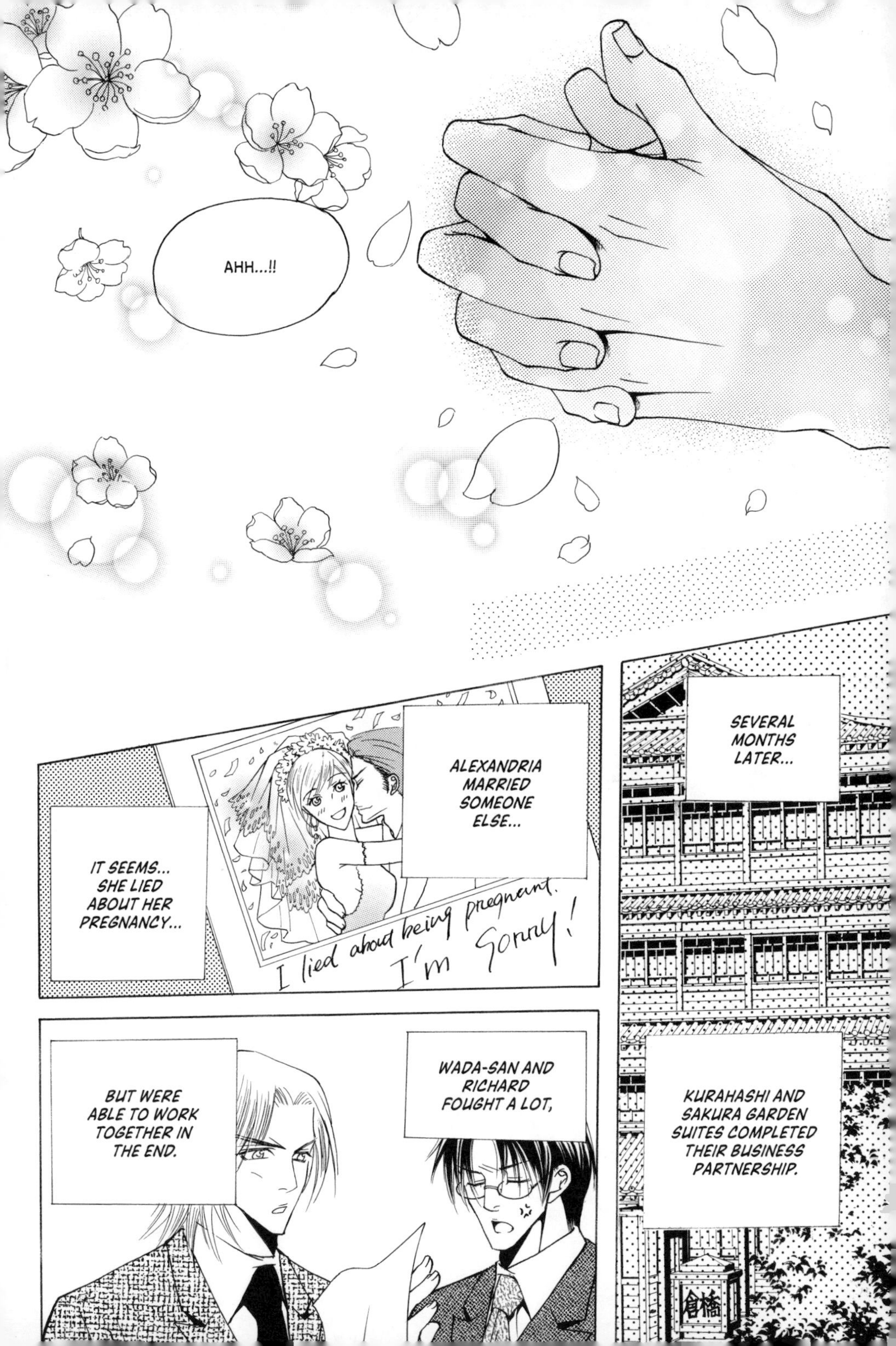
AHH...!!
SEVERAL MONTHS LATER...
KURAHASHI AND SAKURA GARDEN SUITES COMPLETED THEIR BUSINESS PARTNERSHIP.
倉橋
ALEXANDRIA MARRIED SOMEONE ELSE...
IT SEEMS... SHE LIED ABOUT HER PREGNANCY...
I lied about being pregnant. I'm Sorry!
WADA-SAN AND RICHARD FOUGHT A LOT,
BUT WERE ABLE TO WORK TOGETHER IN THE END.

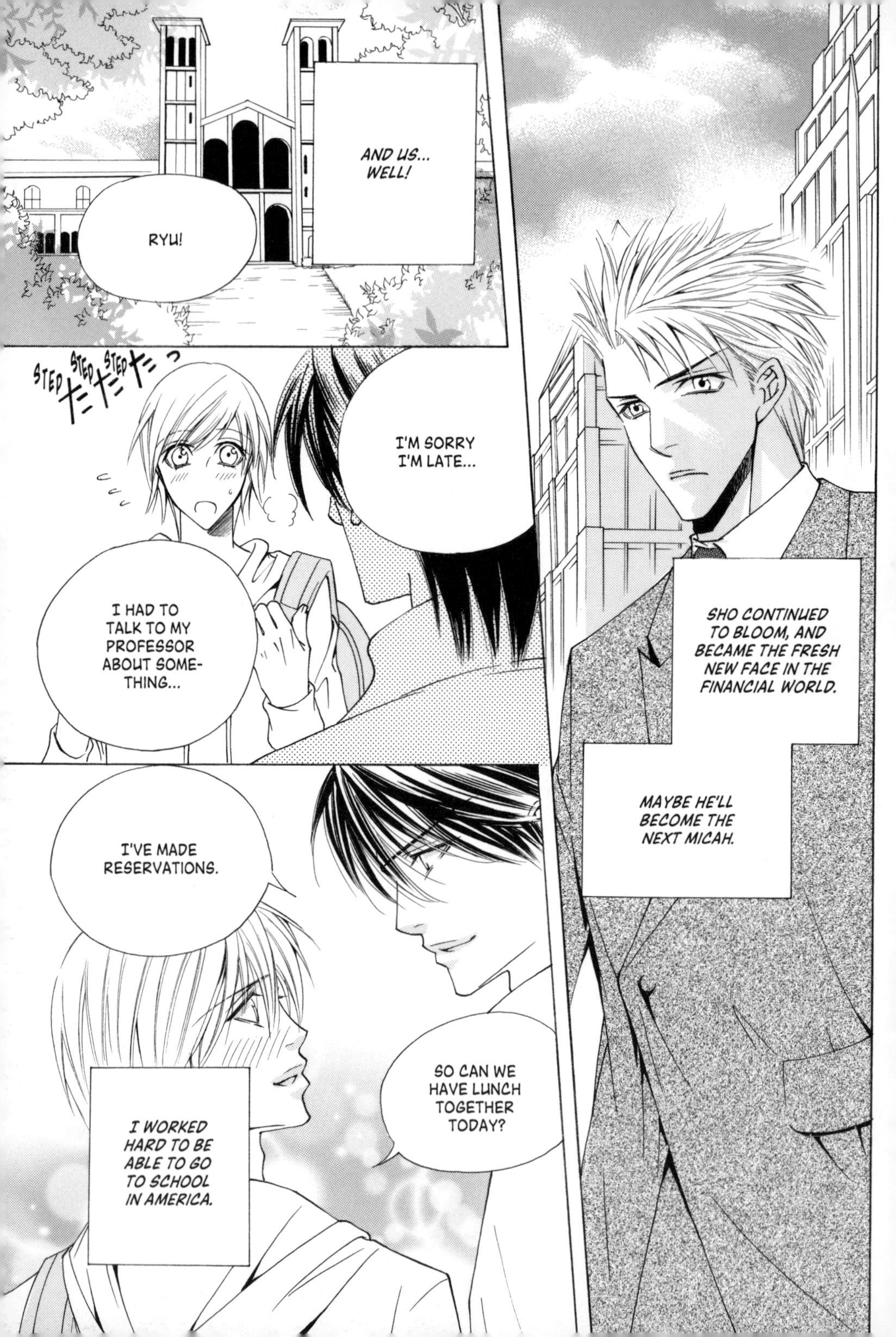
SHO CONTINUED TO BLOOM, AND BECAME THE FRESH NEW FACE IN THE FINANCIAL WORLD.
MAYBE HE'LL BECOME THE NEXT MICAH.
AND US... WELL!
RYU!
I'M SORRY I'M LATE...
STEP STEP STEP
I HAD TO TALK TO MY PROFESSOR ABOUT SOME-THING...
I'VE MADE RESERVATIONS.
SO CAN WE HAVE LUNCH TOGETHER TODAY?
I WORKED HARD TO BE ABLE TO GO TO SCHOOL IN AMERICA.

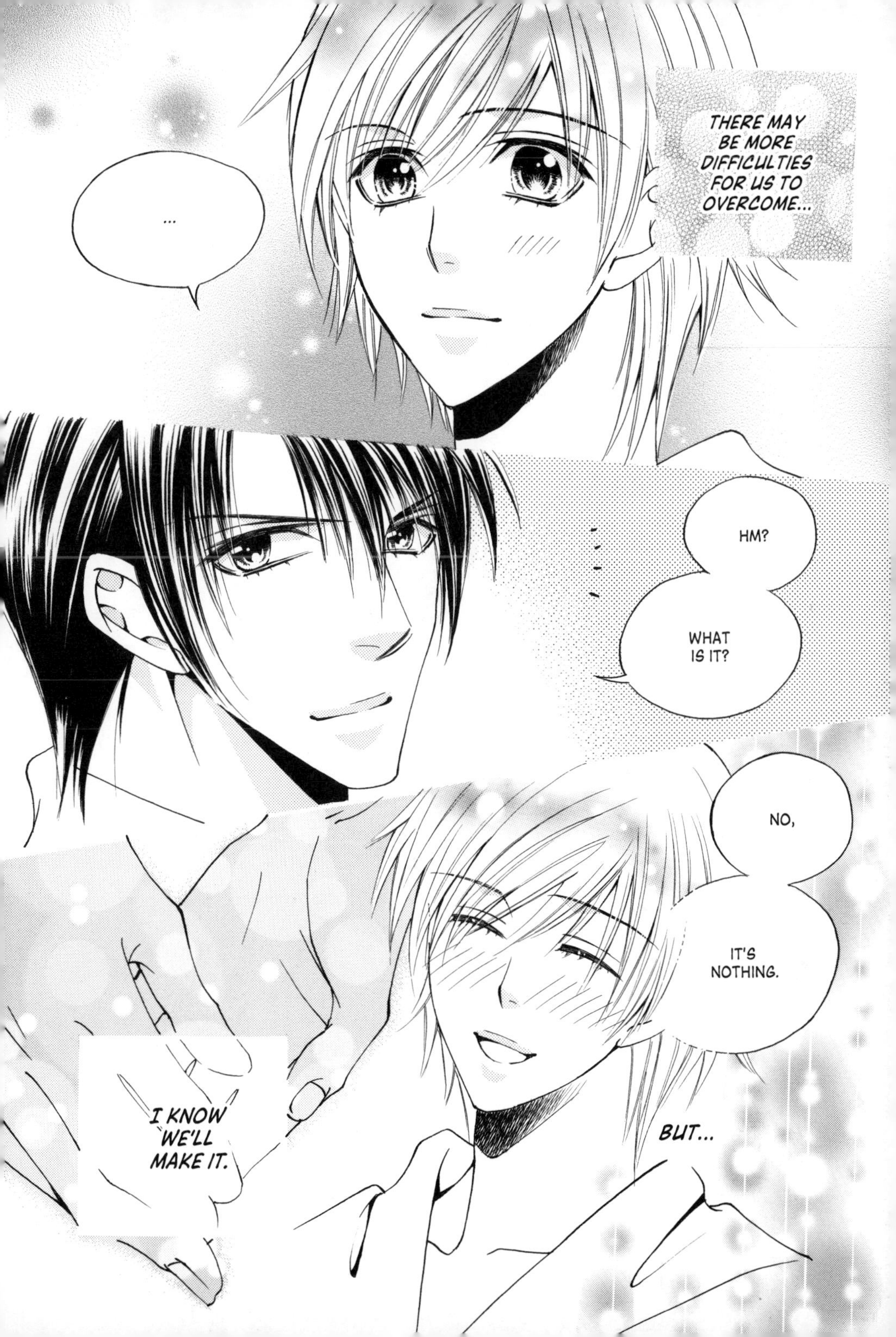
THERE MAY BE MORE DIFFICULTIES FOR US TO OVERCOME...
...
HM?
WHAT IS IT?
NO,
IT'S NOTHING.
BUT...
I KNOW WE'LL MAKE IT.

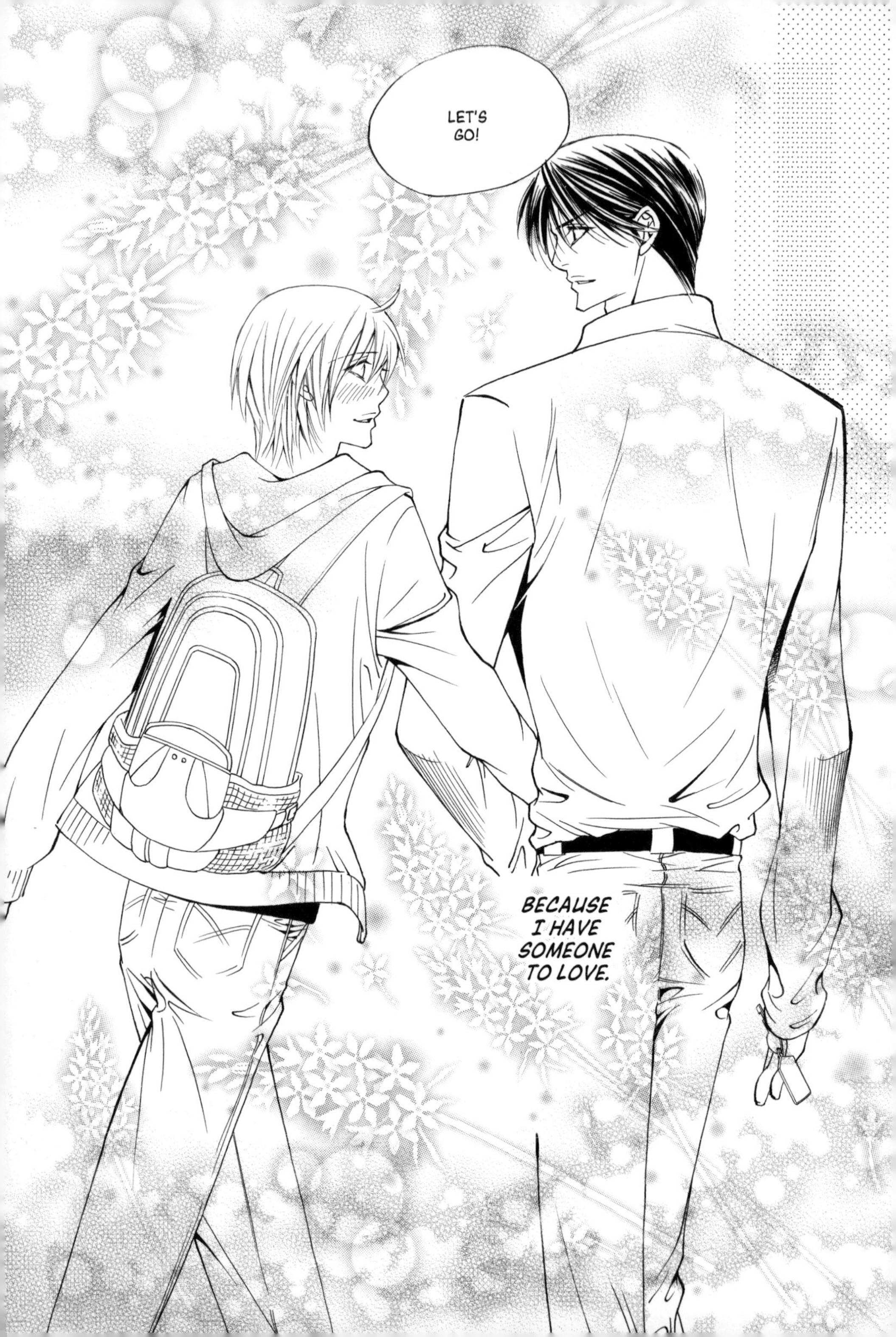
LET'S GO!
BECAUSE I HAVE SOMEONE TO LOVE.

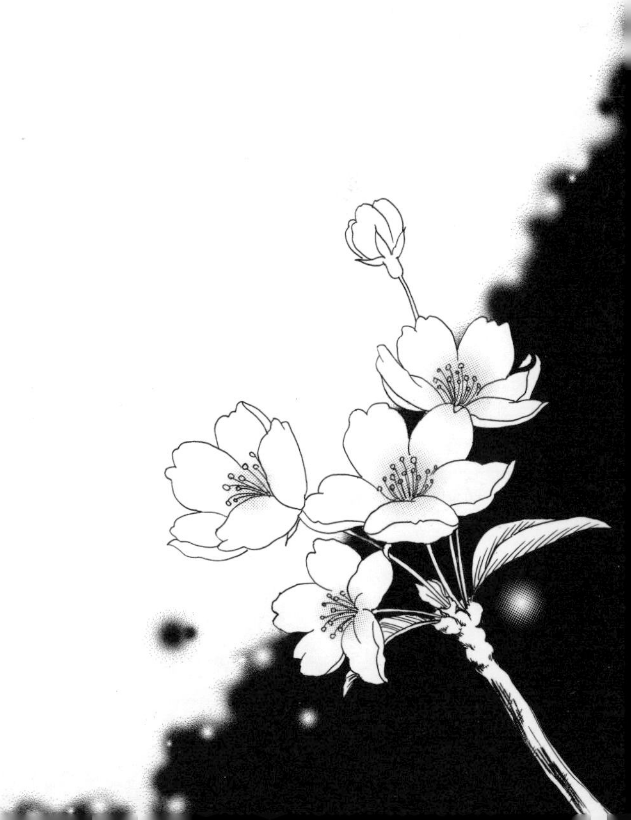

Happy Birthday

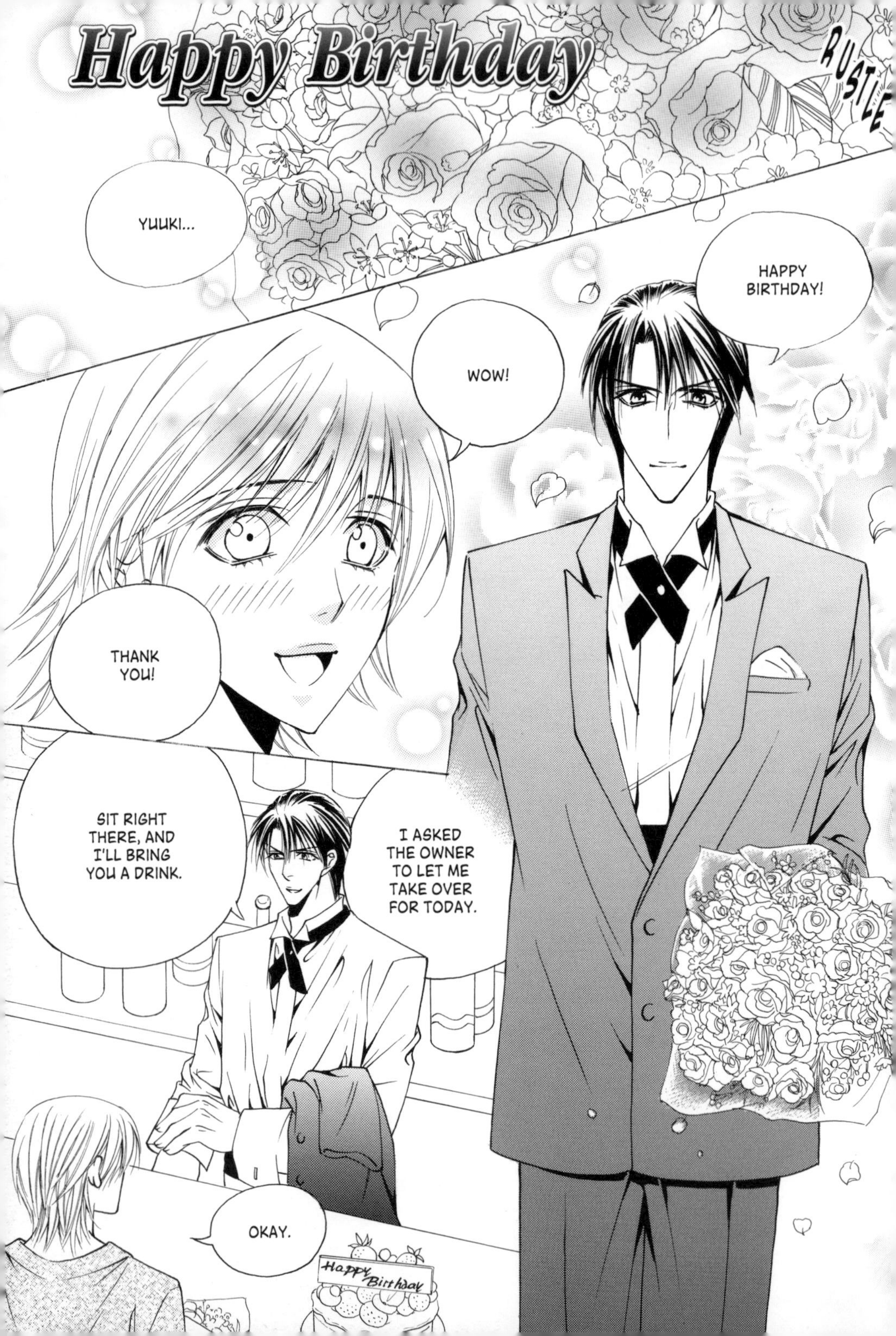
RUSTLE
YUUKI...
HAPPY BIRTHDAY!
WOW!
THANK YOU!
I ASKED THE OWNER TO LET ME TAKE OVER FOR TODAY.
SIT RIGHT THERE, AND I'LL BRING YOU A DRINK.
OKAY.
Happy Birthday

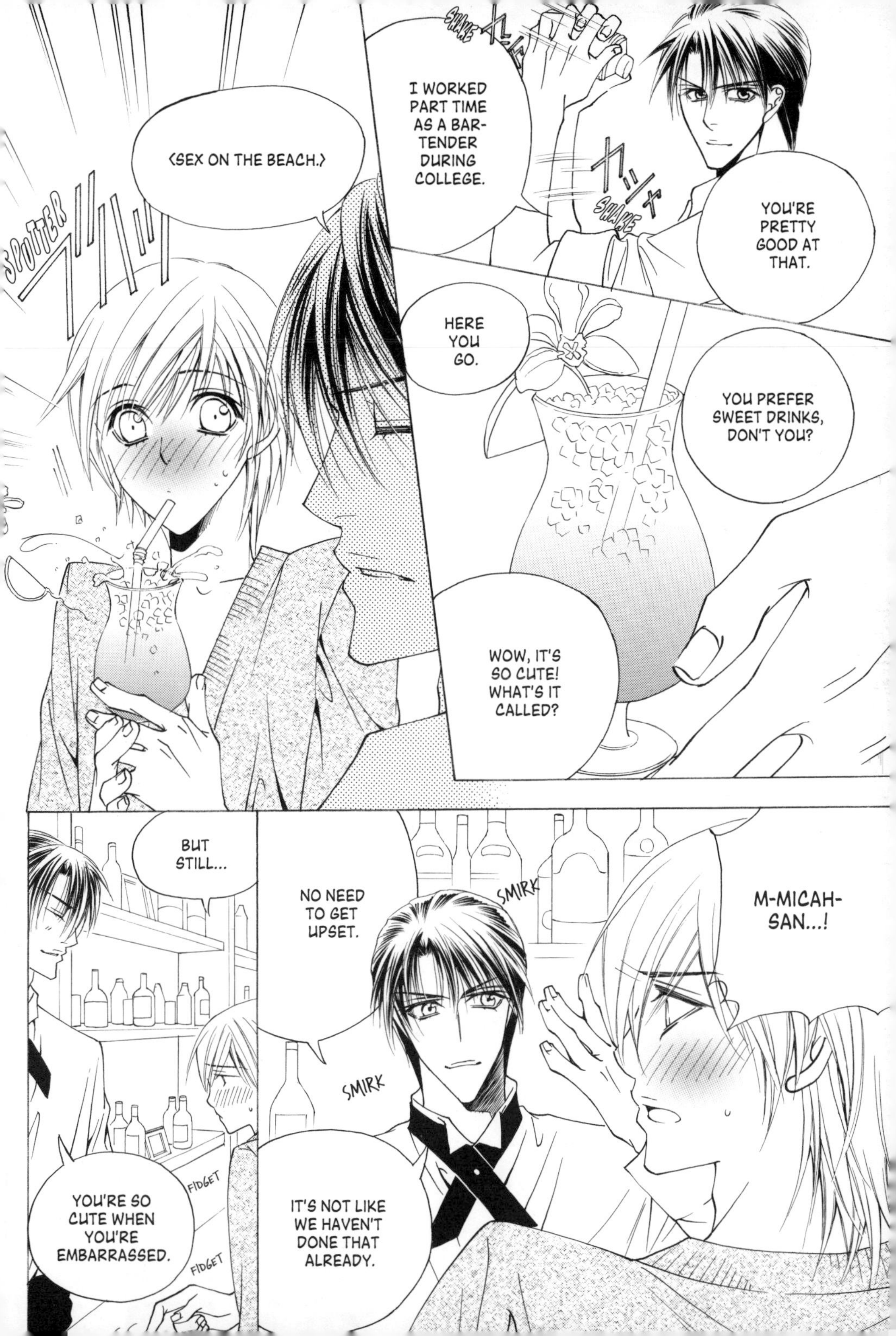
SHAKE
YOU'RE PRETTY GOOD AT THAT.
I WORKED PART TIME AS A BAR-TENDER DURING COLLEGE.
SHAKE
HERE YOU GO.
YOU PREFER SWEET DRINKS, DON'T YOU?
WOW, IT'S SO CUTE! WHAT'S IT CALLED?
⟨SEX ON THE BEACH.⟩
SPOTTER
M-MICAH-SAN...!
SMIRK
NO NEED TO GET UPSET.
SMIRK
IT'S NOT LIKE WE HAVEN'T DONE THAT ALREADY.
BUT STILL...
FIDGET
YOU'RE SO CUTE WHEN YOU'RE EMBARRASSED.
FIDGET

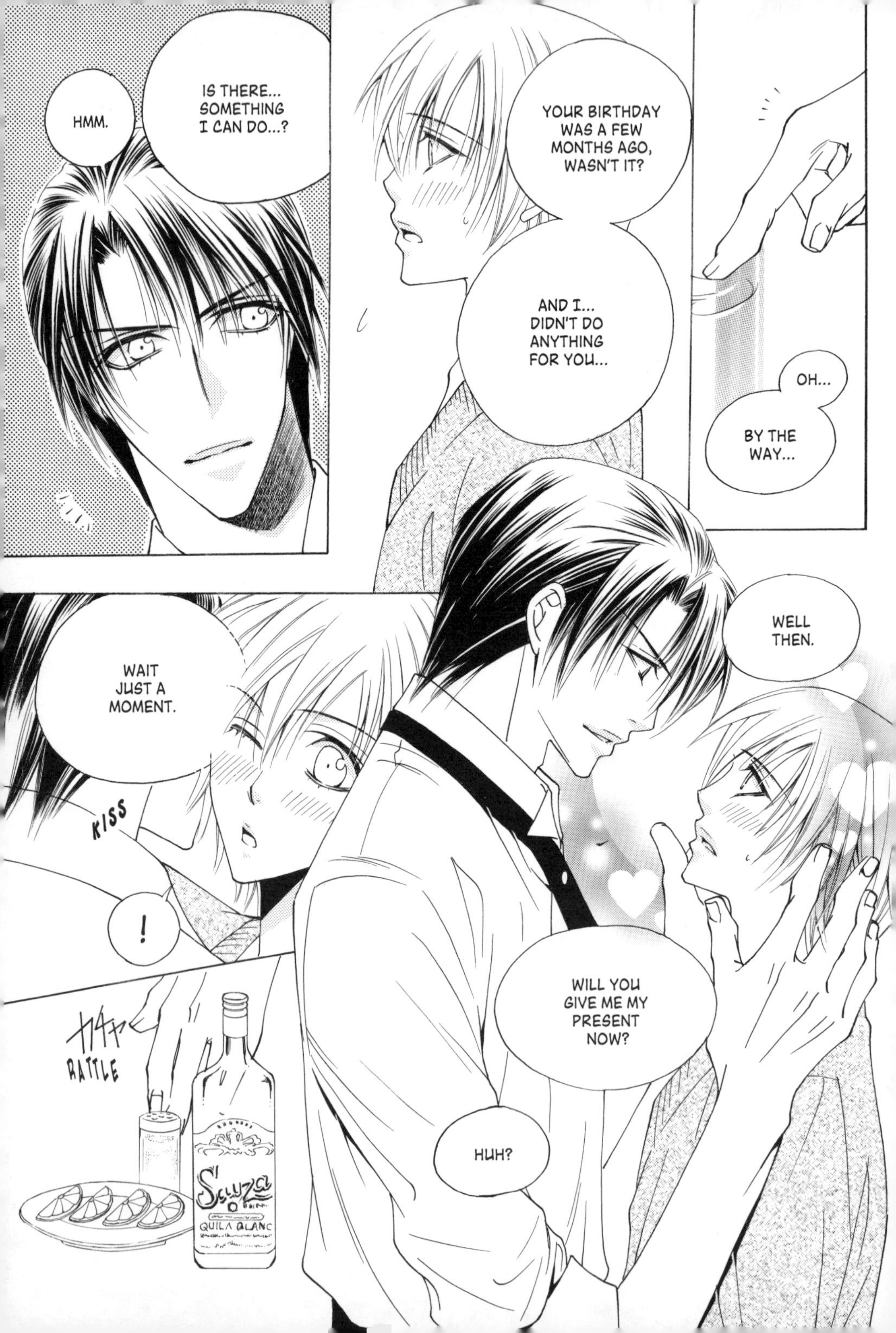
OH...
BY THE WAY...
YOUR BIRTHDAY WAS A FEW MONTHS AGO, WASN'T IT?
AND I... DIDN'T DO ANYTHING FOR YOU...
IS THERE... SOMETHING I CAN DO...?
HMM.
WELL THEN.
WILL YOU GIVE ME MY PRESENT NOW?
HUH?
WAIT JUST A MOMENT.
KISS
!
カチャ
RATTLE

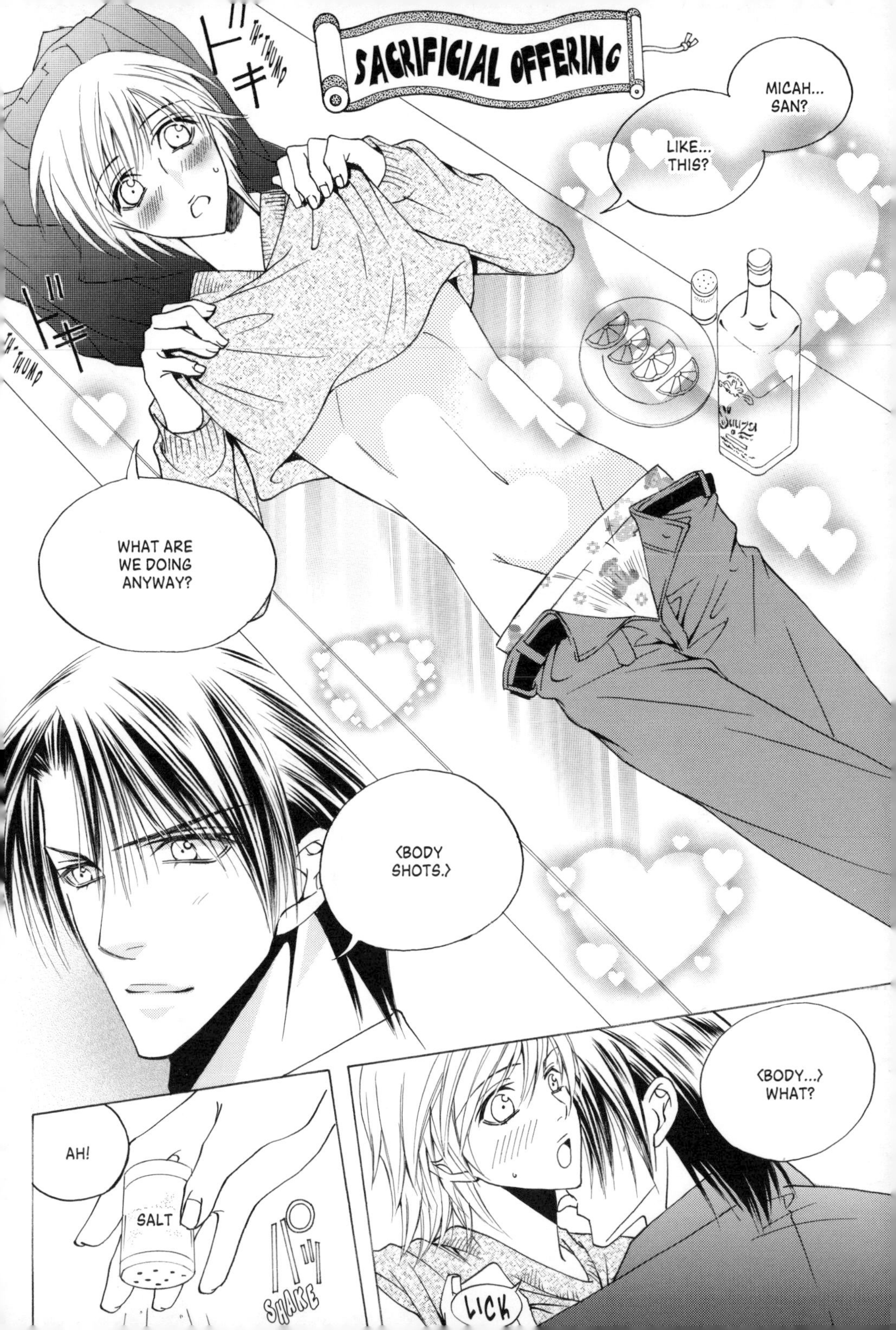
SACRIFICIAL OFFERING
MICAH... SAN?
LIKE... THIS?
ドキ TH-THUMP
ドキ TH-THUMP
WHAT ARE WE DOING ANYWAY?
‹BODY SHOTS.›
‹BODY...› WHAT?
LICK
AH!
SALT
SHAKE

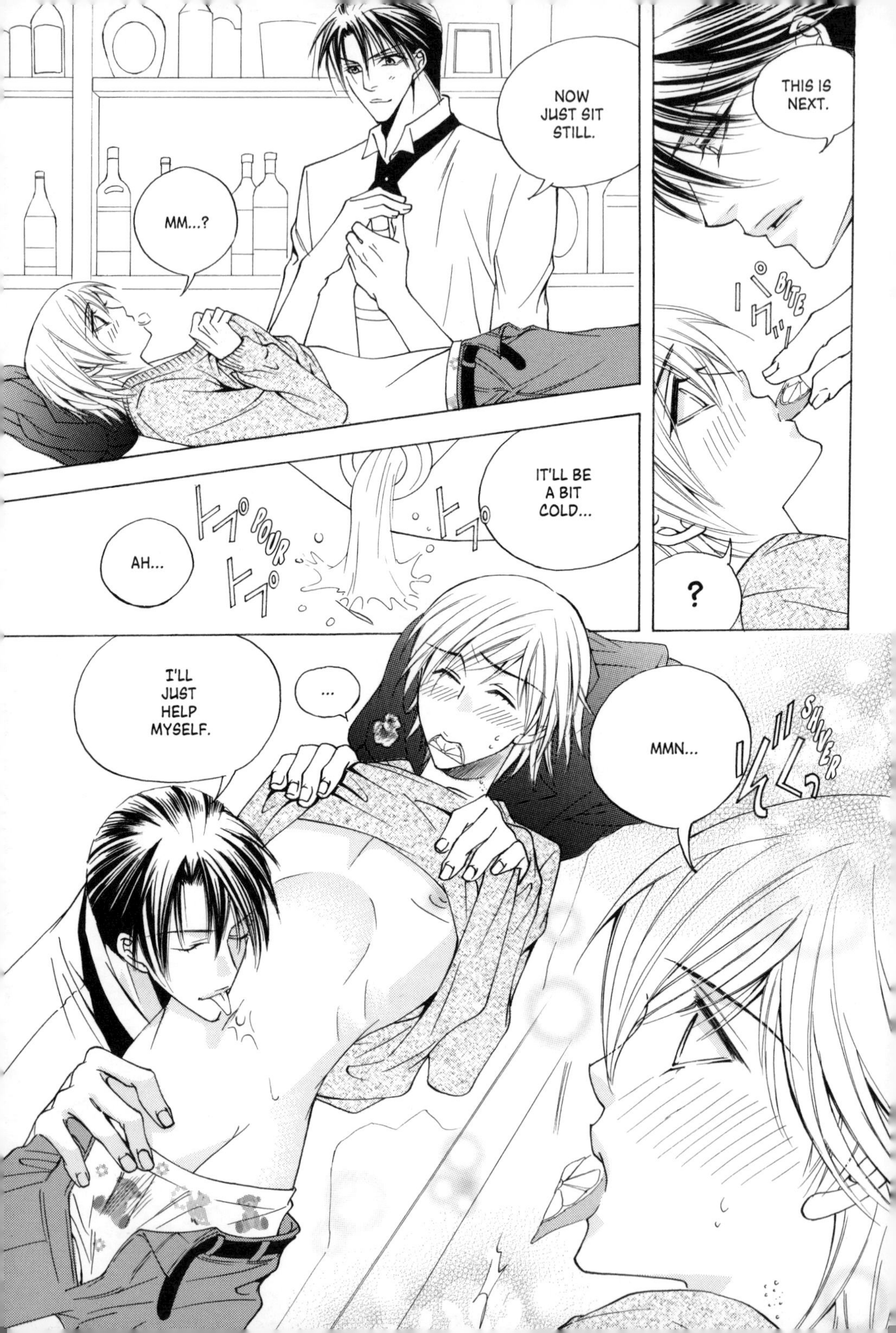
THIS IS NEXT.
BITE
?
NOW JUST SIT STILL.
MM...?
IT'LL BE A BIT COLD...
POUR
AH...
SHIVER
MMN...
...
I'LL JUST HELP MYSELF.

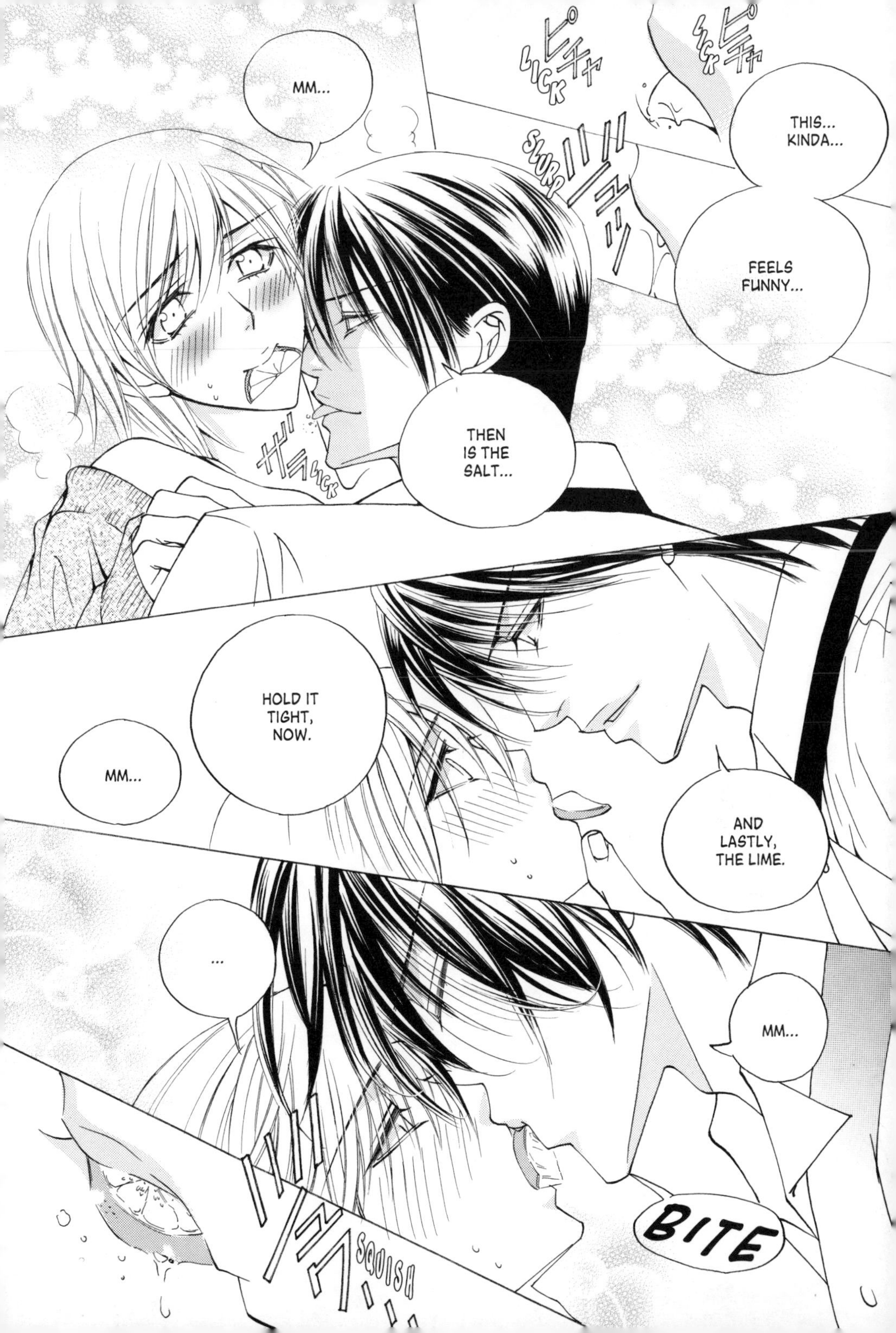
LICK
LICK
SLURP
THIS... KINDA...
FEELS FUNNY...
MM...
THEN IS THE SALT...
LICK
HOLD IT TIGHT, NOW.
MM...
AND LASTLY, THE LIME.
MM...
...
BITE
SQUISH

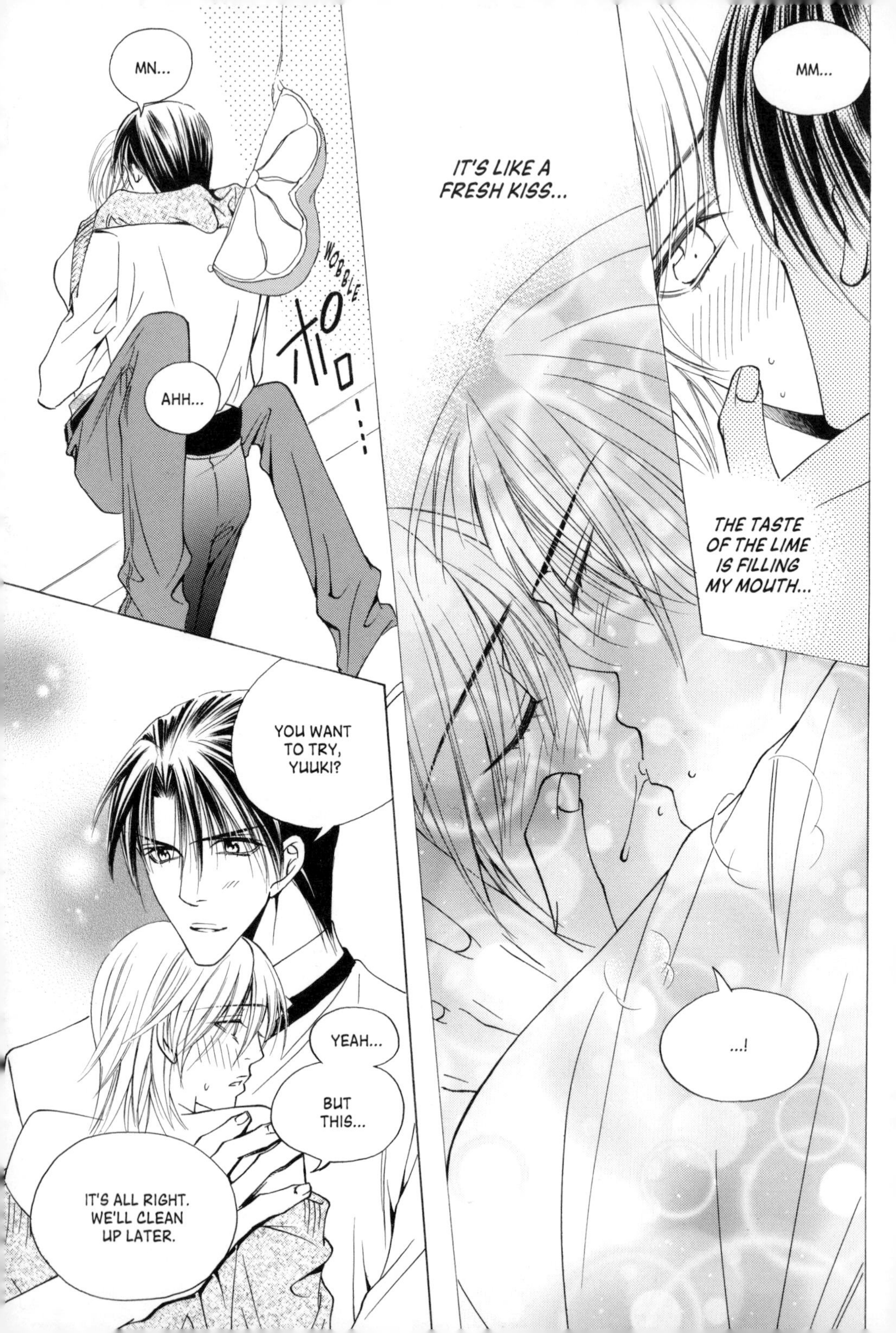
MM...
IT'S LIKE A FRESH KISS...
THE TASTE OF THE LIME IS FILLING MY MOUTH...
...!
MN...
WOBBLE
AHH...
YOU WANT TO TRY, YUUKI?
YEAH...
BUT THIS...
IT'S ALL RIGHT. WE'LL CLEAN UP LATER.

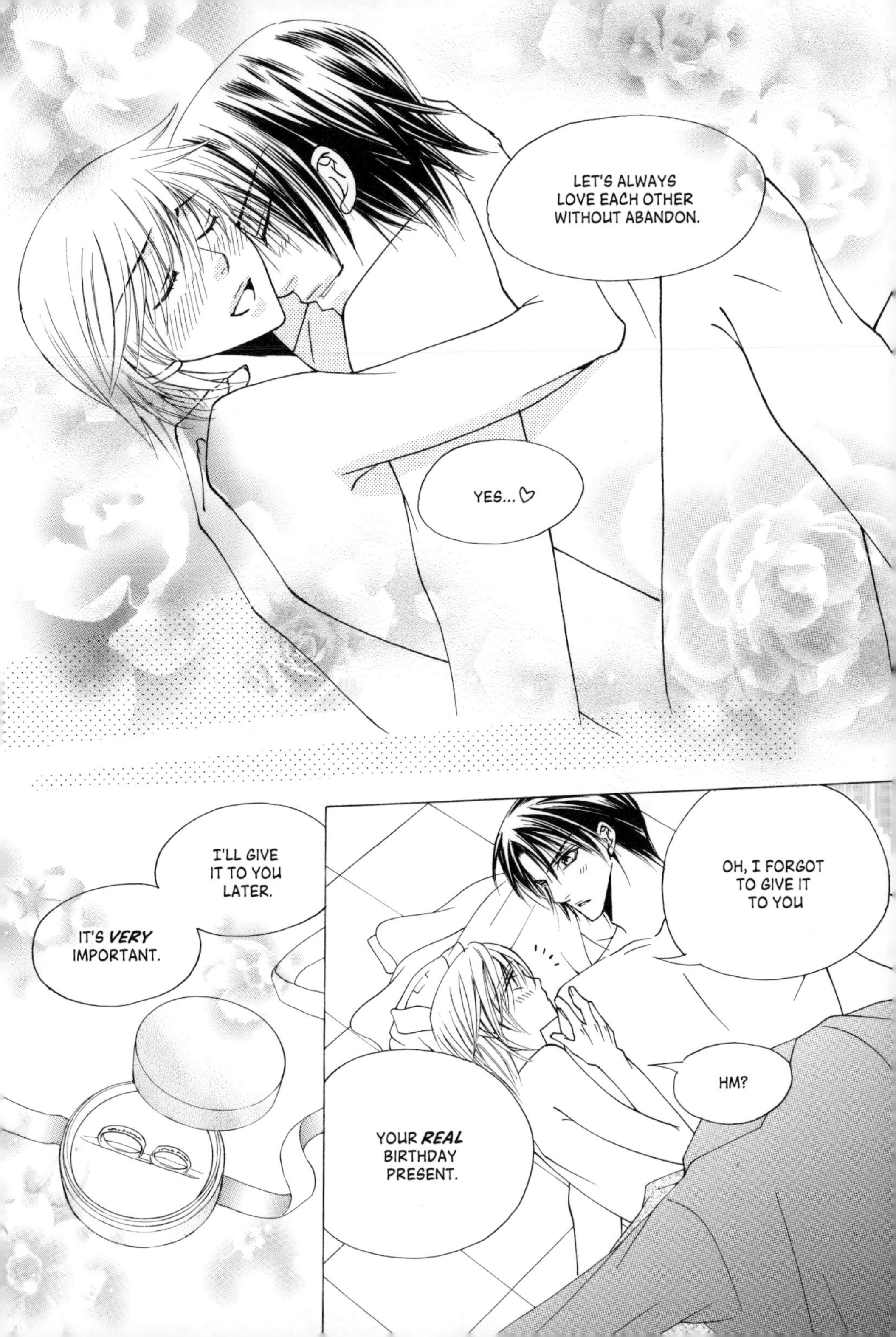
LET'S ALWAYS LOVE EACH OTHER WITHOUT ABANDON.
YES... ♡
OH, I FORGOT TO GIVE IT TO YOU
HM?
YOUR **REAL** BIRTHDAY PRESENT.
I'LL GIVE IT TO YOU LATER.
IT'S **VERY** IMPORTANT.

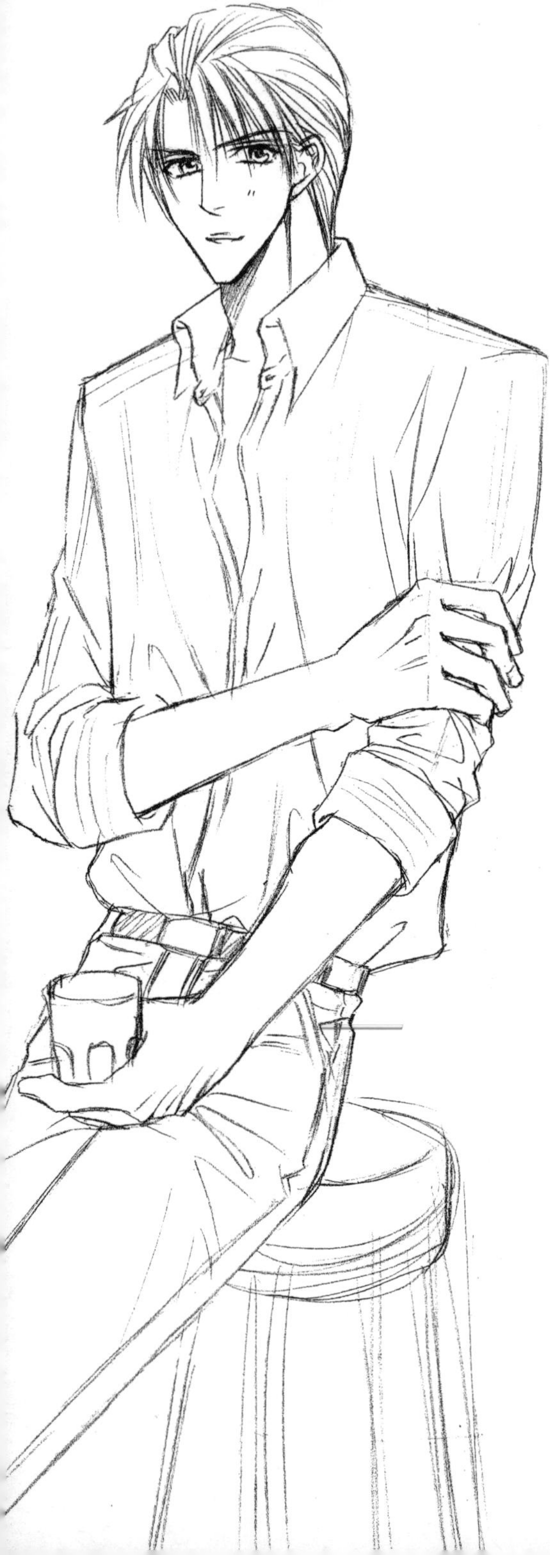

AFTERWORD

HELLO EVERYBODY! I'M YUNO OGAMI. THANK YOU FOR BUYING THIS BOOK. ☆

WHEN I WAS STILL UNSURE ABOUT ACCEPTING THE PROJECT AND DOING "ÉTOILE" OR NOT, I WAS ABOUT TO MOVE TO ANOTHER PLACE, AND MY CONTACT AT DMP TOLD ME "ONCE YOU'RE ALL RESTED FROM THE MOVING, I HAVE HIGH HOPES THAT YOU WILL WANT TO EMBRACE THIS NEW PROJECT IN A BRAND NEW ENVIRONMENT, AND THAT YOU WILL MAKE YOUR FIRST STEP TOWARDS AMERICA."

THOSE WORDS ARE WHAT CONVINCED ME TO DRAW THIS MANGA.

OF COURSE, IT WASN'T A SMOOTH ROAD UNTIL COMPLETION, ESPECIALLY SINCE I WAS DRAWING A SERIES BEING CURRENTLY PUBLISHED IN JAPAN AT THE SAME TIME, AND THUS HAD TO WORK DAY AND NIGHT TO BE ABLE TO DRAW BOTH OF THEM.

AS I DREW, I NOTICED HOW IMMATURE AS A MANGAKA I STILL AM, AND I THINK THIS MIGHT BE THE MANGA WHERE I GREW THE MOST AS I DREW IT.

EVEN NOW THAT I FINISHED DRAWING "ÉTOILE", I STILL HAVE ALL THE CHARACTER PICS PASTED ON MY WALL.

I HOPE THAT MICAH AND YUUKI WILL ALWAYS BE IN LOVE. RICHARD GOT DUMPED, BUT I HOPE HE WILL FIND A NEW LOVE AS WELL. I JUST CAN'T HELP BUT HOPE THAT ALL MY CHARACTERS WILL FIND HAPPINESS. (*LAUGHS*)

THANK YOU SO MUCH TO EVERYBODY WHO GAVE ME SUCH AN OPPORTUNITY, ALL THE WAY FROM THE DMP PRESIDENT, MR. SASAHARA, TO MY CONTACTS, THE TRANSLATION TEAM, EVERYBODY. MY SINCERE THANKS TO EVERYBODY WHO PARTICIPATED IN CREATING THIS MANGA.

THANK YOU ALSO TO EVERYBODY WHO SUPPORTED ME THROUGHOUT THE WHOLE PROCESS, MY FAMILY AND MY CATS INCLUDED.

AND FINALLY, THANK YOU SO MUCH TO YOU ALL WHO ARE READING THIS BOOK!

I HOPE TO BE ABLE TO MEET YOU AGAIN THROUGH ANOTHER MANGA IN THE FUTURE.

THANK YOU VERY MUCH,

YUNO OGAMI

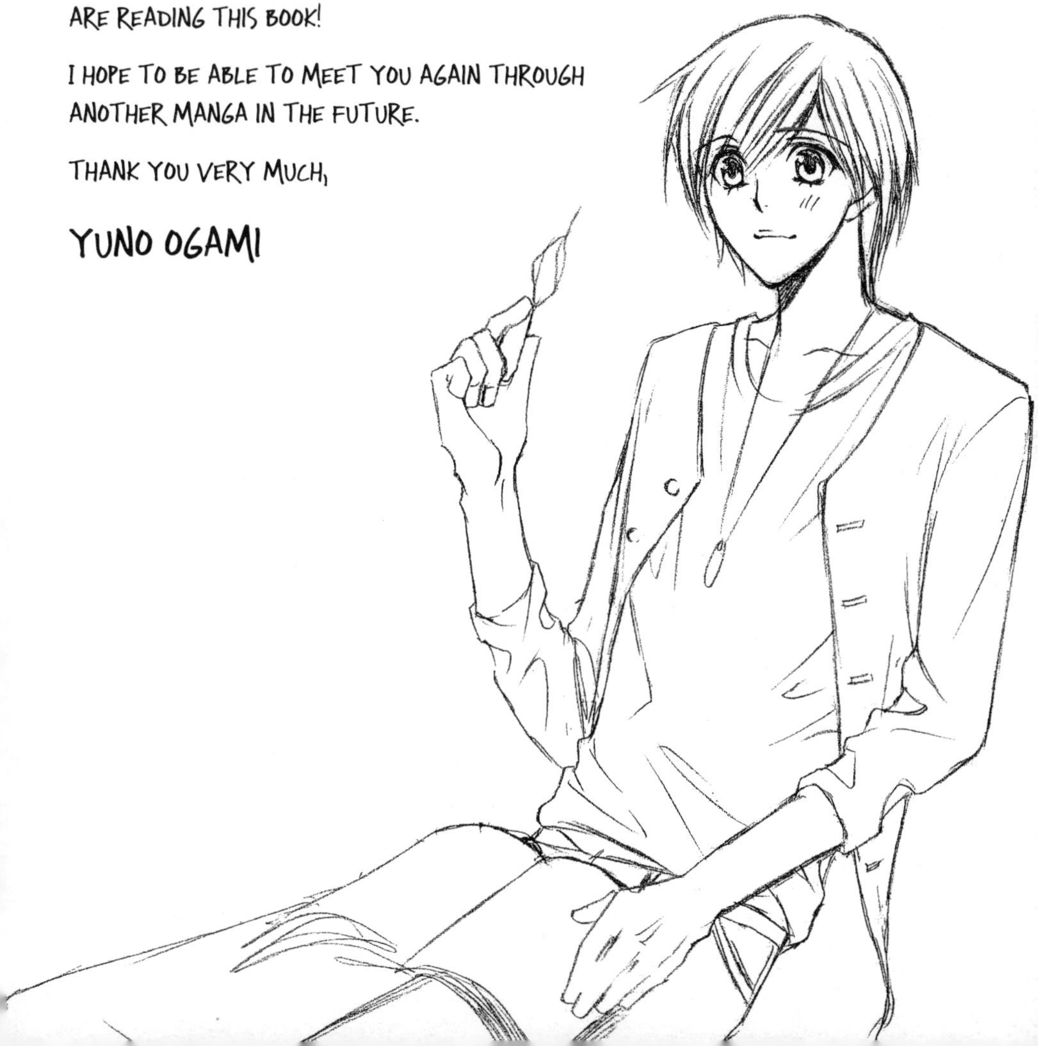

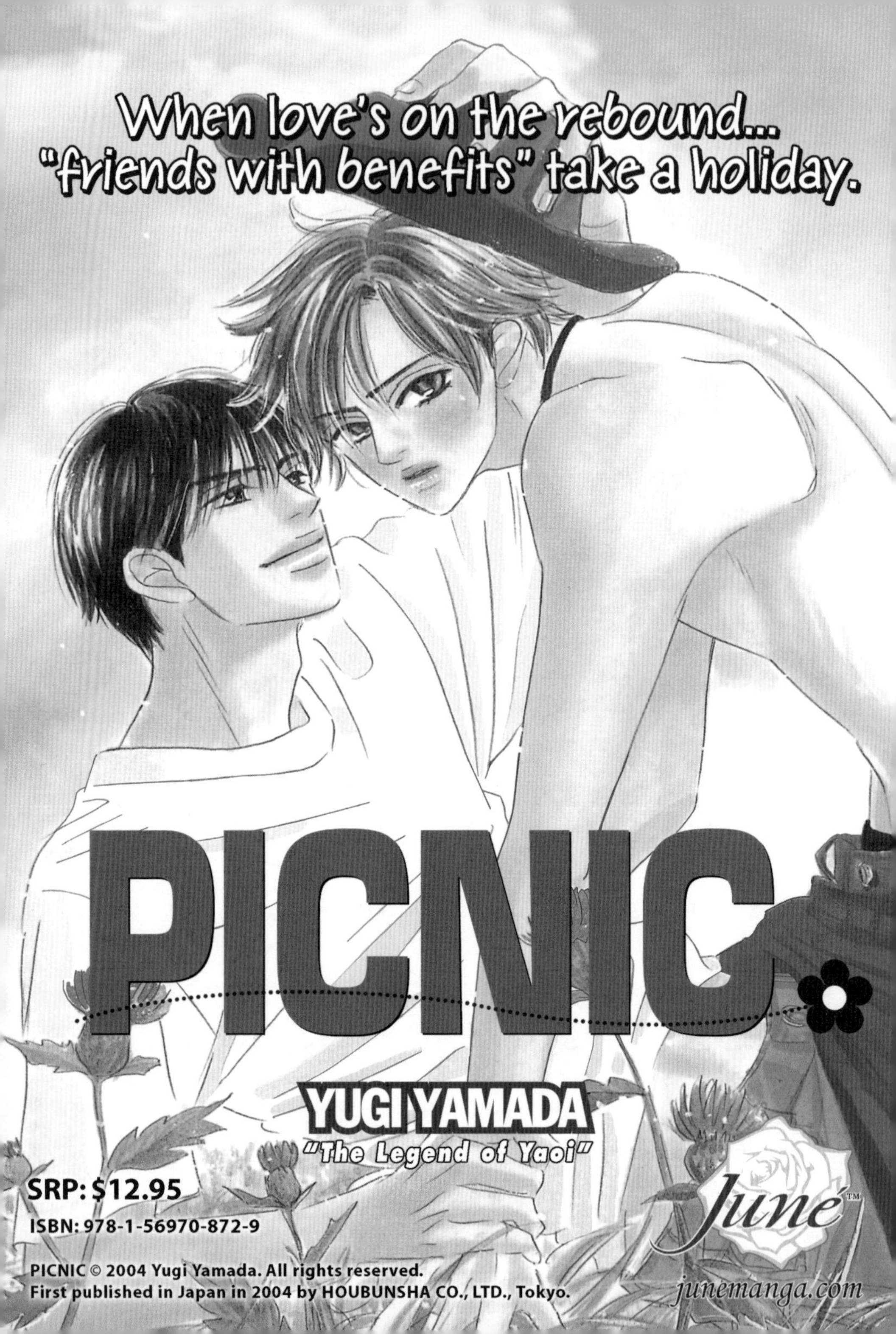

When love's on the rebound...
"friends with benefits" take a holiday.
PICNIC
YUGI YAMADA
"The Legend of Yaoi"
SRP: $12.95
ISBN: 978-1-56970-872-9
PICNIC © 2004 Yugi Yamada. All rights reserved.
First published in Japan in 2004 by HOUBUNSHA CO., LTD., Tokyo.
Juné™
junemanga.com

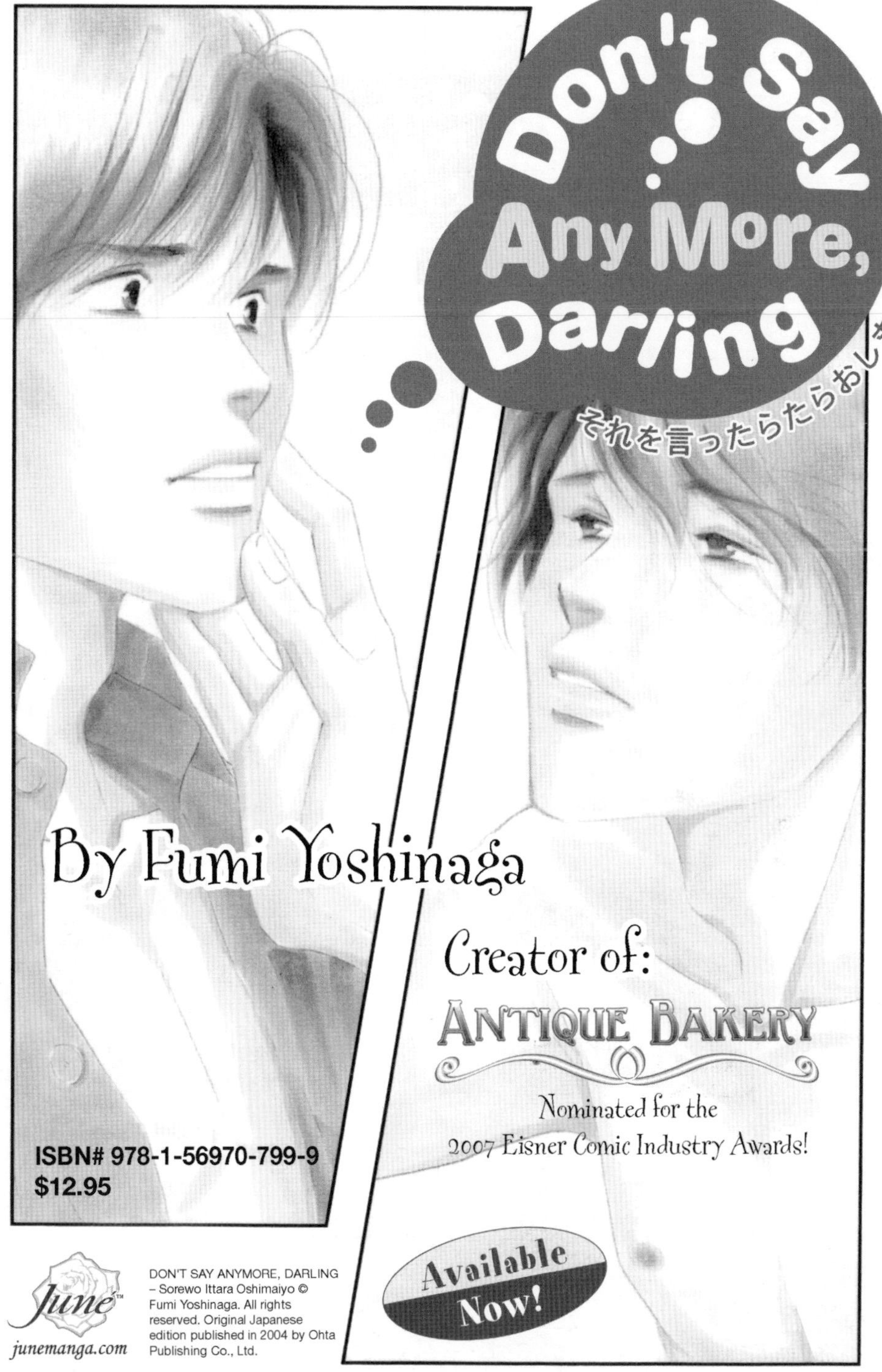
Don't Say Any More, Darling
それを言ったらたらおしまいよ
By Fumi Yoshinaga
Creator of:
ANTIQUE BAKERY
Nominated for the 2007 Eisner Comic Industry Awards!
ISBN# 978-1-56970-799-9
$12.95
Available Now!

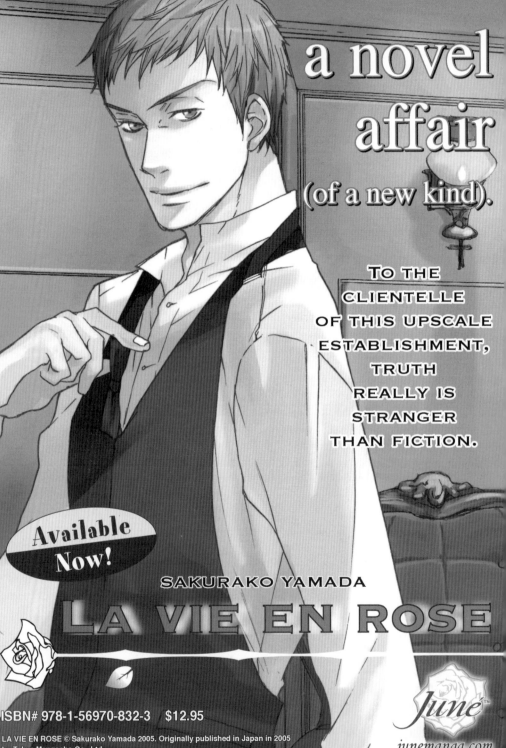

a novel affair (of a new kind).

TO THE CLIENTELLE OF THIS UPSCALE ESTABLISHMENT, TRUTH REALLY IS STRANGER THAN FICTION.

Available Now!

SAKURAKO YAMADA

LA VIE EN ROSE

ISBN# 978-1-56970-832-3 $12.95

LA VIE EN ROSE © Sakurako Yamada 2005. Originally published in Japan in 2005 by Tokyo Mangasha Co., Ltd.

june

junemanga.com

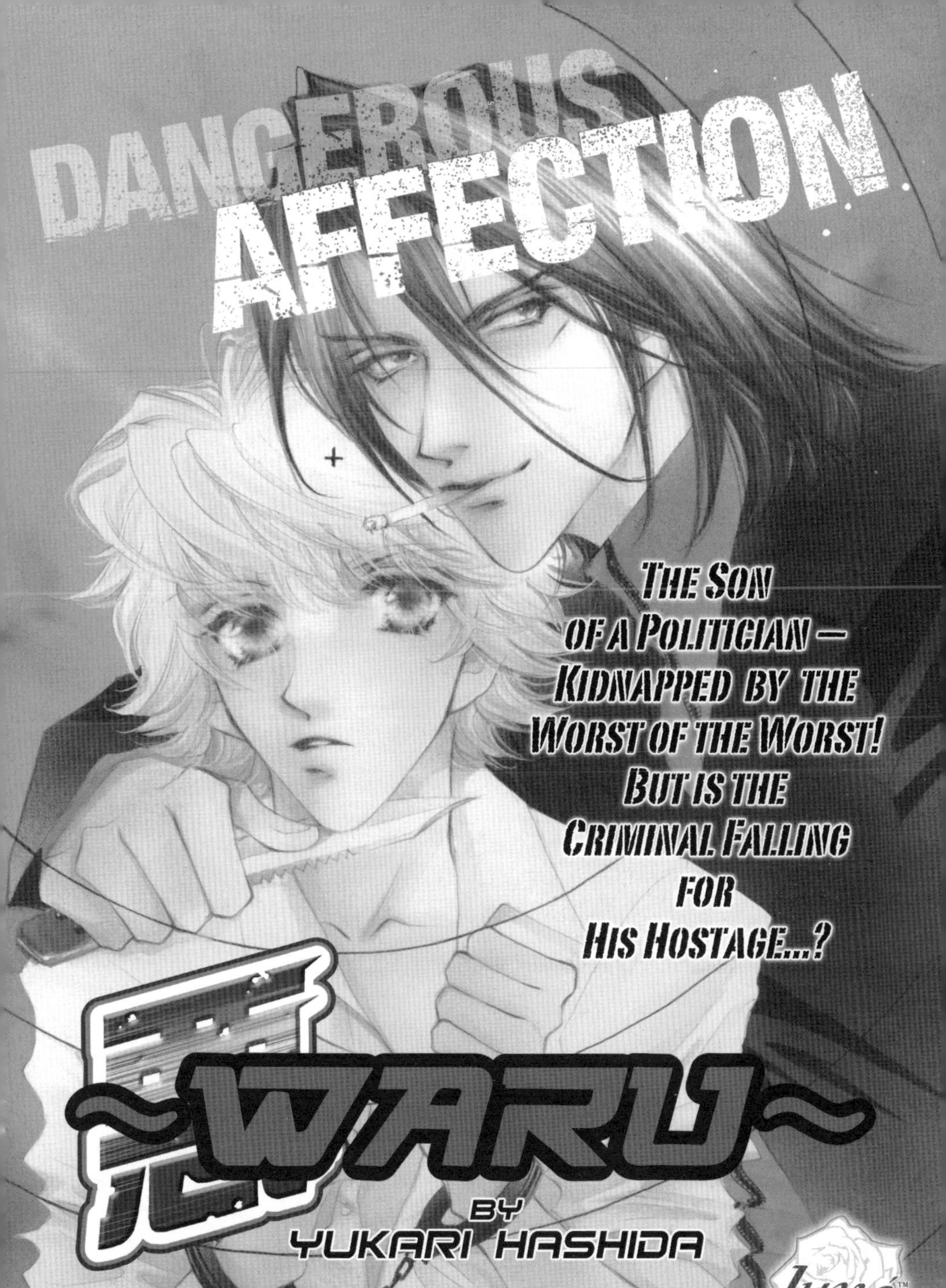
DANGEROUS AFFECTION
THE SON OF A POLITICIAN – KIDNAPPED BY THE WORST OF THE WORST! BUT IS THE CRIMINAL FALLING FOR HIS HOSTAGE...?
~WARU~
BY YUKARI HASHIDA
June™
junemanga.com

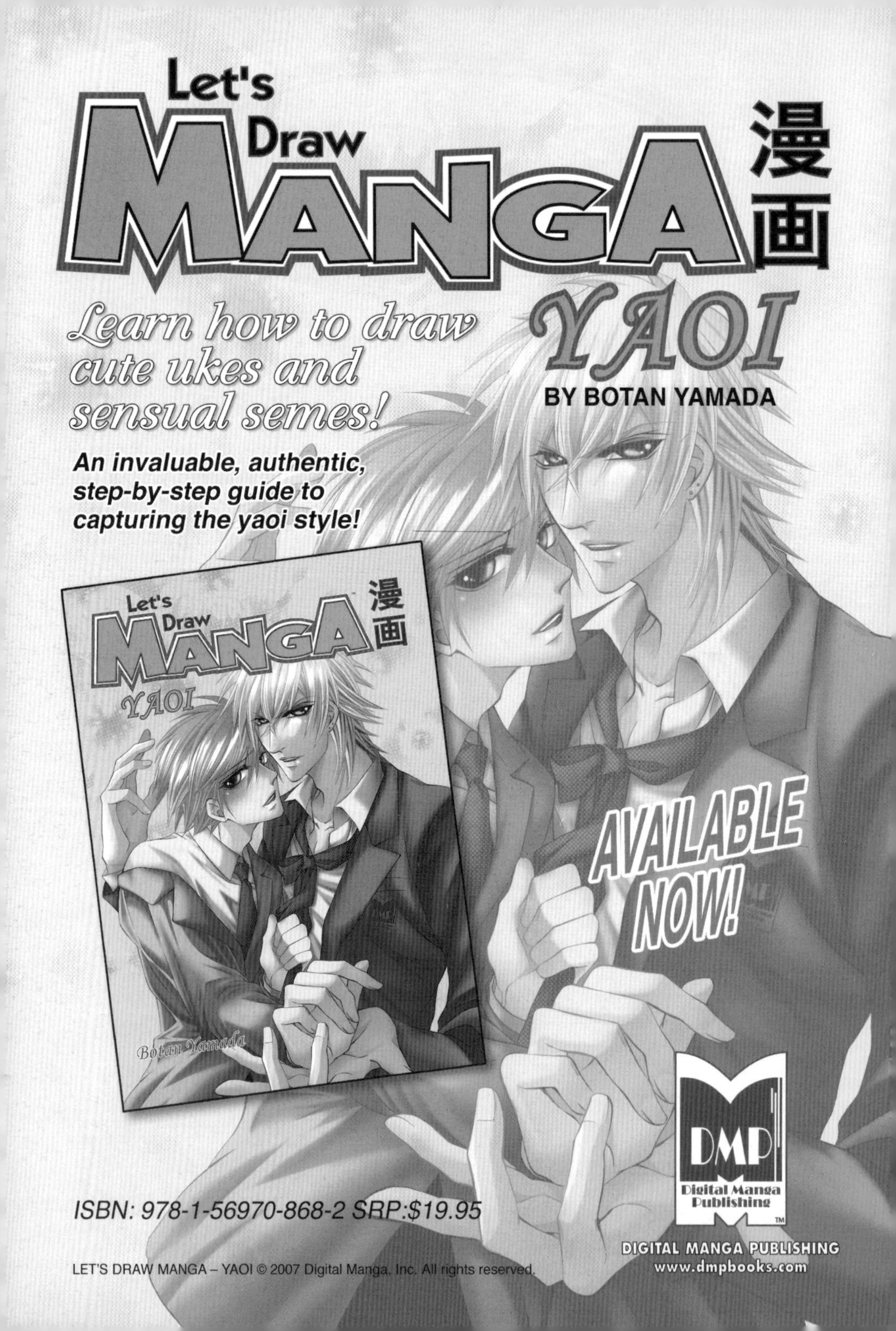
Let's Draw MANGA 漫画
YAOI
BY BOTAN YAMADA
Learn how to draw cute ukes and sensual semes!
An invaluable, authentic, step-by-step guide to capturing the yaoi style!
Let's Draw MANGA 漫画
YAOI
Botan Yamada
AVAILABLE NOW!
DMP
Digital Manga Publishing
TM
ISBN: 978-1-56970-868-2 SRP:$19.95
DIGITAL MANGA PUBLISHING
www.dmpbooks.com
LET'S DRAW MANGA – YAOI © 2007 Digital Manga, Inc. All rights reserved.

STOP

This is the back of the book! Start from the other side.

NATIVE MANGA readers read manga from *right to left*.

1
2
1
3
2
3
5
4
4
6
5
8
7
6

*If you run into our **Native Manga** logo on any of our books... you'll know that this manga is published in it's true original native Japanese right to left reading format, as it was intended. Turn to the other side of the book and start reading from right to left, top to bottom.*

Follow the diagram to see how its done.
Surf's Up!

NATIVE MANGA
READ RIGHT TO LEFT

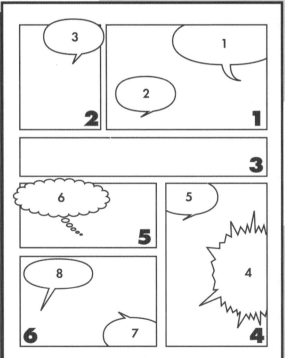

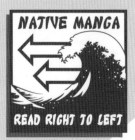